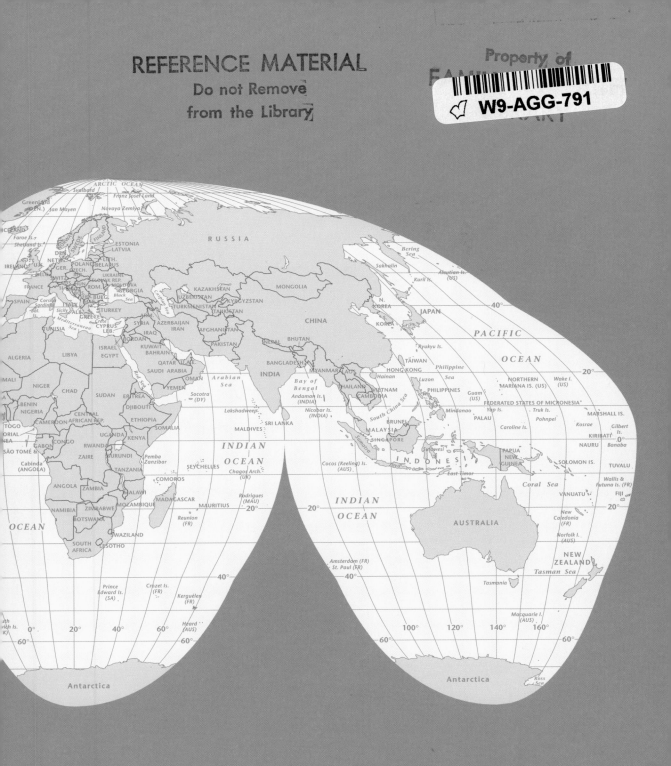

Junior
Worldmark
Encyclopedia
of the

VOLUME 7

Junior Worldmark Encyclopedia of the

Nations

VOLUME 7

Qatar to South Africa

An imprint of Gale Research
An ITP Information/Reference Group Company

Changing the Way the World Learns

NEW YORK • LONDON • BONN • BOSTON • DETROIT
MADRID • MELBOURNE • MEXICO CITY • PARIS
SINGAPORE • TOKYO • TORONTO • WASHINGTON
ALBANY NY • BELMONT CA • CINCINNATI OH

JUNIOR WORLDMARK ENCYCLOPEDIA OF THE NATIONS

Timothy L. Gall and Susan Bevan Gall, *Editors*
Rosalie Wieder, *Senior Editor*
Deborah Baron and Daniel M. Lucas, *Associate Editors*
Brian Rajewski and Deborah Rutti, *Graphics and Layout*
Cordelia R. Heaney, *Editorial Assistant*
Dianne K. Daeg de Mott, Janet Fenn, Matthew Markovich,
    Ariana Ranson, and Craig Strasshofer, *Copy Editors*
Janet Fenn and Matthew Markovich, *Proofreaders*
Maryland Cartographics, Inc., *Cartographers*

U•X•L Staff

Jane Hoehner, *U•X•L Developmental Editor*
Sonia Benson and Rob Nagel, *Contributors*
Thomas L. Romig, *U•X•L Publisher*
Mary Beth Trimper, *Production Director*
Evi Seoud, *Assistant Production Manager*
Shanna Heilveil, *Production Associate*
Cynthia Baldwin, *Product Design Manager*
Barbara J. Yarrow, *Graphic Services Supervisor*
Mary Krzewinski, *Cover Designer*
Margaret McAvoy-Amoto, *Permissions Associate (Pictures)*

Library of Congress Cataloging-in-Publication Data
Junior Worldmark encyclopedia of the nations / edited by Timothy Gall
    and Susan Gall.
            p.   cm.
    Includes bibliographical references and index.
    ISBN 0-7876-0741-X (set)
    1. Geography--Encyclopedias, Juvenile. 2. History--Encyclopedias,
Juvenile. 3. Economics--Juvenile literature. 4. Political science--
Encyclopedia, Juvenile. 5. United Nations--Encyclopedias,
Juvenile. I. Gall, Timothy L. II. Gall, Susan B.
G63.J86 1995
910'.3--dc20   95-36739
                                                             CIP

ISBN 0-7876-0741-X (set)
ISBN 0-7876-0742-8 (vol. 1)   ISBN 0-7876-0743-6 (vol. 2)   ISBN 0-7876-0744-4 (vol. 3)
ISBN 0-7876-0745-2 (vol. 4)   ISBN 0-7876-0746-0 (vol. 5)   ISBN 0-7876-0747-9 (vol. 6)
ISBN 0-7876-0748-7 (vol. 7)   ISBN 0-7876-0749-5 (vol. 8)   ISBN 0-7876-0750-9 (vol. 9)

 U•X•L is an imprint of Gale Research Inc.,
an International Thomson Publishing Company.
ITP logo is a trademark under license.

CONTENTS

Guide to Country Articles

Every country profile in this encyclopedia includes the same 35 headings. Also included in every profile is a map (showing the country and its location in the world), the country's flag and seal, and a table of data on the country. The country articles are organized alphabetically in nine volumes. A glossary of terms is included in each of the nine volumes. This glossary defines many of the specialized terms used throughout the encyclopedia. A keyword index to all nine volumes appears at the end of Volume 9.

Flag color symbols

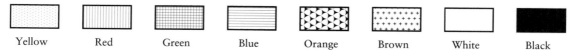

| Yellow | Red | Green | Blue | Orange | Brown | White | Black |

Alphabetical listing of sections

Agriculture	21	Income	18
Armed Forces	16	Industry	19
Bibliography	35	Judicial System	15
Climate	3	Labor	20
Domesticated Animals	22	Languages	9
Economy	17	Location and Size	1
Education	31	Media	32
Energy and Power	27	Migration	7
Environment	5	Mining	25
Ethnic Groups	8	Plants and Animals	4
Famous People	34	Political Parties	14
Fishing	23	Population	6
Foreign Trade	26	Religions	10
Forestry	24	Social Development	28
Government	13	Topography	2
Health	29	Tourism/Recreation	33
History	12	Transportation	11
Housing	30		

Sections listed numerically

1	Location and Size	19	Industry
2	Topography	20	Labor
3	Climate	21	Agriculture
4	Plants and Animals	22	Domesticated Animals
5	Environment	23	Fishing
6	Population	24	Forestry
7	Migration	25	Mining
8	Ethnic Groups	26	Foreign Trade
9	Languages	27	Energy and Power
10	Religions	28	Social Development
11	Transportation	29	Health
12	History	30	Housing
13	Government	31	Education
14	Political Parties	32	Media
15	Judicial System	33	Tourism/Recreation
16	Armed Forces	34	Famous People
17	Economy	35	Bibliography
18	Income		

Abbreviations and acronyms to know

GMT= Greenwich mean time. The prime, or Greenwich, meridian passes through Greenwich, England (near London), and marks the center of the initial time zone for the world. The standard time of all 24 time zones relate to Greenwich mean time. Every profile contains a map showing the country and its location in the world.

These abbreviations are used in references to famous people:
b.=born
d.=died
fl.=flourished (lived and worked)
r.=reigned (for kings, queens, and similar monarchs)

A dollar sign ($) stands for US$ unless otherwise indicated.

QATAR

State of Qatar
Dawlat Qatar

CAPITAL: Doha (Ad-Dawhah).

FLAG: Maroon with white serrated border at the hoist.

ANTHEM: *Qatar National Anthem.*

MONETARY UNIT: The Qatar riyal (QR) of 100 dirhams was introduced on 13 May 1973. There are coins of 1, 5, 10, 25, and 50 dirhams, and notes of 1, 5, 10, 50, 100, and 500 riyals. QR1 = $0.2747 (or $1 = QR3.64).

WEIGHTS AND MEASURES: The metric system is the legal standard, although some British measures are still in use.

HOLIDAYS: Emir's Succession Day, 22 February; Independence Day, 3 September. Muslim religious holidays include 'Id al-Fitr, 'Id al-'Adha', and Milad an-Nabi.

TIME: 3 PM = noon GMT.

1 LOCATION AND SIZE

The State of Qatar, a peninsula projecting northward into the Persian Gulf, has an area of 11,000 square kilometers (4,247 square miles), slightly smaller than the state of Connecticut. Qatar also includes a number of islands.

Qatar's capital city, Doha, is located on the Persian Gulf coast.

2 TOPOGRAPHY

The terrain is generally flat and sandy, rising gradually from the east to a central limestone plateau. Extensive salt flats at the base of the peninsula support the theory that Qatar was once an island.

3 CLIMATE

Qatar's summer is extremely hot. Mean temperatures in June are 42°C (108°F), dropping to 15°C (59°F) in winter. Rainfall is minimal.

4 PLANTS AND ANIMALS

Vegetation is generally sparse. Jerboas (desert rats) and an occasional fox are found. Birds include the flamingo, cormorant, osprey, kestrel, plover, and lark. Reptiles include monitors (large lizards) and land snakes.

5 ENVIRONMENT

Conservation of oil supplies, preservation of the natural wildlife heritage, and increasing the water supply through desalination (removing salt) are high on Qatar's environmental priority list. As of 1987, the hawksbill and green sea turtle were considered endangered species, and protection was afforded to a group of rare white oryx (type of antelope).

6 POPULATION

The 1990 population was estimated at 486,000. Average population density was 46 persons per square kilometer (119 per square mile). A population of 542,000 was projected for the year 2000.

7 MIGRATION

In 1993, the number of immigrant workers was about 85,000, including Pakistanis, Indians, and Iranians.

8 ETHNIC GROUPS

The native population (about 100,000) descends from Bedouin tribes. Pakistanis, Indians, Iranians, and Gulf and Palestinian Arabs are among the leading immigrant groups.

9 LANGUAGES

Arabic is the national language, but English is widely spoken, and Farsi is used by smaller groups in Doha.

10 RELIGIONS

Islam is the official religion of Qatar and is practiced by the great majority of the people. The Qataris are mainly Sunni Muslims of the Wahhabi sect. There are also small populations of Christians, Hindus, and Baha'is.

11 TRANSPORTATION

As of 1991 there were an estimated 1,500 kilometers (932 miles) of highways. In 1991, there were 115,149 passenger cars and 47,228 commercial vehicles registered. Doha International Airport, served by more than a dozen international airlines, serviced an estimated 1.1 million passengers in 1990. Qatar maintains modern deepwater ports at Doha and Umm Sa'id. In 1991, the merchant fleet consisted of 23 vessels with 474,000 gross registered tons.

12 HISTORY

The ath-Thani family, forebears of the present rulers, arrived in Qatar in the eighteenth century from what is now Sa'udi Arabia. During the same century, the al-Khalifah family, who currently rule Bahrain, arrived from Kuwait.

In 1868, the Perpetual Maritime Truce terminated the Bahraini claim to Qatar in exchange for a tribute payment (payment by one ruler of a nation to another to acknowledge submission). In 1872, however, Qatar fell under Ottoman occupation, and Turkish rule lasted until the outbreak of World War I. Qatar then established its independence. In 1916 it signed a treaty with the United Kingdom providing for British protection in exchange for a central role for the United Kingdom in Qatar's foreign affairs. High-quality oil was discovered at Dūkhan in 1940, but full-scale use of the discovery did not begin until 1949.

In January 1968, the United Kingdom announced its intention to withdraw its forces from the Persian Gulf states by the end of 1971. On 3 September 1971, the independent State of Qatar was declared. A new treaty of friendship and cooperation was signed with the United Kingdom, and Qatar was soon admitted to membership in the 20-member Arab League (also known as the League of Arab States) and the United Nations.

On 22 February 1972, Sheikh Khalifa bin Hamad ath-Thani seized power in a peaceful coup, deposing his cousin, Sheikh Ahmad. Since his accession, Sheikh Khalifa has pursued a vigorous program of economic and social reforms, including the transfer of royal income to the state.

Qatar's boundary disputes with Bahrain disrupted relations between the two countries in the mid-1980s. In 1992, there was a minor clash between Qatari and Sa'udi troops over a disputed border. That quarrel was resolved with a boundary agreement signed in December 1992.

13 GOVERNMENT

Qatar is a monarchy ruled by an emir (ruler of an Islamic country). A Basic Law, including a bill of rights, provides for a 9-member executive Council of Ministers (cabinet) and a 30-member legislative Advisory Council. No electoral system has been instituted, and no provisions for voting have been established.

14 POLITICAL PARTIES

There are no organized political parties.

15 JUDICIAL SYSTEM

The legal system is based on the Shari'ah (canonical Muslim law). The Basic Law of 1970, however, provided for the creation of an independent judiciary, including the Court of Appeal, which has final jurisdiction in civil and criminal matters; the Higher Criminal Court, which judges major criminal cases; the Lower Criminal

LOCATION: 26°23′ to 24°31′N; 50°43′ to 51°41′E. **BOUNDARY LENGTHS:** Persian Gulf coastline, 563 kilometers (350 miles); United Arab Emirates, 45 kilometers (28 miles); Sa'udi Arabia, 60 kilometers (38 miles). **TERRITORIAL SEA LIMIT:** 3 miles.

Court; the Civil Court; and the Labor Court, which judges claims involving employees and their employers.

16 ARMED FORCES

The Qatar security force consists of 6,000 army, 700 naval, and 800 air force personnel. Defense spending may be as high as $934 million.

17 ECONOMY

Until recent decades, the Qatar peninsula was an impoverished area with a scant living provided by pearl diving, fishing, and nomadic herding. In 1940, oil was discovered at Dūkhan, and since then it has dominated the Qatari economy. The recent discovery of a vast field of natural gas promises to add a new dimension to the economy.

18 INCOME

In 1992, Qatar's gross national product (GNP) was $8,511 million at current prices, or about $17,022 per person.

19 INDUSTRY

In 1989, the Qatar Fertilizer Company produced 714,000 tons of ammonia and 780,000 tons of urea; and the Qatar Petrochemical Company had an output of 295,000 tons of ethylene, 181,000 tons of polyethylene, and 52,00 tons of sulphur.

20 LABOR

About 70% of the economically active population is engaged in industry (largely oil-related), commerce, and services. Of the remainder, about 10% work in the

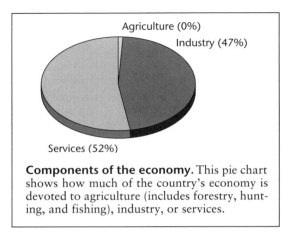

Agriculture (0%)
Industry (47%)
Services (52%)

Components of the economy. This pie chart shows how much of the country's economy is devoted to agriculture (includes forestry, hunting, and fishing), industry, or services.

agricultural sector and another 20% in government.

21 AGRICULTURE

In 1992, 6,000 tons of dates were produced, mostly for local consumption. Rice is also grown for the domestic market.

22 DOMESTICATED ANIMALS

According to 1992 estimates, Qatar had 11,000 head of cattle, 132,000 sheep, 103,000 goats, and 29,000 camels. Output in 1992 included about 5,000 tons of beef and mutton, and 4,000 chickens.

23 FISHING

Fish and shellfish production in 1991 totaled 8,136 tons, meeting more than 80% of local needs.

24 FORESTRY

There are no forests in Qatar.

25 MINING

Aside from petroleum and natural gas, Qatar has few exploitable minerals. In 1991, estimated production of cement was 336,000 tons; limestone, 850,000 tons; and sulfur, 53,000 tons.

26 FOREIGN TRADE

Crude oil exports were $3.74 billion in 1992. The main destinations of crude oil exports are Japan, Singapore, Brazil, and Taiwan. Principal non-oil products are fertilizers and basic metals.

Imports amounted to $2 billion in 1992. Main imports include food, industrial supplies, machinery, and transport equipment. The most important suppliers are Japan, the United Kingdom, the United States, Germany, Italy, and France.

27 ENERGY AND POWER

Qatar's substantial oil reserves, estimated at 3.7 billion barrels in 1993, dominate the country's economy. Production was 485,000 barrels per day in 1992. Qatar's gas reserves are estimated at 227 trillion cubic feet (6.4 trillion cubic meters); output was estimated at 330,000 million cubic feet (9,340 million cubic meters) in 1992. Qatar's electrical power production in 1991 reached 4.7 billion kilowatt hours.

28 SOCIAL DEVELOPMENT

The Ministry of Labor and Social Affairs provides help to orphans, widows, and other Qatari nationals in need of assistance. Both law and Islamic customs closely restrict the activities of Qatari women, who are largely limited to roles within the home.

29 HEALTH

In 1990 there were 2.9 hospital beds per 1,000 inhabitants. There is about 1 doctor per 665 people. In 1991, 100% of the population had access to health care services. Life expectancy is 72 years.

30 HOUSING

A "popular housing" scheme provides dwellings through interest-free loans and repayment on easy terms. Between 1988 and 1990, 100% of urban and 85% of rural dwellers had sanitation facilities.

31 EDUCATION

Literacy in 1982 stood at about 51%. Over the next decade, literacy increased to about 76%. As of 1991, there were 157 schools with 4,598 teachers and 48,785 pupils at the primary level. There are about 11 students per teacher in most primary schools. Secondary level schools had 3,724 teachers and 31,120 pupils.

The leading higher educational institution is the University of Qatar. Enrollment in all higher level institutions in 1989 was 6,469 pupils with 451 teaching staff.

32 MEDIA

There were an estimated 134,823 telephones in 1991, up from 29,000 in 1982. Radio transmissions include 12 hours per day of English-language service. Two television channels transmit mostly in Arabic. In 1991 there were 195,000 radios and 198,000 television sets.

Selected Social Indicators

These statistics are estimates for the period 1988 to 1993. For comparison purposes, data for the United States and averages for low-income countries and high-income countries are also given.

Indicator	Qatar	Low-income countries	High-income countries	United States
Per capita gross national product†	**$17,022**	$380	$23,680	$24,740
Population growth rate	**2.6%**	1.9%	0.6%	1.0%
Population growth rate in urban areas	**2.9%**	3.9%	0.8%	1.3%
Population per square kilometer of land	**46**	78	25	26
Life expectancy in years	**72**	62	77	76
Number of people per physician	**665**	>3,300	453	419
Number of pupils per teacher (primary school)	**11**	39	<18	20
Illiteracy rate (15 years and older)	**24%**	41%	<5%	<3%
Energy consumed per capita (kg of oil equivalent)	**16,196**	364	5,203	7,918

† The gross national product (GNP) is the total dollar value of all goods and services produced by a country in a year. The per capita GNP is calculated by dividing a country's GNP by its population. The World Bank defines low-income countries as those with a per capita GNP of $695 or less. High-income countries have a per capita GNP of $8,626 or more. Less than 14% of the world's 5.5 billion people live in high-income countries, while almost 60% live in low-income countries.

> = greater than   < = less than

Sources: World Bank, *Social Indicators of Development 1995,* Baltimore: Johns Hopkins University Press, 1995. Central Intelligence Agency, *World Fact Book,* Washington, D.C.: Government Printing Office, 1994.

Publications available in Qatar (with 1991 circulation figures) include the daily newspapers *Al-'Arab* (45,000), *Ar-Rayah* (70,000), *Al-Sharq* (25,000), *Al-Usbun* (15,000), and *Gulf Times* (30,000).

33 TOURISM AND RECREATION

Most visitors to Qatar are business travelers; a convention center managed by the Sheraton Hotel Group opened in 1982. Qatar's remoteness and a ban on alcohol have kept tourism weak. In 1991, there were 143,000 tourist arrivals at hotels. Rooms numbered 1,729, with a 29.3% occupancy rate.

34 FAMOUS QATARIS

Sheikh Khalifa bin Hamad ath-Thani (b.1932) became emir (leader of an Islamic state) of Qatar in 1972. His heir-apparent and minister of defense is Sheikh Hamad bin Khalifa ath-Thani (b.1948).

35 BIBLIOGRAPHY

Abu Saud, Abeer. *Qatari Women, Past and Present.* New York: Longman, 1984.

Zahlan, Rosemarie Said. *The Creation of Qatar.* London: Croom Helm, 1979.

ROMANIA

Romania

CAPITAL: Bucharest (Bucuresti).

FLAG: The national flag, adopted in 1965, is a tricolor of blue, yellow, and red vertical stripes.

ANTHEM: *Trei culori (Three Colors).*

MONETARY UNIT: The leu (L) is a paper currency of 100 bani. There are coins of 25 bani and 1, 3, 5, 10, 20, 50, and 100 lei, and notes of 10, 25, 50, 100, 200, 500, 1,000, and 5,000 lei. L1 = $0.0006 (or $1 = L1,650).

WEIGHTS AND MEASURES: The metric system is the legal standard.

HOLIDAYS: New Year's Day, 1 January; International Labor Day, 1–2 May; Liberation Day, 23 August; National Day, 1 December; Christmas Day, 25 December.

TIME: 2 PM = noon GMT.

1 LOCATION AND SIZE

Situated in eastern Europe, north of the Balkan Peninsula, Romania has a total area of 237,500 square kilometers (91,699 square miles), slightly smaller than the state of Oregon. Its total boundary length is 2,744 kilometers (1,702 miles). Romania's capital city, Bucharest, is located in the south central part of the country.

2 TOPOGRAPHY

The backbone of Romania is formed by the Carpathian Mountains, which swing southeastward and then westward through the country. The southern limb of this arc-shaped system is known as the Transylvanian Alps, whose compact, rugged peaks rise to 2,543 meters (8,343 feet) in Mt. Moldoveanu, Romania's highest mountain. On the eastern and southern fringes of the Carpathian arc are low plateaus and plains. On the inside of the Carpathian arc is the Transylvanian Basin, a hilly region divided by the wide, deep valleys of the Mures and Somes rivers. Between the lower Danube (Dunùrea) and the Black Sea is an eroded plateau with average elevations of 400–600 meters (1,310–1,970 feet).

An earthquake that struck Romania on 4 March 1977 left more than 34,000 families homeless. The shock, measuring 7.2 on the open-ended Richter scale, was the most severe in Europe since a series of shocks in October–November 1940, also in Romania.

3 CLIMATE

Romania is exposed to northerly cold winds in the winter and moderate westerly winds from the Atlantic Ocean in the summer. Average January temperatures range from –4°C to 0°C (25–32°F). During the summer, the highest temperatures are recorded in the Danube (Dunùrea) River Valley (24°C/75°F). Precipitation averages between 100 and 125 centimeters (about 40 and 50 inches) annually in the mountains and about 38 centimeters (15 inches) in the delta.

4 PLANTS AND ANIMALS

Natural vegetation consists mainly of grasslands in the northeast lowlands. The Carpathian mountains are covered with forests, with deciduous trees at lower elevations and conifers at altitudes above 1,070–1,220 meters (3,500–4,000 feet). Alpine meadows occupy the highest parts of the mountains.

Wild animals, including the Carpathian deer, wolves, hares, marten, brown bear, lynx, boar, and fox, are found in the Carpathians. Water birds flourish in the Mouths of the Danube (Dunùrea) River area, and sturgeon abound in the waters of the lower Danube (Dunùrea) River. Carp, bream, and pike populate the lakes.

5 ENVIRONMENT

Rapid industrialization since World War II has caused widespread water and air pollution, particularly in the region where oil is refined. Acid rain originating in Hungary and radioactivity from the 1986 nuclear power plant accident at Chernobyl, Ukraine, pose additional environmental problems.

Air pollution is heaviest in the nation's cities where industry produces hazardous levels of sulfur dioxide. Romania uses 59% of its available water to support farming, and 33% for industrial purposes.

In 1994, two of Romania's mammal species, 18 of its bird species, and 67 plant types were endangered. Romania has 12 national parks.

6 POPULATION

According to the 1992 census, Romania's total population was 22,810,035; the population was estimated at 23,777,056 in mid-1994. A population of 24,039,000 was projected for the year 2000. The average density as of 1995 was 96 persons per square kilometer (248 per square mile). Bucharest, the capital and principal city, had a population of 2,067,545 in 1992.

7 MIGRATION

Population shifts numbering in the millions occurred as a result of the two world wars and the 1947 Communist takeover. In the late 1970s and early 1980s, labor unrest caused some 120,000 ethnic Germans to leave Romania between 1978 and 1988. Some 40,000 ethnic Hungarians fled in 1987 alone. In 1990, 80,346 people left: 78% to Germany, and 9% to Hungary. Approximately 44,160 Romanians emigrated in 1991 and 31,152 in 1992. In 1992, 103,787 Romanians were given asylum in Germany, but in September of that year Germany returned 43,000 refugees, over half of whom were Gypsies.

LOCATION: 48°15′06″ to 43°37′07″N; 20°15′44″ to 29°41′24″E. **BOUNDARY LENGTHS:** Ukraine 531 kilometers (329 miles); Moldova, 450 kilometers (279 miles); Black Sea coastline, 234 kilometers (145 miles); Bulgaria, 608 kilometers (377 miles); Serbia, 476 kilometers (295 miles); Hungary, 445 kilometers (277 miles). **TERRITORIAL SEA LIMIT:** 12 miles.

8 ETHNIC GROUPS

Romanians constitute by far the majority group (89.5%, according to the 1992 census), but the population includes two important ethnic minorities: Hungarians (7.1% of the total population) and Germans (0.5%), both concentrated in the Transylvania region. The number of Gypsies, which is officially 401,087, may be as high as 2.3 million. Smaller minorities include Ukrainians, Turks, Russians, Serbs, Croats, Jews, Poles, Bulgarians, Czechs, Greeks, Armenians, Tatars, and Slovaks.

Since 1989 Gypsies have been targets of an organized campaign of violence throughout Romania.

9 LANGUAGES

Romanian is the official language. It is a Romance language derived from the Latin spoken in the Eastern Roman Empire. In the 2,000 years of its development, the language was also influenced by contacts with Slavonic, Albanian, Hungarian, Greek, and Turkish. Hungarian is spoken by a large percentage of the inhabitants of Transylvania.

10 RELIGIONS

The great majority of Romanians (estimated at 87% in 1993) are affiliated with the Romanian Orthodox Church.

There are 13 other legally recognized denominations. About 3.2 million persons belonged to the Roman Catholic Church in 1993. There were about 17,500 Jews in 1988. Other denominations include the Reformed (Calvinist) Church of Romania, with an estimated 600,000 members; the German-minority Evangelical Church of the Augsburg Confession, 150,000; and the Unitarian Church (mostly Hungarian), 60,000. There are small numbers of Baptists, Seventh-Day Adventists, Pentecostals, and Muslims.

11 TRANSPORTATION

The length of Romania's railroad network in 1991 was 10,860 kilometers (6,750 miles) of standard-gauge track and 45 kilometers (28 miles) of broad-gauge track. There were 72,799 kilometers (45,235 miles) of roads at the end of 1991.

In 1992, there were 1,593,029 passenger cars and 378,677 commercial vehicles in use.

Only the Danube (Dunùrea) and Prut rivers are suitable for inland navigation. The main Danube ports include Galaţi, Bràila, and Giurgiu. The Romanian merchant fleet is based in Constanţa, the nation's chief Black Sea port.

Romanian Air Transport (Transporturile Aeriene Române—TAROM) and Romanian Air Lines (Liniile Aeriene Române—LAR) are the primary air carriers. Otopeni International Airport, near Bucharest, is the nation's principal international air terminal.

12 HISTORY

Present-day Romania was known as the kingdom of Dacia at the end of the first millennium (1000 years) BC. It reached the highest stage of its development toward the end of the first century AD, but fell to the Roman Emperor Trajan in AD 106. The withdrawal of the Romans in AD 271 left the Romanians a partly Christianized Dacian-Roman people, speaking Latin and living in towns and villages built in the Roman style.

In the following centuries, as Dacia was overrun by waves of invaders, the early Romanians are believed to have sought refuge in the mountains or to have migrated south of the Danube (Dunùrea) River. There the Dacian-Romanians, assimilating Slavic influences, became known by the seventh century as Vlachs (Walachians). The Vlachs apparently remained independent of their neighbors, but came under Mongol domination in the thirteenth century.

The kingdoms of Walachia and Moldavia were established in the late thirteenth and early fourteenth centuries. Walachia came under Turkish control in 1476 and Moldavia in 1513; thirteen years later, Transylvania, which had been under Hungarian control since 1003, also passed into Turkish hands.

The tide of Ottoman (Turkish) domination began to ebb under Russian pressure in the second half of the seventeenth century. The Congress of Paris in 1856 ended the Crimean War (1853–56), in which Russia fought against Turkey, Britain, and France. As a result, the self-rule of the principalities of Walachia and Moldavia was guaranteed. Russia was forced to return the southernmost part of Bessarabia to Moldavia.

At the Congress of Berlin in 1878, Romania obtained full independence from Turkey but returned southern Bessarabia to Russia. Under the rule of Carol I, Romania developed into a modern political state.

In World War I (1914–18), Romania joined the Allies, and as a result acquired Bessarabia from Russia, Bukovina from Austria, and Transylvania from Hungary. The establishment of a greatly expanded Romania was confirmed in 1919–20 by the treaties of St. Germain, Trianon, and Neuilly. In 1930 Carol II, who had earlier renounced his right of succession, returned to Romania and established a royal dictatorship.

World War II

As economic conditions deteriorated, Fascism (a dictatorial and oppressive political philosophy) and anti-Semitism (discrimination toward Jews) became increasingly powerful. Carol II sought to satisfy both Germany and the Soviet Union. However, with Germany moving towards war with the Soviet Union, Romania would eventually have to pick sides. In 1940, Romania gave up territory to the Soviet Union, Hungary, and Bulgaria. In the same year, German troops entered Romania, and Romania joined the Axis (Germany and Italy) against the Allies in 1941 in World War II (1939–45).

Soviet forces drove into Romania in 1944. A coup (forced takeover) overthrew the wartime regime of General Ion Antonescu. Romania switched sides, joining the Allies against Germany. The Allies would eventually defeat Germany.

After World War II, a Communist-led coalition government under Premier Petru Groza was set up. On 30 December 1947, the Romanian People's Republic was proclaimed.

In international affairs, Romania followed a distinctly pro-Soviet line, becoming a member of the alliance of socialist countries known as the Council for Mutual Economic Assistance (CMEA) and the Warsaw Pact for mutual defense.

Romania Under Ceausescu

During the 1960s, however, and especially after the emergence of Nicolae Ceausescu as Communist Party and national leader,

Romanian citizens walk by the People's House in Bucharest. Former dictator Ceausescu built this huge palace during his ruling period. The building is open now to the Romanian public.

Romania followed a more independent course, increasing its trade with Western nations. In 1968, Romania denounced the intervention by the Soviet Union in Czechoslovakia. In December 1973, President Ceausescu visited Washington, where he signed a joint declaration on economic, industrial, and technical cooperation with the United States.

In contrast to some other East European countries, there was relatively little political dissent in Romania during the first 30 years of Communist rule. In 1977, however, about 35,000 miners in the Jiu Valley, west of Bucharest, went on strike because of economic grievances. In the early and mid-1980s, there were a number of work stoppages and strikes caused by food and energy shortages. In early 1987, Ceausescu indicated that Romania would not follow the reform trend initiated by Mikhail Gorbachev in the Soviet Union.

When the Securitate, Romania's dreaded secret police, attempted to deport Laszlo Toekes, a popular clergyman and leading spokesperson for the local Hungarians, thousands of people took to the streets. Troops were summoned, and two days of rioting ensued, during which several thousand citizens were killed.

Upon Ceausescu's return from a visit to Iran, he convened a mass rally at which he attempted to portray his opponents as advocating dictatorship. However, the rally turned into an anti-government demonstration, in which the army sided with the demonstrators. Ceausescu and his wife attempted to flee the country, but were detained, tried, and executed on 25 December 1989.

Political and Economic Reform

A hastily assembled Council of National Salvation took power. The Council's president was Ion Iliescu, a former secretary of the Communist Party. In February 1990, Iliescu agreed to ban the Communist Party, replacing the 145-member Council of National Salvation with a 241-member Council of National Unity, which included members of opposition parties, national minorities, and former political prisoners.

Parliamentary elections were held in May 1990 against a background of continued civil unrest, especially in the Hungarian west. Iliescu was elected president, with about 85% of the votes, and was reelected in the general elections of September 1992.

Continued political instability and the slow pace of economic change, have kept foreign investment quite low. Because of this, Romania has had to rely upon loans from Western sources, especially the International Monetary Fund (IMF), piling up foreign debt at the rate of about $1 billion a year.

Romanians began the 1990s as among the poorest people in Europe, and their economy has only grown worse. Inflation for 1992 was 210%, and more than 300% for 1993, while unemployment was almost 10%. Most significantly, production has fallen consistently, dropping 22% in 1993 against the preceding year.

13 GOVERNMENT

The Council for National Unity enacted a new constitution for Romania in November 1991, but the document is similar to Soviet-era constitutions.

The present government has a directly elected president, who is head of state. The legislature is made up of two houses, the Senate, with 143 seats, and the Assembly of Deputies, with 341 seats. Although the legislature has the formal duty to propose and pass laws, in practice the bodies have been weak; so that much of the country's function appears still to be conducted by decrees and orders, as in the past.

Romania is divided into 40 counties, as well as the municipality of Bucharest.

14 POLITICAL PARTIES

After the overthrow of Nicolae Ceausescu in 1989, some 80 political parties appeared. The dominant party in the 1990 elections proved to be the National Salvation Front (NSF). Due to disagreements over supporting its leader, Ion Iliescu, the NSF has since split into the Party of Social Democracy in Romania (PSDR), the Democratic National Salvation Front, and the Front for National Salvation.

The second-largest party in the 1992 elections was a coalition, called the Democratic Convention of Romania (DCR), which incorporated such parties as the National Peasant Party Christian Democratic, the Movement of Civic Alliance, the Party of Civic Alliance, Liberal Party '93, and the Social Democratic Party.

Smaller parties include the Magyar Democratic Union, the Agrarian Democratic Party, the National Unity Party, Democratic National Salvation Front, and others. There are two ultra-nationalist parties, the Party of Romanian National Unity and the Greater Romania Party, and the Communists have been reborn as the Socialist Labor Party.

15 JUDICIAL SYSTEM

The 1992 law on reorganization of the judiciary establishes a four-level legal system. The four levels consist of courts of first instance, intermediate appeallate level courts, a Supreme Court, and a Constitutional Court. The Constitutional Court has responsibility for judicial review of constitutional issues. The intermediate appeallate courts had not yet been established as of 1993 due to lack of personnel and funding.

16 ARMED FORCES

The revolution of 1989–90 destroyed the Communist armed forces and security establishment. Reorganization continues. In 1993, the armed forces numbered about 200,000 officers and men: 161,000 in the army, 19,000 in the navy, and 20,000 in the air force, which had 486 combat aircraft and 220 armed helicopters.

Military service is compulsory, and all able-bodied men at the age of 20 may be drafted into the armed forces for 12–18 months. Romania's budgeted defense

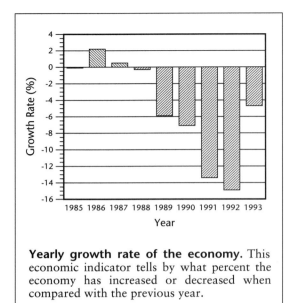

Yearly growth rate of the economy. This economic indicator tells by what percent the economy has increased or decreased when compared with the previous year.

expenditures in 1991 may have been as high as $1 billion.

17 ECONOMY

Before World War II, the economy was mainly agricultural. Under the Communists, industry was developed rapidly and surpassed agriculture in importance. Heavy industry, particularly machine-building, was emphasized as opposed to consumer goods. During the late 1970s and 1980s, the continued emphasis on industrial expansion and consequent neglect of agriculture led to food shortages and rationing.

The transition to a market economy has also proved extremely painful. In 1992, grain production was only two-thirds of the 1989 level, and in 1993 industrial output had fallen to 47% of the

1989 level. After price controls were lifted, the consumer price index soared to 32 times the 1969 level, more than tripling in 1992 and almost quadrupling in 1993. Unemployment, formerly almost nonexistent, reached 10.5% of the labor force in 1993.

18 INCOME

In 1992, the gross national product (GNP) was $24,865 million at current prices, or about $1,090 per person. For the period 1985–92 the average inflation rate was 30.9%, resulting in a real growth rate in per person GNP of −5.5%.

19 INDUSTRY

In 1993, industrial production was at only 47% of the 1989 level. The leading industries in 1993 were food and drink (14.7%), metallurgy (10.6%), electric power (10.9%), chemicals and synthetic fibers (8.9%), and machines and equipment (7.5%).

Steel production fell to 5,376,000 tons in 1992. Chemical production in 1992 included 372,000 tons of caustic soda, 572,000 tons of sulfuric acid, and 1,398,000 tons of chemical fertilizers. Other industrial products in 1992 were 74,000 automobiles, seagoing vessels, 481 million square meters of woven goods, 113,000 tons of artificial fibers, 36,000 tons of synthetic rubber, and 44,000,000 pairs of footwear.

20 LABOR

An estimated 10,785,800 people were employed in 1991, of whom 29.8% worked in agriculture (compared with

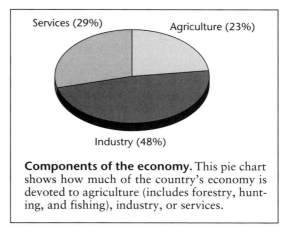

Services (29%)   Agriculture (23%)

Industry (48%)

Components of the economy. This pie chart shows how much of the country's economy is devoted to agriculture (includes forestry, hunting, and fishing), industry, or services.

57.1% as of a 1966 census); 35.2% in industry (including mining and public utilities); 14.8% in trade, transportation, and communications; 4.6% in construction; and 15.6% in other sectors. Officially, unemployment was at 8.4% in 1992.

21 AGRICULTURE

Although under Communism the emphasis had been on industrialization, Romania is still largely an agricultural country. Of the total land area, 64% was devoted to agriculture in 1991. The Land Reform of 1991 returned 80% of agricultural land to private ownership. Romania now has some 5,500,000 farmers on farms of up to 10 hectares (25 acres).

The 1992 production totals (in thousand of tons) for major crops included wheat and rye, 3,261; corn, 6,829; sugar beets, 2,875; and potatoes, 2,600. Romania is an important grape producer. Grape production in 1992 was 906,000 tons; wine output in 1992 reached 750,000 tons. The 1992 harvest also included

2,075,000 tons of fruit and 3,140,000 tons of vegetables.

22 DOMESTICATED ANIMALS

Since the overthrow of the Ceausescu regime in 1989, the government has begun returning grazing land to private ownership. In 1992 there were 4,355 head of cattle, 10,954 hogs, 13,879 sheep, and 106,000 poultry.

Output of livestock products for 1992 comprised 1,397,000 tons (live weight) of meat, including 846,000 tons of pork, 131,000 tons of beef, and 330,000 tons of poultry; 2.8 million tons of milk; 340,000 tons of eggs; and 10,000 tons of honey. Some 53,000 tons of wool were also produced.

23 FISHING

About 32% of the fish comes from the Danube (Dunùrea) floodlands and delta and from the Black Sea, and the rest is from fishing operations in the Atlantic. In 1991, the total catch was 124,933 tons.

24 FORESTRY

Forests, representing 29% of the total area of Romania, are found mainly in the Carpathian Mountains. Roundwood production in 1991 was 14,760,000 cubic meters. Between 1976 and 1985, 580,000 hectares (1,433,200 acres) were reforested.

25 MINING

Output of coal, mainly of the lignite variety, fell from 61.3 million tons in 1989 to 37.4 million tons in 1991. In addition to fuels, Romania mines iron ore (2 million

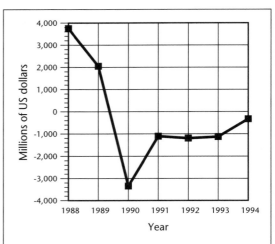

Yearly balance of trade measured in millions of US dollars. The balance of trade is the difference between what a country sells to other countries (its exports) and what it buys (its imports). If a country imports more than it exports, it has a negative balance of trade (a trade deficit). If exports exceed imports there is a positive balance of trade (a trade surplus).

tons in 1991), as well as copper, gold, silver, nonferrous metals, and uranium. Romania is a leading salt producer (6,500,000 tons in 1991—ninth in the world). Barite, bentonite, diatomite, feldspar, graphite, gypsum, kaolin, limestone, and other industrial minerals were also mined at about 60 deposits throughout the country.

26 FOREIGN TRADE

The major export categories in 1992 were minerals, metals, and fuels (30.4% in 1992); machinery and electric equipment (11%); textiles (10.6%), transport vehicles and equipment (10.4%), and chemicals and products (9.8%). Principal import cat-

Selected Social Indicators

These statistics are estimates for the period 1988 to 1993. For comparison purposes, data for the United States and averages for low-income countries and high-income countries are also given.

Indicator	Romania	Low-income countries	High-income countries	United States
Per capita gross national product†	$1,090	$380	$23,680	$24,740
Population growth rate	0.2%	1.9%	0.6%	1.0%
Population growth rate in urban areas	1.0%	3.9%	0.8%	1.3%
Population per square kilometer of land	96	78	25	26
Life expectancy in years	70	62	77	76
Number of people per physician	536	>3,300	453	419
Number of pupils per teacher (primary school)	17	39	<18	20
Illiteracy rate (15 years and older)	2%	41%	<5%	<3%
Energy consumed per capita (kg of oil equivalent)	1,785	364	5,203	7,918

† The gross national product (GNP) is the total dollar value of all goods and services produced by a country in a year. The per capita GNP is calculated by dividing a country's GNP by its population. The World Bank defines low-income countries as those with a per capita GNP of $695 or less. High-income countries have a per capita GNP of $8,626 or more. Less than 14% of the world's 5.5 billion people live in high-income countries, while almost 60% live in low-income countries.

> = greater than   < = less than

Sources: World Bank, *Social Indicators of Development 1995,* Baltimore: Johns Hopkins University Press, 1995. Central Intelligence Agency, *World Fact Book,* Washington, D.C.: Government Printing Office, 1994.

egories during the same year were minerals, metals, and fuels (36.6%); machinery and equipment (15.3%); textiles (9.5%); and chemicals (7%).

The republics of the former Soviet Union remain Romania's most important supplier and customer, followed by Germany. Trade with Eastern Europe has declined sharply. Trade with the European countries, especially Germany, has increased greatly, mostly because of Romania's need for advanced technology and equipment; it accounted for 32.6% of exports and 37.5% of imports in 1992.

27 ENERGY AND POWER

Electric power generation totaled 56.9 billion kilowatt hours in 1991. Before the 1989 revolution, there were frequent power shortages and strict energy rationing measures. Two nuclear reactors being built at Cernavoda, near Constanta, were scheduled to begin operation in 1985, but as of 1991, only one reactor was 50% completed.

In 1991, oil output was 6.8 million tons. Romania has had to import oil since 1979. A major fuel source is natural gas. Output fell from 37.4 billion cubic meters in 1987 to 24.4 billion cubic meters in

1991. Reserves of natural gas were estimated at 485 billion cubic meters in 1991.

28 SOCIAL DEVELOPMENT

Social security covers all wage earners. Workers' compensation and unemployment insurance are also provided. Families with children under age 16 receive family allowances and a birth grant for each child.

Legally, women have the same rights and privileges as men, although they face employment discrimination in Romania's harsh economic climate.

29 HEALTH

In 1989, Romania had 41,938 physicians. There is 1 doctor for every 536 people, and 8.9 hospital beds per 1,000 people. Through social insurance, all workers and employees, pensioners, and their dependents are covered for medical care and medicine. Total health care expenditures were $1,455 million.

Photo credit: AP/Wide World Photos

A Gypsy family is trying to make extra money selling snow flake flowers near one of the Bucharest revolution memorials.

The general health of the population has improved, with several previously serious diseases eliminated (recurrent fever, malaria) or greatly reduced (diphtheria, tuberculosis). Major causes of death in 1990 were communicable diseases, non-communicable diseases, and injuries. Average life expectancy in 1992 was 70 years.

30 HOUSING

Romanian housing suffered from the 1940 earthquake, war damage, neglect, and inadequate repair and maintenance after the war. An increase in the urban population caused by industrialization worsened the problem. Since 1987, construction of new housing units has fallen from 110,400 to 60,400 in 1989 and 28,000 in 1991. The total number of houses was 7,839,000 in 1991.

31 EDUCATION

Average adult illiteracy is about 2% (males, 1% and females, 4%). Since 1968, 10 years of education has been required. Romania's educational system consists of preschool (ages 3–6), primary school (grades 1–4), gymnasium (grades 5–8), lyceum or college in two steps (each consisting of 2 years), vocational schools, higher education, and postgraduate education.

In 1991, there were 13,730 general education schools (primary schools and gymnasiums), with 2,608,914 students and 153,187 teachers. The total number of secondary level students were 1,208,630 with 58,413 teachers. Over 44 institutions of higher learning had 164,507 students and 11,696 teachers in 1989. There are universities in Bucharest, Brasov, Craiova, Galati, Iasi, and Timisoara.

32 MEDIA

There were 12 AM and 5 FM radio broadcasting stations in 1990 and 13 TV stations. In 1991, there were 4,620,000 radios and 1,840,000 television sets. There were 2.3 million telephone subscribers in 1990. In 1991 there were 34 daily newspapers with a total annual circulation of 3,648,000. The leading daily newspapers (with 1991 circulation figures) are *Adevarul* (380,000); *Romania Libera* (300,000); *Libertatea* (250,000); and *Tineretul Liber* (200,000).

33 TOURISM AND RECREATION

The Carpathian Mountains, the Black Sea coast, and the Danube (Dunùrea) river region are being developed to attract and accommodate larger numbers of tourists. In 1991, visitor arrivals (including same day visitors) numbered 5,360,128; 40% came from the republics of the former Soviet Union, 15% from Bulgaria, and 14% from Hungary. There were 87,100 hotel rooms with 166,268 beds.

Major tourist attractions include many old cities and towns (Braşov, Constanţa, Sibiu, Sighişoara, Suceava, Timişoara, and others) and more than 120 health resorts and spas. Castle Dracula, the castle of Prince Vlad of Walachia, has been a tourist attraction since the 1970s.

Popular sports are soccer, skiing, hiking, swimming, canoeing, wrestling, handball, and gymnastics. Between 1965 and 1984, Romanian athletes won 176 Olympic medals.

34 FAMOUS ROMANIANS

Perhaps the most famous historical figure in what is now Romania was Vlad (1431?–76), a prince of Walachia who resisted the Turkish invasion and was called Tepes ("the impaler") and Dracula ("son of the devil") because of his practice of impaling his enemies on stakes; he was made into a vampire by Bram Stoker in his novel *Dracula*. Nicolae Ceausescu (1918–89) was head of state from 1967 to 1989.

The nation's greatest playwright was Ion Luca Caragiale (1852–1912). Playwright Eugène Ionesco (b.1912) settled in Paris in 1938. Romanian-born Elie Wiesel (b.1928), in the United States from 1956, is a writer on Jewish subjects, especially the Holocaust, and a winner of the Nobel Peace Prize in 1986. Romanian-born Mircea Eliade (1907–86) was a scholar in comparative religion and comparative mythology, in the United States from 1948.

Romanian-born Tristan Tzara (1896–1963), a literary and artistic critic who settled in Paris, was one of the founders of Dadaism. Sculpture was greatly advanced by Constantin Brâncusi (1876–1957). Famous musicians include violinist and composer Georges Enescu (1881–1955) and pianist Dinu Lipatti (1917–50). A prominent tennis player is Ilie Nastase (1946–94); gymnast Nadia Comaneci (b.1961) won three gold medals at the 1976 Olympics.

35 BIBLIOGRAPHY

Bachman, Ronald D., ed. *Romania: A Country Study*. 2d ed. Washington, D.C.: Library of Congress, 1991.

Carran, B. *Romania*. Chicago: Children's Press, 1988.

Castellan, Georges. *A History of the Romanians*. New York: Columbia University Press, 1989.

Fischer-Galati, Stephen A. *Twentieth Century Romania*. 2d ed. New York: Columbia University Press, 1991.

RUSSIA

Russian Federation

Rossiyskaya Federatsiya

CAPITAL: Moscow

FLAG: Equal horizontal bands of white (top), blue, and red.

ANTHEM: *Patriotic Song.*

MONETARY UNIT: The rouble (R) is a paper currency of 100 kopecks. There are coins of 1, 2, 3, 5, 10, 15, 20, and 50 kopecks and 1 rouble, and notes of 100, 200, 500, 1,000, 5,000, 10,000 and 50,000 roubles.

WEIGHTS AND MEASURES: The metric system is the legal standard.

HOLIDAYS: New Year's Day, 1–2 January; Christmas, 7 January; Women's Day, 8 March; Spring and Labor Day, 1–2 May; Victory Day, 9 May; State Sovereignty Day, 12 June; Socialist Revolution Day, 7 November.

TIME: 3 PM Moscow = noon GMT.

1 LOCATION AND SIZE

Russia is located in northeastern Europe and northern Asia. It is the largest country in the world—slightly more than 1.8 times the size of the United States, with a total area of 17,075,200 square kilometers (6,592,771 square miles). Russia's capital city, Moscow, is located in the eastern part of the country.

2 TOPOGRAPHY

The topography of Russia features a broad plain with low hills west of the Ural Mountains and vast coniferous forests and tundra in Siberia. Northernmost is the so-called arctic desert zone, which includes most of the islands of the Arctic Ocean and the seacoast of the Taymyr Peninsula (Poluostrov Taymyr).

South of the tundra is the vast forest zone, or taiga, covering half the country. Farther south is the forest-steppe zone, a narrow band bounded by the Great Russian plain and the West Siberian low country. There are uplands and mountains along the southern border region.

3 CLIMATE

Most of the country has a continental climate, with long, cold winters and brief summers. January temperatures range from 6°C (45°F), on the southeastern shore of the Black Sea, to as low as –71°C (–96°F) in northeastern Siberia. The lowest temperatures of any of the world's inhabited regions are found in Siberia. Precipitation varies from 53 centimeters (21 inches) at Moscow to between 20 and 25 centimeters (8–10 inches) in eastern Siberia.

4 PLANTS AND ANIMALS

Vegetation ranges from an almost complete absence of plant cover in the arctic desert zone to spruce, pine, fir, and cedar and some deciduous trees in the forested areas, and oak, birch, and aspen in the forest-steppe areas.

Birds and mammals associated with the sea (sea calf, seal, and walrus) are found in the northernmost part of the country. The arctic fox, reindeer, white hare, and lemming inhabit the tundra. Wildlife in the taiga (forest zone) includes moose, Russian bear, reindeer, lynx, sable, squirrel, and among the birds, capercaillie, hazelgrouse, owl, and woodpecker. European wild boar, deer, roe deer, red deer, mink, and marten are found in the broadleaf woods.

5 ENVIRONMENT

Decades of Soviet rule resulted in severe pollution of land, air, rivers, and seacoasts. Air pollution is especially bad in the Ural Mountains, where vast populations are exposed to hazardous emissions from metal-processing plants. About 75% of Russia's surface water is unsuitable for drinking. Lake Baikal (Ozero Baykal), the largest fresh water reservoir in the world, has been heavily polluted through agricultural and industrial development.

6 POPULATION

The population of Russia was 147,021,869 in 1989. It was estimated at 148,673,000 in 1993. The population was projected at 155,240,000 in 2000. The estimated population density in 1993 was 9 persons per square kilometer (23 per square mile). The biggest city is Moscow, the capital, with an estimated population at the beginning of 1990 of 8,801,000. The 1990 population of St. Petersburg (formerly Leningrad) was 4,468,000.

7 MIGRATION

During the period from 1979 to 1988, Russia (then part of the Union of Soviet Socialist Republics [USSR]) gained 1,747,040 people through net migration from other Soviet republics. In 1989, net migration was 83,000, and in 1991, 164,000. Since then, Russian refugees from other parts of the former Soviet Union have flooded the country—at least 1,500,000 in 1993 alone, according to one account. Official figures reported that 73,742 people emigrated from (left) Russia in 1991. Since Germany reports taking in 156,299 former Soviet Germans in 1991, emigration is probably underreported.

8 ETHNIC GROUPS

In 1989, 81.5% of the population was Russian. Minorities included Tartars, 3.8%, Ukrainians, 3%, and a wide variety of other peoples.

9 LANGUAGES

Russian is a member of the eastern group of Slavic languages. It is highly inflected, with nouns, pronouns, and adjectives having six grammatical cases. The language has been written in the Cyrillic alphabet of 33 letters since about 1000 AD. A variety of other Slavic, Finno–Ugric, Turkic, Mongol, Tungus, and Paleo–Asiatic languages are also spoken.

LOCATION: 60°0′N; 30°0′E. **BOUNDARY LENGTHS:** Total land boundary lengths, 20,139 kilometers (12,514 miles); Azerbaijan, 284 kilometers (177 miles); Belarus, 959 kilometers (596 miles); China (southeast), 3,605 kilometers (2,240 miles); China (south), 40 kilometers (25 miles); Estonia, 290 kilometers (180.2 miles); Finland, 1,313 kilometers (816 miles); Georgia, 723 kilometers (450 miles); Kazakhstan, 6,846 kilometers (4,254 miles); North Korea, 19 kilometers (12 miles); Latvia, 217 kilometers (135 miles); Lithuania, 227 kilometers (141 miles); Mongolia, 3,441 kilometers (2,138 miles); Norway, 167 kilometers (104 miles); Poland 432 kilometers (268 miles); Ukraine, 1,576 kilometers (980 miles); total coastline 37,653 kilometers (23,398 miles).

10 RELIGIONS

Russians are mostly Russian Orthodox, followed by Protestant and Roman Catholic, Jewish, and Moslem. Since the breakup of the former Soviet Union, thousands of churches have been reopened; freedom of religion was incorporated into the draft constitution of 1993.

11 TRANSPORTATION

Russia's transportation system is extensive, but much has fallen into disrepair.

Railroads have long been an important means of transportation in Russia. Railways in 1993 extended some 140,000 kilometers (87,000 miles). There were 879,100 kilometers (546,200 miles) of

Photo credit: Susan D. Rock

Pedestrians on St. Petersburg's busiest street, Nevsky Prospekt.

highways in 1990. Compared with other developed countries, Russia has few passenger cars on the road. Russia's ratio of population per car is four times that of Europe.

Marine transport has been important to Russia ever since the construction of St. Petersburg. Other important maritime ports include Novorossiysk, on the Black Sea; and Vladivostok and Nakhodka, both on the Sea of Japan. Major inland ports include Nizhniy Novgorod, Krasnoyarsk, Samara, Moscow, Rostov, and Volgograd. The merchant fleet consisted in 1991 of 842 ships. Almost three-fifths of the merchant fleet consists of cargo vessels.

12 HISTORY

The history of Russia is usually dated from the ninth century AD when a loose federation of the eastern Slavic tribes was achieved under the legendary Rurik, with its center at Kiev. By the eleventh century, it had united all the eastern Slavs. However, over the next two centuries, its dominance was eroded by other Slavic and non-Slavic groups.

Russia Under the Tsars

The Mongol conquest of Russia marked the fall of Kiev as a center of power. When Mongol power declined in the fourteenth and fifteenth centuries, it was Moscow that emerged as the new Russian capital.

In 1547, Grand Duke Ivan IV was crowned as the first "Tsar (ruler) of All the Russias."

In 1618, the first of the Romanovs was crowned tsar. In the seventeenth century, Russia expanded across Siberia to the Pacific Ocean. Under Peter I (r. 1682–1725), its power was extended to the Baltic Sea, and the Russian capital was moved from Moscow to St. Petersburg. The Russians expanded their territory farther into Europe and Asia during the eighteenth century.

The French Emperor, Napoleon, attacked Russia in 1812. Despite significant advances, he was forced to withdraw from Russia and retreat across Europe in 1814. By the end of the Napoleonic wars in 1815, Russia had acquired Bessarabia (Moldova), Finland, and eastern Poland. In the nineteenth century, Russia completed its conquest of the Caucasus, Central Asia, and what became its Maritime Province (Vladivostok).

Alexander II (r. 1855–81) emancipated (freed) the serfs (farm workers bound to a landowner) of Russia in 1861. He appeared to be embarking on a course of political reform involving elections when he was assassinated in 1881. His son, Alexander III (r. 1881–94) ended political reform efforts and returned to absolute rule.

By the reign of the last tsar, Nicholas II (r. 1894–1917), many had begun to oppose the powerful ruling tsars. A socialist revolutionary movement began in 1905. The Tsarist regime was weak from its defeat in the 1905 Russo-Japanese War. Revolutionary "soviets," or councils, seized power in parts of St. Petersburg and Moscow.

The government was able to appease (calm) the rebels by promising to form an elected Duma (parliament). Four Dumas were convened between 1906 and 1917. While the Third Duma made some progress in economic and social reform, the tsar and his ministers kept firm control over the government.

It was Russia's disastrous involvement in World War I that led to the end of the monarchy. In response to a number of defeats by German forces and continued dictatorship by the tsar, riots broke out in the major cities in March 1917. The tsar attempted to dissolve the Fourth Duma but failed. "Soviets" again rose up in Petrograd (formerly St. Petersburg) and Moscow. Nicholas II was forced to abdicate (give up his ruling power) on 15 March 1917.

The Russian Bolshevik Revolution

A temporary government, based on the old Fourth Duma, was declared, but its authority was challenged. On the night of 6 November 1917, the Bolsheviks (extreme socialists), led by Vladimir Lenin, seized control of St. Petersburg. When the newly elected Constituent Assembly convened on 18 January 1918, it was prevented from meeting by Bolshevik forces. Lenin and the Socialists took over the government.

After taking power, Lenin moved quickly to end Russia's involvement in World War I, signing a peace treaty in

March 1918, and the Bolsheviks moved the capital back to Moscow. From 1918 to 1921, they fought a civil war against a large number of opponents, whom they defeated. Except for Finland, Poland, the Baltic states, and Bessarabia (Moldova), Lenin's forces succeeded in regaining the territories they had given up in the treaty of 1918.

The Bolshevik regime was based on a Marxist-Leninist ideology. They sought to overthrow the rule of the aristocracy (ruling class) and the bourgeoisie (middle class) in favor of the proletariat (working class). Theoretically, power in the Communist Party (the Bolshevik's political group) was vested in an elected party congress and smaller elected groups. In truth, the top party leadership—Lenin and his colleagues—maintained dictatorial control.

The Stalin Era and World War II

After Lenin died on 21 January 1924, a power struggle among the top Communist leaders broke out. By 1928, Joseph Stalin had eliminated all his rivals and achieved full power. He ushered in a brutal period of political repression and forced industrialization and organization of agriculture into communes. Stalin's rule was especially harsh in the republics other than Russia. Scholars estimate that as many as 20 million Soviet citizens died during the 1928–38 period because of either famine or persecution by the state.

In August 1939, as World War II approached, The Soviets signed an agreement with Adolph Hitler's Nazis in Germany that divided Eastern Europe between them. But on 22 June 1941, Hitler's forces invaded the Soviet Union, advancing until they reached the outskirts of Moscow. With the help of massive arms shipments from the United States and other western European countries, Soviet forces were able to drive the Germans back.

By the end of World War II in May 1945, the Soviet Union had reconquered everything it lost to Germany in their 1939 pact. The Red Army (Communist Army) was in Eastern Europe. Stalin was able to establish satellite Communist regimes in Poland, Czechoslovakia, Hungary, Romania, Bulgaria, and East Germany.

Khrushchev and the Cold War

Stalin died in 1953 and the power struggle to succeed him was eventually won by Nikita Khrushchev. Khrushchev ended the terror of the Stalin years. During Khrushchev's era, the "Cold War" (tension between countries involving diplomatic tactics, but no military force) with the United States intensified.

The Soviet Union launched an unmanned satellite before the United States had done so. This action encouraged a competitive "Space Race" between the two countries, which drew public attention and government spending through the 1960s. However, basic features of Stalin's system (Communist Party monopoly on power; centralized economy allowing for little private initiative; limited opportunities for free expression) remained until Mikhail Gorbachev came to power in March 1985.

The Break Up of the Soviet Union

Gorbachev sought to reform the Communist system. However, he was unwilling to implement changes that would weaken Communist Party control. The intense division within the government on how to solve the problems faced by them led ultimately to the break up of the nation into its separate republics in 1991.

For the first time since 1917, free multiparty elections were held in Russia in March 1990. On 12 June 1991, the first elections to the Russian presidency were won by Boris Yeltsin. On 8 December 1991, Yeltsin, together with the leaders of Ukraine and Belarus, formed the nucleus of the Commonwealth of Independent States (CIS). This spelled the end of the Union of Soviet Socialist Republics (USSR) later that month. Like the other former Soviet republics, Russia had become an independent sovereign state.

In early 1992, Yeltsin sought to reform the economy, but prices rose rapidly and public opposition to his reforms grew. Much of Russian politics in 1993 consisted of bitter squabbling between Yeltsin and the legislature. No progress was made on drafting a new constitution to replace the much amended Soviet-era constitution that still governed Russia.

On 21 September 1993, Yeltsin dissolved the Supreme Soviet and introduced rule by presidential decree until new parliamentary elections and a referendum on his draft constitution could be held on 12

Photo credit: Susan D. Rock

Jazz musicians perform near Red Square, Moscow.

December. After anti-Yeltsin legislators barricaded themselves inside the parliament building, a state of emergency was declared for a brief period.

The referendum and parliamentary elections were held as planned. The electorate approved the new constitution, which called for a strong presidency. In the parliamentary elections, ten parties won seats. Both Communist and nationalist forces won representation.

13 GOVERNMENT

A new constitution for Russia was approved in a referendum held 12 December 1993. The constitution established a two-chamber legislature known as the Federal Assembly. The lower house (State Duma) consists of 450 elected deputies while the 178-member upper house (Council of the Federation) is composed of representatives of the provinces and autonomous republics that make up Russia. The president is elected separately for a five-year term.

The president appoints the cabinet members and other top government posts subject to confirmation by the legislature. The president may declare war or a state of emergency on his own authority. Impeachment of the president is provided for in the constitution, but is very difficult.

The State Duma has jurisdiction over the budget and economic policy. The Council has jurisdiction over issues affecting the provinces and autonomous republics, including border changes and the use of force within the Russian Federation.

14 POLITICAL PARTIES

In the elections to the State Duma held 12 December 1993, the party to receive the largest number of seats (76) was the radical reformist Russia's Choice led by Yeltsin's former acting prime minister, Egor Gaidar. The centrist New Regional Policy group won 65. Vladimir Zhirinovsky's ultra-nationalist, anti-democratic Liberal Democratic Party won 63. The pro-Communist Agrarian Party won 55 seats, while the Communist Party of the Russian Federation won 45. Six other parties or blocs (some of which were also formed after the election) won between 12 and 30 seats each.

15 JUDICIAL SYSTEM

A Constitutional Court has been established to rule on disputes between the executive and legislative branches. The Supreme Court reviews charges brought against the executive and legislative branches.

16 ARMED FORCES

The Russian army has 1.4 million soldiers, of whom perhaps one million are draftees. The 400,000 officers and non-commissioned officers are highly skilled military personnel. The air force claims 300,000 airmen (about half draftees) of whom 25,000 are assigned to the strategic nuclear air forces. The Russian navy of 320,000 retains the vast majority of the combat capability of the former Soviet navy. It remains organized in four major fleets with regional and global missions. The fleets are stationed in Arctic Russia, four Baltic bases, three Black Sea bases, and Vladivostok.

Russia remains the world's second most formidable nation, when it comes to nuclear weapons, after the United States. The Strategic Rocket Forces (144,000) control 1,400 silo-based and mobile intercontinental ballistic missiles (ICBMs) with 6,620 warheads, and provide ground defense forces to defend ICBM launch sites and warhead storage facilities.

In addition to troops remaining in Europe and Commonwealth of Independent States (CIS) member nations, Russia maintains major military missions or units in Cuba, Algeria, Libya, India, Cambodia, Syria, Yemen, Mongolia, and Vietnam.

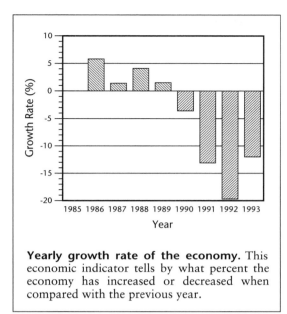

Yearly growth rate of the economy. This economic indicator tells by what percent the economy has increased or decreased when compared with the previous year.

Russian units participate in seven separate peacekeeping missions, five sponsored by the United Nations. Russia has assumed the treaty responsibilities of the former Soviet Union to reduce its strategic arsenal and conventional forces in Europe.

17 ECONOMY

Russia's economic situation has deteriorated steadily since the break-up of the Soviet Union in 1991. It is undergoing a transformation from a centrally planned economy to a market-oriented one, with limited public ownership. There is a serious demand for goods that is not being met, especially for consumer goods. By the end of 1993, unofficial figures placed unemployment at over 10%.

18 INCOME

In 1992, the gross national product (GNP) was $397,786 million at current prices, or about $2,688 per person. For the period 1985–92 the average inflation rate was 13.6%.

19 INDUSTRY

Major manufacturing industries include crude steel, cars and trucks, aircraft, chemicals (including fertilizers), plastics, cement and other building materials, paper, television sets, and appliances. Military production, which dominated industrial output in the former Soviet Union, is being replaced by other types of manufacturing, often consumer goods and food processing.

20 LABOR

In 1993, the labor force was estimated at 75 million, of which production and economic services employees accounted for 83.9%, and government workers 16.1%. Women accounted for about 50% of the work force, but were 90% of the unemployed in 1992. As reforms progress, the role of unions is expected to grow as a reaction to widespread unemployment.

21 AGRICULTURE

In 1992, gross agricultural output dropped by 8% (mostly from a decline in livestock production), whereas grain production grew by 20% due to favorable weather. The 1992 harvest included (in 1,000 tons): wheat, 46,000; potatoes, 37,800, barley, 25,500; sugar beets, 25,500; rye, 13,900; vegetables and melons, 12,500; oats, 11,500; dry peas,

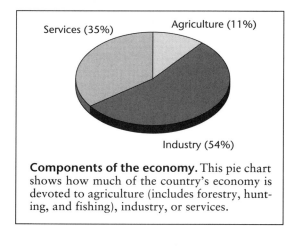

Services (35%)　　Agriculture (11%)

Industry (54%)

Components of the economy. This pie chart shows how much of the country's economy is devoted to agriculture (includes forestry, hunting, and fishing), industry, or services.

3,800; sunflower seeds, 3,070; soybeans, 50; and grapes, 520.

22 DOMESTICATED ANIMALS

Russia's pastures occupy about the same amount of land as those of all the other nations of Europe combined. As of 1992, the livestock population included: cattle, 54,677,000; sheep, 52,535,000; pigs, 35,384,000; goats, 2,765,000; horses, 2,610,000; chickens, 628,000,000; and turkeys, 24,000,000.

In 1992, livestock production dropped sharply, causing gross agricultural output to fall by about 8%. The 1992 meat production amounts included (in 1,000 tons): beef, 3,500; pork, 2,700; mutton, 280; and poultry, 1,577. Milk production in 1992 totaled 46.9 million tons, and egg production amounted to 2.4 million tons in 1992.

23 FISHING

Russia's fishing fleet is second only to Japan's in size. The total catch in 1992 was 5.4 million tons, down 22% from 1991. Exports of fish in 1991 accounted for 2.4% of total exports. Overfishing and pollution of territorial waters have forced fishermen farther away from traditional fishing waters. While fish exports in 1992 totaled 2.5 million tons, exports in 1993 were expected to reach only 1.5 million tons.

24 FORESTRY

Russia's forested areas are vast. In the early 1980s an estimated 760 million hectares (1,878 million acres) were forested—an area about as large as the total land area of Australia. The forests in Russia are 80% coniferous, consisting mainly of spruce, fir, larch, and pine in sub-arctic areas. Deciduous trees (oak, ash, maple, elm) grow farther south. From 1917 to 1980, the area covered by forests declined by only about 16%.

As of April 1993, early estimates predicted production declines of 23% for commercial timber, 27% for sawn timber, 25% for plywood, 29% for particleboard, 23% for paper, and 33% for paperboard from 1992 levels.

25 MINING

Russia has plentiful and varied mineral resources. Mining activities are concentrated near the Arctic Circle (nickel, cobalt, phosphate, uranium, gold, tin, and mercury); in the Ural Mountains region (titanium, vanadium, nickel-cobalt, soda ash, asbestos, magnesite, vermiculite, talc, bauxite, copper, bismuth, beryllium, lead, zinc, and iron ore); and in Siberia (tungsten, molybdenum, fluorospar, mica,

Photo credit: Susan D. Rock

Lining up for snacks at a kiosk in a St. Petersburg park.

asbestos, diamond, talc, iron ore, gold, tin, lead, and zinc).

Iron alloy production in 1991 amounted to 1.7 million tons. Russian gold production was estimated at 147,000 kilograms that year. Iron ore production was 90.9 million tons in 1991.

26 FOREIGN TRADE

Principal exports have traditionally been oil, gas, minerals, military equipment and weapons, gold, shipping, and transport services. Trade with other former republics of the Soviet Union accounted for 51% of imports and 68% of exports. Almost half of Russia's trade in 1992 was with the Baltics (Lithuania, Latvia, Estonia) and Eastern Europe, followed by Germany, France, Spain, and Switzerland.

27 ENERGY AND POWER

Russia possesses enormous reserves of oil, natural gas, and coal. Oil production was 396 million tons in 1992 (about 8 million barrels per day), when Russia ranked third in total oil production, after Sa'udi Arabia and the United States. At the end of 1992, Russia had some 6.6 billion tons (48.4 billion barrels) of proven oil reserves.

In 1992, Russia produced 604 billion cubic meters (21.3 trillion cubic feet) of natural gas. Proven reserves at the end of 1992 totaled 1,681.2 trillion cubic feet (47.6 trillion cubic meters), or 34.4% of the world's total reserves.

Coal production in 1993 was estimated at 278 million tons. In 1992, natural gas contributed 48% to Russia's primary energy consumption; oil, 27%; coal, 20%; nuclear energy, 3.3%; and hydroelectric power, 1.7%.

28 SOCIAL DEVELOPMENT

The Russian Republic had enacted its own pension legislation in November 1990, before the collapse of the Soviet Union. While it followed the Soviet Union model in many respects, it linked pensions to a "minimum subsistence" figure instead of to the minimum wage. However, rapid price increases in 1992 pressured the Yeltsin government into once again tying pensions to the minimum wage.

Selected Social Indicators

These statistics are estimates for the period 1988 to 1993. For comparison purposes, data for the United States and averages for low-income countries and high-income countries are also given.

Indicator	Russia	Low-income countries	High-income countries	United States
Per capita gross national product†	$2,688	$380	$23,680	$24,740
Population growth rate	0.6%	1.9%	0.6%	1.0%
Population growth rate in urban areas	1.1%	3.9%	0.8%	1.3%
Population per square kilometer of land	9	78	25	26
Life expectancy in years	67	62	77	76
Number of people per physician	222	>3,300	453	419
Number of pupils per teacher (primary school)	n.a.	39	<18	20
Illiteracy rate (15 years and older)	2%	41%	<5%	<3%
Energy consumed per capita (kg of oil equivalent)	4,411	364	5,203	7,918

† The gross national product (GNP) is the total dollar value of all goods and services produced by a country in a year. The per capita GNP is calculated by dividing a country's GNP by its population. The World Bank defines low-income countries as those with a per capita GNP of $695 or less. High-income countries have a per capita GNP of $8,626 or more. Less than 14% of the world's 5.5 billion people live in high-income countries, while almost 60% live in low-income countries.

n.a. = data not available   > = greater than   < = less than

Sources: World Bank, *Social Indicators of Development 1995,* Baltimore: Johns Hopkins University Press, 1995. Central Intelligence Agency, *World Fact Book,* Washington, D.C.: Government Printing Office, 1994.

29 HEALTH

In 1992, there were 5 physicians per 1,000 people, or about 1 doctor for 222 people. In 1991, there were 13.8 hospital beds per 1,000 population. Average life expectancy is 67 years.

30 HOUSING

In 1989, 46.7% of all privately owned urban housing had running water, 36.3% had central heating, and 17.2% had hot water. In 1990, Russia had 16.4 square meters of housing space per capita and, as of 1 January 1991, 9,456,000 households (25.6%) were on waiting lists for urban housing.

31 EDUCATION

The illiteracy rate is estimated at about 2%, with males at 0.4%, and females at 2.1%. Education, mostly free and state funded, is also compulsory for 10 years. The state provides a stipend for higher education. There were 42 universities with a total enrollment of 2,824,500 students in 1990–91 school year.

32 MEDIA

Broadcasting is overseen by All-Russian State Television and Radio (Ostankino). There are 1,050 radio stations and 310 television stations. Russia has about 36 million telephone lines.

Photo credit: International Labour Office

Kindergarten children go for a walk with their teacher.

In 1991 there were over 720 daily newspapers with a total circulation of almost 134,000,000. In 1992, Russia's major newspapers, all published in Moscow, were (with circulation figures): *Komsomalskaya Pravda* (3,400,000); *Trud* (3,100,000); *Krasnaya Zvezda* (2,500,000); *Moskovski Komsomolyets* (1,200,000); and *Selskaya Zhizn* (1,200,000).

33 TOURISM AND RECREATION

In September 1992, Russia lifted its travel restrictions on foreigners, opening the entire country to visitors and tourists. Tourist attractions in Moscow include the Kremlin, monasteries and churches, museums, and other cultural attractions, including opera and ballet at the world-famous Bolshoi Theater. Nearby tourist destinations include St. Petersburg (formerly Leningrad) and Kiev.

34 FAMOUS RUSSIANS

Notable among the rulers of pre-revolutionary Russia were Ivan III (the Great, 1440–1505), who established Moscow as a sovereign state; Peter I (the Great, 1672–1725), a key figure in the modernization of Russia; and Alexander II (1818–81), a social reformer who freed the serfs. The founder of the Soviet state was Lenin (Vladimir Illyich Ulyanov, 1870–1924).

Russia's greatest poet Aleksandr Pushkin (1799–1837) was also a brilliant writer of prose. Ivan Turgenev (1818–83) is noted for his sketches, short stories, and the novel *Fathers and Sons*. Fyodor Dostoyevsky (1821–81) wrote outstanding psychological novels (*Crime and Punishment, The Brothers Karamazov).* Leo (Lev) Tolstoy (1828–1910), perhaps the greatest Russian novelist (*War and Peace, Anna Karenina*), also wrote plays, essays and short stories. The playwright and short-story writer Anton Chekhov (1860–1904) was the greatest Russian writer of the late 19th century. The novels, stories, and plays of Maxim Gorky (Aleksey Peshkov, 1868–1936) bridged the tsarist and Soviet periods.

Great Russian composers include Modest Mussorgsky (1839–81), Pyotr Ilyich Tchaikovsky (1840–93), Nikolay Rimsky-Korsakov (1844–1908), Sergei Rachmaninov (1873–1943), Igor Stravinsky (1882–1971), Sergei Prokofiev (1891–1953), and Dmitry Shostakovich (1906–75).

Outstanding figures in the ballet are the impresario Sergey Diaghilev (1872–1929) and the ballet dancers Vaslav Nijinsky (1890–1950) and Anna Pavlova (1881–1931). Famous figures in the theater include Konstantin Stanislavsky (Alekseyev, 1863–1938), director and actor. The most famous film director is Sergey Eisenstein (1898–1948).

Varfolomey (Bartolomeo Francesco) Rastrelli (1700–71) designed many of the most beautiful buildings in St. Petersburg. Modern Russian artists whose work is internationally important include the Suprematist painters Kasimir Malevich (1878–1935) and El (Lazar) Lissitzky (1890–1941). Famous Russian-born artists who left their native country to work abroad include the painters Vasily Kandinsky (1866–1944) and Marc Chagall (1897–1985).

Prominent Russian scientists of the 19th and 20th centuries included the chemist Dmitry Ivanovich Mendeleyev (1834–1907), inventor of the periodic table; Ivan Petrovich Pavlov (1849–1936), expert on the human and animal nervous systems, who received the Nobel Prize in 1904; and Konstantin Eduardovich Tsiolkovsky (1857–1935), scientist and inventor in the fields of rocket engines, interplanetary travel, and aerodynamics.

35 BIBLIOGRAPHY

Belt, Don. "The World's Great Lake." *National Geographic,* June 1992, 2–39.

Clark, Miles. "A Russian Voyage." *National Geographic,* June 1994, 114–138.

Edwards, Mike. "A Broken Empire." *National Geographic,* March 1993, 4–53.

———. "Mother Russia on a New Course." *National Geographic,* February 1991, 2–38.

———. "Siberia: In from the Cold." *National Geographic,* March 1990, 2–39.

Nagel, Rob, and Anne Commire. "Catherine II, the Great." In *World Leaders, People Who Shaped the World.* Volume II: Europe. Detroit: U*X*L, 1994.

———. "Vladimir Lenin." In *World Leaders, People Who Shaped the World.* Volume II: Europe. Detroit: U*X*L, 1994.

Quigley, Howard B. "Saving Siberia's Tigers." *National Geographic,* July 1993, 38–47.

Resnick, A. *The Union of Soviet Socialist Republics: A Survey from 1917 to 1991.* Chicago: Children's Press, 1992.

Yeltsin, Boris Nikolayevich. *The Struggle for Russia.* New York: Times Books, 1994.

RWANDA

Republic of Rwanda
Republika y'u Rwanda

CAPITAL: Kigali.

FLAG: The national flag is a tricolor of red, yellow, and green vertical stripes. The letter "R" in black, appears in the center of the yellow stripe.

ANTHEM: Rwanda Rwacu (Our Rwanda).

MONETARY UNIT: The Rwanda franc (RFr) is a paper currency. There are coins of 1, 5, 10, 20, and 50 francs and notes of 100, 500, 1,000, and 5,000 francs. RFr1 = $0.0135 (or $1 = RFr74.086).

WEIGHTS AND MEASURES: The metric system is the legal standard.

HOLIDAYS: New Year's Day, 1 January; Democracy Day, 28 January; Labor Day, 1 May; Independence Day, 1 July; Peace and National Unity Day, 5 July; Assumption, 15 August; Anniversary of 1961 Referendum, 25 September; Armed Forces' Day, 26 October; All Saints' Day, 1 November; Christmas, 25 December. Movable religious holidays include Easter Monday, Ascension, and Pentecost Monday.

TIME: 2 PM = noon GMT.

1 LOCATION AND SIZE

Rwanda, a landlocked country in east-central Africa, has an area of 26,340 square kilometers (10,170 square miles), slightly smaller than the state of Maryland. It has a total boundary length of 893 kilometers (555 miles). Rwanda's capital city, Kigali, is located near the center of the country.

2 TOPOGRAPHY

Rwanda lies on the great East African plateau. To the west, the land drops sharply to Lake Kivu in the Great Rift Valley; to the east, the land falls gradually across the central plateau to the swamps and lakes on the country's eastern border. The highest peak, Mt. Karisimbi at 4,507 meters (14,787 feet), is snowcapped. The Kagera River forms much of Rwanda's eastern border.

3 CLIMATE

The high altitude of Rwanda provides the country with a pleasant tropical highland climate. At Kigali, on the central plateau, the average temperature is 20°C (68°F). A long rainy season lasts from February to May and a short one from November through December. Annual rainfall averages as much as 160 centimeters (63 inches) in the west.

4 PLANTS AND ANIMALS

Rwanda is one of the most eroded and deforested countries in all of tropical Africa; there is little forest left. The most common trees are eucalyptus, acacia, and oil palm. Wildlife includes elephants, hippopotamuses, buffalo, cheetahs, lions, zebras, leopards, monkeys, gorillas, hyena,

Photo credit: Cynthia Bassett

Rwandan people gather to watch native dances.

wild boar, antelope, crocodiles, partridges, ducks, geese, quail, and snipe.

5 ENVIRONMENT

The war in Rwanda, beginning in 1990, has damaged the environment. Soil erosion and overgrazing are also serious problems, and the remaining forested area has been reduced by uncontrolled cutting for fuel. Sixteen percent of the nation's city dwellers and 33% of the rural people do not have safe water.

In northeastern Rwanda the beautiful Kagera National Park is a game reserve, sheltering many types of wildlife. Rwanda is one of the last existing habitats of the mountain gorilla, which numbered 280 in 1986, up from 250 five years earlier. As of 1994, 11 of the nation's mammal species and 7 of its bird species were threatened with extinction.

6 POPULATION

Rwanda is the most densely populated country on the African continent. In 1994, it had an estimated population of 8,846,620, according to the United States Census Bureau. The estimated population density is 279 persons per square kilometer (722 per square mile). A population of 9,766,000 was projected by the United Nations for the year 2000. Kigali, the capital and largest city, has grown rapidly, from 15,000 in 1969 to 219,000 in 1990.

RWANDA

7 MIGRATION

The Hutu and Tutsi are ethnic groups in Rwanda. Their political quarrels have caused numerous Tutsi to flee their homeland. Many of them have gone to Burundi, where there were 245,600 refugees at the end of 1992. At the end of 1992, there were some 85,800 Rwandan refugees in Uganda; 50,900 in Zaire; and 50,000 in Tanzania (mostly Tutsis). At the same time Rwanda was harboring 25,200 refugees from Burundi, mainly Hutus. Renewed violence in 1994 spawned a new exodus from Rwanda. As many as 2.2 million refugees fled the county, many to Zaire.

8 ETHNIC GROUPS

The population is about 85% Hutu. The Hutu are a Bantu-speaking people who are traditionally farmers. The Tutsi, a warrior people, once made up about 14% of the total population, but many have fled into neighboring territories for refuge. There are also some Twa, a Pygmy tribe of hunters, as well as small numbers of Asians and Europeans.

9 LANGUAGES

The main language is Kinyarwanda, a member of the Bantu language family. The official languages are Kinyarwanda and French.

10 RELIGIONS

In 1988, an estimated 74% of Rwandans were Christian, and in 1993 an estimated 44% were Roman Catholic. As much as one-half the population follows traditional African religion as well. Muslims made up

LOCATION: 1°4′ to 2°50′s; 28°51′ to 30°55′E. BOUNDARY LENGTHS: Uganda, 169 kilometers (105 miles); Tanzania, 217 kilometers (135 miles); Burundi, 290 kilometers (180 miles); Zaire, 217 kilometers (135 miles).

approximately 8%, and there were also small groups of Baha'is and Hindus.

11 TRANSPORTATION

In 1991, Rwanda had 4,885 kilometers (3,036 miles) of road, but only about 9% were paved. In 1992, there were 7,868 automobiles. Rwanda has no railroads. There is ship traffic on Lake Kivu to Zaire from Gisenyi, Kibuye, and Cyangugu. There are international airports at Kigali and at Kamembe. In 1991, Air Rwanda flew 10,100 passengers some 900,000 kilometers (559,000 miles).

12 HISTORY

Stone Age habitation, as far back as 35,000 years, has been reported in the region now called Rwanda. Between the seventh and tenth centuries AD, the Bantu-speaking Hutu people, who followed a settled, agricultural way of life, arrived, probably from the region of the Congo River basin. Between the fourteenth and fifteenth centuries, the Tutsi, herdsmen of Nilotic (Nile River) origin, entered from the north.

At the end of the fifteenth century, the Tutsi formed a state, and, in the sixteenth century, began a process of expansion that continued into the late nineteenth century. The ownership of land and cattle was gradually transferred from the Hutu tribes to the Tutsi, and a feudal system was created between the two peoples. The ownership of cattle was controlled by the Tutsi, who regulated their use by the Hutu. The Hutu did the farming and grew the food, but had no part in government, while the Tutsi did no manual labor.

In 1871, explorers Sir Henry Morton Stanley and David Livingstone landed at Bujumbura (now the capital of neighboring Burundi) and explored the Ruzizi River region. After the Berlin Conference of 1884–85, the German zone of influence in East Africa was extended to include Rwanda and Burundi. The mwami, (Tutsi ruler), submitted to German rule without resistance in 1899. The Germans administered the territory until their defeat in World War I (1914–18). During the war the area was occupied by Belgium. After the war, the League of Nations awarded Belgium a mandate to rule the region, and in 1946, Ruanda-Urundi (present-day Rwanda and Burundi) became a United Nations trust territory.

Ethnic Conflict and Independence

Liberation movements in other African countries after World War II (1939–45) led the Hutu to demand social and political equality with the Tutsis. In November 1959, a Hutu revolution began, continuing sporadically for the next few years. Many Tutsi either were killed or fled to neighboring territories. On 27 June 1962, the United Nations General Assembly passed a resolution providing for the independent states of Rwanda and Burundi, and on 1 July, Rwanda became an independent country. In December 1963, following an unsuccessful invasion by Tutsi refugees from Burundi, a massacre of the remaining resident Tutsi population caused the death of an estimated 12,000 Tutsi and more fled into neighboring countries.

In January 1964, the economic union that had existed between Burundi and Rwanda was terminated. This resulted in severe economic difficulties and internal unrest. The unstable political and economic situation led the Rwandan army to overthrow the government in July 1973. Major General Juvénal Habyarimana assumed the presidency. In 1975, his military regime created a one-party state under the National Revolutionary Movement for Development (MRND). A system of ethnic quotas was introduced that formally limited the Tutsi minority to 14% of the positions in the workplace and in the schools.

Popular discontent grew through the 1980s. In October 1990, over 1,000 Tutsi refugees invaded Rwanda from Uganda; government forces retaliated by massacring Tutsi. In spite of cease-fires negotiated between the government and Tutsi rebels in 1991 and 1992, tensions remained high.

On the political front, Habyarimana liberalized his government in the early 1990s. A power sharing agreement between Hutus and Tutsis was signed in Tanzania in January 1993 but failed to end the fighting. The United Nations Security Council authorized a peacekeeping force, but unrest continued.

In 1994, a total breakdown occurred. In February, the minister of public works was assassinated. In April, a rocket downed an airplane carrying the presidents of Rwanda and Burundi. The president was a Hutu. They were returning to Kigali from regional peace talks in Tanzania. All aboard were killed. From that point on, Rwanda became a killing field, as members of the Rwandan army and other bands of armed Hutu set out to murder all the Tutsi they could find. Hundreds of thousands, mostly Tutsi, were killed.

In July of 1994, Tutsi rebels gained control of the government, prompting Hutus to flee to refugee camps in Tanzania, Zaire, and Burundi. The estimated 2.2 million refugees are afraid to return to Rwanda for fear of reprisals by the now Tutsi dominated government.

13 GOVERNMENT

A new constitution adopted on 18 June 1991 legalized independent parties. The executive branch consisted of an elected president and a prime minister and a Council of Ministers chosen from the legislature. The single-chamber legislature continued the name, National Development Council.

14 POLITICAL PARTIES

The Tutsi-based Rwandan Patriotic Front (RPF), an army once in exile, is now firmly entrenched within Rwanda.

The estimated 2.2 million Hutu refugees have formed the Return and Democracy in Rwanda (RDR) organization which operates in the refugee camps in Zaire and Tanzania. It advocates a safe return of the Hutu refugees to Rwanda.

15 JUDICIAL SYSTEM

There are district courts, provincial courts, and courts of appeal. Also functioning are a constitutional court, a court of accounts, which examines public accounts, and a court of state security for treason and national security cases.

16 ARMED FORCES

Rwanda's armed forces totaled 5,200 in 1993, including an army of 5,000, mostly infantry. An air corps, with 200 personnel and a total of 15 aircraft, is administered by the army. The national police numbers 1,200.

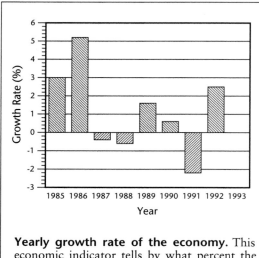

Yearly growth rate of the economy. This economic indicator tells by what percent the economy has increased or decreased when compared with the previous year.

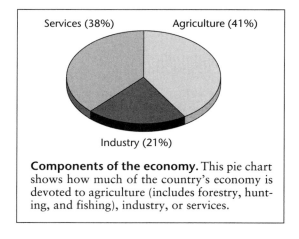

Components of the economy. This pie chart shows how much of the country's economy is devoted to agriculture (includes forestry, hunting, and fishing), industry, or services.

[17] ECONOMY

Rwanda has an agricultural economy with relatively few mineral resources. The manufacturing base is limited to a few basic products. Soil erosion has limited growth in the agricultural sector. Poor markets, lack of natural resources, and difficult transportation problems all painted a discouraging picture for the economy. However, these problems are insignificant in comparison to those brought about in 1994 by the civil war.

[18] INCOME

In 1992 Rwanda's gross national product (GNP) was $1,813 million at current prices, or about $210 per person. For the period 1985–92 the average inflation rate was 2.4%, resulting in a real growth rate in per person GNP of –2.8%.

[19] INDUSTRY

Rwanda has light industry which produces sugar, coffee, tea, flour, cigars, beer, wine, soft drinks, metal products, and assembled radios. There are also has textile mills, soap factories, auto repair shops, a match factory, a pyrethrum (insecticide) refinery, and plants for producing paint, pharmaceuticals, and furniture. Industrial production in 1990 included soap, 9,000 metric tons; cement, 57,000 tons; radios, 2,000; cigarettes, 331 million; beer, 915,000 hectoliters; soft drinks, 101,000 hectoliters; and plastic shoes, 24,000 pairs.

[20] LABOR

According to official 1989 estimates, about 90% of workers were engaged in agriculture, forestry, hunting and fishing; 3% in mining, manufacturing, construction, and utilities; and 4% in services. The government is the largest single employer of wage laborers. About 75% of the small industrial work force is unionized.

21 AGRICULTURE

In 1991, about 1.1 million hectares (2.8 million acres) were under cultivation. In 1992, the principal food crops (in tons) were plantains, 2,900,000; sweet potatoes, 770,000; cassava, 400,000; potatoes, 280,000; dry beans, 200,000; and sorghum, 175,000. The corn crop came to 100,000 tons and the sugarcane crop to 52,000 tons. Coffee is the chief export crop; in 1990, 45,579 tons were exported; in 1992 exports decreased to 33,851 tons. Tea production came to about 14,000 tons in 1992. Coffee and tea together generally contribute 80% to export earnings.

22 DOMESTICATED ANIMALS

Most farmers also raise livestock. In 1992 there were 610,000 head of cattle, 1,100,000 goats, 395,000 sheep, and 142,000 pigs. In 1992, there were an estimated one million chickens. Beekeeping is another important activity, with 15 tons of honey produced in 1992. About 135,000 cattle were slaughtered in 1992, providing 14,000 tons of meat.

23 FISHING

Fishing in the lakes and rivers is principally for local consumption. In 1991, Rwanda produced an estimated catch of 3,551 tons.

24 FORESTRY

In 1991, woodlands and forests covered an estimated 551,000 hectares (1,361,000 acres). Roundwood removals came to an estimated 5,620,000 cubic meters in 1991, almost all for fuel.

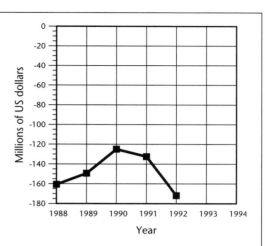

Yearly balance of trade measured in millions of US dollars. The balance of trade is the difference between what a country sells to other countries (its exports) and what it buys (its imports). If a country imports more than it exports, it has a negative balance of trade (a trade deficit). If exports exceed imports there is a positive balance of trade (a trade surplus).

25 MINING

In 1991, estimated mineral production included 730 tons of cassiterite (tin ore), 175 tons of tungsten ore, 60,000 tons of cement, and 150 tons of columbite and tantalite. Gold mine output was 700 kilograms.

26 FOREIGN TRADE

The major exports are coffee and tea. Imports consist chiefly of food and clothing, manufactured goods, transportation equipment, machinery and tools, and petroleum products. Germany took 21.3% of Rwanda's exports in 1991, followed by the Netherlands (18.8%) and Belgium (11.8%). Imports came from Bel-

Selected Social Indicators

These statistics are estimates for the period 1988 to 1993. For comparison purposes, data for the United States and averages for low-income countries and high-income countries are also given.

Indicator	Rwanda	Low-income countries	High-income countries	United States
Per capita gross national product†	$210	$380	$23,680	$24,740
Population growth rate	2.6%	1.9%	0.6%	1.0%
Population growth rate in urban areas	4.4%	3.9%	0.8%	1.3%
Population per square kilometer of land	279	78	25	26
Life expectancy in years	47	62	77	76
Number of people per physician	73,796	>3,300	453	419
Number of pupils per teacher (primary school)	58	39	<18	20
Illiteracy rate (15 years and older)	50%	41%	<5%	<3%
Energy consumed per capita (kg of oil equivalent)	27	364	5,203	7,918

† The gross national product (GNP) is the total dollar value of all goods and services produced by a country in a year. The per capita GNP is calculated by dividing a country's GNP by its population. The World Bank defines low-income countries as those with a per capita GNP of $695 or less. High-income countries have a per capita GNP of $8,626 or more. Less than 14% of the world's 5.5 billion people live in high-income countries, while almost 60% live in low-income countries.

> = greater than   < = less than

Sources: World Bank, *Social Indicators of Development 1995,* Baltimore: Johns Hopkins University Press, 1995. Central Intelligence Agency, *World Fact Book,* Washington, D.C.: Government Printing Office, 1994.

gium (17.1%), Kenya (13.4%), France (6.8%), and Germany (6.0%).

27 ENERGY AND POWER

Rwanda imports all of its petroleum products from Kenya. Petroleum imports included, in 1990, 301,000 barrels of gasoline, 92,000 barrels of kerosene, and 176,000 barrels of gas-diesel oils.

Rwanda has an estimated 60 billion cubic meters of natural gas reserves and 6 billion cubic meters of peat reserves, which could also be used as a domestic energy resource. Rwanda's electrical energy derives chiefly from hydroelectric

sources. Electricity production in 1991 totaled 179 million kilowatt hours.

28 SOCIAL DEVELOPMENT

Old age pensions for workers, family allowances, and payments for those injured on the job are provided for all wage earners.

There are government- and missionary-sponsored mutual aid societies, which increasingly supply the many social services once provided by the clan and family under Rwanda's traditional social structure.

Friendly Rwandan children poured out of their homes to greet the photographer.

29 HEALTH

In normal times, malnutrition is the greatest health problem in Rwanda. Kwashiorkor, a protein-calorie deficiency, is common, increasing the severity of other prevalent diseases, among them pneumonia, tuberculosis, measles, whooping cough, and dysentery. In 1987, Kigali was reported to have one of the world's highest rates of HIV (the virus that causes AIDS) infection. Average life expectancy is 47 years.

In 1990, there were 1.7 hospital beds per 1,000 inhabitants. There is about 1 doctor per 73,796 people. Total health care expenditures were $74 million in 1990, and in 1992, 80% of the population had access to health care services.

30 HOUSING

The basic type of housing in the rural areas is made of mud bricks and poles, and covered with thatch. These residences are dispersed in the collines, or family farms.

31 EDUCATION

In 1990, adult literacy was estimated at 50% (males, 63.9% and females, 37.1%). Education is free and compulsory for all children aged 7 to 15. In 1990, there were 1,671 primary schools, with 19,183 teachers and 1,100,437 pupils attending. There are about 58 students per teacher in the primary schools. In 1990 there were 70,400 pupils and 2,802 teachers in secondary schools. The National University of Rwanda is located at Butare. Other known institutions are the African and Mauritian Institute of Statistics and Applied Economics in Kigali. In 1989, all higher level institutions had 3,389 pupils and 646 teaching staff.

32 MEDIA

Telephone service is limited to Kigali and a few other important centers; there were 12,593 telephones in 1991. The government-operated Radio of the Rwandan Republic broadcasts in French, Swahili, and Kinyarwanda. In 1991 there were about 467,000 radios. There is no television in Rwanda. A French-language daily press bulletin provides news of government activities.

33 TOURISM AND RECREATION

Tourism declined after 1990 due to war and economic factors. Tourists are drawn by Rwanda's mountain gorillas, wild game preserve, and by hiking opportunities in the Volcano National Park.

34 FAMOUS RWANDANS

Kigeri IV Rwabugiri (d.1895) was a famous ruler of precolonial Rwanda. Grégoire Kayibanda (1924–76) was the first president of independent Rwanda. Juvénal Habyarimana (b.1937) became president in July 1973, a position he held into the 1990s.

35 BIBLIOGRAPHY

Nyrop, Richard F. *Rwanda: A Country Study.* Washington, D.C.: The American University, 1982.

ST. KITTS AND NEVIS

Federation of Saint Kitts and Nevis

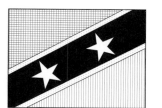

CAPITAL: Basseterre.

FLAG: Two thin diagonal yellow bands flanking a wide black diagonal band separate a green triangle at the hoist from a red triangle at the fly. On the black band are two white five-pointed stars.

ANTHEM: *National Anthem,* beginning "O land of beauty."

MONETARY UNIT: The East Caribbean dollar of 100 cents is the national currency. There are coins of 1, 2, 5, 10, and 25 cents and 1 East Caribbean dollar, and notes of 5, 10, 20, and 100 East Caribbean dollars. EC$1 = US$0.3704 (US$1 = EC$2.70).

WEIGHTS AND MEASURES: The imperial system is used.

HOLIDAYS: New Year's Day, 1 January; Labor Day, 1st Monday in May; Bank Holiday, 1st Monday in August; Independence Day, 19 September; Prince of Wales's Birthday, 14 November; Christmas, 25 December; Boxing Day, 26 December; Carnival, 30 December. Movable religious holidays include Good Friday and Whitmonday.

TIME: 8 AM = noon GMT.

1 LOCATION AND SIZE

St. Kitts is situated in the Leeward Islands. It has a total area of 269 square kilometers (104 square miles), slightly more than 1.5 times the size of Washington, D.C. Nevis lies southeast of St. Kitts, across a channel called The Narrows; it has a land area of 93 square kilometers (36 square miles). The capital city, Basseterre, is located on St. Kitts.

2 TOPOGRAPHY

St. Kitts and Nevis are of volcanic origin. In the northwest of St. Kitts is Mt. Liamuiga (Mt. Misery), the island's highest peak at 1,156 meters (3,792 feet). Nevis's highest elevation is the central peak of Mt. Nevis (Nevis Pk.), at 985 meters (3,231 feet); it is usually cloud-capped. There is a black sand beach on the northwest coast.

3 CLIMATE

Temperatures range from 20°C (68°F) to 29°C (84°F) all year long. Northeast tradewinds are constant. Rain usually falls between May and November, averaging 109 centimeters (43 inches) a year.

4 PLANTS AND ANIMALS

Coconut palms, poincianas, and palmettos are abundant on the upper slopes of Mt. Nevis. Lemon trees, bougainvillea, hibiscus, and tamarind are common on both islands. There are some black-faced vervet monkeys in St. Kitts.

5 ENVIRONMENT

Deforestation has affected the nation's wildlife and contributed to soil erosion. Erosion, in turn, produces silt, which is harmful to marine life on the coral reefs. The nation's water quality is threatened by uncontrolled dumping of sewage and pollution from cruise ships.

6 POPULATION

The 1980 census counted 43,309 residents; St. Kitts had 33,881, and Nevis 9,428. Estimated population in 1994 was 40,980. The estimated population density overall was 116 persons per square kilometer (300 per square mile), with the density of St. Kitts twice that of Nevis.

7 MIGRATION

Emigration has declined since the 1950s, largely because the economy enjoys almost full employment during the tourist and harvest seasons. During the off-season, some people migrate to other islands in search of work.

8 ETHNIC GROUPS

The population is mainly of African descent. As of 1985, roughly 95% of the population was black, about 5% was considered to be mulatto, 3% Indo-Pakistani, and 1.5% European.

9 LANGUAGES

English, sprinkled with local expressions, is the universal language.

10 RELIGIONS

The Anglican Church, the largest church on the island, claims more than a third of the population. Other principal religious groups are the Church of God, the Methodist Church (33% in 1985), the Moravians, the Baptists, the Seventh-day Adventists, the Pilgrim Holiness Church, and the Roman Catholic Church (10.7% in 1985).

11 TRANSPORTATION

A light, narrow-gauge railway of 58 kilometers (36 miles) on St. Kitts is operated by the government to transport sugarcane from fields to factory, and processed sugar to coast for export. In 1991 there were 300 kilometers (186 miles) of roads on the island; the main roads circle each island. In 1985 there were 3,540 automobiles registered. Basseterre is the principal port. A state-run motorboat service is maintained between St. Kitts and Nevis. Golden Rock International Airport serves Basseterre; several small airlines fly to a landing strip at Newcastle, on Nevis.

12 HISTORY

Arawak Indians, followed by Caribs, were the earliest known inhabitants of the islands. Discovered by Columbus in 1493 and named St. Christopher, St. Kitts was the first of the British West Indies to be settled. Sir Thomas Warner established a settlement on St. Kitts in 1623 and led a colonial expedition to Nevis in 1628.

By the 1660s there were some 4,000 Europeans engaged in the sugar trade, based on a plantation system with slaves imported from Africa. The French gained control of the island and held it until it was retaken by the British in 1713. After another French takeover in 1782, the Treaty of Versailles (1783) again returned St. Kitts to Britain. By the late eighteenth century, the thermal baths on Nevis were attracting thousands of international tourists. Although the slaves were emancipated in 1834, many continued to work on the sugar plantations, so the sugar-based economy did not decline as rapidly as elsewhere in the West Indies.

St. Kitts, Nevis, and Anguilla (the most northerly island of the Leeward chain) were incorporated with the British Virgin Islands into a single colony in 1816. The territorial unit of St. Kitts-Nevis-Anguilla became part of the Leeward Islands Federation in 1871 and belonged to the Federation of the West Indies from 1958 to 1962. In 1967, the three islands became an associated state with full internal autonomy under a new constitution. After the Anguilla islanders rebelled in 1969, British paratroopers intervened, and Anguilla was allowed to secede in 1971.

St. Kitts and Nevis became an independent federated state within the Commonwealth on 19 September 1983. Under the arrangement, Nevis was given its own legislature and the power to secede from the federation. The People's Action Movement/Nevis Reformation Party coalition won a majority of seats in the 1984 and 1989 elections.

13 GOVERNMENT

St. Kitts-Nevis is a federation of the two islands. Under the 1983 constitution, the British monarch is head of state and is rep-

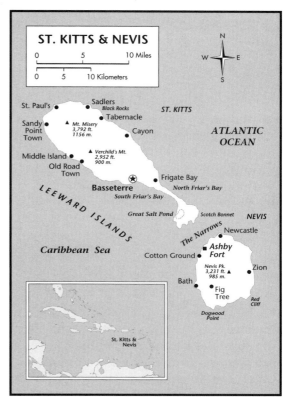

LOCATION: 17°10′ to 17°20′N; 62°24′ to 62°45′W.
TOTAL COASTLINE: 135 kilometers (84 miles).
TERRITORIAL SEA LIMIT: 12 miles.

resented by a governor-general. The nation is governed under a parliamentary system, with legislative power vested in the single-chamber House of Assembly, consisting of the speaker, three appointed senators, and 11 elected members. Nevis also has its own legislative assembly and the right to secede under certain conditions. St. Kitts is divided into nine parishes and Nevis into five.

14 POLITICAL PARTIES

The four political parties holding seats in the House of Assembly are the Labour

Party (also known as the Workers' League), the People's Action Movement, the Nevis Reformation Party, and the Concerned Citizen's Movement.

15 JUDICIAL SYSTEM

The Eastern Caribbean Supreme Court, established on St. Lucia, administers the judicial system. Magistrates' courts deal with petty criminal and civil cases.

16 ARMED FORCES

Antigua and Barbuda, Dominica, Grenada, St. Kitts and Nevis, St. Lucia, and St. Vincent and the Grenadines created a Regional Security System in 1985.

17 ECONOMY

The economy is based on tourism and agriculture, particularly on sugar, which generated some 55% of export revenues in 1994. The government has been making efforts to attract foreign investment, to diversify the economy industrially, to expand tourism, and to improve local food production.

18 INCOME

In 1992, St. Kitts and Nevis's gross national product (GNP) was US$181 million, or about US$4,410 per person. For the period 1985–92 the average inflation rate was 8.8%, resulting in a real growth rate in per person GNP of 5.3%.

19 INDUSTRY

The principal manufacturing plant and largest industrial employer is the St. Kitts Sugar Manufacturing Corp., which grinds and processes sugarcane for export. St.

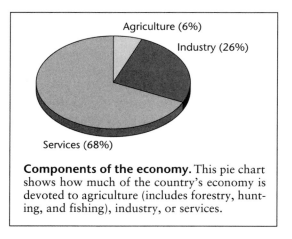

Agriculture (6%)

Industry (26%)

Services (68%)

Components of the economy. This pie chart shows how much of the country's economy is devoted to agriculture (includes forestry, hunting, and fishing), industry, or services.

Kitts and Nevis has transformed small electronic plants into the largest electronics assembly industry in the Eastern Caribbean. Its apparel assembly industry has also become very successful in recent years.

20 LABOR

A 1991 estimate placed the labor force at 20,000. In 1991, the unemployment rate was 13.5%.

21 AGRICULTURE

The principal agricultural product of St. Kitts is sugarcane. Sugar production increased to 20,483 tons in 1992. Peanut production now ranks second. On Nevis, sea island cotton and coconuts are the major commodities.

22 DOMESTICATED ANIMALS

Pasture areas are small, covering some 2.7% of the islands. Estimates of livestock in 1992 were cattle, 5,000 head; sheep, 15,000; pigs, 2,000; and goats, 10,000.

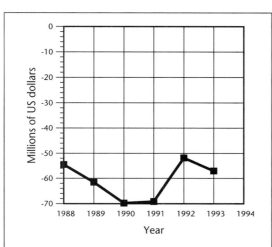

Yearly balance of trade measured in millions of US dollars. The balance of trade is the difference between what a country sells to other countries (its exports) and what it buys (its imports). If a country imports more than it exports, it has a negative balance of trade (a trade deficit). If exports exceed imports there is a positive balance of trade (a trade surplus).

23 FISHING

Fishing is a traditional occupation that has not expanded to any great extent; the catch in 1991 was 1,750 tons.

24 FORESTRY

Both islands have small areas of virgin tropical forest, with palms, poincianas, and palmettos.

25 MINING

Local quarrying of some materials is used to supplement the construction industry.

26 FOREIGN TRADE

Sugar, beer and ale, lobsters, electrical equipment, and margarine and shortening are the main exports. Imports include food, manufactured goods, machinery and transportation equipment, and mineral fuels. In 1991, major trade partners were the United Kingdom, the United States, the Caribbean Community and Common Market (CARICOM) states, and Japan.

27 ENERGY AND POWER

In 1991, 40 million kilowatt hours of electricity were produced, entirely from conventional sources. St. Kitts and Nevis has no fossil fuels, and all petroleum products must be imported.

28 SOCIAL DEVELOPMENT

Effective 1978, a social security system replaced the existing fund as the provider of old age, disability, survivor, sickness, and maternity benefits. The Ministry of Women's Affairs promotes women's rights and provides counseling for abused women.

29 HEALTH

The average life expectancy is 66 years. There were 2.7 hospital beds per 1,000 people and a total of 43 doctors in 1990. The country's health care expenditures were estimated at US$46.7 million that year.

30 HOUSING

The Housing Authority began a program of low-cost home construction in 1977.

31 EDUCATION

The literacy rate is about 98%. Education is free and compulsory for 12 years. In 1991, there were 32 primary schools with 350 teachers and 7,236 students. At the

---

Selected Social Indicators

These statistics are estimates for the period 1988 to 1993. For comparison purposes, data for the United States and averages for low-income countries and high-income countries are also given.

Indicator	St. Kitts and Nevis	Low-income countries	High-income countries	United States
Per capita gross national product†	$4,410	$380	$23,680	$24,740
Population growth rate	1.0%	1.9%	0.6%	1.0%
Population growth rate in urban areas	2.3%	3.9%	0.8%	1.3%
Population per square kilometer of land	116	78	25	26
Life expectancy in years	66	62	77	76
Number of people per physician	953	>3,300	453	419
Number of pupils per teacher (primary school)	21	39	<18	20
Illiteracy rate (15 years and older)	2%	41%	<5%	<3%
Energy consumed per capita (kg of oil equivalent)	476	364	5,203	7,918

† The gross national product (GNP) is the total dollar value of all goods and services produced by a country in a year. The per capita GNP is calculated by dividing a country's GNP by its population. The World Bank defines low-income countries as those with a per capita GNP of $695 or less. High-income countries have a per capita GNP of $8,626 or more. Less than 14% of the world's 5.5 billion people live in high-income countries, while almost 60% live in low-income countries.   > = greater than   < = less than

Sources: World Bank, *Social Indicators of Development 1995,* Baltimore: Johns Hopkins University Press, 1995. Central Intelligence Agency, *World Fact Book,* Washington, D.C.: Government Printing Office, 1994.

eight secondary-level schools, there were 294 teachers and 4,396 students enrolled. At the postsecondary level, there were 38 teachers and 325 students enrolled.

32 MEDIA

In 1991 there were some 27,000 radios and 9,000 television sets in use. There were 3,805 telephones in the same year. There is one newspaper: the *Labour Spokesman,* published twice weekly with a circulation of 2,000.

33 TOURISM AND RECREATION

The chief historic attraction on St. Kitts is Brimstone Hill fortress, which towers 230 meters (750 feet) above the Caribbean. Nevis has many beaches and historic plantations. In 1991, 83,903 stayover tourists arrived on the islands, 75,513 from the Americas.

34 FAMOUS KITTSIANS AND NEVISIANS

Sir Thomas Warner (d.1649) established the first colony on each island. US statesman Alexander Hamilton (1757–1804) was born in Charlestown.

35 BIBLIOGRAPHY

Lowenthal, David. *West Indian Societies.* London: Oxford University Press, 1972.
Williams, Eric Eustace. *From Columbus to Castro: The History of the Caribbean, 1492–1969.* London: Deutsch, 1970.

ST. LUCIA

CAPITAL: Castries.

FLAG: On a blue background is a yellow triangle surmounted by a black arrowhead whose outer edges are bordered in white.

ANTHEM: *Sons and Daughters of St. Lucia.*

MONETARY UNIT: The East Caribbean dollar (EC$) of 100 cents is the national currency. There are coins of 1, 2, 5, 10, and 25 cents and 1 dollar, and notes of 5, 10, 20, and 100 East Caribbean dollars. EC$1 = US$0.3704 (or US$1 = EC$2.70).

WEIGHTS AND MEASURES: The metric system has been introduced, but imperial measures are still commonly employed.

HOLIDAYS: New Year's Day, 1 January; Carnival, 8–9 February; Independence Day, 22 February; Labor Day, 1 May; Queen's Official Birthday, 5 June; Bank Holiday, 1st Monday in August; Thanksgiving Day, 1st Monday in October; St. Lucia Day, 13 December; Christmas Day, 25 December; Boxing Day, 26 December. Movable religious holidays include Good Friday, Easter Monday, Whitmonday, and Corpus Christi.

TIME: 8 AM = noon GMT.

1 LOCATION AND SIZE

The Caribbean island of St. Lucia, part of the Windward Islands group of the Lesser Antilles, has a total area of 620 square kilometers (239 square miles), slightly less than 3.5 times the size of Washington, D.C. The capital city, Castries, is located on St. Lucia's northwest coast.

2 TOPOGRAPHY

St. Lucia is a volcanic island, with a mountainous southern half and a hilly northern half. The highest mountain, Mt. Gimie, rises 950 meters (3,116 feet) above sea level. Peaks on the southern coast, including Grand Piton (Gros Piton) at 798 meters (2,618 feet) are among the scenic highlights of the West Indies. The island has beautiful beaches, some with black volcanic sand.

3 CLIMATE

The average yearly temperature on St. Lucia is 26°C (79°F). The average rainfall at sea level is 231 centimeters (91 inches) a year. Like the rest of the West Indies, St. Lucia is vulnerable to hurricanes.

4 PLANTS AND ANIMALS

Abundant tropical plants include hibiscus, orchids, jasmine, and bougainvillea. There are no large mammals on St. Lucia. Bats are common, and there are several species of small snakes. About a hundred species of birds are found, including flycatchers, hummingbirds, and pigeons. The

Photo credit: Corel Corporation.

The Spanish Hogfish (Bodianus rufus) is found in many of the reef areas of the Caribbean. The warm climate of St. Lucia supports a large variety of tropical plants and animals.

surrounding sea contains lobster, turtle, and conch, as well as many types of fish.

5 ENVIRONMENT

St. Lucia's forests are gradually being depleted by agricultural and commercial interests, and the loss of forest cover contributes to soil erosion. The water supply has been polluted by agricultural chemicals and sewage. Two small areas have been set aside as nature preserves. As of 1987, endangered species included the tundra peregrine falcon and common iguana.

6 POPULATION

In 1991, the population of St. Lucia was 136,041. Some 51,994 persons lived in Castries, the capital, in 1991, when the nation's population density was 225 persons per square kilometer (583 per square mile).

7 MIGRATION

Overcrowding has resulted in emigration to neighboring countries, including Trinidad, Guyana, and the French Caribbean islands, with lesser numbers going to the United Kingdom, Canada, and the United States.

8 ETHNIC GROUPS

Reliable statistics on ethnic groups are unavailable. It is estimated, however, that 90.5% of the population consists of descendants of slaves brought from Africa in the seventeenth and eighteenth centuries. Some 5.5% is mulatto and 3.2% East Indian. Approximately 0.8% of the population is of European descent.

9 LANGUAGES

English is the official language of St. Lucia. Nearly 20% of the population cannot speak it, however. Almost all the islanders also speak a French patois (dialect) based on a mixture of African and French grammar and a vocabulary of mostly French with some English and Spanish words.

10 RELIGIONS

The vast majority of the population (about 79%) was Roman Catholic in 1991. There are also Anglican, Methodist, Baptist, and Seventh-day Adventist churches. The small East Indian community is divided between Hindus and Muslims.

11 TRANSPORTATION

Hewanorra International Airport is located on the southern tip of the island. The smaller Vigie Airport, located near Castries, is used for flights to and from neighboring Caribbean islands. St. Lucia has two important ports: Castries, in the north, and Vieux Fort, to the south, from which ferries link St. Lucia with St. Vincent and the Grenadines. All of the island's towns, villages, and main residential areas are linked by 760 kilometers (472 miles) of all-purpose roads. Motor vehicles numbered 18,938 in 1992.

LOCATION: 13°53′N; 60°58′W. **TOTAL COASTLINE:** 158 kilometers (98 miles). **TERRITORIAL SEA LIMIT:** 12 miles.

12 HISTORY

Arawak and Carib Amerindians were the earliest known inhabitants of what is now St. Lucia. According to tradition, Colum-

An aerial view of the town and harbor of Soufrière.

bus sighted St. Lucia on St. Lucy's Day (December 13) in 1498. It was not settled until the mid-seventeenth century because the Caribs defended the islands successfully for years. The French first settled the island, but it changed hands between the British and the French no fewer than 14 times, until in 1814, the British took permanent possession. In 1838, St. Lucia came under the administration of the Windward Islands government set up by Great Britain.

Unlike other islands in the area, sugar did not monopolize commerce on St. Lucia. Instead, it was one product among many others including tobacco, ginger, and cotton. Small farms rather than large plantations continued to dominate agricultural production into the twentieth century. After slavery was abolished in 1834, East Indian indentured workers were brought to the island during the late 1800s.

St. Lucia established full internal self-government in 1967 and on 22 February 1979 became an independent member of the Commonwealth of Nations.

The first three years of independence were marked by political turmoil and civil strife, as leaders of rival parties fought bitterly. In 1982, the conservative United Workers' Party (UWP) won 14 of 17 seats in the House of Assembly. Party leader and prime minister John Compton became Prime Minister at independence and has governed ever since. In 1992, the UWP controlled 11 parliamentary seats.

13 GOVERNMENT

Under the 1979 constitution, the British monarch, as official head of government, is represented by a governor-general. Executive power is exercised by the prime minister and cabinet. There is a two-chamber parliament consisting of a Senate with 11 members and a House of Assembly with 17 representatives.

14 POLITICAL PARTIES

Since 1982, the majority party has been the United Workers' Party (UWP), led by John Compton. The St. Lucia Labour Party (SLP), led by Julian Hunte, is the other major party in St. Lucia.

15 JUDICIAL SYSTEM

The lowest court is the district or magistrate's court, above which is the Court of Summary Jurisdiction. The Eastern Caribbean Supreme Court, with international jurisdiction, is seated in Castries.

16 ARMED FORCES

As of 1985 there were no armed forces; the police department numbered 300. A regional defense pact provides for joint defense and disaster contingency plans.

17 ECONOMY

Agriculture has traditionally been the main economic activity on St. Lucia, which is the leading producer of bananas in the Windward Islands group. Tourism

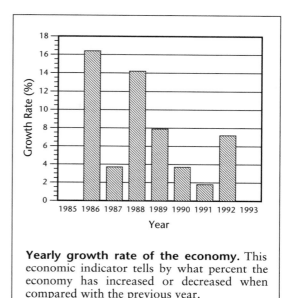

Yearly growth rate of the economy. This economic indicator tells by what percent the economy has increased or decreased when compared with the previous year.

has recently become an equally important economic activity.

18 INCOME

In 1992, the gross national product (GNP) was US$453 million at current prices, or about US$3,380 per person. For the period 1985–92, the average inflation rate was 3.6%, resulting in a real growth rate in per person GNP of 5.2%.

19 INDUSTRY

St. Lucia's manufacturing industry is the largest in the Windward Islands, with many assembly plants producing apparel, electronic components, plastic products, and paper and cardboard boxes.

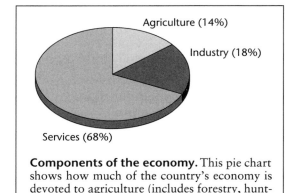

Agriculture (14%)

Industry (18%)

Services (68%)

Components of the economy. This pie chart shows how much of the country's economy is devoted to agriculture (includes forestry, hunting, and fishing), industry, or services.

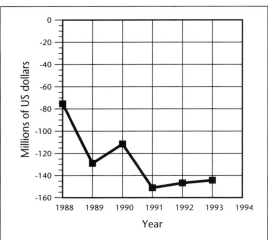

Yearly balance of trade measured in millions of US dollars. The balance of trade is the difference between what a country sells to other countries (its exports) and what it buys (its imports). If a country imports more than it exports, it has a negative balance of trade (a trade deficit). If exports exceed imports there is a positive balance of trade (a trade surplus).

[20] LABOR

In 1991, the labor force was estimated at 52,200, or about 38% of the population. Unemployment was unofficially estimated at 16% in 1991.

[21] AGRICULTURE

The production of bananas, St. Lucia's most important crop, totaled 137,500 tons in 1992. The second most important crop is coconuts, exported as oil and copra; about 25,000 tons were produced in 1992.

[22] DOMESTICATED ANIMALS

Production of almost every category of domesticated animals is insufficient to satisfy local demand. There are only 12,000 head of cattle on the island; milk production covers only about 25% of local demand.

[23] FISHING

St. Lucia meets its own fresh fish needs. In 1991, the total catch was 910 tons.

[24] FORESTRY

A small timber industry processes mahogany, pine, and blue mahoe. About 13% of total available land consists of forest and woodlands.

[25] MINING

There is no regular commercial mining in St. Lucia, but there is some quarrying.

[26] FOREIGN TRADE

At year end 1992, exports included bananas, clothing, cardboard boxes, and coconut products. Imports consisted mainly of manufactured goods, foodstuffs, machinery, fuels, and chemicals. St. Lucia's major trade partners were the

Selected Social Indicators

These statistics are estimates for the period 1988 to 1993. For comparison purposes, data for the United States and averages for low-income countries and high-income countries are also given.

Indicator	St. Lucia	Low-income countries	High-income countries	United States
Per capita gross national product†	$3,380	$380	$23,680	$24,740
Population growth rate	1.6%	1.9%	0.6%	1.0%
Population growth rate in urban areas	2.5%	3.9%	0.8%	1.3%
Population per square kilometer of land	225	78	25	26
Life expectancy in years	69	62	77	76
Number of people per physician	2,306	>3,300	453	419
Number of pupils per teacher (primary school)	29	39	<18	20
Illiteracy rate (15 years and older)	28%	41%	<5%	<3%
Energy consumed per capita (kg of oil equivalent)	373	364	5,203	7,918

† The gross national product (GNP) is the total dollar value of all goods and services produced by a country in a year. The per capita GNP is calculated by dividing a country's GNP by its population. The World Bank defines low-income countries as those with a per capita GNP of $695 or less. High-income countries have a per capita GNP of $8,626 or more. Less than 14% of the world's 5.5 billion people live in high-income countries, while almost 60% live in low-income countries.

> = greater than   < = less than

Sources: World Bank, *Social Indicators of Development 1995*, Baltimore: Johns Hopkins University Press, 1995. Central Intelligence Agency, *World Fact Book*, Washington, D.C.: Government Printing Office, 1994.

United Kingdom, the United States, Caribbean Community and Common Market (CARICOM), Japan, and Canada.

27 ENERGY AND POWER

Electric power production, totaling 105 million kilowatt hours in 1991, is provided by two main diesel generating centers.

28 SOCIAL DEVELOPMENT

The National Insurance Scheme provides all workers from age 16 to 60 with old age, disability, survivor, sickness, and maternity coverage, as well as workers' compensation. Efforts have been made to improve the status of women, especially in employment.

29 HEALTH

There were 5 hospitals on St. Lucia with 528 beds in 1988. In 1991, there were 59 doctors, or about one doctor per 2,306 inhabitants. Malnutrition and intestinal disorders are the main health problems. The average life expectancy is 69 years.

30 HOUSING

The demand for private ownership of homes far exceeds the supply. In 1980, the majority of housing (74%) was built of wood.

31 EDUCATION

In 1993, the literacy rate was estimated at over 72%, an improvement over the average of 67% from 1988–93. In 1988 there were 88 primary schools with 1,137 teaching staff and 33,148 students. There are about 28 students per teacher in the primary schools. There were 352 secondary teachers and 6,391 students. Institutions of higher learning include a branch of the University of the West Indies and the Sir Arthur Lewis Community College.

32 MEDIA

Three newspapers are published in St. Lucia: The *Voice of St. Lucia* (circulation 8,000), the *Crusader* (4,000), and the *Star* (5,000). There were an estimated 20,000 telephones in service in 1993, when there were 2 AM and 2 FM radio stations and 3 TV stations. In 1991 there were 103,000 radios and 26,000 TV sets in use.

33 TOURISM AND RECREATION

Dramatic tropical scenery, beautiful beaches, and excellent water-sports facilities are St. Lucia's principal tourist attractions. Of special interest are the Sulphur Springs (the world's only drive-in volcano). Some 165,987 tourists visited St. Lucia in 1991, of whom 105,338 were from the Americas and 58,763 were from Europe. The hotel occupancy rate in 1991 was 65.9%.

34 FAMOUS ST. LUCIANS

John G.M. Compton (b.1926), trained as a barrister and one of the founders of the United Workers' Party, has been prime minister since 1982. The writer Derek Walcott (b.1930) is best known for his epic autobiographical poem *Another Life*.

35 BIBLIOGRAPHY

Breen, Henry Hegart. *St. Lucia: Historical, Statistical, and Descriptive*. London: F. Cass, 1970.
Eggleston, Hazel. *Saint Lucia Diary*. Greenwich, Conn.: Devin-Adair, 1977.

ST. VINCENT AND THE GRENADINES

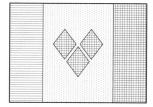

CAPITAL: Kingstown.

FLAG: Three vertical bands of blue, yellow, and green; centered on the yellow band are three green diamonds arranged in a v-pattern.

ANTHEM: *National Anthem,* beginning "St. Vincent! Land so beautiful."

MONETARY UNIT: The East Caribbean dollar (EC$) of 100 cents is the national currency. There are coins of 1, 2, 5, 10, and 25 cents and 1 dollar, and notes of 5, 10, 20, and 100 East Caribbean dollars. EC$1 = US$0.3704 (US$1 = EC$2.70).

WEIGHTS AND MEASURES: The imperial measures are used.

HOLIDAYS: New Year's Day, 1 January; Labor Day, 1 May; CARICOM Day, 5 July; Carnival, 6 July; Bank Holiday, 1st Monday in August; Independence Day, 27 October; Christmas Day, 25 December; Boxing Day, 26 December. Movable religious holidays include Good Friday, Easter Monday, and Whitmonday.

TIME: 8 AM = noon GMT.

1 LOCATION AND SIZE

St. Vincent is located in the Windward Islands group of the Lesser Antilles. Scattered between St. Vincent and Grenada are more than 100 small islands called the Grenadines, half of which belong to St. Vincent and the other half to Grenada. The land area of St. Vincent is 347 square kilometers (134 square miles). The total land area of the country is 340 square kilometers (131 square miles), slightly less than twice the size of Washington, D.C. The capital city, Kingstown, is located on the southeast coast of the island of St. Vincent.

2 TOPOGRAPHY

St. Vincent is a rugged island of volcanic formation, and the Grenadines are formed by a volcanic ridge running north–south between St. Vincent and Grenada, its neighbor to the southwest. The highest peak on St. Vincent is Soufrière, an active volcano with an altitude of 1,234 meters (4,048 feet). The low-lying Grenadines have wide beaches and shallow bays and harbors, but most have no source of fresh water except rainfall.

3 CLIMATE

The islands enjoy a pleasant tropical climate all year round, with a yearly average temperature of 26°C (79°F). The warmest month is September, with an average temperature of 27°C (81°F); the coolest is January, with an average temperature of 25°C (77°F). The average yearly rainfall on St. Vincent is 231 centimeters (91 inches).

4 PLANTS AND ANIMALS

The shallow waters of the Grenadines abound with marine life. Lobsters, conch, fish of all varieties, and turtles can be found. Whales are frequently sighted, and large iguana can be found on some of the waterless rocks and cays. In Kingstown, on St. Vincent, there is a famous botanical garden. Some of the many birds found in St. Vincent are the trembler, the bananaquit, and the Antillean crested hummingbird.

5 ENVIRONMENT

The principal recurring threat to the environment comes from the Soufrière volcano. In April 1979, the volcano was active for weeks, covering mountains, forests, and plantation fields with volcanic ash.

The central highlands of St. Vincent have been set aside as a natural preservation area for the St. Vincent parrot, wren, and solitaire. In the Grenadines, the hawksbill, green sea, and leatherback turtles are endangered.

6 POPULATION

As of 1991 St. Vincent and the Grenadines had a population of 107,598, of whom 98,842 lived on the main island and 8,756 lived in the Grenadines. The population of Kingstown, the capital, was 15,670, with another 10,872 in the suburbs. Overall, the islands had a population density in 1991 of 279 persons per square kilometer (717 per square mile).

7 MIGRATION

Although no reliable statistics are available, emigration is known to take place to Trinidad, Guyana, Guadeloupe, and Martinique.

8 ETHNIC GROUPS

About 65% of the islanders are black; about 20% are of mixed origin; roughly 5.5% are East Indians, of Asian descent; 3.5% are of European descent; and about 2% of the people are Amerindians. Of the mixed group, about 1,000 persons, identified as Black Caribs, descend from the intermarriage of runaway or shipwrecked slaves and Amerindians.

9 LANGUAGES

English is the official language of St. Vincent and the Grenadines. Some islanders speak a French patois (dialect), representing a mixture of African and French grammar, with a mostly French vocabulary and some English and Spanish words. A few islanders speak French as their first language.

10 RELIGIONS

The majority of the population is Protestant, with about 36% Anglican and 40% members of other Protestant churches; but there is a significant Roman Catholic minority (10%). Members of the East Indian community are either Hindus or Muslims.

11 TRANSPORTATION

St. Vincent is on the main air routes of the Caribbean, with direct flights to Trinidad and Barbados as well as the other islands to the north. The international airport is located on the southern tip of the island, near Kingstown. Small airports are located on Union, Canouan, and Mustique islands.

All of the Grenadines have excellent harbors served by a ferry service operating out of Kingstown. The main road of St. Vincent connects all the main towns with the capital. As of 1991, the islands had about 300 kilometers (185 miles) of all-weather roads. About 7,000 vehicles were registered in 1992, including 5,000 passenger cars.

12 HISTORY

The Arawak Amerindians, who migrated from South America, are the earliest known inhabitants of St. Vincent and the Grenadines. The Caribs inhabited the islands when Christopher Columbus reached St. Vincent on 22 January 1498.

St. Vincent was left to the Carib Amerindians by British and French agreement in 1660 and continued to have a sizable Amerindian population until the early eighteenth century. The island was taken formally by the British in 1763, who ruled from then on, except for a period of French rule from 1779 to 1783.

The island changed its ethnic character during the next century. When the remaining Amerindian and mixed-blood population rebelled against the British in 1795, most were expelled from the island. Those who remained were decimated by an eruption of the Soufrière volcano in 1812. They were replaced by African slaves, who were freed in 1834; Madeiran Portuguese,

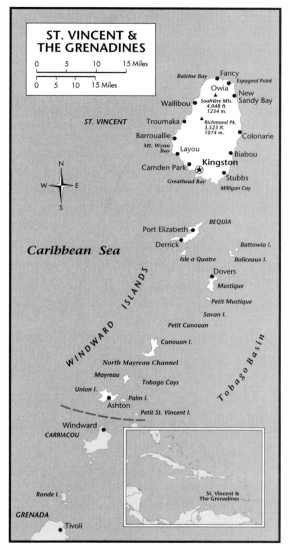

LOCATION: St. Vincent—13°6′ to 14°35′ N; 61°6′ to 61°20′ W. **TOTAL COASTLINE:** 84 kilometers (52 miles). **TERRITORIAL SEA LIMIT:** 12 miles.

who immigrated in 1848 because of a labor shortage; and Asian indentured laborers, who arrived later in the nineteenth century.

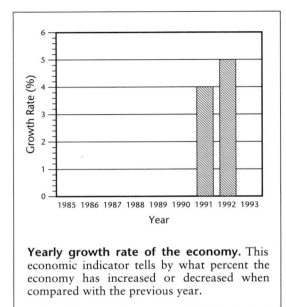

Yearly growth rate of the economy. This economic indicator tells by what percent the economy has increased or decreased when compared with the previous year.

St. Vincent was administered as a crown colony within the Windward Islands group from 1833 until 1960, when it joined the Federation of the West Indies. The federation fell apart in 1962, and St. Vincent became a self-governing state in association with the United Kingdom seven years later. On 27 October 1979, St. Vincent and the Grenadines achieved full independence as a member of the Commonwealth of Nations.

During the first months of independence, the young nation faced a rebellion by a group of Rastafarians (semi-political, semi-religious cult based in Jamaica) attempting to secede. The revolt was put down with help from neighboring Barbados. Otherwise, the political system has had few disruptions. The government at independence under the St. Vincent Labor Party gave way to the New Democratic Party (NDP) in 1984, with the NDP renewing its electoral majority in 1989.

13 GOVERNMENT

The British monarch, represented by a governor-general, is formally head of the government. Executive power is in the hands of the prime minister and cabinet, who are members of the majority party in the legislature. The single-chamber legislature is a 21-seat House of Assembly consisting of 15 elected representatives and six appointed senators. The nation is divided into eight local districts, two of which cover the Grenadines.

14 POLITICAL PARTIES

There are two major parties and three minor parties on the islands. The majority party is the New Democratic Party (NDP), led by Prime Minister James FitzAllen Mitchell. The St. Vincent Labour Party (SVLP) was in power at independence and governed the nation until the July 1984 elections.

15 JUDICIAL SYSTEM

The islands are divided into three judicial districts, each with its own magistrate's court. Appeals may be carried to the East Caribbean Supreme Court, based in St. Lucia.

16 ARMED FORCES

There are no armed forces except those of the police department. A regional defense pact provides for joint coast-guard operations, military exercises, and disaster contingency plans.

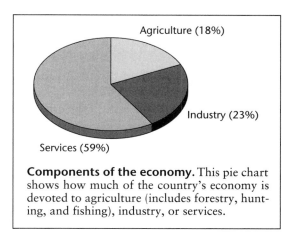

Components of the economy. This pie chart shows how much of the country's economy is devoted to agriculture (includes forestry, hunting, and fishing), industry, or services.

Agriculture (18%)

Industry (23%)

Services (59%)

17 ECONOMY

In recent years, tourism and manufacturing have been expanding steadily. However, as of 1994, St. Vincent and the Grenadines continues to rely heavily on agriculture for its economic progress.

18 INCOME

In 1992, the gross national product (GNP) was US$217 million at current prices, or about US$2,017 per person. For the period 1985–92, the average inflation rate was 4.3%, resulting in a real growth rate in per person GNP of 4.7%.

19 INDUSTRY

A large amount of industrial activity centers on the processing of agricultural products. Nonagricultural industries include several garment factories, a furniture factory, an electronics plant, and a corrugated cardboard box plant.

20 LABOR

Some 37,800 persons make up the work force. Unemployment was 30% in 1991. One of the first authentic labor unions in the West Indies was formed in St. Vincent in 1935, during the Great Depression.

21 AGRICULTURE

About half of St. Vincent is devoted to crop growing. Bananas constitute the main crop; vegetables, coconut, spices, and sugar are also important. In 1992, 76,095 tons of bananas were exported. Other crops in 1992 included coconuts, 23,000 tons; sugar cane, 2,000 tons; sweet potatoes, 2,000 tons; and plantains, 3,000 tons.

22 DOMESTICATED ANIMALS

Rough estimates of the livestock population in 1992 include 6,000 head of cattle, 9,000 hogs, 12,000 sheep, 6,000 goats, and 100,000 poultry of all types.

23 FISHING

At one time, St. Vincent and Bequia were the centers for a thriving whaling industry, but only six humpback whales were captured from 1982 to 1991. In 1991, the total fish catch amounted to 7,665 tons. Technical assistance and training to fisherman and fisheries staff is being sponsored by the Canadian Fisheries Development Project.

24 FORESTRY

There is practically no commercial forestry. Some local timber is used for residential and boat construction.

25 MINING

There is no commercial mining. Some sand is extracted for local construction projects.

26 FOREIGN TRADE

Exports of goods include bananas, flour, and sweet potatoes. Imports are composed of food, beverages, tobacco, machinery and equipment, and manufactured goods.

27 ENERGY AND POWER

Two hydroelectric plants provide 76% of the electricity generated. In 1991, total power generation amounted to 51 million kilowatt hours.

28 SOCIAL DEVELOPMENT

The social security system provides benefits for old age, disability, death, sickness, and maternity. Employers fund a compulsory workers' compensation program. St. Vincent has an extensive program of community development, and a national family planning program. A new law requiring that women receive equal pay for equal work went into effect in 1990.

29 HEALTH

As of 1988, Kingstown had a general hospital with 204 beds, and there were 3 rural hospitals. Approximately 34 outpatient clinics provide medical care throughout the nation. In 1990 there were an estimated 2.7 hospital beds per 1,000 inhabitants. In 1991 there were 55 doctors. Estimated health care expenditures were US$46.7 million in 1990.

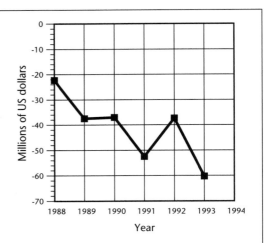

Yearly balance of trade measured in millions of US dollars. The balance of trade is the difference between what a country sells to other countries (its exports) and what it buys (its imports). If a country imports more than it exports, it has a negative balance of trade (a trade deficit). If exports exceed imports there is a positive balance of trade (a trade surplus).

Gastrointestinal diseases continue to be a problem, although they are less so than in the past. Life expectancy is 72 years.

30 HOUSING

The government has undertaken housing renewal projects in both rural and urban areas and has sought to provide housing for workers on industrial estates. Another government program supplies building materials at low cost to working people.

31 EDUCATION

Primary education, which lasts for seven years, is free but not compulsory. There are 64 primary schools. In 1990, enrollment in primary schools was 22,030 with

ST. VINCENT AND THE GRENADINES

Selected Social Indicators

These statistics are estimates for the period 1988 to 1993. For comparison purposes, data for the United States and averages for low-income countries and high-income countries are also given.

Indicator	St. Vincent and the Grenadines	Low-income countries	High-income countries	United States
Per capita gross national product†	**$2,017**	$380	$23,680	$24,740
Population growth rate	**0.9%**	1.9%	0.6%	1.0%
Population growth rate in urban areas	**3.6%**	3.9%	0.8%	1.3%
Population per square kilometer of land	**279**	78	25	26
Life expectancy in years	**72**	62	77	76
Number of people per physician	**1,956**	>3,300	453	419
Number of pupils per teacher (primary school)	**20**	39	<18	20
Illiteracy rate (15 years and older)	**4%**	41%	<5%	<3%
Energy consumed per capita (kg of oil equivalent)	**200**	364	5,203	7,918

† The gross national product (GNP) is the total dollar value of all goods and services produced by a country in a year. The per capita GNP is calculated by dividing a country's GNP by its population. The World Bank defines low-income countries as those with a per capita GNP of $695 or less. High-income countries have a per capita GNP of $8,626 or more. Less than 14% of the world's 5.5 billion people live in high-income countries, while almost 60% live in low-income countries.

> = greater than   < = less than

Sources: World Bank, *Social Indicators of Development 1995,* Baltimore: Johns Hopkins University Press, 1995. Central Intelligence Agency, *World Fact Book,* Washington, D.C.: Government Printing Office, 1994.

1,119 teaching staff. There are about 20 students per teacher in primary schools. In secondary schools the same year, there were 10,719 students and 431 teachers. The government-assisted School for Children with Special Needs serves handicapped students.

At the postsecondary level there are a teachers' training college, affiliated with the University of the West Indies, and a technical college. Adult education classes are offered by the Ministry of Education. Literacy is estimated at 96%. In 1989, stu-dents at the university and all higher-level institutions numbered 677 with 96 teaching staff.

32 MEDIA

There is one weekly newspaper, the *Vincentian News,* appearing on Friday, with a circulation of 8,000.

There are 2 radio stations, and 1 television station. In 1991 there were 75,000 radios and 15,000 television sets. There were 12,000 telephones on the islands in 1983.

33 TOURISM AND RECREATION

Tourism is oriented toward yachting, with havens located on most of the Grenadines. Posh resorts have been created on many of the smaller Grenadines, with villas and cottages built alongside small private beaches.

There are a total of 1,164 hotel rooms. The number of tourist arrivals totaled 51,629 in 1991, of whom 36,088 were from the Americas and 14,013 were from Europe.

34 FAMOUS ST. VINCENTIANS

Robert Milton Cato (b.1915) was prime minister from independence until 1984; James FitzAllen Mitchell (b.1931) has been prime minister since then. Sir Fred Albert Phillips (b.1918) is a specialist on constitutional and international law.

35 BIBLIOGRAPHY

Potter, Robert B. *St. Vincent and the Grenadines.* Santa Barbara, Calif.: Clio, 1992.

Shephard, Charles. *An Historical Account of the Island of Saint Vincent.* London: F. Cass, 1971.

St. Vincent and the Grenadines. Washington, D.C.: U.S. Dept. of Commerce, International Trade Administration, n.d.

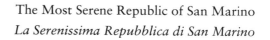

The Most Serene Republic of San Marino
La Serenissima Repubblica di San Marino

CAPITAL: San Marino.

FLAG: The flag is divided horizontally into two equal bands, sky blue below and white above, with the national coat of arms superimposed in the center.

ANTHEM: *Onore a te, onore, o antica repubblica (Honor to You, O Ancient Republic).*

MONETARY UNIT: San Marino principally uses the Italian lira (L) as currency; Vatican City State currency is also honored. The country issues its own coins in standard Italian denominations in limited numbers as well. Coins of San Marino may circulate in both the republic and in Italy. L1 = $0.0006 (or $1 = L1,611.3).

WEIGHTS AND MEASURES: The metric system is the legal standard.

HOLIDAYS: New Year's Day, 1 January; Epiphany, 6 January; Anniversary of St. Agatha, second patron saint of the republic, and of the liberation of San Marino (1740), 5 February; Anniversary of the Arengo, 25 March; Investiture of the Captains-Regent, 1 April and 1 October; Labor Day, 1 May; Fall of Fascism, 28 July; Assumption and August Bank Holiday, 14–16 August; Anniversary of the Foundation of San Marino, 3 September; All Saint's Day, 1 November; Commemoration of the Dead, 2 November; Immaculate Conception, 8 December; Christmas, 24–26 December; New Year's Eve, 31 December. Movable religious holidays include Easter Monday and Ascension.

TIME: 1 PM = noon GMT.

1 LOCATION AND SIZE

San Marino is the third-smallest country in Europe, with an area of 60 square kilometers (232 square miles), about one-third the size of Washington, D.C. It is a landlocked state completely surrounded by Italy, with a total boundary length of 39 kilometers (24 miles).

2 TOPOGRAPHY

The town of San Marino is on the slopes and at the summit of Mt. Titano (Monte Titano) at 739 meters (2,425 feet), which has three peaks. Level areas around the base of Mt. Titano provide land for agricultural use.

3 CLIMATE

The climate is that of northeastern Italy: rather mild in winter, but with temperatures frequently below freezing, and warm and pleasant in the summer, reaching a maximum of 26°C (79°F). Annual rainfall averages about 89 centimeters (35 inches).

4 PLANTS AND ANIMALS

The republic has the same native plants and animals as northeastern Italy.

5 ENVIRONMENT

Information on the environment is not available.

6 POPULATION

The resident population was 23,719 at the 1992 census. Population density was 388 persons per square kilometer (1,004 per square mile). At the end of 1990, 4,185 people lived in the capital, also called San Marino.

7 MIGRATION

Immigrants come chiefly from Italy; emigration is mainly to Italy, the United States, France, and Belgium.

8 ETHNIC GROUPS

The native population is mostly of Italian origin.

9 LANGUAGES

Italian is the official language.

10 RELIGIONS

With few exceptions, the population is Roman Catholic, and Roman Catholicism is the official religion.

11 TRANSPORTATION

Streets and roads within the republic total about 220 kilometers (140 miles), and there is regular bus service between San Marino and the Italian city of Rimini. Motor vehicle registrations in 1991 included 20,508 passenger cars and 3,357 commercial vehicles.

12 HISTORY

San Marino is the oldest republic in the world. It is the sole survivor of the independent states that existed in Italy at various times, from the downfall of the western Roman Empire to the proclamation of the Kingdom of Italy in 1861.

According to tradition, the republic was founded in the fourth century AD by Marinus, a Christian stonecutter who fled from Dalmatia (across the Adriatic Sea from Italy in present-day Croatia) to avoid religious persecution. Later canonized (declared a saint), St. Marinus is known in Italian as San Marino. There was a monastery in San Marino in existence at least as early as 885.

Because of the poverty of the region and the mountainous terrain, San Marino was rarely disturbed by outside powers. It was briefly held by Cesare Borgia (an Italina military and church leader) in 1503, but in 1549 its sovereignty (independence) was confirmed by Pope Paul III. In 1739, a military force under Cardinal Giulio Alberoni occupied San Marino. In the following year, Pope Clement II terminated the occupation and signed a treaty of friendship with the tiny republic. Napoleon allowed San Marino to retain its liberty.

In 1849, Giuseppe Garibaldi, the liberator of Italy, took refuge from the Austrians in San Marino. San Marino and Italy entered into a treaty of friendship in 1862, which is still in effect. In 1922–43, during the period of Benito Mussolini's rule in Italy, San Marino adopted a Fascist (dictatorial) type of government. Despite its claim to neutrality in World War II, San Marino was bombed by Allied (United Kingdom, United States and their allies) planes on 26 June 1944. The raid caused heavy damage, especially to the railway line, and killed a number of persons.

Since 1945, government control has shifted between parties of the right and left, often in coalitions. In 1986, a Communist–Christian Democratic coalition came to power.

LOCATION: 12°27′E and 43°56′N.

13 GOVERNMENT

Legislative power is exercised by the Grand and General Council of 60 members, regularly elected every five years by universal vote at age 18. The Council elects from among its members a State Congress of ten members, which makes and carries out most administrative decisions. Two members of the Council are named every six months to head the executive branch of the government; one represents the town of San Marino and the other the countryside.

14 POLITICAL PARTIES

The political parties in San Marino have close ties with the corresponding parties in Italy: the Christian Democrats (Partito Democratico Cristiano Sammarinese—DCS), Communists (Partito Communista Sammarinese—PCS), Socialists (Partito Socialista Sammarinese—PSS), and Social Democrats (Partito Socialista Democratico Independente Sammarinese—PSDIS).

15 JUDICIAL SYSTEM

There is a civil court, a criminal court, and a superior court. Most criminal cases are tried before Italian magistrates because, with the exception of minor civil suits, the judges in cases in San Marino are not allowed to be citizens of San Marino. The highest appellate court is the Council of Twelve.

16 ARMED FORCES

The San Marino militia officially consists of all able-bodied citizens between the ages of 16 and 55, but the armed forces are principally for purposes of ceremonial display.

17 ECONOMY

Farming was formerly the principal occupation, but it has been replaced in importance by light manufacturing. However, the main sources of income are tourism and payments by citizens of San Marino (Sanmarinese) living abroad. Some government revenue comes from the sale of postage stamps and coins and from a subsidy by Italy.

18 INCOME

In 1992, San Marino's gross domestic product (GDP) was $465 million at current prices, or $29,605 per person. In 1992 the average inflation rate was 5%.

19 INDUSTRY

Manufacturing is limited to light industries such as textiles, bricks and tiles, leather goods, clothing, and metalwork. Cotton textiles are woven at Serravalle; bricks and tiles are made in La Dogana, which also has a dyeing plant; and cement factories and a tannery are located in Acquaviva, as well as a paper-making plant. Synthetic rubber is also produced. The pottery of Borgo Maggiore is well known. Gold and silver souvenirs are made for the tourist trade. Other products are Moscato wine, olive oil, and baked goods.

20 LABOR

Most of the inhabitants are farmers or stock raisers. The wage labor force in 1991 totaled about 13,322 persons, most of whom worked in manufacturing or service occupations. There is little unemployment (493 persons in 1991).

21 AGRICULTURE

Annual crop production includes wheat and grapes, as well as other grains, vegetables, fruits, and livestock feed.

22 DOMESTICATED ANIMALS

Livestock raising uses some 1,400 hectares (3,500 acres), or about 23% of the total area. Cattle, hogs, sheep, and horses are raised.

23 FISHING

There is no significant fishing.

24 FORESTRY

Small quantities of wood are cut for local use.

25 MINING

San Marino has no commercial mineral resources.

26 FOREIGN TRADE

Principal exports are wine, textiles, furniture, quarried stone, ceramics, and handicrafts. The chief imports are raw materials and a wide variety of consumer goods. San Marino has a customs union (agreement allowing for import and export) with Italy.

27 ENERGY AND POWER

Electric power is imported from Italy.

28 SOCIAL DEVELOPMENT

The government maintains a comprehensive social insurance program, including disability, family supplement payments, and old-age pensions. In 1982, Sanmarinese women who married foreign citizens were given the right to keep their citizenships.

29 HEALTH

Public health institutions include the State Hospital, a dispensary for the poor, and a laboratory of hygiene and prophylaxis. All citizens receive free, comprehensive medical care. Estimated average life expectancy in 1992 was 77 years.

30 HOUSING

In 1986, San Marino had 7,926 dwellings, nearly all with electricity and piped-in water. Most new construction is financed privately.

31 EDUCATION

Primary education is compulsory for all children between the ages of 6 and 14; the adult literacy rate is about 98%. The program of instruction is patterned after Italy's.

In 1991, there were 14 elementary schools, with 1,200 students and 218 teachers; middle and upper-secondary schools enrolled 1,158 pupils during the same year. San Marino students (Sanmarinese) are able to enroll at Italian universities.

32 MEDIA

There are no local radio or television stations, but there were 14,000 radios and 8,000 television sets in 1991. A telephone system integrated into Italy's system served 11,707 telephones in 1986.

Daily newspapers are not published in San Marino, but political papers are issued by the political parties: the Christian Democratic *San Marino,* the Social Democratic *Riscossa Socialista,* the Socialist *Il Nuovo Titano,* and the Communist *La Scintilla.*

33 TOURISM AND RECREATION

The government has promoted tourism so successfully that during summer months, the number of San Marino residents is often exceeded by the number of visitors. In 1987, an estimated three million people visited San Marino. There were 22 hotels and 35 restaurants in 1986.

Growth in the tourist industry has increased the demand for San Marino's stamps and coins, gold and silver souvenirs, handicrafts, and pottery.

Principal attractions are the three medieval fortresses at the summit of Mt. Titano (Monte Titano), the magnificent view of the Italian city of Rimini, and the Italian coast of the Adriatic Sea.

34 FAMOUS SANMARINESE

Well-known Italians associated with San Marino include Cardinal Giulio Alberoni

(1664–1752), who attempted to subject the republic to papal domination in 1739–40; and Giuseppe Garibaldi (1807–82), the great Italian patriot, who obtained refuge from the Austrians in San Marino in 1849.

35 BIBLIOGRAPHY

Bent, James Theodore. *A Freak of Freedom; or, The Republic of San Marino*. Port Washington, N.Y.: Kennikat Press, 1970 (orig. 1879).

Johnson, Virginia Wales. *Two Quaint Republics: Andorra and San Marino*. Boston: Estes, 1913.

SÃO TOMÉ AND PRÍNCIPE

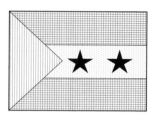

Democratic Republic of São Tomé and Príncipe
República Democrática de São Tomé e Príncipe

CAPITAL: São Tomé.

FLAG: The flag consists of three unequal horizontal stripes of green, yellow, and green; there is a red triangle at the hoist, and two black stars on the yellow stripe.

ANTHEM: *Independéncia Total (Total Independence).*

MONETARY UNIT: The dobra (Db) is equal to 100 centimos. There are coins of 50 centimos and 1, 2, 5, 10, and 20 dobras, and notes of 50, 100, 500, and 1,000 dobras. Db 1 = $0.0306 (or $1 = Db32.6394)

WEIGHTS AND MEASURES: The metric system is used.

HOLIDAYS: New Year's Day, 1 January; Martyrs' Day, 4 February; Labor Day, 1 May; Independence Day, 12 July; Armed Forces Day, first week in September; Farmers' Day, 30 September. The principal Christian holidays are also observed.

TIME: GMT.

1 LOCATION AND SIZE

São Tomé and Príncipe, the smallest country in Africa, lies in the Gulf of Guinea off the west coast of Gabon.

The nation has an area of 960 square kilometers (371 square miles), of which São Tomé comprises 855 square kilometers (330 square miles), and Príncipe 109 square kilometers (42 square miles). Comparatively, the nations' combined area is slightly less than 5.5 times the size of Washington, D.C.

São Tomé has a coastline of 141 kilometers (88 miles); Príncipe's shoreline is 209 kilometers (130 miles). The capital city, São Tomé, is located on the northeast coast of the island of São Tomé.

2 TOPOGRAPHY

The islands form part of a chain of extinct volcanoes and are both quite mountainous. Pico Kabumbé, at 1,403 meters (4,603 feet) is one of the highest peaks on São Tomé; Pico de Príncipe is Príncipe's tallest mountain.

3 CLIMATE

Coastal temperatures average 27°C (81°F), but the mountain regions average only 20°C (68°F). From October to May, São Tomé and Príncipe receive between 380 and 510 centimeters (150–200 inches) of rain.

4 PLANTS AND ANIMALS

Except for the coastal flatlands, where cocoa and coffee plantations predominate,

São Tomé and Príncipe are dominated by forestland. There is little livestock, but domestic fowl are abundant.

5 ENVIRONMENT

The nation lacks an adequate water treatment system, and its forests are threatened by overuse. The cities have inadequate sewage treatment. Soil erosion and exhaustion are other major environmental problems.

6 POPULATION

In 1994, the estimated population of São Tomé and Príncipe was 140,321, of whom all but about 9,000 lived on São Tomé. In 1994, the estimated population density was 125 persons per square kilometer (324 persons per square mile). The capital city, São Tomé, had an estimated 50,000 inhabitants in 1990.

7 MIGRATION

After independence in 1975, almost all the 3,000–4,000 European settlers, and most Cape Verdeans, left the islands.

8 ETHNIC GROUPS

Most of the islands' permanent residents are Fôrros, descendants of the Portuguese colonists and their African slaves. The Angolares, descendants of shipwrecked Angolan slaves, live along the southeast coast of São Tomé.

9 LANGUAGES

Portuguese, the official language, is spoken in a Creole dialect that reveals the heavy influence of African Bantu languages.

10 RELIGIONS

Roman Catholicism is the dominant religion, with professing Catholics estimated at 82.5% in 1993. Traditional African religions are also practiced, and there is a small Protestant minority.

11 TRANSPORTATION

There are about 200 kilometers (125 miles) of surfaced roads. São Tomé and Santo António are the main ports. The international airport at São Tomé serviced an estimated 23,000 passengers in 1991.

12 HISTORY

São Tomé and Príncipe were probably uninhabited volcanic islands when the Portuguese landed there in 1471. They were declared a concession (a grant of land in exchange for services) of Portugal in 1485. The islands were completely taken over by the Portuguese crown in 1522 and 1573. By the mid-sixteenth century, the islands were Africa's leading exporter of sugar. By 1908 São Tomé had become the world's largest producer of cocoa. Plantation slavery or slavelike contract labor remained the basis of island labor for hundreds of years, even after slavery formally ended.

The Committee for the Liberation of São Tomé and Príncipe (later renamed the Movement for the Liberation of São Tomé and Príncipe—MLSTP) was formed in 1960 and recognized by Portugal in 1974 as the sole legitimate representative of the people of São Tomé and Príncipe. On 12 July 1975, the islands achieved full independence. On the same day, Manuel Pinto da Costa, the secretary-general of the

MLSTP, became the country's first president. In 1979, Prime Minister Miguel dos Anjos da Cunha Lisboa Trovoada was arrested and charged with attempting to seize power. By 1985, São Tomé and Príncipe had begun to establish closer ties with the West.

In 1990, a new policy of *abertura*, or political and economic "opening," led to the legalization of opposition parties and direct elections with secret balloting. A number of groups united as the Party of Democratic Convergence-Group of Reflection (PDC-GR), led by former prime minister Miguel Trovoada, who was elected president on 3 March 1991.

13 GOVERNMENT

A new constitution was adopted by the People's Assembly in April 1990. The president is chosen for a maximum of two five-year terms. The People's Assembly, now composed of 55 members, is elected to four-year terms. Voting is universal at age 18.

14 POLITICAL PARTIES

On 15 October 1974, the government of Portugal recognized the Movement for the Liberation of São Tomé and Príncipe (Movimento de Libertação de São Tomé e Príncipe—MLSTP) as the sole legitimate representative for the islands. After independence, the MLSTP became the only political party. With the legalization of opposition party activity, Miguel Trovoada, an MLSTP founder who had been exiled, formed the Democratic Convergence Party-Group of Reflection (PCD-GR). Other parties include The Demo-

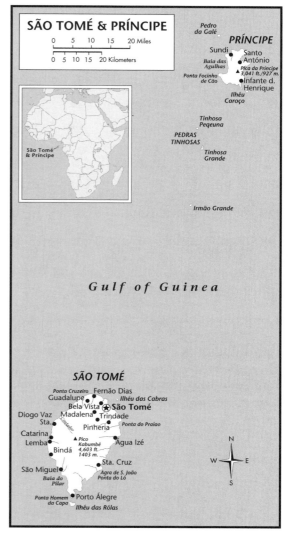

LOCATION: São Tomé: 0°13′N and 6°37′E. Príncipe: 1°37′N and 7°24′E. **TERRITORIAL SEA LIMIT:** 12 miles.

cratic Opposition Coalition (CODO) and the Christian Democratic Front (FDC).

15 JUDICIAL SYSTEM

The highest court is the Supreme Tribunal, which is named by and responsible to the People's Assembly. The constitution

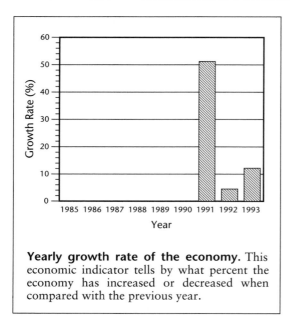

Yearly growth rate of the economy. This economic indicator tells by what percent the economy has increased or decreased when compared with the previous year.

doned socialist-style economic policies in favor of market-style policies.

18 INCOME

In 1992, gross domestic product (GDP) was estimated at $41.4 million. Of that, the agricultural sector accounted for 28.9%, trade 16.9%, and transport 3.7%.

19 INDUSTRY

São Tomé has very little industry. Soap, beverages, finished wood and furniture, bread, textiles, bricks and ceramics, garments, and palm oil are produced on the islands.

20 LABOR

Agriculture and fishing supported over half the population in 1991. Laborers for the plantation sector come from mainland Africa and Cape Verde on a contract basis. Workers may organize and bargain collectively.

21 AGRICULTURE

About half of all cultivated land is used for cocoa production. Production of cocoa was believed to be about 2,000 tons in 1992. Copra (dried coconut meat used to produce coconut oil) is the second most important crop; production in 1992 totaled about 3,000 tons. Other agricultural products in 1992 were palm kernels, 500 tons; bananas, 3,000 tons; cassava, 5,000 tons; and coconuts, 42,000 tons.

22 DOMESTICATED ANIMALS

The livestock sector, largely pigs, was plagued by African swine fever in 1992, necessitating the destruction of the entire

affords parties in civil cases the right to a fair public trial and a right to appeal. The constitution also affords criminal defendants a public trial before a judge as well as legal representation.

16 ARMED FORCES

A small citizen's army was formed in 1975 by the Movement for the Liberation of São Tomé and Príncipe (MLSTP) government after Portuguese troops were withdrawn.

17 ECONOMY

São Tomé and Príncipe is one of the poorest countries in the world. The economy is based on cocoa-producing plantation agriculture, but the fall of cocoa prices since the early 1980s has created serious problems for the government, which aban-

herd of some 30,000 animals. In 1992 there were an estimated 4,000 head of cattle, 2,000 sheep, 4,000 goats, and 3,000 pigs.

23 FISHING

The Angolare (descendants of ship-wrecked slaves) community of São Tomé supplies fish to the domestic market. In 1991, the catch was 3,500 tons.

24 FORESTRY

Wood is used on the plantations for fuel to dry cocoa beans and elsewhere as a building material. Roundwood removals are estimated at 9,000 cubic meters a year.

25 MINING

Mineral wealth remains largely unexplored, although lime deposits are exploited for the local market.

26 FOREIGN TRADE

São Tomé and Príncipe's trade balance depends on price levels for cocoa, which accounts for about 85% of export earnings. Copra (dried coconut meat used to produce coconut oil) is also exported. The leading imports are foodstuffs, fuels, textiles, and machinery. The leading purchasers of exports are the Netherlands and Germany.

27 ENERGY AND POWER

About 8 million of São Tomé's 15 million kilowatt hours of electric power in 1991 were produced by hydroelectricity; the rest was thermal. Only a quarter of the nation's households have electricity.

28 SOCIAL DEVELOPMENT

Before independence in 1975, social welfare was handled largely by the plantation corporations, missionaries, and private agencies. After independence, the government assumed responsibility for fostering community well-being.

29 HEALTH

Malnutrition continues to plague the country. There were an estimated 220 cases of tuberculosis per 100,000 people reported in 1990. Life expectancy is 67 years. In 1983 there were 16 hospitals and dispensaries, and, by 1989, 61 doctors.

30 HOUSING

Housing on the islands varies greatly, from the estate houses of the plantation headquarters to the thatch huts of the plantation laborers. Some town buildings are wooden; others are mud block with timber, as are plantation-labor dormitories.

31 EDUCATION

Schooling is compulsory for three years only. Primary education is for four years and secondary has two stages: the first four years are followed by three years.

In 1989 there were 19,822 pupils in 64 primary schools with 559 teachers; in general secondary schools, there were 318 teachers and 7,446 pupils. In the mid-1990s, adult literacy was estimated at 77%.

32 MEDIA

The *Diario da Republica* (1991 circulation: 500) is published weekly by the gov-

Selected Social Indicators

These statistics are estimates for the period 1988 to 1993. For comparison purposes, data for the United States and averages for low-income countries and high-income countries are also given.

Indicator	São Tomé and Príncipe	Low-income countries	High-income countries	United States
Per capita gross national product†	**$296**	$380	$23,680	$24,740
Population growth rate	**2.0%**	1.9%	0.6%	1.0%
Population growth rate in urban areas	**4.0%**	3.9%	0.8%	1.3%
Population per square kilometer of land	**125**	78	25	26
Life expectancy in years	**67**	62	77	76
Number of people per physician	**2,295**	>3,300	453	419
Number of pupils per teacher (primary school)	**35**	39	<18	20
Illiteracy rate (15 years and older)	**23%**	41%	<5%	<3%
Energy consumed per capita (kg of oil equivalent)	**189**	364	5,203	7,918

† The gross national product (GNP) is the total dollar value of all goods and services produced by a country in a year. The per capita GNP is calculated by dividing a country's GNP by its population. The World Bank defines low-income countries as those with a per capita GNP of $695 or less. High-income countries have a per capita GNP of $8,626 or more. Less than 14% of the world's 5.5 billion people live in high-income countries, while almost 60% live in low-income countries.

> = greater than   < = less than

Sources: World Bank, *Social Indicators of Development 1995*, Baltimore: Johns Hopkins University Press, 1995. Central Intelligence Agency, *World Fact Book*, Washington, D.C.: Government Printing Office, 1994.

ernment. *Noticias Sao Tome e Principe* is a quarterly, with a 1991 circulation of 2,000. The national radio station broadcasts in Portuguese; there were an estimated 32,000 radios in 1991. A television station broadcasts two days a week. In 1991 there were 2,800 telephones in use.

33 TOURISM AND RECREATION

São Tomé and Príncipe's scenic beauty, wildlife, and unique historic architecture have the potential to attract tourists, but tourist facilities are minimal. The first tourist hotel opened in 1986.

34 FAMOUS SÃO TOMÉANS

Rei Amador (d.1596), who rebelled against the Portuguese, is a national hero. Alda de Espírito Santo (b.1926) is a poet and nationalist leader. Manuel Pinto da Costa (b.1937) became the country's first president on 12 July 1975.

35 BIBLIOGRAPHY

Hodges, Tony. *Sao Tome and Principe: from Plantation Colony to Microstate*. Boulder, Colo.: Westview Press, 1988.

Nevinson, Henry Wood. *A Modern Slavery*. With an introduction by Basil Davidson. London: Daimon Press, 1963 (orig. 1906).

SA'UDI ARABIA

Kingdom of Sa'udi Arabia

Al-Mamlakah al-'Arabiyah as-Sa'udiyah

CAPITAL: Riyadh (Ar-Riyad).

FLAG: The national flag bears in white on a green field the inscription, in Arabic, "There is no god but Allah, and Mohammad is the messenger of Allah." There is a long white sword beneath the inscription; the sword handle is toward the fly.

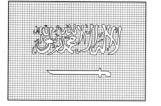

ANTHEM: The National Anthem is a short instrumental selection.

MONETARY UNIT: The Sa'udi riyal (SR) is divided into 20 qursh (piasters), in turn divided into 5 halalah. There are coins of 1, 5, 10, 25, 50, and 100 halalah and notes of 1, 5, 10, 50, 100, and 500 riyals. SR1 = $0.2670 (or $1 = SR3.7450).

WEIGHTS AND MEASURES: The metric system has been officially adopted.

HOLIDAYS: Muslim religious holidays include 1st of Muharram (Muslim New Year), 'Id al-Fitr, and 'Id al-'Adha'.

TIME: 3 PM = noon GMT.

1 LOCATION AND SIZE

Sa'udi Arabia, the third-largest country in Asia, constitutes about four-fifths of the Arabian Peninsula in Southwest Asia. Its precise area is difficult to specify because several of its borders are incompletely marked out. According to United Nations estimates, the nation has an area of 1,960,582 square kilometers (756,985 square miles), slightly less than one-fourth the size of the United States, with a total estimated boundary length of 7,055 kilometers (4,384 miles).

Sa'udi Arabia's capital city, Riyadh, is located in the east central part of the country.

2 TOPOGRAPHY

A narrow plain, the Tihamat ash Sham, parallels the Red Sea coast, as do the Hijaz Mountains (Al Hijaz), which rise sharply from the sea. The highest mountains are in the south. East of the Hijaz, the mountains give way to the central uplands. The Dahna (Ad Dahna), a desert region, separates the uplands from the low plateau to the east, which, in turn, gives way to the low-lying Persian Gulf region.

At least one-third of the total area is sandy desert. There are no lakes, and except for artesian wells (wells where water flows to the surface naturally) in the eastern oases, there is no constant flowing water.

3 CLIMATE

From May to September, the hottest period, daytime temperatures reach 54°C (129°F) in the interior and are among the highest recorded anywhere in the world.

From October through April, the climate is more moderate, with evening temperatures between 16° and 21°C (61° and 70°F). Average annual rainfall is 9 centimeters (3.5 inches).

4 PLANTS AND ANIMALS

The date palm, mangrove, tamarisk, and acacia are common. Wild mammals include the oryx, jerboa, fox, lynx, wildcat, monkey, panther, and jackal. The favorite game bird is the bustard. The country is renowned for its camels and Arabian horses. Fish abound in the coastal waters, and insects, scorpions, lizards, and snakes are numerous.

5 ENVIRONMENT

The dumping of up to six million barrels of oil in the surrounding waters and the destruction of Kuwait's oil wells by fire during the Persian Gulf War polluted Sa'udi Arabia's air and water. Sa'udi Arabia uses 47% of its water for farming and 8% for industrial purposes.

In 1994, 9 of the nation's mammal species and 12 types of birds were endangered. Two type of plants were threatened with extinction.

6 POPULATION

A 1992 census recorded the population as 16,929,294. A population of 20,667,000 was projected for the year 2000. There is much debate as to the reliability of official census figures, and it is possible that the actual Sa'udi population in 1990 was no more than six million persons.

The estimated population density in 1992 was 8 persons per square kilometer (20 per square mile). Riyadh, the capital, had 1,975,000 inhabitants in 1990–91.

7 MIGRATION

Palestinian Arabs, displaced by the establishment of the state of Israel, are the chief immigrant group. In the early 1990s there were significant numbers of foreign workers from the United States, European countries, Turkey, Jordan, Syria, Jordan, Kuwait, Yemen, the Republic of Korea (ROK), Pakistan, India, Sri Lanka, and the Philippines. In 1990 when Iraq invaded Kuwait, Sa'udi Arabia reacted by expelling Palestinians, as well as workers from Jordan and Yemen, for their countries' support of Iraq. The foreign population was 4,624,459 in 1992 (27% of the total population). There were some 25,000 Iraqi refugees in Sa'udi Arabia at the end of 1993.

8 ETHNIC GROUPS

The great majority of the Sa'udis have a common Arabian ancestry. Traces of descent from Turks, Iranians, Indonesians, Pakistanis, Indians, various African groups, and other non-Arab Muslim peoples appear in the Hijaz mountains.

9 LANGUAGES

Arabic, the native language of the native population, is a Semitic language related to Hebrew and Aramaic. The language is written in a cursive script from right to left. Most business people and merchants in oil-producing areas and commercial

SA'UDI ARABIA

SAUDI ARABIA

0   100   200 Miles

0   100   200 Kilometers

ISRAEL

JORDAN

Al'Aqabah

Turayf

SYRIAN

DESERT

An Najaf

Al Jawf

IRAQ

Tigris

Euphrates

Al Başrah

KUWAIT

Kuwait

IRAN

N
W — E
S

Jabal al Lawz
8,464 ft.
2580 m.

Tabūk

Al A'sad

An Nafūd

JABAL SHAMMAR

Ḥā'il

Ad Dahnā'

Ra's al Mish'āb

Manifah

Abū'Ali

Persian

Al Wajh

Hamd

Umm Urūmah

Al
HIJĀZ

Buraydah

'Unayzah

Al Faydah

Miskah

Al Jubaylah

Rimah

Al Qaṭif

Aẓ Ẓahrān

Al Hufūf

Riyadh

Al Kharj

Ad Dammām

BAHRAIN

QATAR

Doha

Gulf

Abu Dhabi

Red

Sea

*Yanbu'
al Baḥr*

Al Madinah
(Medina)

Haraḍ

Al Ḥillah

Tihāmat

Jeddah
(Jiddah)

Makkah (Mecca)

Aṭ Ṭā'if

ash

Qal'at Bishah

JABAL TUWAYQ

Al Kharfah

Sabkhai Maṭṭi
(salt flat)

Al'Ubaylah

UNITED
ARAB
EMIRATES

Umm as
Samim
(salt flat)

AR RUB' AL KHĀLĪ

As Sulayyil

Port Sudan

Dawqah

Al Qunfudhah

Jabal Sawda
10,279 ft.
3133 m.

Khamis Mushayṭ

Ash Sharawrah

OMAN

SUDAN

Abhā

Tihām

Najrān

Jizān

Jazā'ir
Farasān

ERITREA

Asmara

Şan'ā

YEMEN

ETHIOPIA

Saudi Arabia

LOCATION: 16°23′ to 32°14′N; 34°30′ to 56°22′w. **BOUNDARY LENGTHS:** Jordan, 728 kilometers (455 miles); Iraq, 814 kilometers (505 miles); Kuwait, 222 kilometers (138 miles); Persian Gulf coastline, 751 kilometers (468 miles); Qatar, 60 kilometers (37 miles); UAE, 457 kilometers (285 miles); Oman, 676 kilometers (420 miles); Yemen 1,458 kilometers (906 miles); Red Sea coastline, 1,889 kilometers (1,170 miles). **TERRITORIAL SEA LIMIT:** 12 miles.

centers understand English. Government correspondence must be written in Arabic.

10 RELIGIONS

About 85% of the people of Sa'udi Arabia are Sunni Muslims. Most other Sa'udis are Shi'ite Muslims. The holy city of Mecca (Makkah) is the center of Islam and the site of the sacred Ka'bah sanctuary, toward which all Muslims face at prayer. There are several thousand foreign Christian workers—mostly Arab, American, and European.

11 TRANSPORTATION

In 1991 there were 74,000 kilometers (45,880 miles) of highways. In 1991, motor vehicle registrations totaled 4.5 million. Railroad lines totaled 886 kilometers (551 miles) of track in 1991.

Jiddah (Jeddah), on the Red Sea, is the chief port of entry for Muslim pilgrims going to Mecca; other ports include Ad-Dammam, Yanbu 'al Bahr, and Jizan. The government-owned Sa'udi Arabian Airlines (Saudia) operates regular domestic and foreign flights to major cities. There are major airports at Jiddah, Riyadh, and 20 other cities.

12 HISTORY

For several thousand years, Arabia has been inhabited by nomadic Semitic tribes. Towns were established at various oases and along caravan routes. During the seventh century AD, followers of Mohammad expanded beyond the Mecca-Medina region and within a century conquered most of the Mediterranean region between Persia (present-day Iran) in the east and Spain in the west.

Although Arabs were dominant in many parts of the Muslim world and there was a great medieval flowering of Arab civilization, the Arabian Peninsula itself (except for the holy cities of Mecca and Medina [Al Madinah]) declined in importance and remained virtually isolated for almost a thousand years. Throughout this period, Arabia was little less than a province of successive Islamic kingdoms *(caliphates)* that established their capitals in Damascus, Baghdad, Cairo, and Constantinople (now Istanbul).

The Birth of the Sa'udi Kingdom

The foundations of the kingdom of Sa'udi Arabia were laid in the eighteenth century in a program of religious reform and territorial expansion by the Sa'ud family and Mohammad bin 'Abd al-Wahhab, who preached a return to the fundamentals of Islam. First the central uplands, and then the Hijaz mountains were brought under Sa'udi control, as well as the holy city of Mecca. A long struggle with the Ottoman Turks (1811–18) finally resulted in Sa'udi defeat.

Under Faisal (Faysal, r. 1843–67), the Sa'udis regained control of the region. They lost it to the Ibn-Rashids in 1891, but succeeded in breaking the Rashidi power in 1906. In December 1915, the Sa'udi leader Ibn-Sa'ud signed a treaty with the British that placed Sa'udi foreign relations under British control in return for a sizable subsidy.

Prophet's Mosque, Al Madinah Al Munawarah.

In the 1920s, Ibn-Sa'ud consolidated his power, defeating challenges by Hussein ibn-'Ali (Husayn ibn-'Ali), the sharif (of noble ancestry in an Islamic country) of Mecca, and capturing At Ta'if, Mecca, and Medina, as well as Jiddah. On 22 September 1932, the various parts of the realm were combined into the Kingdom of Sa'udi Arabia, with much the same boundaries that exist today.

Oil and the Modern Sa'udi State

With the discovery of oil in the 1930s, the history of Sa'udi Arabia was changed forever. Reserves have proved vast—about one-fourth of the world's total—and production, begun in earnest after World War II (1939–45), has provided a huge income, much of it expended on construction and social services. Sa'udi Arabia's petroleum-derived wealth has considerably enhanced the country's influence in world economic and political forums.

Since the 1980s, the government has regulated its petroleum production to stabilize the international oil market and has used its influence as the most powerful moderate member of the Organization of Petroleum Exporting Countries (OPEC) to restrain the more radical members.

Political life in Sa'udi Arabia has remained basically stable in recent decades, despite several abrupt changes of leadership. Crown Prince Fahd ibn-'Abd al-'Aziz as-Sa'ud ascended the throne in 1982 after his half-brother, King Khaled, died of a heart attack. King Fahd has encouraged continuing modernization while seeking to preserve the nation's social stability and Islamic heritage.

Sa'udi Arabia's wealth and selective generosity have given it great political influence throughout the world and especially in the Middle East. It suspended aid to Egypt after that country's peace talks with Israel at Camp David, Maryland, but renewed relations in 1987. It secretly contributed substantial funds to United States President Ronald Reagan's administration for combating Communist regimes in Central America. It actively supported Iraq during the war with Iran and tried, in vain, to prevent Iraq's conflict with Kuwait.

When Iraq invaded Kuwait in 1990, Sa'udi Arabia, fearing Iraqi aggression, radically altered its traditional policy to permit the stationing of foreign troops on its soil. Riyadh made substantial contributions of arms, oil, and funds to the allied victory, cutting off subsidies to and expelling Palestinians and workers from Jordan, Yemen, and other countries that had supported Iraq in the period after the invasion.

Sa'udi Arabia and the United States consult closely on political, economic, commercial, and security matters.

13 GOVERNMENT

Sa'udi Arabia is a religiously-based monarchy in which the sovereign's dominant powers are regulated according to Muslim law (*Shari'ah*), tribal law, and custom. There is no written constitution; laws must be compatible with Islamic law. The Council of Ministers is appointed by the king to advise on policy, originate legislation, and supervise the growing bureaucracy. In 1992, King Fahd announced the creation of the Majlis al Shura, an advisory body that would provide a forum for public debate.

The kingdom is divided into 14 emirates (state in an Islamic nation), each headed by a crown-appointed governor.

14 POLITICAL PARTIES

There are no political parties in Sa'udi Arabia.

15 JUDICIAL SYSTEM

The king acts as the highest court of appeal and has the power of pardon. The judiciary consists of lower courts that handle misdemeanors and minor civil cases; high courts of Islamic law (Shari'ah), and courts of appeal. An 11-member Supreme Council of Justice reviews all sentences of execution, cutting, or stoning.

16 ARMED FORCES

Sa'udi Arabia's armed forces totaled 102,500 personnel in 1993, having doubled in size to meet the Iraqi threat. The army had 73,000 personnel, 700 main battle tanks, 700 armored fighting vehicles, and 33 batteries of surface-to-air missiles. The navy's strength was about 11,000 personnel (1,500 marines), who manned 8 frigates and 12 other combat-

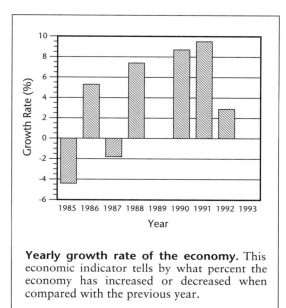

Yearly growth rate of the economy. This economic indicator tells by what percent the economy has increased or decreased when compared with the previous year.

ants. The air force had 18,000 personnel and 273 combat aircraft.

In 1992 Sa'udi Arabia spent $14.5 billion on its own forces, as well as contributing $17 billion for United States Gulf War costs.

17 ECONOMY

The economy is heavily dependent on oil production. The increase in oil prices in 1990 as well as higher oil production levels were largely responsible for the $16 billion increase in oil export revenues that boosted the Saudi economy in 1990.

The government has tried to diversify the economy by developing industries using petroleum, including steel and petrochemical manufacture. Defense accounts for 31% of the budget.

18 INCOME

Sa'udi Arabia's gross national product (GNP) was $126,355 million at current prices, or about $7,810 per person. For the period 1985–92 the average inflation rate was 1.5%, resulting in a real growth rate in per person GNP of 1.3%.

19 INDUSTRY

The country is attempting to diversify its manufacturing. In 1985, some 1,800 operating factories turned out cement, steel, glass, metal manufactures, automotive parts, building materials, and other industrial products, along with petroleum refinery products and petrochemicals. Production of refined oil products totaled 415,255,000 barrels in 1985.

20 LABOR

In 1991, about three million foreigners worked in Sa'udi Arabia, mostly in the oil and construction sector; the total labor force stood at five million, with 34% in government, 28% in industry and oil, 22% in services, and 16% in agriculture. No labor unions exist, but there are professional and trade guilds.

21 AGRICULTURE

Agriculture employed 569,000 persons in 1990. Only about 1.1% of Sa'udi Arabia's land area is cultivated, although 40% is suitable for grazing. Agricultural irrigation accounts for 90% of total water needs, with wheat production alone using about one-third of the country's annual water supply.

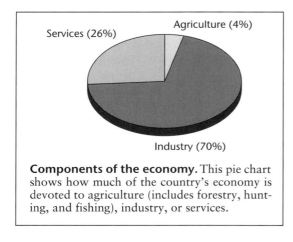

Services (26%)　　Agriculture (4%)

Industry (70%)

Components of the economy. This pie chart shows how much of the country's economy is devoted to agriculture (includes forestry, hunting, and fishing), industry, or services.

Although Sa'udi Arabia has more than seven million date palms and provides about 15% of the world's supply of dates (an estimated 545,000 tons in 1992), the growing of dates has declined in recent decades in favor of wheat, corn, sorghum, tomatoes, onions, grapes, and a variety of other fruits and vegetables. Wheat output was 4,100,000 tons in 1992.

22 DOMESTICATED ANIMALS

As of 1992, Sa'udi Arabia had an estimated 6,008,000 sheep, 3,350,000 goats, 419,000 camels, 216,000 head of cattle, and 102,000 donkeys. Donkeys and mules are still valued as pack animals, and the northern Persian Gulf coast area is well known for its white donkeys. Goats are kept for milk; their hair is used in rugs and tents, and the skins serve as water bags. The output of poultry and eggs doubled during 1975–80, and in 1992, Sa'udi Arabia had an estimated 83 million poultry.

23 FISHING

Fishing provides employment and self-sufficiency to communities on both Sa'udi coasts, although cash earnings are negligible. The fish catch was estimated at 43,251 tons in 1991.

24 FORESTRY

The principal varieties of forest growth—acacia, date, juniper, wild olive, sidr, tamarind, and tamarisk—are generally not useful for timber, but some wood from date palms is used for construction.

25 MINING

Mining experts suspect that Sa'udi Arabia has substantial national reserves of gold, iron ore (up to four million tons), silver, copper, zinc, lead, pyrites, phosphate, magnesite, barite, marble, and gypsum. An intensive search for these deposits is being carried on by Sa'udi and foreign companies. Production of metal concentrate and bullion in 1991 included copper, 900 tons; gold, 6,400 kilograms (crude bullion); and silver, 16,400 kilograms.

26 FOREIGN TRADE

Total exports were valued at $43.9 billion in 1990, and at $47.8 billion in 1991. Oil export revenues in those years averaged $41.5 billion annually, compared with $24 billion in 1989. Non-oil exports included dates, pearls, jewelry, mineral products, and hides and skins.

Sa'udi Arabia's total imports in 1990 were valued at $21.1 billion. The major categories of imports included machinery and electrical appliances, grains and other

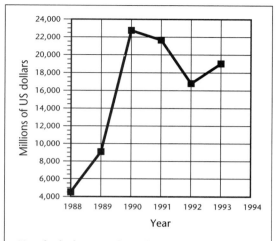

Yearly balance of trade measured in millions of US dollars. The balance of trade is the difference between what a country sells to other countries (its exports) and what it buys (its imports). If a country imports more than it exports, it has a negative balance of trade (a trade deficit). If exports exceed imports there is a positive balance of trade (a trade surplus).

food imports, transportation equipment, and basic metals.

In 1989, Western European countries accounted for 21.3% of Sa'udi Arabia's exports and supplied 39.8% of imports. Japan took 17.5% of exports and supplied 14.2% of imports. The United States accounted for 25.8% of exports and 18.2% of imports.

27 ENERGY AND POWER

With the dissolution of the former Soviet Union in December 1991, Sa'udi Arabia became the world's largest oil producer. Proven reserves of crude oil were estimated at 257.8 billion barrels (35.1 billion tons), or about one-fourth of the world's known deposits, in 1992. In 1992, an estimated 8.4 million barrels of crude oil were produced per day, up from 8.1 million in 1991 and 6.4 million in 1990.

Natural gas production was 34,600 million cubic meters (1,211 billion cubic feet) in 1992. Reserves of natural gas were estimated at 5.2 trillion cubic meters (182.6 trillion cubic feet) in 1992, or 3.7% of the world's total.

Sa'udi Arabia has limited waterpower resources, and oil-powered diesel engines generate most of its electric power. Electrical service reached 92% of the population by 1992. Electric power production in 1991 amounted to 47,710 million kilowatt hours. Solar energy is becoming increasingly important as an alternative to diesel power.

28 SOCIAL DEVELOPMENT

Social welfare in Sa'udi Arabia is traditionally provided through the family or tribe. Those with no family or tribal ties have recourse to the traditional Islamic religious foundations or may request government relief. Social insurance provides health care, disability, death, old age pension, and survivor benefits for workers and their families. A large company with many employees in Sa'udi Arabia, ARAMCO, has a welfare plan for its employees that includes pension funds, accident compensation, and free medical care.

In 1993, only 5% of the labor force was female. Extreme modesty of dress is required, and women are not permitted to drive motor vehicles.

Selected Social Indicators

These statistics are estimates for the period 1988 to 1993. For comparison purposes, data for the United States and averages for low-income countries and high-income countries are also given.

Indicator	Sa'udi Arabia	Low-income countries	High-income countries	United States
Per capita gross national product†	**$7,810**	$380	$23,680	$24,740
Population growth rate	**2.2%**	1.9%	0.6%	1.0%
Population growth rate in urban areas	**2.9%**	3.9%	0.8%	1.3%
Population per square kilometer of land	**8**	78	25	26
Life expectancy in years	**70**	62	77	76
Number of people per physician	**708**	>3,300	453	419
Number of pupils per teacher (primary school)	**16**	39	<18	20
Illiteracy rate (15 years and older)	**38%**	41%	<5%	<3%
Energy consumed per capita (kg of oil equivalent)	**4,552**	364	5,203	7,918

† The gross national product (GNP) is the total dollar value of all goods and services produced by a country in a year. The per capita GNP is calculated by dividing a country's GNP by its population. The World Bank defines low-income countries as those with a per capita GNP of $695 or less. High-income countries have a per capita GNP of $8,626 or more. Less than 14% of the world's 5.5 billion people live in high-income countries, while almost 60% live in low-income countries.

> = greater than   < = less than

Sources: World Bank, Social Indicators of Development 1995, Baltimore: Johns Hopkins University Press, 1995. Central Intelligence Agency, World Fact Book, Washington, D.C.: Government Printing Office, 1994.

29 HEALTH

In 1990, hospital beds per 1,000 people equaled 3.35. Health personnel in 1990 included 21,110 physicians (about 1.82 per 1,000 people), 1,967 dentists, and 48,066 nurses (about 3.8 per 1,000).

The public health care system is supplemented by a small but generally excellent private health sector. In 1992, 97% of the population had access to health care services. Total health care expenditures in 1990 were $4,784 million.

Sa'udi Arabia still suffers from severe health problems. A major cause of disease is malnutrition, leading to widespread scurvy, rickets, night blindness, and anemia, as well as low resistance to tuberculosis. Dysentery attacks all ages and classes, and trachoma is common.

A government campaign was successful in eradicating malaria; typhoid is widespread, but acquired immunity prevents serious outbreaks of this disease.

In 1991, 95% of the population had access to safe water and 86% had adequate sanitation. In 1960, life expectancy at birth was 43 years; it averaged 70 years by 1992.

Photo credit: Information Office, Royal Embassy of Saudi Arabia

General view of H ā'il.

30 HOUSING

The continuing inflow of rural people to towns and cities, coupled with the rise in levels of expectation among the urban population, has created a serious housing problem; improvement in urban housing is one of Sa'udi Arabia's foremost economic needs. Some 506,800 dwelling units were built during 1974–85. In 1984, 78,884 building permits were issued, 84% of these for concrete dwellings and 8% for housing units of blocks and bricks.

31 EDUCATION

The literacy rate was 62% in 1990. In 1990 there were 9,097 primary schools, with 1,876,916 pupils and 119,881 teach-

ers. There are about 16 students per teacher in primary schools. Secondary schools had 892,585 students and 71,149 teachers. Higher education was pursued in 99 institutions, with 84,740 students and 9,512 instructors. The principal universities are King Sa'ud University (formerly Riyadh University) and King 'Abd al-'Aziz University of Jiddah. All higher level institutions had 153,967 pupils and 13,260 teachers in 1990.

32 MEDIA

The telephone system was greatly expanded in the late 1970s, and in 1991 some 1,752,204 telephones were in use. The number of radios was estimated at 4.7

million, and the number of television sets at 4.1 million in 1991.

Newspapers are privately owned; criticism of the fundamental principles of Islam and of basic national institutions, including the royal family, is not permitted. The largest Arabic daily papers (with 1991 circulations) are *Asharq Al-Awsat* (175,000); *Al-Jazirah* (90,000); and *Al-Bilad* (90,000). Leading English-language dailies are the *Arab News* (50,000) and *Saudi Gazette* (50,000).

33 TOURISM AND RECREATION

Sa'udi Arabia is one of the hardest places in the world to visit. Tourist visas are not issued, and foreign visitors must show letters of invitation from Sa'udi employers or sponsors to enter the country. Every year, however, there is a great influx of pilgrims to Mecca (Mekkah) and Medina (Al Madinah), cities that non-Muslims are forbidden to enter. In 1991 the number of pilgrims totaled 720,000. Total visitor arrivals totaled 2.3 million.

Traditional sports include hunting with salukis (tall, swift, slender hunting dogs), falconry, and horse and camel racing. Modern sports facilities include the Riyadh Stadium, complete with Olympic-standard running tracks and soccer fields.

34 FAMOUS SA'UDIS

Sa'udi Arabia is heir to an Islamic civilization that developed from the teachings of Mohammad (570–632), founder of Islam, born of the tribe of Quraysh in Mecca. The branch of Islam which claims most contemporary Sa'udis is that preached by Mohammad bin 'Abd al-Wahhab (1703?–91), a fundamentalist reformer.

The Sa'udi who has gained greatest renown outside the modern kingdom of Sa'udi Arabia is 'Abd al-'Aziz ibn 'Abd ar-Rahman al-Faysal as-Sa'ud, better known as Ibn-Sa'ud (1880–1953), considered the father of his country. In 1964, Faisal (Faysal ibn-'Abd al-'Aziz as-Sa'ud, 1906–75) was proclaimed king. Upon his assassination in March 1975, he was succeeded as king and prime minister by Khaled (Khalid ibn-'Abd al-'Aziz, 1913–82). Ahmad Zaki Yamani (b.1930), a former minister of petroleum and mineral resources, gained an international reputation as a spokesman for the oil-exporting countries.

35 BIBLIOGRAPHY

Alireza, Marianne. "Women of Arabia." *National Geographic,* October 1987, 423–453.

Foster, L. *Saudi Arabia.* Chicago: Children's Press, 1993.

Kostiner, Joseph. *The Making of Sa'udi Arabia, 1916–1936: from Chieftancy to Monarchical State.* New York: Oxford University Press, 1993.

Lawrence, T. E. *Seven Pillars of Wisdom.* New York: Penguin, 1976 (orig. 1926).

Metz, Helen Chapin, ed. *Sa'udi Arabia: A Country Study.* 5th ed. Washington, D.C.: Library of Congress, 1993.

Nagel, Rob, and Anne Commire. "Muhammad." In *World Leaders, People Who Shaped the World.* Volume I: Africa and Asia. Detroit: U*X*L, 1994.

SENEGAL

Republic of Senegal
République du Sénégal

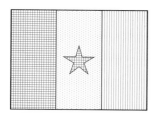

CAPITAL: Dakar.

FLAG: The flag is a tricolor of green, yellow, and red vertical stripes; at the center of the yellow stripe is a green star.

ANTHEM: Begins "Pincez, tous, vos koras, frappez les balafons" ("Pluck your koras, strike the balafons").

MONETARY UNIT: The Communauté Financière Africaine franc (CFA Fr) is the national currency. There are coins of 1, 2, 5, 10, 25, 50, 100, and 500 CFA francs, and notes of 50, 100, 500, 1,000, 5,000, and 10,000 CFA francs. CFA Fr1 = $0.0018 (or $1 = CFA Fr571).

WEIGHTS AND MEASURES: The metric system is the legal standard.

HOLIDAYS: New Year's Day, 1 January; Independence Day, 4 April; Labor Day, 1 May; Day of Association, 14 July; Assumption, 15 August; All Saints' Day, 1 November; Christmas, 25 December. Movable religious holidays include 'Id al-Fitr, 'Id al-'Adha', Milad an-Nabi, Good Friday, Easter Monday, Ascension, and Pentecost Monday.

TIME: GMT.

1 LOCATION AND SIZE

Situated on the western bulge of Africa, Senegal has a land area of 196,190 square kilometers (75,749 square miles), slightly smaller than the state of South Dakota. The total boundary length of Senegal is 3,171 kilometers (1,970 miles). Senegal's capital city, Dakar, is located on the Atlantic coast.

2 TOPOGRAPHY

There are dunes in the northern part of the Senegal coast. Behind the coast is a sandy plain. The Casamance River region in the south is low but more varied, while to the southeast lie the Tamgué foothills. Much of the northwest of Senegal (known as the Ferlo) is desert-like, but the center and most of the south are open savanna, or tropical grasslands. The major rivers are the Senegal, Saloum, Gambia, and Casamance.

3 CLIMATE

The average annual rainfall ranges from 34 centimeters (13 inches) in the extreme north to 155 centimeters (61 inches) in the southwest. Temperatures vary according to the season. At Dakar, during the cool season (December–April), the average daily maximum is 26°C (79°F) and the average minimum is 17°C (63°F). During the hot season (May–November), the averages are 30°C (86°F) and 20°C (68°F).

4 PLANTS AND ANIMALS

The most tropical part of southern Senegal has mangrove swamps and remnants of high forest, including oil palms, bamboo, African teak, and the silk-cotton tree. The dry thornland of the northeast has spiny shrubs, especially acacia, including the gum-bearing species. Most of Senegal is savanna, or tropical grassland. The lion and leopard are occasionally found in the northeast, as are chimpanzees, elephants, hippopotamuses, and buffalo. The wild pig, hare, guinea fowl, quail, and bustard are widely distributed. Insects and birds are abundant, and there are numerous lizards, snakes, and other reptiles.

5 ENVIRONMENT

In much of Senegal, increasing amounts of land are turning to desert (in a process called desertification) because of overgrazing, inadequately controlled cutting of forests for fuel, and soil erosion from overcultivation. Dakar, the capital, suffers from such typical urban problems as improper sanitation (especially during the rainy season, when sewers overflow) and air pollution from motor vehicles. Thirty-five percent of the nation's city dwellers and 74% of the people living in rural areas do not have pure water. Senegal's cities produce 0.6 million tons of solid waste per year. Senegal has six national parks. In 1994, 11 mammal species and 5 bird species are endangered, and 32 types of plants are threatened with extinction.

6 POPULATION

Senegal's estimated 1994 population was 8,718,693. A population of 9,581,000 was projected by the United Nations for the year 2000. The average estimated population density was 40 persons per square kilometer (104 per square mile). Dakar, the capital and principal city, had a population of about 1,613,000 in 1990.

7 MIGRATION

There is seasonal migration between the Gambia and Senegal in connection with cultivation and harvesting of peanuts. There are perhaps 20,000 French and more than 18,000 Lebanese in the country, about a third of whom have Senegalese nationality. Senegal was home to 66,500 Mauritanian refugees at the end of 1992, and 5,000 from Guinea-Bissau. There were 12,200 Senegalese refugees in Guinea-Bissau.

8 ETHNIC GROUPS

The largest ethnic group is the Wolof, who made up 44% of the total population in 1988. Closely related are the Sérer (15%), in west-central Senegal, and the Lebu, concentrated in the Dakar area. Other important groups are the Tukulor, the Fulani (Peul) and Bambara, the Maelinkó or Mandingo, and the Diola.

9 LANGUAGES

French, the official language, is the language of administration and of the schools. Wolof was spoken by 71% of the people in Senegal in 1988; Poular, 21%; Sérer, 14%; Mandingue, 6%; Diola, 6%; and Sarakhole/Sohinke, 1.4%.

10 RELIGIONS

The constitution provides for religious freedom. In 1989, 93% of the people professed Islam. About 6% of Senegalese are Christians, mainly Roman Catholics, with

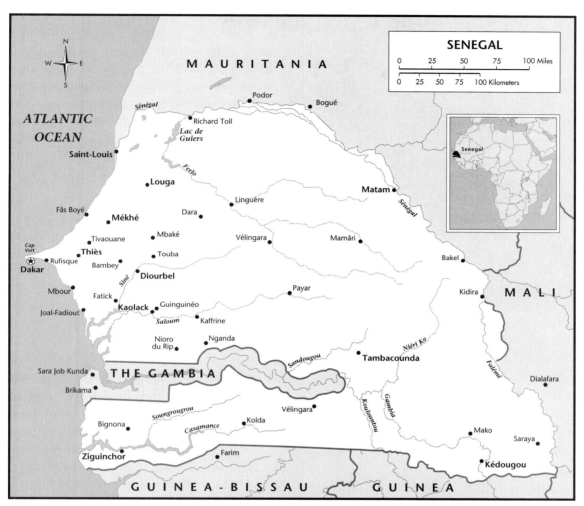

LOCATION: 11°30′ to 17°30′w; 12° to 17°N. **BOUNDARY LENGTHS:** Mauritania, 813 kilometers (505 miles); Mali, 419 kilometers (260 miles); Guinea, 330 kilometers (205 miles); Guinea-Bissau, 338 kilometers (210 miles); Atlantic coastline, 531 kilometers (330 miles); the Gambia, 740 kilometers (460 miles). **TERRITORIAL SEA LIMIT:** 12 miles.

the rest (4%) observing African traditional religions.

11 TRANSPORTATION

Senegal has 1,034 kilometers (642 miles) of railroads, all owned by the government. Of Senegal's 14,007 kilometers (8,705 miles) of classified roads in 1991, some 3,777 kilometers (2,347 miles) were tarred, and 10,230 kilometers (6,358 miles) were laterite or improved earth. In 1991 there were 137,000 vehicles.

Favorably located at the westernmost point of the continent and possessing up-to-date equipment, Dakar is one of the

Photo credit: Cynthia Bassett

Senegalese boy dressed in a typical Senegalese cotton garment.

great ports of Africa. The port, which can accommodate ships of up to 100,000 tons, handled 5 million tons of cargo in 1988. Gross weight of the 3 ships of the merchant fleet came to 10,000 tons in 1991. The Senegal, Saloum, and Casamance rivers are all navigable, to varying degrees. Dakar's Yoff International Airport, a West African air center, is served by many foreign airlines.

12 HISTORY

Between the tenth and fifteenth centuries AD, the Wolof and Sérer peoples entered Senegal from the northeast. The four-teenth century saw the emergence of the Jolof empire, controlling the six Wolof states of Jolof, Kayor, Baol, Walo, Sine, and Salum. Toward the end of the seventeenth century Jolof power declined, due, at least partly, to struggles between the states. European activities in Senegal began with the Portuguese arrival at the Cap Vert Peninsula and the mouth of the Senegal River in 1444–45.

The Portuguese enjoyed a monopoly on trade in slaves and gold until the seventeenth century, when they were succeeded by the Dutch, who virtually dominated all trade by 1650. The later seventeenth century brought the beginnings of the rivalry between the English and the French, which dominated the eighteenth century in Senegal and elsewhere in Africa.

Peanut cultivation, the foundation of Senegal's modern economy, began around 1850. Between 1895 and 1904, a series of decrees consolidated eight territories into a French West Africa federation, of which Dakar became the capital. In 1920, a Colonial Council, partly elected by the citizens of the towns and partly consisting of chiefs from the rest of Senegal, was established. All the elected bodies were suppressed in 1940 but restored at the end of World War II (1939–45). Under the constitution of 1946, Senegal was given two deputies in the French parliament, and a Territorial Assembly was established. The following year, Senegal accepted the new French constitution and became a self-governing republic within the French Community.

In June 1960 Senegal joined the Mali Federation together with Mali and French Sudan, but conflicting views soon led to its breakup; a month later the Legislative Assembly of Senegal proclaimed Senegal's national independence. A new constitution was adopted, and on 5 September 1960, Léopold-Sédar Senghor was elected president and Mamadou Dia became prime minister, retaining the position he had held since 1957 as head of the government. In 1962, the legislature overthrew Dia's government, and Senghor was elected by unanimous vote as head of government. Less than three months later, the electorate approved a new constitution that abolished the post of prime minister and made the president both chief of state and head of the executive branch.

Having been reelected in 1968, 1973, and 1978, Senghor resigned as president at the end of 1980 and was succeeded by Abdou Diouf. In February 1982, Senegal and the Gambia formed the Confederation of Senegambia with Diouf as president. The two countries pledged to integrate their armed and security forces, form an economic and monetary union, and coordinate foreign policy and communications.

Diouf was elected to a full term as president of Senegal on 27 February 1983. He reformed the government, making it less corrupt and more efficient. In the 1988 national elections, Diouf carried 77% of the vote. In April 1989, a nationwide state of emergency was declared and a curfew imposed in Dakar after rioters, enraged by reports of the killing of hundreds of Senegalese in Mauritania, killed dozens of Mauritanians. Relations with Mauritania were broken and armed clashes along the border and internal rioting led to the expulsion of most Mauritanians residing in Senegal. Diplomatic relations were reestablished in April 1992 and the northern border along the Senegal River was reopened.

Diouf again won reelection in February 1993.

In the southernmost province of Casamance, a separatist group, the Movement of Democratic Forces of the Casamance (MFDC), has challenged the armed forces for years. A July 1993 ceasefire agreement appears to be holding, although there are numerous charges of human rights abuses by both sides, and hundreds have been killed. From 1990 to 1993, Senegalese armed forces played a major role in the peacekeeping effort in Liberia.

13 GOVERNMENT

Under the 1963 constitution, as amended, the president of the republic determines national policy and has the power to dissolve the National Assembly. If the president asks the Assembly to reconsider a measure it has enacted, the bill must be passed again by a three-fifths majority before it becomes law. Legislative power is exercised by a 120-member National Assembly, elected for five years simultaneously with the president. The Assembly elects the 16 members of the High Court of Justice from among its ranks.

14 POLITICAL PARTIES

Since independence in 1960, the UPS (Union Progressiste Sénégalaise—UPS) has been the dominant political party. In 1976, the UPS changed its name to the Senegalese Socialist Party (Parti Socialiste Sénégalais—PS), after joining the Socialist International. There was no legal opposition party from 1966 until 1974, when the Senegalese Democratic Party (Parti Démocratique Sénégalais—PDS) was formed in order to meet the constitutional requirement for a responsible opposition. In 1981, the constitution, which had restricted the number of political parties to four, was amended to end all restrictions. Seven parties contested the National Assembly elections of 9 May 1993, including the Jappoo Leggeeyal ("Let Us Unite") Party, the Democratic League, the Independence and Labor Party (PIT), and the Senegalese Democratic Union/Renewal Party.

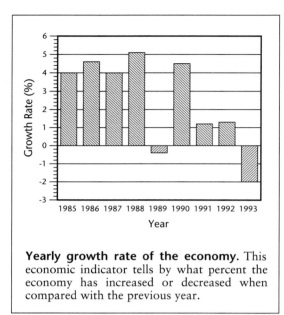

Yearly growth rate of the economy. This economic indicator tells by what percent the economy has increased or decreased when compared with the previous year.

15 JUDICIAL SYSTEM

The High Council of the Magistrature, founded in 1960 and headed by the president, determines the constitutionality of laws and international commitments and decides when members of the legislature and the executive have exceeded their authority. A 16-member High Court of Justice, founded in 1962 and elected by the National Assembly from among its own members, presides over impeachment proceedings. The Supreme Court, founded in 1960, is made up of members appointed by the president of the republic on the advice of the High Council of the Magistrature.

16 ARMED FORCES

Senegal's armed forces totaled about 9,700 men in 1993. The army of 8,500 men included 9 infantry or armored battalions, 1 artillery battalion, and 1 engineering battalion. The navy of 700 had 10 patrol craft and small landing craft, and the air force of 500 had 9 aircraft. Military outlays in 1993 were about $100 million. France maintains a reinforced marine regiment of 1,200 in Senegal.

17 ECONOMY

Senegal's economy is based on its agricultural sector, primarily peanut production, and a modest industrial sector. Agriculture is highly vulnerable to declining rainfall, expansion of the desert onto farm land, and changes in world food prices. When the first of a series of droughts struck in the latter part of the 1960s, the economy deteriorated rapidly. Today, 30 years after achieving independence, Senegal's resource-poor economy remains fragile and dependent upon foreign donors.

18 INCOME

In 1992 Senegal's gross national product (GNP) was $6,124 million at current prices, or about $750 per person. For the period 1985–92 the average inflation rate was 1.7%, resulting in a real growth rate in per person GNP of 1.3%.

19 INDUSTRY

In French-speaking West Africa, Senegal's manufacturing sector is second only to that of the Côte d'Ivoire (Ivory Coast). Processing of agricultural products (oil mills, sugar refineries, fish canneries, flour mills, bakeries, beverage and dairy processing, and tobacco manufacturing) plays a key role. Especially important are the four groundnut-processing mills, which produced 108,100 tons of groundnut oil in 1985. Textiles, leather goods, chemicals, paper, wood products, and building materials are also important manufactures. The textile industry includes four cotton-ginning mills, factories for weaving, dyeing, and printing cloth, and plants that produce mattresses, thread, and hats. Other industrial products include plywood, boats, bicycles, soap, paints, acetylene, sulfuric acid, phosphoric acid, phosphate fertilizer, and cigarettes.

20 LABOR

About 70% of the total work force was in agriculture in 1992. Senegal's fundamental labor legislation provides for collective agreements between employers and trade unions, for the fixing of basic minimum

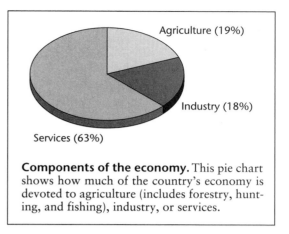

Components of the economy. This pie chart shows how much of the country's economy is devoted to agriculture (includes forestry, hunting, and fishing), industry, or services.

Agriculture (19%)

Industry (18%)

Services (63%)

wages by the government on recommendation of advisory committees, and for a 40- to 48-hour work week. The right to strike is recognized by law, and there are special labor courts. In 1992 there were 19 strikes involving 3,954 workers.

21 AGRICULTURE

Senegal is predominantly an agricultural country, with about 70% of its working population involved in farming. Only about 12% of Senegal's total land area is cultivated; peanuts took up 39% of the cultivated land in 1992. Production of unshelled peanuts varies widely because of periodic drought, and it is frequently underreported because of unauthorized sales to processors in neighboring countries. In 1992, the reported production was 578,000 tons, most for export. Cotton is Senegal's other major export crop. Seed cotton production was 51,000 tons in 1992; lint cotton output was an estimated 20,000 tons during 1992.

Photo credit: Cynthia Bassett

Fishing has surpassed peanuts as Senegal's number one foreign export.

Production of food crops, some of which are grown in rotation with peanuts, does not meet Senegal's needs. Millet and sorghum production was 671,000 tons in 1991 and 563,000 tons in 1992; output of paddy rice during the same period fell from 194,000 to 177,000 tons, but corn increased from 103,000 to 115,000 tons. Cassava output was about 46,000 tons in 1992. About 8,000 hectares (19,700 acres) yielded 837,000 tons of sugarcane in 1992.

22 DOMESTICATED ANIMALS

Raising livestock is a primary activity in the northern section of Senegal and a secondary one for farmers in the southern and central regions. In 1992, the estimated livestock population included 2,800,000 head of cattle, 3,600,000 sheep, 2,400,000 goats, 730,000 horses and donkeys, 310,000 hogs, 15,000 camels, and 19 million poultry. The slaughter in 1992 yielded an estimated 43,000 tons of beef and veal and 20,000 tons of sheep and goat meat. Hides are exported or used in local shoe production and handicrafts.

23 FISHING

Senegal has a flourishing fishing industry, and Dakar is one of the most important Atlantic tuna ports. In 1990, fish exports accounted for 22.4% ($200 million) of total exports. The total catch in 1991 was 319,693 tons, half of which was sardines.

24 FORESTRY

Senegal has about 10.5 million hectares (25.9 million acres) of classified woodland and forest, most of it in the southern Casamance region. Timber production is small, with firewood and charcoal being the most important forest products. About 5,098,000 cubic meters of roundwood were cut in 1991, of which about 88% went for fuel.

25 MINING

Mining, especially of phosphates at a deposit some 80 kilometers (50 miles) northeast of Dakar, has taken on added importance for Senegal's economy in the postindependence era. Production of aluminum phosphate stood at 92,000 tons in 1991. Calcium phosphate output reached 1,741,000 tons in 1991, and mining of sea salt rose to about 102,000 tons.

26 FOREIGN TRADE

Food products are about 38% of Senegal's exports, followed by groundnut oil and cakes. Petroleum refinery products, phosphates, and chemicals were also important exports. The leading imports are industrial products, machinery and transport equipment, and food products. France is Senegal's principal trading partner. Senegal sends about 10% of its exports to India. Its imports came from the United States, Côte d'Ivoire, Spain, Nigeria, Japan, Italy, and Germany.

27 ENERGY AND POWER

Electric power generation is almost entirely thermal. Production in 1991 totaled 756 million kilowatt hours, 98%

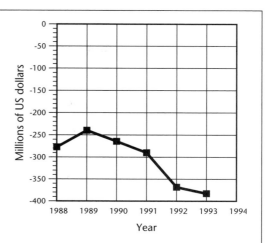

Yearly balance of trade measured in millions of US dollars. The balance of trade is the difference between what a country sells to other countries (its exports) and what it buys (its imports). If a country imports more than it exports, it has a negative balance of trade (a trade deficit). If exports exceed imports there is a positive balance of trade (a trade surplus).

of it in public plants. There are extensive reserves of peat along the coast between Dakar and Saint-Louis. An oil refinery near Dakar, with an annual capacity of 1,200,000 tons, produces petroleum products from imported crude oil. Production was 773,900 tons in 1991. In 1990, Senegal imported 769,900 tons of crude oil from Nigeria and Gabon.

28 SOCIAL DEVELOPMENT

Since 1956, a system of family allowances for wage earners has provided small maternity and child benefits. Shared equally by employer and employee is a 6% contribution to a fund for general medical and hospital expenses. In addition,

Selected Social Indicators

These statistics are estimates for the period 1988 to 1993. For comparison purposes, data for the United States, and averages for low-income countries and high-income countries are also given.

Indicator	Senegal	Low-income countries	High-income countries	United States
Per capita gross national product†	$750	$380	$23,680	$24,740
Population growth rate	2.5%	1.9%	0.6%	1.0%
Population growth rate in urban areas	3.7%	3.9%	0.8%	1.3%
Population per square kilometer of land	40	78	25	26
Life expectancy in years	50	62	77	76
Number of people per physician	17,508	>3,300	453	419
Number of pupils per teacher (primary school)	59	39	<18	20
Illiteracy rate (15 years and older)	62%	41%	<5%	<3%
Energy consumed per capita (kg of oil equivalent)	115	364	5,203	7,918

† The gross national product (GNP) is the total dollar value of all goods and services produced by a country in a year. The per capita GNP is calculated by dividing a country's GNP by its population. The World Bank defines low-income countries as those with a per capita GNP of $695 or less. High-income countries have a per capita GNP of $8,626 or more. Less than 14% of the world's 5.5 billion people live in high-income countries, while almost 60% live in low-income countries.

> = greater than   < = less than

Sources: World Bank, Social Indicators of Development 1995, Baltimore: Johns Hopkins University Press, 1995. Central Intelligence Agency, World Fact Book, Washington, D.C.: Government Printing Office, 1994.

employers contribute 4.8% of gross salary to a retirement fund and employees 3.2%; the retirement age is 65.

29 HEALTH

In 1992, there were 5 doctors per 100,000 people, and in 1990, there were 0.8 hospital beds per 1,000 people. Since 1988, there has been about 1 doctor for every 17,508 people. Still, in 1992, only 40% of the population had access to health care services. Total health care expenditures in 1990 were $214 million.

Major health problems include measles and, to a lesser extent, meningitis, along with water-related diseases such as malaria and schistosomiasis. In 1991, only 48% of the population had access to safe water and only 55% had adequate sanitation. Life expectancy is 50 years.

30 HOUSING

Most housing in Dakar is like that of a European city. Elsewhere, housing ranges from European-type structures to the circular mud huts with thatched roofs common in villages. Since World War II, the growth of Dakar and other towns has been rapid, with government activity largely concentrated on improvement of urban housing and sanitation.

31 EDUCATION

Education is compulsory at the primary level between ages 6 and 12; however, because of a lack of facilities, just over half the children in this age group attend school. In 1990, there were 2,640 primary schools in which 708,448 students were enrolled. There are about 59 students per teacher in the primary schools. At the secondary level, 181,170 students were attending schools the same year. The University of Dakar has two graduate schools and numerous research centers. A polytechnic college opened at Thiès in 1973. Other colleges include a national school of administration at Dakar and a school of sciences and veterinary medicine for French-speaking Africa. Universities and equivalent institutions had 16,764 students in 1989. Literacy rates are low: in 1990, 38% of adults were literate (52% of men and 25% of women).

32 MEDIA

Telephone and telegraph services, publicly owned and operated, are highly efficient by African standards, particularly in the coastal area and in the main centers of peanut production.

The two national radio networks based in Dakar broadcast mostly in French, while the regional stations in Rufisque, Saint-Louis, Tambacounda, Kaolack, and Ziguinchor, which originate their own programs, broadcast primarily in six local languages. There were 860,000 radios in 1991. Transmission of educational televi-

Photo credit: International Labour Office

A worker painting pottery on a wheel.

sion programs began in 1973, and by 1991 there were 273,000 television sets in use. There was one daily newspaper in 1991, *Le Soleil du Sénégal,* the Senegalese Socialist Party (PS) newspaper, with an estimated 19,000 circulation.

33 TOURISM AND RECREATION

The comfortable climate, variety of cultural attractions, physical features such as the coastal beaches and the 5,996-square kilometer (2,315-square mile) Niokolo-Koba National Park, and the relative proximity to Europe have combined to make Senegal an increasingly popular vacation area, and international conference center. Fishing is popular, and hunting is allowed from December to May on an 80,000-hectare (198,000-acre) reserve.

In 1991, 233,512 foreign tourists arrived at hotels and other facilities; 56% came from France, 21% from other European countries, and 16% from Africa. There were 6,826 hotel rooms with a 34% occupancy rate.

34 FAMOUS SENEGALESE

Blaise Diagne (1872–1934) was the first African to be elected to the French parliament. Léopold-Sédar Senghor (b.1906), president of Senegal from 1960 until his retirement in 1980, is a French-language poet of distinction. Abdou Diouf (b.1935) became president of Senegal in 1981 after serving as Senghor's prime minister from 1970 through 1980. Senegalese writers include David Diop (1927–60), an internationally known poet. Ousmane Sembene (b.1923) is a film director and writer of international repute.

35 BIBLIOGRAPHY

Gellar, Sheldon. *Senegal: An African Nation between Islam and the West.* London: Gower, 1983.

Nagel, Rob, and Anne Commire. "Léopold Sédar Senghor." In *World Leaders, People Who Shaped the World.* Volume I: Africa and Asia. Detroit: U*X*L, 1994.

Senegal in Pictures. Minneapolis: Lerner, 1988.

Vaillant, Janet G. *Black, French, and African: A Life of Leopold Sedar Senghor.* Cambridge, Mass.: Harvard University Press, 1990.

SERBIA AND MONTENEGRO

Federal Republic of Yugoslavia
Federativna Republika Jugoslavija

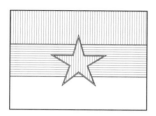

CAPITAL: Belgrade.

FLAG: The flag is a tricolor of blue, white, and red horizontal stripes with a star in the center.

MONETARY UNIT: The new dinar replaced the dinar on 24 January 1994. The new dinar is fixed on par with the German mark.

WEIGHTS AND MEASURES: The metric system is in force.

HOLIDAYS: National Day, 27 April; Assumption, 15 August; All Saints' Day, 1 November; Christmas Day, 25 December. Movable holidays are Easter Sunday and Monday.

TIME: 1 PM = noon GMT.

1 LOCATION AND SIZE

Serbia and Montenegro is located in southern Europe between Bosnia and Herzegovina and Bulgaria. It borders on the Adriatic Sea. Its total area is 102,350 square kilometers (39,500 square miles), slightly larger than the state of Kentucky, and a total boundary length of 2,433 kilometers (1,520 miles).

2 TOPOGRAPHY

In the north, Serbia and Montenegro consists of rich, fertile plains. The east and southeast feature mountains and hills, while the southwest is the high shoreline of the Adriatic Sea, with no islands. The largest lake in the former Yugoslavia, Lake Scutari, is in Serbia and Montenegro.

3 CLIMATE

In the north, the climate features hot, humid summers and cold winters, with well distributed rainfall. To the south, the summers are hot and dry. Inland areas experience heavy snowfall.

4 PLANTS AND ANIMALS

No information is available on the native plants and animals of Serbia and Montenegro.

5 ENVIRONMENT

Coastal waters are polluted from sewage outlets, especially in tourist areas. Around Belgrade and other cities, air pollution is a problem. Serbia and Montenegro is vulnerable to destructive earthquakes. About 25% of the land area is forest and woodland.

6 POPULATION

As of 1993, the population was estimated at 10,699,539.

7 MIGRATION

No official information is available on migration of people within Serbia and Montenegro, nor are there statistics on immigration to or emigration from the country.

8 ETHNIC GROUPS

The population is comprised of 63% ethnic Serbs, 14% is Albanians, 6% Montenegrins, and 4% is Hungarians. Of the remaining 13%, various European ethnicities are represented.

9 LANGUAGES

About 95% of the population speaks the Slavic language, Serbo-Croatian; the remaining 5% speaks Albanian.

10 RELIGIONS

An estimated 65% of the population is Eastern Orthodox (a form of Christianity); 19% Muslim; 4% Roman Catholic; and 1% Protestant.

11 TRANSPORTATION

Serbia and Montenegro controls one of the major land routes from western Europe to Turkey, occupying a strategic location on the Adriatic Coast. As of 1990, there were 46,019 kilometers (28,760 miles) of roads, about 60% of which were paved. Serbia and Montenegro had 44 ships, including 17 cargo, 5 container, 19 bulk, 2 combination tanker/ore carriers, and 1 passenger. Most fly under the flags of Malta, Panama, or Saint Vincent and the Grenadines. There are 48 airports, 16 with permanent surface runways.

12 HISTORY

SERBIA

Origins and Middles Ages

Around the seventh century, the Serbs began settling in the areas now known as Bosnia and Montenegro, straddling the line that divided the eastern and western halves of the Roman Empire since 395. The Serbs organized several principalities made up of a number of clans. Between the ninth and twelfth centuries, several Serbian principalities evolved, among them Raška in the mountainous north of Montenegro and southern Serbia, and Zeta (southern Montenegro along the Adriatic coast).

In 863, the two Greek scholars Constantine (Cyril) and Methodius learned the area's Slavic language and translated the Holy Scriptures into Slavic using an original alphabet of their own invention. These texts were to be used by missionaries to convert people to Christianity. Thus, the liturgy in the Slavic language was introduced in Bulgaria, Macedonia, and Serbia in competition with the usual liturgy in Greek.

The medieval Serbian empire, under Stephen Dušan the Mighty (1331–55) controlled—aside from the central Serbian lands—Macedonia, parts of present-day Greece, and Albania. Dušan, who was

crowned Tsar of "the Serbs and Greeks" in 1346, gave Serbia its first code of laws based on a combination of Serbian customs and Byzantine law. His attempt to conquer the throne of Byzantium failed, however, when the Byzantines called on the advancing Ottoman Turks for help in 1345.

Under Ottoman Rule

Dušan's heirs could not hold his empire together against the Turks of the Ottoman Empire. Following a series of wars between the Turks and the Serbs, Hungarians, Albanians, Venetians, and other Europeans, the Turks succeeded in over-taking Constantinople in 1453 and all of Serbia by 1459. For the next three-and-a-half centuries, Serbs and others had to learn how to survive under Ottoman rule. Non-Turks had to pay a tax for defense support, and were subjected to the practice of forceful wrenching of Christian boys between the age of eight and twenty from their families to be converted to Islam and trained as government administrators. Over the two centuries after 1459 many Serbs left their lands and settled north of the Sava and Danube Rivers in Hungary and Austria.

In 1805, the Serbs defeated the Turks and gained control of the Belgrade region. The Turks reoccupied Serbia by 1813 and revenged themselves with a terrible reign of terror. Turk retaliation included pillaging, looting, and enslaving women and children, while killing all males over age 15 and torturing any captured leader that was not able to escape.

By 1830, Serbia had gained its autonomy and was accepted internationally as a virtually independent state. Through the rest of the 19th century, Serbians continued to strive for increased territory and autonomy. Late in the century, there was a period of stable political and economic development, interrupted by the 1908 Austrian annexation of Bosnia and Herzegovina, the 1912 and 1913 Balkan Wars, and World War I (1914–18).

The War Decades

With the backing of Russia, the Balkan countries (Serbia, Bulgaria, Montenegro, and Greece) formed the Balkan League, agreed provisionally among themselves on territorial divisions, and attacked Turkey in 1912. The League quickly defeated the Turks. The second Balkan War in 1913 ended with the defeat of Bulgaria by Serbia, Montenegro, Greece, Romania, and Turkey itself, which gained back Adrianople and Thrace.

Austria viewed Serbian expansion with great alarm. Naturally, the large Serbian population in Bosnia and Herzegovina looked at Serbia with great hopes for their liberation. In Serbia and Bosnia, secret organizations were operating in support of pro-Serbian and terrorist acts. The Austro-Hungarian political and military leadership, bent on war against Serbia, needed only a spark to ignite a conflagration. The spark was provided by the 28 June 1914 assassination of Austria's Archduke Ferdinand and his wife in Sarajevo. Austria presented an ultimatum to Serbia on 23 July with ten requests that were accepted by Serbia in a desperate effort to avoid a war. Austria, however, declared war on Serbia on 28 July 1914. They began bombing Belgrade the same day, and sent armies across the Danube and Sava Rivers to invade Serbia on 11 August 1914, taking the Serbs by total surprise. The Serbian army twice repelled the Austrian forces in 1914, with tremendous losses in men and materials and civilian refugees. Eventually, they were successful in driving the Austrian forces out of Serbia in October 1918.

The Corfu Declaration of 20 July 1917 consisted of 14 points delineating the future joint state of Yugoslavia, comprised of Serbs, Croats, and Slovenes while treating both Macedonians and Montenegrins as Serbs. But this first Yugoslavia, born out of the distress of World War I, had no time to consolidate and work out its problems. On 6 April 1941, Yugoslavia was attacked by Germany, Italy, Hungary, Romania, and Bulgaria, resulting in its occupation and division among Germany and its allies. Southeast Serbia was taken by Bulgaria, while Hungary occupied the Vojvodina area. Germans controlled the rest of Serbia. In the fall of 1941 Josip Broz Tito was leading the Communist partisan movement to conquer Yugoslavia for Communism.

After the end of World War II (1939–45), the Communist-led forces took control of Serbia and Yugoslavia and instituted a violent dictatorship that committed systematic crimes and human rights violations on an unexpectedly large scale. Thousands upon thousands sent back to Yugoslavia from Austria were tortured and massacred.

Communist Yugoslavia

The second Yugoslavia was formed as a Federative People's Republic of five nations (Slovenes, Croats, Serbs, Macedonians, and Montenegrins) with their individual republics and Bosnia and Herzegovina as a buffer area with its mix of Serb, Muslim, and Croat populations. Tito attempted a balancing act to satisfy most of the nationality issues that were carried over, unresolved, from the first Yugoslavia. However, he failed to satisfy anyone. The official position of the Marxist Yugoslav regime was that national rivalries and conflicting interests would gradually diminish through their absorbtion into a new Socialist order. Without capitalism, nationalism was supposed to fade away.

The elections of 11 November 1945—boycotted by the non-communist coalition parties—gave the Communist-led People's Front 90% of the vote. A Constituent Assembly met on 29 November, abolished the monarchy and established the Federative People's Republic of Yugoslavia. In January 1946, a new constitution was adopted based on the 1936 Soviet constitution. Tito quickly nationalized the economy through a policy of forced industrialization, supported by the collectivization of the agriculture. Yugoslavia began to develop a foreign policy independent of the Soviet Union.

The nonaligned position served Tito's Yugoslavia well by allowing Tito to draw on economic and political support from the Western powers while neutralizing any aggression from the Soviet bloc. Overall, in the 1970s and 1980s, Yugoslavia maintained fairly good relations with its neighboring states by solving disputes and developing cooperative projects and trade.

Meanwhile, Slobodan Miloševic had become the head of the Communist Party in Serbia in early 1987. He was able to take control of the leadership in Montenegro and to impose Serbian control over Kosovo. The League of Communists of Yugoslavia convened in January 1990 to review proposed reforms such as free multiparty elections and freedom of speech. In April 1990 the first free elections since before World War II were held in Slovenia.

Yugoslavia's Dissolution

The collapse of Communist regimes in Eastern Europe in 1989 had a deep impact in Yugoslavia. In Slovenia, the Communist Party agreed to shed its monopoly of power and lost in the first multiparty elections in April 1990. In Serbia and Montenegro, the Communists won on 9 December 1990 on the basis of their strong Serbian nationalism. The Serbian determination to maintain a unitary Yugoslavia hardened, while the determination of the Slovenes and Croats to gain their independence grew stronger.

The new constitution proclaimed by Serbia in September 1990 provided for a unicameral legislature of 250 seats and the elimination of autonomy for Vojvodina and Kosovo. The first elections were held on 9 December 1990. More than 50 parties and 32 presidential candidates participated. Slobodan Miloševic's Socialist Party of Serbia received two thirds of the votes and 194 out of the 250 seats. Having gained control of Serbia, Montenegro, Kosovo, and Vojvodina, Miloševic controlled four of the eight votes in the collective presidency of Yugoslavia.

Slovenia and Croatia proceeded with their declarations of independence on 25 June 1991. Increased fighting from July 1991 caused tremendous destruction of entire cities (Vukovar), and large scale damage to the medieval city of Dubrovnik.

On 27 April 1992, Serbia and Montenegro formed their own Federal Republic of Yugoslavia. The United Nations, convinced that Serbia and Montenegro was supporting the aggression against Bosnia and Herzegovina, imposed economic sanctions. In spite of the sanctions, Miloševic's Socialist Party won the elections of 22 December 1992. The desperate economic situation of Serbia caused by its assistance to the Bosnian Serbs and the UN-imposed sanctions finally forced Miloševic to disassociate Serbia from the Bosnian Serbs and to close the borders with Bosnia in September 1994. Even with the eventual settlement of hostilities in Bosnia and Herzegovina, Serbia will face serious internal political problems in addition to its ruined economy: the tradition of independence in Montenegro, the Albanian majority in Kosovo, the Muslims of the Sandžak area, the Hungarians in Vojvodina, and independent Macedonia.

MONTENEGRO

Montenegro's name came from the Venetian meaning "Black Mountain." Living in a very harsh mountain territory, the Montenegrins were natural and fierce fighters and not even the large Turkish armies could conquer them. In 1516, Montenegro became a theocracy, and for the next three centuries, until 1851, Montenegro was ruled by its bishops. The Montenegro area was an almost impregnable mountain fortress with some limited access from the Adriatic coast where the Turks had taken hold. The population was comprised of Slav and Albanian Muslims.

Following the 1913 Balkan War, Montenegro and Serbia became neighbor states, both primarily populated by Serbs. Montenegro also gained access to the Adriatic Sea south of Lake Scutari (Skadarsko Jezerol), which was divided in 1913 between Montenegro and the newly formed Albanian state.

Between 1880 and 1912, Montenegro took advantage of an era of relative peace to develop roads, education, agriculture, postal services, and banks, mostly with foreign investment especially from Italy. For higher education, most Montenegrins studied at the University of Belgrade and came back home with progressive and democratic ideas, along with deep and personal ties and commitment to the Serbian goals of national unification.

The first Montenegrin parliament met in 1905, with 62 elected and 14 ex-officio members. By 1914, Serbia and Montenegro proposed a union in which they would share their armed forces, foreign policy, and customs while maintaining their separate royal dynasties. World War I (1914–18) interrupted this process. Montenegro's poor defense against Austrian attacks led to Austrian occupation for the better part of the war. Thus Montenegro ceased to officially participate in the war as an ally of Serbia and the Western Powers against Austria.

Montenegro became part of the first Yugoslavia on 1 December 1918, not as Montenegro, but as part of the Kingdom of Serbia. Montenegrins participated very actively in Yugoslavia's political life, mostly supporting the centralist Serbian positions. During World War II (1939–45), Italy controlled Montenegro. In the post-World War II Socialist Federative Yugoslavia, Josip Broz Tito reestablished Montenegro as a separate republic to balance the influence of Serbs in general. Most Montenegrins took the side of the Serbian centralists and, in the late 1980s and early 1990s, supported Slobodan Milosevic. With the demise of Yugoslavia, Montenegro joined Serbia in forming the Federal Republic of Yugoslavia. Being a less-developed area, Montenegro depends heavily on Serbian assistance—difficult to obtain under the impact of economic sanctions. It is in the interest of Serbia to avoid any direct clash with Hungary. Serbia and Montenegro are isolated and facing adversary states.

13 GOVERNMENT

The government of Serbia and Montenegro was established when the state declared its independence on 11 April 1992. The constitution was enacted on 27 April 1992. A bicameral (two-house) Federal Assembly consists of a 40-seat (20 Serbian, 20 Montenegrin) Chamber of Republics (upper house) and a 138-seat (108 Serbian, 30 Montenegrin) Chamber of Deputies or Citizens (lower house). The last election for the Federal Assembly was in mid-1992; the next election had not been scheduled as of late 1995, but will probably be held in 1996. The president, elected by the Federal Assembly, has been Zoran Lilic since 1993; while Slobodan Milossvic has been president of Serbia, and Momir Bulatovic has been president of Montenegro, both since December 1990. Since December 1992, the prime minister has been Radoje Kontic. He is assisted by three deputy prime ministers. Voting is universal at age 18 (at age 16, if employed).

14 POLITICAL PARTIES

The main political parties operating in Serbia and Montenegro are the Serbian Socialist Party (SPS—formerly the Communist Party), led by Slobodan Milossvic; Serbian Radical Party (SRS); Serbian Renewal Party (SPO); Democratic Party (DS); Democratic Party of Serbia; Democratic Party of Socialists (DSSCG); People's Party of Montenegro (NS); Liberal Alliance of Montenegro; Democratic Community of Vojvodina Hungarians (DZVM); League of Communists-Movement for Yugoslavia (SK-PJ); and Serbian Democratic Movement (DEMOS), a coalition of opposition parties.

15 JUDICIAL SYSTEM

There is a Federal Court (*Savezni Sud*), and a Constitutional Court.

16 ARMED FORCES

Serbia and Montenegro maintains a People's Army—Ground Forces (for internal and border patrols); Naval Forces; Air and Air Defense Forces; Frontier Guard; Territorial Defense Force; and Civil Defense.

17 ECONOMY

Serbia and Montenegro faces serious economic problems. In 1991, when the former Yugoslavia collapsed, Serbia lost many of its trade links with the other former Yugoslav republics. In Serbia and Montenegro, the continuation in office of a Communist government has emphasized political and military reform, not economic reform. In 1992, the United Nations imposed economic sanctions on Serbia and Montenegro, further aggravating the difficult economic situation.

18 INCOME

In 1992, the estimated gross domestic product (GDP) was $27–37 billion, or about $2,500–3,500 per person. The inflation rate in 1991 was approximately 81%.

19 INDUSTRY

Industrial output fell by an estimated 20% in 1991. Industries include machine building, metallurgy, mining, and production of consumer goods, electronics, petroleum products, chemicals, and pharmaceuticals.

20 LABOR

In 1991, the unemployment rate was estimated at 25–40%. In 1990, the labor force was 2,640,909; about 40% were engaged in industry or mining, and about 5% in agriculture.

21 AGRICULTURE

Serbia and Montenegro produces about 80% of the cereal output of the former

Yugoslavia. It also produces cotton, oil-seeds, and chicory. Fodder (animal feed) crops to support intensive beef and dairy production are grown; the central regions produce fruit, grapes, and livestock, due to the long growing season. Along the Adriatic Sea, small amounts of olives, citrus fruit, and rice are cultivated.

22 DOMESTICATED ANIMALS

Serbia and Montenegro produce livestock, including sheep, goats, and beef cattle. Dairy farming also prospers in the central regions.

23 FISHING

There is little reliable data on fishing.

24 FORESTRY

Although 25% of the area is forest and woodland, there is little reliable data on forestry practices.

25 MINING

Serbia and Montenegro's mineral resources include oil, gas, coal, antimony, copper, lead, zinc, nickel, gold, pyrite, and chromium. Metallurgy (steel, aluminum, copper, lead, zinc, chromium) and mining (coal, bauxite, and limestone) contribute to industrial output.

26 FOREIGN TRADE

In 1990, exports were $4.4 billion, and were comprised of machinery and transport equipment, 29%; manufactured goods, 28.5%; other manufactured articles, 13.5%; chemicals, 11%; food and live animals, 9%; raw materials, 6%; fuels and lubricants, 2%; beverages and tobacco, 1%. Imports, valued at about $6.4 billion in 1990, included machinery and transport equipment, 26%; fuels and lubricants, 18%; manufactured goods, 16%; chemicals, 12.5%; food and live animals, 11%; miscellaneous manufactured items, 8%; raw materials, including coking coal for the steel industry, 7%; beverages, tobacco, and edible oils, 1.5%. The United Nations Security Council, convinced that Serbia and Montenegro was contributing to the ongoing civil strife in Bosnia and Herzegovina, imposed trade sanctions on Serbia and Montenegro in May 1992. Prior to the sanctions, main trading partners were the other former Yugoslav republics, Italy, Germany, the republics of the former Soviet Union, and the United States.

27 ENERGY AND POWER

In 1992, electric capacity was 8.85 million kilowatts; energy use is about 3,950 kilowatt hours per person.

28 SOCIAL DEVELOPMENT

Reliable information about social programs in Serbia and Montenegro was unavailable.

29 HEALTH

Reliable information about the health care system in Serbia and Montenegro was unavailable.

30 HOUSING

Reliable information about housing in Serbia and Montenegro was unavailable.

31 EDUCATION

Reliable information about the educational system in Serbia and Montenegro was unavailable.

32 MEDIA

There are 700,000 telephones in Serbia and Montenegro; there are 35 radio stations, 26 AM and 9 FM, and about 2 million radios. There are 18 television stations, and approximately 1 million television sets.

33 TOURISM AND RECREATION

Due to the political instability and economic difficulties, tourism is not a factor in the economy of Serbia and Montenegro as of the mid-1990s.

34 FAMOUS SERBS AND MONTENEGRINS

Stephen Dusan (r.1331–55) was ruler of the medieval Nemanjid dynasty empire. Prince Lazar (d.1389) was beheaded after losing the Battle of Kosovo against the Turks. Karageorge "Black George" (d.1817) was the leader of a Serbian revolt against the Turks. Peter I, was the last king of Serbia. Nicholas I, was the last king of Montenegro. Marshal Josip Broz Tito (1892–1980) was president of Yugoslavia from 1953 until his death.

35 BIBLIOGRAPHY

Banac, Ivo. *The Nationality Question in Yugoslavia.* Ithaca, NY: Cornell University Press, 1984.

Glenny, Michael. *The Fall of Yugoslavia: The Third Balkan War.* New York: Penguin, 1992.

Stankovic, Slobodan. *The End fo the Tito Era.* Stanford, Cal.: Hoover Institution Press, 1981.

SEYCHELLES

Republic of Seychelles

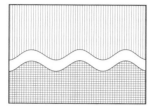

CAPITAL: Victoria.

FLAG: The flag is red above and green below, divided horizontally by a white wave pattern.

ANTHEM: Begins "Seychellois both staunch and true."

MONETARY UNIT: The Seychelles rupee (R) is a paper currency of 100 cents. There are coins of 5, 10, and 25 cents and 1, 5, 10, 20, 25, 50, 100, 1,000, and 1,500 rupees and notes of 10, 25, 50, and 100 rupees. R1 = $0.1940 (or $1 = R5.1318).

WEIGHTS AND MEASURES: The metric system is the legal standard.

HOLIDAYS: New Year's, 1–2 January; Labor Day, 1 May; National Day, 5 June; Independence Day, 29 June; Assumption, 15 August; All Saints' Day, 1 November; Immaculate Conception, 8 December; Christmas, 25 December. Movable religious holidays include Good Friday, Easter Monday, Corpus Christi, and Ascension.

TIME: 4 PM = noon GMT.

1 LOCATION AND SIZE

Seychelles, an archipelago in the Indian Ocean, consists of an estimated 115 islands, most of which are not permanently inhabited. The second-smallest country in Africa, Seychelles has an area of 455 square kilometers (176 square miles), slightly more than 2.5 times the size of Washington, D.C. The capital city of Seychelles, Victoria, is located on the island of Mahé.

2 TOPOGRAPHY

One of two main clusters of islands, the granitic (made of hard rock) islands rise above the sea surface to form a peak or ridge with rugged crests, towering cliffs, boulders, and domes. The coralline Seychelles are, in contrast, low lying, rising only a few feet above the surface of the sea.

3 CLIMATE

Coastal temperatures are fairly constant at about 27°C (81°F) throughout the year. At higher altitudes, temperatures are lower, especially at night. Mean annual rainfall is 236 centimeters (93 inches) at sea level, as much as 356 centimeters (140 inches) in the mountains, and much lower on the southwestern coral islands, averaging about 50 centimeters (20 inches) a year on Aldabra.

4 PLANTS AND ANIMALS

On Praslin and Curieuse islands, the native forests of coco-de-mer have been protected in small reserves. Its fruit, a huge coconut weighing up to 18 kilograms (40 pounds), is the largest seed in the

Photo credit: Susan D. Rock.

Miniature "Big Ben" in the center of the city of Victoria.

world. Virtually all the broadleaf evergreen rainforest has been cut down. Sharks abound in the surrounding oceans; on land the most noteworthy animal is the giant tortoise, a species now sorely depleted. There is a great variety of bird life.

5 ENVIRONMENT

The monitoring of the environment is complicated by the fact that Seychelles consists of 15 islands distributed over a 1.3 million square kilometer area (501,800 square mile). The nation has a water pollution problem due to industrial by-products and sewage. Fires, landslides, and oil leakage also affect the environment in Seychelles. The Aldabra Island atoll (coral island) is a native wildlife preserve.

6 POPULATION

The population was estimated at 70,671 in mid-1994. A total of 24,324 people lived in Victoria, the capital and principal city at the time of the 1987 census. The estimated average population density in 1985 was 158 persons per square kilometer (409 persons per square mile).

7 MIGRATION

In 1990, 371 new immigrants arrived, and 664 Seychellois departed permanently.

8 ETHNIC GROUPS

The bulk of the population is Seychellois, a mixture of African, French, and Asian strains.

9 LANGUAGES

Creole, a simplified form of French with borrowings from African languages, has been the primary language since 1981 and is the initial language in public schools. English is second, and French, third.

10 RELIGIONS

In 1993, some 90% of the population was Roman Catholic; with 6% Anglicans; and Hindus, Muslims, and Seventh-day Adventists each numbering a few hundred.

11 TRANSPORTATION

The road network totaled 260 kilometers (162 miles) in 1991. There were 4,563 automobiles, and 1,860 commercial vehicles in 1992.

Until the opening of Seychelles International Airport on Mahé in 1971, the Seychelles Islands were entirely dependent on the sea for their links with the rest of the world. Air Seychelles, which also runs domestic flights, carried about 181,000 passengers over the course of nine months in 1992.

12 HISTORY

The Seychelles Islands (then uninhabited) were discovered by the Portuguese explorer Vasco da Gama in 1502. The French began colonization of the islands in 1768, when a party of 22 Frenchmen arrived, bringing with them a number of

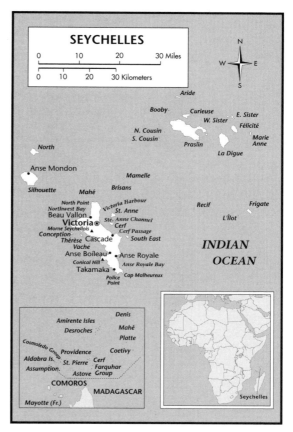

LOCATION: 3°41′ to 10°13′s; 46°12′ to 56°17′e.
TERRITORIAL SEA LIMIT: 12 miles.

slaves. The French and British warred for control of the islands between 1793 and 1813. Under the Treaty of Paris (1814), Seychelles, together with Mauritius, were ceded to Britain. On 31 August 1903, the islands became a British crown colony.

Seychelles achieved independence at 12:05 AM on 29 June 1976. Richard Marie Mancham, leader of the conservative Seychelles Democratic Party, became president on independence, heading a coalition

Boatmen in a secluded beach cove near Victoria.

government that included Seychelles People's United Party (SPUP) leader France Albert René as prime minister. Mancham was overthrown by a coup on 5 June 1977 and went into exile, and René became president. He suspended the constitution, dismissed the legislature, and ruled by decree.

The constitution of March 1979, adopted by referendum, established a one-party state. René was reelected president without opposition in June 1984. Since then, Seychelles has made progress economically and socially. Under rising pressure to democratize, in December 1991, René agreed to reform the system.

Multiparty elections were held in July 1992, and many dissidents, including Mancham, returned from exile. Finally, in June 1993, 73% of the voters approved a new constitution providing for multiparty government. Presidential and National Assembly elections were held 23 July 1993.

13 GOVERNMENT

In June 1993, 73.6% of the voters approved a new constitution drafted by a bipartisan commission. It called for multiparty elections of a president and a National Assembly of 33 members, of which 22 are directly elected and 11 allocated on a proportional basis.

14 POLITICAL PARTIES

The Seychelles People's Progressive Front (SPPF), was established in 1979 as the sole legal party, with the avowed objective of creating a Socialist state. The Seychelles Democratic Party (SDP) was declared to have "disappeared," and there were at least three opposition groups in exile.

After President René's 1991 announcement of a return to multiparty democracy, many dissidents returned from exile and the Democratic Party (DP) was reestablished, as well as the Seychelles Party (PS), the Seychelles Democratic Movement (MSPD), and the Seychelles Liberal Party (SLP).

15 JUDICIAL SYSTEM

Cases are first tried in Magistrates' courts. The Supreme Court hears appeals and takes original jurisdiction of some cases, and the Court of Appeal hears appeals from the Supreme Court. Appointment to the post of chief justice is made by the president of Seychelles.

16 ARMED FORCES

The Seychelles People's Liberation Army (SPLA) was merged with a People's Militia in 1981 to form the Seychelles People's Defense Force (SPDF) of 1,300 men equipped with 6 naval craft, 7 aircraft, and infantry weapons. In 1991 the SPLA spent $15 million on defense.

17 ECONOMY

With the opening of the international airport in 1971, the Seychelles economy began to move away from cash crops to

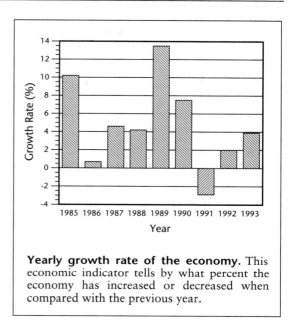

Yearly growth rate of the economy. This economic indicator tells by what percent the economy has increased or decreased when compared with the previous year.

the development of tourism. Seychelles is heavily dependent on imports and financial aid.

18 INCOME

In 1992 Seychelles' gross national product (GNP) was $378 million at current prices, or about $6,280 per person. For the period 1985–92 the average inflation rate was 3.4%, resulting in a real growth rate in per person GNP of 4.1%.

19 INDUSTRY

The largest plant is the tuna cannery, opened in 1987. The rest are small and process local agricultural products, including tea, copra and vanilla. There is a plastics factory, a brewery and soft drink bottler, and a cinnamon distiller.

Selected Social Indicators

These statistics are estimates for the period 1988 to 1993. For comparison purposes, data for the United States and averages for low-income countries and high-income countries are also given.

Indicator	Seychelles	Low-income countries	High-income countries	United States
Per capita gross national product†	$6,280	$380	$23,680	$24,740
Population growth rate	1.1%	1.9%	0.6%	1.0%
Population growth rate in urban areas	2.9%	3.9%	0.8%	1.3%
Population per square kilometer of land	158	78	25	26
Life expectancy in years	69	62	77	76
Number of people per physician	785	>3,300	453	419
Number of pupils per teacher (primary school)	18	39	<18	20
Illiteracy rate (15 years and older)	42%	41%	<5%	<3%
Energy consumed per capita (kg of oil equivalent)	1,681	364	5,203	7,918

† The gross national product (GNP) is the total dollar value of all goods and services produced by a country in a year. The per capita GNP is calculated by dividing a country's GNP by its population. The World Bank defines low-income countries as those with a per capita GNP of $695 or less. High-income countries have a per capita GNP of $8,626 or more. Less than 14% of the world's 5.5 billion people live in high-income countries, while almost 60% live in low-income countries.

> = greater than   < = less than

Sources: World Bank, *Social Indicators of Development 1995,* Baltimore: Johns Hopkins University Press, 1995. Central Intelligence Agency, *World Fact Book,* Washington, D.C.: Government Printing Office, 1994.

20 LABOR

In 1990, formal employment was 23,510. All job vacancies are filled through the government labor office, with preference for the unemployed. Minimum age and other child labor laws are effectively enforced.

21 AGRICULTURE

Production in 1992 included coconuts, 7,000 tons; bananas, about 2,000 tons; and 1,000 tons of copra. Other crops produced for export are cinnamon bark, vanilla, and cloves. Tea planting began in the early 1960s and 1991 exports totaled 1,000 tons.

22 DOMESTICATED ANIMALS

Seychelles is self-sufficient in the production of pork, poultry, and eggs. In 1992, there were about 19,000 hogs, 5,000 goats, and 2,000 head of cattle.

23 FISHING

Fish landings by the domestic fleet totaled 1,501 tons of snapper and 423 tons of mackerel in 1991. The total catch that year was 5,913 tons.

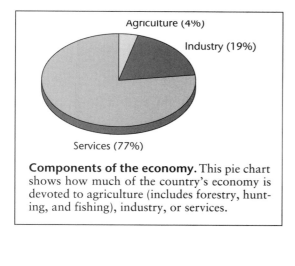

Components of the economy. This pie chart shows how much of the country's economy is devoted to agriculture (includes forestry, hunting, and fishing), industry, or services.

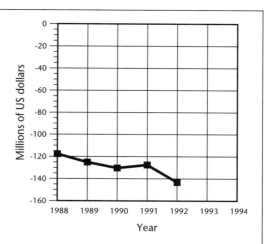

Yearly balance of trade measured in millions of US dollars. The balance of trade is the difference between what a country sells to other countries (its exports) and what it buys (its imports). If a country imports more than it exports, it has a negative balance of trade (a trade deficit). If exports exceed imports there is a positive balance of trade (a trade surplus).

24 FORESTRY

Little natural forest remains. Coconut plantations are the main source of timber, aside from imports.

25 MINING

Mineral production consists of small quantities of rock, coral, and sand for construction.

26 FOREIGN TRADE

The principal exports (95.5% of the total in 1988) are copra (dried coconut meat), cinnamon bark, and frozen fish. Machinery and transport equipment comprised 30.8% of total imports in 1988. Basic manufactures followed at 26.5%; food, beverages, and tobacco at 20.4%; and petroleum products at 14.1%.

In 1988, 56.2% of Seychelles exports went to France and another 11.2% to the United Kingdom. The leading import suppliers were Kuwait (16.7%), the United Kingdom (14.8%), South Africa (13.1%), and Singapore (10.0%).

27 ENERGY AND POWER

Practically the whole of Mahé is now supplied with electricity produced by diesel power in Victoria. Output reached 102 million kilowatt hours in 1991.

28 SOCIAL DEVELOPMENT

The National Provident Fund makes payments for marriage, emigration, disability, survivors, and old age. There is also a workers' compensation scheme. Health services are free for all residents.

29 HEALTH

In 1984, there were 5 hospitals, and, in 1990, 90 doctors. The average life expectancy is 69 years.

30 HOUSING

Most homes are of wood or stone with corrugated iron roofs; many rural houses are thatched.

31 EDUCATION

Public education is free and compulsory for children between the ages of 6 and 15. In 1991, the students in primary schools totaled 14,669. In secondary schools, there were 4,396 students in 1990 and 4,495 in 1991. Seychelles does not provide education at university level, but many students study abroad, especially in the United Kingdom. Adult literacy was estimated at 58% in 1990.

32 MEDIA

The number of telephones in use was 13,937 in 1991. Radio-Television Seychelles broadcasts in English, French, and Creole. There were about 33,000 radios in 1991. Television service began in 1983. There is one daily newspaper—*Seychelles Nation* (1991 circulation about 3,200)—published in English, French, and Creole.

33 TOURISM AND RECREATION

The prosperity of Seychelles depends on tourism. Visitors can enjoy coral beaches, water sports including scuba diving, water skiing, and windsurfing, and boat or yacht tours of the islands. The archipelago's wildlife is also a popular tourist attraction.

There were 98,000 visitor arrivals in 1991, largely from Italy, France, the United Kingdom, and South Africa. Income from tourism was $99 million. The 1,840 hotel rooms were filled to 56% of capacity.

34 FAMOUS SEYCHELLOIS

Sir James Richard Marie Mancham (b.1939), became Seychelles' first president in 1976. He was deposed in 1977 by France Albert René (b.1935).

35 BIBLIOGRAPHY

Doubilet, David. "Journey to Aldabra." *National Geographic,* March 1995, 90–113.
Franda, Marcus. *The Seychelles: Unquiet Islands.* Boulder, Colo.: Westview, 1982.
Vine, Peter. *Seychelles.* London: Immel Publishing Co., 1989.

SIERRA LEONE

Republic of Sierra Leone

CAPITAL: Freetown.

FLAG: The national flag is a tricolor of green, white, and blue horizontal stripes.

ANTHEM: Begins "High we exalt thee, realm of the free, Great is the love we have for thee."

MONETARY UNIT: The leone (Le) is a paper currency of 100 cents. There are coins of 1/2, 1, 5, 10, 20, and 50 cents, and notes of 1, 2, 5, 10, 20, 50, 100, and 500 leones. Le1 = $0.0017 (or $1 = Le577.23).

WEIGHTS AND MEASURES: The metric system is employed.

HOLIDAYS: New Year's Day, 1 January; Independence Day, 27 April; Bank Holiday, August; Christmas, 24–25 December; Boxing Day, 26 December. Movable religious holidays include Good Friday, Easter Monday, Whitmonday, 'Id al-Fitr, 'Id al-'Adha', and Milad an-Nabi.

TIME: GMT.

1 LOCATION AND SIZE

Situated on the west coast of Africa, Sierra Leone has an area of 71,740 square kilometers (27,699 square miles), slightly smaller than the state of South Carolina. It has a total boundary length of 1,364 kilometers (847 miles). In addition to the mainland proper, Sierra Leone also includes the offshore Banana and Turtle islands and Sherbro Island, and other small islands. Sierra Leone's capital city, Freetown, is located on the Atlantic Coast.

2 TOPOGRAPHY

The Sierra Leone peninsula in the extreme west is mostly mountainous, rising to about 884 meters (2,900 feet). Other areas in the west consist of coastal mangrove swamps. To the east, there are coastal plains with many navigable rivers and, far-

ther eastward, a plateau. The highest peak is Loma Mansa in the Loma Mountains, at 1,948 meters (6,390 feet).

3 CLIMATE

Temperatures and humidity are high, and rainfall is heavy. The mean temperature is about 27°C (81°F) on the coast and almost as high on the eastern plateau. There are distinct wet and dry seasons, with rainfall averaging more than 315 centimeters (125 inches) a year in most of the country.

4 PLANTS AND ANIMALS

There are savanna, or grasslands, in the north, while low bush is found in the south-central area, and forest or high bush in the southeast. There are also swamplands, and 3–5% of the land is rainforest. Sierra Leone is West Africa's only remaining habitat for the emerald cuckoo, which has been described as the most beautiful bird in Africa. Many birds that breed in Europe winter in Sierra Leone. Crocodiles and hippopotamuses are native to the coastal plain.

5 ENVIRONMENT

Water pollution is a significant problem in Sierra Leone due to mining by-products and sewage. The nation has 38.4 cubic miles of water, of which 89% is used for farming and 4% for industrial purposes. Twenty percent of the nation's city dwellers and 80% of those living in rural areas do not have pure water. The nation's cities produce 0.3 million tons of solid waste per year.

Forestland is being converted to agricultural land due to the need for food by a population that increased by 80% during the period between 1963 and 1990. Hunting for food has reduced the stock of wild mammals. Cutamba Killimi National Park, which has some wildlife species found only in this part of West Africa, is exploited by poachers. As of 1994, 13 of Sierra Leone's mammal species and 7 bird species were endangered. Twelve of the nation's plant species were also threatened.

6 POPULATION

The population of Sierra Leone was 4,619,433, according to a 1994 estimate, with an average density of 61 persons per square kilometer (167 per square mile). A population of 5,395,000 was projected for the year 2000. Freetown, the capital, had an estimated population of 669,000 in 1990.

7 MIGRATION

Historically, there has been considerable movement over the borders to and from Guinea and Liberia. At the end of 1992, 5,900 Africans were refugees in Sierra Leone. At the end of 1991, 236,000 people in Sierra Leone had been driven from their homes by the spillover of the Liberian civil war. Many of them fled to Guinea, which had more than 120,000 refugees from Sierra Leone at the end of 1992.

8 ETHNIC GROUPS

The African population of Sierra Leone is composed of some 18 ethnic groups, the 2 largest being the Mende (about 34% of the population) and Temne (about 31%). Other peoples are the Bullom, Fulani, Gola, Kissi, Kono, Koranko, Krim, and Kru. There are also 40,000–80,000 Creoles, descendants of settlers from Europe, the West Indies, and other regions.

9 LANGUAGES

The Mende and Temne languages are widely spoken in the south and north, respectively. The common language is Krio, the mother tongue of the Creoles. English is the official language.

10 RELIGIONS

Approximately one-half of the population followed African traditional religions in the early 1990s, and about 10% were Christian.

11 TRANSPORTATION

In the early 1970s, following a World Bank recommendation, Sierra Leone dismantled most of its rail system and replaced it with new roadways; in the mid-1980s, only 84 kilometers (52 miles) of narrow-gauge railway remained. Sierra Leone has about 7,400 kilometers (4,600 miles) of roads. In 1991 there were 47,659 registered motor vehicles, including 35,870 automobiles, and 11,789 commercial vehicles.

Freetown has one of the finest natural harbors in the world. Sierra Leone has many rivers, but most are navigable only over short distances for about three months of the year, during the rainy season. An international airport at Lungi is connected by ferry to Freetown, across the bay. Domestic air service operates from Hastings Airfield, 22 kilometers (14 miles) from Freetown, linking the capital to nearly all the large provincial towns.

12 HISTORY

Archaeological research indicates that by AD 800 the use of iron had been introduced into what is now Sierra Leone and that by AD 1000 the coastal peoples were practicing agriculture. Beginning perhaps in the thirteenth century, migrants arrived from the north. European contact began in 1462 with the Portuguese explorer Pedro da Cintra, who gave the mountainous peninsula the name Sierra Leone ("Lion Mountains"). From the sixteenth to the early nineteenth century, the region was raided for slaves for the Atlantic trade, and later in the nineteenth century it was ravaged by African war leaders and slavers. The colony of Sierra Leone was founded by the British as a home for Afri-

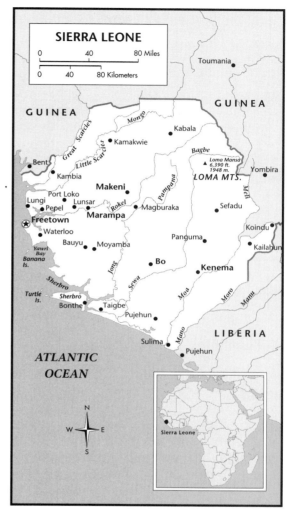

LOCATION: 6°55′ to 10°N; 10°16′ to 13°18′w. **BOUNDARY LENGTHS:** Guinea, 652 kilometers (405 miles); Liberia, 306 kilometers (190 miles); Atlantic coastline, 406 kilometers (252 miles). **TERRITORIAL SEA LIMIT:** 12 miles.

can slaves freed in England. The first settlers arrived in 1787.

The Sierra Leone Company was formed in 1791 to administer the settlement, but the burden of defense and settlement proved too heavy for the company, and

Sierra Leone was transferred to the British crown in 1808. The colony received additions of land up to 1861 through various treaties from the local chiefs. After 1807, when the British Parliament passed an act making the slave trade illegal, the new colony was used as a base from which the act could be enforced. In 1896, a British protectorate was declared over the hinterland of Sierra Leone, which was separate from the colony. A 1924 constitution provided for the election of three members to a Legislative Council, and the constitution of 1951 provided for an elected majority, resulting in African rule. In 1958, Milton Margai became Sierra Leone's first prime minister; in 1960, he led a delegation to London, England, to establish conditions for full independence.

Independence

Sierra Leone became an independent country within the British Commonwealth of Nations on 27 April 1961. After the 1967 national elections, there were two successive military coups, and a state of emergency was declared in 1970. In 1971, a new constitution was adopted, and the country was declared a republic on 19 April 1971. Siaka Stevens, then prime minister, became the nation's first president. An alleged plot to overthrow Stevens failed in 1974, and in March 1976 he was elected without opposition for a second five-year term as president. In 1978, a new constitution was adopted, making the country a one-party state.

Stevens did not run for reelection as president in 1985, yielding power to his handpicked successor, Major General Joseph Saidu Momoh, the armed forces commander. By 29 April 1992, Momoh was overthrown in a military coup and fled to Guinea. A National Provisional Ruling Council (NPRC) was created but, shortly afterward, the head of the five-member junta, Lieutenant Colonel Yahya, was arrested by his colleagues and replaced by Captain Valentine Strasser, who was formally designated head of state.

The Strasser government soon limited the status of the 1991 constitution by a series of decrees and public notices. The NPRC (National Provisional Ruling Council) dissolved parliament and political parties and ruled by decree. There was fighting in the southeast, where the forces of the National Patriot Front of Liberia and Sierra Leone dissidents were fighting with Sierra Leone armed forces. Forces from the Economic Community of West African States (ECOWAS) Monitoring Group sought to create a ceasefire zone along the boundary between the two countries. In November 1993, Strasser announced a unilateral ceasefire and an amnesty for rebels. In November 1993, Strasser issued a timetable for a transition to democracy to culminate in general elections in late 1995. A month later, the NPRC released a "Working Document on the Constitution" to serve as the basis for public debates leading to a constitutional referendum in May 1995.

However, by late 1995, the war between Sierra Leone and Liberia was continuing; since fighting broke out in 1989, more than 150,000 have died. Ironically, it seems that no one can remember the reason for the conflict. Guerillas, known as the Revolutionary United Front, appear to perpetuate the fighting for the chance to use weapons and behave violently.

13 GOVERNMENT

A new constitution came into force on 1 October 1991, but it was superseded by the military junta established after the 29 April 1992 coup. Shortly thereafter, the parliament and political parties were dissolved and the NPRC (National Provisional Ruling Council) now rules by decree through a Supreme Council of State (SCS) and a Council of State Secretaries (CSS-Cabinet). In November 1993, they announced a timetable leading to multiparty democracy and general elections in 1995.

14 POLITICAL PARTIES

The sole parliamentary party held power from 1967 until April 1992. It was formed in 1960 by Siaka Stevens, who was president of Sierra Leone from 1971 to 1985. Prior to that, the Sierra Leone People's Party (SLPP), formed in 1951, ruled the country from its inception until 1967. In September 1970, another opposition group, the United Democratic Party, was formed. Shortly afterward, a state of emergency was declared, and on 8 October the party was banned. After the April 1992 military coup, all political parties were banned and parliament was dissolved. Currently the National Provisional Ruling Council (NPRC), the military junta that rules by decree, is planning to turn power over to a civilian government after multiparty elections in late 1995.

15 JUDICIAL SYSTEM

Magistrates hold court in the various districts and in Freetown, administering the English-based code of law. Appeals from magistrates' courts are heard by the High Court, which also has unlimited original civil and criminal jurisdiction. Appeals from High Court decisions may be made to the Court of Appeal and finally to the Supreme Court, consisting of a chief justice and not fewer than three other justices. The National Provisional Ruling Council (NPRC) formed after the 1992 military coup has not altered the previously existing judicial system, but it has set up special commissions of inquiry to handle some cases.

16 ARMED FORCES

In 1993, the Sierra Leone armed services had about 6,150 members, including 6,000 ground troops in one brigade group and 150 naval (coast guard) personnel, in addition to an 800-member state security force. Military service is voluntary. The military was expanded in 1992 to respond to the attack by Liberians and Sierra Leone guerillas.

17 ECONOMY

Although Sierra Leone is a potentially rich country with diverse resources, which include diamonds, gold, rutile, bauxite, and a variety of agricultural products, the economy has been severely depressed over the past two decades. Currently, agriculture employs 70% of the labor force.

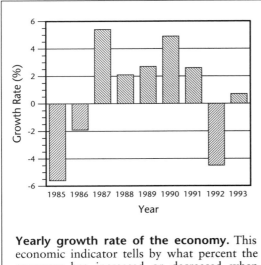

Yearly growth rate of the economy. This economic indicator tells by what percent the economy has increased or decreased when compared with the previous year.

[18] INCOME

In 1992 Sierra Leone's gross national product (GNP) was $726 million at current prices, or about $140 per person. For the period 1985–92 the average annual inflation rate was 75.3%, resulting in no real growth in per person GNP.

[19] INDUSTRY

The Wellington Industrial Estate, covering 46 hectares (113 acres) just east of Freetown, was developed in the 1960s by the government to encourage investments. Its factories produce a variety of products, including cement, nails, shoes, oxygen, cigarettes, beer and soft drinks, paint, and knitted goods. Timber for prefabricated buildings is milled, and another factory produces modern furniture.

[20] LABOR

Agriculture is the occupation of at least two-thirds of the labor force; manufacturing engages only 2% of the labor force. Only 70,200 Sierra Leoneans were wage earners as of 1988 (in establishments with six or more workers). The 1991 constitution provides for the right of association, and all workers have the right to join trade unions of their choice.

Minimum age laws exist to regulate child labor, but they are not enforced; children routinely work in agriculture and in small businesses.

[21] AGRICULTURE

Agriculture is the primary occupation in Sierra Leone, employing two-thirds of the labor force. Rice is the most important subsistence crop and, along with millet in the northeast, is a food staple; an estimated 420,000 tons were produced in 1992. Other domestic food crops include cassava, yams, peanuts, corn, pineapples, coconuts, tomatoes, and pepper. Agricultural exports include coffee, cocoa, palm kernels, piassava, kola nuts, and ginger. Coffee exports rose to about 8,200 tons in 1990. Piassava, a raffia palm fiber used for broom and brush bristles, is grown in the swampy areas of the extreme south.

[22] DOMESTICATED ANIMALS

Estimates of livestock in 1992 were 333,000 head of cattle, 275,000 sheep, 152,000 goats, and 50,000 hogs. Large numbers of cattle are kept, mainly by nomads in the grasslands area of the northeast. Poultry farmers had an estimated 6 million chickens in 1992.

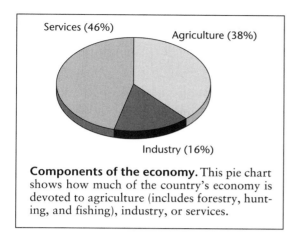

Services (46%) Agriculture (38%)

Industry (16%)

Components of the economy. This pie chart shows how much of the country's economy is devoted to agriculture (includes forestry, hunting, and fishing), industry, or services.

diamonds close to the earth's surface are smuggled out of the country.

Production of 1,288,000 tons of bauxite was reported in 1991. Rutile output rose from 46,000 tons in 1980–81 to a record 154,000 tons in 1991. A zircon recovery plant opened in April 1991, and in that year, production was a reported 1,119 tons. Production of alluvial (deposited by running water) gold was 26 kilograms in 1991. Other known minerals are antimony, cassiterite, columbite, corundum, fluorspar, ilmenite, lead, lignite, magnetite, molybdenum, monazite, platinum, silver, tantalite, tin, titanium, tungsten, and zinc.

23 FISHING

The fishing industry includes industrial, freshwater, and shellfish fisheries. Total fish and shellfish production in 1991 was 50,000 tons. Shrimp is the main export.

24 FORESTRY

Although much of Sierra Leone was once forested, intensive farming gradually eliminated most of the forest area. There are still about 2 million hectares (4.9 million acres) of forests and woodland. In 1991, an estimated total of 3.1 million cubic meters of roundwood was harvested, 96% of it for fuel.

25 MINING

Diamonds, first discovered in 1930, are widely scattered over a large area but particularly along the upper Sewa River. Production was reported at 243,000 carats in 1991, of which 160,000 carats were of gem quality. It is believed that many of the

26 FOREIGN TRADE

Sierra Leone exports primary minerals and agricultural commodities, and it imports food and machinery. The trade balance recovered in 1993 after a deficit in 1992. The principal exports in 1993 were rutile, bauxite, diamonds, coffee, and cocoa. In the same year, the principal imports were foodstuffs, machinery and transport equipment, and chemicals.

Sierra Leone's leading export partner in 1993 was the United States (30.6%), followed by Germany (12.2%) and the United Kingdom (8.8%). Imports to Sierra Leone came from the United Kingdom (14.2%), Germany (10.9%), and China (10.1%).

27 ENERGY AND POWER

Total national production of electricity increased to 230 million kilowatt hours in 1991, of which about 60% was generated

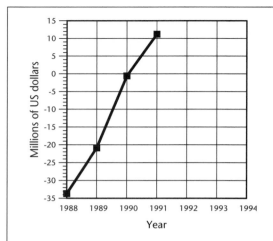

Yearly balance of trade measured in millions of US dollars. The balance of trade is the difference between what a country sells to other countries (its exports) and what it buys (its imports). If a country imports more than it exports, it has a negative balance of trade (a trade deficit). If exports exceed imports there is a positive balance of trade (a trade surplus).

by public utilities. Installed capacity in 1991 was 126,000 kilowatts. Apart from wood, lignite is the only natural fuel found, but known deposits are not being economically mined.

28 SOCIAL DEVELOPMENT

Since 1946, the Welfare Department has sponsored child welfare and domestic affairs programs, promoted youth groups, and set up programs for the care of the aged, the blind, and the mentally handicapped. In 1955, these services were reorganized into the Ministry of Social Welfare. A National Coordinating Committee concerned with community development and social services has also been set up. The government allows the Planned Parenthood Association to provide services but does not actively encourage family planning and population limitation.

29 HEALTH

In 1985, Sierra Leone had 52 hospitals and 263 dispensaries and health-treatment centers. There is 1 doctor per 13,640 people. In 1990, there was 1 hospital bed per 1,000 inhabitants. In 1992, only 38% of the population had access to health care services.

With technical assistance from World Health Organization (WHO) and United Nations Children's Fund (UNICEF), a disease-control unit reduced the incidence of sleeping sickness and yaws and began a leprosy-control campaign. Malaria, tuberculosis, and schistosomiasis remain serious health hazards, however, as is malnutrition, with the calorie supply meeting only 83% of minimum requirements in 1992. Life expectancy is only 39 years, one of the lowest in the world. The country spent $22 million on health care in 1990.

30 HOUSING

Many of the older two-story wooden houses in Freetown are being replaced by structures built largely of concrete blocks, with corrugated iron or cement-asbestos roofs. Building is controlled in the major towns, and designs are subject to approval. Village houses in the provinces are traditionally made of sticks, with mud walls and thatch or grass roofs, and they may be circular or rectangular in shape.

Selected Social Indicators

These statistics are estimates for the period 1988 to 1993. For comparison purposes, data for the United States and averages for low-income countries and high-income countries are also given.

Indicator	Sierra Leone	Low-income countries	High-income countries	United States
Per capita gross national product†	$140	$380	$23,680	$24,740
Population growth rate	2.5%	1.9%	0.6%	1.0%
Population growth rate in urban areas	4.8%	3.9%	0.8%	1.3%
Population per square kilometer of land	61	78	25	26
Life expectancy in years	39	62	77	76
Number of people per physician	13,640	>3,300	453	419
Number of pupils per teacher (primary school)	34	39	<18	20
Illiteracy rate (15 years and older)	79%	41%	<5%	<3%
Energy consumed per capita (kg of oil equivalent)	72	364	5,203	7,918

† The gross national product (GNP) is the total dollar value of all goods and services produced by a country in a year. The per capita GNP is calculated by dividing a country's GNP by its population. The World Bank defines low-income countries as those with a per capita GNP of $695 or less. High-income countries have a per capita GNP of $8,626 or more. Less than 14% of the world's 5.5 billion people live in high-income countries, while almost 60% live in low-income countries.

> = greater than   < = less than

Sources: World Bank, *Social Indicators of Development 1995,* Baltimore: Johns Hopkins University Press, 1995. Central Intelligence Agency, *World Fact Book,* Washington, D.C.: Government Printing Office, 1994.

31 EDUCATION

In 1990, Sierra Leone's 1,795 primary schools had 10,850 teachers and a total enrollment of 367,426 pupils, and secondary schools had 102,474 pupils and 5,969 teachers. The ultimate goal of the government is to provide free primary school facilities for every child. In 1990, the adult literacy rate was estimated to be 21%: males, 30.7% and females, 11.3%.

Fourah Bay College, the oldest institution of higher learning in West Africa, was founded in 1827 by the Church Missionary Society, primarily to provide theological training. In 1967, the University of Sierra Leone was chartered with two constituent colleges, Fourah Bay (in Freetown) and Njala University College (in Moyamba District). In 1990, all higher level institutions were reported to have 4,742 pupils and 600 teaching personnel.

32 MEDIA

Radio Sierra Leone, the oldest broadcasting service in English-speaking West Africa, broadcasts mainly in English, with regular news and discussion programs in several native languages, and a weekly program in French. In 1991 there were 4 radio transmitters and about 950,000

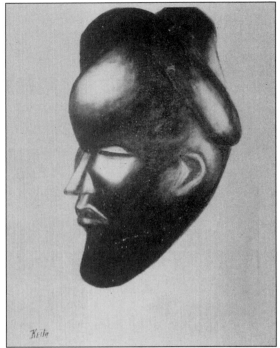

Portrait or Mask, *an oil on canvasboard by artist Keita.*

radio receivers, as well as 2 television transmitters and about 43,000 television receivers. International cablegram, telex, and telephone services are provided by Sierra Leone External Telecommunications.

The only daily newspaper is the government-owned *Daily Mail* (with a 1986 circulation of about 10,000), but there were several privately owned weekly newspapers in 1991.

33 TOURISM AND RECREATION

Sierra Leone has magnificent beaches, including Lumley Beach on the outskirts of Freetown, perhaps the finest in West Africa. Natural scenic wonders include the Loma Mountains. There are several modern hotels in Freetown, as well as a luxury hotel and casino at Lumley Beach. The main provincial towns have smaller hotels, and a number of government rest houses are located throughout the country. International tourist arrivals numbered about 118,000 in 1991, but the ongoing guerilla warfare since 1992 has seriously curtailed tourism. In January 1995 the guerillas took nine Europeans hostage, and warned all foreign visitors to expect a similar fate.

34 FAMOUS SIERRA LEONEANS

Sir Samuel Lewis (1843–1903) was a member of the Legislative Council for more than 20 years and the first mayor of Freetown. Sir Milton Augustus Strieby Margai (1895–1964) was the first prime minister of Sierra Leone, a post he held until his death. Siaka Probyn Stevens (b.1905), founder of the APC political party, was prime minister from 1968 to 1971 and became the republic's first president from 1971 to 1985.

35 BIBLIOGRAPHY

Alie, Joe A. D. *A New History of Sierra Leone.* New York: St. Martin's, 1990.

Binns, Margaret. *Sierra Leone.* Oxford, England; Santa Barbara, Calif.: Clio Press, 1992.

Foray, Cyril P. *Historical Dictionary of Sierra Leone.* Metuchen, N.J.: Scarecrow, 1977.

Fyfe, Christopher. *A Short History of Sierra Leone.* New York: Longman, 1979.

Greene, Graham. *The Heart of the Matter.* New York: Viking, 1948.

White, E. Frances. *Sierra Leone's Settler Women Traders: Women on the Afro-European Frontier.* Ann Arbor: University of Michigan Press, 1987.

SINGAPORE

Republic of Singapore

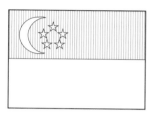

CAPITAL: Singapore.

FLAG: The flag consists of a red stripe at the top and a white stripe on the bottom. On the red stripe, at the hoist, are a white crescent opening to the fly and five white stars.

ANTHEM: *Long Live Singapore.*

MONETARY UNIT: The Singapore dollar (s$) of 100 cents is a freely convertible currency. There are coins of 1, 5, 10, 20, and 50 cents and 1 dollar and notes of 2, 5, 10, 20, 50, 100, 500, 1,000, and 10,000 dollars. s$1 = us$0.6373 (or us$1 = s$1.5692).

WEIGHTS AND MEASURES: The metric system is in force, but some local measures are used.

HOLIDAYS: Major Western, Chinese, Malay, and Muslim holidays are celebrated, some of which fall on annually variable dates because of the calendars used. Major holidays include New Year's Day, 1 January; Chinese New Year; Good Friday; Vesak Day (Buddhist festival); Labor Day, 1 May; Hari Raya Puasa (Muslim festival); National Day, 9 August; Hari Raya Haji (Malay Muslim festival); Dewali; Christmas, 25 December.

TIME: 8 PM = noon GMT.

1 LOCATION AND SIZE

The Republic of Singapore, the second smallest country in Asia, consists of Singapore Island and several smaller adjacent islets. Situated in the Indian Ocean off the southern tip of the Malay Peninsula, Singapore has an area of 632.6 square kilometers (244.2 square miles), slightly less than 3.5 times the size of Washington, D.C. Singapore is connected to the nearby western portion of Malaysia by a causeway across the narrow Johore Strait. Singapore's capital city, Singapore, is located on the country's southern coast.

2 TOPOGRAPHY

Singapore Island is mostly low-lying, green, rolling country with a small range of hills at the center. The highest point of the island is Timah Hill (176 meters/577 feet). There are sections of rainforest in the center and large mangrove swamps along the coast. Singapore's harbor is wide, deep, and well protected.

3 CLIMATE

The climate is tropical, with heavy rainfall and high humidity. The range of temperature is slight; the average annual maximum is 31°C (88°F), and the average minimum 24°C (75°F). The annual rainfall of 237 centimeters (93 inches) is distributed fairly evenly throughout the year, ranging from 39 centimeters (15 inches) in December to 28 centimeters (11 inches) in May. It rains about every other day.

4 PLANTS AND ANIMALS

The dense tropical forest that originally covered Singapore has mostly been cleared. There is some rainforest in the central area of the island, however, as well as extensive mangrove (trees with dense roots) swamps along the coast.

5 ENVIRONMENT

Air pollution from transportation vehicles is a problem in the nation's growing urban areas. Singapore does not have enough water to support the needs of its people. The nation uses 4% of its water for farming and 51% for industrial purposes. Pollution from the nation's oil industry is also a significant problem. Waste water is treated and recycled to conserve water supplies.

In 1994, 19 plant species were considered to be in danger of extinction.

6 POPULATION

Singapore's mid-1993 estimated population was projected at 2,874,000; it was 2,705,115 at the time of the 1990 census. The projected population for the year 2000 is 2,976,000. The population density, estimated at 4,454 persons per square kilometer (11,539 per square mile) in 1993, is the highest of any nation in the world (excluding Monaco).

7 MIGRATION

Immigration, rather than natural increase, was the major factor in Singapore's fast population growth through the mid-twentieth century. In November 1965, following separation from Malaysia, Singapore's newly independent government introduced measures to restrict the flow of Malaysians entering the country in search of work, who had averaged 10,000 a year up to 1964. Immigration is now generally restricted to those with capital or with special skills.

8 ETHNIC GROUPS

The people of Singapore are mainly of Chinese origin. Of an estimated 1992 population of 2,818,200, about 2,187,200 (77.6%) were ethnic Chinese (most of them, however, born in Singapore or in neighboring Malaysia). Some 399,400 (14.2%) were Malays; 199,600 (7.1%) were South Asian, (including Indians, Pakistanis, Bangladeshis, and Sri Lankans).

9 LANGUAGES

There are four official languages: Chinese (Mandarin dialect), Malay, English, and Tamil. English is the principal language of government and is widely used in commerce. Malay is the national language. In 1990, Chinese dialects were the first language of 36.7% of the population and Mandarin of 26%. English was used by nearly 20%.

10 RELIGIONS

The Chinese for the most part (54% in 1991) adhere in varying degrees to Buddhism, Taoism, and Confucianism. Malays and persons with origins in the Pakistani and Bangladeshi portions of the Indian subcontinent—about 16% of the population—are almost exclusively Muslims. Most of the Indian minority are Hindus. The Christian population was estimated in 1991 at 13%.

11 TRANSPORTATION

With a natural deepwater harbor that is open year-round, Singapore now ranks as the largest container port in the world, with facilities that can accommodate supertankers. Ships of some 600 shipping lines, flying the flags of nearly all the maritime nations of the world, regularly call at Singapore. In 1991, Singapore itself had the fourteenth largest merchant fleet, with 478 ships totaling 8,684,350 gross registered tons.

There are two major airports: Singapore Changi International Airport and Seletar Airport. Singapore Airlines carried 8,477,300 passengers in 1992, including about 50% of all visitors who came by air.

In 1991, there were 415,442 motor vehicles, of which 285,298 were automobiles. They traveled on 2,644 kilometers (1,643 miles) of roads. Singapore's sole rail facility is a 26-kilometer (16-mile) section of the Malayan Railways, which links Singapore to Kuala Lumpur, Malaysia.

12 HISTORY

Singapore is thought to have been a thriving trading center in the thirteenth and fourteenth centuries, until it was devastated by a Javanese (island of present-day Indonesia) attack in 1377. However, it was an almost uninhabited island when Sir Stamford Raffles, in 1819, established a trading station there of the British East India Company. In 1826 it was incorporated with Malacca (Melaka, Malaysia)

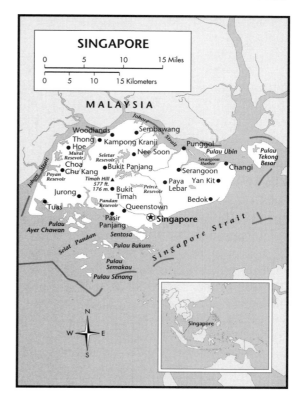

LOCATION: 1°9′ to 1°29′N; 103°38′ to 104°6′E.
TERRITORIAL SEA LIMIT: 3 miles.

and Penang (Pinang, Malaysia) to form the Straits Settlements, which was the form of its legal status and administration up to World War II (1939–45). The trading center grew into the city of Singapore and attracted large numbers of Chinese, many of whom became merchants, until it became a largely Chinese-populated community.

A Nation Built on Trade

With its excellent harbor, Singapore also became a flourishing commercial center and the leading seaport of Southeast Asia, handling the vast export trade in tin and rubber from British-ruled Malaya (present-day Malaysia). In 1938, the British completed construction of a large naval base on the island, which the Japanese captured in February 1942 during World War II, following a land-based attack from the Malay Peninsula to the north.

Recaptured by the United Kingdom in 1945, Singapore was detached from the Straits Settlements to become a separate crown colony in 1946. In 1959, Singapore became a self-governing state, and on 16 September 1963, it joined the new Federation of Malaysia (formed by bringing together the previously independent Malaya and Singapore and the formerly British-ruled northern Borneo territories of Sarawak and Sabah).

Independence

However, Singapore, with its mostly urban Chinese population and highly commercial economy, found itself at odds with the Malay-dominated central government of Malaysia. Frictions mounted, and on 9 August 1965, Singapore separated from Malaysia to become wholly independent in its own right as the Republic of Singapore. Singapore, Indonesia, Malaysia, the Philippines and Thailand formed the Association of South-East Asian Nations (ASEAN) in 1967. Brunei became a member of ASEAN in 1984. Harry Lee Kuan Yew, a major figure in the move toward independence, served as Singapore's first prime minister.

The People's Action Party (PAP) founded in 1954 has been the dominant political party, winning every general election since 1959. The PAP's popular support has rested on economic growth and improved standards of living along with unrelenting repression of opposition leaders. The PAP won all parliamentary seats in the general elections from 1968 to 1980.

In May and June 1987, the Government detained 22 persons for alleged involvement in a "Marxist conspiracy." These detentions triggered an international response on human rights critical of the detentions without trial and allegations of torture of the detainees. Most of the alleged conspirators were released by December, but eight were rearrested in April 1988 after issuing a joint press statement regarding the circumstances of their detention.

On 28 November 1990, Lee Kuan Yew, Prime Minister of Singapore for over thirty-one years, transferred the prime ministership to Goh Chock Tong, the former first deputy prime minister. Singapore's first direct presidential elections were held on 28 August 1993, and Ong Teng Cheong became the first elected president.

A Nation of Strict Laws

Laws are strictly enforced in Singapore. An incident that garnered worldwide attention was the Singapore government's arrest in October 1993 of nine foreign youths charged with vandalism of some 70 cars which were spray painted. Michael Fay, an American student suspected of being the leader, admitted his guilt under police interrogation and was sentenced to four months in prison, a fine of US$2,230, and six strokes of the cane.

On 7 March 1994 President Bill Clinton urged Singapore to reconsider the flogging of Fay, but Fay's appeal was dismissed. A plea to the president for clemency (mercy) was rejected, but as a "goodwill gesture towards President Clinton," the sentence of caning was reduced from six strokes to four. The sentence was carried out on 5 May 1994.

13 GOVERNMENT

The constitution of the Republic of Singapore provides for a single-chamber parliamentary form of government. Singapore practices universal suffrage, and voting has been compulsory for all citizens over 21 since 1959. In 1993, the unicameral legislature consisted of an 81 elected-member parliament and six nominated members (NMPs) appointed by the president.

The prime minister, who commands the confidence of a majority of parliament, acts as effective head of government, and appoints the cabinet. The president is elected for a term of six years.

Singapore has no local government divisions.

14 POLITICAL PARTIES

There were 22 registered political parties at the beginning of 1993. The ruling People's Action Party (PAP) of former Prime Minister Lee Kuan Yew has dominated the country since 1959. The main opposition parties are the Singapore Democratic

Photo credit: Corel Corporation.

Worshippers at Sri Veeramakaliamman Temple, Singapore.

Party (SDP) and the Workers' Party (WP). Smaller minority parties are the United People's Front, the Singapore Malays' National Organization, and the Singapore Solidarity Party. The Malay Communist Party and the underground Malayan National Liberation Front are illegal.

15 JUDICIAL SYSTEM

The judiciary includes the Supreme Court as well as district, magistrate, and special courts. Minor cases are heard in the country's ten magistrate courts and in district courts (two civil and four criminal), each presided over by a district judge. The

Supreme Court is headed by a chief justice and is divided into the High Court, the Court of Appeal, and the Court of Criminal Appeal. In its appeals jurisdiction, the High Court hears criminal and civil appeals from the magistrate and district courts.

16 ARMED FORCES

Compulsory national military service has been in effect since 1967. Male citizens are called up for 24 months' full-time military service at age 18. Singapore's armed forces are small, but they are well trained and equipped, and their reserve strength (250,000 in 1993) is substantial.

In 1993, the army had an estimated 45,000 personnel, including one combined arms division; the navy had 4,500 personnel and a fleet of 30 ships, including 6 corvettes and 6 missile gunboats. The air force had 6,000 personnel and more than 192 combat and transport aircraft. The 1990 defense budget was US$1.7 billion.

17 ECONOMY

Historically, Singapore's economy was based primarily on its role as a trading center for neighboring countries, which developed from its strategic geographic location. Its most significant natural resource is a deep-water harbor. By the early 1980s, Singapore had built a strong, diversified economy, giving it an economic importance in Southeast Asia out of proportion to its small size.

In the late 1980s, Singapore began to further diversify its economy, making it capable of providing manufacturing,

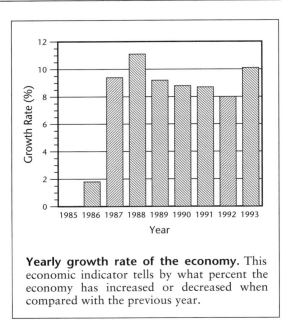

Yearly growth rate of the economy. This economic indicator tells by what percent the economy has increased or decreased when compared with the previous year.

financial, and communications facilities for multinational firms. One of the fastest-growing sectors of Singapore's economy was international banking and finance, ranking Singapore behind Tokyo and Hong Kong among financial service centers in Southeast Asia region.

The inflation rate based on consumer prices in 1992 was 2.3%. The exodus of professional and skilled labor remained a problem; in 1992, the number of Singaporeans who left the country for overseas work grew by an estimated 10–15%. Manufacturing was dominated by the production of computer peripherals and oil processing. Since 1992, property prices have doubled and residential property prices were still climbing in mid-1994. The main constraints on Singapore's economic performance are labor shortages, rising labor costs, and erosion of productivity.

18 INCOME

In 1992, Singapore's gross national product (GNP) was US$44,315 million at current prices, or about US$19,850 per person. For the period 1985–92 the average annual inflation rate was 2.7%, resulting in a real growth rate in per person GNP of 5.9%.

19 INDUSTRY

Manufacturing grew by an average annual rate of about 20% during the 1962–74 period, and it registered an average annual increase of over 10% from 1975–81. Manufacturing in 1992 employed some 27.5% of the work force.

Petroleum refining is a well-established industry in Singapore. After Rotterdam, the Netherlands, and Houston, Texas, Singapore is the world's third-largest refining center. Production capacity is one million barrels a day. Other major industries are electronics, oil drilling equipment, rubber processing and rubber products, processed food and beverages, ship repair, entrepôt (intermediary) trade, financial services, and biotechnology.

20 LABOR

In 1992, Singapore's employed work force totaled 1,576,200. Of this number, 27.5% were employed in manufacturing; 22.6% in commerce; 21.5% in community, social, and personal services; 10% in transportation, storage, and communications; 6.5% in construction; 10.9% in finance, insurance, real estate, and busi-

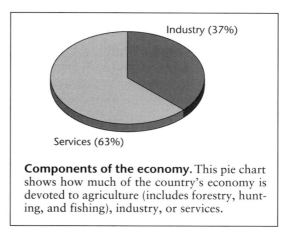

Components of the economy. This pie chart shows how much of the country's economy is devoted to agriculture (includes forestry, hunting, and fishing), industry, or services.

ness services; and 1% in other sectors. The unemployment rate was 1.9% in mid-1991.

There is no minimum wage legislation. At the end of 1991, the average real weekly earnings for a semi-skilled factory worker were US$146.20. In 1992, there were 83 registered trade unions in Singapore.

21 AGRICULTURE

Urbanization and industrialization have taken almost all the land away from agricultural activity in post-World War II Singapore. Many of the rubber and coconut plantations that dominated Singapore's landscape before the war have disappeared altogether. Housing for a growing population—and factories for its employment—stand where rubber and coconut trees used to grow. Still, agriculture remains a small part (<.05%) of Singapore's total economic activity.

Only about 1.6% of the land area is used for farming. In 1992, production of fresh vegetables totaled 5,000 tons, resulting in a decreased need to rely on foreign produce imports. Despite this improvement, the value of Singapore's agricultural imports still far exceeded the value of its agricultural products. Orchids are grown for export.

22 DOMESTICATED ANIMALS

Singapore has been self-sufficient (or nearly so) in the production of pork, poultry, and eggs since 1964. However, hog farming is being phased out because of environmental pollution; domestic pork requirements are increasingly being met by imports. In 1992, the livestock population included 3 million chickens, 280,000 pigs, and 1,000 goats. That year also, about 15,000 tons of eggs, 69 tons of sheepskins, and 42 tons of cattle hides were produced.

The Pig and Poultry Research and Training Institute and Lim Chu Kang Veterinary Experimental Station conduct research on feeding, housing, breeding, management, and disease control.

23 FISHING

Local fishermen operate chiefly in inshore waters, but some venture into the South China Sea and the Indian Ocean. Traditional fishing methods are used along coastal waters, but there is a trend toward mechanization in both offshore and deep-sea fishing. In 1991, Singapore's fishermen caught 13,054 tons of fish.

Aquaculture (fish-raising) concentrates on the breeding of grouper, sea bass, mussels, and shrimp. By the end of 1985, 60 marine fish farms were in operation. By 1990, Singapore was contributing 1.5% to the world's total exports of fresh, chilled, and frozen fish.

24 FORESTRY

There is little productive forestry left on the island, but Singapore continues to have a fairly sizable sawmilling industry, processing timber imported largely from Malaysia (with some additional imports from Indonesia). Both Malaysia and Indonesia are expanding their processing capacities, however, and the industry is declining in Singapore in the face of the government's policy shift to high-technology industries.

25 MINING

There is no mining in Singapore.

26 FOREIGN TRADE

Since World War II (post-1945), Singapore has changed from a trading center for its neighbors in Southeast Asia to an exporting country in its own right. Machinery and transport equipment constituted the leading import and also headed the export list, followed by mineral fuels.

Singapore's main trading partners are the ASEAN group (principally Malaysia), the United States, and Japan.

27 ENERGY AND POWER

Electricity generated in 1991 totaled 16.5 billion kilowatt hours. All power was generated thermally, largely from imported

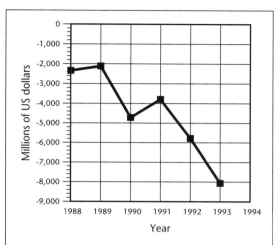

Yearly balance of trade measured in millions of US dollars. The balance of trade is the difference between what a country sells to other countries (its exports) and what it buys (its imports). If a country imports more than it exports, it has a negative balance of trade (a trade deficit). If exports exceed imports there is a positive balance of trade (a trade surplus).

mineral fuels. Singapore, a major petroleum-refining center, produced gasoline in 1991 at a rate of 86,000 barrels per day; distillate fuel oil, 239,000; residual fuel oil, 232,000; jet fuel, 168,000; and kerosene, 55,000. The total output of 945,000 barrels per day ranked Singapore fifth in the Far East in 1991, after Japan, China, South Korea (Republic of Korea), and India.

28 SOCIAL DEVELOPMENT

Besides institutionalized care, the Ministry of Community Development administers foster and homemaker service schemes for needy young persons. In January 1986, the government operated 88 child care centers and three welfare homes for aged and destitute persons. Social welfare assistance is also provided by mutual-benefit organizations and voluntary services.

The Central Provident Fund, a public pension and retirement program, provides lump-sum benefits for old age, disability, death, sickness, and maternity. Employers fund workers' compensation benefits for job-related injuries.

The government's family planning program was so successful that by 1976 the fertility rate was down to replacement level, and in early 1984 the government mounted a campaign to encourage the well-educated to bear more children.

Women's legal rights are equal to those of men in most areas, including civil liberties, employment, business, and education. Women comprise over half the labor force and are well-represented in the professions. However, they still fill most low-paying clerical positions, and their average salary is only 70% that of men.

29 HEALTH

Singapore's population enjoys one of the highest health levels in all of Southeast Asia due largely to good housing, sanitation, and water supply, as well as the best hospitals and other medical facilities in the region. Fully 100% of the population has access to safe drinking water, and 99% has adequate sanitation. Nutritional standards are among the highest in Asia. Life expectancy in 1992 was 75 years.

In 1990, there were 19 hospitals. In 1989, there were 9,801 hospital beds in Singapore (3.5 per 1,000 people). In 1991,

Selected Social Indicators

These statistics are estimates for the period 1988 to 1993. For comparison purposes, data for the United States and averages for low-income countries and high-income countries are also given.

Indicator	Singapore	Low-income countries	High-income countries	United States
Per capita gross national product†	$19,850	$380	$23,680	$24,740
Population growth rate	1.0%	1.9%	0.6%	1.0%
Population growth rate in urban areas	1.0%	3.9%	0.8%	1.3%
Population per square kilometer of land	4,454	78	25	26
Life expectancy in years	75	62	77	76
Number of people per physician	837	>3,300	453	419
Number of pupils per teacher (primary school)	26	39	<18	20
Illiteracy rate (15 years and older)	14%	41%	<5%	<3%
Energy consumed per capita (kg of oil equivalent)	5,563	364	5,203	7,918

† The gross national product (GNP) is the total dollar value of all goods and services produced by a country in a year. The per capita GNP is calculated by dividing a country's GNP by its population. The World Bank defines low-income countries as those with a per capita GNP of $695 or less. High-income countries have a per capita GNP of $8,626 or more. Less than 14% of the world's 5.5 billion people live in high-income countries, while almost 60% live in low-income countries.

> = greater than   < = less than

Sources: World Bank, *Social Indicators of Development 1995,* Baltimore: Johns Hopkins University Press, 1995. Central Intelligence Agency, *World Fact Book,* Washington, D.C.: Government Printing Office, 1994.

there were 3,779 doctors and 10,240 nurses. There was 1 doctor per 837 people in 1992. In the same year, 100% of the population had access to health care services.

The principal causes of death are heart disease and cancer. Other leading causes of death are communicable diseases and maternal/perinatal causes, noncommunicable diseases, and injuries.

30 HOUSING

In 1985, as a result of government-sponsored efforts, 2,148,720 persons—or 84% of the total population of Singapore—lived in 551,767 apartments under the management of the Housing and Development Board. Some 397,180 units had been sold to the public. In 1990, 84% of all housing units were apartments, 7% were bungalows and terrace houses, 5% were condominiums, and 1% were dwellings with attap or zinc roofs. The total number of housing units in 1992 was 758,000.

31 EDUCATION

Average literacy is 86%: 93% for men and 79% for women. All children who are citizens are entitled to free primary education. Primary schooling is available in all four official languages. Upon completion of primary school, students can receive vocational training, or if they qualify, they can take four or five years of secondary schooling leading to two-year courses in junior colleges or three-year courses in school centers at the pre-university level.

In 1989, there were 203 primary schools in Singapore and 145 secondary schools and junior colleges. The total school population was 257,833 primary and 199,076 secondary and pre-university students. Fifteen vocational institutes offered training courses in the metal, woodworking, electrical, electronic, and building trades. There were 9,998 teachers in primary schools, and 9,236 at secondary and pre-university levels.

The National University of Singapore was established on 8 August 1980 through the merger of the University of Singapore and Nanyang University. In addition, there are the Singapore Technical Institute, Ngee Ann Polytechnic, Singapore Polytechnic, and Nanyang Technological Institute.

32 MEDIA

Postal, telephone, and telegraph services in Singapore are among the most efficient in Southeast Asia. In 1985, there were 77 post offices and 48 postal agencies. Service is available on a 24-hour basis for worldwide telegraph, telephone, and telex communication. There were 1,219,604 telephones in 1991, or 45.59 telephones per 100 people.

The Singapore Broadcasting Corp., created in 1980, operates radio and television

Photo credit: Corel Corporation.

Teenage girl dressed for a parade, Singapore.

services. Radio Singapore broadcasts in Chinese, Malay, English, and Tamil. Television Singapore, inaugurated in 1963, operates daily on three channels. There were 1,770,000 radios and 1,035,000 television sets in 1991.

Singapore has eight daily newspapers, with at least one printed in each of the four official languages. The total circulation of daily papers in 1991 was 858,000. The oldest and most widely circulated daily is the English-language *Straits Times,* founded in 1845.

Although freedom of the press is guaranteed by law, the International Press

Institute has on various occasions cited Singapore for interference with press freedom. In August 1986, parliament passed a bill enabling the government to restrict sales and distribution of foreign publications "engaging in domestic politics." Two months later, the government announced that the distribution of *Time* magazine would be reduced because the magazine had refused to print the entire text of a letter from a government official. In 1987, similar distribution restrictions were placed on the *Asian Wall Street Journal*.

In 1991 Singapore's largest newspapers, with their estimated daily circulations, were the *Straits Times* (English, 300,000); *Lian He Zao Bao* (Chinese, 191,000); *Lian He Wan Bao* (Chinese, 107,000); *Shin Min Daily News* (Chinese, 102,000); *Berita Harian* (Malay, 47,000); and the *Business Times* (English, 24,000).

33 TOURISM AND RECREATION

Singapore's tourist volume has increased steadily. In 1991, 5,414,651 tourists visited Singapore, 3,326,331 from East Asia and 1,157,562 from Europe. That year Singapore earned a record US$5.02 billion from tourism, and there were a total of 25,592 hotel beds, filled to 76.8% of capacity.

Shopping, with bargaining the usual practice, is a major tourist attraction. Points of interest include the Van Kleef Aquarium at Fort Canning Park, the Singapore Zoological and Botanical Gardens, and the resort island of Sentosa. Singapore has a number of tourist attractions, including an amusement park at Haw Pav Village, site of historic Chinese statues, and the restored Alkaff Mansion.

Singapore has many sports clubs and associations, notably in the areas of badminton (in which Singaporeans have distinguished themselves internationally), basketball, boxing, cricket, cycling, golf, hockey, horse racing, motoring, polo, swimming, tennis, and yachting.

34 FAMOUS SINGAPOREANS

Sir Thomas Stamford Bingley Raffles (1781–1826) played a major role in the establishment of a British presence on Singapore Island in 1819, introducing policies that greatly enhanced Singapore's wealth and suppressing the slave trade. The English writer and educator Cyril Northcote Parkinson (b.1909), formerly a professor at the University of Singapore, became internationally known as the originator of Parkinson's Law. Singapore's dominant contemporary figure is Lee Kuan Yew (b.1923), prime minister of the Republic of Singapore since 1965.

35 BIBLIOGRAPHY

Brown, M. *Singapore*. Chicago: Children's Press, 1989.

Chew, Ernest, and Edwin Chew, eds. *A History of Singapore*. New York: Oxford University Press, 1991.

Jayapal, Maya. *Old Singapore*. New York: Oxford University Press, 1992.

LePoer, Barbara Leitch, ed. *Singapore: A Country Study*. 2d ed. Washington, D.C.: Library of Congress, 1991.

Minchin, James. *No Man Is an Island: A Portrait of Singapore's Lee Kuan Yew*. 2d ed. Sydney: Allen & Unwin, 1990.

SLOVAKIA

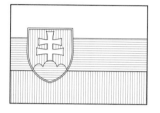

Slovak Republic
Slovenska Republic

CAPITAL: Bratislava

FLAG: Horizontal bands of white (top), blue, and red superimposed with a crest of white double cross on three blue mountains.

ANTHEM: *Nad Tatru sa blyska (Over Tatra it lightens).*

MONETARY UNIT: The currency of the Slovak Republic is the Slovak koruna (Sk) consisting of 100 hellers, which replaced the Czechoslovak Koruna (Kcs) on 8 February 1993. There are coins of 10, 20, and 50 hellers and 1, 2, 5, and 10 korun, and notes of 20, 50, 100, 500, 1,000 and 5,000 korun.

WEIGHTS AND MEASURES: The metric system is the legal standard.

HOLIDAYS: New Year's Day, 1 January; May Day, 1 May; Anniversary of Liberation, 8 May; Day of the Slav Apostles, 5 July; Anniversary of the Slovak National Uprising, 29 August; Reconciliation Day, 1 November; Christmas, 24–26 December. Movable holiday is Easter Monday.

TIME: 1 PM = noon GMT.

1 LOCATION AND SIZE

Slovakia, a landlocked country located in Eastern Europe, is about twice the size of the state of New Hampshire with a total area of 48,845 square kilometers (18,859 square miles). It has a total boundary length of 1,355 kilometers (842 miles). Slovakia's capital city, Bratislava, is located on the southwestern border of the country.

2 TOPOGRAPHY

The topography of Slovakia features rugged mountains in the central and northern part of the country, and lowlands in the south. Over one-third of the land is forest. The Tatry Mountains along the Polish border are surrounded by many lakes and deep valleys.

3 CLIMATE

In July the mean temperature is 21°C (70°F). January's mean temperature is –1°C (30°F). Rainfall averages roughly 49 centimeters (19.3 inches) a year, and can exceed 200 centimeters (80 inches) annually in the Tatry mountains.

4 PLANTS AND ANIMALS

There are areas of steppe grassland. Mammals include fox, rabbits, and wild pig. A wide variety of birds inhabit the valleys of Slovakia. Carp, pike, and trout are found in the country's rivers, lakes, and streams.

5 ENVIRONMENT

Both Slovakia and its neighbor, the Czech Republic, suffer from air, water, and land pollution caused by industry, mining, and agriculture. The air in both nations is contaminated by sulfur dioxide emissions. The two republics use 9% of available water for farming and 68% for industry. The land has suffered from the loss of forest cover, erosion, and acid rain.

In 1994, 2 mammal species and 18 types of birds were endangered, and 29 types of plants were threatened with extinction.

6 POPULATION

The population of Slovakia was 5,274,335 in 1991. The US Bureau of the Census has projected a population of 5,584,684 for the year 2000. The population density in 1991 was 108 persons per square kilometer (279 per square mile). Bratislava, the capital, had a population of 442,197 in 1991.

7 MIGRATION

The former Czechoslovakia (present-day Czech Republic and Slovakia) received 5,782 immigrants in 1991, while emigrants totaled 3,896. No statistics were available for migration in Slovakia, an independent nation since 1992.

8 ETHNIC GROUPS

The population was 85% Slovak in 1991. Hungarians, heavily concentrated in southern border areas, totaled 11.5%; Romany Gypsies, 1.5%; Ruthenians, 1%; and Czechs, 1%. There were smaller numbers of Germans, Poles, and Ukrainians.

9 LANGUAGES

Slovak is the official language. It belongs to the western Slavic group and is written in the Roman alphabet. There are only slight differences between Slovak and Czech. Minority languages include Hungarian.

10 RELIGIONS

In 1993 an estimated 74% of the population was Roman Catholic, although estimates vary widely, with some as low as 46%. Other churches with substantial memberships are the Slovak Evangelical Church of the Augsburg Confession (329,000 members in 1991) and the Orthodox Church (54,000 members in 1991). In the same year there were also 3,300 Jews, a remnant of what had been a much larger population prior to the World War II.

11 TRANSPORTATION

There were some 3,669 kilometers (2,280 miles) of railroads in 1990. The road system totaled 17,737 kilometers (11,022 miles) in 1992. As an inland country, Slovakia relies on the Danube (Dunaj) River for transportation of goods. Bratislava and Komárno are the major ports on the Danube (Dunaj). Air service in Slovakia is primarily through Ivanka Airport at Bratislava. In 1991, Ivanka Airport handled 155,000 passengers.

12 HISTORY

The first recorded inhabitants of the present-day Slovak Republic settled there about 50 BC. Early ethnic groups included Celts, Slavs, and Franks. The Moravian Empire thrived in parts of Slovakia but was destroyed at the end of the ninth century by invading Magyars (Hungarians).

LOCATION: 47°44' to 49°37'; 16°51' to 22°34'ᴇ. **BOUNDARY LENGTHS:** Total boundary lengths, 1,355 kilometers (842 miles); Austria, 91 kilometers (57 miles); Czech Republic, 215 kilometers (134 miles); Hungary, 515 kilometers (320 miles); Poland, 444 kilometers (275 miles); Ukraine, 90 kilometers (56 miles).

Although the first Christian missionaries active in the area were Orthodox, it was the Roman church that eventually established dominance. Some contact with the Czechs, who speak a closely related language, began in the early fifteenth century, as refugees from the Hussite (nationalist and religious movement founded by John Huss) religious wars in Bohemia moved east.

In 1526, the Kingdom of Hungary was divided into three parts. "Royal Hungary," which included Slovakia, came under the rule of the Habsburg dynasty.

Bratislava was the Habsburg capital until the end of the seventeenth century. Slovak nationalism gained force in the late eighteenth century, with the attempt by the Habsburg rulers to spread the German language and customs throughout the empire, and again during the 1848 Revolution.

When World War I began in 1914, the Slovaks joined with the Czechs and other oppressed nationalities of the Austro-Hungarian Empire in demanding their own states. The Czechs declared independence on 28 October 1918, and the Slovaks seceded from Hungary two days later, to create the Czecho-Slovak Republic.

The relationship between the two parts of the new state was an uneasy one. The Czech lands were more developed economically, and Czechs dominated the political system. Many Slovak nationalists wanted complete independence.

World War II

After first occupying what is now the north Czech Republic in 1938, German leader Adolf Hitler took over the remainder of the Czechoslovakian lands on 15 March 1939, ending the first republic. Slovak nationalists argued that once the breakup of Czechoslovakia had begun, they too should secede. When Hitler's forces seized Prague, a separate Slovak state was declared, but it, too, immediately fell under Hitler's Nazi domination.

During World War II (1939–45), Slovak leaders like Stefan Osusky and Juraj Slavik cooperated with Edward Benes's Czechoslovak government-in-exile, headquartered in London. In December 1943, a Slovak National Council was formed in opposition to the government, with both democratic and communist members. In 1945, negotiations between the Czech leaders Benes and Klement Gottwald and the Soviet Union's Josef Stalin led to the formation of a postwar Czechoslovakian government.

Communism and Soviet Influence

The new National Front government ran Czechoslovakia as a democracy until 1948, when a military coup with Soviet backing forced President Benes to accept a government headed by Klement Gottwald, a Communist. A wave of purges and arrests rolled over the country from 1949 to 1954. Gottwald died a few days after Stalin, in March 1953. His successors clung to harsh Stalinist (dictatorial) methods of control, holding Czechoslovakia in a tight grip until well into the 1960s.

Soviet leader Nikita Khrushchev led a movement of liberalization in the Soviet Union. This atmosphere encouraged liberals within the Czechoslovak party to try to emulate his leadership style. In January 1968, Alexander Dubček was named head of the Czechoslovak Communist Party, the first Slovak ever to hold the post. Under Dubček, Czechoslovakia embarked on a radical liberalization, termed "socialism with a human face." The leaders of the Soviet Union and other eastern bloc (communist) nations viewed these developments —termed the "Prague Spring"— with alarm. Communist leaders issued warnings to Dubček.

Finally, on the night of 20–21 August 1968, military units from almost all the Warsaw Pact (communist) nations invaded Czechoslovakia, to "save it from counter-revolution." Dubček and other officials were arrested, and the country was placed under Soviet control. A purge of liberals followed, and Dubček was expelled from the Communist Party. Between 1970 and 1975 nearly one-third of the party was dismissed, as the new Communist Party leader, Gustav Husak, consolidated his power, reuniting the titles of party head and republic president.

In the 1980s, liberalization in the Soviet Union (under the concepts of "perestroika" and "glasnost") once again set off political change in Czechoslovakia. After ignoring Soviet leader Mikhail Gorbachev's calls for Communist Party reform, in 1987 Husak announced his retirement. His replacement was Milos Jakes.

The Velvet Revolution

In November 1989, thousands gathered in Prague's Wenceslas Square, demanding free elections. This "velvet revolution," so-called because it was not violent, ended on 24 November, when Jakes and all his government resigned. Vaclav Havel, a Czech playwright and dissident, was named president on 29 December 1989, while Dubček was named leader of the national assembly.

There was less enthusiasm for returning to an economic system of private ownership in Slovakia than among the Czechs. Vladimir Meciar, the Slovak premier, was a persuasive voice for growing Slovak separatism from the Czechs. In July 1992, the new Slovak legislature issued a declaration of sovereignty and adopted a new constitution as an independent state, to take effect 1 January 1993. By the end of 1992, it was obvious that separation was inevitable. The two prime ministers, Klaus and Meciar, agreed to the peaceful separation—the so-called "velvet divorce," which took effect 1 January 1993.

The new Slovak constitution created a 150-seat National Assembly, which elects the head of state, the president. The

Photo credit: Dusan Keim.

Old town in Bratislava, capital of Slovakia.

Meciar government rejected the political and economic liberalization which the Czechs were pursuing, attempting instead to retain a socialist-style government. Swift economic decline, especially compared to the Czechs' growing prosperity, caused him to lose a vote of no-confidence in March 1994.

The new prime minister is Jozef Moravcik, representing a coalition of five parties.

13 GOVERNMENT

The constitution which the Slovak National Assembly adopted in July 1992 created a single-chamber legislature of 150 members. The government is formed by the leading party, or coalition of parties, and headed by a prime minister. The president is head of state. Slovakia is currently divided into 38 districts.

14 POLITICAL PARTIES

The single most popular party is Meciar's Movement for a Democratic Slovakia. Common Choice, the Christian Democratic Movement, and Prime Minister Jozef Moravcik's Democratic Left Party are other leading parties.

15 JUDICIAL SYSTEM

The judicial system consists of a republic-level Supreme Court; regional courts in Bratislava, Banská Bystrica, and Košice; and 38 local courts responsible for individual districts. The highest judicial body, the ten-judge Constitutional Court in Košice, rules on the constitutionality of laws as well as the decisions of lower level courts.

16 ARMED FORCES

The armed forces of Slovakia are still being reorganized. They will probably include an active duty army and air force of around 80,000, recruited through a draft and armed with weapons from communist countries.

17 ECONOMY

The economy of Slovakia is highly industrialized, although the industrial structure is less developed than that of the Czech Republic. Agriculture, which had been the most important area of the economy

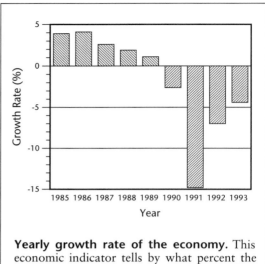

Yearly growth rate of the economy. This economic indicator tells by what percent the economy has increased or decreased when compared with the previous year.

before the communist era, now plays a smaller role than industry.

18 INCOME

In 1992, Slovakia's gross national product (GNP) was $10,249 million at current prices, or $1,950 per person. For the period 1985–92 the average annual inflation rate was 7.6%, resulting in a real growth rate in per person GNP of –7.0%.

19 INDUSTRY

Major industries include heavy engineering, armaments, iron and steel production, nonferrous metals, and chemicals.

20 LABOR

Agriculture and industry accounted for 11% and 43% of employment, respectively, in 1991. Registered unemployment

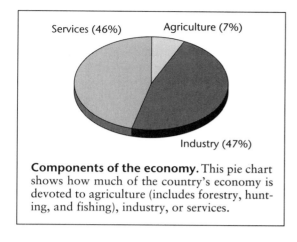

Components of the economy. This pie chart shows how much of the country's economy is devoted to agriculture (includes forestry, hunting, and fishing), industry, or services.

- Services (46%)
- Agriculture (7%)
- Industry (47%)

was estimated at 14.5% in 1993. About 78% of all workers are members of one of Slovakia's 22 unions. There is a minimum employment age of 14 years.

21 AGRICULTURE

Some 43% of the total land area is under cultivation. Important crops in Slovakia in 1990 (in thousands of tons) included: wheat, 2,083; rye, 178; corn, 370; barley, 914; potatoes, 779; and sugar beets, 1,581. Barley and hops are important agricultural exports of the new republic.

22 DOMESTICATED ANIMALS

Some 16.5% of the total area is classified as meadow and pasture. In 1990, there were about 1,563,000 head of cattle, 2,521,000 pigs, 16,478,000 chickens, 600,000 sheep, and 14,000 horses.

23 FISHING

Fishing is only a minor source of the domestic food supply.

24 FORESTRY

Slovakian forest product exports include paper, wood, and furniture. In 1990, paper production amounted to 333,649 tons. Forests cover an estimated 40% of Slovakia.

25 MINING

Nonfuel mineral resources include antimony ore, mercury, iron ore, copper, lead, zinc, precious metals, magnesite, limestone, dolomite, gravel, brick soils, ceramic materials, and stonesalt.

26 FOREIGN TRADE

The Czech Republic accounts for roughly half of Slovakia's foreign trade. Trade with the republics of the former Soviet Union has declined in importance and has been replaced more and more by Organization for Economic Cooperation and Development (OECD) trade, which accounts for almost half of all Slovak exports. Countries of Western Europe, the United States, and Australia are OECD members.

27 ENERGY AND POWER

Over 50% of total electricity production is generated by nuclear power plants. As of 1992, of the total 5,666,000 kilowatts of electrical generating capacity, nuclear plants accounted for 1,760,000 kilowatts; thermal power plants, 1,990,000 kilowatts; and hydroelectric plants, 1,916,000 kilowatts. Coal mining produces some 4.6 million tons per year. There are petroleum refineries at Bratislava, Strážske, and Zvolen.

SLOVAKIA

Selected Social Indicators

These statistics are estimates for the period 1988 to 1993. For comparison purposes, data for the United States and averages for low-income countries and high-income countries are also given.

Indicator	Slovakia	Low-income countries	High-income countries	United States
Per capita gross national product†	$1,950	$380	$23,680	$24,740
Population growth rate	0.4%	1.9%	0.6%	1.0%
Population growth rate in urban areas	1.2%	3.9%	0.8%	1.3%
Population per square kilometer of land	108	78	25	26
Life expectancy in years	71	62	77	76
Number of people per physician	286	>3,300	453	419
Number of pupils per teacher (primary school)	22	39	<18	20
Illiteracy rate (15 years and older)	<1%	41%	<5%	<3%
Energy consumed per capita (kg of oil equivalent)	n.a.	364	5,203	7,918

† The gross national product (GNP) is the total dollar value of all goods and services produced by a country in a year. The per capita GNP is calculated by dividing a country's GNP by its population. The World Bank defines low-income countries as those with a per capita GNP of $695 or less. High-income countries have a per capita GNP of $8,626 or more. Less than 14% of the world's 5.5 billion people live in high-income countries, while almost 60% live in low-income countries.

n.a. = data not available   > = greater than   < = less than

Sources: World Bank, Social Indicators of Development 1995, Baltimore: Johns Hopkins University Press, 1995. Central Intelligence Agency, World Fact Book, Washington, D.C.: Government Printing Office, 1994.

28 SOCIAL DEVELOPMENT

Slovak law guarantees the equality of all citizens and prohibits discrimination. Health care, retirement benefits, and other social services are provided regardless of race, sex, religion, or disability. Women and men are equal under the law, enjoying the same property, inheritance, and other rights, and receiving equal pay for equal work.

29 HEALTH

Life expectancy in 1992 was 71 years, and infant mortality was 12 per 1,000 live births. In 1992, most children up to one year old were immunized. The country had 17,419 physicians in 1992 and 61,573 hospital beds.

30 HOUSING

With a shortage of 500,000 apartments, the Slovak Republic planned to build 200,000 new ones by the year 2000. As of 1992, 80,000 people were on waiting lists.

31 EDUCATION

Slovakia has an estimated adult literacy rate of more than 99%. Education is compulsory for 10 years, approximately up to the age of 18.

Photo credit: Dusan Keim.

Horses in the scenic countryside of Slovakia.

In the school year 1989–90, approximately 721,687 children attended the elementary schools. Nearly 55,648 pupils attended the 132 general secondary schools while 237,130 pupils attended the 493 specialized and technical secondary schools.

Slovakia has 13 universities, with the oldest being Cornenius (Komensky) University in Bratislava. In 1989–90, nearly 54,350 students were enrolled at the universities.

32 MEDIA

There is one radio station (Slovak Radio Bratislava) and one television station (Slovak Television). There are 12 major daily newspapers in Bratislava and one each in Košice and Banská Bysterica. Major newspapers, with their estimated 1991 circulations, are *Prácal* (230,000) and *Smena* (132,000).

33 TOURISM AND RECREATION

Slovakia's outdoor tourist attractions include mountains (the most famous being the Tatry Mountains), forests, cave formations, and over 1,000 mineral and hot springs. In addition, tourists can visit ancient castles, monuments, chateaux, museums, and galleries. There are over 1,000 hotels in Slovakia.

34 FAMOUS SLOVAKS

The greatest Slovak poet, Pavel Hviezdoslav (1849–1921), contributed to the awakening of Slovak nationalism. The Robin Hood of the Slovaks, Juraj Jánošík (1688–1713), fought the Hungarians. Milan Rastislav Štefánik (1880–1919) was a famous military leader. Alexander Dubček (1921–92) was first secretary of the Czechoslovak Communist Party (1968–69) until the invasion of Czechoslovakia by the Warsaw Pact (communist) nations in 1968. In 1989 he was elected the Federal Assembly's first speaker.

35 BIBLIOGRAPHY

Mikus, Joseph A. *Slovakia and the Slovaks.* Washington, D.C.: Three Continents Press, 1977.

Momatiuk, Yva, and John Eastcott. "Slovakia's Spirit of Survival." *National Geographic,* January 1987, 120–146.

Palickar, Stephen Joseph. *Slovakian Culture in the Light of History, Ancient, Medieval and Modern.* Cambridge, Mass.: Hampshire Press, 1954.

SLOVENIA

Republic of Slovenia
Republika Slovenije

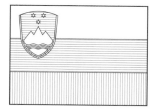

CAPITAL: Ljubljana

FLAG: Equal horizontal bands of white (top), blue, and red with seal superimposed on upper hoist side.

ANTHEM: *Zive naj vsi narodi.* (The national anthem begins, "Let all nations live . . .")

MONETARY UNIT: The currency of Slovenia is the tolar (Slt), which consists of 100 stotinov. There are coins of 50 stotinov and 1, 2, and 5 tolars, and notes of 10, 20, 50, and 200 tolars.

WEIGHTS AND MEASURES: The metric system is in force.

HOLIDAYS: New Year, 1–2 January; Prešeren Day, Day of Culture, 8 February; Resistance Day, 27 April; Labor Days, 1–2 May; National Statehood Day, 25 June; Assumption, 15 August; Reformation Day, 31 October; All Saints' Day, 1 November; Christmas Day, 25 December; Independence Day, 26 December. Movable holidays are Easter Sunday and Monday.

TIME: 1 PM = noon GMT.

1 LOCATION AND SIZE

Located in central Europe, Slovenia is slightly larger than the state of New Jersey with a total area of 20,296 square kilometers (7,836 square miles). Slovenia has a total boundary length of 999 kilometers (621 miles). The capital city, Ljubljana, is located near the center of the country.

2 TOPOGRAPHY

The topography of Slovenia features a small coastal strip on the Adriatic Sea, an alpine region adjacent to Italy, and mixed mountains and valleys with numerous rivers in the east.

3 CLIMATE

Slovenia's climate is Mediterranean on the coast, and continental in the plateaus and valleys to the east. July's mean temperature is 22°C (72°F). The mean temperature in January is 1°C (31°F). Rainfall averages 62 centimeters (24 inches) a year.

4 PLANTS AND ANIMALS

Ferns, flowers, mosses, and common trees populate the landscape. Wild animals include deer, brown bear, rabbit, fox, and wild boar. Farmers plant vineyards on the hillsides and raise livestock in the fertile lowlands of the country.

5 ENVIRONMENT

The Sava River is polluted with domestic and industrial waste; heavy metals and toxic chemicals can be found along coastal water near Koper. Metallurgical and chemical emissions have damaged the forests.

6 POPULATION

The population of Slovenia was 1,974,839 in 1991. A population of 2.1 million was projected by the World Bank for 2010. The population density in 1991 was 95 persons per square kilometer (246 per square mile). Ljubljana, the capital, had a population of 276,133 in 1991.

7 MIGRATION

In 1990, the number of immigrants was 6,842 and the number of emigrants, 4,720. Slovenia, a republic of the former Yugoslavia, was harboring 47,000 refugees at the end of 1992. Most of them were from other republics of the former Yugoslavia.

8 ETHNIC GROUPS

In 1991, the population was 88% Slovene. Croats comprised 3%; Serbs, 2%; and Muslims, 1%.

9 LANGUAGES

Like Serbo-Croatian, Macedonian, and Bulgarian, Slovene is a language of the southern Slavic group. It is closest to Serbo-Croatian. Slovene is written in the Roman alphabet.

10 RELIGIONS

Membership in the Roman Catholic Church was estimated in 1993 at 84% of the population. There is also a Slovenian Old Catholic Church and some Eastern Orthodox Churches. The only well-established Protestant group is the Evangelical Lutheran Church of Slovenia, with some 18,900 members in 1993.

11 TRANSPORTATION

As of March 1993, there were some 1,200 kilometers (746 miles) of railway tracks. With over 150 passenger stations and 140 freight stations, almost every town in Slovenia can be reached by train. In 1991, Slovenia had 14,553 kilometers (9,045 miles) of roads. Slovenia has two expressways: one connects Ljubljana and Postojna with the coastal region; the other links Ljubljana with Kranj and the Karawanken tunnel to Austria.

The principal marine port is Koper. Slovenian owners control 21 vessels (1,000 gross registered tons or over) totaling 334,995 gross registered tons.

12 HISTORY

The Slovenes are one of a large group of Slavic nations. An agricultural people, the Slovenes settled from around AD 550 in the Roman Noricum (present-day Austria and Germany) area of the eastern Alps and in the western Pannonian plains (present-day Hungary). Part of the Slavic Kingdom of Samo in the mid-seventh century, the settlement continued its existence as a Duchy of the Slovenes after Samo's death in AD 659, eventually coming under the control of the numerically stronger Bavarians (southern Germans).

The eastward expansion of the Franks (west Germans) in the ninth century brought all Slovene lands under Frankish control. Under the feudal system, various families of mostly Germanic nobility were granted fiefdoms (areas of control) over Slovene lands and competed among themselves to increase their holdings.

SLOVENIA

| 0 | 10 | 20 | 30 | 40 Miles |
| 0 | 10 | 20 | 30 | 40 Kilometers |

AUSTRIA

HUNGARY

Murska Sobota

Drava

Mura

Lendava

Maribor

Ljutomer

POHORJE

KARAWANKEN

Jesenice

Bled

Mt. Triglav
9,396 ft.
2863 m.

Grintavec
8,392 ft.
2558 m.

Mozirje

Slovenska Bistrica

Ptuj

Zaga

Bohinjsko Jezero

Soča

Kranj

Savinja

Celje

Rogatec

Dravinja

Varaždin

Železniki

ITALY

JULIAN ALPS

Domžale

Trbovlje

Pregrada

Dobrovo

Ljubljana ✪

Sava

CROATIA

Idrija

Sevnica

Udine

Nova Gorica

Krka

Novo Mesto

Krško

Soula

Podnanos

Cerknica

Krka

Kras Plateau

Postojna

Stari Trg

Žumberačka Gora

Gulfo di Trieste

Veliki Snežnik
5,892 ft.
1796 m.

Kočevje

Piran

Trieste

Crni Kal

Črnomelj

Koper

Kupa

CROATIA

Slovenia

LOCATION: 46°15′N; 15°10′E. **BOUNDARY LENGTHS:** Total boundary lengths, 999 kilometers (621 miles); Austria 262 kilometers (163 miles); Croatia, 455 kilometers (283 miles); Italy, 199 kilometers (124 miles); Hungary, 83 kilometers (52 miles).

The Austrian Habsburgs grew steadily in power and by the fifteenth century became the leading feudal family in control of most Slovene lands. Rebellions by Slovene and Croat peasants in the fifteenth to eighteenth centuries were cruelly repressed.

The Protestant Reformation (mid-1500s) gave a boost to the Slovenians' sense of national identity through the efforts of Protestant Slovenes to provide printed Slovenian language materials to support their cause. When the ideas of the French Revolution (late 1700s) spread through Europe and Napoleon Bonaparte seized power at the end of the eighteenth century, the Slovenes were ready to join in the effort to eliminate the aristocracy.

When Napoleon defeated Austria, Slovenia became part of his Illyrian Provinces (1809–13). The Slovene language was encouraged in the schools and also used, along with French, as an official language. Austria, however, regained the Illyrian Provinces in 1813 and reestablished its direct control over the Slovene lands.

The 1848 "spring of nations" brought about various demands for national freedom of Slovenes and other Slavic nations of Austria. The revolts of 1848 were repressed after a few years and dictatorial regimes kept under control any movements in support of national rights.

In 1867, the region's German and Hungarian majorities agreed to the reorganization of the state into a "Dualistic" Austro-Hungarian Monarchy in order to better control the minority elements in each half of the empire. However, the addition of Bosnia and Herzegovina to Austria through occupation and annexation increased the power of the region's Slovenes, Croats, and Serbs in an arrangement that eventually would allow these South Slavic groups ("Yugoslavs") to form their own joint nation state. However, the German leadership's policies prevented any compromise, and nationalist strife in the region helped to ignite World War I (1914–18).

World War I brought about the breakup of centuries-old ties between the Slovenes and the Austrian Monarchy, and the Croats/Serbs and the Hungarian Crown. On 29 October 1918, the National Council for all Slavs of former Austro-Hungary proclaimed the separation of the South Slavs from Austro-Hungary and the formation of a new state of Slovenes, Croats, and Serbs.

Creation of Yugoslavia

A united "Kingdom of Serbs, Croats, and Slovenes" was declared on 1 December 1918, and it included a strongly centralized government ruled, after 1921, by King Alexander of Serbia. However, the Slovenes and Croats, while freed from Austro-Hungarian domination, did not win the political and cultural self-rule for which they had hoped.

The period between 1921 and 1929 was a confused one, with a series of 23 governments. On 6 January 1929, the king dissolved the parliament, abolished the 1921 constitution, and established his own personal dictatorship as a temporary arrangement. On 3 October 1929, the country was renamed the Kingdom of Yugoslavia. King Alexander was assassinated in Marseille, France, on 9 October 1934 by agents of the extreme Croatian nationalist group, the Ustaša.

Hitler unleashed German forces on Yugoslavia on 6 April 1941, bombing Belgrade and other cities without any warning or formal declaration of war. The Yugoslav government fled the country, and the Nazis set up a government run by Ustaša, who initiated a bloody orgy of mass murders of Serbs.

Slovenia was divided in 1941 among Germany, Italy, and Hungary. Resistance movements were initiated by nationalist groups and by Communist-dominated Partisans. Spontaneous resistance to the Partisans by the non-Communist peasantry led to a bloody civil war in Slovenia. The other Yugoslav states also suffered civil war. All were now largely under foreign occupiers, who encouraged the bloodshed.

With the entry of Soviet armies into Yugoslav territory in October 1944, the

Partisans swept over Yugoslavia in pursuit of the retreating German forces. The Partisans took over Croatia, launching a campaign of executions and large-scale massacres.

All of the republics of the former Federal Socialist Republic of Yugoslavia share a common history between 1945 and 1991, the year of Yugoslavia's break-up. The World War II (1939–45) Partisan resistance movement, controlled by the Communist Party of Yugoslavia and led by Marshal Josip Broz Tito, won a civil war waged against nationalist groups.

A conflict erupted between Tito and the Russian leader Josef Stalin in 1948, and Tito was expelled from the Soviet Bloc (communist countries allied with the Soviet Union). Yugoslavia then developed its own brand of communism based on workers' councils and self-management of enterprises and institutions. Yugoslavia became the leader of the nonaligned group of nations (those countries who were neither allies of the United States nor the Soviet Union).

The Yugoslav Communist regime relaxed its central controls somewhat. This allowed for the development of more liberal wings of Communist parties, especially in Croatia and Slovenia. Also, nationalism reappeared, with tensions especially strong between Serbs and Croats in the Croatian republic. This led Tito to repress the Croatian and Slovenian "springs" (freedom movements like the one in Czechoslovakia in 1968) in 1970–71.

Independence for Yugoslavia

The 1974 constitution shifted much of the decision-making power from the federal level to the republics, further decentralizing the political process. Following Tito's death in 1980, there was an economic crisis. Severe inflation and inability to pay the nation's foreign debts led to tensions between the different republics and demands for a reorganization of the Yugoslav federation into a confederation of sovereign states.

Pressure towards individual autonomy for the regions, as well as a market economy, grew stronger, leading to the formation of non-Communist political parties. By 1990 these parties were able to win majorities in multiparty elections in Slovenia and then in Croatia, ending the era of Communist Party monopoly of power.

Slovenia and Croatia declared their independence on 25 June 1991. On 27 June 1991, the Yugoslav army tried to seize control of Slovenia but was met by heavy resistance from Slovenian "territorial guards." The "guards" surrounded Yugoslav army tank units, isolated them, and engaged in close combat. In most cases, the Yugoslav units surrendered to the Slovenian forces. Over 3,200 Yugoslav army soldiers surrendered and were well-treated by the Slovenes, who gained favorable publicity by having the prisoners call their parents all over Yugoslavia to come to Slovenia and take their sons back home.

The war in Slovenia ended in ten days due to the intervention of the European Community (nations of Europe), which negotiated a ceasefire. Thus Slovenia was

Children play on an abandoned field gun in the refugee center of Bloke, about 40 miles southwest of Ljubljana, Slovenia. The center currently has 474 refugees from Bosnia; 250 of them are children under 16.

able to remove itself from Yugoslavia with a minimum of casualties, although the military operations caused considerable damage to property estimated at almost $3 billion.

On 23 December 1991, a new constitution was adopted by Slovenia establishing a parliamentary democracy with a two-chamber legislature. International recognition came first from Germany on 18 December 1991, from the European Community (EC) on 15 January 1992, and finally from the United States on 7 April 1992. Slovenia was accepted as a member of the United Nations on 23 April 1992 and has since become a member of many other international organizations.

In December 1992, a coalition government was formed by the Liberal Democrats, Christian Democrats, and the United List Group of Leftist Parties. Dr. Milan Kučan was elected president and Dr. Janez Drnovšek became prime minister.

In the 1970s, in the region of Slovenia, the standard of living was close to the one in neighboring Austria and Italy. However, the burdens imposed by the cost of maintaining a large Yugoslav army and the repayments on a $20 billion international debt caused a lowering of its living standard over the 1980s. The situation worsened with the trauma of secession from Yugoslavia, the war damages suffered, and the loss of the former Yugoslav markets.

In spite of all these problems Slovenia has made good progress since independence in improving its productivity, controlling inflation, and reorienting its exports to western Europe.

13 GOVERNMENT

Slovenia is a republic based on a constitution adopted on 23 December 1991. The president is Dr. Milan Kučan, elected in December 1992. The prime minister is Dr. Janez Drnovšek.

The constitution provides for a National Assembly as the highest legislative authority with 90 seats. Deputies are elected to four-year terms of office. The National Council, with 40 seats, has an advisory role. Council members are elected to five-year terms of office and may propose laws to the National Assembly, request it to review its decisions, and may demand the calling of a constitutional referendum.

The executive branch consists of a President of the Republic who is also Supreme Commander of the Armed Forces, and is elected to a five-year term of office, limited to two consecutive terms. The president calls for elections to the National Assembly, proclaims the adopted laws, and proposes candidates for prime minister to the National Assembly. Since 1993, the government has consisted of 15 ministries instead of the previous 27.

The National Assembly is attempting to reform the inefficient local government system inherited from the former Yugoslavia.

14 POLITICAL PARTIES

As of July 1994, the government was a coalition of three parties: Liberal Democrats, Christian Democrats, and The United List. Of the 16 members of the Council of Ministers, 6 are Liberal Democrats, 4 are Christian Democrats, 3 are from the United List, 1 from the Greens, and 2 are not party members.

15 JUDICIAL SYSTEM

The judicial system consists of local and district courts and a Supreme Court which hears appeals. A nine-member Constitutional Court resolves jurisdictional disputes and rules on the constitutionality of legislation and regulations. The Constitutional Court also acts as a final court of appeal in cases requiring constitutional interpretation.

The Constitution guarantees the independence of judges. Judges are appointed to permanent positions subject to an age limit. The Constitution affords criminal defendants a presumption of innocence, open court proceedings, the right to an appeal, a prohibition against double jeopardy, and a number of other due process protections.

16 ARMED FORCES

The Slovenian armed forces number 15,000 active duty soldiers and 85,000 reservists who are required to give seven months of service. The paramilitary police has 4,500 actives and 5,000 reserves.

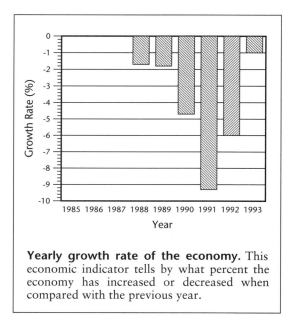

Yearly growth rate of the economy. This economic indicator tells by what percent the economy has increased or decreased when compared with the previous year.

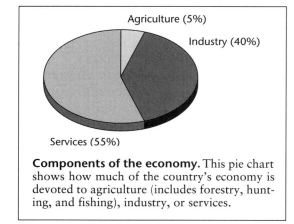

Components of the economy. This pie chart shows how much of the country's economy is devoted to agriculture (includes forestry, hunting, and fishing), industry, or services.

Defense spending is probably around $170 million (1991).

17 ECONOMY

Before its independence, Slovenia was the most highly developed and wealthiest republic of Yugoslavia, with a per person income more than double that of the Yugoslav average, and nearly comparable to levels in neighboring Austria and Italy. The painful transition to a market-based economy has been aggravated by the disruption of intra-Yugoslav trade.

Slovenia deregulated prices and in November 1992 adopted a law which has enabled private businesses to expand. As of mid-1992, 78% of all enterprises were privately owned (up from 67% in 1990).

18 INCOME

In 1992, Slovenia's gross national product (GNP) was $12,744 million at current prices, or about $6,490 per person. In 1992 the average inflation rate was 93%, resulting in a real growth rate in per person GNP of –7%.

19 INDUSTRY

Manufacturing is the most prominent economic activity and is widely diversified. Important manufacturing areas include electrical and non-electrical machinery, metal processing, chemicals, textiles and clothing, wood processing and furniture, transport equipment, and food processing. Industrial production fell by 12% in 1991 and an estimated 13% in 1992, due in part to the international sanctions against Serbia, a major trading partner.

20 LABOR

In March 1991, the total economically active population (employees, self-employed, and unpaid family workers over age 15) totaled 945,766. As of the end of 1992, there were some 789,810 persons employed, excluding the armed forces. Of all employees, 41% were in manufacturing; 21% in community, social, and personal services; 11% in commerce; 6% in transportation and communication; 5% in construction; 9% in agriculture; and 7% in other sectors.

About 47% of those employed in 1992 were women. Unemployment stood at 12% in 1992. The 1991 Constitution provides that the establishment, activities, and recruitment of members of labor unions shall be unrestricted. There are three main labor federations, with branches throughout the society.

Minimum age laws governing child labor are generally respected and enforced, except in some agricultural areas.

21 AGRICULTURE

Some 247,000 hectares (610,300 acres), or 12% of the total land area, were in use as cropland in 1991. Slovenia was the least agriculturally active of all the republics of Yugoslavia. Major crops produced in 1992 included wheat, 186,000 tons; corn, 207,000 tons; potatoes, 368,000 tons; sugar beets, 97,000 tons; and fruit, 340,000 tons (of which grapes accounted for 63%). Food industry products contributed 3% to total exports in 1992.

22 DOMESTICATED ANIMALS

As of 1991, about 565,000 hectares (1,396,000 acres), or 28% of the total land area, were permanent pastureland. Sheep and cattle breeding, as well as dairy farming, dominate the agricultural part of the economy. In 1992, the livestock population included cattle, 484,000; sheep, 28,000; pigs, 529,000; chickens, 12,000,000; and horses, 11,000. Meat production in 1992 included 50,000 tons of beef, 75,000 tons of pork, and 53,000 tons of poultry. Productivity rates for livestock and dairy farming are comparable to much of Western Europe. In 1992, 352,000 tons of milk and 15,800 tons of eggs were produced.

23 FISHING

As of 1991, fishing and agriculture accounted for 5% of GDP. As of 1991, the fishing sector accounted for less than 1% of foreign investment in Slovenia.

24 FORESTRY

In 1991, forests and woodlands covered just over 50% of the total area; they are Slovenia's most important natural resource. In 1992, wood processing accounted for 4% of manufacturing; paper production for 9%. Paper, paperboard, and related products amounted to 5% of exports in 1992. The furniture-making industry is a major consumer of Slovenia's forest products.

25 MINING

Slovenia's nonfuel mineral resources include lead-zinc and mercury (mined and smelted in Idrija). Imported ore is needed for the aluminum plant at Kidričevo, and for the iron and steel producing facilities at Jesenice.

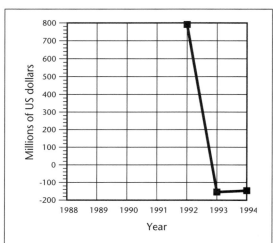

Yearly balance of trade measured in millions of US dollars. The balance of trade is the difference between what a country sells to other countries (its exports) and what it buys (its imports). If a country imports more than it exports, it has a negative balance of trade (a trade deficit). If exports exceed imports there is a positive balance of trade (a trade surplus).

26 FOREIGN TRADE

Slovenia has reoriented much of its trade away from its former Yugoslav neighbors toward Western Europe. Sanctions imposed by the United Nations on trade with Serbia severed Slovenia from its largest foreign market. In 1992, 55% of Slovenia's exports were sent to the European Union, and only 30% to Croatia and the other former Yugoslav republics.

In 1990, Slovenian exports included transport equipment and machinery which accounted for 38% of total exports; other manufactured goods, 44%; chemicals, 9%; food and live animals, 5%; raw materials, 3%; and beverages and tobacco products, less than 1%.

Imports in 1990 included machinery and transport equipment which accounted for 35% of the total; other manufactured goods, 27%; chemicals, 15%; raw materials, 9%; fuels and lubricants, 7%; and food and live animals, 6%.

The European Union (EU) signed a cooperation agreement with Slovenia in April 1993, which provided for greater access to the EU market. Slovenia also entered into trade agreements with Hungary, the Czech Republic, and Slovakia in 1993 that will gradually eliminate most trade barriers.

27 ENERGY AND POWER

In 1991, total electricity production amounted to 12,250 million kilowatt hours. Slovenia is relatively well supplied with hydroelectricity. Several thermal plants and one nuclear power plant also supply electricity. Slovenia imports oil from the republics of the former Soviet Union and the developing world to supply a refinery at Lendava. Coal is mined at Velenje; the mine had an annual capacity of 5 million tons in 1991. Natural gas is used extensively for industry and is supplied by the former Soviet Union and Algeria via 305 kilometers (190 miles) of natural gas pipelines.

28 SOCIAL DEVELOPMENT

The constitution provides for special protection against economic, social, physical, or mental exploitation or abuse of children. Women and men have equal status under the law. Discrimination against women or minorities in housing, jobs, or other areas, is illegal. Officially, both

Selected Social Indicators

These statistics are estimates for the period 1988 to 1993. For comparison purposes, data for the United States and averages for low-income countries and high-income countries are also given.

Indicator	Slovenia	Low-income countries	High-income countries	United States
Per capita gross national product†	$6,490	$380	$23,680	$24,740
Population growth rate	0.4%	1.9%	0.6%	1.0%
Population growth rate in urban areas	1.9%	3.9%	0.8%	1.3%
Population per square kilometer of land	95	78	25	26
Life expectancy in years	73	62	77	76
Number of people per physician	n.a.	>3,300	453	419
Number of pupils per teacher (primary school)	18	39	<18	20
Illiteracy rate (15 years and older)	n.a.	41%	<5%	<3%
Energy consumed per capita (kg of oil equivalent)	1,531	364	5,203	7,918

† The gross national product (GNP) is the total dollar value of all goods and services produced by a country in a year. The per capita GNP is calculated by dividing a country's GNP by its population. The World Bank defines low-income countries as those with a per capita GNP of $695 or less. High-income countries have a per capita GNP of $8,626 or more. Less than 14% of the world's 5.5 billion people live in high-income countries, while almost 60% live in low-income countries.

n.a. = data not available   > = greater than   < = less than

Sources: World Bank, *Social Indicators of Development 1995,* Baltimore: Johns Hopkins University Press, 1995. Central Intelligence Agency, *World Fact Book,* Washington, D.C.: Government Printing Office, 1994.

spouses are equal in marriage, and the Constitution asserts the state's responsibility to protect the family. Women are well represented in business, academia, and government, although they still hold a disproportionate share of lower-paying jobs.

29 HEALTH

No recent information is available.

30 HOUSING

No recent information is available.

31 EDUCATION

Slovenia has a high literacy rate. There are 842 primary schools and 149 secondary schools; 5% of the population are pupils and the teacher-student ratio is 1:18.

In Slovenia there are two universities, located at Ljubljana and Maribor. The University of Ljubljana, founded in 1919, had 26,190 pupils enrolled in 1993, including 300 students from foreign countries. The University of Maribor had 12,000 students enrolled in 1992.

32 MEDIA

In 1989, Slovenia had 630,000 telephones, 21 radio stations, and 2 television channels. In 1991, there were 710,000 radios and 560,000 televisions.

In 1989, there were 3 daily and 425 other newspapers and 250 periodicals. A total of 1,932 book titles were published in the same year.

33 TOURISM AND RECREATION

There are 75,000 beds available in hotels and other types of accommodations. Slovenia has convention centers in Ljubljana and three other cities, and international airports in Ljubljana and two other cities. Popular recreational activities include tennis, golf, mountain-climbing, canoeing, and fishing.

34 FAMOUS SLOVENIANS

Milan Kučan and Janez Drnovšek have been president and prime minister of Slovenia since 1992. In 1551, Primož Trubar translated the New Bible into Slovene. The poet Valentin Vodnik (1754–1819) wrote poems in praise of Napoleon. Slovenian tennis star Mima Jausovec (b.1956) won the Italian Open in 1976 and the French Open in 1977.

35 BIBLIOGRAPHY

Cerar, Miro, and Janez Kranjc, eds. *Constitution of the Republic of Slovenia*. Ljubljana: Uradni list Republike Slovenije, 1992.

Glenny, Michael. *The Fall of Yugoslavia: The Third Balkan War*. New York: Penguin, 1992.

Gobetz, Edward, and Ruth Lakner, eds. *Slovenian Heritage*. Willoughby Hills, Ohio: Slovenian Research Center of America, 1980.

Harriman, Helga H. *Slovenia Under Nazi Occupation, 1941–1945*. New York: Studia Slovenica, 1977.

SOLOMON ISLANDS

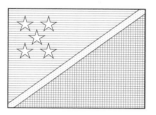

CAPITAL: Honiara.

FLAG: The flag consists of two triangles, the upper one blue, the lower one green, separated by a diagonal gold stripe; on the blue triangle are five white five-pointed stars.

ANTHEM: *God Save the Queen.*

MONETARY UNIT: The Solomon Islands dollar (SI$), a paper currency of 100 cents, was introduced in 1977, replacing the Australian dollar, and became the sole legal tender in 1978. There are coins of 1, 2, 5, 10, 20, and 50 cents and 1 dollar, and notes of 2, 5, 10, 20, and 50 dollars. SI$1 = US$0.3064 (or US$1 = SI$3.2637).

WEIGHTS AND MEASURES: The metric system is in force.

HOLIDAYS: New Year's Day, 1 January; Queen's Birthday, June; Independence Day, 7 July; Christmas, 25 December; Boxing Day, 26 December. Movable religious holidays include Good Friday, Easter Monday, and Whitmonday.

TIME: 11 PM = noon GMT.

1 LOCATION AND SIZE

The Solomon Islands consist of a chain of six large and numerous small islands situated in the South Pacific. The Solomon Islands have an area of 28,450 square kilometers (10,985 square miles), slightly larger than the state of Maryland.

The largest island is Guadalcanal, covering 5,302 square kilometers (2,047 square miles). The total coastline of the Solomon Islands is 5,313 kilometers (3,301 miles).

The capital city, Honiara, is located on the island of Guadalcanal.

2 TOPOGRAPHY

The topography varies from the volcanic peaks of Guadalcanal to low-lying coral atolls. The highest peak is Mt. Popomana-

siu, at 2,447 meters (8,023 feet), on Guadalcanal. Extensive coral reefs and lagoons surround the island coasts.

3 CLIMATE

The annual mean temperature is 27°C (81°F); annual rainfall averages 305 centimeters (120 inches); humidity is about 80%. Damaging cyclones occur periodically.

4 PLANTS AND ANIMALS

Dense rainforest covers about 90% of the islands, with extensive mangrove swamps and coconut palms along the coasts. The islands abound in small reptiles, birds, mammals, and insects. There are over 230 kinds of orchids.

5 ENVIRONMENT

Most of the coral reefs surrounding the islands are dead or dying. United Nations sources estimate that the islands' forests will be exhausted in 10–15 years. Some 42% of the islands' rural people do not have pure water. Sources of pollution include sewage, pesticides, and mining by-products. In 1994, two mammal species and 20 bird species were endangered, as well as 28 types of plants.

6 POPULATION

The population at the 1986 census was 285,796. It was estimated at 342,000 in 1992 and was projected by the United Nations at 444,000 in 2000. The estimated overall population density in 1992 was 12 persons per square kilometer (32.1 per square mile). Honiara, on Guadalcanal, is the largest town and chief port, with an estimated 1989 population of 33,749.

7 MIGRATION

Since 1955, immigrants from the Gilbert Islands (now Kiribati) have settled in underpopulated areas. Movements from the countryside to Honiara and north Guadalcanal have created overcrowding in those two areas.

8 ETHNIC GROUPS

According to the 1986 census, Melanesians numbered 268,536, or 94% of the total population. Also counted were 10,661 Polynesians, 3,929 Micronesians, 1,107 Europeans, 379 Chinese, and 564 others.

9 LANGUAGES

Pidgin English is the common language, but English is the official language. Some 87 local languages and dialects are spoken. Melanesian languages are spoken by about 85% of the population, Papuan languages by 9%, and Polynesian languages by 4%.

10 RELIGIONS

Christianity is the principal organized religion. As of the 1986 census, 33.9% of the islanders were Anglicans, 23.5% were Evangelical Protestants, and 19.2% were Roman Catholics. Native religions are practiced by up to 5% of the population, and there is a small Baha'i community.

11 TRANSPORTATION

In 1991 there were about 2,100 kilometers (1,300 miles) of roads in the Solomons. Honiara is the principal port. Government vessels provide interisland connections and handle freight. There are two permanent-surface air runways. Solomon Airlines provides regular flights between islands and to nearby Papua New Guinea and Vanuatu.

12 HISTORY

The Solomons were first sighted in 1567 by the Spanish explorer Alvaro de Mendaña, who named them Islas de Salomon for King Solomon's gold mines. The islands were visited by the English navigator Philip Carteret in 1767. The period 1845–93 saw the arrival of missionaries, traders, and "blackbirders," who captured native people and sold them into forced labor, often on colonial sugar plantations in Fiji, Hawaii, Tahiti, or Queensland.

In 1893, the British government established a protectorate over parts of the Solomons, including Guadalcanal, Malaita, San Cristobal, and the New Georgia group. The remainder had by this time fallen under German dominion; some of these, including Choiseul and Santa Isabel, were transferred by treaty to the United Kingdom in 1900.

During World War II (1939–45), the Solomons saw some of the most bitter fighting of the Pacific war after Japanese troops invaded and occupied Guadalcanal in 1942. The Battle of Guadalcanal cost the lives of about 1,500 American soldiers and 20,000 Japanese.

In the decades after the war, the Solomons moved gradually toward independence. The islands achieved internal self-government in 1976 and became an independent member of the Commonwealth of Nations on 7 July 1978.

Francis Billy Hilly became the Solomon Islands' new prime minister in June 1993. Hilly has worked with the Melanesian Spearhead Conference to ease tension between the Solomon Islands and Papua New Guinea.

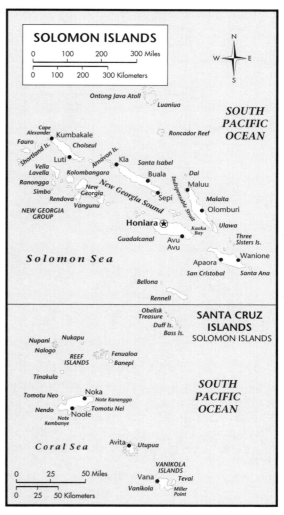

LOCATION: 5° to 12°30′s; 155° to 170°E. **TERRITORIAL SEA LIMIT:** 12 miles.

13 GOVERNMENT

The Solomon Islands are a parliamentary democracy with a prime minister and a single-chamber 47-member National Parliament. The islands are divided into eight administrative districts.

14 POLITICAL PARTIES

Parties have included the People's Alliance Party (PAP), the National Democratic Party (NDP), and the Nationalist Front for Progress. The Group for National Unity and Reconciliation (GNUR), led by

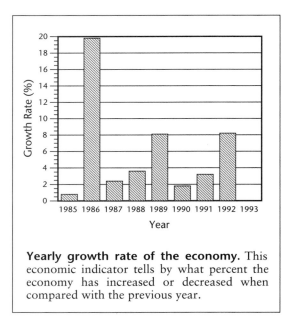

Yearly growth rate of the economy. This economic indicator tells by what percent the economy has increased or decreased when compared with the previous year.

Solomon Mamaloni, gained the most seats in the 1993 election. Other parties receiving seats were the National Action Party, the Labour Party, and the Christian Fellowship Group.

15 JUDICIAL SYSTEM

The judicial system consists of the High Court, magistrate courts, and local courts. Appeals from magistrate courts go to the High Court; customary land appeals courts hear appeals from the local courts.

16 ARMED FORCES

The Solomon Islands have no military forces.

17 ECONOMY

At least 80% of the population is tied to farming. The economy depends on the export of copra (dried coconut meat), timber, and fish. Production of other cash commodities—particularly cocoa, spices, and palm oil—has grown in recent years. Cyclone Namu in 1986 caused serious economic damage.

18 INCOME

In 1992, Solomon Islands' gross national product (GNP) was $237 million at current prices, or about $740 per person. For the period 1985–92 the average inflation rate was 11.2%, resulting in a real growth rate in per person GNP of 2.7%.

19 INDUSTRY

The leading industries are fish processing and timber milling; soaps are made from palm oil and coconut oil. Small firms produce goods for local consumption, including biscuits, tobacco products, rattan furniture, and baskets and mats.

20 LABOR

About 90% of Solomon Islanders engage in farming. The wage labor force in 1990 totaled 26,122. The country suffers from an acute shortage of skilled workers. Minimum age laws regulate the use of child labor.

21 AGRICULTURE

Copra (dried coconut meat) is the dominant export and the economic lifeline of the Solomons; 1992 production was 38,500 tons. Other agricultural products in 1992 included cocoa, 4,453 tons; palm oil, 31,000 tons; and palm kernels, 6,900 tons.

The major food crops are coconuts, yams, taro, sweet potatoes, cassava, and green vegetables.

22 DOMESTICATED ANIMALS

There were 13,000 head of cattle and 54,000 pigs on the islands in 1992. About 3,000 tons of meat were produced in 1992.

23 FISHING

In 1991, the total catch reached a record high of 69,292 tons. In 1992, the annual catch of skipjack and yellowfin tuna was just over 39,000 tons.

24 FORESTRY

Forests cover about 90% of the total area, providing an estimated timber yield in 1992 of 640,000 cubic meters, of which about 580,000 cubic meters were exported as logs. About 8,500 cubic meters of sawn timber were also exported.

25 MINING

In addition to gold, deposits of bauxite, nickel, copper, chromite, and manganese ores have also been found.

26 FOREIGN TRADE

Copra (dried coconut meat) accounted for only 5% of export value in 1986 due to the effects of Cyclone Namu. In that year, wood and lumber made up 31% of the total, and fish 46%. In 1992, timber accounted for 37% of exports.

In 1991, Japan, the Solomons' most important trade partner, received close to 50% of the islands' exports. Other important trade partners are Australia, the United Kingdom, the Netherlands, Thailand, Singapore, New Zealand, and the United States.

27 ENERGY AND POWER

In 1991, electrical output was 30 million kilowatt hours. Honiara accounts for 90% of electricity consumption.

28 SOCIAL DEVELOPMENT

A National Provident Fund provides old age, disability, and survivor benefits. Most organized welfare services are provided by church missions. Much assistance is traditionally provided through the extended family.

29 HEALTH

Malaria and tuberculosis are widespread. In 1985 there were 38 doctors, 6 government hospitals, a mission hospital, and 124 clinics. Average life expectancy was 71 years for both men and women.

30 HOUSING

The government has built low-cost housing projects in Honiara to help ease congestion. Outside Honiara, housing is primitive, with overcrowding a problem. As of 1990, 82% of urban and 58% of rural dwellers had access to a public water supply, while 73% of the urban population had access to sanitation services.

31 EDUCATION

About 60% of the adult population is estimated to be literate. In 1991 there were 520 primary schools, with 1 teacher for every 24 pupils. Secondary schools had 5,607 pupils and 298 teachers in 1987.

Selected Social Indicators

These statistics are estimates for the period 1988 to 1993. For comparison purposes, data for the United States and averages for low-income countries and high-income countries are also given.

Indicator	Solomon Islands	Low-income countries	High-income countries	United States
Per capita gross national product†	$740	$380	$23,680	$24,740
Population growth rate	3.4%	1.9%	0.6%	1.0%
Population growth rate in urban areas	6.6%	3.9%	0.8%	1.3%
Population per square kilometer of land	12	78	25	26
Life expectancy in years	71	62	77	76
Number of people per physician	6,581	>3,300	453	419
Number of pupils per teacher (primary school)	24	39	<18	20
Illiteracy rate (15 years and older)	40%	41%	<5%	<3%
Energy consumed per capita (kg of oil equivalent)	164	364	5,203	7,918

† The gross national product (GNP) is the total dollar value of all goods and services produced by a country in a year. The per capita GNP is calculated by dividing a country's GNP by its population. The World Bank defines low-income countries as those with a per capita GNP of $695 or less. High-income countries have a per capita GNP of $8,626 or more. Less than 14% of the world's 5.5 billion people live in high-income countries, while almost 60% live in low-income countries.

> = greater than   < = less than

Sources: World Bank, *Social Indicators of Development 1995,* Baltimore: Johns Hopkins University Press, 1995. Central Intelligence Agency, *World Fact Book,* Washington, D.C.: Government Printing Office, 1994.

Higher education is provided by the Solomon Islands Teachers College, the Honiara Technical Institute, and the University of the South Pacific.

32 MEDIA

There were an estimated 40,000 radios in 1991. There are no daily newspapers. The two weeklies are the *Solomon Star* (1992 circulation, 3,000) and the *Solomon Toktok* (3,000).

33 TOURISM AND RECREATION

In 1991, 11,105 tourists visited the Solomon Islands, 36% from Australia, 14% from New Zealand, and 9% from the United States. Popular pastimes include rugby football, soccer, and water sports.

34 FAMOUS SOLOMON ISLANDERS

Sir Peter Kenilorea (b.1943), Solomon Mamaloni (b.1943), and Ezekiel Alebua (b.1947) were the Solomons' political and government leaders from independence to the 1990s.

35 BIBLIOGRAPHY

Diamond, J. *Solomon Islands.* Chicago: Children's Press, 1995.

White, Geoffrey M. *Identity through History: Living Stories in a Solomon Islands Society.* New York: Cambridge University Press, 1991.

SOMALIA

Somali Democratic Republic

Jamhuriyadda Dimugradiga Somaliya

CAPITAL: Mogadishu (Muqdisho).

FLAG: The national flag is light blue with a five-pointed white star in the center.

ANTHEM: *Somalia Hanolato (Long Live Somalia)*.

MONETARY UNIT: The Somali shilling (SH) of 100 cents is a paper currency. There are coins of 1, 5, 10, and 50 cents and 1 shilling, and notes of 5, 10, 20, 100, 500, and 1,000 shillings. SH1 = $0.01 (or $1 = SH100).

WEIGHTS AND MEASURES: The metric system is in use.

HOLIDAYS: New Year's Day, 1 January; Labor Day, 1 May; National Independence Day, 26 June; Foundation of the Republic, 1 July. Muslim religious holidays include 'Id al-Fitr, 'Id al-Adha', 'Ashura, and Milad an-Nabi.

TIME: 3 PM = noon GMT.

1 LOCATION AND SIZE

Situated on the horn of East Africa, Somalia has an area of 637,660 square kilometers (246,202 square miles), slightly smaller than the state of Texas. It has a total boundary length of 5,391 kilometers (3,350 miles). Somalia's capital city, Mogadishu, is located on the Indian Ocean coast.

2 TOPOGRAPHY

The northern region is somewhat mountainous, and there are plateaus to the northeast, south and west. The region between the Jubba and Shabeelle (Webi Shabeelle) rivers is low agricultural land. The Jubba and Shabeelle rivers originate in Ethiopia and flow toward the Indian Ocean. Despite its lengthy shoreline, Somalia has only one natural harbor, Berbera.

3 CLIMATE

Somalia has a tropical climate, and there is little seasonal change in temperature. In the low areas, the mean temperature ranges from about 24°C to 31°C (75°F to 88°F). Rain falls in two seasons of the year, and average annual rainfall is estimated at less than 28 centimeters (11 inches).

4 PLANTS AND ANIMALS

Acacia thorntrees, aloes, baobab, candelabra, and incense trees are native to the drier regions. Mangrove, kapok, and papaya grow along the rivers. Animal life includes the elephant, lion, wildcat, giraffe, zebra, hyena, and hippopotamus. The most common birds are the ostrich, duck, guinea fowl, partridge, green pigeon, sand grouse, and heron.

5 ENVIRONMENT

In 1985, expansion of the desert into forest areas had affected 134 square kilometers (52 square miles) of land in Somalia. Fifty percent of the nation's city dwellers and 71% of the people living in rural areas do not have pure water. The nation's cities produce 500,000 tons of solid waste per year.

Somalia in the early 1980s still had one of the most abundant and varied stocks of wildlife in Africa. The hunting and trapping of antelopes and gazelles for their skins was banned in 1969. However, many species continued to be harmed by the advance of livestock and human settlement into their habitats, and the cutting of bush vegetation and tree cover. In 1994, 17 of the country's mammal species and 7 bird species were endangered; 52 types of plants were threatened with extinction.

6 POPULATION

In 1994, Somalia had a population estimated by the US Census Bureau at 7,400,107. But the United Nations, which apparently included refugees in its count while the Census Bureau did not, estimated the 1995 population at 10,173,000. A population of 11,864,000 was projected by the United Nations for the year 2000. The largest city and its estimated 1990 population is Mogadishu, the capital, with 779,000.

7 MIGRATION

Since about half of all Somalis are nomadic herdsmen, there is much movement back and forth across the frontiers as a normal part of grazing activities. By 1993, it was estimated that three-quarters of the population had been driven from their homes by civil war since 1988. The political violence in Somalia was so extreme that about 700,000 people fled the country between 1988 and 1991. At the end of 1992, there were 406,100 refugees in Ethiopia, 285,600 in Kenya, 20,000 in Djibouti, and 4,900 in Egypt.

8 ETHNIC GROUPS

The Somalis are classified as a Hamitic people with a Cushitic culture. Ethnic Somalis, who made up about 98.8% of the population in 1985, are divided into two main clan families: the Samaal—approximately 70% of the population—who are principally nomadic herdsmen; and the Saab—about 20% of the population—who are primarily farmers and settled herders. The nonnative population consists primarily of Arabs, Italians, Pakistanis, and Indians.

9 LANGUAGES

Somali, classified as a lowland Eastern Cushitic language, is spoken by all Somalis, with dialectal differences that follow clan divisions. In 1973, a written form of Somali, with a script based on the Latin alphabet, was adopted as the nation's main official language, with Arabic a secondary language.

SOMALIA

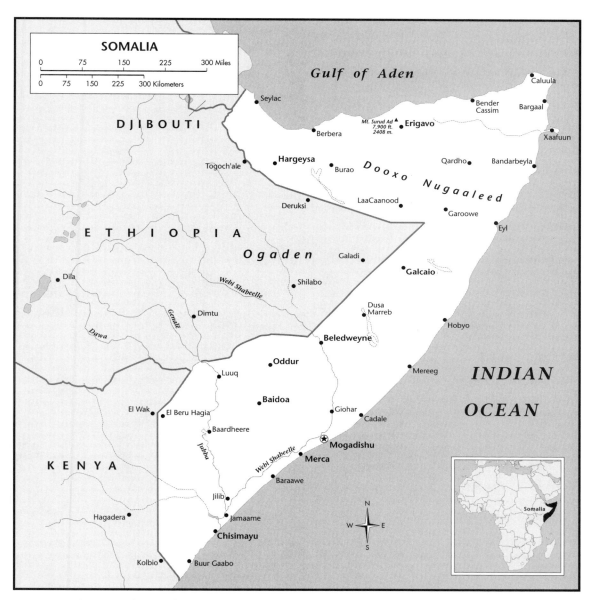

SOMALIA

| 0 | 75 | 150 | 225 | 300 Miles |
| 0 | 75 | 150 | 225 | 300 Kilometers |

Gulf of Aden

DJIBOUTI

Caluula
Seylac
Bender Cassim
Bargaal
Berbera
Mt. Surud Ad
7,900 ft.
2408 m.
Erigavo
Xaafuun

Togoch'ale
Hargeysa
Burao
Qardho
Bandarbeyla

Dooxo Nugaaleed

ETHIOPIA
Deruksi
LaaCaanood
Garoowe
Eyl

Ogaden
Galadi
Galcaio

Dila
Shilabo

Webi Shabeelle
Dusa Marreb
Hobyo

Genalē
Dimtu

Dawa
Beledweyne

Mereeg

INDIAN
OCEAN

Oddur
Luuq

Baidoa

El Wak
El Beru Hagia
Giohar
Cadale

Baardheere
Mogadishu
Merca

Jubba
Webi Shabeelle

KENYA
Baraawe

Jilib

Hagadera
Jamaame

Chisimayu
N
W E
S

Kolbio
Buur Gaabo

Somalia

LOCATION: 12°N to 1°39′s; 41°30′ to 51°E. **BOUNDARY LENGTHS:** Total coastline, 3,025 kilometers (1,874 miles); Kenya, 682 kilometers (424 miles); Ethiopia, 1,626 kilometers (1,016 miles); Djibouti, 58 kilometers (36 miles). **TERRITORIAL SEA LIMIT:** 200 miles.

10 RELIGIONS

The Somalis are Sunni Muslims of the Shafi'i sect, and Islam is the religion of the state. Christian mission schools closed in 1972, and foreign Protestant missionaries were expelled in 1976. Protestants and Catholics make up less than 1% of the population.

11 TRANSPORTATION

Of 22,000 kilometers (13,650 miles) of roads in Somalia in 1991, 12% were paved. Motor vehicles in use in 1991 numbered 22,500. There are no railways and no commercial water transport facilities. The ports of Mogadishu, Chisimayu, and Berbera are served by vessels from many parts of the world. The major airfields are in Mogadishu and Berbera.

12 HISTORY

Ancient Egyptians came to Somalia's northern shores for incense and aromatic herbs. In the ninth or tenth century, Somalis began pushing south from the Gulf of Aden coast. About this time, Arabs and Persians established settlements along the Indian Ocean coast.

European Influence

During the fifteenth and sixteenth centuries, Portuguese explorers attempted without success to establish Portuguese rule over the Somali coast. After the British armed forces occupied Aden in 1839, they developed an interest in the northern Somali coast, and the British signed a number of treaties with Somali chiefs of the northern area to make Somalia a British protectorate. From 1899 to 1920, British rule was constantly disrupted by the "holy war" waged by 'Abdallah bin Hasan (generally known in English literature as the "Mad Mullah").

Italian expansion in Somalia began in 1885, and by 1889 Italy established protectorates over the eastern territories that were officially ruled by the sultans of Obbia and of Alula. Direct administrative control of the territory known as Italian Somaliland was not established until 1905. Italy's Fascist (dictatorial) government, which came to power under Benito Mussolini in 1922, increased Italian authority by its extensive military operations. During the Italian-Ethiopian conflict (1934–36), Somalia was a staging area for Italy's invasion and conquest of Ethiopia. From 1936 to 1941, Somalia and the Somali-inhabited portion of Ethiopia, the Ogaden, were combined in an enlarged province of Italian East Africa.

In 1940–41, the British conquered Italian Somaliland from Italian troops, who were allied with Nazi Germany. The Ogaden was returned to Ethiopia in 1948, and British administration over the rest of Italian Somaliland continued until 1950, when Italy, through the United Nations, gained administrative control again. However, in 1949 the UN General Assembly resolved that Italian Somaliland would receive its independence in 1960.

A United Somalia

By the end of 1956, Somalis were in almost complete charge of domestic affairs. Meanwhile, Somalis in British Somaliland were demanding self-govern-

Photo credit: AP/Wide World Photos/Kathy Willens

Hassan Riyole, left, plays on a tree branch with other children from his tiny village of Dheeray, Somalia.

ment. As Italy agreed to grant independence on 1 July 1960 to its trust territory, the United Kingdom gave its protectorate independence on 26 June 1960, thus enabling the two Somali territories to join in a united Somali Republic on 1 July 1960. On 20 July 1961, the Somali people ratified a new constitution, drafted in 1960, and one month later confirmed Aden 'Abdullah Osman Daar as the nation's first president.

Military Rule

Somalia was involved in many border clashes with Ethiopia and Kenya. Soviet influence in Somalia grew after Moscow agreed in 1962 to provide substantial military aid. Abdirashid 'Ali Shermarke, who was elected president in 1967, was assassinated on 15 October 1969. Six days later, army commanders seized power with the support of the police. The military leaders dissolved parliament, suspended the constitution, arrested members of the cabinet, and changed the name of the country to the Somali Democratic Republic. Major General Jalle Mohamed Siad Barre, commander of the army, was named chairman of a 25-member Supreme Revolutionary Council (SRC) that assumed the powers of the president, the Supreme Court, and the National Assembly. Siad Barre was later named president.

In 1970, President Siad Barre proclaimed "scientific socialism" as the republic's guiding ideology. Controversy arose in the mid-1970s over Somalia's links to the Soviet Union and its support of the Western Somali Liberation Front in Ethiopia's Ogaden region.

In January 1986, Siad Barre met three times with Ethiopia's head of state in an effort to improve relations between the two countries, but no agreement was reached. In addition, internal dissent continued to mount.

Civil War Leads to Mass Starvation

In February 1987, relations between Somalia and Ethiopia worsened following an Ethiopian attack. By 1990, the Somali regime was losing control. Armed resistance from guerrilla groups was turning the Somali territory into a death trap.

In 1990, Barre was ousted and, in January 1991, he fled Mogadishu. The United Somali Congress (USC) seized the capital. The economy broke down and the country turned into chaos as armed groups terrorized the population and disrupted shipments of food. Several hundred thousand people were killed, and far more were threatened by starvation. Over a half million fled to Kenya. As the starvation and total breakdown of public services was publicized in the western media, calls for the United Nations to intervene mounted.

The United Nations Intervenes

Late on 3 December 1992, the UN Security Council passed a resolution to deploy a massive US-led international military intervention (UNITAF-United Task Force) to safeguard relief operations. By the end of December, faction leaders Muhammad Farrah Aideed and Ali Maludi Muhammad had pledged to stop fighting. The UNITAF spread throughout the country, and violence decreased dramatically.

Although the problem of relief distribution had largely been solved, there was no central government, few public institutions, and local warlords and their forces became increasingly bold. By early 1993, over 34,000 troops from 24 United Nations members—75% from the United States—were deployed. Starvation was virtually ended, and some order had been restored. Yet, little was done to achieve a political solution or to disarm the factions. From January 1993 until 27 March, 15 armed factions met in Addis Ababa, Ethiopia, to end hostilities and form a transitional National Council for a two-year period to serve as the political authority in Somalia.

On 4 May 1993, Operation Restore Hope, as the relief effort was labeled, was declared successful, and US force levels were sharply reduced. A second relief effort, UNOSOM II, featured Pakistani, American, Belgian, Italian, Moroccan, and French troops, commanded by a Turkish general. On 23 June 1993, 23 Pakistani solders were killed in an ambush. General Aideed's forces were blamed and a $25,000 bounty was placed on Aideed's head. Mogadishu became a war zone.

In early October 1993, 18 US Army Rangers were killed and 75 were wounded in a firefight. American public opinion and

Photo credit: AP/Wide World Photos/Kathy Willens

Hassan Riyole, 10, recites prayers from the Koran with his father Osman inside their straw hut in Dheeray, Somalia. Hassan's father says he would like Hassan to attend school, but Hassan cannot read or write yet.

politicians pressured President Bill Clinton to withdraw American troops. New discussions in Kenya and in Mogadishu reached agreements that teetered on collapse. After the withdrawal of the foreign peacekeeping troops, General Muhammad Farrah Aideed became Somalia's "self-declared" president. However, his rivals refuse to bow to his authority and the country remains in a precarious position.

13 GOVERNMENT

Since the overthrow of President Siad Barre in June 1991, Somalia has had no viable central government. Some 15 armed factions have been fighting, except for the relatively peaceful early months of UN-US administration from December 1992 until around June 1993.

14 POLITICAL PARTIES

President Siad Barre's SRSP (Somali Revolutionary Socialist Party) was the sole legal party at the time of his overthrow in January 1991. The Somali National Movement (SNM) has seized control of the north. Armed factions have divided up the territory as they fight and negotiate to expand their influence. Although many of them bear the titles of political parties, such as the Somali Democratic Movement, the Somali National Union, and the United

Somali Congress (USC), they do not have national bases of support. The USC controlled Mogadishu and much of central Somalia until late in 1991 when it split into two major factions, Aideed's Somali National Alliance (SNA) and Ali Mahdi's Somali Salvation Alliance.

15 JUDICIAL SYSTEM

As a result of the civil disorder in recent years, most of the structure for the administration of justice has collapsed. Islamic law and traditional courts continue to be applied to settle disputes over property and criminal offenses.

16 ARMED FORCES

The regular armed forces disintegrated in the revolution of 1991. Clan gangs armed with imported weapons terrorized the country and continue to fight among themselves.

17 ECONOMY

Since 1990, Somalia's primarily agricultural economy has fallen apart due to drought and a drawn-out civil war which has left the country without central authority. By early 1992, virtually all trade, industry, and agriculture had stopped, large numbers of people were forced from their homes, and more than 6 million were at risk of starvation. In 1993 donors pledged $130 million toward Somalia's reconstruction, and good rains and increased stability eased the food situation. However, floods in 1995 destroyed crops and malnutrition once again became a problem.

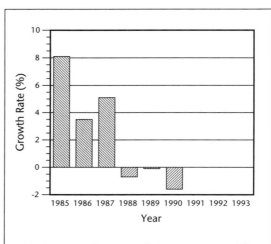

Yearly growth rate of the economy. This economic indicator tells by what percent the economy has increased or decreased when compared with the previous year.

18 INCOME

In 1987, the last year for which the United Nations has statistics, Somalia's gross domestic product (GDP) in current prices was $1,686 million, or less than $695 per person.

19 INDUSTRY

Industries mainly serve the domestic market and, to a lesser extent, provide some of the needs of Somalia's agricultural exports, such as the manufacture of crates for packing bananas. The most important industries are the petroleum refinery, the state-owned sugar plants, an oilseed-crushing mill, and a soap factory. Newer industries manufacture corrugated iron, paint, cigarettes and matches, aluminum utensils, cardboard boxes and polyethylene bags, and textiles.

20 LABOR

In 1992, workers' rights vanished amid the civil chaos and fighting. Nomadic shepherds made up about 60% of the working population in the mid-1980s; some 22% were farmers. About 19% of the labor force was in government, trade, and services and 9% in industry in the late 1980s.

While children are not generally employed, they often are part of the armed militia groups that are fighting for control of Somalia.

21 AGRICULTURE

In 1991, only 1.6% of Somalia's total land area was cultivated, and 69% was permanent pasture. There are two main types of agriculture, one native and the other introduced by European settlers. Somali and Italian farmers operating the banana farms practice modern European-style techniques, as do some of the newly created Somali cooperatives. Bananas constitute the nation's major commercial crop; output was 55,000 tons in 1992. Sugarcane production in 1992 totaled some 50,000 tons. Somalia is the world's leading producer of frankincense.

22 DOMESTICATED ANIMALS

The majority of Somalis raise livestock; in some areas, particularly in the north, this is the only livelihood. The national livestock herd was estimated at 10 million head at the end of 1992. Livestock exports included 40,000 sheep and goats, 20,000

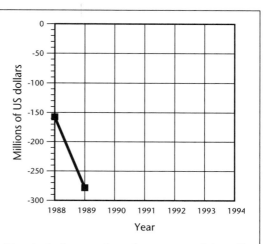

Yearly balance of trade measured in millions of US dollars. The balance of trade is the difference between what a country sells to other countries (its exports) and what it buys (its imports). If a country imports more than it exports, it has a negative balance of trade (a trade deficit). If exports exceed imports there is a positive balance of trade (a trade surplus).

cattle, and other animals with a combined value of $31.5 million. The export of hides and skins is also important.

23 FISHING

Fish-processing plants produced fish flour, inedible oil, and semirefined edible oil. In 1985, fish—tuna, sardines, mackerel, and lobster—and fish products accounted for 10.7% of exports. The catch in 1991 was 16,100 tons.

24 FORESTRY

Somalia is one of the few areas in the world where frankincense is produced; incense trees of the genus Boswellia are found in the northeast. Gum arabic in

Selected Social Indicators

These statistics are estimates for the period 1988 to 1993. For comparison purposes, data for the United States and averages for low-income countries and high-income countries are also given.

Indicator	Somalia	Low-income countries	High-income countries	United States
Per capita gross national product†	<$695	$380	$23,680	$24,740
Population growth rate	0.6%	1.9%	0.6%	1.0%
Population growth rate in urban areas	1.8%	3.9%	0.8%	1.3%
Population per square kilometer of land	14	78	25	26
Life expectancy in years	47	62	77	76
Number of people per physician	15,825	>3,300	453	419
Number of pupils per teacher (primary school)	19	39	<18	20
Illiteracy rate (15 years and older)	76%	41%	<5%	<3%
Energy consumed per capita (kg of oil equivalent)	7	364	5,203	7,918

† The gross national product (GNP) is the total dollar value of all goods and services produced by a country in a year. The per capita GNP is calculated by dividing a country's GNP by its population. The World Bank defines low-income countries as those with a per capita GNP of $695 or less. High-income countries have a per capita GNP of $8,626 or more. Less than 14% of the world's 5.5 billion people live in high-income countries, while almost 60% live in low-income countries.

> = greater than   < = less than

Sources: World Bank, *Social Indicators of Development 1995,* Baltimore: Johns Hopkins University Press, 1995. Central Intelligence Agency, *World Fact Book,* Washington, D.C.: Government Printing Office, 1994.

small quantities is also produced. Roundwood production was estimated at 7,326,000 cubic meters.

25 MINING

In 1991, the only nonfuel minerals being exploited were materials quarried for construction—cement, gypsum, and limestone—and 5,000 tons of marine salt. Small amounts of sepiolite (meerschaum) were also reportedly extracted in 1991.

26 FOREIGN TRADE

Bananas, followed closely by live animal sales, are the nation's leading export (1988), while petroleum is the leading import. The single greatest purchaser of Somalia's exports in 1985 was Sa'udi Arabia, accounting for 34.2% of total exports. The leading import supplier was Italy, accounting for 25.8% of all imports.

27 ENERGY AND POWER

Installed electrical capacity in 1991 was 60,000 kilowatts, almost entirely thermal; total production was 110 million kilowatt hours. There were four 200 kilowatt windmills in operation. As of 1991, Somalia was entirely dependent on imports to fill its oil needs. In 1985, 240,000 tons of crude oil were imported. The only immediately exploitable domestic sources of energy are firewood and charcoal.

28 SOCIAL DEVELOPMENT

The internal fighting and widespread drought conditions between 1989 and late 1992 have totally destroyed the government's provision of social services. Private humanitarian agencies tried to fill the needs but fighting, extortion, and the activities of armed factions and looters chased many of them away. The United Nations is also trying to fill the needs but it, too, finds its operation difficult.

29 HEALTH

Because of the ongoing civil strife, hospitals are without drugs and illnesses are on the rise. Malaria and intestinal parasites are widespread. Water has been cut off to the capital city of Mogadishu leaving the people to rely on well water which is scarce and often contaminated. Major operations are often performed without anesthetic.

30 HOUSING

Development schemes aided by United Nations and foreign assistance programs have helped alleviate housing shortages in Mogadishu and Hargeysa. The typical Somali house is either a round or a rectangular hut with a thatched or metal roof.

31 EDUCATION

During 1992, Somalia was in a state of anarchy and not only did the country's economy collapse, but its educational system did as well. Few schools were operat-

Photo credit: AP/Wide World Photos/Kathy Willens

Ten year old Hassan Riyole, right, walks with his best friend Osman Abdow, also ten, in the village of Dheeray, Somalia. Disruption of food supplies during Somalia's civil war brought Hassan to the brink of starvation. He was rescued by the Red Cross and placed in a hospital in Lafoole. He has since returned to his village with his father and his friends.

ing, and even the Somali National University was closed in 1991. In 1990, the United Nations Educational, Scientific and Cultural Organization (UNESCO) estimated the adult literacy rate to be 24% (males, 36% and females, 14%).

32 MEDIA

As of 1992, the government published a daily newspaper in Somali, *Xiddigta*

Oktobar, and a weekly newspaper in English, *Heegan.* The Somali National News Agency (SONNA) provides news information for radio and press, supplies information to foreign correspondents in Somalia, and publishes a daily news bulletin, *October Star,* in Somali and English.

Somalia had an estimated 6,000 telephones in 1985. In 1992, it had two radio stations—Radio Mogadishu and Radio Hargeisa—both government-owned, and an estimated 330,000 radio receivers. A television service, limited to the Mogadishu area, was inaugurated in 1983; it broadcasts in Somali and Arabic. There were 108,000 television sets in 1991.

33 TOURISM AND RECREATION

Somalia's modest tourist industry has been stagnant since the civil war began. Before the war, Somalia offered lovely beaches, excellent skin diving, and numerous species of East African wildlife. About 39,000 tourists visited Somalia from abroad in 1985.

34 FAMOUS SOMALIS

The most important historical figure in Somali history was Muhammad 'Abdallah bin Hasan (known popularly in the English-speaking world as the "Mad Mullah"), who resisted British rule and also was one of Somalia's greatest poets. Aden 'Abdullah Osman Daar (b.1908) is regarded as the Somali most responsible for bringing about the transition of the Somali territory from dependence to independence; he was the nation's first president.

Major General Jalle Mohamed Siad Barre (b.1921) was the leader of the bloodless coup that took over the government after the assassination of Abdirashid 'Ali Shermarke (1919–69), Somalia's first prime minister after independence. Jalle later became president of the Somali Democratic Republic.

35 BIBLIOGRAPHY

Burton, Richard F. *First Footsteps in Eastern Africa.* London: Longman, Brown, Green and Longmans, 1856.

Jardine, D. *The Mad Mullah of Somaliland.* Westport, Conn.: Negro Universities Press, 1969 (orig. 1924).

Loughran, Katheryne S. et al., eds. *Somalia in Word and Image.* Bloomington: Indiana University Press, 1986.

SOUTH AFRICA

Republic of South Africa

Republiek van Suid-Afrika

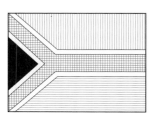

CAPITAL: Cape Town (legislative); Pretoria (administrative); Bloemfontein (judicial).

FLAG: The national flag, adopted in 1994, consists of a blue-black triangle placed vertical to the hoist and bordered in gold-yellow. Bands of red, white, green, white, and blue appear horizontally.

ANTHEM: Two anthems are currently in use: the official anthem, *Die Stem van Suid-Afrika (The Call of South Africa),* and *Nkosi Sikelel' Afrika (God Bless Africa),* a hymn adopted by most liberation groups.

MONETARY UNIT: The South African rand (R) is a paper currency of 100 cents. It is used throughout the South African monetary area, which includes all the black homelands. There are coins of 1, 2, 5, 10, 20, and 50 cents and 1 rand, and notes of 2, 5, 10, 20, and 50 rand. R1 = $0.2874 (or $1 = R3.4795).

WEIGHTS AND MEASURES: The metric system is in use.

HOLIDAYS: New Year's Day, 1 January; Republic Day, 31 May; Kruger Day, 10 October; Day of the Vow, 16 December; Christmas, 25 December; Goodwill Day, 26 December. Movable religious holidays include Good Friday and Ascension; Family Day is a movable secular holiday.

TIME: 2 PM = noon GMT.

1 LOCATION AND SIZE

The area of South Africa is 1,321,219 square kilometers (510,125 square miles). Comparatively, the area occupied by South Africa is slightly less than twice the size of the state of Texas.

South Africa also controls two small islands, Prince Edward and Marion, which lie some 1,920 kilometers (1,200 miles) southeast of Cape Town.

South Africa's capital city, Pretoria, is located in the northeastern part of the country.

2 TOPOGRAPHY

South Africa has a mean altitude of about 1,200 meters (3,900 feet). Parts of Johannesburg are more than 1,800 meters (6,000 feet) above sea level. There are three major zones: the outside regions, including the eastern and western plateau slopes; a vast saucer-shaped interior plateau, separated from the outside regions by an area of higher elevation, and a desert in the northcentral region near the border with Botswana. The land rises steadily from west to east to the Drakensberg Mountains, the tallest of which is Champagne Castle (3,375 meters/11,072 feet), on the border with Lesotho.

Photo credit: Cynthia Bassett

Lionesses at Kruger National Park, Africa's first wildlife reserve.

The two most important rivers draining the interior plateau are the Orange, which flows into the Atlantic Ocean, and the Limpopo, which empties into the Indian Ocean through Mozambique.

3 CLIMATE

South Africa lies almost wholly within the southern temperate zone. In February, the average daily minimum temperature at Durban, on the east coast, ranges from 11°C (52°F) in July to 21°C (70°F), while on the west coast, at Port Nolloth, the range is from 7°C (45°F) to 12°C (54°F). Temperatures are cooler in the highlands: at Johannesburg, the average daily mini-mum is 4°C (39°F) in June and July and 14°C (57°F) in January. While the mean annual rainfall is 46 centimeters (18 inches), 21% of the country receives less than 20 centimeters (8 inches) and 31% gets more than 60 centimeters (24 inches).

4 PLANTS AND ANIMALS

The variety of South Africa's climate and altitude accounts for its diversified plant and animal life. Of the 200 natural orders of plants in the world, over 140 are repre-sented, and South Africa has over 25,000 species of plants, including a plant king-dom found nowhere else. There are more than 500 species of grass in the Cape Prov-ince alone. Wildflowers (including the protea, South Africa's national flower) abound throughout the Cape region.

Aardvark, jackal, lion, elephant, wild buffalo, hippopotamus, and various kinds of antelope are still found in some parts of the country. So great is the variety both of smaller mammals and of plants that they have not yet all been identified. The num-ber of different kinds of birds is approxi-mately 900; that of snakes, 200. The number of species of insects is estimated at 40,000, and there are about 1,000 kinds of fish.

5 ENVIRONMENT

Industry and urban life have taken their toll on the South African environment, as have such agricultural practices as veld fires, overgrazing of livestock, and inten-sive use of pesticides. Three hundred to four hundred million tons of soil per year are lost due to erosion and the expansion of the desert into farm land. Mine drain-

SOUTH AFRICA

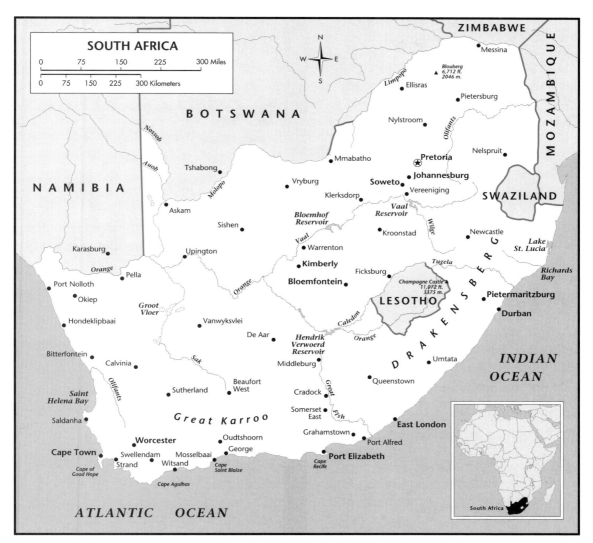

SOUTH AFRICA

0   75   150   225   300 Miles

0   75   150   225   300 Kilometers

ZIMBABWE

MOZAMBIQUE

Messina

Blouberg
6,712 ft.
2046 m.

BOTSWANA

Limpopo

Ellisras

Pietersburg

Nylstroom

Olifants

Nelspruit

Mmabatho

Pretoria ✪

Johannesburg

SWAZILAND

NAMIBIA

Tshabong

Soweto

Vereeniging

Vryburg

Klerksdorp

Vaal
Reservoir

Wilge

Newcastle

Lake
St. Lucia

Askam

Bloemhof
Reservoir

Kroonstad

Sishen

Vaal

Warrenton

Champagne Castle ▲
11,072 ft.
3,375 m.

Richards
Bay

Karasburg

Upington

Kimberly

Ficksburg

Tugela

Orange

Pella

Bloemfontein

LESOTHO

Pietermaritzburg

Port Nolloth

Okiep

Groot
Vloer

Vanwyksvlei

Caledon

Durban

Hondeklipbaai

De Aar

Orange

Bitterfontein

Calvinia

Sak

Hendrik
Verwoerd
Reservoir

Middleburg

Umtata

INDIAN
OCEAN

Saint
Helena Bay

Olifants

Sutherland

Beaufort
West

Cradock

Queenstown

Saldanha

Great Karroo

Somerset
East

Great Fish

East London

Worcester

Oudtshoorn

George

Grahamstown

Port Alfred

Cape Town

Swellendam

Mosselbaai

Port Elizabeth

Strand

Witsand

Cape
Saint Blaize

Cape
Recife

Cape of
Good Hope

Cape Agulhas

ATLANTIC   OCEAN

DRAKENSBERG

Nossob

Auob

Molopo

Orange

South Africa

LOCATION: 16°28' to 32°54'E; 22°8' to 34°50's. **BOUNDARY LENGTHS:** Botswana, 1,778 kilometers (1,105 miles); Zimbabwe, 225 kilometers (140 miles); Mozambique, 491 kilometers (305 miles); Swaziland, 449 kilometers (279 miles); total coastline, 2,954 kilometers (1,836 miles, including Transkei and Ciskei); Namibia (South West Africa), 1,078 kilometers (670 miles); Lesotho, 909 kilometers (565 miles). **TERRITORIAL SEA LIMIT:** 12 miles.

age has endangered South Africa's limited water resources. The country has 12.0 cubic miles of water, of which 67% is used for farming and 17% for industrial activity. The country's cities produce 4.2 million tons of solid waste per year. Air pollution in urban areas stems primarily from coal burning and motor vehicle exhausts. The level of emissions per person is twice the world average.

As of 1994, 25 mammal species and 13 bird species were endangered. Plant species numbering 1,116 were also endangered. About 3% of the total land area is allocated to wildlife preservation, and there are numerous nature and game reserves and national parks. Some 120 rare Addo elephants are protected in Addo Elephant National Park, 56 kilometers (35 miles) north of Port Elizabeth; Mountain Zebra National Park (near Cradock, in Cape Province) is a refuge for several hundred rare mountain zebras and springbok; and Kruger National Park has almost every species of South African wildlife in its natural habitat.

6 POPULATION

South Africa's population was estimated by the US Census Bureau at 43,942,832 in 1994. Excluding the "sovereign" black homelands (areas set aside for people of a specific race or culture) of Bophuthatswana, Ciskei, Transkei, and Venda, the 1991 population was 26,288,390 according to that year's census. This was considered an undercount, however, and the population (excluding the homelands) was estimated by the government at 31,917,000 in 1992. It was projected by the United Nations at 47,912,000 for the year 2000 (including all homelands). Estimated average population density was 32 persons per square kilometer (83 per square mile). However, more than a third of the people live on only 4% of the land area.

The largest city, the commercial and industrial center of Johannesburg, had a 1991 census population of 1,907,229; the legislative capital, Cape Town, had 1,869,144; and Pretoria, the administrative capital, had 1,025,790. At the 1991 census, 8,402,192 people lived in the Bantu homelands (excluding Bophuthatswana, Ciskei, Transkei, and Venda. The four formerly independent homelands had an estimated population of 6,700,000 in 1991).

7 MIGRATION

Between 1980 and 1984, some 72,528 residents of Zimbabwe (formerly Rhodesia) emigrated to South Africa, after black rule was instituted in Zimbabwe. Since then, immigration has fallen, and, perhaps as a consequence, the white population actually dropped between 1980 and 1991. Of the 63,495 immigrants between 1986 and 1991, 16,815 came from other African countries, 16,056 from the United Kingdom, 16,512 from other European countries, and 14,112 from other parts of the world. Emigration came to 46,541 during these years.

In 1986, it was estimated that between 1.5 million and 2 million black Africans migrate temporarily to South Africa each year to fulfill work contracts. South Africa was providing informal sanctuary to perhaps 200,000 refugees from Mozambique in 1992; about 8,700 South Africans had been granted refugee status in other African countries.

8 ETHNIC GROUPS

South Africa has one of the world's most complex ethnic patterns. Legal separation of the racial communities—called apartheid—was a cornerstone of government policy through most of the twentieth century and created one of the most rigidly segregated societies in the world. During the 1970s and 1980s, enforcement of separatist policies eased, but the division of the population into four racial communities remained. In 1991, parliament passed measures to repeal the apartheid laws.

As of the 1991 census, blacks formed the largest segment of the population, constituting 68.4% (17,973,320) of the total; this proportion, which excludes the homelands (areas set aside for people of a particular race or culture) Bophuthatswana, Ciskei, Transkei, and Venda, whose populations are almost entirely black, would be 74.8% if those four homelands were included. As of 1991, whites accounted for 17.2% (4,521,873) with the homelands excluded, but only for 13.7% with the homelands included; Cape Coloureds (persons of mixed race), 11.1% (2,929,329); and Asians, 3.3% (863,874).

The black population includes a large number of peoples. According to a 1985 estimate, the largest groups were the Zulu, about 5.3 million; Xhosa, 2.1 million; Northern Sotho, 2.6 million; Southern Sotho, 1.6 million; and Tswana, 1.1 million. The four homelands contained another 3.5 million Xhosa and 1.6 million Tswana.

About 60% of the whites are descendants of Dutch, French Huguenot, and German settlers, and about 40% are of British descent. South Africans of European, especially Dutch, descent are called Afrikaners. The Cape Coloureds are a long-established racial amalgam of white,

Photo credit: Corel Corporation.

Zulu village women in Natal, South Africa.

Hottentot, and other African, Indian, and Malay lineage. The Asians include descendants of Indian, East Indian, and Chinese indentured laborers.

9 LANGUAGES

The interim constitution adopted in 1993 recognized 11 languages as official at the national level: Afrikaans, English, isi Ndebele, Sesotho sa Leboa, Sesotho, isi Swati, Xitsonga, Setswana, Tshivenda, isi Xhosa, and isi Zulu. The African languages spoken in South Africa are of the Niger-Congo family. In general, English is more commonly spoken in the cities, and Afrikaans in the rural areas.

Afrikaans is a variant of the Dutch spoken by the seventeenth-century colonists, and it includes words and phrases from Malay, Portuguese, the Bantu group, Hottentot, and other African languages, as well as from English, French, and German. Afrikaans has borrowed from English words such as *gelling* (gallon), *jaart* (yard), *sjieling* (shilling), and *trippens* (three pence), while English has taken over *kraal*, *veld*, and other Afrikaans words.

More than 70% of South African whites are bilingual. Afrikaans was the mother tongue of 58%, and English of 39%, in 1991. Some 83% of Coloureds spoke Afrikaans as their first language. Asians mostly (95%) spoke English as their first language. Zulu was the most common language of the blacks, and 39% spoke it as their first language.

10 RELIGIONS

In the early 1990s, nearly 70% of the population was Christian, and about 28% followed native tribal religions. Black Christians were found in large numbers in all the European denominations, as well as in some 3,000 separatist sects under their own leaders. Nearly half of white South Africans, including almost all the Afrikaans-speaking population, belonged to the Dutch Reformed churches. The next-largest denomination was the Anglican (Episcopal), with 10% of the white population. About 9% was Methodist, 8% Roman Catholic, and 3% Presbyterian. About 3% of the white population was Jewish.

Most Christian nonwhites were members of the Dutch Reformed, Anglican, Roman Catholic, and other Christian churches. Most Asians retained their Asian religions, principally Hinduism (1.3%) and Islam (1.1%). In 1993, there were about 100,000 Jews in South Africa, and some 8,000 Baha'is.

11 TRANSPORTATION

South Africa's transportation network is among the most modern and extensive on the continent. In 1991, there were 188,309 kilometers (117,035 miles) of national and provincial roads, of which 54,013 kilometers (33,569 miles) were paved. There were 3,488,570 automobiles and 1,899,721 commercial vehicles in 1992.

The South African Transport Service, a government department under the minister of transport affairs, operates the railways, principal harbors, South African Airways, and some road transportation services. In 1991 there were 20,638 kilometers (12,827 miles) of track. South Africa's seven ports, owned and operated by the government, include the deepwater ports of Durban, Port Elizabeth, and Table Bay (at Cape Town).

The government-owned South African Airways, which operates both international and domestic flights, carried 1,957,900 passengers and flew 78 million tons of freight during five months of activity in 1991. Jan Smuts Airport, near Johannesburg, is the major international airport; other international airports are located at Cape Town and Durban.

12 HISTORY

Fossil skulls suggest that South Africa may have been one of the earliest scenes of human evolution. Little is known of the original settlers, but when Europeans first arrived, there were two distinct groups of peoples—the Bushmen, primitive nomadic hunters of the western desert, and the Hottentots, herdsmen who occupied the southern and eastern coastal areas.

European Exploration

Before AD 100, Bantu-speaking peoples entered the Transvaal area (northern region between the Vaal and Limpopo rivers). In 1488, the Portuguese sailor Bartholomeu Dias discovered the Cape of Good Hope, and on Christmas Day of 1497, Vasco da Gama discovered Natal, the area between the Drakensberg Mountains and the Indian Ocean.

The first European settlement at the Cape was made in 1652 under Jan van Riebeeck on behalf of the Dutch East India Company. Because there was a shortage of farm labor, the Dutch imported slaves from West Africa, Madagascar, and the East Indies, and because of the scarcity of European women, mixed marriages took place, eventually producing the Cape Coloured people.

The demand for meat encouraged the development of cattle farming, which in turn led to the need for more grazing land. Settlements were established on the coastal plain, along the valleys, and on the Great Karroo, a plateau in the south. The European population multiplied, but the Bushmen and Hottentots declined in numbers. In 1778, the Cape authorities proclaimed the Great Fish River the boundary between the colonists and the Africans. In 1779, invading Xhosa tribesmen were driven back across the river border. Three more frontier wars were fought by 1812.

British Influence

In 1814, the Cape of Good Hope was turned over to Britain by the Treaty of Vienna. Throughout the rest of the nineteenth century, the United Kingdom expanded its territory to include Natal, Kaffraria (south of Natal on the Indian Ocean), Griqualand West (north of the Orange River), Zululand (northeast of Natal on the Indian Ocean), Tongaland, and Basutoland (now Lesotho). The Transvaal was annexed in 1877 but returned to independence after a revolt in 1880–81.

Because of severe droughts and in reaction to British policy, about 6,000 Boers (Dutch farmers) undertook the Great Trek in 1834–36, migrating northward into the present Orange Free State (between the Orange and Vaal rivers) and the Transvaal.

In 1860, indentured Indians were brought into Natal to work on the sugarcane plantations; by 1911, when India halted the emigration because of what it called "poor working conditions," more than 150,000 Indians had come to South Africa as contract laborers. While pursuing the Indians' claims of injustice in South Africa, Mohandas (Mahatma) Gandhi, a young lawyer who later became famous for leading India to independence, developed his philosophy of nonviolent resistance.

The Boer War

Tension between the Boers and outsiders attracted to Transvaal by the discovery of gold in 1866 was increased by an unsuccessful attempt to capture Johannesburg by Dr. Leander Starr Jameson (Jameson Raid) in 1895–96 and culminated in the South African (or Boer) War in 1899–1902. Ultimately, the Boer republics of Transvaal and the Orange Free State gave up their independence by the Treaty of Vereeniging on 31 May 1902, but shortly thereafter were granted self-government by the British.

The Union of South Africa

A constitution for a united South Africa, which passed the British Parliament as the South Africa Act in 1909, provided for a union of all four territories or provinces, to be known as the Union of South Africa. South Africa fought with the Allies (United States, United Kingdom, and their allies) in World War I (1914–18), signed the Treaty of Versailles, and became a member of the League of Nations. Mining and industrialization advanced in the period between the two wars and led to higher living standards. South Africa sent troops to fight the German Nazis in World War II (1939–45), although many Afrikaners (as the Boers had come to be called) favored neutrality. In 1948, the National Party (NP) took power, enforcing the policy of apartheid, or racial separation of whites and non-whites.

Apartheid

South Africa became a republic on 31 May 1961, and the president replaced the British monarch as head of state. There were mounting pressures on the government because of its apartheid policies. On 21 March 1960, a black demonstration had been staged against the "pass laws," laws requiring blacks to carry identification enabling the government to restrict their movement into urban areas. The demonstration resulted in the killing of 69 black protesters by government troops at Sharpeville in Soweto, and provided a focus for local black protests and for widespread international expressions of outrage. During this period, many black leaders were jailed, including Nelson Mandela, the leader of the African National Congress (ANC), a black nationalist group. The ANC was banned as a political party.

In the mid-1970s, the Portuguese colonial empire disbanded and blacks came to power in Mozambique and Angola. The new black-controlled governments in these countries gave aid and political support to the ANC in South Africa. In response, South Africa aided rebel movements in the two former Portuguese territories.

In June 1976, the worst domestic confrontation since Sharpeville took place in Soweto, where blacks violently protested the compulsory use of the Afrikaans language in schools. Suppression of the riots by South African police left at least 174 blacks dead and 1,139 injured.

During the late 1970s, new protest groups and leaders emerged among the young blacks. After one of these leaders, 30-year-old Steven Biko, died while in police custody on 12 September 1977, there were renewed protests. On 4 November, the United Nations Security Council approved a mandatory arms embargo against South Africa—the first ever imposed on a member nation.

In an effort to satisfy nonwhite and international opinion, the government scrapped many aspects of apartheid in the mid-1980s, including the "pass laws" and the laws barring interracial sexual relations and marriage. These measures failed to satisfy blacks, however, and as political violence mounted the government imposed states of emergency in July 1985 and again in June 1986.

Further repression in the late 1980s included the banning of the United Democratic Front (UDF) and 16 other anti-apartheid organizations, suppression of the alternative newspapers *New Nation* and *Weekly Mail*, and assassination of anti-apartheid leaders by secret hit squads identified with the police and military intelligence.

De Klerk and the End of Apartheid

In 1989, President P.W. Botha resigned as head of the NP (National Party) and was replaced by F. W. de Klerk, who was also named acting state president. After the 6 September general election, de Klerk was elected to a five-year term as president. De Klerk launched a series of reforms in September 1989 that led to the release of ANC leader Nelson Mandela and others on 10 February 1990.

The African National Congress (ANC) and other resistance militants, including the Communist Party, were legalized. Mandela had been in prison 27 years and had become a revered symbol of resistance to apartheid. At that point, the ANC began to organize within South Africa and, in August 1990, suspended its armed struggle. Most leaders of the ANC returned from exile. Still, fighting continued, largely between ANC activists and supporters of the Zulu-dominated Inkatha Freedom Party, strongest in Natal province. More than 6,000 people were killed in political violence in 1990 and 1991. In 1991, parliament passed measures to repeal the apartheid laws—the Land Acts (1913 and 1936), the Group Areas Act (1950), and the Population Registration Act (1950).

Mandela becomes President

In July, the ANC convened its first full conference in South Africa in 30 years. Mandela was elected president, and Cyril Ramaphosa was elected secretary general. Meanwhile, negotiations continued through 1991 and 1992 over a transition to majority rule and an end to factional fighting between the ANC and Inkatha, mostly through the Convention for a Democratic South Africa (CODESA), which began in December 1991.

In February 1993, the government and the ANC reached agreement on plans for a transition to democracy. The broad guidelines were agreed upon by the government, the ANC, and other parties in late December 1993. The Conservative Party and Inkatha boycotted the talks on multiparty government, but just a few days before the scheduled elections, Inkatha agreed to participate. The white right was divided on whether to participate in preelection talks, in the election itself, or whether to take up arms as a last resort. The elections proceeded relatively peacefully and with great enthusiasm, and they were pronounced "free and fair" by international observers.

The ANC was awarded 252 of the 400 seats in parliament. It is the governing party in all but two of the nine regions. Mandela became president and the ANC's Thabo Mbeki and the NP's de Klerk were made deputy presidents. Zulu leader Mangosuthu Buthelezi was persuaded to take a ministerial post in the cabinet.

13 GOVERNMENT

There is a 400-seat National Assembly chosen by proportional representation. There is also a Senate of 90 members, 10 from each province or region, who serve as a legislature and also elect the president and deputy presidents. The president names a cabinet, divided proportionally between parties that have gained at least 5% of the vote. The nine provinces have assemblies based on the total number of votes cast in the general election.

14 POLITICAL PARTIES

Banned in 1960, the African National Congress (ANC) was legalized in 1987 in return for renouncing violence. Headed by Nelson Mandela, it received 62.5% of the vote in the April 1994 elections, making it the ruling party in South Africa.

The National Party (NP), first formed in 1910, was the last party of white rule in South Africa before the 1994 elections, in which it received 20.4% of the vote.

The Inkatha Freedom Party (IFP), headed by Zulu Chief Mangosuthu Buthelezi, captured over 10% of the national vote and won the election for the provincial government in Natal.

Other parties participating in the elections were the Freedom Front (2.2%), the Democratic Party (1.7%), and the Pan-Africanist Congress (1.2%).

15 JUDICIAL SYSTEM

The Supreme Court has a supreme appeals division and provincial and local divisions with both original and appeals jurisdictions. The Court of Appeals, with its seat in Bloemfontein, normally consists of the chief justice and a variable number of appeals judges. In 1986, there were 309 magistrate offices with certain judicial as well as administrative powers. Judges are appointed by the state president. There were no nonwhite judges as of 1987.

16 ARMED FORCES

In 1993, the South African defense force consisted of the permanent force, the citizen force, and the commandos, but it may change with a new government and constitution in 1994. There were 72,400 personnel, of whom 36,400 were draftees. The army had 50,000 troops, and the total strength of the navy was 4,500. The air force, with 16,400 regulars and 3,000 draftees, had 259 combat aircraft and 14–20 armed helicopters. There is also a med-

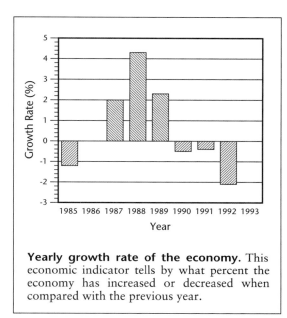

Yearly growth rate of the economy. This economic indicator tells by what percent the economy has increased or decreased when compared with the previous year.

ical corps of 8,000. In 1993, there were 135,000 active members of the citizen force and 140,000 commandos. In 1993, South Africa spent $3.5 billion on defense.

17 ECONOMY

The opening of the political process to all South Africans and the election of a new multiracial government in 1994 have marked a turning point in South Africa's economic history. With modest agriculture, fabulous mineral wealth, and diverse manufacturing, South Africa's influence extends well beyond its borders.

Before the 1994 elections, there were a number of state-owned enterprises existing jointly with a strong private sector. For the past five years, the economy has been in recession with recovery dependent on the world economy, continued growth

in the country's exports, and greater access to foreign capital following the lifting of trade and financial sanctions.

18 INCOME

In 1992 South Africa's gross national product (GNP) was $106.019 billion at current prices, or about $2,980 per person. For the period 1985–92 the average annual inflation rate was 14.4%, resulting in a real growth rate in per person GNP of −1.3%.

19 INDUSTRY

Manufacturing is the largest contributor to South Africa's economy. Industry is located mainly in the southern Transvaal, western Cape, Durban-Pinetown and Port Elizabeth-Uitenhage areas. The largest industrial area is the metal products and engineering sector. The steel industry supplies a large motor vehicle sector. The food, beverage, and tobacco industry is expanding, employing 16% of the manufacturing labor force, and the clothing and textiles sector produces 90% of local needs. The chemical sector centers on fertilizer production and an explosives factory. The synthetic fuels production industry, with three plants in operation, serves 40% of the nation's motor fuels demand.

20 LABOR

In 1992, unemployment reached an estimated 42%, with over 100,000 jobs lost in manufacturing, mining, and construction. As of mid-1991, 11,624,000 persons were classified as economically active; the labor force is expected to grow by nearly

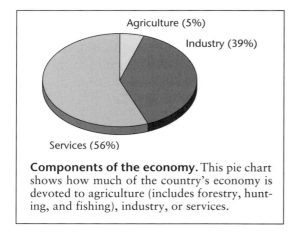

Agriculture (5%)

Industry (39%)

Services (56%)

Components of the economy. This pie chart shows how much of the country's economy is devoted to agriculture (includes forestry, hunting, and fishing), industry, or services.

working conditions and accident prevention measures. Workers' compensation, financed by employers, covers employees killed or injured at work, and compensation is payable in the case of occupational diseases. Unemployment insurance is paid to some contributing employees.

Minimum age laws regulate the use of child labor in business and industry but not in agriculture or the informal economy, where abuses are common.

21 AGRICULTURE

The worst drought of this century in southern Africa resulted in near to total crop failure in 1991–92. Many farmers subsequently abandoned the countryside for urban areas. During 1992, total agricultural production fell by 16.8%. Production levels for specific crops fell as much as 75%. Nevertheless, except for rice, tea, coffee, and cocoa, the country is typically self-sufficient in essential food production.

The principal crop of both whites and blacks is corn ("mealies")—the staple diet of the blacks. Output totaled 3,125,000 tons in 1992. Wheat can be grown only in winter; production of wheat totaled 1,269,000 tons in 1992. A native sorghum ("Kaffir corn") is used by the blacks to make beer and is an important source of protein in their diet. Less important, but planted in considerable quantities, are the other winter cereals—barley, oats, and rye. Potatoes are produced in large quantities. Sugarcane production totaled 18,500,000 tons in 1992.

50% during the rest of the decade, reaching 18 million by 2000. In 1991, there were 1,417,127 workers in manufacturing, the majority of whom were nonwhite. In that year, of the 840,747 persons employed in mining, the great majority was black. In 1982, an estimated 2,168,000 blacks from the ten black homelands (including the formerly "independent" homelands) worked in South Africa as commuters or legal migratory workers.

At the end of 1992, there were 200 registered trade unions. Black trade unions were not officially recognized until 1979, when the law was modified to allow blacks not assigned to black homelands to join black trade unions. The number of strikes increased with the growth of black participation in unions. In 1988 there were 1,025 strikes, involving 161,679 workers. In 1992, there were 789 strikes involving 137,946 workers.

Hours of work vary from 40 to 46 per week. Employers must provide satisfactory

22 DOMESTICATED ANIMALS

The country's sheep breeds consist mainly of Merino for wool and Dorpes for mutton. Cattle breeds include the Hereford and Aberdeen Angus as well as the indigenous Afrikaner. Dairy cows are mostly Fresian, forming a well-developed dairy industry. The livestock in 1992 included 32,110,000 sheep, 13,585,000 head of cattle, 5,900,000 goats, 1,490,000 hogs, and 40 million chickens. Total estimated output of livestock products in 1992 included meat, 1,392,000 tons; milk, 2,390,000 tons; eggs, 221,200,000 tons; and wool, 145,500 tons.

23 FISHING

South Africa is Africa's most important fishing nation. In 1993, about 22,000 people were employed in the fishing industry. In 1991, the fish catch amounted to 498,884 tons. Abalone, hake, kingklip, rock lobster, pilchard, anchovy, oysters, mussels, octopus, and shark were the main varieties caught. Hake accounts for 70% of all domestic white fish sales. Major fishery products are fish meal, canned fish, and fish oil. About 1,835 tons of rock lobster were caught in 1991, with much of it processed into frozen lobster tails for export.

24 FORESTRY

South Africa is sparsely wooded, with a wooded and forested area of about 4.5 million hectares (11.1 million acres), or less than 4% of the land area. Commercial forestry covers 1.2 million hectares (3 million acres), with pine and commercial softwoods, eucalyptus, and wattle the principal timbers produced. Domestic timber production satisfies 90% of domestic needs.

25 MINING

Since the latter part of the nineteenth century, the South African economy has been based on the production and export of minerals. Taxation of mining enterprises has supported South African agriculture and financed many of the country's administrative and social needs. The railways were built mainly to transport mineral products, and minerals still form a major part of rail freight.

As of 1991, South Africa produced 28% of the world's gold metal, 38% of its chrome ore, 36% of manganese, and 8% of diamonds. South Africa leads the world in the production of gem diamonds and ferrochromium. It is also a leading producer of platinum-group metals, uranium, vermiculite, antimony, industrial diamonds, and asbestos. Other minerals produced include corundum, nickel, talc, copper, tin, and silver. The country also has much coal and iron ore and all the materials needed for alloying steel, a factor of great importance for its industrial development.

In 1991, iron ore production rose to nearly 29 million tons, and coal output increased to 178 million tons. In 1991, 83 gold mines were in production. Gold production totaled 601 tons in 1991. South Africa claims 75% of the world's chromite reserves; production in 1991 totaled 5.1 million tons. South Africa's diamond production in 1991 totaled 8,421,000 carats. Dimension stone is also quarried and

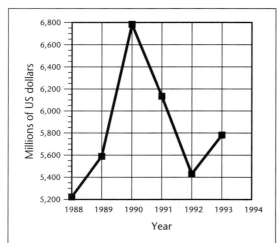

Yearly balance of trade measured in millions of US dollars. The balance of trade is the difference between what a country sells to other countries (its exports) and what it buys (its imports). If a country imports more than it exports, it has a negative balance of trade (a trade deficit). If exports exceed imports there is a positive balance of trade (a trade surplus).

exported (500,000 tons in 1991). The value of all exported minerals in 1991 was $12.5 billion, representing more than 52% of total exports.

26 FOREIGN TRADE

Gold and other metals and minerals are the most valuable export commodities. In the 1980s, both the United States and the European Economic Community (EEC) banned a number of South African imports to protest South Africa's racial policies. These bans were lifted as progress was made toward the 1994 transition to a multiracial government.

The principal exports in 1992 were base metals, precious stones, and mineral products. By far the largest expenditures on imports are for machinery (28.8%), chemicals, and motor vehicles. The leading buyer of South African exports in 1991 was Switzerland (8.9%), followed by the United Kingdom (7.8%), Japan (6.3%), the United States (6.2%) and Germany (5.3%). Imports came from Germany (17.6%), the United States (13.7%), Japan (10.6%), and the United Kingdom (10.3%).

27 ENERGY AND POWER

South Africa produces at least half of all electricity generated on the African continent. Coal supplies about 80% of the country's primary energy needs. Electric generation totaled 163,500 million kilowatt hours in 1991. South Africa's electricity consumption is 147 billion kilowatt hours (1990). Seventeen coal-fired plants accounted for 88.5% of installed capacity; nuclear power, 5.1%; and hydroelectric power, 1.5%. Net generating capacity totaled 26,500 megawatts at the end of 1991.

South Africa produces no crude oil, but does have four crude oil refineries whose current combined annual distillation capacity is about 21.5 million tons. Africa's only nuclear power station, at Koeburg near Cape Town, began operating in 1984.

28 SOCIAL DEVELOPMENT

South Africa has a comprehensive system of social legislation, which includes unemployment insurance, industrial accident insurance, old age pensions, disability pensions, war veterans' pensions, pensions for

Selected Social Indicators

These statistics are estimates for the period 1988 to 1993. For comparison purposes, data for the United States and averages for low-income countries and high-income countries are also given.

Indicator	South Africa	Low-income countries	High-income countries	United States
Per capita gross national product†	**$2,980**	$380	$23,680	$24,740
Population growth rate	**2.3%**	1.9%	0.6%	1.0%
Population growth rate in urban areas	**2.9%**	3.9%	0.8%	1.3%
Population per square kilometer of land	**32**	78	25	26
Life expectancy in years	**63**	62	77	76
Number of people per physician	**610**	>3,300	453	419
Number of pupils per teacher (primary school)	**n.a.**	39	<18	20
Illiteracy rate (15 years and older)	**24%**	41%	<5%	<3%
Energy consumed per capita (kg of oil equivalent)	**2,399**	364	5,203	7,918

† The gross national product (GNP) is the total dollar value of all goods and services produced by a country in a year. The per capita GNP is calculated by dividing a country's GNP by its population. The World Bank defines low-income countries as those with a per capita GNP of $695 or less. High-income countries have a per capita GNP of $8,626 or more. Less than 14% of the world's 5.5 billion people live in high-income countries, while almost 60% live in low-income countries.

n.a. = data not available   > = greater than   < = less than

Sources: World Bank, *Social Indicators of Development 1995,* Baltimore: Johns Hopkins University Press, 1995. Central Intelligence Agency, *World Fact Book,* Washington, D.C.: Government Printing Office, 1994.

the blind, and maternity grants. In addition, there are about 25 major private welfare organizations partly subsidized by government funds. A variety of pension funds also have been established by railways, commercial and business firms, and the gold-mining industry for the protection of employees and their families.

The current African National Congress (ANC) "government of national unity" is seeking to provide more social services for its black constituents within the context of the constraints of a weakened economy. Its first priorities are housing, health, education, and the creation of more jobs in the formal economic sector.

29 HEALTH

As of 1992, the South African government increased its spending in the public and private sectors of health care.

South Africa's governmental policy has been directed toward a more streamlined and equitable public health service to bridge the country's social and ideological divisions. With apartheid dissolved and a new 1994 government in place, other new programs may come into being. Provincial administrations maintain most major hos-

Photo credit: Cynthia Bassett

A typical early 19th century house with black thatch roofing and wood doors and trim.

pitals and receive subsidies from the national government. Hospital care is free for those unable to bear the costs, including nonwhites, but medical treatment is generally conducted on a private basis.

In 1990, there were 684 hospitals, with Baragwanath Hospital near Johannesburg the largest in southern Africa (nearly 3,000 beds). Private health care equaled 35% of total health care expenditures in 1990 ($5.7 billion) and was growing fast. In 1989 there were 22,260 physicians and, in 1992, there was 1 doctor per 610 people. There are medical schools at six universities in South Africa.

The most prevalent infectious diseases reported in South Africa in 1984 were tuberculosis, measles, typhoid, malaria, and viral hepatitis. Circulatory disorders are the leading causes of death. By 1990, leprosy had been reduced to less than 1 per 100,000, but malaria and tuberculosis still cause serious problems. In 1990, there were 250 cases of tuberculosis per 100,000 people and 650 cases of AIDS. Average life expectancy was 63 years in 1992.

30 HOUSING

In 1994, the housing backlog was estimated to be 1.2 million homes for the black population, while there is a surplus of white housing units of 83,000. Experts in South Africa forecast that almost 3 million homes will have to be provided by the year 2000 in the urban areas of the country. Recently, there has been an explosive growth of shacks and shantytowns surrounding South Africa's major urban areas. An estimated 66% of the country's population have no access to electricity, and in most black townships there is only one water tap per several thousand people.

31 EDUCATION

Systems of primary, secondary, and university education are generally provided in separate English-language and Afrikaans-language institutions. Adult literacy was close to 100% for whites and about 50% for blacks in the mid-1980s. After the Soweto riots of 1976, the national government has greatly increased expenditures for black education, and black student enrollment rose sharply. The government reported in 1991 that primary and secondary schools combined had 1,021,442 white students, 5,794,100 blacks, 874,315 coloured, and 225,529 Asians.

In 1991, there were 21 universities and even those universities that were not admitting students from other races prior to the 1980s started admitting them. In 1984, there were 198,675 students enrolled in these universities, including about 7,500 nonwhites. In that year, 19,231 students were enrolled in the four black universities. The University of the Western Cape is for Coloureds, and the University of Durban-Westville is for Indians. In 1984, 11,160 students were enrolled at these two universities. In 1991, all university-level students were estimated as follows: 157,432 whites; 110,130 blacks; 19,575 coloureds; and 21,035 Asians.

32 MEDIA

The government operates the postal, telegraph, and telephone services through the Department of Posts and Telecommunications. In 1992, there were over 4.5 million telephones. The South African Broadcasting Corporation (SABC), a semigovernmental organization, offers transmissions in English, Afrikaans, and nine Bantu languages. The country's first television service was begun in January 1976 under government auspices. In 1981, a separate channel began broadcasting to blacks in native languages. In 1986, there were four commercial broadcasting services, with transmissions in English, Afrikaans, and four Bantu languages. There were an estimated 3,800,000 television sets and 11,800,000 radios in 1991.

The English and Afrikaans populations have their own newspapers, distinguished not only by language but also by the variety and slant of news. Two Sunday newspapers are published in Johannesburg and two in Durban, of which one is in Afrikaans and three are in English. About 150 local newspapers appear weekly or biweekly. Magazines and general periodicals are divided equally between Afrikaans and English.

33 TOURISM AND RECREATION

In 1991, international sanctions against tourism were lifted with the support of the

ANC, and tourist arrivals rose to 1.7 million. There were 45,215 hotel rooms with a 49.6% occupancy rate.

In addition to the principal cities and many ocean beaches, popular attractions include the Kruger National Park, situated in the northeast on the Mozambique and Zimbabwe borders, and several game reserves; the Castle of Good Hope fortress at Cape Town (built during 1666–82); and the Kimberley Mine Museum at the site of the famous Big Hole diamond mine. Entertainment facilities include symphony halls, theaters, movies, nightclubs, and discos. Among popular pastimes are golf, tennis, bowls, hunting, horse racing, rugby, soccer, cricket, and water sports.

34 FAMOUS SOUTH AFRICANS

Among the most famous tribal leaders in what is now South Africa were Shaka (1773–1828), who built the Zulu into a powerful nation, and Cetewayo (d.1884), who led the Zulu in an unsuccessful war against the British in 1879. Jan Christiaan Smuts (1870–1950) was a renowned statesman and military leader.

Among the best-known South African writers in the English language was Olive (Emily Albertina) Schreiner (1855–1920), whose *Story of an African Farm* has become a classic. Well-known authors and poets in the Afrikaans language are Cornelis Jacob Langenhoven (1873–1932), author of the national anthem; and N.P. van Wyk Louw (1906–70). Breyten Breytenbach (b.1939) has earned international recognition as an important Afrikaans poet. V. (J.E.A.) Volschenck (1853–1935) is sometimes called the "father of South African art." Christiaan Neething Barnard (b.1922) pioneered open heart surgery.

South Africa's first Nobel Prize winner (for peace in 1961) was Chief Albert John Luthuli (1898–1967), a former president of the ANC. Desmond Mpilo Tutu (b.1931), the secretary general of the South African Council of Churches during 1979–84 and an outspoken foe of apartheid, received the 1984 Nobel Prize for peace. Nelson R. Mandela (b.1918), a prominent leader of the ANC, was sentenced to life imprisonment in 1964; he was released in 1990 and elected president of South Africa in April 1994.

35 BIBLIOGRAPHY

Brink, André. "The Afrikaners." *National Geographic,* October 1988, 556–585.
Cobb, Charles E., Jr. "The Twilight of Apartheid." *National Geographic,* February 1993, 66–94.
Davenport, T. R. H. *South Africa: A Modern History.* 3d ed. Toronto: University of Toronto Press, 1987.
Mandela, Nelson. *The Struggle Is My Life.* Rev. ed. New York: Pathfinders, 1986.
Stein, R. *South Africa.* Chicago: Children's Press, 1986.
Smith, David Marshall. *Apartheid in South Africa, 3d ed.* Cambridge; New York: Cambridge University Press, 1990.
Thompson, Leonard Monteath. *A History of South Africa.* New Haven: Yale University Press, 1990.
Watson, R. L. *South Africa in Pictures.* Minneapolis: Lerner Publications Co., 1988.
Woods, Donald. *Biko.* 3d rev. ed. New York: H. Holt, 1991.

aboriginal: The first known inhabitants of a country. A species of animals or plants which originated within a given area.

acid rain: Rain (or snow) that has become slightly acid by mixing with industrial air pollution.

adobe: A brick made from sun-dried heavy clay mixed with straw, used in building houses. A house made of adobe bricks.

adult literacy: The ability of adults to read and write.

afforestation: The act of turning arable land into forest or woodland.

agrarian economy: An economy where agriculture is the dominant form of economic activity. A society where agriculture dominates the day-to-day activities of the population is called an agrarian society.

air link: Refers to scheduled air service that allows people and goods to travel between two places on a regular basis.

airborne industrial pollutant: Pollution caused by industry that is supported or carried by the air.

allies: Groups or persons who are united in a common purpose. Typically used to describe nations that have joined together to fight a common enemy in war.

In World War I, the term Allies described the nations that fought against Germany and its allies. In World War II, Allies described the United Kingdom, United States, the USSR and their allies, who fought against the Axis Powers of Germany, Italy, and Japan.

aloe: A plant particularly abundant in the southern part of Africa, where leaves of some species are made into ropes, fishing lines, bow strings, and hammocks. It is also a symbolic plant in the Islamic world; anyone who returns from a pilgrimage to Mecca (Mekkah) hangs aloe over his door as a token that he has performed the journey.

Altaic language family: A family of languages spoken in portions of northern and eastern Europe, and nearly the whole of northern and central Asia, together with some other regions. The family is divided into five branches: the Ugrian or Finno-Hungarian, Smoyed, Turkish, Mongolian, and Tunguse.

althing: A legislative assembly.

amendment: A change or addition to a document.

Amerindian: A contraction of the two words, American Indian. It describes native peoples of North, South, or Central America.

amnesty: An act of forgiveness or pardon, usually taken by a government, toward persons for crimes they may have committed.

Anglican: Pertaining to or connected with the Church of England.

animism: The belief that natural objects and phenomena have souls or innate spiritual powers.

annual growth rate: The rate at which something grows over a period of 12 months.

annual inflation rate: The rate of inflation in prices over the course of a year.

anthracite coal: Also called hard coal, it is usually 90 to 95 percent carbon, and burns cleanly, almost without a flame.

anti-Semitism: Agitation, persecution, or discrimination (physical, emotional, economic, political, or otherwise) directed against the Jews.

apartheid: The past governmental policy in the Republic of South Africa of separating the races in society.

appeasement: To bring to a state of peace.

appellate: Refers to an appeal of a court decision to a high authority.

applied science: Scientific techniques employed to achieve results that solve practical problems.

aquaculture: The culture or "farming" of aquatic plants or other natural produce, as in the raising of catfish in "farms."

aquatic resources: Resources that come from, grow in, or live in water, including fish and plants.

aquifer: An underground layer of porous rock, sand, or gravel that holds water.

arable land: Land that can be cultivated by plowing and used for growing crops.

arbitration: A process whereby disputes are settled by a designated person, called the arbitrator, instead of by a court of law.

archipelago: Any body of water abounding with islands, or the islands themselves collectively.

archives: A place where records or a collection of important documents are kept.

arctic climate: Cold, frigid weather similar to that experienced at or near the north pole.

aristocracy: A small minority that controls the government of a nation, typically on the basis of inherited wealth.

armistice: An agreement or truce which ends military conflict in anticipation of a peace treaty.

artesian well: A type of well where the water rises to the surface and overflows.

ASEAN *see* Association of Southeast Asian Nations

Association of Southeast Asian Nations: ASEAN was established in 1967 to promote political, economic, and social cooperation among its six member countries: Indonesia, Malaysia, the Philippines, Singapore, Thailand, and Brunei. ASEAN headquarters are in Jakarta, Indonesia. In January 1992, ASEAN agreed to create the ASEAN Free Trade Area (AFTA).

atheist: A person who denies the existence of God or of a supreme intelligent being.

atoll: A coral island, consisting of a strip or ring of coral surrounding a central lagoon.

atomic weapons: Weapons whose extremely violent explosive power comes from the splitting of the nuclei of atoms (usually uranium or plutonium) by neutrons in a rapid chain reaction. These weapons may be referred to as atom bombs, hydrogen bombs, or H-bombs.

austerity measures: Steps taken by a government to conserve money or resources during an economically difficult time, such as cutting back on federally funded programs.

Australoid: Pertains to the type of aborigines, or earliest inhabitants, of Australia.

Austronesian language: A family of languages which includes practically all the languages of the Pacific Islands—Indonesian, Melanesian, Polynesian, and Micronesian sub-families. Does not include Australian or Papuan languages.

authoritarianism: A form of government in which a person or group attempts to rule with absolute authority without the representation of the citizens.

autonomous state: A country which is completely self-governing, as opposed to being a dependency or part of another country.

autonomy: The state of existing as a self-governing entity. For instance, when a country gains its independence from another country, it gains autonomy.

average inflation rate: The average rate at which the general prices of goods and services increase over the period of a year.

average life expectancy: In any given society, the average age attained by persons at the time of death.

Axis Powers: The countries aligned against the Allied Nations in World War II, originally applied to Nazi Germany and Fascist Italy (Rome-Berlin Axis), and later extended to include Japan.

bagasse: Plant residue left after a product, such as juice, has been extracted.

Baha'i: The follower of a religious sect founded by Mirza Husayn Ali in Iran in 1863.

Baltic states. The three formerly communist countries of Estonia, Latvia, and Lithuania that border on the Baltic Sea.

Bantu language group: A name applied to the languages spoken in central and south Africa.

banyan tree: An East Indian fig tree. Individual trees develop roots from the branches that descend to the ground and become trunks. These roots support and nourish the crown of the tree.

Baptist: A member of a Protestant denomination that practices adult baptism by complete immersion in water.

barren land: Unproductive land, partly or entirely treeless.

barter: Trade practice where merchandise is exchanged directly for other merchandise or services without use of money.

bedrock: Solid rock lying under loose earth.

bicameral legislature: A legislative body consisting of two chambers, such as the U.S. House of Representatives and the U.S. Senate.

bill of rights: A written statement containing the list of privileges and powers to be granted to a body of people, usually introduced when a government or other organization is forming.

bituminous coal: Soft coal; coal which burns with a bright-yellow flame.

black market: A system of trade where goods are sold illegally, often for excessively inflated prices. This type of trade usually develops to avoid paying taxes or tariffs levied by the government, or to get around import or export restrictions on products.

bloodless coup: The sudden takeover of a country's government by hostile means but without killing anyone in the process.

boat people: Used to describe individuals (refugees) who attempt to flee their country by boat.

bog: Wet, soft, and spongy ground where the soil is composed mainly of decayed or decaying vegetable matter.

Bolshevik Revolution. A revolution in 1917 in Russia when a wing of the Russian Social Democratic party seized power. The Bolsheviks advocated the violent overthrow of capitalism.

bonded labor: Workers bound to service without pay; slaves.

border dispute: A disagreement between two countries as to the exact location or length of the dividing line between them.

Brahman: A member (by heredity) of the highest caste among the Hindus, usually assigned to the priesthood.

broadleaf forest: A forest composed mainly of broadleaf (deciduous) trees.

Buddhism: A religious system common in India and eastern Asia. Founded by and based upon the teachings of Siddhartha Gautama, Buddhism asserts that suffering is an inescapable part of life. Deliverance can only be achieved through the practice of charity, temperance, justice, honesty, and truth.

buffer state: A small country that lies between two larger, possibly hostile countries, considered to be a neutralizing force between them.

bureaucracy: A system of government that is characterized by division into bureaus of administration with their own divisional heads. Also refers to the inflexible procedures of such a system that often result in delay.

Byzantine Empire: An empire centered in the city of Byzantium, now Istanbul in present-day Turkey.

CACM *see* Central American Common Market.

candlewood: A name given to several species of trees and shrubs found in the British West Indies, northern Mexico, and the southwestern United States. The plants are characterized by a very resinous wood.

canton: A territory or small division or state within a country.

capital punishment: The ultimate act of punishment for a crime, the death penalty.

capitalism: An economic system in which goods and services and the means to produce and sell them are privately owned, and prices and wages are determined by market forces.

Caribbean Community and Common Market (CARICOM): Founded in 1973 and with its headquarters in Georgetown, Guyana, CARICOM seeks the establishment of a common trade policy and increased cooperation in the Caribbean region. Includes 13 English-speaking Caribbean nations: Antigua and Barbuda, the Bahamas, Barbados, Belize, Dominica, Grenada, Guyana, Jamaica, Montserrat, Saint Kitts-Nevis, Saint Lucia, St. Vincent/Grenadines, and Trinidad and Tobago.

CARICOM *see* Caribbean Community and Common Market.

carnivore: Flesh-eating animal or plant.

carob: The common English name for a plant that is similar to and sometimes used as a substitute for chocolate.

cartel: An organization of independent producers formed to regulate the production, pricing, or marketing practices of its members in order to limit competition and maximize their market power.

cash crop: A crop that is grown to be sold rather than kept for private use.

cassation: The reversal or annulling of a final judgment by the supreme authority.

cassava: The name of several species of stout herbs, extensively cultivated for food.

caste system: One of the artificial divisions or social classes into which the Hindus are rigidly separated according to the religious law of Brahmanism. Membership in a caste is hereditary, and the privileges and disabilities of each caste are transmitted by inheritance.

Caucasian: The white race of human beings, as determined by genealogy and physical features.

Caucasoid: Belonging to the racial group characterized by light skin pigmentation. Commonly called the "white race."

cease-fire: An official declaration of the end to the use of military force or active hostilities, even if only temporary.

CEMA *see* Council for Mutual Economic Assistance.

censorship: The practice of withholding certain items of news that may cast a country in an unfavorable light or give away secrets to the enemy.

census: An official counting of the inhabitants of a state or country with details of sex and age, family, occupation, possessions, etc.

Central American Common Market (CACM): Established in 1962, a trade alliance of five Central American nations. Participating are Costa Rica, El Salvador, Guatemala, Honduras, and Nicaragua.

Central Powers: In World War I, Germany and Austria-Hungary, and their allies, Turkey and Bulgaria.

centrally planned economy: An economic system all aspects of which are supervised and regulated by the government.

centrist position: Refers to opinions held by members of a moderate political group; that is, views that are somewhere in the middle of popular thought between conservative and liberal.

cession: Withdrawal from or yielding to physical force.

chancellor: A high-ranking government official. In some countries it is the prime minister.

cholera: An acute infectious disease characterized by severe diarrhea, vomiting, and, often, death.

Christianity: The religion founded by Jesus Christ, based on the Bible as holy scripture.

Church of England: The national and established church in England. The Church of England claims continuity with the branch of the Catholic Church that existed in England before the Reformation. Under Henry VIII, the spiritual supremacy and jurisdiction of the Pope were abolished, and the sovereign (king or queen) was declared head of the church.

circuit court: A court that convenes in two or more locations within its appointed district.

CIS *see* Commonwealth of Independent States

city-state: An independent state consisting of a city and its surrounding territory.

civil court: A court whose proceedings include determinations of rights of individual citizens, in contrast to criminal proceedings regarding individuals or the public.

civil jurisdiction: The authority to enforce the laws in civil matters brought before the court.

civil law: The law developed by a nation or state for the conduct of daily life of its own people.

civil rights: The privileges of all individuals to be treated as equals under the laws of their country; specifically, the rights given by certain amendments to the U.S. Constitution.

civil unrest: The feeling of uneasiness due to an unstable political climate, or actions taken as a result of it.

civil war: A war between groups of citizens of the same country who have different opinions or agendas. The Civil War of the United States was the conflict between the states of the North and South from 1861 to 1865.

climatic belt: A region or zone where a particular type of climate prevails.

Club du Sahel: The Club du Sahel is an informal coalition which seeks to reverse the effects of drought and the desertification in the eight Sahelian zone countries: Burkina Faso, Chad, Gambia, Mali, Mauritania, Niger, Senegal, and the Cape Verde Islands. Headquarters are in Ouagadougou, Burkina Faso.

CMEA *see* Council for Mutual Economic Assistance.

coalition government: A government combining differing factions within a country, usually temporary.

coastal belt: A coastal plain area of lowlands and somewhat higher ridges that run parallel to the coast.

coastal plain: A fairly level area of land along the coast of a land mass.

coca: A shrub native to South America, the leaves of which produce organic compounds that are used in the production of cocaine.

coke: The solid product of the carbonization of coal, bearing the same relation to coal that charcoal does to wood.

cold war: Refers to conflict over ideological differences that is carried on by words and diplomatic actions, not by military action. The term is usually used to refer to the tension that existed between the United States and the USSR from the 1950s until the breakup of the USSR in 1991.

collective bargaining: The negotiations between workers who are members of a union and their employer for the purpose of deciding work rules and policies regarding wages, hours, etc.

collective farm: A large farm formed from many small farms and supervised by the government; usually found in communist countries.

collective farming: The system of farming on a collective where all workers share in the income of the farm.

colloquial: Belonging to ordinary, everyday speech: often especially applied to common words and phrases which are not used in formal speech.

colonial period: The period of time when a country forms colonies in and extends control over a foreign area.

colonist: Any member of a colony or one who helps settle a new colony.

colony: A group of people who settle in a new area far from their original country, but still under the jurisdiction of that country. Also refers to the newly settled area itself.

COMECON *see* Council for Mutual Economic Assistance.

commerce: The trading of goods (buying and selling), especially on a large scale, between cities, states, and countries.

commercial catch: The amount of marketable fish, usually measured in tons, caught in a particular period of time.

commercial crop: Any marketable agricultural crop.

commission: A group of people designated to collectively do a job, including a government agency with certain law-making powers. Also, the power given to an individual or group to perform certain duties.

commodity: Any items, such as goods or services, that are bought or sold, or agricultural products that are traded or marketed.

common law: A legal system based on custom and decisions and opinions of the law courts. The basic system of law of England and the United States.

common market: An economic union among countries that is formed to remove trade barriers (tariffs) among those countries, increasing economic cooperation. The European Community is a notable example of a common market.

commonwealth: A commonwealth is a free association of sovereign independent states that has no charter, treaty, or constitution. The association promotes cooperation, consultation, and mutual assistance among members.

Commonwealth of Independent States: The CIS was established in December 1991 as an association of 11 republics of the former Soviet Union. The members include: Russia, Ukraine, Belarus (formerly Byelorussia), Moldova (formerly Moldavia), Armenia, Azerbaijan, Uzbekistan, Turkmenistan, Tajikistan, Kazakhstan, and Kirgizstan (formerly Kirghiziya). The Baltic states—Estonia, Latvia, and Lithuania—did not join. Georgia maintained observer status before joining the CIS in November 1993.

Commonwealth of Nations: Voluntary association of the United Kingdom and its present dependencies and associated states, as well as certain former dependencies and their dependent territories. The term was first used officially in 1926 and is embodied in the Statute of Westminster (1931). Within the Commonwealth, whose secretariat (established in 1965) is located in London, England, are numerous subgroups devoted to economic and technical cooperation.

commune: An organization of people living together in a community who share the ownership and use of property. Also refers to a small governmental district of a country, especially in Europe.

communism: A form of government whose system requires common ownership of property for the use of all citizens. All profits are to be equally distributed and prices on goods and services are usually set by the state. Also, communism refers directly to the official doctrine of the former U.S.S.R.

compulsory: Required by law or other regulation.

compulsory education: The mandatory requirement for children to attend school until they have reached a certain age or grade level.

conciliation: A process of bringing together opposing sides of a disagreement for the purpose of compromise. Or, a way of settling an international dispute in which the disagreement is submitted to an independent committee that will examine the facts and advise the participants of a possible solution.

concordat: An agreement, compact, or convention, especially between church and state.

confederation: An alliance or league formed for the purpose of promoting the common interests of its members.

Confucianism: The system of ethics and politics taught by the Chinese philosopher Confucius.

coniferous forest: A forest consisting mainly of pine, fir, and cypress trees.

conifers: Cone-bearing plants. Mostly evergreen trees and shrubs which produce cones.

conscription: To be required to join the military by law. Also known as the draft. Service personnel who join the military because of the legal requirement are called conscripts or draftees.

conservative party: A political group whose philosophy tends to be based on established traditions and not supportive of rapid change.

constituency: The registered voters in a governmental district, or a group of people that supports a position or a candidate.

constituent assembly: A group of people that has the power to determine the election of a political representative or create a constitution.

constitution: The written laws and basic rights of citizens of a country or members of an organized group.

constitutional monarchy: A system of government in which the hereditary sovereign (king or queen, usually) rules according to a written constitution.

constitutional republic: A system of government with an elected chief of state and elected representation, with a written constitution containing its governing principles. The United States is a constitutional republic.

consumer goods: Items that are bought to satisfy personal needs or wants of individuals.

continental climate: The climate of a part of the continent; the characteristics and peculiarities of the climate are a result of the land itself and its location.

continental shelf: A plain extending from the continental coast and varying in width that typically ends in a steep slope to the ocean floor.

copra: The dried meat of the coconut; it is frequently used as an ingredient of curry, and to produce coconut oil. Also written *cobra, coprah,* and *copperah.*

Coptic Christians: Members of the Coptic Church of Egypt, formerly of Ethiopia.

cordillera: A continuous ridge, range, or chain of mountains.

corvette: A small warship that is often used as an escort ship because it is easier to maneuver than larger ships like destroyers.

Council for Mutual Economic Assistance (CMEA): Also known as Comecon, the alliance of socialist economies was established on 25 January 1949 and abolished 1 January 1991. It included Afghanistan*, Albania, Angola*, Bulgaria, Cuba, Czechoslovakia, Ethiopia*, East Germany, Hungary, Laos*, Mongolia, Mozambique*, Nicaragua*, Poland, Romania, USSR, Vietnam, Yemen*, and Yugoslavia. Nations marked with an asterisk were observers only.

counterinsurgency operations: Organized military activity designed to stop rebellion against an established government.

county: A territorial division or administrative unit within a state or country.

coup d'ètat or coup: A sudden, violent overthrow of a government or its leader.

court of appeal: An appellate court, having the power of review after a case has been decided in a lower court.

court of first appeal: The next highest court to the court which has decided a case, to which that case may be presented for review.

court of last appeal: The highest court, in which a decision is not subject to review by any higher court. In the United States, it could be the Supreme Court of an individual state or the U.S. Supreme Court.

cricket (sport): A game played by two teams with a ball and bat, with two wickets (staked target) being defended by a batsman. Common in the United Kingdom and Commonwealth of Nations countries.

criminal law: The branch of law that deals primarily with crimes and their punishments.

crown colony: A colony established by a commonwealth over which the monarch has some control, as in colonies established by the United Kingdom's Commonwealth of Nations.

Crusades: Military expeditions by European Christian armies in the eleventh, twelfth, and thirteenth centuries to win land controlled by the Muslims in the middle east.

cultivable land: Land that can be prepared for the production of crops.

Cultural Revolution: An extreme reform movement in China from 1966 to 1976; its goal was to combat liberalization by restoring the ideas of Mao Zedong.

Cushitic language group: A group of Hamitic languages that are spoken in Ethiopia and other areas of eastern Africa.

customs union: An agreement between two or more countries to remove trade barriers with each other and to establish common tariff and nontariff policies with respect to imports from countries outside of the agreement.

cyclone: Any atmospheric movement, general or local, in which the wind blows spirally around and in towards a center. In the northern hemisphere, the cyclonic movement is usually counter-clockwise, and in the southern hemisphere, it is clockwise.

Cyrillic alphabet: An alphabet adopted by the Slavic people and invented by Cyril and Methodius in the ninth century as an alphabet that was easier for the copyist to write. The Russian alphabet is a slight modification of it.

decentralization: The redistribution of power in a government from one large central authority to a wider range of smaller local authorities.

deciduous species: Any species that sheds or casts off a part of itself after a definite period of time. More commonly used in reference to plants that shed their leaves on a yearly basis as opposed to those (evergreens) that retain them.

declaration of independence: A formal written document stating the intent of a group of persons to become fully self-governing.

deficit: The amount of money that is in excess between spending and income.

deficit spending: The process in which a government spends money on goods and services in excess of its income.

deforestation: The removal or clearing of a forest.

deity: A being with the attributes, nature, and essence of a god; a divinity.

delta: Triangular-shaped deposits of soil formed at the mouths of large rivers.

demarcate: To mark off from adjoining land or territory; set the limits or boundaries of.

demilitarized zone (DMZ): An area surrounded by a combat zone that has had military troops and weapons removed.

demobilize: To disband or discharge military troops.

democracy: A form of government in which the power lies in the hands of the people, who can govern directly, or can be governed indirectly by representatives elected by its citizens.

denationalize: To remove from government ownership or control.

deportation: To carry away or remove from one country to another, or to a distant place.

depression: A hollow; a surface that has sunken or fallen in.

deregulation: The act of reversing controls and restrictions on prices of goods, bank interest, and the like.

desalinization plant: A facility that produces freshwater by removing the salt from saltwater.

desegregation: The act of removing restrictions on people of a particular race that keep them socially, economically, and, sometimes, physically, separate from other groups.

desertification: The process of becoming a desert as a result of climatic changes, land mismanagement, or both.

détente: The official lessening of tension between countries in conflict.

devaluation: The official lowering of the value of a country's currency in relation to the value of gold or the currencies of other countries.

developed countries: Countries which have a high standard of living and a well-developed industrial base.

development assistance: Government programs intended to finance and promote the growth of new industries.

dialect: One of a number of regional or related modes of speech regarded as descending from a common origin.

dictatorship: A form of government in which all the power is retained by an absolute leader or tyrant. There are no rights granted to the people to elect their own representatives.

diplomatic relations: The relationship between countries as conducted by representatives of each government.

direct election: The process of selecting a representative to the government by balloting of the voting public, in contrast to selection by an elected representative of the people.

disarmament: The reduction or depletion of the number of weapons or the size of armed forces.

dissident: A person whose political opinions differ from the majority to the point of rejection.

dogma: A principle, maxim, or tenet held as being firmly established.

domain: The area of land governed by a particular ruler or government, sometimes referring to the ultimate control of that territory.

domestic spending: Money spent by a country's government on goods used, investments, running of the government, and exports and imports.

dominion: A self-governing nation that recognizes the British monarch as chief of state.

dormant volcano: A volcano that has not exhibited any signs of activity for an extended period of time.

dowry: The sum of the property or money that a bride brings to her groom at their marriage.

draft constitution: The preliminary written plans for the new constitution of a country forming a new government.

Druze: A member of a Muslim sect based in Syria, living chiefly in the mountain regions of Lebanon.

dual nationality: The status of an individual who can claim citizenship in two or more countries.

duchy: Any territory under the rule of a duke or duchess.

due process: In law, the application of the legal process to which every citizen has a right, which cannot be denied.

durable goods: Goods or products which are expected to last and perform for several years, such as cars and washing machines.

duty: A tax imposed on imports by the customs authority of a country. Duties are generally based on the value of the goods (*ad valorem* duties), some other factors such as weight or quantity (specific duties), or a combination of value and other factors (compound duties).

dyewoods: Any wood from which dye is extracted.

dynasty: A family line of sovereigns who rule in succession, and the time during which they reign.

earned income: The money paid to an individual in wages or salary.

Eastern Orthodox: The outgrowth of the original Eastern Church of the Eastern Roman Empire, consisting of eastern Europe, western Asia, and Egypt.

EC *see* European Community

ecclesiastical: Pertaining or relating to the church.

echidna: A spiny, toothless anteater of Australia, Tasmania, and New Guinea.

ecological balance: The condition of a healthy, well-functioning ecosystem, which includes all the plants and animals in a natural community together with their environment.

ecology: The branch of science that studies organisms in relationship to other organisms and to their environment.

economic depression: A prolonged period in which there is high unemployment, low production, falling prices, and general business failure.

economically active population: That portion of the people who are employed for wages and are consumers of goods and services.

ecotourism: Broad term that encompasses nature, adventure, and ethnic tourism; responsible or wilderness-sensitive tourism; soft-path or small-scale tourism; low-impact tourism; and sustainable tourism. Scientific, educational, or academic tourism (such as biotourism, archetourism, and geotourism) are also forms of ecotourism.

elected assembly: The persons that comprise a legislative body of a government who received their positions by direct election.

electoral system: A system of choosing government officials by votes cast by qualified citizens.

electoral vote: The votes of the members of the electoral college.

electorate: The people who are qualified to vote in an election.

emancipation: The freeing of persons from any kind of bondage or slavery.

embargo: A legal restriction on commercial ships to enter a country's ports, or any legal restriction of trade.

emigration: Moving from one country or region to another for the purpose of residence.

empire: A group of territories ruled by one sovereign or supreme ruler. Also, the period of time under that rule.

enclave: A territory belonging to one nation that is surrounded by that of another nation.

encroachment: The act of intruding, trespassing, or entering on the rights or possessions of another.

endangered species: A plant or animal species whose existence as a whole is threatened with extinction.

endemic: Anything that is peculiar to and characteristic of a locality or region.

Enlightenment: An intellectual movement of the late seventeenth and eighteenth centuries in which scientific thinking gained a strong foothold and old beliefs were challenged. The idea of absolute monarchy was questioned and people were gradually given more individual rights.

enteric disease: An intestinal disease.

epidemic: As applied to disease, any disease that is temporarily prevalent among people in one place at the same time.

Episcopal: Belonging to or vested in bishops or prelates; characteristic of or pertaining to a bishop or bishops.

ethnolinguistic group: A classification of related languages based on common ethnic origin.

EU *see* European Union

GLOSSARY

European Community: A regional organization created in 1958. Its purpose is to eliminate customs duties and other trade barriers in Europe. It promotes a common external tariff against other countries, a Common Agricultural Policy (CAP), and guarantees of free movement of labor and capital. The original six members were Belgium, France, West Germany, Italy, Luxembourg, and the Netherlands. Denmark, Ireland, and the United Kingdom became members in 1973; Greece joined in 1981; Spain and Portugal in 1986. Other nations continue to join.

European Union: The EU is an umbrella reference to the European Community (EC) and to two European integration efforts introduced by the Maastricht Treaty: Common Foreign and Security Policy (including defense) and Justice and Home Affairs (principally cooperation between police and other authorities on crime, terrorism, and immigration issues).

exports: Goods sold to foreign buyers.

external migration: The movement of people from their native country to another country, as opposed to internal migration, which is the movement of people from one area of a country to another in the same country.

fallout: The precipitation of particles from the atmosphere, often the result of a ground disturbance by volcanic activity or a nuclear explosion.

family planning: The use of birth control to determine the number of children a married couple will have.

Fascism: A political philosophy that holds the good of the nation as more important than the needs of the individual. Fascism also stands for a dictatorial leader and strong oppression of opposition or dissent.

federal: Pertaining to a union of states whose governments are subordinate to a central government.

federation: A union of states or other groups under the authority of a central government.

fetishism: The practice of worshipping a material object that is believed to have mysterious powers residing in it, or is the representation of a deity to which worship may be paid and from which supernatural aid is expected.

feudal estate: The property owned by a lord in medieval Europe under the feudal system.

feudal society: In medieval times, an economic and social structure in which persons could hold land given to them by a lord (nobleman) in return for service to that lord.

final jurisdiction: The final authority in the decision of a legal matter. In the United States, the Supreme Court would have final jurisdiction.

Finno-Ugric language group: A subfamily of languages spoken in northeastern Europe, including Finnish, Hungarian, Estonian, and Lapp.

fiscal year: The twelve months between the settling of financial accounts, not necessarily corresponding to a calendar year beginning on January 1.

fjord: A deep indentation of the land forming a comparatively narrow arm of the sea with more or less steep slopes or cliffs on each side.

fly: The part of a flag opposite and parallel to the one nearest the flagpole.

fodder: Food for cattle, horses, and sheep, such as hay, straw, and other kinds of vegetables.

folk religion: A religion with origins and traditions among the common people of a nation or region that is relevant to their particular life-style.

foreign exchange: Foreign currency that allows foreign countries to conduct financial transactions or settle debts with one another.

foreign policy: The course of action that one government chooses to adopt in relation to a foreign country.

Former Soviet Union: The FSU is a collective reference to republics comprising the former Soviet Union. The term, which has been used as both including and excluding the Baltic republics (Estonia, Latvia, and Lithuania), includes the other 12 republics: Russia, Ukraine, Belarus, Moldova, Armenia, Azerbaijan, Uzbekistan, Turkmenistan, Tajikistan, Kazakhstan, Kyrgizstan, and Georgia.

fossil fuels: Any mineral or mineral substance formed by the decomposition of organic matter buried beneath the earth's surface and used as a fuel.

free enterprise: The system of economics in which private business may be conducted with minimum interference by the government.

free-market economy: An economic system that relies on the market, as opposed to government planners, to set the prices for wages and products.

frigate. A medium-sized warship.

fundamentalist: A person who holds religious beliefs based on the complete acceptance of the words of the Bible or other holy scripture as the truth. For instance, a fundamentalist would believe the story of creation exactly as it is told in the Bible and would reject the idea of evolution.

game reserve: An area of land reserved for wild animals that are hunted for sport or for food.

GDP *see* gross domestic product.

Germanic language group: A large branch of the Indo-European family of languages including German itself, the Scandinavian languages, Dutch, Yiddish, Modern English, Modern Scottish, Afrikaans, and others. The group also includes extinct languages such as Gothic, Old High German, Old Saxon, Old English, Middle English, and the like.

glasnost: President Mikhail Gorbachev's frank revelations in the 1980s about the state of the economy and politics in the Soviet Union; his policy of openness.

global greenhouse gas emissions: Gases released into the atmosphere that contribute to the greenhouse effect, a condition in which the earth's excess heat cannot escape.

global warming: Also called the greenhouse effect. The theorized gradual warming of the earth's climate as a result of the burning of fossil fuels, the use of man-made chemicals, deforestation, etc.

GMT *see* Greenwich Mean Time.

GNP *see* gross national product.

grand duchy: A territory ruled by a nobleman, called a grand duke, who ranks just below a king.

Greek Catholic: A person who is a member of an Orthodox Eastern Church.

Greek Orthodox: The official church of Greece, a self-governing branch of the Orthodox Eastern Church.

Greenwich (Mean) Time: Mean solar time of the meridian at Greenwich, England, used as the basis for standard time throughout most of the world. The world is divided into 24 time zones, and all are related to the prime, or Greenwich mean, zone.

gross domestic product: A measure of the market value of all goods and services produced within the boundaries of a nation, regardless of asset ownership. Unlike gross national product, GDP excludes receipts from that nation's business operations in foreign countries.

gross national product: A measure of the market value of goods and services produced by the labor and property of a nation. Includes receipts from that nation's business operation in foreign countries

groundwater: Water located below the earth's surface, the source from which wells and springs draw their water.

guano: The excrement of seabirds and bats found in various areas around the world. Gathered commercially and sold as a fertilizer.

guerrilla: A member of a small radical military organization that uses unconventional tactics to take their enemies by surprise.

gymnasium: A secondary school, primarily in Europe, that prepares students for university.

hardwoods: The name given to deciduous trees, such as cherry, oak, maple, and mahogany.

harem: In a Muslim household, refers to the women (wives, concubines, and servants in ancient times) who live there and also to the area of the home they live in.

harmattan: An intensely dry, dusty wind felt along the coast of Africa between Cape Verde and Cape Lopez. It prevails at intervals during the months of December, January, and February.

heavy industry: Industries that use heavy or large machinery to produce goods, such as automobile manufacturing.

hoist: The part of a flag nearest the flagpole.

Holocaust: The mass slaughter of European civilians, the vast majority Jews, by the Nazis during World War II.

Holy Roman Empire: A kingdom consisting of a loose union of German and Italian territories that existed from around the ninth century until 1806.

home rule: The governing of a territory by the citizens who inhabit it.

homeland: A region or area set aside to be a state for a people of a particular national, cultural, or racial origin.

homogeneous: Of the same kind or nature, often used in reference to a whole.

Horn of Africa: The Horn of Africa comprises Djibouti, Eritrea, Ethiopia, Somalia, and Sudan.

housing starts: The initiation of new housing construction.

human rights activist: A person who vigorously pursues the attainment of basic rights for all people.

human rights issues: Any matters involving people's basic rights which are in question or thought to be abused.

humanist: A person who centers on human needs and values, and stresses dignity of the individual.

humanitarian aid: Money or supplies given to a persecuted group or people of a country at war, or those devastated by a natural disaster, to provide for basic human needs.

hydrocarbon: A compound of hydrogen and carbon, often occurring in organic substances or derivatives of organic substances such as coal, petroleum, natural gas, etc.

hydrocarbon emissions: Organic compounds containing only carbon and hydrogen, often occurring in petroleum, natural gas, coal, and bitumens, and which contribute to the greenhouse effect.

hydroelectric potential: The potential amount of electricity that can be produced hydroelectrically. Usually used in reference to a given area and how many hydroelectric power plants that area can sustain.

hydroelectric power plant: A factory that produces electrical power through the application of waterpower.

IBRD *see* World Bank.

illegal alien: Any foreign-born individual who has unlawfully entered another country.

immigration: The act or process of passing or entering into another country for the purpose of permanent residence.

imports: Goods purchased from foreign suppliers.

indigenous: Born or originating in a particular place or country; native to a particular region or area.

Indo-Aryan language group: The group that includes the languages of India; also called Indo-European language group.

Indo-European language family: The group that includes the languages of India and much of Europe and southwestern Asia.

industrialized nation: A nation whose economy is based on industry.

infanticide: The act of murdering a baby.

infidel: One who is without faith or belief; particularly, one who rejects the distinctive doctrines of a particular religion.

inflation: The general rise of prices, as measured by a consumer price index. Results in a fall in value of currency.

installed capacity: The maximum possible output of electric power at any given time.

insurgency: The state or condition in which one rises against lawful authority or established government; rebellion.

insurrectionist: One who participates in an unorganized revolt against an authority.

interim government: A temporary or provisional government.

interim president: One who is appointed to perform temporarily the duties of president during a transitional period in a government.

internal migration: Term used to describe the relocation of individuals from one region to another without leaving the confines of the country or of a specified area.

International Date Line: An arbitrary line at about the 180th meridian that designates where one day begins and another ends.

Islam: The religious system of Mohammed, practiced by Moslems and based on a belief in Allah as the supreme being and Mohammed as his prophet. The spelling variations, Muslim and Muhammed, are also used, primarily by Islamic people. Islam also refers to those nations in which it is the primary religion.

isthmus: A narrow strip of land bordered by water and connecting two larger bodies of land, such as two continents, a continent and a peninsula, or two parts of an island.

Judaism: The religious system of the Jews, based on the Old Testament as revealed to Moses and characterized by a belief in one God and adherence to the laws of scripture and rabbinic traditions.

Judeo-Christian: The dominant traditional religious makeup of the United States and other countries based on the worship of the Old and New Testaments of the Bible.

junta: A small military group in power of a country, especially after a coup.

khan: A sovereign, or ruler, in central Asia.

khanate: A kingdom ruled by a khan, or man of rank.

kwashiorkor: Severe malnutrition in infants and children caused by a diet high in carbohydrates and lacking in protein.

kwh: The abbreviation for kilowatt-hour.

labor force: The number of people in a population available for work, whether actually employed or not.

labor movement: A movement in the early to mid-1800s to organize workers in groups according to profession to give them certain rights as a group, including bargaining power for better wages, working conditions, and benefits.

land reforms: Steps taken to create a fair distribution of farmland, especially by governmental action.

landlocked country: A country that does not have direct access to the sea; it is completely surrounded by other countries.

least developed countries: A subgroup of the United Nations designation of "less developed countries;" these countries generally have no significant economic growth, low literacy rates, and per person gross national product of less than $500. Also known as undeveloped countries.

leeward: The direction identical to that of the wind. For example, a *leeward tide* is a tide that runs in the same direction that the wind blows.

leftist: A person with a liberal or radical political affiliation.

legislative branch: The branch of government which makes or enacts the laws.

leprosy: A disease that can effect the skin and/or the nerves and can cause ulcers of the skin, loss of feeling, or loss of fingers and toes.

less developed countries (LDC): Designated by the United Nations to include countries with low levels of output, living standards, and per person gross national product generally below $5,000.

literacy: The ability to read and write.

Maastricht Treaty: The Maastricht Treaty (named for the Dutch town in which the treaty was signed) is also known as the Treaty of European Union. The treaty creates a European Union by: (a) committing the member states of the European Economic Community to both European Monetary Union (EMU) and political union; (b) introducing a single currency (European Currency Unit, ECU); (c) establishing a European System of Central Banks (ESCB); (d) creating a European Central Bank (ECB); and (e) broadening EC integration by including both a common foreign and security policy (CFSP) and cooperation in justice and home affairs (CJHA). The treaty entered into force on November 1, 1993.

Maghreb states: The Maghreb states include the three nations of Algeria, Morocco, and Tunisia; sometimes includes Libya and Mauritania.

maize: Another name (Spanish or British) for corn or the color of ripe corn.

majority party: The party with the largest number of votes and the controlling political party in a government.

mangrove: A tree which abounds on tropical shores in both hemispheres. Characterized by its numerous roots which arch out from its trunk and descend from its branches, mangroves form thick, dense growths along the tidal muds, reaching lengths hundreds of miles long.

manioc: The cassava plant or its product. Manioc is a very important food-staple in tropical America.

maquis. Scrubby, thick underbrush found along the coast of the Mediterranean Sea.

marginal land: Land that could produce an economic profit, but is so poor that it is only used when better land is no longer available.

marine life: The life that exists in, or is formed by the sea.

maritime climate: The climate and weather conditions typical of areas bordering the sea.

maritime rights: The rights that protect navigation and shipping.

market access: Market access refers to the openness of a national market to foreign products. Market access reflects a government's willingness to permit imports to compete relatively unimpeded with similar domestically produced goods.

market economy: A form of society which runs by the law of supply and demand. Goods are produced by firms to be sold to consumers, who determine the demand for them. Price levels vary according to the demand for certain goods and how much of them is produced.

market price: The price a commodity will bring when sold on the open market. The price is determined by the amount of demand for the commodity by buyers.

Marshall Plan: Formally known as the European Recovery Program, a joint project between the United States and most Western European nations under which $12.5 billion in U.S. loans and grants was expended to aid European recovery after World War II.

Marxism *see* Marxist-Leninist principles.

Marxist-Leninist principles: The doctrines of Karl Marx, built upon by Nikolai Lenin, on which communism was founded. They predicted the fall of capitalism, due to its own internal faults and the resulting oppression of workers.

Marxist: A follower of Karl Marx, a German socialist and revolutionary leader of the late 1800s, who contributed to Marxist-Leninist principles.

massif: A central mountain-mass or the dominant part of a range of mountains.

matrilineal (descent): Descending from, or tracing descent through, the maternal, or mother's, family line.

Mayan language family: The languages of the Central American Indians, further divided into two subgroups: the Maya and the Huastek.

mean temperature: The air temperature unit measured by the National Weather Service by adding the maximum and minimum daily temperatures together and diving the sum by 2.

Mecca (Mekkah): A city in Saudi Arabia; a destination of pilgrims in the Islamic world.

Mediterranean climate: A wet-winter, dry-summer climate with a moderate annual temperature range.

mestizo: The offspring of a person of mixed blood; especially, a person of mixed Spanish and American Indian parentage.

migratory birds: Those birds whose instincts prompt them to move from one place to another at the regularly recurring changes of season.

migratory workers: Usually agricultural workers who move from place to place for employment depending on the growing and harvesting seasons of various crops.

military coup: A sudden, violent overthrow of a government by military forces.

military junta: The small military group in power in a country, especially after a coup.

military regime: Government conducted by a military force.

military takeover: The seizure of control of a government by the military forces.

militia: The group of citizens of a country who are either serving in the reserve military forces or are eligible to be called up in time of emergency.

millet: A cereal grass whose small grain is used for food in Europe and Asia.

minority party: The political group that comprises the smaller part of the large overall group it belongs to; the party that is not in control.

missionary: A person sent by authority of a church or religious organization to spread his religious faith in a community where his church has no self-supporting organization.

Mohammed (or Muhammedor Mahomet): An Arabian prophet, known as the "Prophet of Allah" who founded the religion of Islam in 622, and wrote *The Koran,* the scripture of Islam. Also commonly spelled Muhammed, especially by Islamic people.

monarchy: Government by a sovereign, such as a king or queen.

money economy: A system or stage of economic development in which money replaces barter in the exchange of goods and services.

Mongol: One of an Asiatic race chiefly resident in Mongolia, a region north of China proper and south of Siberia.

Mongoloid: Having physical characteristics like those of the typical Mongols (Chinese, Japanese, Turks, Eskimos, etc.).

Moors: One of the Arab tribes that conquered Spain in the eighth century.

Moslem (Muslim): A follower of Mohammed (spelled Muhammed by many Islamic people), in the religion of Islam.

mosque: An Islam place of worship and the organization with which it is connected.

mouflon: A type of wild sheep characterized by curling horns.

mujahideen (mujahedin or mujahedeen): Rebel fighters in Islamic countries, especially those supporting the cause of Islam.

mulatto: One who is the offspring of parents one of whom is white and the other is black.

municipality: A district such as a city or town having its own incorporated government.

Muslim: A frequently used variation of the spelling of Moslem, to describe a follower of the prophet Mohammed (also spelled Muhammed), the founder of the religion of Islam.

Muslim New Year: A Muslim holiday. Although in some countries 1 Muharram, which is the first month of the Islamic year, is observed as a holiday, in other places the new year is observed on Sha'ban, the eighth month of the year. This practice apparently stems from pagan Arab times. Shab-i-Bharat, a national holiday in Bangladesh on this day, is held by many to be the occasion when God ordains all actions in the coming year.

NAFTA (North American Free Trade Agreement): NAFTA, which entered into force in January 1994, is a free trade agreement between Canada, the United States, and Mexico. The agreement progressively eliminates almost all U.S.-Mexico tariffs over a 10–15 year period.

nationalism: National spirit or aspirations; desire for national unity, independence, or prosperity.

nationalization: To transfer the control or ownership of land or industries to the nation from private owners.

native tongue: One's natural language. The language that is indigenous to an area.

NATO *see* North Atlantic Treaty Organization

natural gas: A combustible gas formed naturally in the earth and generally obtained by boring a well. The chemical makeup of natural gas is principally methane, hydrogen, ethylene compounds, and nitrogen.

natural harbor: A protected portion of a sea or lake along the shore resulting from the natural formations of the land.

naturalize: To confer the rights and privileges of a native-born subject or citizen upon someone who lives in the country by choice.

nature preserve: An area where one or more species of plant and/or animal are protected from harm, injury, or destruction.

neutrality: The policy of not taking sides with any countries during a war or dispute among them.

Newly Independent States: The NIS is a collective reference to 12 republics of the former Soviet Union: Russia, Ukraine, Belarus (formerly Byelorussia), Moldova (formerly Moldavia), Armenia, Azerbaijan, Uzbekistan, Turkmenistan, Tajikistan, Kazakhstan, and Kirgizstan (formerly Kirghiziya), and Georgia. Following dissolution of the Soviet Union, the distinction between the NIS and the Commonwealth of Independent States (CIS) was that Georgia was not a member of the CIS. That distinction dissolved when Georgia joined the CIS in November 1993.

news censorship *see* censorship

Nonaligned Movement: The NAM is an alliance of third world states that aims to promote the political and economic interests of developing countries. NAM interests have included ending colonialism/neo-colonialism, supporting the integrity of independent countries, and seeking a new international economic order.

Nordic Council: The Nordic Council, established in 1952, is directed toward supporting cooperation among Nordic countries. Members include Denmark, Finland, Iceland, Norway, and Sweden. Headquarters are in Stockholm, Sweden.

North Atlantic Treaty Organization (NATO): A mutual defense organization. Members include Belgium, Canada, Denmark, France (which has only partial membership), Greece, Iceland, Italy, Luxembourg, Netherlands, Norway, Portugal, Spain, Turkey, United Kingdom, United States, and Germany.

nuclear power plant: A factory that produces electrical power through the application of the nuclear reaction known as nuclear fission.

nuclear reactor: A device used to control the rate of nuclear fission in uranium. Used in commercial applications, nuclear reactors can maintain temperatures high enough to generate sufficient quantities of steam which can then be used to produce electricity.

OAPEC (Organization of Arab Petroleum Exporting countries): OAPEC was created in 1968; members include: Algeria, Bahrain, Egypt, Iraq, Kuwait, Libya, Qatar, Saudi Arabia, Syria, and the United Arab Emirates. Headquarters are in Cairo, Egypt.

OAS (Organization of American States): The OAS (Spanish: Organizaciûn de los Estados Americanos, OEA), or the Pan American Union, is a regional organization which promotes Latin American economic and social development. Members include the United States, Mexico, and most Central American, South American, and Caribbean nations.

OAS *see* Organization of American States

oasis: Originally, a fertile spot in the Libyan desert where there is a natural spring or well and vegetation; now refers to any fertile tract in the midst of a wasteland.

occupied territory: A territory that has an enemy's military forces present.

official language: The language in which the business of a country and its government is conducted.

oligarchy: A form of government in which a few people possess the power to rule as opposed to a monarchy which is ruled by one.

OPEC *see* OAPEC

open economy: An economy that imports and exports goods.

open market: Open market operations are the actions of the central bank to influence or control the money supply by buying or selling government bonds.

opposition party: A minority political party that is opposed to the party in power.

Organization of Arab Petroleum Exporting Countries *see* OAPEC

organized labor: The body of workers who belong to labor unions.

Ottoman Empire: An Turkish empire founded by Osman I in about 1603, that variously controlled large areas of land around the Mediterranean, Black, and Caspian Seas until it was dissolved in 1918.

overfishing: To deplete the quantity of fish in an area by removing more fish than can be naturally replaced.

overgrazing: Allowing animals to graze in an area to the point that the ground vegetation is damaged or destroyed.

overseas dependencies: A distant and physically separate territory that belongs to another country and is subject to its laws and government.

Pacific Rim: The Pacific Rim, referring to countries and economies bordering the Pacific Ocean.

pact: An international agreement.

Paleolithic: The early period of the Stone Age, when rough, chipped stone implements were used.

panhandle: A long narrow strip of land projecting like the handle of a frying pan.

papyrus: The paper-reed or -rush which grows on marshy river banks in the southeastern area of the Mediterranean, but more notably in the Nile valley.

paramilitary group: A supplementary organization to the military.

parasitic diseases: A group of diseases caused by parasitic organisms which feed off the host organism.

parliamentary republic: A system of government in which a president and prime minister, plus other ministers of departments, constitute the executive branch of the government and the parliament constitutes the legislative branch.

parliamentary rule: Government by a legislative body similar to that of Great Britain, which is composed of two houses—one elected and one hereditary.

parochial: Refers to matters of a church parish or something within narrow limits.

patriarchal system: A social system in which the head of the family or tribe is the father or oldest male. Kinship is determined and traced through the male members of the tribe.

patrilineal (descent): Descending from, or tracing descent through, the paternal or father's line.

pellagra: A disease marked by skin, intestinal, and central nervous system disorders, caused by a diet deficient in niacin, one of the B vitamins.

per capita: Literally, per person; for each person counted.

perestroika: The reorganization of the political and economic structures of the Soviet Union by president Mikhail Gorbachev.

periodical: A publication whose issues appear at regular intervals, such as weekly, monthly, or yearly.

petrochemical: A chemical derived from petroleum or from natural gas.

pharmaceutical plants: Any plant that is used in the preparation of medicinal drugs.

plantain: The name of a common weed that has often been used for medicinal purposes, as a folk remedy and in modern medicine. *Plaintain* is also the name of a tropical plant producing a type of banana.

poaching: To intrude or encroach upon another's preserves for the purpose of stealing animals, especially wild game.

polar climate: Also called tundra climate. A humid, severely cold climate controlled by arctic air masses, with no warm or summer season.

political climate: The prevailing political attitude of a particular time or place.

political refugee: A person forced to flee his or her native country for political reasons.

potable water: Water that is safe for drinking.

pound sterling: The monetary unit of Great Britain, otherwise known as the pound.

prefect: An administrative official; in France, the head of a particular department.

prefecture: The territory over which a prefect has authority.

prime meridian: Zero degrees in longitude that runs through Greenwich, England, site of the Royal Observatory. All other longitudes are measured from this point.

prime minister: The premier or chief administrative official in certain countries.

private sector: The division of an economy in which production of goods and services is privately owned.

privatization: To change from public to private control or ownership.

protectorate: A state or territory controlled by a stronger state, or the relationship of the stronger country toward the lesser one it protects.

Protestant Reformation: In 1529, a Christian religious movement begun in Germany to deny the universal authority of the Pope, and to establish the Bible as the only source of truth. (*Also see* Protestant)

Protestant: A member or an adherent of one of those Christian bodies which descended from the Reformation of the sixteenth century. Originally applied to those who opposed or protested the Roman Catholic Church.

proved reserves: The quantity of a recoverable mineral resource (such as oil or natural gas) that is still in the ground.

province: An administrative territory of a country.

provisional government: A temporary government set up during time of unrest or transition in a country.

pulses: Beans, peas, or lentils.

purge: The act of ridding a society of "undesirable" or unloyal persons by banishment or murder.

Rastafarian: A member of a Jamaican cult begun in 1930 as a semi-religious, semi-political movement.

rate of literacy: The percentage of people in a society who can read and write.

recession. A period of reduced economic activity in a country or region.

referendum: The practice of submitting legislation directly to the people for a popular vote.

Reformation *see* Protestant Reformation.

refugee: One who flees to a refuge or shelter or place of safety. One who in times of persecution or political commotion flees to a foreign country for safety.

revolution: A complete change in a government or society, such as in an overthrow of the government by the people.

right-wing party: The more conservative political party.

Roman alphabet: The alphabet of the ancient Romans from which the alphabets of most modern western European languages, including English, are derived.

Roman Catholic Church: The designation of the church of which the pope or Bishop of Rome is the head, and that holds him as the successor of St. Peter and heir of his spiritual authority, privileges, and gifts.

romance language: The group of languages derived from Latin: French, Spanish, Italian, Portuguese, and other related languages.

roundwood: Timber used as poles or in similar ways without being sawn or shaped.

runoff election: A deciding election put to the voters in case of a tie between candidates.

Russian Orthodox: The arm of the Orthodox Eastern Church that was the official church of Russia under the czars.

sack: To strip of valuables, especially after capture.

Sahelian zone: Eight countries make up this dry desert zone in Africa: Burkina Faso, Chad, Gambia, Mali, Mauritania, Niger, Senegal, and the Cape Verde Islands. *Also see* Club du Sahel.

salinization: An accumulation of soluble salts in soil. This condition is common in desert climates, where water evaporates quickly in poorly drained soil due to high temperatures.

Samaritans: A native or an inhabitant of Samaria; specifically, one of a race settled in the cities of Samaria by the king of Assyria after the removal of the Israelites from the country.

savanna: A treeless or near treeless plain of a tropical or subtropical region dominated by drought-resistant grasses.

schistosomiasis: A tropical disease that is chronic and characterized by disorders of the liver, urinary bladder, lungs, or central nervous system.

secession: The act of withdrawal, such as a state withdrawing from the Union in the Civil War in the United States.

sect: A religious denomination or group, often a dissenting one with extreme views.

segregation: The enforced separation of a racial or religious group from other groups, compelling them to live and go to school separately from the rest of society.

seismic activity: Relating to or connected with an earthquake or earthquakes in general.

self-sufficient: Able to function alone without help.

separation of power: The division of power in the government among the executive, legislative, and judicial branches and the checks and balances employed to keep them separate and independent of each other.

separatism: The policy of dissenters withdrawing from a larger political or religious group.

serfdom: In the feudal system of the Middle Ages, the condition of being attached to the land owned by a lord and being transferable to a new owner.

Seventh-day Adventist: One who believes in the second coming of Christ to establish a personal reign upon the earth.

shamanism: A religion of some Asians and Amerindians in which shamans, who are priests or medicine men, are believed to influence good and evil spirits.

shantytown: An urban settlement of people in flimsy, inadequate houses.

Shia Muslim: Members of one of two great sects of Islam. Shia Muslims believe that Ali and the Imams are the rightful successors of Mohammed (also commonly spelled Muhammed). They also believe that the last recognized Imam will return as a messiah. Also known as Shiites. (*Also see* Sunnis.)

Shiites *see* Shia Muslims.

Shintoism: The system of nature- and hero-worship which forms the indigenous religion of Japan.

shoal: A place where the water of a stream, lake, or sea is of little depth. Especially, a sand-bank which shows at low water.

sierra: A chain of hills or mountains.

Sikh: A member of a politico-religious community of India, founded as a sect around 1500 and based on the principles of monotheism (belief in one god) and human brotherhood.

Sino-Tibetan language family: The family of languages spoken in eastern Asia, including China, Thailand, Tibet, and Burma.

slash-and-burn agriculture: A hasty and sometimes temporary way of clearing land to make it available for agriculture by cutting down trees and burning them.

slave trade: The transportation of black Africans beginning in the 1700s to other countries to be sold as slaves—people owned as property and compelled to work for their owners at no pay.

Slavic languages: A major subgroup of the Indo-European language family. It is further subdivided into West Slavic (including Polish, Czech, Slovak and Serbian), South Slavic (including Bulgarian, Serbo-Croatian, Slovene, and Old Church Slavonic), and East Slavic (including Russian Ukrainian and Byelorussian).

social insurance: A government plan to protect low-income people, such as health and accident insurance, pension plans, etc.

social security: A form of social insurance, including life, disability, and old-age pension for workers. It is paid for by employers, employees, and the government.

socialism: An economic system in which ownership of land and other property is distributed among the community as a whole, and every member of the community shares in the work and products of the work.

socialist: A person who advocates socialism.

softwoods: The coniferous trees, whose wood density as a whole is relatively softer than the wood of those trees referred to as hardwoods.

sorghum (also known as Syrian Grass): Plant grown in various parts of the world for its valuable uses, such as for grain, syrup, or fodder.

Southeast Asia: The region in Asia that consists of the Malay Archipelago, the Malay Peninsula, and Indochina.

staple crop: A crop that is the chief commodity or product of a place, and which has widespread and constant use or value.

state: The politically organized body of people living under one government or one of the territorial units that make up a federal government, such as in the United States.

steppe: A level tract of land more or less devoid of trees, in certain parts of European and Asiatic Russia.

student demonstration: A public gathering of students to express strong feelings about a certain situation, usually taking place near the location of the people in power to change the situation.

subarctic climate: A high latitude climate of two types: *continental subarctic*, which has very cold winters, short, cool summers, light precipitation and moist air; and *marine subarctic*, a coastal and island climate with polar air masses causing large precipitation and extreme cold.

subcontinent: A land mass of great size, but smaller than any of the continents; a large subdivision of a continent.

subsistence economy: The part of a national economy in which money plays little or no role, trade is by barter, and living standards are minimal.

subsistence farming: Farming that provides the minimum food goods necessary for the continuation of the farm family.

subtropical climate: A middle latitude climate dominated by humid, warm temperatures and heavy rainfall in summer, with cool winters and frequent cyclonic storms.

subversion: The act of attempting to overthrow or ruin a government or organization by stealthy or deceitful means.

Sudanic language group: A related group of languages spoken in various areas of northern Africa, including Yoruba, Mandingo, and Tshi.

suffrage: The right to vote.

Sufi: A Muslim mystic who believes that God alone exists, there can be no real difference between good and evil, that the soul exists within the body as in a cage, so death should be the chief object of desire, and sufism is the only true philosophy.

sultan: A king of a Muslim state.

Sunni Muslim: Members of one of two major sects of the religion of Islam. Sunni Muslims adhere to strict orthodox traditions, and believe that the four caliphs are the rightful successors to Mohammed, founder of Islam. (Mohammed is commonly spelled Muhammed, especially by Islamic people.) (*Also see* Shia Muslim.)

Taoism: The doctrine of Lao-Tzu, an ancient Chinese philosopher (about 500 B.C.) as laid down by him in the *Tao-te-ching.*

tariff: A tax assessed by a government on goods as they enter (or leave) a country. May be imposed to protect domestic industries from imported goods and/ or to generate revenue.

temperate zone: The parts of the earth lying between the tropics and the polar circles. The *northern temperate zone* is the area between the tropic of Cancer and the Arctic Circle. The *southern temperate zone* is the area between the tropic of Capricorn and the Antarctic Circle.

terracing: A form of agriculture that involves cultivating crops in raised banks of earth.

terrorism: Systematic acts of violence designed to frighten or intimidate.

thermal power plant: A facility that produces electric energy from heat energy released by combustion of fuel or nuclear reactions.

Third World: A term used to describe less developed countries; as of the mid-1990s, it is being replaced by the United Nations designation Less Developed Countries, or LDC.

topography: The physical or natural features of the land.

torrid zone: The part of the earth's surface that lies between the tropics, so named for the character of its climate.

totalitarian party: The single political party in complete authoritarian control of a government or state.

trachoma: A contagious bacterial disease that affects the eye.

treaty: A negotiated agreement between two governments.

tribal system: A social community in which people are organized into groups or clans descended from common ancestors and sharing customs and languages.

tropical monsoon climate: One of the tropical rainy climates; it is sufficiently warm and rainy to produce tropical rainforest vegetation, but also has a winter dry season.

tsetse fly: Any of the several African insects which can transmit a variety of parasitic organisms through its bite. Some of these organisms can prove fatal to both human and animal victims.

tundra: A nearly level treeless area whose climate and vegetation are characteristically arctic due to its northern position; the subsoil is permanently frozen.

undeveloped countries *see* least developed countries.

unemployment rate: The overall unemployment rate is the percentage of the work force (both employed and unemployed) who claim to be unemployed.

UNICEF: An international fund set-up for children's emergency relief: United Nations Children's Fund (formerly United Nations International Children's Emergency Fund).

universal adult suffrage: The policy of giving every adult in a nation the right to vote.

untouchables: In India, members of the lowest caste in the caste system, a hereditary social class system. They were considered unworthy to touch members of higher castes.

urban guerrilla: A rebel fighter operating in an urban area.

urbanization: The process of changing from country to city.

USSR: An abbreviation of Union of Soviet Socialist Republics.

veldt: In South Africa, an unforested or thinly forested tract of land or region, a grassland.

Warsaw Pact: Agreement made 14 May 1955 (and dissolved 1 July 1991) to promote mutual defense between Albania, Bulgaria, Czechoslovakia, East Germany, Hungary, Poland, Romania, and the USSR.

Western nations: Blanket term used to describe mostly democratic, capitalist countries, including the United States, Canada, and western European countries.

wildlife sanctuary: An area of land set aside for the protection and preservation of animals and plants.

workers' compensation: A series of regular payments by an employer to a person injured on the job.

World Bank: The World Bank is a group of international institutions which provides financial and technical assistance to developing countries.

world oil crisis: The severe shortage of oil in the 1970s precipitated by the Arab oil embargo.

wormwood: A woody perennial herb native to Europe and Asiatic Russia, valued for its medicinal uses.

yaws: A tropical disease caused by a bacteria which produces raspberry-like sores on the skin.

yellow fever: A tropical viral disease caused by the bite of an infected mosquito, characterized by jaundice.

Zoroastrianism: The system of religious doctrine taught by Zoroaster and his followers in the Avesta; the religion prevalent in Persia until its overthrow by the Muslims in the seventh century.

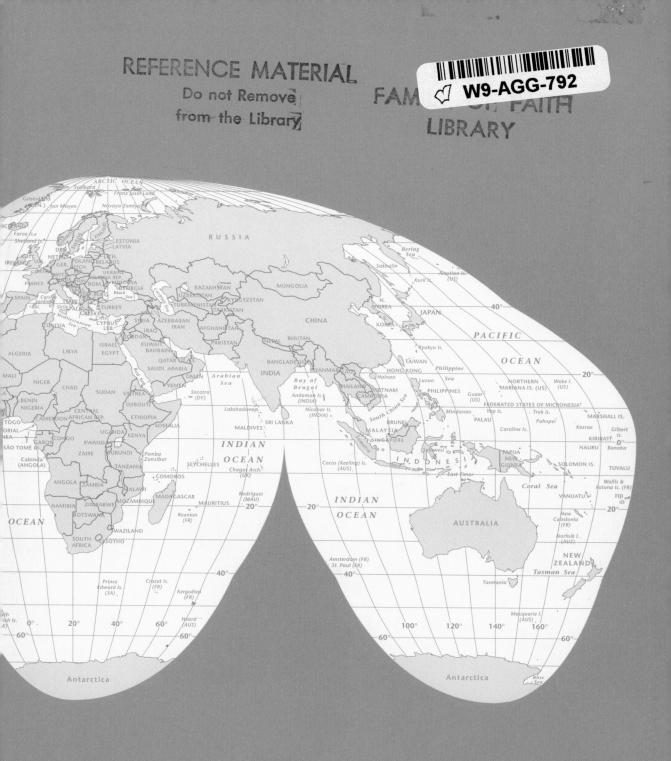

Junior
Worldmark
Encyclopedia
of the

VOLUME 8

Junior
Worldmark
Encyclopedia
of the

VOLUME 8

Spain to Tuvalu

An imprint of Gale Research
An ITP Information/Reference Group Company

Changing the Way the World Learns

NEW YORK • LONDON • BONN • BOSTON • DETROIT
MADRID • MELBOURNE • MEXICO CITY • PARIS
SINGAPORE • TOKYO • TORONTO • WASHINGTON
ALBANY NY • BELMONT CA • CINCINNATI OH

JUNIOR WORLDMARK ENCYCLOPEDIA OF THE NATIONS

Timothy L. Gall and Susan Bevan Gall, *Editors*
Rosalie Wieder, *Senior Editor*
Deborah Baron and Daniel M. Lucas, *Associate Editors*
Brian Rajewski and Deborah Rutti, *Graphics and Layout*
Cordelia R. Heaney, *Editorial Assistant*
Dianne K. Daeg de Mott, Janet Fenn, Matthew Markovich,
    Ariana Ranson, and Craig Strasshofer, *Copy Editors*
Janet Fenn and Matthew Markovich, *Proofreaders*
Maryland Cartographics, Inc., *Cartographers*

U•X•L Staff

Jane Hoehner, *U•X•L Developmental Editor*
Sonia Benson and Rob Nagel, *Contributors*
Thomas L. Romig, *U•X•L Publisher*
Mary Beth Trimper, *Production Director*
Evi Seoud, *Assistant Production Manager*
Shanna Heilveil, *Production Associate*
Cynthia Baldwin, *Product Design Manager*
Barbara J. Yarrow, *Graphic Services Supervisor*
Mary Krzewinski, *Cover Designer*
Margaret McAvoy-Amoto, *Permissions Associate (Pictures)*

Library of Congress Cataloging-in-Publication Data
Junior Worldmark encyclopedia of the nations / edited by Timothy Gall
and Susan Gall.
        p.   cm.
    Includes bibliographical references and index.
    ISBN 0-7876-0741-X (set)
    1. Geography--Encyclopedias, Juvenile. 2. History--Encyclopedias,
Juvenile. 3. Economics--Juvenile literature. 4. Political science--
Encyclopedia, Juvenile. 5. United Nations--Encyclopedias,
Juvenile. I. Gall, Timothy L. II. Gall, Susan B.
G63.J86   1995
910'.3--dc20   95-36739
                                                           CIP

ISBN 0-7876-0741-X (set)
ISBN 0-7876-0742-8 (vol. 1)   ISBN 0-7876-0743-6 (vol. 2)   ISBN 0-7876-0744-4 (vol. 3)
ISBN 0-7876-0745-2 (vol. 4)   ISBN 0-7876-0746-0 (vol. 5)   ISBN 0-7876-0747-9 (vol. 6)
ISBN 0-7876-0748-7 (vol. 7)   ISBN 0-7876-0749-5 (vol. 8)   ISBN 0-7876-0750-9 (vol. 9)

 ITP™   U•X•L is an imprint of Gale Research Inc.,
an International Thomson Publishing Company.
ITP logo is a trademark under license.

CONTENTS

Guide to Country Articles

Every country profile in this encyclopedia includes the same 35 headings. Also included in every profile is a map (showing the country and its location in the world), the country's flag and seal, and a table of data on the country. The country articles are organized alphabetically in nine volumes. A glossary of terms is included in each of the nine volumes. This glossary defines many of the specialized terms used throughout the encyclopedia. A keyword index to all nine volumes appears at the end of Volume 9.

Flag color symbols

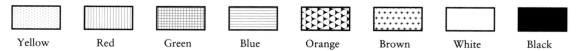

| Yellow | Red | Green | Blue | Orange | Brown | White | Black |

Alphabetical listing of sections

Agriculture	21
Armed Forces	16
Bibliography	35
Climate	3
Domesticated Animals	22
Economy	17
Education	31
Energy and Power	27
Environment	5
Ethnic Groups	8
Famous People	34
Fishing	23
Foreign Trade	26
Forestry	24
Government	13
Health	29
History	12
Housing	30

Income	18
Industry	19
Judicial System	15
Labor	20
Languages	9
Location and Size	1
Media	32
Migration	7
Mining	25
Plants and Animals	4
Political Parties	14
Population	6
Religions	10
Social Development	28
Topography	2
Tourism/Recreation	33
Transportation	11

Sections listed numerically

1	Location and Size
2	Topography
3	Climate
4	Plants and Animals
5	Environment
6	Population
7	Migration
8	Ethnic Groups
9	Languages
10	Religions
11	Transportation
12	History
13	Government
14	Political Parties
15	Judicial System
16	Armed Forces
17	Economy
18	Income

19	Industry
20	Labor
21	Agriculture
22	Domesticated Animals
23	Fishing
24	Forestry
25	Mining
26	Foreign Trade
27	Energy and Power
28	Social Development
29	Health
30	Housing
31	Education
32	Media
33	Tourism/Recreation
34	Famous People
35	Bibliography

Abbreviations and acronyms to know

GMT= Greenwich mean time. The prime, or Greenwich, meridian passes through Greenwich, England (near London), and marks the center of the initial time zone for the world. The standard time of all 24 time zones relate to Greenwich mean time. Every profile contains a map showing the country and its location in the world.

These abbreviations are used in references to famous people:
b.=born
d.=died
fl.=flourished (lived and worked)
r.=reigned (for kings, queens, and similar monarchs)

A dollar sign ($) stands for US$ unless otherwise indicated.

SPAIN

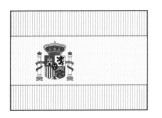

CAPITAL: Madrid.

FLAG: The national flag, adopted in 1785, consists of three horizontal stripes: a yellow one—equal in size to the other two combined—between two red ones, with the coat of arms on the yellow stripe.

ANTHEM: *Marcha Real Granadera (March of the Royal Grenadier).*

MONETARY UNIT: The peseta (P) is a paper currency of 100 centimos. There are coins of 50 centimos and 1, 5, 25, 50, and 100 pesetas, and notes of 1,000, 2,000, 5,000, and 10,000 pesetas. P1 = $0.0073 (or $1 = P137.38).

WEIGHTS AND MEASURES: The metric system is the legal standard.

HOLIDAYS: New Year's Day, 1 January; St. Joseph's Day, 19 March; Epiphany, 31 March; Day of St. Joseph the Artisan, 1 May; St. James's Day, 25 July; Assumption, 15 August; National Day and Hispanic Day, 12 October; All Saints' Day, 1 November; Immaculate Conception, 8 December; Christmas, 25 December. Movable religious holidays include Holy Thursday, Good Friday, Easter Monday, and Corpus Christi.

TIME: 1 PM = noon GMT.

1 LOCATION AND SIZE

Occupying the greater part of the Iberian Peninsula, Spain is the third-largest country in Europe, with an area of 504,750 square kilometers (194,885 square miles). Comparatively, Spain is slightly more than twice the size of the state of Oregon. Spain has a total boundary length of 7,885 kilometers (4,899 miles). Spain has long claimed Gibraltar, a narrow peninsula on the south coast.

Spain's capital city, Madrid, is located in the center of the country.

2 TOPOGRAPHY

Continental Spain is divided into five general topographic regions: (1) the northern coastal belt, a mountainous region with fertile valleys; (2) the central plateau, or Meseta; (3) Andalucía, which covers the whole of southern and southwestern Spain; (4) the Levante, on the Mediterranean coastal belt; and (5) Catalonia (Cataluña) and the Ebro Valley in the northeast.

Principal mountain ranges are the Pyrenees; the Cordillera Cantábrica; the Montes de Toledo; the Sierra Morena; the Serranías Penibéticas; and the Sistema Ibérico. The main rivers are the Tagus (Tajo), Duero, Guadiana, Guadalquivir, and the Ebro.

Also part of Spain are the Canary Islands, a group of 13 islands in the Atlantic Ocean west of Morocco, and the picturesque Balearic Islands in the western Mediterranean, which combine steep mountains with rolling, fertile ranges.

3 CLIMATE

The northern coastal regions are cool and humid, with an average annual temperature of 14°C (57°F); temperatures at Bilbao ranged in 1981 from an average of 10°C (50°F) in January–March to 19°C (66°F) during July–September. The central plateau is cold in the winter and hot in the summer; Madrid has a winter average of about 8°C (46°F) and a summer average of 23°C (73°F). In Andalucía and the Levante, the climate is temperate except in summer, when temperatures sometimes reach above 40°C (104°F) in the shade.

The northern coastal regions have an average annual rainfall of 99 centimeters (39 inches); the southern coastal belt has 41–79 centimeters (16–31 inches); and the interior central plain averages no more than 50 centimeters (20 inches) annually.

4 PLANTS AND ANIMALS

Because of its wide variety of climates, Spain has more different types of natural plant life than any other European country; some 8,000 species are known. Nevertheless, plant life is generally thin. In the humid areas of the north there are deciduous trees (including oak, chestnut, elm, beech, and poplar), as well as varieties of pine. Pine, juniper, and other evergreens, particularly the ilex and cork oak, and drought-resistant shrubs make up most of the plant life in the dry southern region.

The Canary Islands, named for the wild dogs (*canariae insulae*) once found there, have both Mediterranean and African plants. A small, yellow-tinged finch on the islands has given the name "canary" to a variety of yellow songbirds widely bred as house pets. Wild animals have been driven out of Spain by the number of people living there. Very few wild species remain.

5 ENVIRONMENT

Centuries of uncontrolled cutting have thinned out Spain's forests. Fire destroys 700,000 to 1,000,000 hectares (1,730,000 to 2,470,000 acres) of forestland each year. During the 1980s, an average of 92,000 hectares (227,000 acres) were reforested each year.

Air pollution is also a problem in Spain. Hydrocarbon emissions amount to 929 tons per year. Spain is also vulnerable to oil pollution from tankers which travel the shipping routes near the nation's shores. Spain's cities produce 13.8 million tons of solid waste per year.

In 1994, 6 of the country's mammal species and 23 bird species were endangered.

6 POPULATION

The population of Spain in 1991 was 39,433,942. Population density in 1991 was 78 persons per square kilometer (202 persons per square mile). A population of 39,640,000 is projected for the year 2000. An estimated 81% of the population lived in cities in 1995, compared with 52.6% in 1950. Madrid is the largest city, with 3,010,492 inhabitants in 1985.

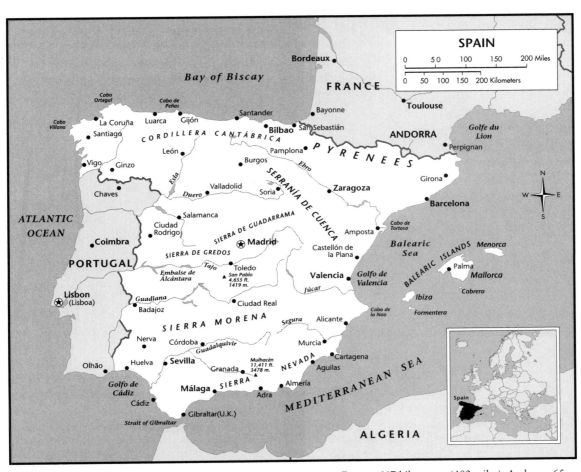

LOCATION: 36° to 43°47′N; 3°19′E to 9°30′W. **BOUNDARY LENGTHS:** France, 647 kilometers (402 miles); Andorra, 65 kilometers (40 miles); Mediterranean coastline, 1,670 kilometers (1,038 miles); Gibraltar, 1 kilometers (0.6 miles); Portugal, 1,232 kilometers (766 miles); Atlantic and Bay of Biscay coastlines, 2,234 kilometers (1,388 miles). The Balearic Islands extend from 1°12′ to 4°19′E and 38°38′ to 40°5′N; coastline, 910 kilometers (565 miles). The Canary Islands, 1,400 kilometers (900 miles) to the southwest, extend from 13°20′ to 18°19′W and 27°38′ to 29°25′N; coastline, 1,126 kilometers (700 miles). **TERRITORIAL SEA LIMIT:** 12 miles.

7 MIGRATION

More than 1.7 million Spanish citizens lived outside the country in 1987. In 1991, Spain had 360,655 foreign residents. Some come there to retire, others to work. There were 75,422 British in 1991 and 49,513 Moroccans. Germans, French, Portuguese, and Argentinians were also well represented. In addition there were an estimated 300,000 illegal immigrants in Spain.

Internal migration was 685,966 in 1990. Rural-to-urban and urban-to-rural migration is now roughly equal.

Photo credit: Susan D. Rock

The tourist area of Tenerife, Canary Islands.

8 ETHNIC GROUPS

An unmixed Latin stock is found in three-fourths of the country. The people moving to the cities, the coast, and the islands has caused some mixing of ethnic characteristics.

The Basques, Galicians, and Catalans consider themselves separate nations within Spain. They enjoy a fair amount of cultural, economic, and political independence. Estimates of the Gypsy population range from 50,000 to 450,000.

9 LANGUAGES

According to the 1978 constitution, Spanish is the national language. Castilian, the dialect of the central and southern regions, is spoken by most Spaniards and is used in the schools and courts.

Regional languages include Catalan, a neo-Latin tongue; Galician, which is close to Portuguese; Bable, a form of Old Castilian; and Valencian, a dialect of Catalan. Basque, spoken in northern Spain, is a pre-Roman language unrelated to any other known tongue and using an ancient script.

10 RELIGIONS

In 1993, at least 95% of the population (about 38 million) was Roman Catholic (organized into more than 21,000 congregations). Protestants numbered 250,000 in 1993. There are more than 15,000 Jews.

In addition, about 200,000 who observe Roman Catholicism still keep some Jewish practices. These people are descendants of the Marranos, the Spaniards who officially converted to Christianity but secretly practiced Judaism for centuries after all practicing Jews had been expelled from Spain in 1492. In 1993, Muslims numbered approximately 300,000 and there were small Baha'i and Buddhist communities.

11 TRANSPORTATION

In 1991, Spain had 150,839 kilometers (198,211 miles) of highways. State-operated national roads comprised 82,513 kilometers (51,273 miles). There were 15,152,132 vehicles in 1991, including 2,495,226 trucks and 46,604 buses. The National Spanish Railway Network in 1991 was made up of 12,691 kilometers (7,886 miles) of broad-gauge track.

The largest ports are Barcelona, Tarragona, and Cartagena on the Mediterranean, Algeciras on the Strait of Gibraltar, La Coruña on the Atlantic, and Las Palmas and Santa Cruz de Tenerife in the Canaries. In 1991, the merchant fleet totaled 267 vessels, with 2,713,000 gross registered tons, less than half what it was in 1985.

Spain has 61 airports, the most important being Madrid-Barajas, Barcelona-Prat, and Palma-Son San Juan. The state-owned Iberia Air Lines flew 194,800,000 kilometers (121,050,000 miles), carrying some 15,411,600 passengers in 1991.

12 HISTORY

Beginning in about 1000 BC, the prehistoric Iberian culture of present-day Spain was changed by Celtic, Phoenician, and Greek invaders. From the sixth to the second century BC, Carthage controlled the Iberian Peninsula up to the Ebro River. From 133 BC until the barbarian invasions of the fifth century AD, Rome ruled Hispania (from which the name Spain is derived). During the Roman period, cities and roads were built, and Christianity and Latin were introduced. The Spanish language grew out of Latin.

In the fifth century, the Visigoths settled in Spain, ruling the country until 711, when it was invaded by the Moors. All of Spain, except for a few northern districts, was under Moorish Muslim rule for periods ranging from 300 to 800 years. A rich civilization arose, characterized by prosperous cities, industries, and agriculture and by brilliant intellectual figures, including Jews as well as Muslims. Throughout this period (711–1492), however, Christian Spain waged periodic wars against the Moors. By the thirteenth century, Muslim rule was restricted to the south of Spain.

In 1492, Spain was unified under Ferdinand II of Aragón and Isabella I of Castile, the "Catholic Sovereigns." Moors and Jews were driven out of Spain. Those who chose to convert to Catholicism and stay in Spain were terrorized by officials of the Inquisition to be sure they were no longer practicing their old religions. Also in 1492, Christopher Columbus sailed to the Americas with Ferdinand and Isabella's backing. In 1519, Ferdinand Magellan, a

Portuguese in the service of Spain, began the first voyage to sail around the world, completed in 1522 by Juan Sebastián Elcano.

The Rise of Spanish Power

The sixteenth century was the golden age of Spain: its empire in the Americas produced vast wealth; its arts flourished; its fleet ruled the high seas; and its armies were the strongest in Europe. By the second half of the sixteenth century, however, religious wars in Europe and the flow of people and resources to the New World had drained the strength of the Spanish nation. In 1588, the "invincible" Spanish Armada was defeated by England.

Spain's power on land was ended by wars with England, the Netherlands, and France in the seventeenth century and by the War of the Spanish Succession (1701–14), which established the Bourbon dynasty in Spain.

Much of the nineteenth and early twentieth centuries was spent in passionate struggles between the monarchy and those who wanted Spain to be a republic. Abroad, Spain lost most of its lands in the West to colonial rebellions during the first half of the nineteenth century. Cuba, Puerto Rico, and the Philippines were lost as a result of the Spanish-American War in 1898. Spain remained neutral in World War I (1914–18) but in the postwar period fought to keep its colonial possessions in Morocco.

Civil War

The Spanish general and dictator Primo de Rivera, who successfully ended the fighting in Morocco in 1927, remained in power under the monarchy until 1930. In 1931, after a public vote, King Alfonso XIII left Spain and a republic was established. Neither right-wing nor left-wing groups had a parliamentary majority, and on the whole the coalition governments were ineffective.

Between 17 July 1936 and 31 March 1939, Spain was ravaged by civil war. The two opposing parties were the Republicans, made up partly of democrats and partly of left-wing groups, and the rebels (Nationalists), who favored the establishment of a right-wing dictatorship. Germany and Italy furnished soldiers and weapons to the Nationalists, while the Soviet Union, Czechoslovakia, and Mexico supported the Republicans. Finally the Republicans were defeated, and General Francisco Franco formed a new government. Under the Franco dictatorship, Spain gave aid to the Axis powers in World War II (1939–45) but was not an active participant.

The Postwar Years

Spain was admitted to the United Nations in 1955. However, the repressive nature of the Franco regime kept Spain apart from the main social, political, and economic currents of postwar Western Europe. On 20 November 1975, General Franco died at the age of 82, ending a career that had dominated nearly four decades of Spanish history. Two days later, Juan Carlos I was sworn in as king. Labor groups and Catalan and Basque separatists protested the new government. A sharp rise in living costs caused even more political unrest.

On 15 June 1977, the first democratic elections in Spain in 40 years took place. The Union of the Democratic Center (Unión de Centro Democrático—UCD), headed by Adolfo Suárez González won a majority in the new Cortes (parliament). The Cortes prepared a new constitution, which was approved by popular vote and by the king in December 1978.

When Suárez announced his resignation in January 1981, the king named Leopoldo Calvo Sotelo y Bustelo to the premiership. In 1982, 1986, and 1989, the Spanish Socialist Worker's Party (Partido Socialista Obrero Español—PSOE), headed by Felipe González Márquez, won absolute majorities in both houses of parliament. The PSOE failed to win a majority in 1993 but governed with the support of the Basque and Catalan nationalist parties. Political violence, especially murders and kidnappings in the Basque region, has been a continuing problem since the late 1960s. Spain joined the North Atlantic Treaty Organization in 1982, a controversial move that was approved by a majority of Spanish voters in 1986. On 1 January of that year, Spain became a full member of the European Community.

13 GOVERNMENT

A new constitution, approved by the Cortes (parliament) on 31 October 1978, confirmed Spain as a parliamentary monarchy. The king is the head of state. Legislative power rests in the Cortes Generales, consisting of two chambers: the Congress

Photo credit: Susan D. Rock

An intricately carved entrance to a cathedral in Barcelona.

of Deputies (350 members in 1994) and the Senate (254 members). All deputies and 208 senators are popularly elected to four-year terms under universal adult suffrage. The remaining senators (46) are chosen by the assemblies in the 17 autonomous regions. The president, vice-president, and ministers are all appointed by the king and answerable to Congress.

14 POLITICAL PARTIES

The Spanish political scene is characterized by changing parties and shifting alliances. The Spanish Socialist Worker's Party (*Partido Socialista Obrero*

Español—PSOE) won absolute majorities in both chambers of the Cortes in 1982, 1986, and 1989. It finished 17 seats short of a parliamentary majority in 1993.

The right-wing element is represented by the People's Alliance (CP), also known as the Popular Party or PP, a coalition made up of the Alianza Popular, the Christian Democratic Partido Demócrata Popular, and the Partido Liberal.

In the 1986 election, the Communist Party (*Partido Comunista*—PC) formed part of the United Left coalition (*Izquierda Unida*—IU), which included a rival Communist faction and several socialist parties. Nationalist parties function in Catalonia, Andalucía, the Basque provinces, and other areas.

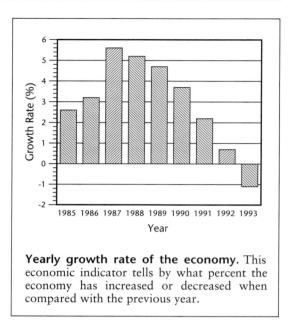

Yearly growth rate of the economy. This economic indicator tells by what percent the economy has increased or decreased when compared with the previous year.

15 JUDICIAL SYSTEM

The highest judicial body is the seven-member Supreme Court (*Tribunal Supremo*). Territorial high courts (*audiencias*) are the courts of last appeal in the 15 regions of the country. Provincial *audiencias* serve as appeals courts in civil matters and provide the first hearing for criminal cases. The National High Court (*Audiencia Nacional*), created in 1977, has jurisdiction over criminal cases that cross regional boundaries and over civil cases involving the central state administration.

16 ARMED FORCES

Spain has a 9-month compulsory military service system but is moving toward a smaller, volunteer force. In 1993, the armed forces totaled 217,000, of whom 158,100 were draftees. The 146,000-man army was organized into divisions and special purpose brigades. The navy had 36,000 men. The air force had 35,000 men and about 207 combat aircraft. The Guardia Civil numbered about 65,000. In 1991 Spain spent $8.7 billion on defense. Spain contributes 164 observers to two United Nations missions.

17 ECONOMY

Agriculture, livestock, and mining used to be the main supports of the economy. In order to offset the damage suffered during the Civil War, however, the Franco regime concentrated its efforts on industrial expansion. So industry now provides most of the jobs and exports from Spain.

In terms of per person income, Spain still ranks among the lowest in Western Europe. From 1974 through the early

1980s, the Spanish economy was hurt by international factors, especially oil price increases. Consumer prices rose 25.1% between 1989 and 1993, and unemployment rose from 17.3% to 22.7%.

18 INCOME

In 1992, Spain's gross national product (GNP) was $547,947 million at current prices, or $13,590 per person. For the period 1985–92, the average inflation rate was 6.9%, resulting in a real growth rate in per person GNP of 3.8%.

19 INDUSTRY

The chief industries are food and beverages, energy, and transport materials. Chemical production, particularly of superphosphates, sulfuric acid, dyestuffs, and pharmaceutical products, is also significant. Of the heavy industries, iron and steel (1992 production 12,271,000 tons) is the most important. Petroleum refinery production in 1991 totaled 54.8 million tons, and in 1992, 24.6 million tons of cement were produced. Other important products in 1992 included automobiles, 1,795,620; and commercial vehicles, 372,842.

20 LABOR

In 1991, civilian employment totaled 12,609,400, distributed as follows: services, 7,100,700; industry, 2,890,100; fishing and agriculture, 1,345,100; and construction, 1,273,500. Fewer and fewer work in agriculture; many former farm workers have gone into construction and industry. The service sector has grown the most in recent years. Unemployment aver-

Photo credit: Susan D. Rock

Open air produce market on a plaza in Barcelona.

aged about 17% during 1991. The minimum age for employment is 16, or 18 for night-shift, overtime, or dangerous work.

21 AGRICULTURE

Farm land in 1991 covered 20,089,000 hectares (49,640,000 acres), of which 76% was used for field crops, and 24% planted with olive trees, vineyards, and orchards.

Agricultural production, in 1992, included (in millions of tons) barley, 6.0; potatoes, 5.2; wheat, 4.5; corn, 2.6; tomatoes, 2.6; oats, 0.3; and rice, 0.5. Fruit and nut production for 1992 (in thousands of tons) included oranges, 2,724; apples, 1,027; tangerines, 1,488; peaches, 964;

lemons, 661; pears, 602; bananas, 355; almonds, 288; apricots, 193; plums, 141; and hazelnuts, 27.

Other significant crops were grapes, 5,676,000 tons, and olives, 2,831,000 tons. Grapes are cultivated in every region; in 1992, 3,472,000 tons of wine were produced. Olive oil remains a major agricultural product, with 597,000 tons produced during 1992.

22 DOMESTICATED ANIMALS

Sheep are by far the most important domestic animals. In 1992, Spain's livestock population (in thousands) included sheep, 24,625; hogs, 17,240; cattle, 4,924; goats, 3,000; horses, 240; donkeys 130; and mules, 100. In 1992, milk production was 5.8 million tons; egg production was an estimated 597,400 tons.

23 FISHING

Fishing is important, especially along the northern coastline. In 1991, the fish catch was 1,350,000 tons.

24 FORESTRY

Spain's forested area in 1991 was 15,858,000 hectares (39,185,000 acres). Roundwood production in 1991 totaled 17,272,000 cubic meters. Spain is one of the largest producers of cork, its main commercial forest product. Scotch and maritime pine, as well as radiata pine, are the main softwood lumber species produced in Spain; eucalyptus and poplar are the principal hardwood species.

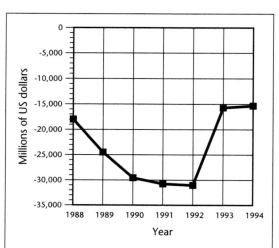

Yearly balance of trade measured in millions of US dollars. The balance of trade is the difference between what a country sells to other countries (its exports) and what it buys (its imports). If a country imports more than it exports, it has a negative balance of trade (a trade deficit). If exports exceed imports there is a positive balance of trade (a trade surplus).

25 MINING

Almost all known minerals are found in Spain, and mining is still important in the Spanish economy. Total iron ore reserves are estimated at 6 million tons, with 3.9 million tons of ore produced in 1991. Coal reserves are estimated at 500 million tons.

In 1991, 16 million tons of lignite, 14 million tons of bituminous coals, and 5.8 million tons of anthracite were produced. In 1991, the output of potash salts was 760,000 tons; lead, 50,000 tons; and mercury, 992 tons of processed metal, second only to the Soviet Union.

Selected Social Indicators

These statistics are estimates for the period 1988 to 1993. For comparison purposes, data for the United States and averages for low-income countries and high-income countries are also given.

Indicator	Spain	Low-income countries	High-income countries	United States
Per capita gross national product†	$13,590	$380	$23,680	$24,740
Population growth rate	0.2%	1.9%	0.6%	1.0%
Population growth rate in urban areas	0.5%	3.9%	0.8%	1.3%
Population per square kilometer of land	78	78	25	26
Life expectancy in years	78	62	77	76
Number of people per physician	278	>3,300	453	419
Number of pupils per teacher (primary school)	21	39	<18	20
Illiteracy rate (15 years and older)	5%	41%	<5%	<3%
Energy consumed per capita (kg of oil equivalent)	2,373	364	5,203	7,918

† The gross national product (GNP) is the total dollar value of all goods and services produced by a country in a year. The per capita GNP is calculated by dividing a country's GNP by its population. The World Bank defines low-income countries as those with a per capita GNP of $695 or less. High-income countries have a per capita GNP of $8,626 or more. Less than 14% of the world's 5.5 billion people live in high-income countries, while almost 60% live in low-income countries.

n.a. = data not available   > = greater than   < = less than

Sources: World Bank, *Social Indicators of Development 1995,* Baltimore: Johns Hopkins University Press, 1995. Central Intelligence Agency, *World Fact Book,* Washington, D.C.: Government Printing Office, 1994.

26 FOREIGN TRADE

Traditionally, exports consisted mainly of agricultural products (chiefly wine, citrus fruits, olives and olive oil, and cork) and minerals. While agricultural products and minerals remain important, they have been overtaken by industrial exports since the 1960s.

Imports always exceed exports by a large margin, resulting in a serious trade deficit.

Principal trade partners in 1992 were France, Germany, Italy, and Britain.

27 ENERGY AND POWER

Production of electricity in 1991 reached 155 billion kilowatt hours. Per person consumption increased from 420 kilowatt hours in 1955 to 3,972 kilowatt hours in 1991. In the same year, 46% of production was conventional thermal, 37% nuclear, and 17% hydroelectric in origin (up from 4.8% in 1981). Coal production in 1992 totaled 33.9 million tons; known reserves were estimated at 500 million tons of hard coal in 1991.

In 1992, Spanish oil wells were producing an estimated 20,000 barrels of crude oil per day. Consumption, however, totaled 1,065,000 barrels daily in 1992. Spain imports much of its natural gas from Algeria and Libya.

28 SOCIAL DEVELOPMENT

All employed persons aged 14 and older must pay into the national social security program. The program provides for health and maternity insurance, old age and incapacity insurance, a family subsidy, workers' compensation, and job-related disability payments.

One-third more women now work outside the home than a decade ago, but employment levels for women are still relatively low.

29 HEALTH

In 1991, there were a total of 175,375 hospital beds. In 1990, Spain had 148,717 doctors. In 1992, there were 3.60 doctors per 1,000 people.

Average life expectancy for the period 1988–93 was 78 years. Leading causes of death in 1990 were categorized as follows: communicable diseases and maternal/perinatal causes (45 per 100,000 people); noncommunicable diseases (410 per 100,000); and injuries (42 per 100,000).

30 HOUSING

Construction has generally fallen short of the 336,000 units needed each year to keep pace with population growth and the deterioration of old buildings. In 1989, 233,063 units were completed and the total number of dwellings in 1991 was 15,974,000.

31 EDUCATION

Elementary education is compulsory and free. During 1989, there were 19,331 schools with 140,285 teachers and 2,961,953 pupils. General secondary schools had 3,657,391 pupils with 187,934 teachers. The adult literacy rate was estimated at 95% for the period 1988-93 (79% for women and 93% for men in 1985). Students in higher education numbered 1,169,141 in 1989 and there were 59,136 instructors.

32 MEDIA

In 1991, radio transmissions were broadcast over more than 500 stations by four government, six private networks, and four state-owned television networks. In the same year, Spaniards had some 12.1 million radios and 15.6 million television sets. There were 15,476,775 telephone lines in 1991.

There were 102 daily newspapers in 1991. Sunday editions have become increasingly common, with circulations often double the weekday runs. English-language papers are now printed in Madrid and Palma de Mallorca. There are also some 3,000 magazines, bulletins, and journals. The leading Spanish dailies, with 1991 circulations, included *El Pais* (875,800); *ABC* (800,000); *El Periódico* (230,000); *La Vanguardia Española* (225,000); and *Diario 16* (200,000).

33 TOURISM AND RECREATION

Tourism has become an important industry. In 1991, Spain was the world's third most popular tourist destination, and

Europe's second. In that year, 53.4 million people visited Spain, 22% from France, 19% from Portugal, and 14% from Germany. Tourism receipts totaled $19 billion.

Many are attracted to Spain by its warm climate, beaches, and relatively low costs. Among the principal tourist attractions are Madrid, with its museums, the Escorial Palace, and the nearby Valley of the Fallen (dead in the Civil War); Toledo, with its churches and its paintings by El Greco; the Emerald Coast around San Sebastián; the Costa Brava on the coast of Catalonia, north of Barcelona; Granada, with the Alhambra and the Generalife; Sevilla, with its cathedral and religious processions; and the Canary and Balearic islands. There were 627,055 hotel rooms in 1991, with 1,146,473 beds.

Soccer is the most popular sport in Spain, and many cities have large soccer stadiums; Spain was host to the World Cup competition in 1982. Barcelona was the site of the 1992 Summer Olympics. In the same year, an International Exposition was held in Sevilla. Among traditional attractions are the bullfights, held in Madrid from April through October, and *pelota*, an indoor ball game in which spectators bet on the outcome.

34 FAMOUS SPANIARDS

Important Spanish thinkers of the Middle Ages included Averroës (Ibn Rushd; 1126–98), a Muslim philosopher, and Maimonides (Moses ben Maimon, 1135–1204), a Jewish physician and philosopher. El Cid (Rodrigo Díaz de Vivar,

Photo credit: Susan D. Rock

The monument to Christopher Columbus in Barcelona.

1043?–99) has become the national hero of Spain for his fight against the Moors.

The golden age of Spanish exploration and conquest began with the Catholic Sovereigns, Ferdinand (1452–1516) and Isabella (1451–1504), in the late 15th century. The first great explorer for Spain was Christopher Columbus (Cristoforo Colombo, 1451–1506), who made four voyages of discovery to the Americas. Among the later explorers, Vasco Núñez de Balboa (1475–1517) is noted for his discovery of the Pacific Ocean, and Hernán Cortés (1485–1547) for his conquest of Mexico.

In Spanish art, architecture, and literature, the great age was the 16th century and the early part of the 17th. Among the painters, El Greco (Domenikos Theotokopoulos, b.Crete, 1541–1614) was a leading figure. In literature, the novelist Miguel de Cervantes y Saavedra (1547–1616) wrote the well-known *Don Quixote*. St. Ignatius de Loyola (Iñigo de Oñez y Loyola, 1491–1556) founded the Jesuit order.

The 16th century was also the golden age of Spanish music. Cristóbal de Morales (1500?–53) and Tomás Luis de Vittoria (1549?–1611) were the greatest Spanish masters of sacred vocal polyphony. Leading modern composers are Isaac Albéniz (1860–1909) and Manuel de Falla (1876–1946). World-famous performers include the cellist and conductor Pablo Casals (1876–1973), the guitarist Andrés Segovia (1894–1987), and opera singer Placido Domingo (b.1941).

Francisco Goya y Lucientes (1746–1828) was the outstanding Spanish painter and etcher of his time. Pablo Ruiz y Picasso (1881–1973) was perhaps the most powerful single influence on contemporary art. Another important painter, Salvador Dali (1904-89), like Picasso spent most of his creative life outside Spain. Federico García Lorca (1899–1936) was an internationally acclaimed poet linked to the Spanish civil war. Luis Buñuel (1900–83), who lived in Mexico, was one of the world's leading film directors.

Francisco Franco (1892–1975), the leader of the right-wing rebellion that led to the Spanish Civil War (1936–39), was chief of state during 1939–47 and lifetime regent of the Spanish monarchy after 1947. After Franco's death, King Juan Carlos I (b.1938) guided Spain through the transitional period between dictatorship and democracy. Felipe González Márquez (b.1942), a Socialist, became prime minister in December 1982.

35 BIBLIOGRAPHY

Abercrombie, Thomas J. "Extremadura: Cradle of Conquerors." *National Geographic,* April 1991, 116–134.

Bryson, Bill. "The New World of Spain." *National Geographic,* April 1992, 3–33.

Cross, W., and E. Cross. *Spain.* Chicago: Children's Press, 1985.

Hooper, John. *The Spaniards: A Portrait of the New Spain,* Harmondsworth, Eng.: Penguin Books, 1987.

Nagel, Rob, and Anne Commire. "Isabella I and Ferdinand II." In *World Leaders, People Who Shaped the World.* Volume II: Europe. Detroit: U*X*L, 1994.

Orwell, George. *Homage to Catalonia.* New York: Harcourt Brace Jovanovich, 1969.

Solsten, Eric, and Sandra W. Meditz, eds. *Spain: A Country Study.* 2d ed. Washington, D.C: Library of Congress, 1990.

Thomas, Hugh. *The Spanish Civil War.* Rev. ed. New York: Harper & Row, 1977.

SRI LANKA

Democratic Socialist Republic of Sri Lanka
Sri Lanka Prajathanthrika Samajavadi Janarajaya

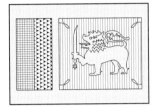

CAPITAL: Colombo.

FLAG: The national flag contains, at the hoist, vertical stripes of green and saffron (orange-yellow) and, to the right, a maroon rectangle with yellow bo leaves in the corners and a yellow lion symbol in the center. The entire flag is bordered in yellow, and a narrow yellow vertical area separates the saffron stripe from the dark maroon rectangle.

ANTHEM: *Sri Lanka Matha (Mother Sri Lanka).*

MONETARY UNIT: The Sri Lanka rupee (R) of 100 cents is a paper currency with one official rate. There are coins of 1, 2, 5, 10, 25, and 50 cents and 1 and 2 rupees, and notes of 10, 20, 50, 100, 500, and 1,000 rupees. R1 = $0.0204 (or $1 = R49.065).

WEIGHTS AND MEASURES: The metric system is the national standard, but British weights and measures and some local units are also used.

HOLIDAYS: Independence Commemoration Day, 4 February; May Day, 1 May; National Heroes Day, 22 May; Bank Holiday, 30 June; Christmas Day, 25 December; Bank Holiday, 31 December. Movable holidays include Maha Sivarathri Day, Milad-an-Nabi, Good Friday, 'Id al-Fitr, Dewali, and 'Id al-'Adha'; in addition, the day of the rise of the full moon of every month of the Buddhist calendar, called a Poya day, is a public holiday.

TIME: 5:30 PM = noon GMT.

1 LOCATION AND SIZE

Sri Lanka (formerly Ceylon) is an island in the Indian Ocean situated south and slightly east of the southernmost point of India, separated from that country by the Palk Strait which is 23 kilometers (14 miles) wide.

Sri Lanka has a total area of 65,610 square kilometers (25,332 square miles), slightly larger than the state of West Virginia, and a total coastline of 1,340 kilometers (833 miles). Sri Lanka's capital city, Colombo, is located on the Gulf of Mannar coast.

2 TOPOGRAPHY

The south-central part of Sri Lanka is a rough plateau cut by a range of mountains whose highest peak is Pidurutalagala, 2,524 meters (8,281 feet). Narrow coastal plains skirt the mountainous section on the east, south, and west. In the north the extensive coastal plain fans out, reaching from the eastern to the western shores of the island. Rivers and streams flow seaward in all directions from the central mountain area. The longest river, flowing northeastward, is the Mahaweli Ganga (335 kilometers/208 miles).

3 CLIMATE

Sri Lanka has neither summer nor winter but only rainy and dry seasons. Average rainfall varies from 63 centimeters (25 inches) to 510 centimeters (200 inches), most of the rain coming during the monsoon season. Average temperature is 27°C (80°F).

4 PLANTS AND ANIMALS

Tree ferns, bamboo, palm, satinwood, ebony, and jak trees are abundant. Water buffalo, deer, bear, elephants, monkeys, and leopards are among the larger animals still present. The Ceylon elk (sambhur) and the polonga snake are unique to Sri Lanka. Birds are numerous, many varieties from colder countries wintering on the island.

5 ENVIRONMENT

Sri Lanka's principal environmental problem has been rapid loss of forest land, leading to soil erosion, destruction of wildlife habitats, and reduction of water flow. In 1985, the total amount of land affected by deforestation was 580 square kilometers (224 square miles).

The nation's water has been polluted by industrial and agricultural by-products along with untreated sewage. As a result, 20% of the nation's city dwellers and 45% of the people living in rural areas do not have pure water. Air pollution from industry and transportation vehicles is another significant environmental concern.

By 1985 there were 37 protected wildlife areas, covering about 10% of the country's total land area. As of 1994,

Photo credit: Cynthia Bassett

Young Buddhists visiting ancient ruins from 1,500 years ago.

seven of Sri Lanka's mammal species and eight of its bird species were endangered.

6 POPULATION

The 1992 population totaled an estimated 17,405,000. A population of 19,438,000 was forecast for the year 2000. The average population density for the period 1988–93 was 269 persons per square kilometer (698 persons per square mile), one of the highest among nonindustrial countries.

Colombo, the commercial capital and chief city, had an estimated population of 615,000 in 1990.

7 MIGRATION

With the increase in conflict between eth-* nic groups in the 1980s, about 230,000 Tamils fled to India. More than 30,000 returned to Sri Lanka in 1992. About 620,000 Sri Lankans remained internally displaced in 1993.

In recent years, many Sri Lankan workers have migrated to work in Middle Eastern countries. Others—over 200,000 in all—have emigrated to Western Europe, Australia, and North America, in part as a result of the Tamil uprising.

8 ETHNIC GROUPS

According to official 1985 data, the Sinhalese constitute the largest population group, numbering 11,719,390 (74% of the total population). Sri Lankan Tamils totaled 1,900,440 (12%); Sri Lankan Moors, 1,140,265 (7.2%); Indian Tamils, 950,220 (6%); Malays, 47,511 (0.3%); and Burghers (descended from the Dutch) and Eurasians, 47,511 (0.3%). A small group of Veddas, an aboriginal tribe, together with other scattered groups, made up the remaining 0.2%.

9 LANGUAGES

The 1978 constitution recognized Sinhala as the official language but also recognized Tamil as a national language. Sinhala is a member of the Indo-Aryan subgroup of the Indo-European language family, related to Pali. Tamil is a Dravidian language spoken in northern and eastern Sri Lanka and in southern India. It became an official language in December 1988.

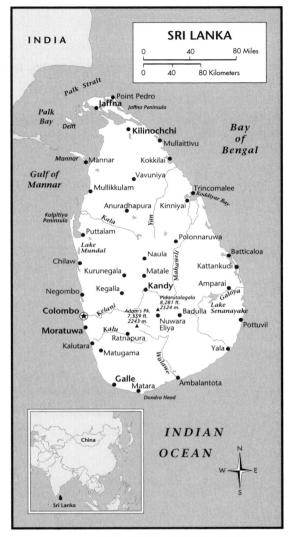

LOCATION: 5°55′ to 9°50′N; 79°42′ to 81°53′E.
TERRITORIAL SEA LIMIT: 12 miles.

10 RELIGIONS

Nearly 70% are Buddhists. Almost all the Buddhists are ethnic Sinhalese. Hindus make up 15% of the total population and are almost exclusively ethnic Tamils. Muslims account for 8% and include the

Moor and Malay communities; and Christians, accounting for 8%, are to be found in the Sinhalese, Burgher/Eurasian, and Sri Lankan Tamil communities.

A majority of Christians are Roman Catholic. There are also many Anglicans and Baptists, the latter the result of American missionary activity in the north in the nineteenth century. The religious atmosphere is traditionally tolerant, and the issues involved in the Tamil insurgency are communal and ethnic rather than religious in origin.

11 TRANSPORTATION

In 1991, the country had about 75,263 kilometers (46,768 miles) of highways. Registered motor vehicles numbered 326,934, including 180,135 passenger cars and 146,799 commercial vehicles. In 1991, there were 1,948 kilometers (1,210 miles) of broad-gauge railroad, state-owned and state operated.

Colombo, the major port, is one of the world's greatest artificial harbors. In 1991, the merchant fleet consisted of 31 ships with a capacity of 321,000 gross registered tons.

The principal international airport is Katunayaka, 39 kilometers (24 miles) north of Colombo. In 1992, Air Lanka handled all of Sri Lanka's international passenger air traffic, with 1,045,600 passengers arriving and departing.

12 HISTORY

Colonial Times–Ceylon

The earliest Indo-European-speaking settlers, the Sinhalese, came late in the sixth century BC, probably from northern India. Later arrivals from India, beginning about 240 BC, brought Buddhism. At cities such as Anuradhapura and Polonnaruwa, the Sinhalese developed a great civilization. Much of that civilization was later destroyed by civil wars and by the invasion of Hindu Dravidian-speakers from across the Palk Strait, who established a Tamil kingdom in the northern part of the island.

The Portuguese East India Company brought the first of Ceylon's European rulers in the early sixteenth century. The Portuguese quickly conquered almost the entire island. By the middle of the seventeenth century, the Portuguese were driven out of Ceylon by the Dutch East India Company, which governed for more than 100 years. They introduced plantation agriculture and developed trade. But they too soon found themselves displaced.

The British laid claim to Ceylon at the end of the eighteenth century after the Netherlands fell under French control. Ceylon was designated a crown colony in 1802, and by 1815, the entire island was united under British rule. The British introduced coffee, tea, coconut, and rubber plantations, and a more efficient government.

Photo credit: Susan D. Rock.

The commercial district of Colombo.

Independence–Sri Lanka

With the development of India's nationalist movement in the twentieth century, nationalists in Ceylon also pressured for greater self-rule. Democratic political reforms were enacted in 1910, 1920, 1924, 1931, and 1947. In 1947 India became independent with little actual struggle, and one year later, Ceylon became a self-governing dominion within the British Commonwealth.

The period from 1948 through 1970 saw the evolution of Ceylon's multiparty parliamentary system in which orderly and constitutional elections and changes of government took place. Beginning in 1970, executive power began to be highly centralized under Prime Minister Sirimavo Bandaranaike. From 1971–77 she ruled through the use of unpopular emergency powers in support of her socialist, pro-Sinhalese policies. She introduced a new constitution in 1972, changing the dominion of Ceylon to the republic of Sri Lanka.

A constitutional amendment in the fall of 1977 established a presidential form of government. Junius Richard Jayewardene of the more moderate United National Party (UNP) became Sri Lanka's first elected executive president in February 1978. Seven months later, a new, more liberal constitution came into effect, rejecting many of the authoritarian features of the 1972 constitution and introducing proportional representation.

1980–1987

Since 1978, rising tensions and violence between the majority (mostly Buddhist) Sinhalese and minority (mostly Hindu) Tamil communities have dominated Sri Lankan political life. By the early 1980s, peaceful efforts by moderate Sri Lankan Tamils to make changes in the government to protect their cultural heritage failed. Their participation in Parliament as a responsible opposition had brought no changes. An outbreak of violence in the summer of 1983 had left hundreds, if not thousands, dead in Colombo and elsewhere. By 1984–85, Sri Lankan Tamil leadership fell into the hands of extremists advocating violence.

Fighting between the Sinhalese-dominated army and well-armed Sri Lankan Tamil separatists grew worse in 1986 and 1987. In the spring of 1987, the government began a war against Tamil forces in the Jaffna Peninsula in the Northern Province. India airlifted food and supplies to the Tamils, creating considerable tension between the two countries.

On 29 July 1987, Jayewardene and Prime Minister Rajiv Gandhi of India signed an agreement by which the Sri Lankan government reluctantly agreed to give official status to the Tamil language, and to create a separate, independently governed area for the Tamils in the Northern and Eastern provinces. An Indian peacekeeping force which eventually grew to more than 100,000 troops was sent to Sri Lanka to make sure the agreement was followed and to enforce a cease-fire.

But it was already too late. In the fall of 1987, Tamil separatists led by the extremist Liberation Tigers of Tamil Ealam (LTTE) resumed their attacks, killing about 300 people. When they refused the protection of the Indian Peacekeeping Force (IPKF), the IPKF attacked the rebel stronghold in Jaffna. Fighting continued between the IPKF and the LTTE for 18 months with heavy casualties on both sides.

1988–1994

Meanwhile, throughout 1988 and 1989, the government was under attack from the militant Sinhalese nationalist JVP, for agreeing to the presence of Indian forces in Sri Lanka. The rebellion was put down firmly and brutally by President Ramasinghe Premadasa, who succeeded Jayewardene in 1988 in a close race against former prime minister Sirimavo Bandaranaike.

By 1990, it was clear that the Indian peacekeeping force was unable to stop the Tamil rebellion (at the cost of an estimated 1200 Indian lives alone). The Indian forces withdrew from Sri Lanka. President Premadasa tried to achieve a negotiated settlement, but new LTTE violence led him to order an all-out war against the north in the second half of 1990. Guerrilla warfare resumed. Through 1991 and 1992, Premadasa's government continued to pursue the possibility of a negotiated settlement, but the LTTE rejected most government terms.

Tamil rebels assassinated President Premadasa on May Day, 1993. The warfare, and the search for a solution, continued under Premadasa's successor, President Wijetunga, with frequently announced cease-fires followed by new outbreaks of fighting. The death toll and the cost, reportedly $1 million per day, continued to build up.

Chandrika Bandaranaike Kumaratunga, daughter of former prime minister Sirimavo Bandaranaike, became prime minister in August 1994. She arranged to partially lift the economic blockade of the rebel-held Jaffna peninsula and offered unconditional talks for a resolution of the dispute. Talks were scheduled for mid-October 1994.

13 GOVERNMENT

The constitution of September 1978 established the Democratic Socialist Republic of Sri Lanka as a free, sovereign, independent state based on universal suffrage at 18 years of age. The president of the republic is directly elected for a six-year term and serves as head of state and as executive head of government, appointing and heading the cabinet of ministers. A prime minister, similarly selected, serves mainly as parliamentary leader. The normal business of legislation is in the hands of a single-chamber parliament consisting of 225 members elected for six-year terms.

Sri Lanka is divided into nine provinces containing a total of 24 districts.

14 POLITICAL PARTIES

The United National Party (UNP) was the main party of the independence movement. Its widely respected leader, D. S. Senanayake, became Ceylon's first prime minister after independence. In 1951, Solomon Bandaranaike left the UNP to form the Sri Lanka Freedom Party (SLFP). Over the years, the SLFP became the island's other major political party. The UNP was friendlier to the West while the SFLP related more to the former Eastern bloc.

After President Premadasa was killed by a Tamil bomber on 1 May 1993, the Parliament unanimously elected Prime Minister Wijetunga as his successor on 7 May 1993. A "snap" election called six months early by President Wijetunga as part of his campaign for re-election backfired on 16 August 1994, when the voters rejected the UNP by a small margin. In its place, they elected to office a seven-party, leftist coalition—now dubbed the People's Alliance—led by the SLFP's Sirimavo Bandaranaike and Chandrika Bandaranaike Kumaratunga, mother and daughter, 80 and 49 years of age, respectively. More vigorous but less experienced, the younger Kumaratunga promptly became prime minister.

15 JUDICIAL SYSTEM

Sri Lanka's judicial system includes district courts, magistrates' courts, courts of request (restricted to civil cases), and rural courts. In criminal cases, the Supreme Court has appeals jurisdiction. Under the 1978 constitution, the other high-level courts are the Court of Appeal, the High Court, and courts of first instance.

16 ARMED FORCES

The defense budget has increased dramatically since 1984 as a result of the Sri Lankan Tamil uprising in the northern half of the island. In 1991, it amounted to $416 million. Between 1983 and 1993 the army expanded from less than 15,000 to 39,000, with reserves adding another 2,500. In 1993, the navy had 8,900 sailors on active duty (with another 1,000 reserves). The air force had 8,000, with another 8,500 reserves.

The armed forces, traditionally lightly armed, have been re-equipped with United States and European weaponry purchased abroad, at a cost of $160 million since 1986. Since 1985 Sri Lanka has increased its police force to 30,000, backed up by a volunteer auxiliary force of 20,000 and a home guard of 15,200.

17 ECONOMY

While Sri Lanka remains a primarily agricultural country, expansion of the economy since 1980 has been fueled by strong growth in industry and services.

In the latter half of the 1980s, the national economy faced several grave problems: rising defense costs as a result of the civil war, a series of droughts, and sharply lowered prices for the country's major export crops, tea and coconut-based goods. These conditions led to a rise in inflation, increasing unemployment, and stagnating economic growth.

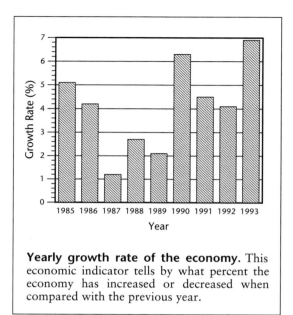

Yearly growth rate of the economy. This economic indicator tells by what percent the economy has increased or decreased when compared with the previous year.

In 1990 the economy rebounded. Though per person income in Sri Lanka remains low at around $600, other social welfare indicators such as adult literacy, school enrollment, infant mortality, and life expectancy compare very favorably with those of countries at much higher income levels.

18 INCOME

In 1992, Sri Lanka's gross national product (GNP) was $9,459 million at current prices, or $600 per person. For the period 1985–92 the average inflation rate was 11.3%, resulting in a real growth rate in per person GNP of 2.2%.

19 INDUSTRY

Since 1977, the government's market-oriented economic policies have encouraged

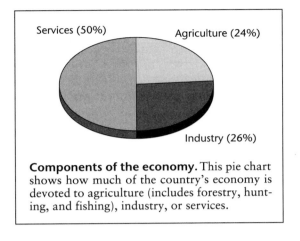

Services (50%)

Agriculture (24%)

Industry (26%)

Components of the economy. This pie chart shows how much of the country's economy is devoted to agriculture (includes forestry, hunting, and fishing), industry, or services.

industrial growth, particularly in textiles, wood products, rubber and plastics, food and beverages, and other consumer goods. Between 1990 and 1992, industrial output increased by an average of 8.4% per year. Textile production showed particularly strong growth with a 30% increase in 1992.

Output from major industries in 1992 include cement, 649,900 tons; paper and paperboard, 25,899 tons; tea, 179,000 tons; cotton fabric, 49 million square meters (59 million square yards); cotton yarn, 8,400 tons; plywood, 7,000 cubic meters; rubber tires, 228,000. In 1988, the state-run Sri Lanka Petroleum Corporation produced 1,141,000 tons of distillate and residual fuel oil, 169,000 tons of gasoline, and 159,000 tons of kerosene.

20 LABOR

In 1992, the number of employable people was about 5,948,226. That year, the agricultural sector accounted for 40%; 19.6% worked in industry and commerce; and

14.4% were sales and service workers. The number of unemployed persons in 1992 was estimated at 789,256, or about 13.3% of those who could potentially be working.

Sri Lanka has minimum wage, safety, health, and welfare laws and legislation dealing with women, young persons, and children in industry, but there are not enough officers to enforce the labor laws. About 250,000 children younger than the minimum age of 14 are estimated to be employed, and they each contribute 30–40% of household income.

The Bureau of Foreign Employment reported 300,000 Sri Lankan workers abroad in 1991, mostly in Saudi Arabia, Kuwait, United Arab Emirates, Singapore, Hong Kong, Bahrain, Qatar, and Oman. Many of them are housemaids and nannies valued for their literacy and English-language skills.

21 AGRICULTURE

Agriculture, the main support of the economy, employs about 40% of the working population. Tea production in 1992 was 179,000 tons; plantings were 210,000 hectares (518,900 acres). Rubber production was 116,000 tons, and coconut production totaled 1,750,000 tons. In 1992, tea exports ($340 million) and rubber exports ($67 million) accounted for 13.5% and 2.7% of total exports, respectively.

Production of paddy (rice), the staple food crop, totaled 2,250,000 tons in 1992; the average yield per hectare on the 790,000 hectares (1,952,000 acres) harvested was 3 tons (1.2 tons per acre).

Lesser crops include sugar, pepper, cinnamon, chilies, sesame, cardamom, tobacco, cashew nuts, betel leaves, coffee, and cocoa.

22 DOMESTICATED ANIMALS

Sri Lanka's livestock population is comparatively small; in 1992 there were 9,000,000 chickens; 1,586,000 head of cattle; 896,000 water buffalo; 502,000 goats; 91,000 hogs; and 17,000 sheep. In 1992, milk output was 194,000 tons, and 45,800 tons of eggs were produced.

23 FISHING

Fishing produces less than the country's needs and yields a meager income to fishers, most of whom use primitive boats and gear in the shallow waters surrounding the island. In 1991, the total fish catch was estimated at 198,063 tons, down from 205,286 tons in 1989.

24 FORESTRY

About one-third of the total land area consists of woodland. In 1991, 9,096,000 cubic meters of roundwood were cut. Forestry products included 5,000 cubic meters of sawn timber and 8,453,000 cubic meters of firewood for domestic use.

25 MINING

The mining industry in Sri Lanka mines mostly gemstones and graphite. Graphite production amounted to 6,381 tons in 1991. The island's gem industry is world-famous. A lapidary (cutting precious stones) industry has been set up for the international marketing of cut and pol-

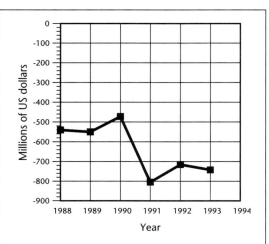

Yearly balance of trade measured in millions of US dollars. The balance of trade is the difference between what a country sells to other countries (its exports) and what it buys (its imports). If a country imports more than it exports, it has a negative balance of trade (a trade deficit). If exports exceed imports there is a positive balance of trade (a trade surplus).

ished precious and semiprecious gemstones.

Rare earth minerals of the cerium, yttrium, zirconium, niobium, tantalum, thorium, and uranium groups have been found; thorianite appears to be widely distributed. Miocene limestone from the Jaffna peninsula is used in the manufacture of cement. In the dry-zone coastal areas, salt is manufactured by solar evaporation (drying by sunlight) of seawater.

26 FOREIGN TRADE

Sri Lanka's principal exports traditionally have been tea, natural rubber, and coconut products, especially dried coconut and coconut oil. However, these three export

Selected Social Indicators

These statistics are estimates for the period 1988 to 1993. For comparison purposes, data for the United States and averages for low-income countries and high-income countries are also given.

Indicator	Sri Lanka	Low-income countries	High-income countries	United States
Per person gross national product†	$600	$380	$23,680	$24,740
Population growth rate	1.3%	1.9%	0.6%	1.0%
Population growth rate in urban areas	2.2%	3.9%	0.8%	1.3%
Population per square kilometer of land	269	78	25	26
Life expectancy in years	72	62	77	76
Number of people per physician	7,807	>3,300	453	419
Number of pupils per teacher (primary school)	29	39	<18	20
Illiteracy rate (15 years and older)	12%	41%	<5%	<3%
Energy consumed per person (kg of oil equivalent)	110	364	5,203	7,918

† The gross national product (GNP) is the total dollar value of all goods and services produced by a country in a year. The per person GNP is calculated by dividing a country's GNP by its population. The World Bank defines low-income countries as those with a per person GNP of $695 or less. High-income countries have a per person GNP of $8,626 or more. Less than 14% of the world's 5.5 billion people live in high-income countries, while almost 60% live in low-income countries.

n.a. = data not available   > = greater than   < = less than

Sources: World Bank, *Social Indicators of Development 1995*, Baltimore: Johns Hopkins University Press, 1995. Central Intelligence Agency, *World Fact Book*, Washington, D.C.: Government Printing Office, 1994.

commodities earned less and less between 1972 and 1992; tea decreased from its 58% share of total export value in 1972 to only 14% in 1992.

Lower percentages of export income for the country's agriculturally-based exports are due to bad weather in recent years as well as rapid growth in the export earnings of industrial products. The textile and garment sector accounted for 48% of total exports in 1992. Textiles, apparel, and petroleum refinery products are now the country's leading foreign exchange earners.

In 1990, the United States, the Federal Republic of Germany (FRG), Britain, and Japan were Sri Lanka's chief export markets. Japan, Iran, the United States, and India were the principal import suppliers.

27 ENERGY AND POWER

In 1991 electric power generation totaled 4,200 million kilowatt hours, or about 250 kilowatt hours per person. Four hydroelectric stations have a combined capacity of 580,000 kilowatts, which accounted for 46% of the total energy generated domestically in 1990.

28 SOCIAL DEVELOPMENT

Despite low per person income, Sri Lankans have enjoyed a relatively high standard of living because of generous social welfare programs. In 1978, the government began a vigorous population control program, combining an emphasis on family planning and voluntary sterilization with tax penalties for larger families.

The government gives monthly payments to the aged, sick, and disabled; to poor widows; and to wives of imprisoned or disabled men. To increase private efforts, the government gives grants to volunteer agencies engaged in various welfare activities, particularly orphanages, homes for the aged, and institutions for the mentally and physically handicapped. Although women have equal rights under law, their rights in family matters, including marriage, divorce, child custody, and inheritance, are often dictated by their ethnic or religious group.

29 HEALTH

The government provides medical service free or at a nominal cost to almost everyone, but its health program is hampered by an increasing shortage of trained personnel and hospital beds. Medical standards, traditionally British, are considered excellent, but in recent years many Sri Lankan physicians and surgeons have moved their practices abroad—particularly to the United States and Britain, where they can make more money.

In 1989, the Department of Health Services had 2,456 physicians, 9,632 nurses, and 5,030 midwives. For the period 1988-93, there was an average of 5,613 people per physician. In 1990, there were 2.8 hospital beds per 1,000 people. About 93% of the population has access to health care services.

Malaria, smallpox, cholera, and plague have been virtually eliminated. Malnutrition, tuberculosis (167 cases per 100,000 people in 1990), and the gastrointestinal group of infectious diseases are the chief medical problems. In 1990, 45% of children under 5 years of age were considered malnourished. Average life expectancy is 72 years.

30 HOUSING

Rapid population increase, along with a slow-down in construction during and immediately following World War II, led to a serious housing shortage, high rents, high building costs, and many unsanitary and unfit houses in Sri Lanka's first decades after independence. Under the United National Party government's urban development program, 184,860 public-sector housing units were built during the 1978–86 period.

The 1981 census showed a total of 2,813,844 housing units, of which 2,084,841 were rural, 511,810 urban, and 217,193 situated on farming estates. The average housing unit had 2.5 rooms. Although about 46% of city homes had electricity and 49% had running water, only 8.3% of rural houses were equipped with electricity and 5.1% supplied with piped-in water.

Photo credit: Cynthia Bassett

These young Sri Lankans attend their local school. Sri Lanka's literacy rate approaches 90 percent.

31 EDUCATION

In 1990, 88% of the adult population was estimated as literate with men estimated at 93.4% and women at 83.5%. All education from kindergarten up to and including university training is free. Education is compulsory for 10 years.

Since 1970, the public educational system has consisted of five years of elementary school, six years of secondary, and two years of higher levels. In 1991, there were 9,590 primary schools, with 2,112,723 students and 72,852 teachers. General secondary schools had 2,106,050 students the same year. For the period 1988-93, there were an average of 29 students per teacher in primary schools. The estimated government expenditure on education in 1985 was $68.5 million. Since 1986, the educational system has been separated into two systems, one which teaches in Sinhala and the other in Tamil.

In 1986 there were nine universities: Colombo, Peradeniya, Moratuwa, Sri Jayawardhanapura, Kelaniya, Jaffna, Ruhuna, Open University, and Batticaloa. Included in the consolidated university system are the former Vidyalankara University, a famous seat of learning for Oriental studies and Buddhist culture; the former Vidyadaya University (established 1959); and the former University of Ceylon (founded 1942). In 1990, universities and other higher-level schools had a total of 2,013 teaching staff and 38,424 students.

32 MEDIA

In 1991 there were about 166,057 telephones. The government operates radio broadcasting services in Sinhala, Tamil, and English and began television service in 1982. There were 3,460,000 radios and 17,100,000 television sets in 1991. The Sri Lanka Broadcasting Corporation airs broadcasts on AM, FM, and shortwave. In 1992, two television broadcasting stations served Sri Lanka.

In 1991, Sri Lanka had 21 daily newspapers. The principal morning and evening dailies (with their 1991 daily circulations) were *Dinamina* (Sinhala, 116,000); *Daily News* (English, 65,000); *Lankadipa* (Sinhala, 75,000); *Virakesari* (Tamil, 45,000); *Dinapathi* (Tamil, 41,200); and *Aththa* (Sinhala, 40,000). Sri Lanka also has more than 100 weekly and monthly publications.

33 TOURISM AND RECREATION

In the 1980s tourism suffered due to the civil war, but it has since recovered. In 1991, 317,703 tourists visited Sri Lanka; 198,413 came from Europe. The country had 10,870 hotel rooms with a 48.4% occupancy rate. Gross earnings from tourism were estimated at $156 million.

Except for areas of conflict between government and rebel forces, all parts of the island are easily reached by train, bus, or rented car. The principal tourist attraction is the sacred city of Anuradhapura, home of Buddhist temples and palaces. Other popular sites include the ancient cities of Polonnaruwa and Kandy, where a sacred tooth relic of the Buddha is preserved in the Dalada Maligawa temple. The botanical gardens near Kandy and the Dehiwela Zoo at Colombo are also popular. Sri Lanka's recreational facilities include the beach resorts of Bentota and Negombo, which, like Colombo, have modern hotels. Popular water sports are swimming, fishing, sailing, surfing, water skiing, and skin diving. The island has excellent facilities for golf, tennis, squash, soccer, rugby, and cricket.

34 FAMOUS SRI LANKANS

Dutugemunu (fl.100 BC) is famous for having saved Ceylon from conquest by Indian invaders. Mahasen, a king in the 3d century AD, built many fine dagobas (monuments that house a relic of Buddha or a Buddhist saint) and other monuments that delight and amaze visiting art lovers. The most famous political figure in modern Ceylon was Don Stephen Senanayake (1884–1952), leader of the independence movement and first prime minister of independent Ceylon.

35 BIBLIOGRAPHY

De Silva, Chandra Richard. *Sri Lanka, a History.* New Delhi: Vikas, 1987.

Fernando, Tissa, and Robert N. Kearney. *Sri Lanka: Profile of an Island Republic.* Boulder, Colo.: Westview, 1986.

Ross, Russell R., and Andrea Matles Savada, eds. *Sri Lanka, a Country Study.* 2d ed. Washington, D.C.: Library of Congress, 1990.

Sri Lanka in Pictures. Minneapolis: Lerner Publications Co., 1988.

Zimmermann, R. *Sri Lanka.* Chicago: Children's Press, 1992.

SUDAN

Republic of Sudan
Jumhuriyat as-Sudan

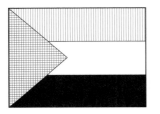

CAPITAL: Khartoum.

FLAG: The national flag consists of a tricolor of red, white, and black horizontal stripes, with a green triangle at the hoist.

ANTHEM: *Jundi al-Allah (Soldiers of God).*

MONETARY UNIT: The Sudanese pound (£s) is a paper currency of 100 piasters (qurush) or 1,000 milliemes. There are coins of 1, 2, 5, and 10 milliemes and 2, 5, 10, and 50 piasters, and notes of 25 and 50 piasters and 1, 5, 10, 20, and 50 Sudanese pounds. £s1 = $0.2625 (or $1 = £s3.81).

WEIGHTS AND MEASURES: The metric system is the legal standard, but a highly diverse system based on Egyptian and British standards is in local use.

HOLIDAYS: Independence Day, 1 January; Unity Day, 3 March; Uprising Day, 6 April; Decentralization Day, 1 July; Christmas, 25 December. Movable Muslim religious holidays include the 1st of Muharram (Muslim New Year), 'Id al-Fitr, 'Id al-'Adha', and Milad an-Nabi.

TIME: 2 PM = noon GMT.

1 LOCATION AND SIZE

Situated in northeast Africa, Sudan is the largest country on the continent. It covers an area of 2,505,810 square kilometers (967,490 square miles), slightly more than one-quarter the size of the United States. Sudan's capital city, Khartoum, is located in the northeastern part of the country.

2 TOPOGRAPHY

Most of Sudan is a vast plain traversed by the northward-flowing Nile River and its tributaries. The northern area is mainly desert, with rock at or near the surface covered by thin soils of low fertility. The most important geographic feature is the Nile River. The highest elevation is Mt. Kinyeti at 3187 meters (10,456 feet),

located along the southern border with Uganda.

3 CLIMATE

Maximum temperatures range from 32°C (90°F) in winter to 42°C (108°F) in summer. Average annual rainfall varies from 120 centimeters (47 inches) in the south to less than 10 centimeters (4 inches) in the north. The most temperate climate occurs in the Red Sea Hills.

4 PLANTS AND ANIMALS

Acacia, desert shrub, and acacia short-grass shrub grow in the northern desert and the grasslands of the west. The broad-leafed tropical woodland and forest region is for the most part in the southwest; grass covers much of the southeast. Date palms line the banks of the Nile. Wildlife includes most of the mammals, birds, and reptiles common to central Africa. Many varieties of fish are found in the rivers and in the coastal waters of the Red Sea.

5 ENVIRONMENT

A shortage of drinkable water limits farming, raising livestock, and human settlement in much of Sudan. Sudan has 7.2 cubic miles of water, of which 99% is used for farming and the remaining 1% is used in homes and businesses. Serious health problems are caused by diseases carried in the water supply; 80% of the nation's rural dwellers do not have pure water. The water on the nation's coasts is also polluted by industrial by-products, oil, and sewage. Sudan's cities produce 1.1 million tons of solid waste per year. The nation's farm land is threatened by the advance of the desert. Current estimates show that the desert overtakes 2–6 miles of land each year. Due to uncontrolled hunting, the nation's wildlife is threatened: 17 mammal species and 8 bird species are endangered, as well as 9 types of plants.

6 POPULATION

The estimated population in 1994 was 29,774,480; a population of 33,166,000 was projected for the year 2000. The average population density for the period 1988–93 was 10 persons per square kilometer (26.81 per square mile). Khartoum, the capital, and its suburbs had a population of more than 1,950,000 in 1990.

7 MIGRATION

Civil war and famine in southern Sudan were estimated to have displaced up to 3.5 million people by early 1990. Many fled abroad: there were 109,400 refugees in Zaire, 92,100 in Uganda, 25,600 in Ethiopia, 21,800 in Kenya, and 17,700 in the Central African Republic, at the end of 1992. As of the end of 1992, the Office of the United Nations High Commissioner of Refugees estimated that there were 725,600 refugees in Sudan; the refugees included 703,500 from Ethiopia, 16,000 from Chad, and 3,800 from Uganda.

8 ETHNIC GROUPS

Native Sudanese include Arabs (an estimated 39% of the population); Nilotic or Negroid peoples, of whom the Dinka form the largest portion and constitute about 10% of the national population; and Beja (6%). In all, there are nearly 600 ethnic groups.

9 LANGUAGES

Arabic, the official language, is the mother tongue of about half the population. Besides standard Arabic there are two major Arabic dialects. There is also a pidgin language (a simplified language used for communication by people who speak different languages) used in the South. English is used widely, in many cases serving as a common language among the southern tribes. In all, more than 400 languages and dialects are spoken.

SUDAN

SUDAN

Scale:
0 — 125 — 250 — 375 Miles
0 — 125 — 250 — 375 Kilometers

N W E S

EGYPT

LIBYA

Libyan Desert

Nile

Wādi Ḥalfā'

Nubian Desert

Halā'ib

Ras Hadarba

Port Sudan

Red Sea

Dunqulah

Suakin

'Aquiq

'Aṭbarah

'Aṭbarah

CHAD

Iriba

Adré

Al Junaynah

Howar

Malik

Nile

Jebel Teljo
6,411 ft.
1954 m.

Al Fāshir

Omdurman

Khartoum

Kassalā

Sebderat

ERITREA

Blue Nile

Wad Madanī

Al Qaḍārif

JEBEL MARRA

Al Ubayyid

Kūstī

Sannār

Nyala

An Nuhūd

NUBA MTS.

Kāduqli

Ad Damazin

Lake Tana

ETHIOPIA

Haraze

Birao

'Arab

Lol

Ghazāl

Malakāl

Nhar Sūbāt

White Nile

Ākobo Wenz

Hosa'ina

Waw

Sue

Jabal

Kangen

Māji

CENTRAL AFRICAN REPUBLIC

Yambio

Juba

*Kinyeti
10,456 ft.
3187 m.*

Kapoeta

ZAIRE

UGANDA

KENYA

Sudan

LOCATION: 23° to 3°N; 22° to 38°E. **BOUNDARY LENGTHS:** Egypt 1,273 kilometers (789 miles); Red Sea coastline, 853 kilometers (529 miles); Ethiopia and Eritrea, 2,221 kilometers (1,377 miles); Kenya, 232km (144 miles); Uganda, 435 kilometers (270 miles); Zaire, 628 kilometers (390 miles); Central African Republic, 1,167 kilometers (725 miles); Chad, 1,360 kilometers (845 miles); Libya, 383 kilometers (238 miles). **TERRITORIAL SEA LIMIT:** 12 miles.

10 RELIGIONS

As an important stop along the route for Mecca-bound African pilgrims, Sudan is closely linked with the Islamic world. The state religion is Islam, whose followers (primarily Sufi) are estimated to constitute up to 70% of the population. The blacks of southern Sudan mainly follow traditional African religions. As a result of missionary work, over 8% of the population are Christians, mostly Roman Catholics. Greek Orthodox, Coptic, and Anglican Christians are found in small numbers in towns.

11 TRANSPORTATION

The 5,500 kilometers (3,418 miles) of railroad track link most of the main towns of Sudan. In 1991, the overall road system, including earth tracks, totaled 20,000 kilometers (12,400 miles), of which 8% was paved. There were 116,000 automobiles and 57,000 commercial vehicles.

River transport services link many communities. Port Sudan, on the Red Sea, is primarily a cargo port, handling all of Sudan's cotton exports as well as most food imports. The international airport is at Khartoum. The state-owned Sudan Airways Corporation, founded in 1947, links the main cities and provides international service.

12 HISTORY

Early History

The most important events in recorded Sudanese history occurred in the northern half of the country, where several kingdoms thrived between ancient and modern times. The kingdom of Kush (or Cush) broke away from Egyptian rule about 1000 BC and was destroyed about AD 350. Maqurra, in northern Sudan, fell in the fifteenth century. Alwa, in central Sudan, was conquered around the beginning of the seventeenth century. The inhabitants of the south, until the twentieth century, lived in primitive tribal isolation, interrupted only by explorers.

In the 1820s, the Ottoman viceroy of Egypt, Muhammad 'Ali, brought Sudan under Turkish-Egyptian rule, which lasted until 1885. By then, most of the Sudanese tribes had rebelled against the harshness and corruption of the regime and joined together under the leadership of Muhammad Ahmad bin 'Abdallah. He proclaimed himself the Mahdi (Rightly Guided One), whose victory for Islam had been prophesied in Muslim tradition. The Mahdi installed himself as head of a theocratic (religion-based) state, which survived until 1898. The Mahdi's successor, the Khalifa ('Abdallah bin Muhammad), was defeated that year by an Anglo-Egyptian invasion force under General Horatio Herbert Kitchener in the battle of Omdurman. The French then attempted to seize parts of Sudan. They were prevented from doing so by Kitchener at Fashoda (now Kodok) in an incident that almost started a war between France and Great Britain. The British did much to restore law and order, stop slave trading, and bring modern government and economic stability to Anglo-Egyptian Sudan, as it was then called.

The Republic of Sudan

Sudanese nationalism grew after World War I (1914–18) and during World War II (1939–45). After failed attempts to join Egypt and Sudan in a dual monarchy, the new Republic of the Sudan, under a parliamentary government, was proclaimed on 1 January 1956. On 17 November 1958, a military dictatorship seized power, headed by Lieutenant General Ibrahim Abboud, after a bloodless coup that had the support of some party leaders. President Abboud's military regime was overthrown on 26 October 1964, and civilian politicians ruled for the next five years.

A revolutionary council led by Colonel Gaafar Mohammed Nimeiri (Ja'far Muhammad Numayri) overthrew the government in another bloodless coup on 25 May 1969 and established the Democratic Republic of the Sudan. On 25 May 1971, he proclaimed that Sudan would become a one-party state, with the Sudanese Socialist Union the sole political organization. Nimeiri, running unopposed, was elected president in September. One of his most significant acts was to bring an end to the civil war that had plagued Sudan since independence. In February 1972, the Sudanese government and the South Sudan Liberation Front (the Anyanya rebels) agreed on a cease-fire and on self-rule for the southern provinces. Nimeiri was reelected without opposition in 1977 and 1983, but his regime had to survive considerable turmoil both on the home-front and in relations with neighboring countries, especially Libya.

Nimeiri declared a state of emergency in April 1984 to cope with protests over rising prices and government policies. The state of emergency ended in September 1984, but by then a new rebellion was under way in the south, which was unhappy with Nimeiri's efforts to restrict its actions and apply Shari'ah (Muslim law). Riots broke out in the spring of 1985 when Nimeiri's economic policies caused prices to rise. On 7 April 1985 Nimeiri was replaced by a military council headed by General Abdel-Rahman Swar ad-Dhahab. The country was renamed the Republic of Sudan, the ruling Sudanese Socialist Union was abolished, political and press freedom was restored, and food prices were lowered. Sudan returned to a foreign policy of nonalignment, backing away from its close ties with Egypt and the United States.

Unrest in the South

General elections held in April 1986 resulted in a moderate civilian coalition government headed by Prime Minister Sadiq al-Mahdi. The government began searching for a way to unite the country with the Sudanese People's Liberation Army (SPLA). The SPLA controlled much of the south, blocking air traffic (including food relief) to the south and opposing major projects vital to the economy.

In March 1989, a new government composed of Ummah Party and Democratic Unionist Party (DUP) ministers agreed to work with the SPLA. However, on 30 June 1989, a group of army officers led by Brigadier Omar Hassam al-Bashir overthrew the civilian government. The coup makers created a National Salvation Revolutionary Command Council (RCC), a junta (a group of people who run a government, particularly after a coup) composed of 15 military officers assisted by a civilian cabinet. They suspended the 1985 transitional constitution, took away press freedoms, and dissolved all parties and trade unions.

On 23 April 1990, Bashir declared a state of emergency and dissolved parliament because of an alleged coup attempt. The following day, 28 officers were court-martialed and executed. Yet none of these reforms seemed to make southern leaders happy. Peace talks sponsored by ex-United States president Jimmy Carter, Nigeria, and others broke down with few positive results.

Bashir's Islamic government is dominated by the fundamentalist National Islamic Front (NIF), under the leadership of Hassan al-Turabi. Bashir remains president, chief of state, prime minister, and chief of the armed forces. Sudan has given sanctuary to Muslim rebels from Tunisia and Algeria, to the Hezbollah (Party of God), and to Abu Nidal's Palestinian rebels. The regime has eliminated all non-Muslims from the civil service, the armed forces, the judiciary and the educational system. With the fall of Ethiopia's Marxist government in 1991, the SPLA lost its chief ally. The government is still fighting rebels in the south. In 1992 it reduced rebel-held territory but increased casualties and displaced persons (who number, at times, over two million). As the fighting grows, so does famine. Private and United Nations relief efforts have been held off from time to time after attacks by rebels. Fighting between factions of the SPLA adds to the unrest.

Because of its militant Islamic policies, Sudan's allies are limited to Afghanistan, Iran, Libya, and Syria. The United Nations General Assembly condemned Sudan's human rights violations in March 1993.

13 GOVERNMENT

After the 1989 military coup, the 1985 transitional constitution was set aside. In January 1991, Islamic law was imposed in the six northern provinces. Executive and legislative authority was vested in a 15-member Revolutionary Command Council (RCC). Its chairman, acting as prime minister, appointed a 300-member transitional National Assembly. In mid-October 1993, Bashir dissolved the RCC and officially declared himself president of a new civilian government. Elections are planned for 1994 and 1995.

14 POLITICAL PARTIES

The Revolutionary Command Council (RCC), which formed the latest military government, dissolved all parties in 1989. The fundamentalist National Islamic Front (NIF), however, continues to function openly and is the strength behind the government. NIF members and supporters hold most key positions and when Bashir dissolved the RCC in October 1993, the NIF further tightened its grip on the state.

The main opposition to the central government is the Sudan's People's Liberation Army (SPLA) which, in 1993, split into

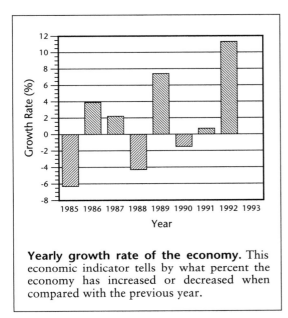

Yearly growth rate of the economy. This economic indicator tells by what percent the economy has increased or decreased when compared with the previous year.

two main groups, the "Torit" faction and the SPLA-United.

15 JUDICIAL SYSTEM

For the Muslim population, justice in personal matters is administered by Muslim law courts, which form the Shari'ah Division of the Sudan judiciary. Civil justice is administered by the Supreme Court, courts of appeal, and lower courts. Criminal justice is administered by major courts, magistrates' courts, and local people's courts, which try civil cases as well.

16 ARMED FORCES

The army has an estimated strength of 75,000, organized into 9 divisions and 29 brigades. The navy, established in 1962, has 1,500 personnel and 2 patrol craft; the

air force has 6,000 personnel and 51 combat aircraft, plus air defense missile units. Estimated defense expenditures in 1989 were $610 million. The Sudanese armed forces face an estimated 50,000 rebels of the Sudanese People's Liberation Army.

17 ECONOMY

Sudan has an agricultural economy with great potential for production with the help of irrigation. The livestock sector is sizable as well. However, droughts have led to recent famines, and civil war has led to the virtual collapse of the economy. In 1993, Sudan's failure to pay its international debt, together with its poor human rights record, led to the World Bank's suspension of financing for 15 development projects, and to the IMF's suspension of Sudan's voting rights in the organization.

18 INCOME

In 1992 Sudan's gross national product (GNP) was $184 per person. For the period 1985–92, the average inflation rate was 150%.

19 INDUSTRY

Sudan's industrial output has decreased since the early 1980s due to problems with trade and production. Before this difficult period, Sudan's industries supplied many items that had formerly been imported, such as cotton textiles, sugar, household appliances, cement, and tires. Textiles are the largest industry. Factories process cotton seed and groundnuts into oil and cake. The Kenana sugar complex is one of the largest sugar plantations and refining installations in the world.

20 LABOR

About two-thirds of the population relied on agriculture in 1991/92. Industry engages less than 10% of the labor force. Unemployment officially stood at 30% in 1990/91. In September 1989, the Sudan Workers Trade Union Federation (with some 800,000 members) was restored under tight government control.

The minimum age for employment is 16, but the law is not well-enforced. Poverty forces many families to send their children to work to bring in extra money for survival.

21 AGRICULTURE

About one-third of the total area of Sudan is suitable for farming. Cotton is the principal export crop and the lifeblood of the country's economy; in 1992, over 76,000 tons of cotton were exported, valued at $116 million (28% of total exports).

Among agricultural products in 1992 were sorghum, 4,320,000 tons; wheat, 895,000 tons; peanuts, 454,000 tons; and sesame, 330,000 tons, (the highest in Africa). Cotton fiber production in 1992 was 87,000 tons. Production in 1992 also included sugarcane, 4,600,000 tons; millet, 424,000 tons; cottonseed, 170,000 tons; tomatoes, 151,000 tons; dates, 142,000 tons; yams, 129,000 tons; corn, 51,000 tons; and cassava, 9,000 tons.

22 DOMESTICATED ANIMALS

In 1992, Sudan's livestock population included 35 million chickens, 22.6 million sheep, 21.6 million cattle, 18.7 million goats, and 2.8 million camels. The national livestock herd was second only to that of Ethiopia in Africa. Livestock products in 1992 included an estimated 3,193,000 tons of milk, 449,000 tons of meat, and 34,500 tons of eggs.

23 FISHING

The Nile River yields some 110 varieties of fish, and the Red Sea is another valuable fishing ground. In 1991, the total catch was 33,303 tons.

24 FORESTRY

About 44 million hectares (108 million acres) of Sudan are covered by woodlands and forests. Sudan supplies over 80% of the world's needs of gum arabic, extracted from the acacia. Production of roundwood, which is almost entirely used for fuel, was estimated at 23.4 million cubic meters in 1991.

25 MINING

Sudan is not rich in mineral resources, although large iron ore reserves have been found near Port Sudan. Estimated mineral production in 1991 included salt, 75,000 tons; chromium ore, 10,000 tons; and crude gypsum and anhydrite, 7,000 tons. Commercial-scale gold mining in the Red Sea Hills began in late 1985; production in 1991 amounted to 50 kilograms (110 pounds).

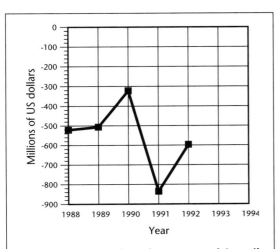

Yearly balance of trade measured in millions of US dollars. The balance of trade is the difference between what a country sells to other countries (its exports) and what it buys (its imports). If a country imports more than it exports, it has a negative balance of trade (a trade deficit). If exports exceed imports there is a positive balance of trade (a trade surplus).

26 FOREIGN TRADE

The main exports are agricultural products including cotton, gum arabic, sesame, millet, and sorghum. The main imports are a broad range of industrial goods, petroleum products, and foodstuffs. In 1987, 49.1% of Sudan's exports went to the countries of the European Community, followed by Japan (6.3%) and the United States (4.7%). Sa'udi Arabia was Sudan's highest import supplier (14.9%, almost entirely petroleum) in 1986.

27 ENERGY AND POWER

In the absence of coal reserves, Sudan has come to rely mainly on waterpower to meet its commercial energy needs. In 1991, production of electricity amounted to 1,329 million kilowatt hours. In 1991, the burning of wood fulfilled 82% of the total energy requirement. Modest petroleum reserves, estimated at 219 million barrels, have been discovered.

28 SOCIAL DEVELOPMENT

Organized social welfare is administered by the central and local governments, labor unions, and fraternal organizations. Social legislation requires business firms to provide benefits for their employees.

Since the military coup in 1989, the fundamentalist Islamic government has removed many of the basic rights and freedoms of women.

Because of the civil war, starvation and malnutrition are widespread.

29 HEALTH

In spite of an improvement in medical services and supervision, such diseases as malaria, schistosomiasis, sleeping sickness, tuberculosis (about 211 cases per 100,000 people in 1990), and various forms of dysentery persist. Food aid was not reaching famine-stricken southern Sudan in the mid-1980s because of civil war.

For the period 1988-93, average life expectancy was estimated at 53 years. Hospital facilities and medical and public health services are free, but only 51% of the population had access to them in 1992. From 1988-93, there were an average of 9,964 people per physician. Total

Selected Social Indicators

These statistics are estimates for the period 1988 to 1993. For comparison purposes, data for the United States and averages for low-income countries and high-income countries are also given.

Indicator	Sudan	Low-income countries	High-income countries	United States
Per person gross national product†	**$184**	$380	$23,680	$24,740
Population growth rate	**2.7%**	1.9%	0.6%	1.0%
Population growth rate in urban areas	**4.5%**	3.9%	0.8%	1.3%
Population per square kilometer of land	**10**	78	25	26
Life expectancy in years	**53**	62	77	76
Number of people per physician	**9,964**	>3,300	453	419
Number of pupils per teacher (primary school)	**34**	39	<18	20
Illiteracy rate (15 years and older)	**73%**	41%	<5%	<3%
Energy consumed per person (kg of oil equivalent)	**68**	364	5,203	7,918

† The gross national product (GNP) is the total dollar value of all goods and services produced by a country in a year. The per person GNP is calculated by dividing a country's GNP by its population. The World Bank defines low-income countries as those with a per person GNP of $695 or less. High-income countries have a per person GNP of $8,626 or more. Less than 14% of the world's 5.5 billion people live in high-income countries, while almost 60% live in low-income countries.

> = greater than   < = less than

Sources: World Bank, *Social Indicators of Development 1995,* Baltimore: Johns Hopkins University Press, 1995. Central Intelligence Agency, *World Fact Book,* Washington, D.C.: Government Printing Office, 1994.

health care expenditures in 1990 were $300 million.

30 HOUSING

As of 1983, 60% of housing units were *gottias*, single rooms with round mud walls and a conical straw roof; 36% were *menzils*, multi-room houses with toilet facilities.

A national housing authority provides low-cost housing to government employees, rural schoolteachers, and persons in low-income groups. Khartoum has a number of modern apartment buildings.

31 EDUCATION

In 1990, 57.3% of the adult male and 88.3% of the adult female population were illiterate. The average literacy rate for the period 1988-93 was estimated at 27%. In the mid-1980s, only 57% of school-age boys and 41% of eligible girls were actually attending primary school; the proportions for secondary school were 23% and 16%, respectively.

In 1990, 7,939 primary schools had 2,042,743 students and 60,047 teachers; secondary schools had 731,624 students and 33,628 teachers.

In 1986, the University of Khartoum's 10 faculties had about 14,000 students. A branch of Cairo University was opened at Khartoum in 1955; by 1986, it had about 20,000 students. Other institutions include the Islamic University of Omdurman and the universities of El-Gezirah (at Wad Madani) and Juba. In 1989, higher level institutions had a total of 2,522 teachers and 60,134 students.

32 MEDIA

In 1991 there were 77,920 telephones. The Sudan Broadcasting Service (the government-controlled radio network) transmits daily in Arabic, English, French, Amharic, Somali, and other languages; 5,375,000 radios were in use in 1991. Television service was began in 1963; by 1991 there were about 2 million sets in use.

When it came to power in June 1989, the al-Bashir government banned all newspapers and magazines except one pro-government military newspaper.

33 TOURISM AND RECREATION

The main tourist attractions are big-game hunting in the jungles of the south, boat excursions down the Nile through the jungle and desert, deep-sea fishing, the Red Sea Hills, the underwater gardens at Port Sudan, and archaeological sites in the north.

Since the civil war and the establishment of Islamic rule, there is practically no tourism in Sudan. There were 1,423 tour-

Photo credit: U.S. National Archives

Head of a Mahdiya Warrior, *an ink drawing by Ibrahim El Salahi.*

ist arrivals in 1991, generating receipts of $8 million.

34 FAMOUS SUDANESE

The one Sudanese to achieve world renown in modern history was the Mahdi (Muhammad Ahmad bin 'Abdallah, 1843–85), the religious leader who led the people of Sudan to overthrow their Egyptian rulers.

Osman Digna ('Uthnab Abu Bakr Digna, c. 1840–1926), an organizer and leader of the Mahdist armies, and Sayyid 'Abd ar-Rahman al-Mahdi (1885–1959), posthumous son of the Mahdi, are revered by Sudanese.

The most influential figure in recent years was Gaafar Mohammed Nimeiri (Ja'far Muhammad Numayri, b.1930), leader of Sudan from the 1969 coup until 1985.

[35] BIBLIOGRAPHY

Holt, P. M. *The History of the Sudan, from the Coming of Islam to the Present Day.* 4th ed. New York: Longman, 1988.

Metz, Helen Chapin, ed. *Sudan: A Country Study.* 4th ed. Washington, D.C.: Library of Congress, 1992.

Sudan in Pictures. Minneapolis: Lerner Publications Co., 1988.

SURINAME

Republic of Suriname
Republiek Suriname

CAPITAL: Paramaribo.

FLAG: A yellow star is at the center of five stripes: a broad red band in the middle, two white bands, and a green stripe at the top and bottom.

ANTHEM: The *Surinaams Volkslied (National Anthem)* begins "God zij met ons Suriname" ("God be with our Suriname").

MONETARY UNIT: The Suriname guilder (Sf) is a paper currency of 100 cents. There are coins of 1, 5, 10, and 25 cents, and notes of 5, 10, 25, 100, and 500 guilders. Sf1 = $0.5602 (or $1 = Sf1.785).

WEIGHTS AND MEASURES: The metric system is used.

HOLIDAYS: New Year's Day, 1 January; Revolution Day, 25 February; Labor Day, 1 May; National Union Day, 1 July; Independence Day, 25 November; Christmas, 25 December; Boxing Day, 26 December. Movable religious holidays include Holi Phagwah, Good Friday, Easter Monday, and 'Id al-Fitr.

TIME: 8:30 AM = noon GMT.

1 LOCATION AND SIZE

Situated on the northeast coast of South America, Suriname is the smallest independent country on the continent, with a total area of 163,270 square kilometers (63,039 square miles). The area occupied by Suriname is slightly larger than the state of Georgia. Suriname has a total boundary length of 2,093 kilometers (1,301 miles). Suriname's capital city, Paramaribo, is located on the Atlantic coast.

2 TOPOGRAPHY

Suriname is divided into three regions. The fertile coastal plain is flat and sometimes as much as 1.5 meters (5 feet) below sea level. A grassy savanna belt lies south of the coastal region. Still farther south are the tropical rainforest of the interior and a mountainous area near the Brazilian border. Several rivers, including the Maroni and the Courantyne, flow northward to the Atlantic Ocean, where a great number of rapids and waterfalls block boat passage.

3 CLIMATE

The climate is tropical and moist. Daytime temperatures range from 28° to 32°C (82–90°F). At night the temperature drops as low as 21°C (70°F). The annual rainfall in Paramaribo is about 230 centimeters (90 inches).

4 PLANTS AND ANIMALS

Covered largely by rainforest, Suriname contains many flowers but is most famous for water lilies and orchids. Tropical shrubs include hibiscus, bougainvillea, and oleander. There are over 184 species of mammals. Among the reptiles are the tortoise, iguana, caiman, and many kinds of snakes. Tropical birds abound, especially the white egret.

5 ENVIRONMENT

Pollutants from the country's mining industry affect the purity of the water; 18% of Suriname's city dwellers and 44% of all rural dwellers do not have pure water.

Suriname's eight nature reserves are managed by the Foundation for Nature Preservation. The Suriname Wildlife Rangers Club, consisting mainly of students 15–20 years old, assists in various nature preservation activities. As of 1994, 11 mammal species and 6 bird species were endangered, as well as 68 types of plants.

6 POPULATION

The population in July 1993 was estimated at 416,321. The United Nations projected a population of 500,000 for the year 2000. Average estimated population density in 1991 was 3 persons per square kilometer (6 per square mile). Paramaribo, the capital, had a population of about 200,000 in 1990.

7 MIGRATION

Emigration increased with Suriname's independence and again after the coup of February 1980. Some 200,000 Surinamese lived in the Netherlands by 1985. An estimated 6,000 fled to French Guiana by 1987, seeking refuge from guerrilla warfare. Some 1,500 were still living in camps there at the end of 1992.

8 ETHNIC GROUPS

Suriname has one of the most diverse populations in the world. The two largest ethnic groups are the Creoles, mixed-race descendents of black plantation slaves (about 35% of the population), and the Hindustanis (about 33%), descendants of indentured laborers from India. The Bushmen (10%) are descended from Africans who escaped from the plantations into the forests of the interior. Other groups include the Javanese (about 16%), Chinese, and Europeans. The Amerindians (3%), Suriname's original inhabitants, include the Arawak, Carib, and Warrau.

9 LANGUAGES

The official language is Dutch, but English is widely spoken. The local people use a common language known as Sranang-Tongo or Takki-Takki, a mixture of Dutch, African, and other languages. Hindi, Javanese, and several Chinese, Amerindian, and African languages and dialects are also spoken.

10 RELIGIONS

The majority of the Asiatic peoples are Muslim (an estimated 19% in 1983). The Creole group is mostly Christian, about 20% Roman Catholic and 18% Protestant. Most Bush Creoles follow traditional African religions, but a small proportion are either Roman Catholic or Moravian. The European sector includes small numbers of Jews, Roman Catholics, Lutherans, Moravians, and members of the Dutch Reformed Church.

11 TRANSPORTATION

Suriname has 1,200 kilometers (746 miles) of navigable waterways. A ferry service across the Courantyne River to Guyana began operating in 1990. There are 166 kilometers (103 miles) of single-track railway. As of 1991, there were an estimated 8,300 kilometers (5,158 miles) of roadways. In 1992, there were 35,000 passenger cars and 15,000 commercial vehicles. Three merchant ships were in service as of the end of 1991. Zanderij International Airport near Paramaribo can handle jet aircraft. Suriname Airways offers regularly scheduled service to the Netherlands and Curaçao.

12 HISTORY

Spaniards came to Suriname in the sixteenth century in search of gold, but did not stay when they found none. The first large-scale colonization took place under Francis, Lord Willoughby, the English governor of Barbados. Willoughby sent an expedition to Suriname in 1650 under Anthony Rowse. In 1660, the British crown granted Willoughby official rights, and it became a flourishing agricultural colony. Settlers included English colonists, African slaves, and Jewish immigrants from the Netherlands, Italy, and Brazil. In the Peace of Breda between England and the United Netherlands in 1667, Suriname became a Dutch colony.

The English held Suriname again between 1799 and 1802 and from 1804 to 1816, when the Dutch resumed control over the colony under the Treaty of Paris. With the final abolition of slavery in 1863, workers were imported from India, Java,

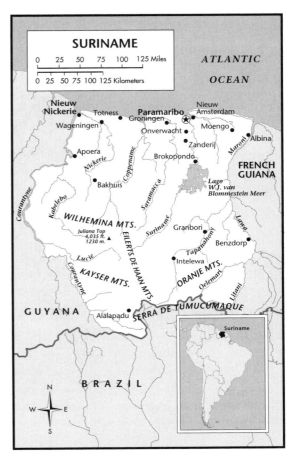

LOCATION: 2° to 6°N; 54° to 58°W. **BOUNDARY LENGTHS:** Atlantic coastline, 386 kilometers (228 miles); French Guiana, 510 kilometers (318 miles); Brazil, 597 kilometers (373 miles); Guyana, 600 kilometers (382 miles). **TERRITORIAL SEA LIMIT:** 12 miles.

and China. In 1954, a new Dutch statute provided for full self-rule for Suriname, except in foreign affairs and defense. Suriname became an independent country on 25 November 1975.

For five years, Suriname was a parliamentary republic under prime minister Henk Arron. On 25 February 1980, the government was overthrown in a military

Photo credit: Anne Kalosh

Maroon (Bushmen) home in Suriname.

The military allowed for elections on 25 November 1987. An anti-Bouterse coalition, the Front for Democracy, won 80% of the vote, but the military gave law-making authority to a new appointed State Council, rather than the elected National Assembly. International pressure mounted, and the military soon gave in, scheduling elections on 25 May 1991. Again, an anti-military coalition swept the election. The leader of the coalition, Ronald Venetiaan, was chosen president on 6 September 1991.

13 GOVERNMENT

The 1987 constitution provides for a single-chamber, 51-member National Assembly directly elected for a four-year term. The executive branch consists of the president, vice-president, and prime minister, all chosen by the National Assembly. There is also a cabinet and an appointed Council of State. The republic is divided into 10 districts.

14 POLITICAL PARTIES

The leading parties are the National Party of Suriname (NPS), led by President Ronald Venetiaan, which draws support from the Creole population; the Progressive Reform Party (VHP), which is East Indian; and the Indonesian Peasant's Party (KTPI). In 1991, these three parties and the Suriname Labor Party (SPA) formed the New Front (NF) and won a solid victory, gaining 30 of 51 Assembly seats.

15 JUDICIAL SYSTEM

The Constitution provides the right to a fair public trial before a single judge, the

coup led by Désiré Bouterse. Parliament was dissolved and the constitution suspended. In 1981 the new government declared itself a Socialist republic.

The military and Bouterse ruled through a series of supposedly civilian governments, while pressure mounted for a return to genuine civilian rule. When the Surinamese Liberation Army (SLA), a guerrilla movement, began operating in the northeast in July 1986, the government responded by killing civilians suspected of supporting the rebels.

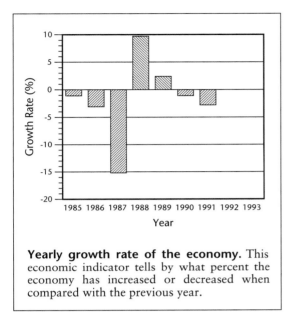

Yearly growth rate of the economy. This economic indicator tells by what percent the economy has increased or decreased when compared with the previous year.

right to legal counsel, and the right to appeal. There is a Supreme Court.

16 ARMED FORCES

The Suriname National Army consists of army, air force, and naval divisions, with a strength of about 1,800 in 1993. Defense spending is below $100 million.

17 ECONOMY

The bauxite industry has traditionally set the pace for Suriname's economy. Next to bauxite, foreign aid is the mainstay of the country's economy.

In February 1987, guerrilla fighters cut off electricity to the bauxite mines, which ten closed while repairs were made. The resulting collapse of bauxite exports in 1987 was a severe blow to the economy. Production of bauxite has not fully recov-

ered and earnings continue to sag. In 1992, average inflation grew to 44%.

18 INCOME

In 1992, the gross national product (GNP) was $1,728 million at current prices. For the period 1988–93, the average per person GNP was $1,180. For the period 1985–92 the average inflation rate was 14.7%, resulting in a real growth rate in per person GNP of –3.2%.

19 INDUSTRY

The major industries are mining and food processing. The bauxite industry over the years has developed into a complex of factories, workshops, power stations, and laboratories. The output of refined aluminum was 28,785 tons in 1985. During the same year, Surinamese factories produced 79,480 tons of cement, 253,313 pairs of shoes, 30 million liters (8 million gallons) of soft drinks, and 14 million liters (3.7 million gallons) of beer.

20 LABOR

Of the total working population (99,010), most are employed in the northern regions, where about 40% are employed in services. Overall, agriculture accounts for about 33% of national civilian employment. About 33% of the total labor force was unemployed in 1990. The minimum age for employment is 16, but the law is not strictly enforced.

21 AGRICULTURE

The chief crops are rice, sugar, plantains and bananas, citrus fruits, coffee, coconuts, and palm oil, in addition to staple food crops. Rice production was 238,000 tons in 1991. Production of sugar in 1992 was 45,000 tons; of bananas, 49,000 tons; of oranges, 11,000 tons; of coconuts, 13,000 tons; and of palm oil, 1,600,000 tons.

22 DOMESTICATED ANIMALS

Most livestock is owned by small farmers who have only a few animals each. Estimated livestock numbers in 1992 included 95,000 head of cattle, 31,000 hogs, 18,000 goats and sheep, and 9,000,000 chickens.

23 FISHING

The chief commercial catch is shrimp, which is exported. In 1991, shrimp production was 790 tons, and the fish catch was about 4,100 tons.

24 FORESTRY

Approximately 95% of Suriname is covered by tropical rainforest, but forest resources have scarcely been touched. Roundwood production was about 140,000 cubic meters in 1991.

25 MINING

Suriname is the sixth-largest producer of bauxite and the fifth-largest producer of alumina in the world. The total quantity of bauxite mined in 1991 was some 3.2 million tons. Suriname's bauxite industry has suffered in recent years from a weak market, foreign competition, and the effects of the guerrilla war, but new mines with higher grade bauxite should be replacing older depleted mines by 1995.

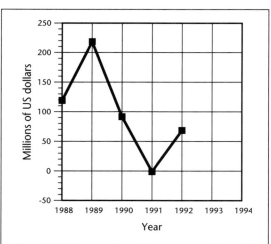

Yearly balance of trade measured in millions of US dollars. The balance of trade is the difference between what a country sells to other countries (its exports) and what it buys (its imports). If a country imports more than it exports, it has a negative balance of trade (a trade deficit). If exports exceed imports there is a positive balance of trade (a trade surplus).

By 1991, gold production had fallen to 30 kilograms (66 pounds).

26 FOREIGN TRADE

In 1992, exports totaled $417 million and consisted mainly of alumina, aluminum, bauxite, rice, shrimp, wood products, and bananas. Imports registered $417 million, including fuel and lubricating oils, cotton, flour, meat, and dairy products, refined petroleum products, machinery and transport equipment, and consumer goods. Suriname exported mainly to Norway, Netherlands, the United States, Germany, France, Brazil, and Venezuela. It imported mostly from the United States, Netherlands, Trinidad and Tobago, Netherlands

Selected Social Indicators

These statistics are estimates for the period 1988 to 1993. For comparison purposes, data for the United States and averages for low-income countries and high-income countries are also given.

Indicator	Suriname	Low-income countries	High-income countries	United States
Per capita gross national product†	$1,180	$380	$23,680	$24,740
Population growth rate	1.2%	1.9%	0.6%	1.0%
Population growth rate in urban areas	2.4%	3.9%	0.8%	1.3%
Population per square kilometer of land	3	78	25	26
Life expectancy in years	70	62	77	76
Number of people per physician	1,217	>3,300	453	419
Number of pupils per teacher (primary school)	23	39	<18	20
Illiteracy rate (15 years and older)	5%	41%	<5%	<3%
Energy consumed per capita (kg of oil equivalent)	1,877	364	5,203	7,918

† The gross national product (GNP) is the total dollar value of all goods and services produced by a country in a year. The per capita GNP is calculated by dividing a country's GNP by its population. The World Bank defines low-income countries as those with a per capita GNP of $695 or less. High-income countries have a per capita GNP of $8,626 or more. Less than 14% of the world's 5.5 billion people live in high-income countries, while almost 60% live in low-income countries.

> = greater than   < = less than

Sources: World Bank, Social Indicators of Development 1995, Baltimore: Johns Hopkins University Press, 1995. Central Intelligence Agency, World Fact Book, Washington, D.C.: Government Printing Office, 1994.

Antilles, Brazil, the United Kingdom, and Venezuela.

27 ENERGY AND POWER

Total electrical power production in 1991 was 1,400 million kilowatt hours. In 1990, the government-owned oil company, Staatsolie, increased production to 4,500 barrels per day. By the mid-1990s, oil production was expected to expand to 6,500 barrels per day.

28 SOCIAL DEVELOPMENT

Welfare programs are largely conducted privately, or through ethnic or religious groups. The privately run Home for Women in Crisis Situations is consistently overcrowded, indicating a national problem in the area of violence against women.

29 HEALTH

Tuberculosis, malaria, and syphilis, once the chief causes of death, have been controlled. In 1993, Suriname's average life expectancy was 70 years. For the period 1988–93, there was an average of 1,217 people per doctor. In 1990, there were an estimated 2.7 hospital beds per 1,000 people and estimated health care expenditures of $46.7 million.

30 HOUSING

Between 1988 and 1990, 82% of the urban and 94% of the rural population had access to a public water supply, while 64% of urban dwellers and 36% of rural dwellers had sanitation services.

31 EDUCATION

In 1988, there were 301 elementary schools, with 2,921 teachers and 65,798 pupils; secondary schools had 34,248 pupils. For the period 1988–93, there was an average of 23 students per teacher in primary schools. Education is compulsory and free for all children aged 6 through 12. The adult literacy rate in 1990 was 95%. Higher education includes four teacher-training colleges, the Technical College, and the University of Suriname. In 1990, higher level institutions reported a total of 495 teaching staff with 4,319 students enrolled.

32 MEDIA

There were 27,500 telephones in 1993. As of the same year there were 6 AM radio stations, 14 FM stations, and 6 state-run television stations. In 1991, 274,000 radios and 56,000 television sets were in use. There are two daily newspapers, the Dutch-language *De Ware Tijd* (circulation 30,000), and *Dagblad de West* (circulation 15,000).

33 TOURISM AND RECREATION

Tourism has fallen sharply since the 1980 coup. In 1991, there were 30,000 tourists. However, Suriname's tropical rainforest is increasingly attracting eco-tourism.

Photo credit: Anne Kalosh

Dining at Eco-tourism Lodge, Kumalu Island, Suriname.

Hotel rooms numbered 1,550, with 3,900 beds, and tourism receipts totaled $11 million.

34 FAMOUS SURINAMESE

Lieutenant Colonel Désiré ("Dési") Bouterse (b.1945) led the coup of February 1980.

35 BIBLIOGRAPHY

Goslinga, Cornelis C. *A Short History of the Netherlands Antilles and Suriname*. Norwell, Mass.: Kluwer Academic Press, 1978.

Hoefte, Rosemarijn. *Suriname*. Santa Barbara, Calif.: Clio Press, 1990.

Lieberg, C. *Suriname*. Chicago: Children's Press, 1995.

SWAZILAND

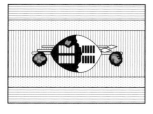

Kingdom of Swaziland

CAPITAL: Mbabane (administrative and judicial); Lobamba (royal and parliamentary).

FLAG: Blue, yellow, crimson, yellow, and blue stripes with the shield and spears of the Emasotsha regiment superimposed on the crimson stripe.

ANTHEM: National Anthem, beginning "O God, bestower of the blessings of the Swazi."

MONETARY UNIT: The lilangeni (pl. emalangeni; E) of 100 cents is a paper currency equal in value to the South African rand, which is also legal tender. There are coins of 1, 2, 5, 10, 20, and 50 cents, 1 lilangeni, and notes of 2, 5, 10, 20, and 50 emalangeni. E1 = $0.2874 (or $1 = E3.4795).

WEIGHTS AND MEASURES: The metric system replaced imperial weights and measures in September 1969.

HOLIDAYS: New Year's Day, 1 January; Commonwealth Day, 2nd Monday in March; National Flag Day, 25 April; Birthday of King Sobhuza II, 22 July; Umhlanga (Reed Dance) Day, last Monday in August; Somhlolo (Independence) Day, 6 September; UN Day, 24 October; Christmas Day, 25 December; Boxing Day, 26 December. Movable religious holidays include Good Friday, Holy Saturday, Easter Monday, Ascension, and the Incwala Ceremony.

TIME: 2 PM = noon GMT.

1 LOCATION AND SIZE

A landlocked country in southern Africa, Swaziland has an area of 17,360 square kilometers (6,703 square miles), slightly smaller than the state of New Jersey. It has a total boundary length of 554 kilometers (344 miles).

Swaziland's capital city, Mbabane, is located in the west central part of the country.

2 TOPOGRAPHY

The country is divided west-to-east into four regions: the high-, middle-, and lowveld, and the Lubombo plain. There are rivers and streams throughout the country, making it one of the best watered areas in southern Africa.

3 CLIMATE

The highveld has a humid climate with about 140 centimeters (55 inches) of mean annual rainfall. The middleveld and Lubombo are somewhat drier, with about 85 centimeters (33 inches) of rain; the lowveld receives about 60 centimeters (24 inches) of rain in an average year. Temperatures range from as low as −3°C (27°F) in winter in the highlands to as high as 42°C (108°F) in summer in the lowlands.

Photo credit: Cynthia Bassett

The black rhino, native to Swaziland, is a browser with a different upper lip and temperament from the white rhino. Both are the same color.

4 PLANTS AND ANIMALS

Grassland, mixed bush, and scrub cover most of Swaziland. There is some forest in the highlands. Native plants include aloes, orchids, and begonias. Large native mammals include the blue wildebeest, kudu, impala, zebra, waterbuck, and hippopotamus. Crocodiles live in the lowland rivers, and bird life is plentiful.

5 ENVIRONMENT

The main environmental problem is soil erosion and destruction. Swaziland has four protected areas for wildlife totaling 40,045 hectares (98,953 acres). There is also air pollution from motor vehicles and from other countries in the area and water pollution from industry, farming, and untreated sewage. Over 90% of the nation's rural people do not have pure water. As of 1994, 5 of the nation's bird species and 25 types of plants were threatened with extinction.

6 POPULATION

According to the 1986 census, Swaziland's population was 681,059. A population of 984,000 was projected by the United Nations for the year 2000. The estimated average density for the period 1988–93 was 45 persons per square kilometer (117 per square mile). Mbabane, the capital, had 47,000 people in 1990.

7 MIGRATION

At the end of 1992, Swaziland harbored 55,600 refugees. About 7,400 of them were South Africans, primarily Swazis fleeing the black homeland of KwaZulu. There were also 48,100 Mozambican refugees. In 1991 there were 49,118 Swaziland-born blacks residing in South Africa.

8 ETHNIC GROUPS

The native African population is Swazi, comprising more than 70 clans, of which the Nkosi Dlamini, the royal clan, is dominant. Other Africans are mainly from Mozambique. There are also Europeans, Asians, and people of mixed race.

9 LANGUAGES

English and Siswati are the official languages.

10 RELIGIONS

About 20% of the population practices traditional African religions. Except for a small Muslim community, the rest of the population is Christian. There is also a small Baha'i presence.

11 TRANSPORTATION

The country had 2,853 kilometers (1,773 miles) of roads in 1991. There were 21,287 passenger cars and 15,874 trucks and buses in use in 1991. The Swaziland Railway is 224 kilometers (139 miles) long. Matsapa Airport, near Manzini, provides service, via Royal Swazi National Airways, to neighboring countries. In all, 90,000 passengers were carried in 1991.

12 HISTORY

Origins

Swaziland was originally occupied by hunting and gathering peoples known as Bushmen. In the sixteenth century, Bantu-speaking peoples inhabited what is now Mozambique. By the beginning of the nineteenth century, the Swazi had broken away from them and emerged as a distinct tribe. In the 1840s, the Swazi made their first formal contact with the British, asking them for help against the Zulu. In 1890, a provisional government was established, representing the Swazi, the British, and the Transvaal. After the South African (Boer) War of 1899–1902, the governing of Swaziland was transferred to the British. This relationship between the Swazi and the British provided the framework within which British rule was conducted for 60 years.

LOCATION: 25°43' to 27°20's; 30°48' to 32°8'E
BOUNDARY LENGTHS: Mozambique, 108 kilometers (67 miles); South Africa (including homelands), 446 kilometers (277 miles).

Independence

In 1963, the subject of independence for Swaziland was opened in London. Swazi-

A market in Mbabane filled with handmade baskets.

land became an independent nation within the British Commonwealth on 6 September 1968. On 12 April 1973, King Sobhuza II repealed the constitution and assumed supreme executive, legislative, and judicial powers. After Sobhuza died in 1982, a long power struggle took place. Eventually it was decided that 15-year-old Makhosetive, one of Sobhuza's 67 sons, would ascend the throne upon reaching adulthood. He was crowned King Mswati III on 25 April 1986. The new king decreased the power of the Liqoqo, the advisory council, and he has ruled through his prime minister and cabinet.

After signing an agreement with South Africa, Swaziland arrested and deported members of the African National Congress (ANC), the leading South African black nationalist group. In late 1985 and 1986, South African commando squads conducted raids on ANC members and supporters in Swaziland. In September and October, 1993, popular elections were held for parliament and a new prime minister, Prince Mbilini, took office.

13 GOVERNMENT

In 1979, a new parliament was created, with a 50-member House of Assembly and a 20-member Senate. To become law, legislation passed by parliament must be approved by the king.

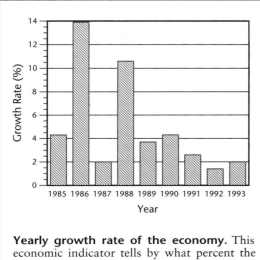

Yearly growth rate of the economy. This economic indicator tells by what percent the economy has increased or decreased when compared with the previous year.

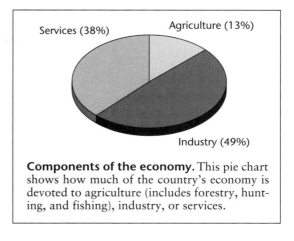

Components of the economy. This pie chart shows how much of the country's economy is devoted to agriculture (includes forestry, hunting, and fishing), industry, or services.

14 POLITICAL PARTIES

Several parties, including the People's United Democratic Movement (Pudemo), the Swaziland United Front, and the Swaziland Progressive Party, operate openly.

15 JUDICIAL SYSTEM

The dual judicial system consists of a set of courts based on a western model and western law, and a set of national courts that follows Swazi law and custom.

16 ARMED FORCES

The Umbutfo Swaziland Defense Force has fewer than 3,000 personnel.

17 ECONOMY

The majority of Swazis are engaged in farming. Swaziland's economy benefited considerably when other nations boycotted South Africa to protest apartheid and made their investments in Swaziland instead.

18 INCOME

In 1992, Swaziland's gross national product (GNP) was $930 million at current prices. The average GNP per person for the period 1988–93 was $1,290. Annual inflation in 1992 was 19.7%.

19 INDUSTRY

The industrial growth of the 1980s slowed in the early 1990s. Textile manufacturing, which flourished when South African tariffs were high, began to wither when they were equalized.

20 LABOR

The domestic wage labor force was about 91,333 in 1989; nearly one-seventh (14%) were engaged in sugar production. The Swaziland Federation of Trade Unions is the major labor organization. The minimum age for employment is 15, except in

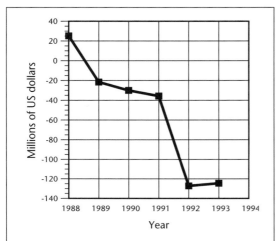

Yearly balance of trade measured in millions of US dollars. The balance of trade is the difference between what a country sells to other countries (its exports) and what it buys (its imports). If a country imports more than it exports, it has a negative balance of trade (a trade deficit). If exports exceed imports there is a positive balance of trade (a trade surplus).

family businesses for which there is no legal minimum.

21 AGRICULTURE

Sugar is the most important cash crop, and corn is the staple crop. Output in 1992 was sugarcane, 3.6 million tons; and corn, 54,000 tons. Citrus production in 1992 was about 87,000 tons. Cotton fiber production in that year was 10,000 tons.

22 DOMESTICATED ANIMALS

In 1992, Swaziland had about 753,000 head of cattle, 406,000 goats, 31,000 hogs, 23,000 sheep, 13,000 horses, and 1,000,000 poultry. The country slaughtered a total of 63,000 head of cattle in 1992.

23 FISHING

By 1982, several commercial fish farms had been established. Annual production is estimated at 105 tons.

24 FORESTRY

Swaziland's forests are among the world's largest planted forests. Roundwood output totaled 2,223,000 cubic meters in 1991.

25 MINING

In 1991, coal production was 122,502 tons, and diamond production was 57,420 carats in 1991.

26 FOREIGN TRADE

More than 95% of imports either come from or pass through South Africa. Principal imports in 1985 included machinery and transport equipment and manufactured goods. Principal exports in 1990 included sugar, timber, and wood pulp.

27 ENERGY AND POWER

In 1991, a total of 155 million kilowatt hours of electricity was generated, and about $10 million of imported electricity came from South Africa. All petroleum products come from South Africa.

28 SOCIAL DEVELOPMENT

The government subsidizes workers whose wages fall below specified minimums, and workers' compensation for injuries on the job is also provided.

Selected Social Indicators

These statistics are estimates for the period 1988 to 1993. For comparison purposes, data for the United States and averages for low-income countries and high-income countries are also given.

Indicator	Swaziland	Low-income countries	High-income countries	United States
Per capita gross national product†	**$1,290**	$380	$23,680	$24,740
Population growth rate	**2.8%**	1.9%	0.6%	1.0%
Population growth rate in urban areas	**6.2%**	3.9%	0.8%	1.3%
Population per square kilometer of land	**45**	78	25	26
Life expectancy in years	**58**	62	77	76
Number of people per physician	**8,857**	>3,300	453	419
Number of pupils per teacher (primary school)	**33**	39	<18	20
Illiteracy rate (15 years and older)	**32%**	41%	<5%	<3%
Energy consumed per capita (kg of oil equivalent)	**283**	364	5,203	7,918

† The gross national product (GNP) is the total dollar value of all goods and services produced by a country in a year. The per capita GNP is calculated by dividing a country's GNP by its population. The World Bank defines low-income countries as those with a per capita GNP of $695 or less. High-income countries have a per capita GNP of $8,626 or more. Less than 14% of the world's 5.5 billion people live in high-income countries, while almost 60% live in low-income countries.

> = greater than   < = less than

Sources: World Bank, *Social Indicators of Development 1995,* Baltimore: Johns Hopkins University Press, 1995. Central Intelligence Agency, *World Fact Book,* Washington, D.C.: Government Printing Office, 1994.

29 HEALTH

Major health problems include bilharzia, typhoid, tapeworm, gastroenteritis, malaria, kwashiorkor, and pellagra. In 1992, average life expectancy was 58 years. In 1990, there were 83 doctors, and about 55% of the population had access to health care services.

30 HOUSING

The government hopes to improve housing conditions for low-income groups through self-help schemes and by providing mortgage assistance. In 1985, 30 residential buildings were completed.

31 EDUCATION

In 1991 there were 514 primary schools with 172,908 pupils and 5,347 teachers. Secondary schools had 44,085 students and 2,430 teachers. For the period 1988–93, the average number of students per teacher in primary school was 33. Higher education is provided by the University of Swaziland and the Swaziland College of Technology. Higher level institutions had a total of 452 teachers and 3,224 students in 1991. The literacy rate is 68%.

32 MEDIA

In 1991 there were 23,905 telephones in service. In 1991 there were about 127,000

Photo credit: Cynthia Bassett

A young woman of Swaziland crossing a busy street.

8,000 and 3,500, respectively. There is also a daily newspaper published in Siswati, *Tikhatsi Temaswati*.

33 TOURISM AND RECREATION

Swaziland offers the tourist a great variety of scenery and casinos at Mbabane, Nhlangano, and Pigg's Peak. In 1991 there were 279,000 tourists; 223,000 were Africans. Tourists spent an estimated $26 million. There were 1,210 hotel rooms with an occupancy rate of 37.4%.

34 FAMOUS SWAZI

Sobhuza II (1899–1982) was king, or *ngwenyama*, of the Swazi nation from 1921 until his death. Mswati III (b.1968) became king in 1986.

35 BIBLIOGRAPHY

Booth, Alan R. *Swaziland: Tradition and Change in a Southern African Kingdom*. Boulder, Colo.: Westview, 1984.

Kuper, Hilda. *An African Aristocracy*. New York: Holmes & Meier, 1980 (orig. 1965).

radios and 15,000 television sets. There are two daily English newspapers, the *Times of Swaziland* and the *Swaziland Observer*, with circulations in 1991 of

SWEDEN

Kingdom of Sweden
Konungariket Sverige

CAPITAL: Stockholm.

FLAG: The national flag, dating from 1569 and employing a blue and gold motif used as early as the mid-14th century, consists of a yellow cross with extended right horizontal on a blue field.

ANTHEM: *Du gamla, du fria, du fjallhöga nord (O Glorious Old Mountain-Crowned Land of the North).*

MONETARY UNIT: The krona (Kr) is a paper currency of 100 öre. There are coins of 50 öre and 1, 2, 5, and 10 kronor, and notes of 5, 10, 20, 50, 100, 500, and 1,000 kronor. Kr1 = $0.1277 (or $1 = Kr7.828).

WEIGHTS AND MEASURES: The metric system is the legal standard, but some old local measures are still in use, notably the Swedish mile (10 kilometers).

HOLIDAYS: New Year's Day, 1 January; Epiphany, 6 January; Labor Day, 1 May; Midsummer Day, Saturday nearest 24 June; All Saints' Day, 5 November; Christmas, 25–26 December. Movable religious holidays include Good Friday, Easter Monday, Ascension, Whitmonday.

TIME: 1 PM = noon GMT.

1 LOCATION AND SIZE

Fourth in size among the countries of Europe, Sweden is the largest of the Scandinavian countries, with about 15% of its total area situated north of the Arctic Circle. Sweden has a total area of 449,964 square kilometers (173,732 square miles), slightly smaller than the state of California. Its total boundary length is 5,423 kilometers (3,370 miles).

Sweden's capital city, Stockholm, is located on the Baltic Sea coast.

2 TOPOGRAPHY

Northern Sweden slopes from the Kjölen Mountains along the Norwegian border to the coast of the Gulf of Bothnia. Its many rivers include the Göta, the Dal, the circle Angerman, the Ume, and the Lule. Central Sweden has several large lakes, of which Vänern, at 5,585 square kilometers (2,156 square miles), is the largest in Europe outside the former Soviet Union. At the southern tip of the country rises a highland area of Smaland. Much of Sweden is composed of ancient rock. The lowlands were once under water. The best, most lime-rich soils are found in Skåne, the leading agricultural region.

3 CLIMATE

Because of ocean winds, Sweden has higher temperatures than its northerly latitude would suggest. Stockholm averages 3°C (26°F) in February and 18°C (64°F) in

July. The climates of northern and southern Sweden differ widely. The north has a winter of more than seven months and a summer of less than three, while the south has a winter of about two months and a summer of more than four.

Annual rainfall averages 61 centimeters (24 inches) and is heaviest in the southwest and along the frontier between Norrland and Norway. There is much snowfall, and in the north snow remains on the ground for about half the year.

4 PLANTS AND ANIMALS

Plant life ranges from Alpine-Arctic types in the north through coniferous forests in the central regions to deciduous trees in the south. Black cock, woodcock, duck, partridge, swan, and many other varieties of birds are abundant. Fish and insects are plentiful.

5 ENVIRONMENT

Sweden's relatively slow population growth and an effective conservation movement have helped preserve the nation's extensive forests. By the end of 1985 there were 19 national parks, 1,215 nature reserves, and 2,016 other protected landscape areas.

Air pollution is a serious problem in Sweden. The list of 2150 pollutants includes nitrogen compounds, oil, VOCs (volatile organic compounds), radon, and methane. The pollution of the nation's water supply is also a significant problem. Airborne sulfur pollutants have made more than 16,000 lakes so acidic that fish can no longer breed in them. By 1992, United Nation reports described acidification as Sweden's most serious environmental problem. Sweden has 42.2 cubic miles of water with 9% used for farming and 55% used for industrial purposes.

In 1994, 1 of the nation's mammal species and 14 bird species were endangered, as well as 10 types of plants.

6 POPULATION

The population of Sweden as of 31 December 1992 was estimated at 8,692,013. The government has projected a population of 8,949,742 for the year 2000. The average population density was 19 persons per square kilometer (49 per square mile) of land area for the period 1988–93. Stockholm, the capital and principal city, had a population of 684,576 at the end of 1992, with 1,517,285 in the greater Stockholm area.

7 MIGRATION

In 1992, 19,622 persons moved to Sweden, representing 41% of the population increase. There were 45,348 immigrants and 25,726 emigrants in 1992. There were 499,072 aliens in 1992 (5.7% of the population). This figure included 111,477 Finns, 39,578 Yugoslavs, 38,996 Iranians, 35,319 Norwegians, 27,176 Danes, 26,547 Turks, 17,872 Chileans, and 16,365 Poles.

8 ETHNIC GROUPS

The Swedes are Scandinavians of Germanic origin. Minorities include about 300,000 Finns in the north and approximately 20,000 Lapps.

9 LANGUAGES

Swedish is the universal language. Swedish is closely related to Norwegian and Danish. Many Swedes speak English and German, and many more understand these languages. The Lapps speak their own language. Some Finnish-speaking people have spread from across the frontier.

10 RELIGIONS

Religious freedom is provided for by the constitution, but Lutheranism is the state religion. Some 88% of the population belonged to the Lutheran Church in 1993. The monarch and cabinet members dealing with church matters must be Lutheran. According to 1991 estimates, Roman Catholicism had 147,414 followers; Pentecostal Church, 95,800; Mission Covenant Church of Sweden, 77,013; and Salvation Army, 26,600. In addition, there were an estimated 21,000 Baptists and 15–20,000 Jews.

11 TRANSPORTATION

As of 1991, the total length of highways was 97,400 kilometers (60,520 miles). At the end of 1991 there were 3,619,000 passenger cars, 310,000 trucks, 15,000 buses, 204,000 vans, and 103,000 motorcycles in service. In 1967, Sweden changed from left- to right-hand traffic.

Sweden's railroad system of 12,000 kilometers (7,450 miles) is operated by the state-owned Statens Järnvagar. Railway passenger traffic declined from 93 million to 88 million between 1982 and 1984.

Göteborg, Stockholm, and Malmö, the three largest ports, and a number of

LOCATION: 55°20′ to 69°4′N; 10°58′ to 24°10′E.
BOUNDARY LENGTHS: Finland, 586 kilometers (364 miles); coastline, 2,746 kilometers (1,706 miles); Norway, 1,619 kilometers (1,006 miles); Gotland Island coastline, 400 kilometers (249 miles); Öland Island coastline, 72 kilometers (45 miles). **TERRITORIAL SEA LIMIT:** 12 miles.

Photo credit: Susan D. Rock

A city street in Helsingborg leading towards the channel.

smaller ports are well-equipped to handle large oceangoing vessels. Sweden has an increasing number of special-purpose vessels, such as fruit tramps, ore carriers, and oil tankers. At the start of 1992, the Swedish merchant fleet consisted of 172 ships with a combined capacity of 2.5 million gross registered tons. Canals in central Sweden have opened the lakes to seagoing craft; inland waterways add up to 2,050 kilometers (1,270 miles).

Principal airports are Arlanda (Stockholm), Bromma (Stockholm), Sturup (Malmö), and Torslanda (Göteborg). The Scandinavian Airlines System (SAS) is operated jointly by Sweden, Denmark, and Norway.

12 HISTORY

Origins

Sweden and the Swedes are first referred to in written records by the Roman historian Tacitus, who, in his *Germania* (AD 98), mentions the Suiones, a people "mighty in ships and arms." In the ninth and tenth centuries, Swedes crossed Russia and entered Constantinople. According to tradition, the descendants of one of their chieftains, Rurik, founded the first Russian state.

Christianity was gradually introduced from the ninth through the eleventh century. Through religious and other crusades, the Swedish kingdom began to expand into the Baltic during the twelfth century, absorbing Finland. During the twelfth century, the monarchy became more centralized and Latin education was introduced.

Norway and Sweden were united in 1319, and all the Scandinavian countries were united under Denmark's Queen Margaret in 1397. For over a century, Sweden resisted Danish rule. In 1523, following a war with Denmark, the Swedes elected Gustaf I, known as Gustavus, to the Swedish throne. A great king and the founder of modern Sweden, Gustavus made Lutheranism the state religion, established a hereditary monarchy, and organized a national army and navy. His successors conquered Estonia and other areas in Eastern Europe. The growth of nationalism and Protestantism contributed to the rise of Sweden in the following century.

Seventeenth–Nineteenth Centuries

In the period of the Thirty Years' War (1618–48), Sweden was the foremost Protestant power in Europe. Renewed wars extended Swedish territory even farther. Under young Charles XII (r.1697–1718), Sweden fought the Great Northern War (1700–1721) against a coalition of Denmark, Poland, Saxony, and Russia. Sweden at first was militarily successful. But after a crushing defeat by Russian forces under Peter the Great (Peter I) in 1709 at the Battle of Poltava, Sweden lost territories to Russia, Prussia, and Hanover. Its status as an international power was reduced.

Throughout the eighteenth century there was internal conflict, mostly over the conflicting policies of the pro-French faction (the Hats) and the pro-Russian faction (the Caps).

Sweden entered the Napoleonic Wars in 1805, allying itself with Great Britain, Austria, and Russia against France. The Russo-Swedish conflict (1808–9) resulted in the loss of Finland. King Gustavus IV was then overthrown by the army, and a more democratic constitution was adopted. In 1810, one of Napoleon's marshals, a Frenchman named Jean Baptiste Jules Bernadotte, was invited to become the heir to the Swedish throne.

In 1814, Norway was united with Sweden and remained tied to the Swedish kings until 1905, when the union was dissolved. Bernadotte assumed the name Charles John (Carl Johan) and succeeded to the Swedish throne in 1818. The Bernadotte dynasty, which has reigned since 1818, gradually gave up almost all of its powers, which were assumed by the Riksdag (parliament). Sweden became one of the most progressive countries in the world.

Twentieth Century

Sweden remained neutral in both world wars. During World War II (1939–45), however, Sweden served as a safe place for refugees from the Nazis and let the Danish resistance movement operate on its soil. After the war, Sweden did not join the North Atlantic Treaty Organization, as did its Scandinavian neighbors Norway and Denmark. It did, however, become a member of the United Nations in 1946. In 1953, Sweden joined with Denmark, Norway and Iceland (and later, Finland) to form the Nordic Council.

Carl XVI Gustaf has been king since 1973. In September 1976, a coalition of three non-Socialist parties won a majority in parliamentary elections, ending 44 years of almost uninterrupted Social Democratic rule that had established a modern welfare state. The country's economic situation worsened, however, and the Social Democrats were returned to power in the elections of September 1982. Prime Minister Olof Palme, leader of the Social Democratic Party since 1969, was assassinated for an unknown reason in February 1986.

The environment and nuclear energy were major political issues in the 1980s. In the 1990s, the major concerns have been conflicts over immigration policies, the economy, and Sweden's relationship to the European Community (EC). In 1991, though many Swedes were against it, Sweden applied for membership in the EC.

In May 1993, the Riksdag changed Sweden's long-standing foreign policy of neutrality. In the future, neutrality would only be followed in time of war. The Riksdag also opened up the possibility of Sweden's participation in defense alliances.

13 GOVERNMENT

Sweden is a constitutional monarchy. Legislative authority rests in the parliament (*Riksdag*). The monarch performs only ceremonial duties and must belong to the Lutheran Church. In 1980, female descendants were granted the right to the throne. The real chief executive is the prime minister, who is proposed by the speaker of the Riksdag and confirmed by the parliamentary parties. The prime minister appoints a cabinet consisting of 18–20 members.

The Riksdag is a single-chamber body of 349 members serving three-year terms. All members of the Riksdag are directly elected by universal suffrage at age 18. The Riksdag has direct control of the Bank of Sweden and the National Debt Office.

The Riksdag elects one or more ombudsmen (four in 1981) who make sure the courts and public officials follow laws properly. The ombudsmen are concerned especially with protecting the civil rights of individual citizens and of religious and other groups. They may warn or prosecute offenders, although prosecutions are rare.

Sweden is divided into 24 counties and about 278 municipalities, each with an elected council.

14 POLITICAL PARTIES

The constitution requires that a party must gain at least 4% of the national popular vote, or 12% in a constituency, to be represented in the Riksdag. Except for a brief period in 1936, the Social Democratic Labor Party was in power almost continuously from 1932 to 1976, either alone or in a coalition with other parties. They lost their parliamentary majority in the elections of September 1976 but returned to power in 1982.

The 1988 election marked a turning point in Sweden with the decline of the Social Democrats and the growth of the Moderates and Liberals. For the first time in 70 years, a new party gained representation in the Riksdag—the Environment Party (MpG) which obtained 20 seats.

The Social Democrats were narrowly defeated in September 1991, and the government of Ingvar Carlsson gave way to that of Carl Bilt (Moderate Party), who headed a minority four-party, center-right coalition composed of Moderates, the Liberals, the Center Party, and the Christian Democratic community.

Other parties include the Christian Democrats, New Democracy, the anti-immigration Progress Party, and the Left Party (VP) in 1990. In 1991, Inegerd Traedsson became the first woman to be elected Speaker of the Riksdag. This post is the second highest ranking office after the monarch.

15 JUDICIAL SYSTEM

Ordinary criminal and civil cases are tried in a local court (*tingsrätt*), consisting of a judge and a panel of citizens appointed by the municipal council. Above these local courts are six courts of appeal (*hovrätter*). The highest court is the Supreme Court (*Högsta Domstolen*), with 24 justices. Special cases are heard by the Supreme Administrative Court and other courts. Capital punishment, last used in 1910, is forbidden by the constitution.

16 ARMED FORCES

Because Sweden is neutral in times of war and, therefore, gets no help from any other country, it must have a strong, modern, and independent defense force. The 1991 budget allocated $6.2 billion for defense.

Swedish military defense is based on general draft of all male citizens between the ages of 18 and 47. In wartime a force of 700,000 reservists can be mobilized within 72 hours. The coastal defense is under the command of the Royal Swedish Navy. Regular armed forces in 1993 totaled 60,500 (38,800 draftees). The army had 43,500 (half draftees). The navy had 9,650 men on active duty (5,900 draftees). The air force, with 7,500 regulars (5,500 draftees), had a total of 499 combat aircraft. Reserves in voluntary defense organizations totaled 40,000.

As part of the civil defense program, nuclear-resistant shelters were built over a 10-year period in the large urban areas. The shelters, completed in 1970, are used

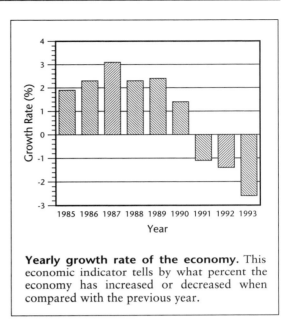

Yearly growth rate of the economy. This economic indicator tells by what percent the economy has increased or decreased when compared with the previous year.

as garages in peacetime and can hold 6.3 million people in a national emergency.

17 ECONOMY

Sweden is a highly industrialized country. The shift from agriculture to industry began in the 1930s and developed rapidly after World War II.

Swedish industry makes high-quality goods and specialized products—ball bearings, high-grade steel, machine tools, glassware—that are in world demand. There is close contact between trade, industry, and finance. Factories are spreading to rural districts. Some natural resources are in good supply, particularly lumber, iron ore, and waterpower. However, Sweden's lack of oil and coal resources makes it dependent on imports for energy production, despite its abundant waterpower.

Swedish living standards and purchasing power are among the highest in the world. However, inflation has been a chronic problem since the early 1970s, with the annual rise in consumer prices peaking at 13.7% in 1980. The rate of price increase declined after that to 9.4% in 1991, then to 2.2% in 1992. Unemployment shot up from 1.7% in 1990 to 8.2% in 1993.

18 INCOME

In 1992, Sweden's gross national product (GNP) was $233,209 million at current prices, or $24,740 per person. For the period 1985–92 the average inflation rate was 6.9%, resulting in a real growth rate in per person GNP of 0.4%.

19 INDUSTRY

The basic resources for industrial development are forests, iron ore, and waterpower. Forest products, machinery, and motor vehicles made up 60% of total export value in 1992.

Since the end of World War II, emphasis has shifted from production of consumer goods to the manufacture of export items. Swedish-made ships, airplanes, and automobiles are considered outstanding in quality. In 1991, 176,937 automobiles and about 75,000 trucks were manufactured. Sweden's motor vehicle producers are Volvo and SAAB-Scania.

As exports, transport equipment and iron and steel have become less important,

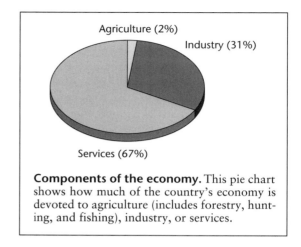

Agriculture (2%)

Industry (31%)

Services (67%)

Components of the economy. This pie chart shows how much of the country's economy is devoted to agriculture (includes forestry, hunting, and fishing), industry, or services.

while exports of machinery, chemicals, and paper have been growing in value.

20 LABOR

The labor force numbered 4,429,000 persons in 1992, of whom 52% were men and 48% women. During that year, the number of employed workers was 4,195,000, of whom 20% were employed in manufacturing, mining, electricity, or water service; 14.3% in wholesale and retail trade, restaurants, and hotels; 9.1% in financial and business services; 7.1% in transport and communications; 6.5% in construction; 3.3% in agriculture, forestry, hunting, and fishing; and 39.7% in other services.

The unemployment rate averaged 4.8% in 1992 and was projected to rise due to cuts in the defense industry and downsizing in government employment.

More and more women work outside their homes. About 71% of all women between the ages of 16 and 74 years par-

"Gamla Stan," an old part of Stockholm.

ticipated in the labor force in 1991. The trade unions have lent their support to closing the wage gap between the sexes; as of 1992, women's wages in manufacturing had risen to 90% of men's.

About 84% of Swedish wage earners are members of trade unions. At the end of 1992 the Swedish Trade Union Confederation, which is closely allied to the Social Democratic Party, had 2.23 million members and was the largest organization of any kind in Sweden.

The minimum age for employment is 16, or 18 for night work. During school vacations, younger children may be hired for simple jobs that last five days or less.

21 AGRICULTURE

Only about 3% of the people earned their living in agriculture in 1992, compared with more than 50% at the beginning of the 20th century and about 20% in 1950.

Grains (particularly oats, wheat, barley, and rye), potatoes and other root crops, vegetables, and fruits are the chief agricultural products. Sugar beet cultivation in Skåne is important and produces almost enough sugar to make Sweden self-sufficient. In 1992, Sweden produced 1,411,000 tons of wheat; 1,261,000 tons of barley; 1,144,000 tons of potatoes; 807,000 tons of oats; and 128,000 tons of rye.

Recently the government has been merging small unprofitable farms into larger units of 10 to 20 hectares (25–50 acres) of land for cultivation with some woodland. This larger unit is the size estimated able to support a farm family at the same living standard as that of an industrial worker.

22 DOMESTICATED ANIMALS

Although the long winters require indoor feeding from October to May, livestock raising is important. About 80% of farm income comes from animal products, especially dairy products. Cattle (2.2 million in 1992) are the most important livestock. Milk production totaled 3,168,000 tons in 1992; cheese, 115,000 tons; and butter, 58,900 tons.

The sheep population was 448,000 in 1992, and pigs numbered 2,280,000. There were 12,000,000 chickens during the same year. Fur farms breed large numbers of mink and some number of fox. In 1992 the reindeer population in Lapp villages was 300,000.

23 FISHING

Fish is an important item in the Swedish diet, and Sweden both imports and exports a great deal of fish. Herring, cod, plaice, flounder, salmon, eel, mackerel, and shellfish are the most important saltwater varieties. Freshwater fish include trout, salmon, and crayfish (a national delicacy). The ocean catch was 239,502 tons in 1991, and the total catch was 245,016 tons.

24 FORESTRY

The forestry industry ranks second in importance in the economy (after metal-based industry). Sweden competes with Canada for world leadership in the export of wood pulp and is the world's leading exporter of cellulose. In 1992, wood and wood products made up about 18% of exports. Forests occupy some 57% of the land area and total 23,500,000 hectares (58,069,000 acres).

Important varieties of wood include spruce, pine, birch, oak, beech, alder, and aspen. Forestry and farming are interdependent everywhere except in the most fertile plains. In northern Sweden, almost one of every two men works in the woods for at least part of the winter.

The total timber felled for sale in 1991 amounted to an estimated 51.7 million cubic meters. Sweden is the world's third largest exporter of paper and board, supplying 13% of the export market, with production amounting to 4% of the world's total.

25 MINING

Since ancient days, mining and the iron industry have been of great importance in the economic life of Sweden. Sweden's iron ore reserves were estimated at 3 billion tons in 1991. Sweden accounts for about 2.2% of the world's iron-ore production and is a leading iron-ore exporter. Iron-ore production in 1991 was estimated at 19.3 million tons. Lead, copper, zinc, gold, silver, bismuth, cobalt, and huge quantities of arsenic are produced in the Skellefte River region. Farther south,

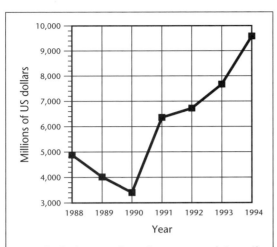

Yearly balance of trade measured in millions of US dollars. The balance of trade is the difference between what a country sells to other countries (its exports) and what it buys (its imports). If a country imports more than it exports, it has a negative balance of trade (a trade deficit). If exports exceed imports there is a positive balance of trade (a trade surplus).

phosphate, tungsten, kyanite, and pyrite are mined. Granite is quarried for domestic use and for export.

26 FOREIGN TRADE

The volume of Sweden's foreign trade has grown very rapidly since World War II.

Principal exports by value in 1992 were nonelectrical machinery; transport equipment; paper and paper products; and chemicals. Principal imports were nonelectrical machinery; chemicals, plastics, and pharmaceuticals; transport equipment; crude oil and petroleum products; and electrical machinery.

In 1992, most of Sweden's foreign trade continued to be with Western Europe. Imports from the European Community (EC) represented 56% of the total, and exports to the EC also accounted for 56%; imports from and exports to fellow members of EFTA were 16% and 17% of the total, respectively.

Principal trade partners in 1985 were Germany, Britain, the United States, Norway, Denmark, Finland, France, and the Netherlands.

27 ENERGY AND POWER

With its many rivers, waterfalls, and lakes, Sweden has a great deal of waterpower. Because of environmental considerations, high production costs, and low world market prices, Sweden has not made use of its large uranium reserves.

Net installed electrical capacity in 1991 was 34,089,000 kilowatts, of which 48% was hydroelectric, 29% nuclear, and 23% conventional thermal. That same year, Sweden's electricity production totaled 147,730 million kilowatt hours.

Oil's share in the total energy supply declined from nearly 70% in 1979 to 40% in 1992. In 1991, electricity accounted for 55% of the total energy requirement; petroleum, 29%; coal, wood, and other solids, 11%; natural gas, 1%; and other sources, 4%.

Sweden began an ambitious nuclear energy program in the 1970's, under which seven nuclear reactors came into operation between 1972 and 1980. By 1986, 12 units offered a capacity of 9.4 million kilowatt hours; but by 2010, all 12 will be shut down, with two reactors closing by 1995. Plants fired by natural gas will replace nuclear energy.

28 SOCIAL DEVELOPMENT

Sweden has been called the model welfare state; every citizen is guaranteed a minimum subsistence income and medical care. Basic benefits are often increased by cost-of-living supplements.

Old-age pensions are paid to everyone 65 years of age or older, but an earlier retirement is possible, with a reduction in pension benefits. The system also contains provisions for pensions to persons totally disabled before retirement age and for family pensions (widows and orphans). Unemployment insurance is the only kind of voluntary social insurance in Sweden. Administered by the trade unions, it provides benefits according to salary to those who voluntarily enroll. More than half of all employees are covered.

Compulsory health service was introduced in 1955. Hospital care is free for up to two years. Medical services and medicines are provided at very low cost or, in some cases, without charge. Costs of pregnancy and childbirth are covered by health insurance. Since the beginning of 1955, workers' compensation for injuries on the job has been coordinated with the national health service scheme. Public assistance is provided for blind or disabled persons confined to their homes and to people who are in sanitariums, special hospitals, or charitable institutions.

The social services help meet the costs of raising children through monthly family allowances for each child under age 16. A housing allowance is also paid to families with children under 16 to help them have modern, roomy dwellings. For 360 days, a parental benefit is paid upon the birth or adoption of a child to the parent who stays home and takes care of the child. Schoolchildren receive free textbooks, and about 75% of public-school children are given free meals.

Women are less likely to get higher paying jobs, and often receive less pay for equal work. The percentage of women in the work force fell in 1993, for the first time since World War II, to 75.9%, possibly as a result of the recession.

29 HEALTH

The national health insurance system, financed by the state and employer contributions, was established in January 1955 and covers all Swedish citizens and alien residents. In 1991 Sweden spent $20,055 million on health care.

In 1990 there were an estimated 28,000 physicians, more than one for every 368 inhabitants. Swedish hospitals, well known for their high standards, had 35,990 short-term beds (hospital) and 85,972 long-term beds (nursing/old-age homes) in 1991.

Many health problems are related to environment and lifestyle (including tobacco smoking, alcohol consumption, and overeating). The most common serious diseases are cardiovascular conditions and cancer. In 1991, there were 137 cases of AIDS.

Selected Social Indicators

These statistics are estimates for the period 1988 to 1993. For comparison purposes, data for the United States and averages for low-income countries and high-income countries are also given.

Indicator	Sweden	Low-income countries	High-income countries	United States
Per capita gross national product†	**$24,740**	$380	$23,680	$24,740
Population growth rate	**0.5%**	1.9%	0.6%	1.0%
Population growth rate in urban areas	**0.5%**	3.9%	0.8%	1.3%
Population per square kilometer of land	**19**	78	25	26
Life expectancy in years	**78**	62	77	76
Number of people per physician	**368**	>3,300	453	419
Number of pupils per teacher (primary school)	**10**	39	<18	20
Illiteracy rate (15 years and older)	**1%**	41%	<5%	<3%
Energy consumed per capita (kg of oil equivalent)	**5,385**	364	5,203	7,918

† The gross national product (GNP) is the total dollar value of all goods and services produced by a country in a year. The per capita GNP is calculated by dividing a country's GNP by its population. The World Bank defines low-income countries as those with a per capita GNP of $695 or less. High-income countries have a per capita GNP of $8,626 or more. Less than 14% of the world's 5.5 billion people live in high-income countries, while almost 60% live in low-income countries.

> = greater than   < = less than

Sources: World Bank, *Social Indicators of Development 1995,* Baltimore: Johns Hopkins University Press, 1995. Central Intelligence Agency, *World Fact Book,* Washington, D.C.: Government Printing Office, 1994.

In 1992, average life expectancy in Sweden was 74.8 years for males and 80.4 years for females. The average general life expectancy for the period 1988-93 was 78 years.

30 HOUSING

The total number of dwellings was 4,043,378 in 1990, most of them having two rooms and a kitchen. Construction of new dwellings totaled 66,886 in 1991. Most houses are built by private contractors, but more than half of new housing is designed, planned, and financed by nonprofit organizations and cooperatives.

To ease the housing shortage, the government subsidizes new construction and reconditioning, helps various groups to get better housing, and gives credit at lower interest rates than those in the open market. In 1987, these interest subsidies totaled $1.6 billion; and housing allowances for low-income families were $1 billion.

31 EDUCATION

Practically the entire adult Swedish population is literate. Education is free and compulsory from age 7 to 17. All students receive the same course of instruction for six years. Beginning in the seventh year, students may choose between a classical and a vocational course. About 80% of all students then enter *gymnasium* (senior high school) or *continuation* schools.

The *gymnasium* specializes in classical or modern languages or science. After the three-year course, students may take a final graduating examination. The continuation schools offer a two-year curriculum that is more practical and specialized than that of the *gymnasium* and leads more quickly to the practice of a trade. In 1991 there were 293,482 students at the primary level, 291,866 at the secondary level, and 206,079 students enrolled in the universities.

More than 25% of secondary-school graduates attend college or university. Sweden's six universities, all largely financed by the state, are at Uppsala, Lund, Stockholm (1877), Göteborg, Umea, and Linköping. There are also more than two dozen specialized schools and institutions at the university level for such subjects as medicine, dentistry, pharmacology, music, economics, commerce, technology, veterinary science, agriculture, and forestry. Tuition is free, except for some special courses.

Sweden has an active adult education movement in which some 3 million persons participate each year.

32 MEDIA

In 1993, the former Swedish Broadcasting Corporation was broken up and its three subsidiaries became independent. One operates the two television networks, and one is responsible for educational radio. The other runs the four national and local radio channels and Radio Sweden, which broadcasts internationally in several languages. In 1991, Swedes owned 7,550,000 radios and 4,030,000 television sets.

The Swedish press is said to be the first to make censorship illegal. There were 107 daily newspapers in Sweden in 1991 with a combined average daily circulation of 4,387,000. There were also 69 nondaily newspapers with a total circulation of 392,000.

Sweden's leading newspapers, with circulation figures for the first half of 1991, are *Expressen* (612,000); *Dagens Nyheter* (423,500); *Aftonbladet* (412,000); and *Svenska Dagbladet* (233,450). In 1988 there were about 46 general interest magazines, with a total circulation of 4,947,000.

33 TOURISM AND RECREATION

Tourism is a major industry in Sweden. The number of foreign tourists to Sweden cannot be counted because of uncontrolled tourist movements across borders within Scandinavia. Approximately 80% of Sweden's tourism is domestic. International tourism is led by Norway and other Nordic countries. In 1991, Sweden had 83,932 hotel rooms with a 27% occupancy rate, and receipts from tourism totaled $2.72 billion.

Principal tourist sites include the Royal Palace in Stockholm, the "garden city" of Göteborg, the resort island of Öland off the Baltic coast, and the lake and mountain country in the north. Cultural centers

Marstrand, a west coast summer resort area.

in Stockholm are the Royal Opera, Royal Dramatic Theater, and Berwald Concert Hall. Popular recreational activities include soccer, skiing, ice skating, swimming, mountain climbing, and gymnastics.

34 FAMOUS SWEDES

Gustaf I, known as Gustavus, was a great king and the founder of modern Sweden. Gustavus made Lutheranism the state religion, established a hereditary monarchy, and organized a national army and navy. Another great king and one of the world's outstanding military geniuses was Gustavus Adolphus (Gustaf II Adolf, r.1611–32). He is generally regarded as the creator of the first modern army.

Esaias Tegnér (1782–1846), considered the national poet of Sweden, and Erik Gustaf Geijer (1783–1847), historian and poet, are the best-known Swedish writers of the early 19th century. August Strindberg (1849–1912) influenced dramatists worldwide with his powerful, socially oriented plays. Swedish winners of the Nobel Prize for literature include Selma Lagerlöf (1858–1940) in 1909, and novelist and short-story writer Pär Lagerkvist (1891–1974) in 1951.

The outstanding Swedish musician of the 19th century was Franz Adolf Berwald (1796–1868), composer of symphonies, operas, and chamber music. The famous soprano Jenny Lind (1820–87) was called the "Swedish nightingale." Birgit Nilsson (b.1918) is an outstanding 20th-century singer.

Famous 18th-century scientists were the astronomer and physicist Anders Celsius (1705–44), who devised the temperature scale named after him; and the botanist Carolus Linnaeus (Carl von Linné, 1707–78), who established the classification schemes of plants and animals named after him. Emanuel Swedenborg (1688–1772) was a scientist, philosopher, and religious writer whose followers founded a religious sect in his name.

Swedish inventors include Alfred Nobel (1833–96), inventor of dynamite and originator of the Nobel Prizes, and Gustaf de Laval (1845–1913), who developed steam turbines. Kai M. Siegbahn (b.1918) shared the 1981 Nobel Prize in physics for developing spectroscopy. Sune Karl Bergström (b.1916) and Bengt Ingemar Samuelsson (b.1934) shared the 1982 prize in medicine for their research on prostaglandins. Bergström has also served as chairman of the Nobel Foundation.

Political economist Karl Gunnar Myrdal (1898–1987) was awarded the 1974 Nobel Prize in economic science. His 1944 book *An American Dilemma* contributed to the discussion of racial segregation in the United States. Dag Hammarskjöld (1905–61) was secretary-general of the United Nations from 1953 until his death and was posthumously awarded the 1961 Nobel Prize for peace.

One of the most noted film directors of modern times is Ingmar Bergman (b.1918). Famous screen personalities have included Greta Garbo (Greta Louisa Gustafsson, 1905–90), Ingrid Bergman (1917–82), and Max Von Sydow (b.1929). Sweden's sports stars include five-time Wimbledon tennis champion Björn Borg (b.1956), and Alpine skiing champion Ingemar Stenmark (b.1956).

35 BIBLIOGRAPHY

Belt, Don. "Sweden." *National Geographic*, August 1993, 2–35.

Bengtsson, Frans G. *The Long Ships*. Glasgow: William Collins Sons & Co., Ltd., 1984

Elstob, Eric. *Sweden: A Popular and Cultural History*. Totowa, N.J.: Rowman & Littlefield, 1979.

Hintz, M. *Sweden*. Chicago: Children's Press, 1985.

Moberg, Vilhelm. *A History of the Swedish People*. New York: Pantheon Books, 1973.

Nagel, Rob, and Anne Commire. "Gustavus Adolphus." In *World Leaders, People Who Shaped the World*. Volume II: Europe. Detroit: U*X*L, 1994.

Sather, Leland B. *Sweden*. Santa Barbara, Calif.: Clio, 1987.

Scott, Franklin Daniel. *Sweden, the Nation's History*. Carbondale: Southern Illinois University Press, 1988.

Sweden in Brief. Stockholm: Swedish Institute, 1981.

SWITZERLAND

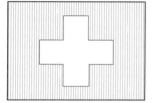

Swiss Confederation

[French:] *Suisse,* [German:] *Schweiz,* [Italian:] *Svizzera,*
[Romanish:] *Svizra,* Swiss Confederation, [French:] *Confédération Suisse,*
[German:] *Schweizerische Eidgenossenschaft,* [Italian:] *Confederazione
Svizzera,* [Romanish:] *Confederaziun Helvetica*

CAPITAL: Bern.

FLAG: The national flag consists of an equilateral white cross on a red background, each arm of the cross being one-sixth longer than its width.

ANTHEM: The Swiss Hymn begins "Trittst in Morgenrot daher, Seh' ich dich in Strahlenmeer" ("Radiant in the morning sky, Lord, I see that Thou art nigh").

MONETARY UNIT: The Swiss franc (SwFr) of 100 centimes, or rappen, is the national currency. There are coins of 1, 5, 10, 20, and 50 centimes and 1, 2, and 5 francs, and notes of 10, 20, 50, 100, 500, and 1,000 francs. SwFr1 = $0.1277 (or $1 = SwFr1.41).

WEIGHTS AND MEASURES: The metric system is the legal standard.

HOLIDAYS: New Year, 1–2 January; Labor Day, 1 May; Christmas, 25–26 December. Movable religious holidays include Good Friday, Easter Monday, Ascension, and Whitmonday.

TIME: 1 PM = noon GMT.

1 LOCATION AND SIZE

A landlocked country in west-central Europe, Switzerland has an area of 41,290 square kilometers (15,942 square miles), slightly more than twice the size of New Jersey. Switzerland has a total boundary length of 1,852 kilometers (1,151 miles).

Switzerland's capital city, Bern, is located in the western part of the country.

2 TOPOGRAPHY

Switzerland is divided into three natural topographical regions: (1) the Jura Mountains in the northwest; (2) the Alps in the south, covering three-fifths of the country's total area; and (3) the central Swiss plateau. The highest point in Switzerland is the Dufourspitze of Monte Rosa, near the border with Italy, at 4,634 meters (15,203 feet). The most celebrated of the Swiss Alps is the Matterhorn (4,478 meters/14,692 feet).

Rivers include the Rhine (Rhein); the Aare; the Rhône; the Ticino; and the Inn. Switzerland has 1,484 lakes and also contains more than 1,000 glaciers.

3 CLIMATE

The climate of Switzerland north of the Alps is temperate; the average annual temperature is 9°C (48°F). The average rainfall varies from 53 centimeters (21 inches) in the Rhône Valley to 170 centimeters (67

Photo credit: Susan D. Rock

Matterhorn during the summer season in the Alps.

inches) in Lugano. Generally, the areas to the west and north of the Alps have a cool, rainy climate, with winter averages near or below freezing and summer temperatures seldom above 21°C (70°F). The region south of the Alps has a Mediterranean climate, and frost is almost unknown. The climate of the Alps and of the Jura uplands is mostly raw, rainy, or snowy, with frost occurring above 1,830 meters (6,000 feet).

4 PLANTS AND ANIMALS

Variation in climate and altitude produces varied plants and animals. At the lowest elevations, chestnut, walnut, cypress, and palm trees grow, as well as figs, oranges, and almonds; up to 1,200 meters (3,940 feet), forests of beech, maple, and oak; around 1,680 meters (5,500 feet), fir and pine; around 2,130 meters (7,000 feet), rhododendron, larches, dwarf and cembra pine, and whortleberries; and above the snow line, more than 100 species of flowering plants, including the edelweiss. Wild animals include the chamois, boar, deer, otter, and fox. There are large birds of prey, as well as snipe, heath cock, and cuckoo. Lakes and rivers are full of fish.

5 ENVIRONMENT

Switzerland's federal forestry law of 1876 is among the world's earliest environmental laws. In 1986, however, the Swiss Federal Office of Forestry issued a report stating that 36% of the country's forests have been killed or damaged by acid rain and other types of air pollution.

Air pollution is a major environmental concern in Switzerland; automobiles and other transportation vehicles are the main causes. Strict standards for exhaust emissions were imposed on new passenger cars manufactured after October 1987. Water pollution is caused by phosphates, fertilizers, and pesticides in the water supply. The country's cities produce 3.1 million tons of solid waste annually.

In 1994, 2 of Switzerland's mammal species and 15 bird species were endangered, and 18 types of plants were endangered. The lynx, once nearly extinct, has been brought back to Switzerland.

On 1 November 1986, as a result of a fire in a chemical warehouse near Basel, some 30 tons of toxic waste flowed into

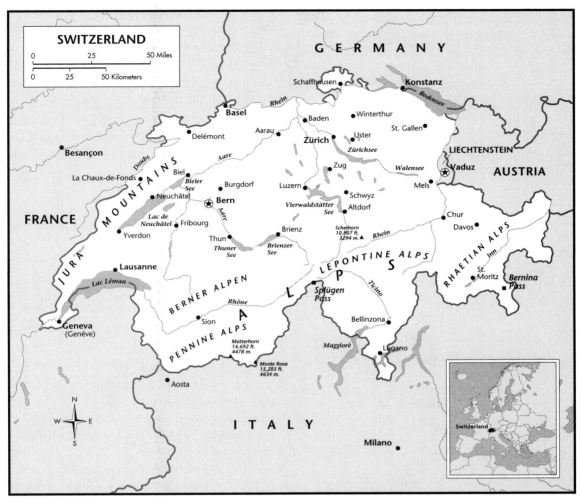

LOCATION: 5°57′24″ to 10°29′36″E; 45°49′8″ to 47°48′35″N. **BOUNDARY LENGTHS:** Germany, 334 kilometers (208 miles); Liechtenstein, 41 kilometers (25 miles); Austria, 164 kilometers (103 miles); Italy, 740 kilometers (460 miles); France, 573 kilometers (355 miles).

the Rhine (Rhein) River, killing an estimated 500,000 fish and eels.

6 POPULATION

As of the census of 4 December 1990, the population of Switzerland was 6,873,700, with a density of 169 persons per square kilometer (438 per square mile). By the year 2000, according to United Nations projections, the population is expected to rise to about 7,156,000. The largest cities at the end of 1991, according to estimates, were as follows: Zürich, 343,106; Basel, 172,768; and Geneva, 167,697.

7 MIGRATION

Total emigration of both Swiss and foreigners in 1992 was 117,034; immigration totaled 157,190, for a net increase in population of 40,156. Foreigners living in Switzerland numbered 1,190,991 (over 17% of the population) at the end of 1991. Nearly a third of all foreigners living in Switzerland were Italian. The next-leading countries of origin were the former Yugoslavia, Spain, Portugal, Germany, and Turkey. There were 61,691 known refugees in 1991. In April 1987, Swiss voters approved a government plan to tighten rules on immigration and political asylum.

Internal migration came to 371,332 in 1992. There was a tendency to move from urban to rural areas and from north to south.

8 ETHNIC GROUPS

There are four distinct ethnic and linguistic groups living in Switzerland: Germanic, French, Italian, and Rhaeto-Romanish.

9 LANGUAGES

Switzerland is a multilingual state with four national languages—German, Italian, French, and Rhaeto-Romanish. As of the 1990 census, 63.6% of the resident population spoke German as their principal language, 19.2% French, 7.6% Italian, and 0.6% Rhaeto-Romansh.

10 RELIGIONS

Of Switzerland's 19 predominantly German-speaking cantons (provinces), 10 are mostly Protestant and 9 are mostly Roman Catholic. Of the 6 predominantly French-speaking cantons, 2 are mostly Protestant and 4 are mostly Roman Catholic. The Italian-speaking canton of Ticino is mainly Roman Catholic.

As of the 1980 census, 50.4% of all residents were Protestant (52.7% in 1960); 43.6% were Roman Catholic (45.6% in 1960); and 8.1% belonged to other faiths. There were some 15,000 Jews in 1990.

11 TRANSPORTATION

There are 5,174 kilometers (3,215 miles) of Swiss railroads. Because of its geographical position, Switzerland is an international railway center. The Swiss road network covered 72,000 kilometers (44,740 miles) in 1991. Vehicles included 3,065,812 passenger cars, and 311,017 commercial vehicles.

Inland waterways are an important part of Swiss transportation. Basel is the only river port. During World War II, the Swiss organized a merchant marine to carry Swiss imports and exports on the high seas. In 1991, 22 ships totaling 360,000 gross registered tons were in use. In 1992, Swissair had 7,433,000 paying passengers.

12 HISTORY

Origins

The Helvetii, a Celtic tribe conquered by Julius Caesar in 58 BC, were the first inhabitants of Switzerland (Helvetia) known by name. Beginning in the third century AD, Switzerland was occupied, first by the Alemanni, then the Burgundians, and then the Franks, all Germanic tribes. Under Frankish rule, Christianity was introduced.

In 1032, Switzerland became part of the Holy Roman Empire. In the thirteenth century, it was placed under the rule of the House of Habsburg. In August 1291, the three forest cantons (provinces) of Schwyz, Uri, and Unterwalden formed an alliance. On 15 November 1315, they won their independence, defeating the Habsburgs at Morgarten Pass. By 1353, five other cantons, Luzern (1332), Zürich (1351), Glarus and Zug (1352), and Bern (1353), had joined the confederacy. All these allies were called Swiss (Schwyzer), after the largest canton. The confederacy was known as the Helvetian Confederation, after the original Celtic name for Switzerland.

The Helvetian Confederation

The Helvetian Confederation continued to grow with the inclusion of Aargau (1415), Thurgau (1460), and Fribourg and Solothurn (1481). Complete independence was secured by the Treaty of Basel (1499) with the Holy Roman Empire. Afterwards, Basel and Schaffhausen joined (1501), and Appenzell (1513). As of 1513, there were 13 cantons and several affiliated cities and regions.

The power of the Confederation was weakened by conflicts stemming from the Protestant Reformation, which began in 1517. Seven cantons resisted the Reformation, causing a long conflict which lasted through the Thirty Years' War (1618–48) and after.

In the following centuries, the Catholic-Protestant conflict continued with varying success for each side. Apart from this struggle, a number of unsuccessful uprisings took place against Switzerland's rulers. In 1798, the Helvetic Republic was proclaimed, under French guidance. During the Napoleonic imperial era, Switzerland was governed as a part of France.

The Swiss Confederation

In 1815, the Congress of Vienna reestablished the independent Swiss Confederation with three additional cantons (for a total of 22) and recognized its neutrality. In 1848, a new federal constitution, quite similar to that of the United States, was adopted. Meanwhile, the struggle between Protestants and Catholics had ended in the Secession (Sonderbund) War of 1847, in which the Protestant cantons quickly defeated the movement to secede of the seven Catholic cantons. As a result of the war, federal authority was greatly strengthened.

In 1874, the constitution was again changed to increase federal authority, especially in fiscal and military affairs. Since the last quarter of the nineteenth century, Switzerland has been concerned primarily with domestic matters, such as social legislation, communications, and industrialization. In foreign affairs, it remained neutral through both world wars, determined to protect its independence with its highly regarded militia. In 1978, Switzerland's 23d canton, Jura, was established by nationwide vote. In 1991, Switzerland celebrated the 700th anniversary of Confederation.

Despite its neutrality, Switzerland has cooperated wholeheartedly in various international organizations, including the League of Nations and the Red Cross. Switzerland has long resisted joining the United Nations, however, partly on the grounds that imposition of sanctions on other countries, as required by various UN resolutions, goes against Switzerland's policy of strict neutrality. However, Switzerland is a member of most specialized United Nations agencies.

13 GOVERNMENT

The Swiss Confederation is a federal union governed under the constitution of 1874, which gave supreme authority to the Federal Assembly (the legislative body) and executive power to the Federal Council.

The Federal Assembly consists of two chambers: the National Council (*Nationalrat*) of 200 members, elected by direct ballot for four-year terms by all citizens 18 years of age or older; and the Council of States (*Ständerat*) of 46 members, 2 appointed by each of the 20 cantons and 1 from each of the 6 half-cantons, and paid by the cantons. Legislation must be approved by both houses.

The seven members of the Federal Council, which has no veto power, are the respective heads of the main departments of the federal government.

The Swiss Confederation consists of 23 cantons, 3 of which are subdivided into half-cantons. The cantons have independent rule in all matters not delegated to the federal government by the constitution.

14 POLITICAL PARTIES

The three strongest parties are the Social Democratic Party, which supports wider state participation in industry and strong social legislation; the Radical Democratic Party, a progressive middle-class party, which favors increased social welfare, strengthening of national defense, and a democratic federally structured government; and the Christian Democrats, which opposes centralization of power.

Other parties include the Center Democratic Union (Swiss People's Party); the League of Independents, a progressive, middle-class consumers' group; the Communist-inclined Workers Party; the Liberal Party; and the Independent and Evangelical Party, which is Protestant and conservative.

15 JUDICIAL SYSTEM

The Federal Court of Justice in Lausanne, composed of 30 permanent members, rules in the majority of cases where a canton or the federal government is involved. It is the highest appeals court for many types of cases. Each canton has its own courts. District courts have three to five members and try lesser criminal and civil cases.

16 ARMED FORCES

The Swiss army is a well-trained citizen's militia, composed of three field army corps and one alpine field corps. Although in 1993 the standing armed forces had only 1,600 regulars and 18,500 conscript trainees, Switzerland can mobilize 625,000 trained militia within 48 hours. All males age 19–20 must serve in the military. Swiss fighting men are world-famous.

Switzerland's civil defense program, begun in the early 1970s, is able to shelter 90% of the population. Swiss volunteers serve in four overseas peacekeeping operations. Switzerland spent $3.5 billion for defense in 1993.

17 ECONOMY

Because of a lack of minerals and other raw materials and limited agricultural production, Switzerland depends upon imports of food and fodder (livestock feed) and of industrial raw materials. It finances these imports with exports of manufactured goods. Swiss manufacturers focus on quality rather than quantity of output. Other important branches of the economy include international banking, insurance, tourism, and transportation.

Switzerland was less affected than most other nations by the worldwide recession of the early 1980s and experienced a strong recovery beginning in 1983. However, gross national product (GNP) fell in 1991, 1992, and 1993. From 1990 to 1992, the annual inflation rate averaged 5.1%. Swiss unemployment has remained consistently low in comparison with other countries, although it reached an unusual high of 4.5% in 1993.

18 INCOME

In 1992, Switzerland's GNP was $248,688 million at current prices. The average per person income for the period 1988–93 was $35,760. For the period

Photo credit: Susan D. Rock

An overhead view of Bern, Switzerland's capital, as seen from the Gothic Cathedral.

1985–92 the average inflation rate was 4.0%, resulting in a real growth rate in per person GNP of 1.1%.

19 INDUSTRY

Swiss industries are chiefly engaged in the manufacture of highly finished goods. Some industries are concentrated in certain regions: the watch and jewelry industry in the Jura Mountains; machinery in Zürich, Geneva, and Basel; the chemical industry (dyes and pharmaceuticals) in Basel; and the textile industry in northeastern Switzerland.

The machine industry, first among Swiss industries today, produces goods ranging from heavy arms and ammunition to fine precision and optical instruments. Watches and machinery represent about 45% of the total Swiss export value. About 10% of the world's medicines are produced by three companies in Basel. Switzerland has also developed a major food industry, relying in part on the country's capacity for milk production. Condensed milk was first developed in Switzerland, as were two other important processed food products: chocolate and baby food.

20 LABOR

In 1992, total civilian employment numbered approximately 3,481,000, of whom about 33.9% were employed in the industrial sector; 5.6% in agriculture, forestry, and fishing; and 60.5% in services and other occupations. Another 9.2% worked in construction. In June 1992, the unemployment rate was 2.7%. Foreign workers account for about 30% of the work force, and 40% of the total unemployed.

Only 29% of the labor force was unionized in 1991. Despite legal requirements, women's wages often fall behind those of men on average by 14%, and in some cases up to 30%. The minimum age for employment is 15, or 13 for some light work. There are strict rules for employment between the ages of 15 and 20, which are well enforced.

21 AGRICULTURE

Some 30,715 square kilometers (11,860 square miles), or about 75% of the coun-

try's total area, is used for farming or grazing. Agricultural production provides only about 60% of the nation's food needs. Some principal crops, with their production figures for 1992, were as follows: sugar beets, 907,000 tons; potatoes, 737,000 tons; wheat, 533,000 tons; barley, 365,000 tons; maize, 192,000 tons; oats, 53,000 tons; and rye, 29,000 tons. In the same year, a total of 137,000 tons of wine were produced, and there were 13,450 hectares (33,235 acres) of vineyards.

22 DOMESTICATED ANIMALS

More than half of Switzerland's productive area is grassland used for hay production and/or grazing. In 1992 there were 1,783,000 head of cattle, 1,707,000 pigs, and 415,000 sheep. Switzerland had 6,000,000 laying chickens in 1992. In 1992, Switzerland produced about 3,845,000 tons of milk and 38,000 tons of butter. Swiss cheeses are world famous. In 1992, 36,100 tons of eggs were produced.

23 FISHING

Fishing is relatively unimportant but is carried on in Swiss rivers and lakes. Local fish supply about 12% of domestic needs.

24 FORESTRY

Forests occupy slightly more than 1 million hectares (2.5 million acres). About 80% of the wood in Swiss forests is coniferous, primarily spruce; the remaining 20% is deciduous, mostly red beech. Forestry production in 1991 amounted to about 1,985,000 cubic meters of sawnwood, 1,218,000 of paper and paper-

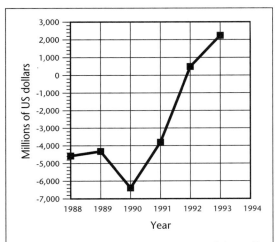

Yearly balance of trade measured in millions of US dollars. The balance of trade is the difference between what a country sells to other countries (its exports) and what it buys (its imports). If a country imports more than it exports, it has a negative balance of trade (a trade deficit). If exports exceed imports there is a positive balance of trade (a trade surplus).

board, and 700,000 cubic meters of firewood.

25 MINING

Mining is of little commercial importance. Minerals produced commercially include salt, lime, iron ore, sulfur, cement, and aluminum (from imported alumina and bauxite).

26 FOREIGN TRADE

Switzerland imports food and raw materials and exports manufactured products. Iron, minerals, and machinery have been the primary imports since 1954, while leading exports have been machinery and watches, pharmaceuticals, precision tools,

and textiles. Swiss cheese and chocolate are important products on the international market.

In 1992, European Community countries purchased 58.9% of Swiss exports and provided 72.2% of the imports. Principal trading partners in 1992 were Germany, France, Italy, the United States, and the United Kingdom.

27 ENERGY AND POWER

Switzerland is heavily dependent on imported petroleum, which supplied 50% of the energy consumed in 1991. Switzerland's electric power plants supplied 37.9% of the energy consumed in 1991. Electricity production totaled 57,802 million kilowatt hours; about 58% was hydroelectric. In 1991 there were five nuclear plants in operation. Natural gas consumption totaled 1.8 billion cubic meters in 1992.

28 SOCIAL DEVELOPMENT

Swiss social legislation has three main components: accident insurance; sickness insurance; and old-age, survivors', and disability insurance. In addition, there are unemployment insurance, military insurance, income insurance, and the farmers' aid organization.

In 1981, a constitutional amendment guaranteeing equal rights to women, particularly in education, work, and the family, was passed by a vote of 797,679 to 525,950. In 1985, 54.7% of voters approved a new law giving women equal rights in marriage.

Selected Social Indicators

These statistics are estimates for the period 1988 to 1993. For comparison purposes, data for the United States and averages for low-income countries and high-income countries are also given.

Indicator	Switzerland	Low-income countries	High-income countries	United States
Per capita gross national product†	$35,760	$380	$23,680	$24,740
Population growth rate	1.1%	1.9%	0.6%	1.0%
Population growth rate in urban areas	1.5%	3.9%	0.8%	1.3%
Population per square kilometer of land	169	78	25	26
Life expectancy in years	78	62	77	76
Number of people per physician	607	>3,300	453	419
Number of pupils per teacher (primary school)	n.a.	39	<18	20
Illiteracy rate (15 years and older)	<1%	41%	<5%	<3%
Energy consumed per capita (kg of oil equivalent)	3,491	364	5,203	7,918

† The gross national product (GNP) is the total dollar value of all goods and services produced by a country in a year. The per capita GNP is calculated by dividing a country's GNP by its population. The World Bank defines low-income countries as those with a per capita GNP of $695 or less. High-income countries have a per capita GNP of $8,626 or more. Less than 14% of the world's 5.5 billion people live in high-income countries, while almost 60% live in low-income countries.

n.a. = data not available   > = greater than   < = less than

Sources: World Bank, *Social Indicators of Development 1995,* Baltimore: Johns Hopkins University Press, 1995. Central Intelligence Agency, *World Fact Book,* Washington, D.C.: Government Printing Office, 1994.

29 HEALTH

Health standards and medical care are excellent. The pharmaceuticals industry ranks as one of the major producers of specialized pharmaceutical products. In 1983, Switzerland had 432 hospitals with 72,605 beds. In 1990, there were 11 hospital beds per 1,000 people. In 1988, there were 11,327 practicing physicians. In the period from 1988–93, there was an average of 641 people per doctor.

There were about 18 cases of tuberculosis per 100,000 people reported in 1990. Life expectancy was averaged at 78 years in 1992.

30 HOUSING

In 1991, a total of 37,597 new homes were built in communities of 2,000 or more inhabitants. The total housing stock in 1991 stood at 3,181,000. As of 1986, 99.5% of all dwellings had a water supply, 97% had a bath or shower, 78% had central heating, and 100% had a private toilet.

31 EDUCATION

Primary education is free, and adult illiteracy is nearly nonexistent. Education at all levels is the responsibility of the cantons. Thus, Switzerland has 26 different systems based on differing education laws and var-

Photo credit: Susan D. Rock

Typical regional hotel in the city of Engadine decorated in sgraffito painting.

ied cultural and linguistic needs. The cantons decide on the types of schools, length of study, teaching materials, and teachers' salaries.

Education is compulsory in most cantons for nine years, and in a few for eight. After primary school, students complete the compulsory portion of their education in various types of secondary Grade I schools, which emphasize vocational or academic subjects to varying degrees.

Switzerland has eight cantonal universities. The largest universities are those of Zürich, Geneva, and Basel; others include those of Lausanne, Bern, Fribourg, and Neuchâtel.

32 MEDIA

Broadcasting is controlled by the Swiss Broadcasting Corp. (SBC). In 1991 there were six SBC radio channels and three television channels. A number of independent local radio stations have been operating on a trial basis since 1983. Radio programs are broadcast in German, French, Italian, and Romanish. In 1991, Switzerland had 2,701,000 licensed radios and 2,476,000 televisions. There were 6,050,926 telephones (90 per 100 population) in the same year.

Switzerland had the world's third highest number of newspapers per 1,000 inhabitants as of 1992. In 1991, Switzerland had 98 daily newspapers with a total circulation of 3,280,000. The *Schweizer Illustrierte* (1991 circulation 175,000) is the most popular illustrated weekly.

33 TOURISM AND RECREATION

Switzerland has long been one of the most famous tourist areas in the world. There are many scenic attractions, and in the Swiss Alps and on the shores of the Swiss lakes there are opportunities for the skier, the swimmer, the hiker, the mountain climber, and the high alpinist. There are approximately 50,000 kilometers (31,000 miles) of marked footpaths and 500 ski lifts. The hotels are among the best in the world; Switzerland pioneered in modern hotel management and in specialized training for hotel personnel. In 1991, Switzerland had 145,677 hotel rooms with a 43.9% occupancy rate.

In 1991, there were about 12.6 million tourists. Of these, 7.94 million were from Europe; 1.02 million from the Americas; and 533,000 from Eastern and Southeast Asia. Tourism receipts totaled $7.06 million.

34 FAMOUS SWISS

World-famous Swiss scientists include the physician and alchemist Philippus Aureolus Paracelsus (Theophrastus Bombastus von Hohenheim, 1493?–1541); the geologist Louis Agassiz (Jean Louis Rodolphe Agassiz, 1807–73), who was active in the United States; and the German-born physicist Albert Einstein (1879–1955, a naturalized Swiss citizen).

Jean-Jacques Rousseau (1712–78), a Geneva-born philosopher who lived in France, was a great figure of the 18th century whose writings profoundly influenced education and political thought. Swiss-born Mme. Germaine de Staël (Anne Louise Germaine Necker, 1766–1817) was famous as a defender of liberty against Napoleon.

Well-known Swiss sculptors and painters include Henry Fuseli (Johann Heinrich Füssli, 1741–1825); Paul Klee (1879–1940); and Alberto Giacometti (1901–66). Le Corbusier (Charles Édouard Jeanneret, 1887–1965) was a leading 20th-century architect.

Swiss religious leaders include Ulrich Zwingli (1484–1531), and French-born John Calvin (Jean Chauvin, 1509–64). Other famous Swiss are Ferdinand de Saussure (1857–1913), founder of modern linguistics; the psychiatrist Carl Gustav Jung (1875–1961); Jean Piaget (1896–1980), authority on child psychology; and the philosopher Karl Jaspers (1883–1969). Swiss winners of the Nobel Prize for peace include Henri Dunant (1828–1910), founder of the Red Cross in 1901.

35 BIBLIOGRAPHY

Hintz. M. *Switzerland.* Chicago: Children's Press, 1986.
Martin, William. *Switzerland from Roman Times to the Present.* New York: Praeger, 1971.
Mehr, Christian. "Are the Swiss Forests in Peril?" *National Geographic,* May 1989, 637–651.
Meier, Heinz K. *Switzerland.* Santa Barbara, Calif.: Clio Press, 1990.
Story, A. T. *Swiss Life in Town and Country.* New York: AMS, 1983.
Switzerland: An Inside View: Politics, Economy, Culture, Society, Nature. Zurich: Der Alltag/ Scalo Verlag, 1992.

SYRIA

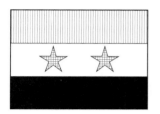

Syrian Arab Republic
Al-Jumhuriyah al-'Arabiyah as-Suriyah

CAPITAL: Damascus (Dimashq).

FLAG: The national flag is a horizontal tricolor of red, white, and black stripes; in the white center stripe are two green five-pointed stars.

ANTHEM: *An-Nashid as-Suri (The Syrian National Anthem)* begins "Protectors of the nation, peace be upon you."

MONETARY UNIT: The Syrian pound (s£) is a paper currency of 100 piasters. There are coins of 25 and 50 piasters and 1 Syrian pound and notes of 1, 5, 10, 25, 50, 100, and 500 Syrian pounds. s£1 = $0.0891 (or $1 = s£11.225).

WEIGHTS AND MEASURES: The metric system is the legal standard, but local units are widely used.

HOLIDAYS: New Year's Day, 1 January; Revolution Day, 8 March; Egypt's Revolution Day, 23 July; Union of Arab Republics Day, 1 September; National Day, 16 November. Muslim religious holidays include 'Id al-Fitr, 'Id al-'Adha', Milad an-Nabi, and Laylat al-Miraj. Christian religious holidays include Easter (Catholic); Easter (Orthodox); and Christmas, 25 December.

TIME: 2 PM = noon GMT.

1 LOCATION AND SIZE

Situated in southwest Asia, at the eastern end of the Mediterranean Sea, Syria has an area of 185,180 square kilometers (71,498 square miles), slightly larger than the state of North Dakota. Included in this total is the Golan Heights region (1,176 square kilometers/454 square miles), which Israel captured in 1967 and annexed on 14 December 1981.

Syria has a total boundary length of 2,446 kilometers (1,520 miles).

2 TOPOGRAPHY

There are five main geographic zones: (1) the narrow coastal plain along the Mediterranean shore; (2) the hill and mountain regions of the northwest, east, and southeast; (3) the cultivated area east of the Anti-Lebanon (Al Jabal Ash Sharqi) ranges; (4) the steppe and desert region, traversed by the Euphrates (Furāt) River; and (5) the northeast region.

The Anti-Lebanon Mountains (Al Jabal Ash Sharqi) extend southward along the Lebanese border. To the north of this range, the mountains slope westward to the Mediterranean.

3 CLIMATE

Average temperatures for Damascus range from about 21° to 43°C (70–109°F) in August and from about –4° to 16°C (25°–61°F) in January. Average rainfall ranges from less than 25 centimeters (10 inches) in the eastern three-fifths of the country to around 125 centimeters (50 inches) in some mountain areas.

4 PLANTS AND ANIMALS

The coastal plain is highly cultivated, with small amounts of wild growth. On the northern slopes of the mountain range are remnants of pine forests, while oak and scrub oak grow in the less well-watered central portion. Terebinth, a small tree used in making turpentine, is native to the low hill country of the steppes, and wormwood grows on the plains.

There are a few bears in the mountains; antelope are found, and there are also deer in some sections. Smaller animals include squirrel, wildcat, otter, and hare. The viper, lizard, and chameleon are found in the desert. Native birds include flamingo and pelican.

5 ENVIRONMENT

Much of Syria's natural plant life has been destroyed by farming, livestock grazing, and cutting of trees for firewood and construction. The thick forests that once covered western Syria have been severely cut back, leading to soil erosion.

Other environmental problems include pollution of coastal waters from oil spills and human wastes, and pollution of inland waterways by industrial wastes and sewage. Thirty-two percent of the people living in rural areas do not have pure water. The nation's cities produce 1.3 million tons of solid waste per year.

In 1994, 2 of Syria's mammal species, 15 of its bird species, and 11 types of plants were endangered.

6 POPULATION

Syria's population was estimated at 12,958,000 in mid-1992, and 17,546,000 was projected for the year 2000. The average population density was estimated at 71 persons per square kilometer (183 per square mile), but most of the population was concentrated in a small area.

Over 70% of Syria's people live in Damascus and the six western provinces. Damascus, the capital, had an estimated population of 1,378,000 in 1990.

7 MIGRATION

There is a great deal of migration across the borders with Lebanon and Jordan. About 150,000 Syrians working in Kuwait returned during 1990–91.

In mid-1991, 289,923 Palestinian refugees were registered with the United Nations Relief and Works Agency (UNRWA), of whom 84,972 were living in 10 camps.

8 ETHNIC GROUPS

It is estimated that Arabs make up about 90% of the population. Other ethnic groups include Kurds (about 9%), Armenians, Turkomans, Circassians, Assyrians, and Jews.

9 LANGUAGES

The language of the majority is Arabic (about 89%), but there are different dia-

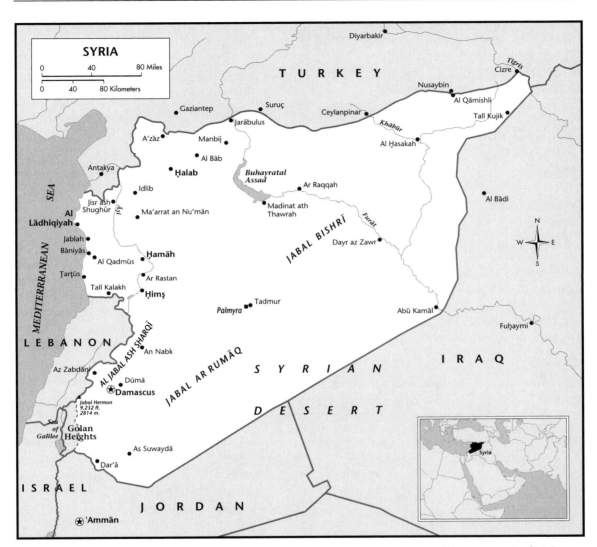

SYRIA

0	40	80 Miles
0	40	80 Kilometers

Diyarbakir

T U R K E Y

Tigris

Cizre

Nusaybin

Gaziantep

Suruç

Al Qāmishli

Ceylanpinar

Tall Kujik

Jarābulus

Khābūr

A'zāz

Manbij

Al Ḥasakah

Antakya

Al Bāb

Ḥalab

Buhayratal
Assad

Idlib

Ar Raqqah

Al Bādi

Jisr ash
Shughūr

Ma'arrat an Nu'mān

Madinat ath
Thawrah

Al
Lādhiqiyah

JABAL BISHRĪ

Furāt

Jablah

Dayr az Zawr

Bāniyās

Ḥamāh

Al Qadmūs

Ṭarṭūs

Ar Rastan

Tall Kalakh

Ḥimṣ

Palmyra

Tadmur

Abū Kamāl

Fuḥaymi

LEBANON

AL JABAL ASH SHARQĪ

An Nabk

S Y R I A N

I R A Q

Az Zabdāni

Dūmā

MEDITERRANEAN

SEA

Damascus

Jabal Hermon
9,232 ft.
2814 m.

JABAL AR RUMĀQ

D E S E R T

Sea
of
Galilee

Golan
Heights

As Suwaydā

ISRAEL

Dar'ā

Syria

JORDAN

'Ammān

LOCATION: (1949): 32°30′ to 37°30′N; 35°50′ to 42°E. **BOUNDARY LENGTHS:** Turkey, 822 kilometers (510 miles); Iraq, 605 kilometers (378 miles). Jordan, 375 kilometers (234 miles). Israel, 76 kilometers (47 miles); Lebanon, 375 kilometers (234 miles). Mediterranean coastline, 193 kilometers (117 miles). **TERRITORIAL SEA LIMIT:** 35 miles.

lects from region to region and even from town to town. Kurdish (6%) and Armenian (3%) are the principal minority languages. Aramaic, the language of Jesus, is still spoken in some villages.

10 RELIGIONS

Islam is the religion of the vast majority. Most of the Muslims are Sunnis; some are Isma'ili Shi'is. The 'Alawis are an important minority in Syria and have a great deal of political power. Also important are the Druze, whose religion is an offshoot of Shi'ite Islam. Orthodox Muslims, Alawis, and Druzes together constituted about 90% of the population in 1993.

The Christian population—including Greek Orthodox, Armenian Catholic, Armenian Orthodox, Syrian Catholic, Syrian Orthodox, Maronite Christian, Protestant, and Nestorian—make up an estimated 9%. The small Jewish population totaled 4,000 in 1984.

11 TRANSPORTATION

The Syrian national railway system consists of 2,035 kilometers (1,265 miles) of standard gauge line. In 1985, Syria had 28,960 kilometers (17,995 miles) of roads, and there were 254,456 motor vehicles in 1991.

Tartus and Al Ladhiqiyah are the main ports. In 1991, the merchant fleet had 31 vessels with a capacity of 87,000 gross registered tons.

Damascus is a connecting point for a number of major airlines. Syrian Arab Airlines flies to other Arab countries and to Europe and Africa, carrying 551,900 passengers in 1992.

12 HISTORY

Origins

Syria was the center of a great Semitic empire extending from the Red Sea north to Turkey and east to Mesopotamia around 2500 BC. (Damascus is considered by many to be the world's oldest continuously occupied city.) Later, an advanced civilization was developed along the Syrian and Lebanese coastlands under the Phoenicians (c.1600–c.800 BC). Trade, industry, and seafaring flourished.

In the fourth century BC, Syria fell to Alexander the Great, the first in a long line of European conquerors. In the first century BC, all of Syria, Lebanon, Palestine, and Transjordan was conquered by the Romans and organized as the province of Syria. Christianity spread throughout the region, especially after the early fourth century AD.

In 637, Damascus fell to the Arabs. Most Syrians were converted to Islam, and Arabic gradually became the language of the area. After a period of Arabic rule, Syria suffered a series of invasions, including those of Byzantines and Crusaders from Western Europe.

During the thirteenth century, Mongols frequently invaded Syria. For 200 years parts of Syria were controlled by Mamluks, who ruled from Egypt through local governors. In 1516, the Ottoman forces of Sultan Selim I defeated the Mamluks, and for the next four centuries, Syria was a province of the Ottoman Empire.

Independence

After World War I (1914–18) and the defeat of the Ottomans, Saudi Arabia's King Faisal and Arab nationalists opposed France's desire to control Syria and claimed independence. However, "geographic Syria" (Lebanon, Palestine, and Transjordan, as well as present-day Syria) was divided between the British and French. The French, who had been given

Photo credit: AP/Wide World Photos

Muslim Syrian men sit outside a street cafe in Damascus waiting for the sun to set so that they can begin to eat and drink again after fasting for the day. The daily fasting will last until the holy month of Ramadan ends in mid-April.

Syria and Lebanon, removed Faisal and set up their own government.

Arab protests continued until the outbreak of World War II (1939–45), during which Free French and British forces took control of Syria from Vichy (Nazi-controlled) France. Two years later, under pressure from Britain and the United States, the French permitted elections and the formation of a nationalist government. Britain and the United States recognized Syria's independence in 1944.

1948–1963

The Palestine War of 1948–49, which ended with the defeat of the Arab armies and the establishment of an Israeli state, caused Syrians to lose faith in their leadership. Several army factions struggled for more than a year to gain control of the Syrian state. Colonel Adib Shishakli ruled for most of the period from December 1949 to March 1954, when he was overthrown by an army coup.

The years from 1954 to 1958 were marked by the growth of pan-Arab (in favor of a united Arab nation) and left-of-center political forces. The strongest of these was the Arab Socialist Ba'th Party, which developed ties with Gamal Abdel Nasser, the president of Egypt, another pan-Arabist. In late 1957, the Arab Socialist Ba'th Party and Nasser agreed to a union of the two countries, and on 1 February 1958, they proclaimed the union of Syria and Egypt as the United Arab Republic (UAR).

A single-party structure replaced the lively Syrian political tradition; decisions were made in Egypt; land reforms were introduced. Syrians became unhappy with Egyptian rule and in September 1961, Syria seceded from the UAR. After a period of political instability, power was seized in 1963 by the Ba'th Party and a radical socialist government was formed.

1967–1980s

Israel gained control of the Golan Heights in the June 1967 war between Israel, on one side, and Syria, Egypt, and Jordan on the other. General Hafez al-Assad, a former chief of the Air Force and Defense Minister, became Syria's chief of state on 16 November 1970. On 6 October 1973, Syrian troops launched a full-scale attack against Israeli forces in the Golan Heights, as the Egyptians attacked Israel in the Suez Canal area.

After the United Nations cease-fire of 24 October 1973, Israel remained in control of the Golan Heights. On 31 May 1974, Syria signed an agreement with Israel, which returned part of the Golan Heights to Syria and created a buffer zone, policed by a United Nations peacekeeping force. This buffer zone was annexed by Israel in 1981.

During the 1980s, Syria intervened militarily in neighboring Arab states for its own political purposes. Syria supported the Palestinians in Jordan's 1970 civil war, aided Christian forces in Lebanon in 1976, and supported Iran in its war against Iraq. After signing a 20-year friendship treaty with the Soviet Union in 1980, Syria placed Soviet antiaircraft missiles in Lebanon's Bekaa Valley. Israel invaded southern Lebanon in June 1982, knocked out the missiles, crippled Syria's Soviet-equipped air force, and trapped Syrian (as well as Palestinian) fighters in Beirut before allowing the Syrians to return home. In the continuing Lebanese civil war, Syria has supported the Druze and Muslim militias against the Maronite Lebanese Forces.

1990s

Syria joined the coalition of forces against Iraq in 1990 and agreed to participate in direct peace talks with Israel in 1991. The collapse of the Soviet Union removed Syria's most important outside support.

Internally, many Syrians dislike the current government because it is not democratic and too much power is given to members of Assad's minority religious sect, the 'Alawis. There has been no serious threat to the regime since the early 1980s, and the Ba'th Party has continued to be used as a means of control throughout the country. In the 1990s, Assad took steps to liberalize economic controls and to permit some political freedoms. About 300 political prisoners were released in 1992 and Syrian Jews were again allowed to travel.

13 GOVERNMENT

The constitution of 12 March 1973 gives strong executive power to the president, who is nominated by the Ba'th Party and elected by popular vote to a seven-year term. The single-chamber People's Council has 250 members who are elected every four years, but who have no real power. Suffrage is universal, beginning at age 18. Syria has been under a state of emergency since 1963 (except for 1973-74).

Syria is divided into 13 provinces (*muhafazat*) and Damascus.

14 POLITICAL PARTIES

The Arab Socialist Ba'th Party is Syria's strongest political force. It is much larger and more influential than the combined strength of its five partners in the National Progressive Front (NPF), an official political alignment that groups the Communist Party of Syria (SCP) and four small leftist parties—the Syrian Arab Socialist Union (ASU), the Socialist Unionist Party (ASUM), the Democratic Socialist Union Party (DSUP), and the Arab Socialist Party (ASP)—with the Ba'th.

15 JUDICIAL SYSTEM

There are civil and criminal appeals courts, the highest being the Court of Cassation. Separate State Security Courts rule in cases affecting the security of the government. In addition, Shari'ah courts apply Islamic law in personal cases. The Druze and non-Muslim communities have their own religious courts.

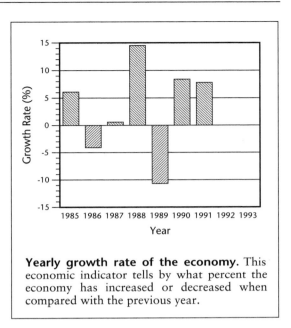

Yearly growth rate of the economy. This economic indicator tells by what percent the economy has increased or decreased when compared with the previous year.

16 ARMED FORCES

In 1993, the army had an estimated 300,000 regular troops (130,000 conscripts) and 300,000 reserves, of whom 50,000 were recalled. The navy had 8,000 men and 8,000 reserves. Naval vessels included 3 submarines, 2 frigates, 30 missile-equipped fast patrol boats, and 2 amphibious landing vessels. The air force had 40,000 men, 639 combat aircraft, and 100 armed helicopters. The air defense command numbered 60,000 with 24 brigades or regiments.

In 1989, budgeted military expenditures totaled $2.5 billion.

17 ECONOMY

Development of the state-owned oil industry and greater use of other mineral resources, particularly phosphates, have helped to expand Syrian industry, which was formerly concentrated in light manufacturing and textiles.

Syria's economy has improved since 1990 due to an increase in oil production, the recovery of the agricultural sector from drought, aid from the Gulf states, and economic reforms which boosted Syrian business. Syria's attempts to improve its economy and living standards have depended heavily on technical aid from Socialist countries, especially the former Soviet Union, and financial aid from Arab oil states.

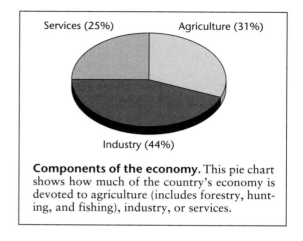

Components of the economy. This pie chart shows how much of the country's economy is devoted to agriculture (includes forestry, hunting, and fishing), industry, or services.

Services (25%) Agriculture (31%) Industry (44%)

18 INCOME

In 1992, Syria's gross national product (GNP) was $14,607 million at current prices, or about $2,300 per person. For the period 1985–92 the average inflation rate was 19.4%, resulting in a real growth rate in per person GNP of 0%.

19 INDUSTRY

In 1965, the textile industry was nationalized and reorganized into 13 large state corporations. Syria's production in 1988 included 24,000 tons of cotton and silk textiles and 642 tons of woolen fabrics, down from 1,673 tons in 1985.

Also important are the chemical and engineering industries, the food industry, and oil refining. The largest component of the chemical and engineering sector is the cement industry, which produced 3.33 million tons in 1988. In the same year, Syria produced 20,000 tons of sugar. Vegetable and olive oils are traditional Syrian products; 109 tons were produced in

1988. Some 15,455 tons of iron bars were produced in 1988, and 21,821 refrigerators were produced.

20 LABOR

It has been estimated that 3,485,368 persons were employed in 1991, of whom 26.3% worked in agriculture, 27.3% in social and personal services, 13.1% in manufacturing, 10.9% in commerce, 9.8% in building and construction, 4.8% in transportation and communication, and 7.8% in other sectors. There is a high level of underemployment, and unemployment was officially reported at 6.8% in 1991.

There are child labor laws setting the minimum age for employment in different types of jobs. But these laws are not well enforced and a great deal of abuse is reported.

21 AGRICULTURE

The principal cash crop is cotton. Other cash crops are cereals, vegetables, fruit, and tobacco. Principal crops and 1992 output (in 1,000 tons) were wheat, 3,046; sugar beets, 1,272; barley, 1,092; olives, 491; tomatoes, 448; and cotton, 215. Fruits include grapes, apples, apricots, and figs.

22 DOMESTICATED ANIMALS

The raising of livestock contributes significantly to the Syrian economy. In 1992 there were 15,782,000 sheep, 986,000 goats, 762,000 head of cattle, and 16,000,000 poultry. Production of milk in 1992 totaled 775,000 tons; cheese, 67,550 tons; butter and ghee, 13,357 tons; and eggs, 65,250 tons.

23 FISHING

There is some fishing off the Mediterranean coast and from rivers and fish farms. The commercial catch is small (5,500 tons in 1991).

24 FORESTRY

Although 730,000 hectares (1,804,000 acres) were officially listed as forest land in 1991, only about 58,000 cubic meters of roundwood was produced that year.

25 MINING

Syria does not have great mineral resources, but deposits of phosphate, iron, and petroleum have been mined in recent years. Production of phosphate rock was 1,359,000 tons in 1991. In 1991, output of salt totaled 127,000 tons; of marble, 18,000 cubic meters.

26 FOREIGN TRADE

Syria's principal exports since 1974 have been crude petroleum and oil products.

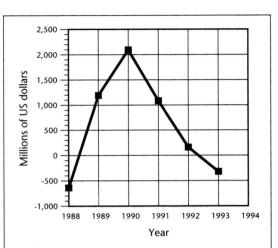

Yearly balance of trade measured in millions of US dollars. The balance of trade is the difference between what a country sells to other countries (its exports) and what it buys (its imports). If a country imports more than it exports, it has a negative balance of trade (a trade deficit). If exports exceed imports there is a positive balance of trade (a trade surplus).

Between 1980 and 1988, Syria's exports to Socialist countries increased from 16.1% of total exports to 41.4%; the Socialist countries supplied 19.0% of Syria's imports in 1988. The European Community countries took 33.8% of exports and supplied 36.1% of imports, while Arab countries took 13.1% of exports and supplied 5.2% of imports.

27 ENERGY AND POWER

Crude oil production was 25.2 million tons in 1992. The proven reserves of Syria's five oil fields amounted to an estimated 1.7 billion barrels (200 million tons) of crude petroleum at the end of 1992. Proven natural gas reserves were officially estimated at 7 trillion cubic feet in 1992.

Thermal production, primarily by oil-fueled plants, supplied 87% of electricity production in 1991. Total electricity production in 1991 was 12,179,000 kilowatt hours.

28 SOCIAL DEVELOPMENT

The Ministry for Social and Labor Affairs was formed in 1956 to protect the interests of the working population, provide clean housing conditions for workers, and support charities. A system of social insurance, introduced in 1959, provides old age pensions and disability and death benefits. Workers' compensation (for injuries on the job) provides temporary and permanent disability benefits, as well as medical and survivor benefits.

Although the government supports equal pay for equal work and encourages education for women, Islamic beliefs which contradict these policies govern many areas of women's lives.

29 HEALTH

Since World War II, malaria has been virtually eliminated with the aid of the World Health Organization (WHO). Intestinal and respiratory diseases caused by poor living conditions are still common, particularly in rural areas. Average life expectancy for the period 1988–93 was 68 years.

In 1990, there were 1.1 hospital beds per 1,000 people. In 1991, there were 10,114 physicians and 11,957 nurses. In 1992, there were approximately 85 doctors per 100,000 people, with a nurse to doctor ratio of 1.2. In 1992, about 83% of the population had access to health care services. Total health care expenditures for 1990 were $283 million.

30 HOUSING

According to the latest available information for 1980–88, total housing units numbered 1,670,000 with 6.4 people per dwelling.

31 EDUCATION

Elementary schooling is free and compulsory for six years. The estimated literacy rate in 1990 was 64% (78.3% for men and 50.8% for women). In 1991 there were 2,539,081 primary-school pupils with 102,617 teachers in 9,934 schools. At the secondary level, there were 902,819 students and 55,029 teachers in 1991. Syria has four universities: the University of Damascus; Tishrin University; the University of Aleppo (Ḥalab); and Al-Ba'th University. In 1991, higher level institutions had a total of 183,079 students enrolled.

32 MEDIA

There were 685,000 telephones in use in 1991. The Syrian Broadcasting Service broadcasts in Arabic and 10 foreign languages. Syrian Arab TV has two stations. There were about 3,270,000 radios and 770,000 television sets in use in 1991.

Syrian newspapers are published by government ministries and popular organizations, and are subject to censorship. Principal dailies in Arabic (with 1991 circulations) include *Al-Ba'th,* the party newspaper (75,000), *Tishrin* (75,000), and

Selected Social Indicators

These statistics are estimates for the period 1988 to 1993. For comparison purposes, data for the United States, and averages for low-income countries and high-income countries are also given.

Indicator	Syria	Low-income countries	High-income countries	United States
Per capita gross national product†	$2,300	$380	$23,680	$24,740
Population growth rate	3.5%	1.9%	0.6%	1.0%
Population growth rate in urban areas	4.4%	3.9%	0.8%	1.3%
Population per square kilometer of land	71	78	25	26
Life expectancy in years	68	62	77	76
Number of people per physician	1,178	>3,300	453	419
Number of pupils per teacher (primary school)	24	39	<18	20
Illiteracy rate (15 years and older)	36%	41%	<5%	<3%
Energy consumed per capita (kg of oil equivalent)	798	364	5,203	7,918

† The gross national product (GNP) is the total dollar value of all goods and services produced by a country in a year. The per capita GNP is calculated by dividing a country's GNP by its population. The World Bank defines low-income countries as those with a per capita GNP of $695 or less. High-income countries have a per capita GNP of $8,626 or more. Less than 14% of the world's 5.5 billion people live in high-income countries, while almost 60% live in low-income countries.

> = greater than   < = less than

Sources: World Bank, Social Indicators of Development 1995, Baltimore: Johns Hopkins University Press, 1995. Central Intelligence Agency, World Fact Book, Washington, D.C.: Government Printing Office, 1994.

Al-Thawrah (75,000) in Damascus, and Al-Jamahir (10,000) in Aleppo (Ḥalab).

33 TOURISM AND RECREATION

In 1991 there were 622,000 tourists, mostly from neighboring Middle Eastern countries. Tourists spent a total of $300 million. As of that year, Syria had 13,960 hotel rooms with an occupancy rate of 34%.

Syria has many famous tourist attractions, such as the Krak des Chevaliers, a Crusaders' castle. Palmyra, the capital of Queen Zenobia, is a fairly well preserved ruin of an Arabo-Hellenic city. The Umayyad Mosque in Damascus, which includes parts of the Byzantine Cathedral of St. John the Baptist, is popular. Syria's mountains and Mediterranean beaches also attract visitors.

34 FAMOUS SYRIANS

Among famous Syrians of an earlier period are the philosopher Al-Farabi (Muhammad bin Muhammad bin Tarkhan abu Nasr al-Farabi, 872–950), considered by the Arab world as second only to Aristotle; and the poet Al-

Mutanabbi (Abu at-Tayyib Ahmad bin al-Husayn al-Mutanabbi, 915–65).

Nureddin (Nur ad-Din, 1118–74), ruler of Aleppo, annexed Damascus and brought Egypt under his control. By unifying Muslim forces against the Crusaders, he made possible the victories of the renowned Saladin (Salah ad-Din, 1138–93), sultan of both Syria and Egypt, whose tomb is in Damascus. Hafez al-Assad (Hafiz al-Asad, b.1928) has ruled Syria since 1970.

35 BIBLIOGRAPHY

Beaton, M. *Syria*. Chicago: Children's Press, 1988.

Castle, Wilfred Thomas Frogatt. *Syrian Pageant: The History of Syria and Palestine, 1000 B.C. to A.D. 1945*. New York: Gordon, 1977.

Collelo, Thomas, ed. *Syria: A Country Study*. 3d ed. Washington, D.C.: Library of Congress, 1988.

Roberts, David. *The Ba'th and the Creation of Modern Syria*. New York: St. Martin's, 1987.

TAIWAN

Republic of China
Chung Hwa Min Kuo

CAPITAL: T'aipei.

FLAG: The flag is red with a 12-pointed white sun on the blue upper left quadrant. The 12 points of the sun represent the 12 two-hour periods of the day in Chinese tradition, and symbolize progress. The colors red, white, and blue represent the Three Principles of the people (San Min Chu I) of Sun Yat-sen, father of the Republic of China, and symbolize the spirit of liberty, fraternity, and equality.

ANTHEM: *Chung Hwa Min Kuo Kuo Ke (Chinese National Anthem).*

MONETARY UNIT: The new Taiwan dollar (NT$) is a paper currency of 100 cents. There are coins of 50 cents and 1, 5, and 10 dollars, and notes of 50, 100, 500, and 1,000 new Taiwan dollars. NT$1 = US$0.0350 (or US$1 = NT$28.54).

WEIGHTS AND MEASURES: The metric system is employed in government and industrial statistics. Commonly used standards of weights and measures are the catty (1.1 lb or 0.4989 kilograms), the li (0.5 kilometers or 0.31 miles), the ch'ih (0.33 meters or 1.09 feet), and the chia (0.97 hectare or 2.39 acres).

HOLIDAYS: New Year's Day and the Founding of the Republic of China (1912), 1 January; Youth Day (formerly known as Martyrs' Day), 29 March; Tomb-Sweeping Day and Anniversary of the Death of Chiang Kai-shek, 5 April; Birthday of Confucius and Teachers' Day, 28 September; National Day (Double Tenth Day), 10 October; Taiwan Retrocession Day, 25 October; Chiang Kai-shek's Birthday, 31 October; Sun Yat-sen's Birthday, 12 November; Constitution Day, 25 December.

TIME: 8 PM = noon GMT.

1 LOCATION AND SIZE

Taiwan, the seat of the Republic of China, lies in the western Pacific Ocean, less than 161 kilometers (100 miles) from the southeast coast of mainland China, from which it is separated by the Taiwan Strait. Besides the island proper, Taiwan comprises 21 small islands in the Taiwan group and 64 islands in the P'enghu Ch'üntoo (Pescadores) group, giving it a total area of 35,980 square kilometers (13,892 square miles), slightly larger than the states of Maryland and Delaware combined.

Also under the control of the Taiwan government are Chinmen and Matsu, two island groups located strategically close to mainland China. Taiwan's capital, T'aipei, is located at the northern end of the country.

2 TOPOGRAPHY

The eastern two-thirds of the island is composed of rugged foothill ranges and massive mountain chains. A low, flat coastal plain, extending from north to south, occupies the western third. Yu Shan, with an elevation of 3,997 meters (13,113 feet), is the highest peak on the island. Mild earthquake tremors are common.

All the rivers flow from the mountains in the central part of the island. The longest river, Choshui, is only 183 kilometers (114 miles) long.

3 CLIMATE

Taiwan enjoys an oceanic, subtropical monsoon climate. The average lowland temperature in January is 16°C (61°F) in the north and 20°C (68°F) in the south. The average July temperature is 28°C (82°F) in both the north and south. The average rainfall is 257 centimeters (101 inches), ranging from 127 centimeters (50 inches) at the middle of the western coast to 635 centimeters (250 inches) and more on exposed mountain slopes.

4 PLANTS AND ANIMALS

Taiwan has almost 190 plant families, and more than 3,800 species. Trees range from mangrove forests in the tidal flats, to palm, teak, and bamboo at heights of up to 2,000 meters (6,600 feet), to pines, cypresses, firs, and junipers in the highest regions.

The mammals so far discovered number more than 60 species. The largest beast of prey is the Formosan black bear.

Foxes, flying foxes, deer, wild boar, bats, squirrels, macaques, and pangolins are some of the mammals seen on the island. There are more than 330 species and sub-species of birds and more than 65 species of reptiles and amphibians.

5 ENVIRONMENT

Water pollution is a significant problem in Taiwan. Outside of the larger hotels and urban centers, the water is likely to be impure. Air pollution is another significant problem, complicated by a high pollen count. In the mid-1980s, the government began tightening emission standards for automobiles and ordered many factories and power plants to install filters and dust collectors.

The nation's marine life is threatened by the use of driftnets in fishing. Endangered species as of 1987 included the Formosan sika, Oriental white stork, and Lan Yü scops owl.

6 POPULATION

According to the 1990 census, Taiwan had a population of 20,352,900. Taiwan had an estimated population of 20,992,000 in 1994. A population of 22,065,000 was forecast for the year 2000. The population density, among the world's highest, was 566 persons per square kilometer (1,466 per square mile) in 1990. T'aipei, the capital and principal city, had a population of 2,696,073 at the end of 1992.

7 MIGRATION

In 1963, the Nationalist government in Taiwan reported that since the Communist conquest of mainland China in 1949–50, a total of 146,772 Chinese refugees had come to Taiwan for resettlement. There may be as many as 100,000 illegal immigrants.

In 1986, the Taiwan government reported that there were 28,714,000 overseas Chinese (25,799,000 in Asia, 2,044,000 in the Americas, 584,000 in Europe, 214,000 in Oceania, and 73,000 in Africa), including those with dual nationality.

8 ETHNIC GROUPS

The term "Taiwanese" is often used when referring to those Chinese who are natives of the island, as distinct from the 2 million "mainlanders" who migrated from China after the end of World War II. Most of the more than 20 million inhabitants of Taiwan are descendants of earlier immigrants from Fujian and Guangdong (Kwangtung) provinces in South China. They form several distinct groups. The Hakka are descendants of refugees and exiles from Guangdong who came to Taiwan before the nineteenth century; the more numerous Fujians are descendants of peasants from Fujian who migrated to Taiwan in the eighteenth and nineteenth centuries.

In 1991 there were 345,523 aborigines, primarily of Indonesian origin. They are divided into nine major tribes, with the Ami, Atayal, Paiwan, and Bunun accounting for about 88%. The remainder is mainly distributed among the Puyuma, Rukai, Saisiyat, Tsou, and Yami. The language and customs of the aborigines suggest a close resemblance to the Malays.

LOCATION: 21°45′25″ to 25°56′39″N; 119°18′3″ to 124°34′30″E. TERRITORIAL SEA LIMIT: 12 miles.

9 LANGUAGES

Most people on Taiwan now speak the Chinese dialect, Mandarin (Peking dialect). It is the official language and is used in administration, law, education, and, to a large extent, in commerce. It has come into increasingly common use during the last three decades.

Native Taiwanese (those born on the island) speak a variety of southern Chinese dialects, but mainly Southern FuKienese, the native tongue of about 70% of the population. It has also influenced the vocabulary of Mandarin spoken on Taiwan. There is also a sizable population of Hakka speakers, the dialect spoken mainly in Kwantung Province on mainland China. As a result of 50 years of Japanese rule (1895–1945), most Taiwanese and aborigines over the age of 60 speak or understand Japanese. Tribal peoples speak dialects of the Malay-Polynesian family which have no written script.

10 RELIGIONS

The Taiwan folk religion is a mixture of ancestor worship, spirit worship, Buddhism, and Taoism. As of 1985, Taiwan had an estimated 10 million folk-religionists, with 4.86 million Buddhists in 1991.

Since the end of World War II, more than 80 Protestant denominations have been established on the island, and the activities of Christian missions, many coming over from the mainland, have become widespread. As of 1991, the Christian population was estimated at 720,000, about 300,000 of whom were Roman Catholics. Muslims numbered about 52,000.

11 TRANSPORTATION

As of 1991, Taiwan had about 4,600 kilometers (2,900 miles) of railroad track. In the same year, Taiwan had 20,041 kilome-ters (12,453 miles) of highways, of which 85% were paved. By the end of 1992 there were 2,781,000 registered motor vehicles, three-fourths of which were passenger cars.

Taiwan has a number of international seaports, including Kaohsiung in the southwest; Chilung, on the north coast; and Hualien on the east coast. At the end of 1991, Taiwan's merchant marine consisted of 211 vessels totaling 5.8 million gross registered tons.

There are two international airports. The main one is Chiang Kai-shek International Airport, southwest of T'aipei. Principal air service is provided by China Air Lines, Taiwan's international airline, and other international carriers, and by Taiwan's leading domestic airline, Far Eastern Air Transport.

12 HISTORY

Although Taiwan can be seen from the China mainland on a clear day, ancient Chinese chronicles contain few references to the island. Chinese emigration to Taiwan probably began as early as the T'ang dynasty (618–907 AD). During the reign of Kublai Khan (1263–94), the first civil administration was established in the neighboring Pescadores (present-day P'enghu). Taiwan itself, however, remained outside the jurisdiction of the Mongol Empire. During the Ming dynasty (1368–1644), Japanese pirates and Chinese outlaws and refugees won the coastal areas from the native aborigines. The Chinese settled in the southwest region, while the Japanese occupied the northern tip of the island. Significant Chinese settlement, by immigrants from Fujian and Guang-dong, began in the seventeenth century.

In 1517, the Portuguese sighted the island and named it Ilha Formosa (Beautiful Island). In the seventeenth century, the Chinese, Portuguese, and Dutch competed for control of the island. By 1656, the Dutch had gained control of it, but in 1661 they were driven out by forces belonging to the Chinese Ming dynasty. In 1683, the Manchus, who had overtaken the Ming dynasty on mainland China in 1661, assumed control of the island as well.

From 1683 to 1885, Taiwan was administered as a part of Fujian Province of mainland China. After the French bombardment and blockade of the island in 1884 during the Sino-French War over Annam, Taiwan's strategic importance was recognized. It was made into a separate province in 1885.

Upon the conclusion of the First Sino-Japanese War between China and Japan in 1895, Taiwan was given to Japan. Under the Japanese, the island's agricultural resources were developed rapidly to supply Japan's needs at home, and transportation was modernized.

After World War II (1939–45), Taiwan was restored to China. On 8 December 1949, as the Chinese Communists were sweeping the Nationalist (non-communist) armies off the mainland, the government of the Republic of China (ROC), led by General Chiang Kai-shek (Jiang Jieshi), was officially transferred to Taiwan.

Photo credit: Corel Corporation.

A girl of the Ami tribe, Taroko, Taiwan.

The Republic of China

When Chiang Kai-Shek moved the ROC government to Taiwan, two million mainland Chinese fled to the island with him. An authoritarian rule began under martial law. Strong government policies contributed to steady economic progress, first in agriculture and then in industry. In the 1950s, with American aid and advice, the ROC undertook a successful program of land redistribution. Japanese investment and the Vietnam War in the 1960s further stimulated economic growth.

The question of which China—the People's Republic of China (PRC), on the

Chinese mainland, or the Republic of China (ROC) in Taiwan—should occupy China's seat at the United Nations was debated by the UN General Assembly for more than two decades, beginning in 1950. Support for Taiwan's representation gradually lessened over the years, and on 25 November 1971 the General Assembly voted 75–36 (with 17 abstentions) to remove recognition from the ROC and recognize the PRC.

In a significant policy reversal, the United States voted with the majority to seat the mainland government. Although maintaining full diplomatic ties with Taiwan, the United States took the occasion of President Richard Nixon's 1972 visit to China to acknowledge, in what became known as the Shanghai communiqué of February 1972, that "all Chinese on either side of the Taiwan Strait maintain there is but one China and that Taiwan is part of China. The United States government does not challenge that position."

By 1975, most nations had shifted recognition from the ROC to the PRC. On 1 January 1979, the United States formally recognized the PRC as the sole legal government of China and severed diplomatic ties with Taiwan. Nonetheless, the United States continued to sell arms to Taiwan, and commercial and cultural contacts were unofficially maintained. Taiwan successfully avoided worldwide political and economic isolation by maintaining a host of similar contacts with other countries.

When President Chiang Kai-shek died at age 87 on 5 April 1975, he was succeeded in office by former Vice-President Yen Chia-kan (Yan Jiagan). While control of the central government had remained in the hands of former mainlanders in the first decades of the Nationalists' rule on Taiwan, native-born Taiwanese Chinese increasingly won elections at local levels. Chiang Ching-kuo instituted a policy of bringing more Taiwanese into the Nationalist Party.

Demonstrations Grow

By the 1980s, economic development had produced a new middle class. The passage of time, together with intermarriage between former mainlanders and Taiwanese, had brought a new generation for which the distinction between mainlander and Taiwanese held less importance. These factors contributed to popular pressure for a more democratic government. Thousands protested the 38th anniversary of martial law in May 1987. And, in March 1990, more than 10,000 demonstrators demanded greater democracy and direct presidential elections.

In 1987 martial law was revoked. Press restrictions were eased, citizens were allowed to visit relatives in mainland China, and it became legal to form political parties. In January 1988, Chiang Ching-kuo died and was succeeded as president by the vice-president, Lee Teng-hui (Li Denghui, 1923–). Lee, a protégé of Chiang Ching-kuo, is a native Taiwanese. In March 1990, Lee was reelected by the National Assembly as president in his own right for a six-year term. In July, he was also named Chairman of the Nationalist Party by the Party Congress.

13 GOVERNMENT

The government of the Republic of China in T'aipei claims to be the central government of all of China. The government gets its powers from the National Assembly, which, according to the constitution, exercises political powers on behalf of the people. In 1990 the National Assembly had 651 members. The Assembly has the power to elect and recall the president and the vice-president, amend the constitution, and approve constitutional amendments proposed by the legislative council (*Legislative Yuan*).

The president is the head of state. His term of office is six years, with eligibility for a second term. The constitutional prohibition against third terms was suspended in March 1960 to permit President Chiang Kai-shek to continue in office. He was reelected in 1972 for a fifth six-year term.

Under the president, there are five government branches known as yuans (councils or departments): Legislative, Executive, Control, Examination, and Judicial. The Legislative Yuan, elected by popular vote, is the highest lawmaking body. The Executive Yuan is comparable to the cabinet in other countries. The Control Yuan, the highest supervisory branch, exercises audit powers over the government and may impeach public officials. It also supervises the government budget. The Examination Yuan is the equivalent of a civil service commission.

14 POLITICAL PARTIES

The Chinese Nationalist Party, better known as the Kuomintang—KMT (Guomindang—GMD), is the dominant political party in Taiwan. The teachings of Sun Yat-sen (Sun Zhongshan), which stress nationalism, democracy, and people's livelihood, form the ideals of the party.

Under martial law, from 1949 through 1986, the formation of new political parties was illegal. In September 1986, a group of "nonpartisans" formed a new opposition party, the Democratic Progressive Party (DPP), which leaned toward the Taiwanese population and advocated "self-determination." In addition to the DPP, new parties include the Labor Party, the Workers Party, and other minor parties. In the first fully competitive, democratic national elections, in December 1992, the KMT won 53% and the DPP 31% of the votes for the Legislative Yuan.

15 JUDICIAL SYSTEM

The Judicial Yuan is Taiwan's highest judicial branch. It interprets the constitution and other laws and decrees, rules on administrative suits, and disciplines public officials. The Supreme Court, the highest court of the land, consists of a number of civil and criminal divisions, each of which is formed by a presiding judge and four associate judges.

In 1993 a separate Constitution Court was established. The new court is charged with resolving constitutional disputes and regulating the activities of political parties.

16 ARMED FORCES

Two years' military service is compulsory for all male citizens. The armed forces totaled 360,000 in 1993. The army had 260,000 members, the navy 30,000, the marines 30,000, and the air force 70,000. In addition, reserves totaled 1.6 million. The navy had 24 destroyers, 4 submarines, 10 frigates, and 93 patrol and coastal combatants. The air force had 486 combat aircraft.

17 ECONOMY

The decade 1971–80 saw the development of the steel, machinery, machine tools, and motor vehicle industries. Such industries, based on imports of raw materials, were encouraged through massive government support for major improvements in roads, railroads, ports, and electricity.

During the 1980s, emphasis was placed on the development of high-technology industries. As a result, between 1981 and 1991, the share of high-technology industries in total manufactures increased from 20% to 29%, making Taiwan the seventh largest producer of computer hardware on the global market. In contrast to Taiwan's industry-led economic growth of previous decades, since the late 1980s the country has undergone a shift towards a services-dominated economy.

The growth rate declined to 4.5% in 1981/82 in the face of worldwide recession, recovering quickly though unevenly in following years. For the 1981–89 period as a whole, the growth rate averaged 8.2% a year. During 1990–92, however, the gross national product (GNP) increased only 6% annually due to declining export growth and poor performances in the mining and agricultural sectors.

Photo credit: Susan D. Rock.

Commercial district of Keelung.

18 INCOME

In 1992, Taiwan's gross national product (GNP) was US$209 billion at current prices, or US$10,202 per person. In 1992 the inflation rate for consumer prices was 4.4% and the national product real growth rate was estimated at 6.7%.

19 INDUSTRY

Industrial production rose spectacularly after the end of World War II (1939–45), especially between 1952 and the early 1980s. Slower economic growth since the mid-1980s and greater investment emphasis on heavy and high-technology industries, as well as services, resulted in declining production figures for some traditional manufactures during the past decade.

Cotton yarn production totaled 197,133 tons in 1992. Production of cotton fabrics peaked at 840 million meters in 1977, declining to 568,639 meters in 1992. Similarly, fertilizer production rose to 2.1 million tons in 1980, but declined to 1.9 million tons in 1992. Television set production declined from 5,748,000 in 1986 to 2,623,000 units in 1992. Caustic soda production fell from 386,505 to 290,348 tons.

Nevertheless, production increases continued to be registered for a number of key products. Cement production grew from 14.8 million tons in 1986 to 21.5 million tons in 1992. Paper production rose from 530,224 in 1986 to 1.0 million tons in 1992. Production of integrated circuits increased from 1,651 million pieces in 1986 to 3,694 million pieces in 1992.

Motor vehicle production rose from 170,923 passenger cars in 1986 to 429,208 units in 1992; steel bars from 6,164,000 to 14,556,298 tons; synthetic fibers from 1,371,000 to 2,163,662 tons; polyvinyl chloride from 795,000 tons to 1,042,564; shipbuilding from 552,294 deadweight tons (dwt) to 1,342,018; sewing machines from 2,675,000 in 1986 to 3,208,430 sets in 1992.

20 LABOR

In 1992, the civilian labor force in Taiwan numbered 8,770,000. About 20% of the labor force is engaged in agriculture, 32%

in services, 41% in industry and commerce, and the remainder in other activities. Only about 1.5% of the labor force was unemployed in 1992.

Most large firms give allowances for transportation, meals, housing, and other benefits, which can increase base pay by 60–80%. Women are entitled to eight weeks of maternity leave at full pay and an extra paid holiday on Woman's Day (8 March). The law does not provide for effective collective bargaining and also prohibits strikes, shutdowns, and walkouts in vital industries.

The minimum age for employment is 15, which is also the age at which most children finish their compulsory education.

21 AGRICULTURE

Although still important as both an export earner and a domestic food source, agriculture has fallen far from the dominant position it long held in the Taiwan economy. In 1993, agriculture accounted for only 3.5% of GNP, down from 28% in 1964. High production costs and low return have driven much of the agricultural work force away to industry.

Rice, the principal food crop, is grown along the western plain and in the south. Other food crops include sweet potatoes, bananas, peanuts, soybeans, and wheat. Sugar, pineapples, citrus fruits, crude tea, and asparagus are plantation-grown and are the principal cash and export crops. Small amounts of Taiwan's world-famous oolong tea, cotton, tobacco, jute, and sisal are also produced. A fast-rising industry, mushroom canning, led to the development of mushroom cultivation, a specialty crop well suited to Taiwan since it is labor-intensive and requires little space and small investment.

22 DOMESTICATED ANIMALS

Hog raising is overtaken in importance only by rice and sugarcane production in Taiwan's rural economy. By 1990, there were some 11 million pigs. Chickens and ducks are raised by most households.

23 FISHING

In 1990, Taiwan accounted for 5.6% of the world's fresh, chilled and frozen fish exports, valued at $742.3 million, and 4.7% of the world's prepared and preserved fish exports, valued at $257.8 million. Bonito, shark, sturgeon, tuna, red snapper, lobster, and shrimp are the main items of the inshore and coastal catch.

24 FORESTRY

Approximately 55% of Taiwan is forested. Production declined from a peak of 1,219,118 cubic meters in 1971 to 474,584 cubic meters in 1985. The decline of timber processing during the 1980s was largely the result of policies which favored conservation.

25 MINING

Coal, oil, and natural gas are the country's most valuable mine products. Dolomite, limestone, and marble are the most important nonfuel mineral commodities. Other minerals produced are small amounts of sulfur, pyrite, gold, silver, copper, manganese, mercury, petroleum, and natural gas.

26 FOREIGN TRADE

To fulfill both production and consumer needs, Taiwan must import large quantities of industrial raw materials and manufactured goods. By 1992, industrial exports (excluding processed agricultural products) had jumped to an overwhelming 95.7% share of the total. With rising consumer wealth within Taiwan as well as recent tariff reductions, imports have risen rapidly.

The United States remains Taiwan's single most important trade partner, although Japan has made major gains, becoming Taiwan's major supplier in the 1970s and 1980s. Trade with mainland China via Hong Kong has expanded rapidly over the past decade.

27 ENERGY AND POWER

Total electric power output reached 76,900 million kilowatt hours in 1991, when about 38% of Taiwan's electricity came from three nuclear plants with a combined installed capacity of 5,144 Megawatts. Total energy requirements have increased to about 365 million barrels in 1991, representing an annual average increase of 7.8%. The principal sources for consumption in 1992 were oil (51%), coal (29%), nuclear energy (15%), natural gas (3.5%), and hydroelectricity (1.5%). Oil is imported from the Middle East, Indonesia, Brunei, and Venezuela.

28 SOCIAL DEVELOPMENT

A social insurance system provides medical, disability, old age, survivor, and other benefits. All enterprises and labor organizations must also furnish welfare funds for

Selected Social Indicators

These statistics are estimates for the period 1988 to 1993. For comparison purposes, data for the United States and averages for low-income countries and high-income countries are also given.

Indicator	Taiwan	Low-income countries	High-income countries	United States
Per capita gross national product†	$10,202	$380	$23,680	$24,740
Population growth rate	1.0%	1.9%	0.6%	1.0%
Population growth rate in urban areas	n.a.	3.9%	0.8%	1.3%
Population per square kilometer of land	566	78	25	26
Life expectancy in years	75	62	77	76
Number of people per physician	831	>3,300	453	419
Number of pupils per teacher (primary school)	n.a.	39	<18	20
Illiteracy rate (15 years and older)	7%	41%	<5%	<3%
Energy consumed per capita (kg of oil equivalent)	2,786	364	5,203	7,918

† The gross national product (GNP) is the total dollar value of all goods and services produced by a country in a year. The per capita GNP is calculated by dividing a country's GNP by its population. The World Bank defines low-income countries as those with a per capita GNP of $695 or less. High-income countries have a per capita GNP of $8,626 or more. Less than 14% of the world's 5.5 billion people live in high-income countries, while almost 60% live in low-income countries.

n.a. = data not available   > = greater than   < = less than

Sources: World Bank, Social Indicators of Development 1995, Baltimore: Johns Hopkins University Press, 1995. Central Intelligence Agency, World Fact Book, Washington, D.C.: Government Printing Office, 1994.

workers and "welfare units," such as cafeterias, nurseries, clinics, and low-rent housing. Government programs include relief for mainland refugees, disaster-relief assistance, and direct assistance to children in needy families.

In the workplace, women tend to receive lower salaries and less frequent promotion, and are often denied federally mandated maternity leave.

29 HEALTH

As a result of improved living conditions and mass vaccinations, significant progress has been made in controlling malaria, tuberculosis, venereal disease, leprosy, trachoma, typhoid, diphtheria, and encephalitis. Life expectancy in 1990 was 75 years. At the end of 1985, Taiwan's public health facilities included 55 general hospitals and 888 health stations. In 1990, there were 22,300 doctors.

30 HOUSING

The evacuation of more than 2 million persons from the mainland to an already densely populated island in 1949 made the development of low-cost housing an early priority. Since the 1970s, government housing programs have focused on the cities, with slum clearance and the construction of high-rise apartment dwellings for low-income groups the major goals. The total housing stock stood at 4,740,000 units in 1992. The number of people per dwelling was 4.3 as of 1988.

31 EDUCATION

Taiwan enjoys one of the world's highest literacy rates because of its emphasis on education. About 93% of the people aged six or older are literate. In 1985, 234,674 children attended 2,210 preschools, 2,321,700 were in 2,486 primary schools, and 1,062,226 attended junior high. After completing nine years of compulsory schooling, 194,757 students chose to attend senior high school, and 421,784 sought vocational training. In 1989–90, there were 116 universities, junior colleges, and independent colleges in Taiwan. Many students attend college in Japan, Europe and the United States.

32 MEDIA

By 1992 there were 7,800,000 telephone subscribers in Taiwan. By 1988 there were about 186 radio broadcasting stations. These stations broadcast in 14 languages and dialects. Television was introduced in 1962. The number of television sets in 1992 was estimated at 6,386,000 and the number of radios at 8,620,000.

In 1991 there were 232 daily newspapers. The leading papers and estimated 1992 daily circulations are *United Daily News* (1,200,000), *China Daily News* (724,915), *China Times* (623,500), and *Central Daily News* (530,000).

33 TOURISM AND RECREATION

In 1991, tourist arrivals totaled an estimated 1,855,000, of whom 1,233,000 were from Eastern and Southeast Asia. In 1991 there were 19,786 hotel rooms with a 54.3% occupancy rate. T'aipei is the chief tourist attraction, with such popular sites as the seat of government in Presidential Square, Lungshan Temple, and the nearby National Palace Museum and famous Yangmingshan Park. Attractions outside the capital include Shihmen Dam recreation area, Lake Tzuhu, and the mausoleum of Chiang Kai-shek. The national sports are baseball, soccer, and basketball.

34 FAMOUS TAIWANESE

Among the many Chinese scholars who have lived in Taiwan since 1949 are Hu Shih (1891–1962), philosopher and president of the Academia Sinica; Li Chi (1896–1979) and Tung Tso-pin (1895–1963), archaeologists, whose discoveries at the Anyang site laid the foundation for modern Chinese archaeology.

The outstanding political and military figure of Nationalist China and postwar Taiwan was Chiang Kai-shek (Chiang Chung-cheng, 1887–1975).

35 BIBLIOGRAPHY

Crome, A. *Taiwan*. Chicago: Children's Press, 1994.

Fairbank, John King. *The United States and China*. Rev. ed. Cambridge, Mass.: Harvard University Press, 1974.

Lin, Zhiling, and Thomas W. Robinson, eds. *The Chinese and their Future: Beijing, Taipei, and Hong Kong*. Washington, D.C.: AEI Press, 1994.

Long, Simon. *Taiwan: China's Last Frontier*. New York: St. Martin's, 1991.

TAJIKISTAN

Republic of Tajikistan
Respublica i Tojikistan

CAPITAL: Dushanbe.

FLAG: The flag consists of a broad white horizontal stripe in the center, with a red stripe at the top and a green stripe at the bottom. The national emblem is centered in the white stripe.

MONETARY UNIT: Ruble. (As of the end of 1993, Tajikistan was the only former Soviet republic still using Soviet rubles as the single currency.)

WEIGHTS AND MEASURES: The metric system is used.

HOLIDAYS: New Year's Day, 1 January; Navruz ("New Day"), 21 March; Independence Day, 9 September.

TIME: 6 PM = noon GMT.

1 LOCATION AND SIZE

Tajikistan is located in southern Asia, between Uzbekistan and China. Comparatively, it is slightly smaller than the state of Wisconsin, with a total area of 143,100 square kilometers (55,251 square miles). Tajikistan's boundary length totals 3,651 kilometers (2,269 miles).

Its capital city, Dushanbe, is located in the western part of the country.

2 TOPOGRAPHY

The Pamir and Alay mountains dominate the landscape.

3 CLIMATE

The climate ranges from desert-like to polar. The mean temperature is 30°C (86°F) in July and 0°C (32°F) in January. Rainfall in the country averages 12.2 centimeters (4.8 inches).

4 PLANTS AND ANIMALS

Wildflowers can be found in the valleys. Marco Polo sheep, yak, and snow leopards can be found in the mountains.

5 ENVIRONMENT

Over the last 30 years, irrigation practices have increased the levels of salt in the soil, threatening its productivity. The nation's water supply is threatened by pollution.

6 POPULATION

The population of Tajikistan was 5,108,576 in 1989. The projection for the year 2000 was 6,871,000. The estimated population density in 1995 was 40 persons per square kilometer (104 per square mile). Dushanbe, the capital, had an estimated population of 602,000 at the beginning of 1990.

7 MIGRATION

About 400,000 to 250,000 Russians migrated during 1992–93 because of political turmoil. About 50,000 displaced people in Dushanbe were forced back to their home regions in the south during 1993.

8 ETHNIC GROUPS

In 1989, Tajiks constituted 62% of the population and Uzbeks (who live in the northwest) 23.5%. Russians comprised 7.6% and Tatars 1.4%.

9 LANGUAGES

Tajik, an Iranian language, was scheduled to become the single official language by 1996. Russian is the language for "inter-ethnic communication."

10 RELIGIONS

Most Tajiks are Sunni Muslims of the Hanafi sect, although the people of the Pamirs are Ismaili. The Russian Orthodox Church is also present, and in 1990 the Jewish population numbered some 11,500.

11 TRANSPORTATION

Some 480 kilometers (298 miles) of railroads are utilized in Tajikistan. In 1990, there were some 29,900 kilometers (18,600 miles) of highways. Air service is underdeveloped. Freight often must be transported by charter plane.

12 HISTORY

The territory of Tajikistan has been continuously inhabited since the early Stone Age. The territory was Persian-controlled from the sixth century BC, until conquered by Alexander the Great in 329 BC. Arabs conquered the area in the eighth century AD, introducing Islam. In 1219–21 Genghis Khan's Mongol troops conquered the entire area, destroying many cities. A series of kingdoms followed one another until present-day Tajikistan was split between the Khanates (kingdoms) of Bukhara and Kokand in the eighteenth and nineteenth centuries.

Photo credit: AP/Wide World Photos

Tajik refugees look through a barbed wire border fence awaiting permission to return to Tajikistan at the Takjik-Afghan border near the town of Pyandzh. In 1992, the Tajik government imposed emergency rules along its southern border with Afghanistan to control the flow of refugees and guns.

TAJIKISTAN

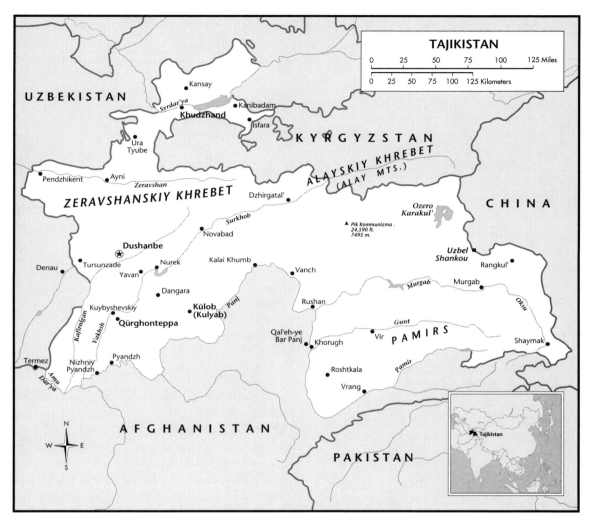

LOCATION: 15°0′N; 39°0′E. **BOUNDARY LENGTHS:** Total boundary lengths, 3,651 kilometers (2,269 miles); Afghanistan, 1,206 kilometers (749.4 miles); China, 414 kilometers (257.3 miles); Kyrgyzstan, 870 kilometers (541 miles); Uzbekistan, 1,161 kilometers (721.4 miles).

In 1863, Russia asserted a right to exercise dominance in Central Iasi, and began the military conquest of the khanates. Bukhara and Samarkand were incorporated into Russia in 1868. Kokand was eliminated in 1876, and the border with Afghanistan was set by accord with England in 1895. At that point, past of Tajikistan was in the Emirate of Bukhara and part was in Turkestan. When the

Tsar's draft call-up of 1916 was announced, rebellions broke out all over Central Asia, including in Tajikistan. These were surpressed, at a great loss of life.

Tajikistan was conquered by the Bolsheviks (Communists) between 1918 and 1920. By 1925, Tajikistan was established as a self-governing republic within the Uzbek Soviet Socialist Republic. It became a full Soviet republic in 1929.

Border delineations were very arbitrary. For several hundred years educated Central Asians had used Persian and Turkic languages essentially equally. Therefore, separation of the population into Turkic-speaking Uzbeks and Persian-speaking Tajiks, as if to create separate nationalities, was primarily administrative. Bukhara and Samarkand, the major Tajik cities, were included in Uzbekistan, while Tajikistan was left only with smaller cities, and little arable land. People were forced to assume one nationality or another.

In the late Soviet period Tajikistan was the poorest and least developed of the republics. It comprised four separate areas, the elites of which competed for power. Traditionally power was held by people from Khojent, which is geographically and culturally closest to Uzbekistan's Fergana valley. They were contested by families and clans from Kuliab. Poorest were people from Badakhshan, most of which is in the unfarmable Pamir Mountains. The final area was Kurgan-Tiube, where the influence of Islam was strong:

public calls for establishing an Islamic state were heard here as early as 1976.

In 1985, Mikhail Gorbachev replaced long-time republic leader Rahmon Nabiev with Makhkamov, whose control never penetrated to the most local levels. Riots in February 1990 exposed his weaknesses, and encouraged a proliferation of political parties and groups. When the August 1991 attempted coup came in the Soviet Union, Makhkamov was the only republic leader to welcome it. When the coup failed, Makhkamov was forced to resign, and Nabiev returned to power.

With the breakup of the Soviet Union, the republic declared independence on 9 September 1991. Rahmon Nabiev was elected president in hotly contested presidential elections conducted on 27 October.

Civil disorder grew throughout 1992. By September, when Nabiev was forced from office at gunpoint by a disgruntled democratic faction, full civil war had erupted, with casualties perhaps as high as 50,000. By October, Uzbekistan and Russia had joined in the effort to help drive the Tajik government and its supporters out of the country, mostly into neighboring Afghanistan.

In November 1992, the post of president was abolished, and Speaker I. Rakhmonov, of Kŭlob (Kulyab), took power, brutally rooting out all opposition. Although he is recognized as a legitimate leader by the outside world, Rakhmonov's control of the republic remains weak. Important opposition leaders have set up bases in Afghanistan, vowing to return to fight. The parts of the republic Rakhmonov controls have become essentially Russian protectorates, relying upon Russian soldiers to keep order and using Russian money to prop up the economy.

13 GOVERNMENT

An 80-member Majlis, or Assembly, replaced the Soviet-era Parliament in May 1992. The office of president has been abolished, and Majlis chairman Imomali Rakhmonov has been declared head of state. The republic is basically controlled by Russia, so many important governmental decisions are made in Moscow, the capital of Russia, or by the Russian military.

14 POLITICAL PARTIES

The principal party is still the Communist Party. In the period preceding the Rakhmonov government, there were several opposition parties, now in exile. The most important were the Democratic Party, Rastokhez (Renaissance), a nationalist party primarily of artists and intellectuals, and the Islamic Renaissance Party.

15 JUDICIAL SYSTEM

The judicial system from the Soviet period remains in place. There are courts at the city, district, regional, and republic levels with a separate but parallel system of military courts.

16 ARMED FORCES

There are Uzbek, Kyrgyz, and Kazakh forces in Tajikistan, as well as two resident Russian divisions.

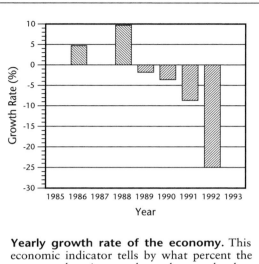

Yearly growth rate of the economy. This economic indicator tells by what percent the economy has increased or decreased when compared with the previous year.

17 ECONOMY

Tajikistan is the poorest of the post-Soviet republics. Agriculture, mainly cotton production, dominates the country's economy. Imports provide practically all of the country's manufactured consumer needs. The outbreak of open civil war in 1992 dashed most hopes for swift economic improvement.

18 INCOME

In 1992, Tajikistan's gross national product (GNP) was $2,723 million at current prices, or about $470 per person.

19 INDUSTRY

Light industry accounted for roughly 45% of industrial production in 1990, and included cotton cleaning, silk processing, textiles production, knitted goods, foot-

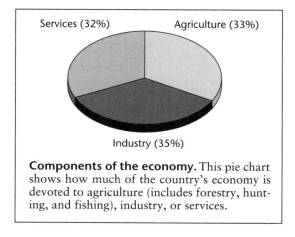

Services (32%) Agriculture (33%)

Industry (35%)

Components of the economy. This pie chart shows how much of the country's economy is devoted to agriculture (includes forestry, hunting, and fishing), industry, or services.

1992 included milk, 475,000 tons; eggs, 18,000 tons; wool, 4,000 tons; and butter and cheese, 4,000 tons.

23 FISHING

Some fishing occurs in the upper Amu Darya River.

24 FORESTRY

Forestry is of little importance.

25 MINING

Mercury and antimony are mined, as well as fluorospar, arsenic, cadmium, tungsten, lead-zinc, uranium, graphite, and gold.

26 FOREIGN TRADE

Trade with former Soviet Union republics accounts for 80–90% of all imports and exports. Aluminum, raw cotton, and textile products comprise about 60% of Tajikistan's exports. Energy, intermediate industrial goods and equipment, manufactured consumer goods, and food are its principal imports. Trade with countries beyond the former Soviet Union in 1990 was dominated by Germany, the former Czechoslovakian republics, and Bulgaria.

27 ENERGY AND POWER

More than 90% of Tajikistan's electricity production is hydropower. In 1991, power production totaled 17,500 million kilowatt hours.

28 SOCIAL DEVELOPMENT

Women are provided with three years' maternity leave and monthly subsidies for each child.

wear, sewing, tanning, and carpet making. The food industry made up 18% of production and included processing domestically harvested fruit, wheat, tobacco, and other agricultural products.

20 LABOR

Over two-thirds of the population relied on agriculture or personal services as a means of support in 1992.

21 AGRICULTURE

Tajik agriculture relies heavily on irrigation. In 1992, about 109,000 tons of cotton were produced. Wheat production in 1992 totaled 200,000 tons, and barley, 40,000 tons.

22 DOMESTICATED ANIMALS

As of 1992, the livestock included 6,000,000 chickens, 2,600,000 sheep, 1,400,000 cattle, 780,000 goats, and 100,000 pigs. Meat production in 1992 included 43,000 tons of beef, 20,000 tons of mutton, 8,000 tons of poultry, and 5,000 tons of pork. Livestock products in

Selected Social Indicators

These statistics are estimates for the period 1988 to 1993. For comparison purposes, data for the United States and averages for low-income countries and high-income countries are also given.

Indicator	Tajikistan	Low-income countries	High-income countries	United States
Per capita gross national product†	$470	$380	$23,680	$24,740
Population growth rate	3.0%	1.9%	0.6%	1.0%
Population growth rate in urban areas	3.0%	3.9%	0.8%	1.3%
Population per square kilometer of land	40	78	25	26
Life expectancy in years	70	62	77	76
Number of people per physician	434	>3,300	453	419
Number of pupils per teacher (primary school)	21	39	<18	20
Illiteracy rate (15 years and older)	2%	41%	<5%	<3%
Energy consumed per capita (kg of oil equivalent)	634	364	5,203	7,918

† The gross national product (GNP) is the total dollar value of all goods and services produced by a country in a year. The per capita GNP is calculated by dividing a country's GNP by its population. The World Bank defines low-income countries as those with a per capita GNP of $695 or less. High-income countries have a per capita GNP of $8,626 or more. Less than 14% of the world's 5.5 billion people live in high-income countries, while almost 60% live in low-income countries.

> = greater than   < = less than

Sources: World Bank, Social Indicators of Development 1995, Baltimore: Johns Hopkins University Press, 1995. Central Intelligence Agency, World Fact Book, Washington, D.C.: Government Printing Office, 1994.

29 HEALTH

Life expectancy is 70 years. In 1992, there was 1 doctor for every 434 people. Total health care expenditures in 1990 were $532 million.

30 HOUSING

In 1990, Tajikistan had 9.3 square meters of housing space per person and, as of 1 January 1991, 90,000 households (or 24.6%) were on waiting lists for urban housing.

31 EDUCATION

The adult literacy rate was estimated at 98% (98.8% for males and 96.6% for females) in 1990. Education is free and compulsory between the ages of 7 and 17 (for 10 years). There are about 21 primary students per teacher. In 1990, all higher level institutions had a total of 68,800 pupils.

32 MEDIA

Tajik Radio and Television broadcast in Russian, Tajik, Persian, and Uzbek. Roughly 90% of Tajikistan's 74 newspapers are published in Tajik.

33 TOURISM AND RECREATION

Tajikistan's potential as a tourist site, already limited by the destruction of most ancient buildings by numerous earthquakes, has been further reduced by civil war.

34 FAMOUS TAJIKISTANIS

Outstanding representatives of Tajik culture are the Tadzhik poet Rudaki (d. 941) and the scientist and poet Avicenna (Hussayn ibn 'Abd' Addallah ibn Sine, 980?–1037), born near Bukhara.

35 BIBLIOGRAPHY

Atkin, Muriel. *The Subtlest Battle: Islam in Soviet Tajikistan*. Philadelphia: Foreign Policy Research Institute, 1989.

Rakowska-Harmstone, Teresa. *Russia and Nationalism in Central Asia: The Case of Tadzhikstan*. Baltimore: Johns Hopkins Press, 1970.

TANZANIA

United Republic of Tanzania

Jamhuri Ya Muungano Wa Tanzania

CAPITAL: Dar es Salaam.

FLAG: The flag consists of a black diagonal stripe running from the lower left-hand corner to the upper right-hand corner, flanked by yellow stripes. The diagonal stripes separate two triangular areas: green at the upper left and blue at the lower right.

ANTHEM: The Tanzanian National Anthem is a setting to new words of the widely known hymn *Mungu Ibariki Afrika (God Bless Africa)*.

MONETARY UNIT: The Tanzanian shilling (Sh) of 100 cents is a paper currency. There are coins of 5, 10, 20, and 50 cents and 1, 5, 10, and 20 shillings, and notes of 10, 20, 50, 100, 200, 500, and 1,000 shillings. Sh1 = $0.0020 (or $1 = Sh494.41).

WEIGHTS AND MEASURES: The metric system is used.

HOLIDAYS: Zanzibar Revolution Day, 12 January; Chama Cha Mapinduzi Day, 5 February; Union Day, 26 April; International Workers' Day, 1 May; Farmers' Day, 7 July; Independence Day, 9 December; Christmas, 25 December. Movable religious holidays include 'Id al-Fitr, 'Id al-'Adha', Milad an-Nabi, Good Friday, and Easter Monday.

TIME: 3 PM = noon GMT.

1 LOCATION AND SIZE

Situated in East Africa just south of the equator, mainland Tanzania lies between the area of the great lakes—Victoria, Tanganyika, and Malawi (Niassa)—and the Indian Ocean. It contains a total area of 945,090 square kilometers (364,901 square miles), slightly larger than twice the size of the state of California. Tanzania has a total boundary length of 5,114 kilometers (3,178 miles). The section of Tanzania known as Zanzibar comprises the islands of Zanzibar and Pemba and all islands within 19 kilometers (12 miles) of their coasts. Tanzania's capital city, Dar es Salaam, is located on the Indian Ocean coast.

2 TOPOGRAPHY

A plateau makes up the greater part of the country. The Pare mountain range is in the northeast, and the Kipengere mountain range is in the southwest. Mt. Kilimanjaro (5,895 meters/19,340 feet) is the highest mountain in Africa. On the borders are three large lakes: Victoria, Tanganyika, and Lake Malawi.

Two-thirds of Zanzibar Island consists of low-lying coral country covered by bush and grass plains. The western side of the island is fertile, and Pemba, apart from a narrow belt of coral country in the east, is fertile and densely populated.

3 CLIMATE

There are four main climatic zones: the coastal area and immediate interior, where conditions are tropical; the central plateau, which is hot and dry; the highland areas; and the high, moist lake regions. The eastern parts of the country average only 75–100 centimeters (30–40 inches of rain, while the western parts receive 200–230 centimeters (80–90 inches). The climate on the islands is tropical, but the heat is tempered by sea breezes.

4 PLANTS AND ANIMALS

Two main types of trees—low-level hardwoods and mountain softwoods—are found on the main mountain masses and in parts of the Lake Victoria Basin. Wooded grasslands are widely scattered throughout the country. The drier central areas include bushlands and thickets. Grasslands and heath are common in the highlands, while the coast has mangrove forests.

The 4 million wild mammals, of 430 species, include antelope, zebra, elephant, hippopotamus, rhinoceros, giraffe, and lion. There are about 1,000 species of birds, ranging in size from ostrich to warbler. Insect life consists of more than 60,000 species, and there are at least 25 species of reptiles and amphibians and 25 poisonous varieties among the 100 species of snakes. Fish are plentiful.

The native plants and animals of Zanzibar and Pemba are varied. Mammals common to both are bats, mongooses, rats, and mice. Zanzibar has the leopard, Syke's monkey, civet, and giant rat.

5 ENVIRONMENT

One of the nation's major concerns is soil destruction as a result of recent droughts. A fourth of the nation's city dwellers and 54% of the people living in rural areas do not have pure water. The nation's cities produce 1.8 million tons of solid waste per year. As of 1994, 30 of Tanzania's mammal species were in danger of extinction; 26 bird species and 158 plant species are also endangered.

6 POPULATION

The population of the entire country was estimated at 29,736,704 in mid-1994. A population of 35,916,000 was projected for the year 2000. Dar es Salaam, the capital, had 1,360,850 people in 1988, and the population of the islands was 640,578.

7 MIGRATION

During the clove harvest, labor moves from the towns to the clove plantations, and from Zanzibar and the mainland to Pemba. At the end of 1992, Tanzania was host to some 292,100 refugees, including 149,500 from Burundi, 75,000 from Mozambique, 21,000 from Rwanda, and 16,000 from Zaire.

8 ETHNIC GROUPS

About 120 peoples in Tanzania have been divided into 5 ethnic groups recognizable by their physical characteristics and languages. Approximately 95% of Tanzanians may be roughly classified as Bantu.

TANZANIA

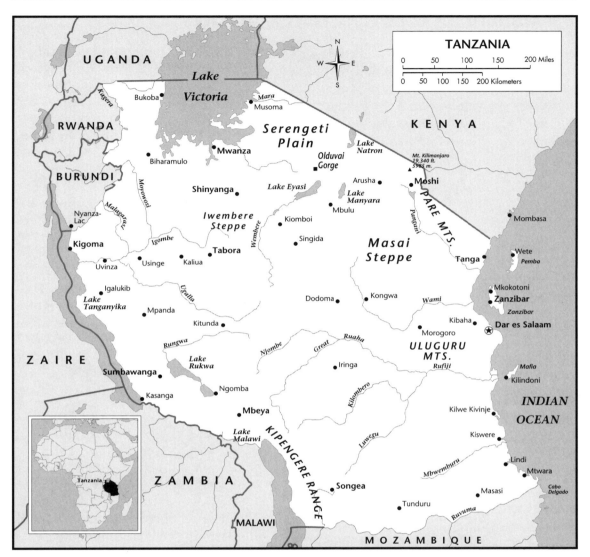

LOCATION: 1° to 11°45's; 29°21' to 40°25'e. **BOUNDARY LENGTHS:** Uganda, 418 kilometers (260 miles); Kenya, 769 kilometers (478 miles); total coastline (including coasts of Zanzibar and Pemba islands), 1,271 kilometers (790 miles); Mozambique, 756 kilometers (470 miles); Malawi, 451 kilometers (280 miles); Zambia, 322 kilometers (200 miles); Zaire, 459 kilometers (285 miles); Burundi, 451 kilometers (280 miles); Rwanda, 217 kilometers (135 miles). **TERRITORIAL SEA LIMIT:** 50 miles.

Other major tribes include the Nyamwezi, Makonde, Haya, and Chagga. The inhabitants of Zanzibar and Pemba are mostly descendants of mainland Africans or are of mixed African and Arab ancestry. Among non-Africans, there are about 70,000 Arabs, 40,000 Asians, and 10,000 Europeans in Tanzania.

9 LANGUAGES

Most Tanzanians speak Bantu languages and dialects. Swahili (or Kiswahili) is the common language. English and Kiunguja, the form of Swahili spoken in Zanzibar, are the official languages. Arabic is widely spoken in Zanzibar and Pemba.

10 RELIGIONS

Many of the mainland peoples follow African traditional beliefs, and religious practices differ from tribe to tribe. About 35% of the population is Muslim and 30% Christian. Almost all of the population (95% in 1993) of the islands is Muslim. Most are orthodox Sunni Muslims of the Shafi school.

11 TRANSPORTATION

The Tanzanian Railways Corporation operates domestic railway services on 3,555 kilometers (2,209 miles) of track. In 1991, Tanzania had 81,900 kilometers (50,900 miles) of roads. In 1991 there were 84,517 motor vehicles, including 46,552 passenger cars.

The principal ports on the mainland are Dar es Salaam, Mtwara, Tanga, and Lindi. Most internal air services are operated by Air Tanzania, which also flies internationally. Foreign airlines provide service from international airports at Dar es Salaam, near Mt. Kilimanjaro, and on Zanzibar, which maintains its own airline, Zanair. Air Tanzania carried 172,800 passengers in 1992.

12 HISTORY

Paleontologists Louis and Mary Leakey, working in northern Tanzania, uncovered fossil evidence that humanlike creatures inhabited the area at least as early as 3.7 million years ago. The hunter-gatherers of the late Stone Age, known as Bushmen, were gradually displaced by Cushitic, Bantu, and Nilotic peoples. By the first millennium (1,000 years) AD, the Iron Age Urewe culture had developed along the western shore of Lake Victoria. Arabs from the Persian Gulf area were engaged in trade along the Indian Ocean coast by the ninth century AD and by the twelfth century had established trading posts on the mainland and the offshore islands. Intermarriage between the Arabs and coastal Bantu-speaking peoples resulted in the creation of the Swahili people and language. (*Swahili* literally means "of the coast.")

In 1498, Portuguese explorer Vasco da Gama rounded the southern tip of Africa, called the Cape of Good Hope. Later the Portuguese established posts on the East African coast. Eventually, however, the Portuguese lost control of the sea routes. The Ibahdis of Oman (a neighbor of Sa'udi Arabia) retained control of East Africa, and there was a profitable trade in slaves and ivory.

Sayyid Sa'id bin Sultan, who ruled Oman from 1806 to 1856, is regarded as the founder of modern Zanzibar. Sa'id first visited Zanzibar in 1828, and in 1840, he made the island his capital. By the time he died in 1856, he had established a large, loosely held empire that

Photo credit: Susan D. Rock.

Sailors at work in "Dhow Harbor," Zanzibar.

included Oman and Zanzibar and the east African coast inland to the Congo.

Beginning with the British Sir Richard Francis Burton and John Hanning Speke in 1857, Europeans began to explore the interior of Tanzania. In 1866, Sultan Majid of Zanzibar began building the coastal town of Dar es Salaam ("Haven of Peace"). Tanganyika (the name for the mainland prior to the 1964 union with Zanzibar) came under German influence in 1884–85, when a charter was granted to the German East Africa Company. In 1890, two treaties between Germany and Great Britain divided what is today known as Tanzania. A British protectorate was established over Zanzibar and Pemba.

Tanganyika and Ruanda-Urundi (now Rwanda and Burundi) became recognized as German East Africa in 1891. As they occupied the interior, the German-led troops put down tribal opposition and uprisings. During World War I (1914–18), a small German force led by General Paul von Lettow-Vorbeck fought a long defensive guerrilla war against British armies, and much of Tanganyika was severely damaged.

Moving Toward Independence

Following Germany's defeat in World War I, the British governed Tanganyika in cooperation with the League of Nations. In 1946, Tanganyika became a United

Nations trust territory. On 9 December 1961, Tanganyika became an independent nation, and a year later, on 9 December 1962, it was established as a republic, headed by Julius Nyerere as president.

On 24 June 1963, Zanzibar attained internal self-government. It became completely independent on 10 December 1963. On 26 April 1964, Tanganyika merged with Zanzibar and became the United Republic of Tanganyika and Zanzibar, with Nyerere as president. In October, the name was changed to Tanzania. Under Nyerere, Tanzania became steadily more socialist.

In international affairs, Tanzania became one of the strongest supporters of majority rule in southern Africa, backing liberation movements in Mozambique and Rhodesia (now Zimbabwe). Growing differences between the East African Community's three members—Kenya, Tanzania, and Uganda—led to the breakup of the 10-year-old group in 1977. In 1978 and 1979 there were military clashes between Tanzania and Uganda. In 1982, Tanzanian troops helped put down an army mutiny in the Seychelles Islands. Ali Hassan Mwinyi followed Nyerere as president of Tanzania in November 1985 and was reelected in 1990.

In February 1992, at a national conference of the ruling party, Chama Cha Mapinduzi (CCM), delegates voted unanimously to introduce a multiparty system. On 17 June 1992, Mwinyi signed into law constitutional amendments that allowed new parties to participate in elections. Tensions between the mainland (Tanganyika) and Zanzibar grew in the 1990s, often linked to the ongoing Christian-Muslim conflicts.

13 GOVERNMENT

The president, who is both chief of state and head of government, is elected for a five-year term by universal adult voting. Before 1992, the president was nominated by the sole legal party, the Chama Cha Mapinduzi (CCM). He is assisted by a prime minister and cabinet. Formerly there were two vice-presidents. In 1993, however, it was agreed to have just one vice-president, the running mate of the winning presidential nominee. As of 1985, the National Assembly consisted of 216 members elected by universal adult voting for five-year terms and 75 appointed members, many of whom serve by virtue of holding other government posts. The prime minister, who is chosen from the Assembly members, heads the Assembly.

The government of Zanzibar has exclusive jurisdiction over internal matters, including immigration, finances, and economic policy. In the 1990s, Zanzibar seems to be moving toward even greater self-rule, if not secession.

14 POLITICAL PARTIES

The Tanganyika African National Union (TANU), established in 1954, and the ruling Afro-Shirazi Party of Zanzibar were merged into the Chama Cha Mapinduzi (CCM) Revolutionary Party. It was the only legal political party in Tanzania until 1995. The CCM officially favors nonracism and African socialism. Its basic aims are social equality, self-reliance, economic cooperation with other African states, and ujamaa (familyhood)—the development of forms of economic activity, particularly in rural areas, based on collective efforts. The 172-member National Executive Committee is the main policymaking and directing body of the CCM.

Although Tanzania amended its constitution in 1992 to become a multiparty state, the CCM still controlled the government. National elections were scheduled in 1995. Of the other parties which have tried to organize, many complain of harassment by government and CCM activists.

15 JUDICIAL SYSTEM

Mainland Tanzanian law is a combination of British and East African customary law. Local courts are presided over by appointed magistrates. They have limited powers, and there is a right of appeal to district courts, headed by either resident or district magistrates. Appeal can be made to the High Court, which consists of a chief justice and 17 judges appointed by the president. Appeals from the High Court can be made to the five-member Court of Appeal. Cases concerning the Zanzibar Constitution are heard only in Zanzibar courts. All other cases may be appealed to the Court of Appeal of the Republic.

16 ARMED FORCES

Tanzania's armed forces totaled 46,800 in 1993. The army had 45,000 members in 8 infantry brigades, 1 tank brigade, and 10 supporting arms battalions. The navy had 800 members and 20 craft, and the air

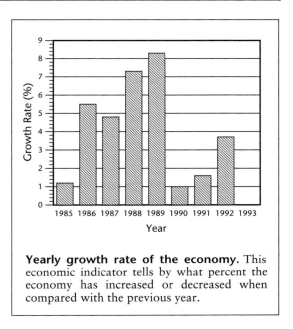

Yearly growth rate of the economy. This economic indicator tells by what percent the economy has increased or decreased when compared with the previous year.

force had 1,000 members and 24 combat aircraft. Police field forces, which include naval and air units, number 1,500. The citizens militia totaled 100,000. Defense spending is around $100 million per year.

17 ECONOMY

Tanzania has an agricultural economy whose chief commercial crops are sisal, coffee, cotton, tea, tobacco, spices, and cashew nuts. The most important minerals are diamonds and coal. Industry is mainly concerned with the processing of raw materials for export and local consumption. Twenty-five years of socialist government achieved important advances in education and health. However, in 1986, the government moved toward a free-market economy.

18 INCOME

In 1992 Tanzania's gross national product (GNP) was $2,561 million at current prices, or $90 per person. For the period 1985–92 the average inflation rate was 25.2%, resulting in a real growth rate in GNP of 1.4% per person.

19 INDUSTRY

Tanzanian industry is centered on the processing of local products. Some products are exported to neighboring countries: textiles and clothes, shoes, tires, batteries, transformers and switchgear, electric stoves, bottles, cement, and paper. Other industries include oil refining, fertilizers, rolling and casting mills, metal working, beer and soft drinks, vehicle assembly, bicycles, canning, industrial machine goods, glass and ceramics, agricultural implements, electrical goods, wood products, bricks and tiles, oxygen and carbon dioxide, and pharmaceutical products.

20 LABOR

Over 90% of Tanzania's working population (680 million in 1992) is engaged in agriculture, 1% in mining, and much of the remainder in public service. A minimum wage is fixed by law. Strikes are illegal without first attempting to settle the dispute before a labor tribunal.

By law, the minimum working age is 12, but this does not apply to children working on family farms or herding livestock. Children between age 12 and age 15 may be employed on a day-to-day basis, but they must have parental permission and they must return to their homes at night. No child or young person may be

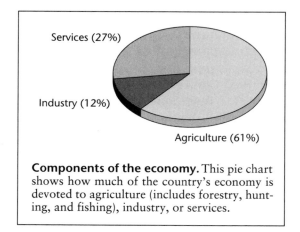

Components of the economy. This pie chart shows how much of the country's economy is devoted to agriculture (includes forestry, hunting, and fishing), industry, or services.

Services (27%)

Industry (12%)

Agriculture (61%)

employed in a business that is unhealthy, dangerous, or otherwise unsuitable. Young people between the ages of 12 and 15 may be employed in industrial work, but only between the hours of 6:00 a.m. and 6:00 p.m. It is believed that the problem of child labor in Tanzania is widespread, although the government lacks the resources to investigate and control the problem.

21 AGRICULTURE

The main food crops are corn, millet, rice, sorghum, and pulses (peas, beans and lentils). The chief cash crops are coffee, cotton, and cashew nuts. Sisal, cloves, sugar, tea, pyrethrum (an insecticide made from the dried heads of certain flowers), and tobacco are also important. Tanzania is one of Africa's leading producers of sisal. In 1992, production was 35,000 tons. Other estimated agricultural production in 1992 included manioc, 7,111,000 tons; corn, 2,226,000 tons; sorghum, 587,000 tons; rice, 392,000 tons; and millet,

263,000 tons. Production in 1992 also included coffee, 56,000 tons; cotton, 73,000 tons; cashew nuts, 40,150 tons; tea, 18,000 tons; tobacco, 17,000 tons; sweet potatoes, 257,000 tons; white potatoes, 200,000 tons; and 65,000 tons of peanuts. Sugarcane production in that year was an estimated 1,410,000 tons; bananas and plantains, 794,000 tons each; dry beans, 195,000 tons; seed cotton, 218,000 tons; and cottonseed, 142,000 tons.

Tanzania was once the leading producer of cloves, which are grown mostly on Pemba. It is also an important producer of coconuts (365,000 tons in 1992), mostly from the island of Zanzibar. Production of copra (dried coconut meat) was around 34,000 tons in 1992.

Photo credit: Susan D. Rock.

Produce vendor in Old Stone Town, Zanzibar.

22 DOMESTICATED ANIMALS

The estimated livestock population in 1992 included 13.2 million head of cattle, 3.7 million sheep, and 25 million poultry. About 285,000 tons of meat were produced in 1992. Milk production was 460,000 tons in the same year.

23 FISHING

Inland fishing, especially on Lake Tanganyika, holds an important place in the economy. The total catch was 400,300 tons in 1991.

24 FORESTRY

There are about 13,000,000 hectares (32,000,000 acres) of permanent forest reserves. Production in 1991 included about 35.5 million cubic meters of round-wood and about 156,000 cubic meters of sawn wood.

25 MINING

Tanzania's known mineral resources include diamonds, gold, mica, salt, tin, tungsten, coal, iron, phosphates, lead, copper, and uranium. Salt output was 64,419 tons in 1991. Gold production was 2,779 kilograms in 1991. Production of apatite, a phosphate mineral, was 22,419 tons in 1991. Diamond output in 1991 was 99,763 carats. Lime production in 1991 was 870 tons. Gypsum production was 35,263 tons.

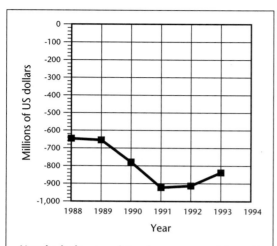

Yearly balance of trade measured in millions of US dollars. The balance of trade is the difference between what a country sells to other countries (its exports) and what it buys (its imports). If a country imports more than it exports, it has a negative balance of trade (a trade deficit). If exports exceed imports there is a positive balance of trade (a trade surplus).

26 FOREIGN TRADE

Agricultural products are Tanzania's main export items: coffee, cotton, cloves, sisal, cashew nuts, and pyrethrum (an insecticide made from the dried heads of certain flowers). Diamonds, gemstones, textiles, hides, extracts, instant coffee, timber, fish and prawns, fresh fruit and vegetables, and honey are also exported.

The chief imports are transport equipment and intermediate and industrial goods machinery. Imports have led exports in value, resulting in sizeable trade deficits (1988–90).

In 1988, Tanzania's leading export partner was Germany (14.2%) followed by the United Kingdom (10.1%), and India (6.4%). Imports came primarily from the United Kingdom (17.3%), Japan (12.5%), Germany (11.8%), and Italy (7.8%).

27 ENERGY AND POWER

Tanzania imports all of its crude oil. The refinery at Dar es Salaam refined about 600,000 tons in 1991 and exported petroleum products to Rwanda and Burundi. Electrical production was 901 million kilowatt hours in 1991.

28 SOCIAL DEVELOPMENT

The government concentrates on community development (including health, labor, and literacy programs) rather than on welfare programs. The elderly, widows, and the physically and mentally handicapped normally are provided for by the traditional tribal system. Orphaned and abandoned children usually are cared for similarly, but missions and voluntary agencies also are active in this field.

29 HEALTH

An estimated 76% of the population had access to health care services in 1992, and, in 1990, total health care expenditures were $109 million. Life expectancy was 52 years in 1992.

In 1992, there were 3,000 rural health facilities, 17 regional hospitals, and 3 national medical centers. There is 1 physician for every 28,271 people. Special disease control programs have been carried out with the assistance of the World Health Organization (WHO) and the United Nations Children's Fund (UNICEF) for

Selected Social Indicators

These statistics are estimates for the period 1988 to 1993. For comparison purposes, data for the United States and averages for low-income countries and high-income countries are also given.

Indicator	Tanzania	Low-income countries	High-income countries	United States
Per capita gross national product†	$90	$380	$23,680	$24,740
Population growth rate	3.1%	1.9%	0.6%	1.0%
Population growth rate in urban areas	6.3%	3.9%	0.8%	1.3%
Population per square kilometer of land	29	78	25	26
Life expectancy in years	52	62	77	76
Number of people per physician	28,271	>3,300	453	419
Number of pupils per teacher (primary school)	36	39	<18	20
Illiteracy rate (15 years and older)	21%	41%	<5%	<3%
Energy consumed per capita (kg of oil equivalent)	35	364	5,203	7,918

† The gross national product (GNP) is the total dollar value of all goods and services produced by a country in a year. The per capita GNP is calculated by dividing a country's GNP by its population. The World Bank defines low-income countries as those with a per capita GNP of $695 or less. High-income countries have a per capita GNP of $8,626 or more. Less than 14% of the world's 5.5 billion people live in high-income countries, while almost 60% live in low-income countries.

> = greater than   < = less than

Sources: World Bank, *Social Indicators of Development 1995*, Baltimore: Johns Hopkins University Press, 1995. Central Intelligence Agency, *World Fact Book*, Washington, D.C.: Government Printing Office, 1994.

most major diseases, including malaria, tuberculosis, sleeping sickness, schistosomiasis, poliomyelitis, and yaws.

30 HOUSING

Tanzania has developed a serious urban housing shortage as a result of the migration of people to the towns. The government in 1951 began a low-cost housing program, which has been continued since that time. As of 1978, 41% of dwellings were constructed with mud and poles, 23% with mud bricks and blocks, and 18% with concrete and stone.

31 EDUCATION

Education is compulsory for children aged 7 to 14. In 1991, there were a total of 3,512,347 students and 98,174 teachers in the 10,437 primary schools. In the same year, there were 183,109 students and 9,904 teachers in the 193 secondary schools. Higher education facilities include the University College in Dar es Salaam, the Sokoine University of Agriculture, the Dar es Salaam Technical College, and the College of African Wildlife Management. Literacy was estimated at 79% in 1987, a rate second only to Mauritius among African countries. In 1989, all higher level

Photo credit: International Labour Office

Two young girls pound corn in large hand mill

institutions had 5,254 students and 1,206 teaching staff.

32 MEDIA

Radio Tanzania broadcasts internally in Swahili and English and abroad in English, Afrikaans, and several native African languages. Radio Tanzania Zanzibar broadcasts in Swahili. Television is broadcast only from Zanzibar. In 1991 there were 660,000 radios and 42,000 television sets. In the same year, there were 130,504 telephones in use.

The press is government-controlled. The largest dailies are the *Daily News* (in English), with a circulation of about 80,000 in 1992, and the *Uhuru* (in Swahili), with a circulation of 100,000. *Kipanga* (in Swahili) is published on Zanzibar by the government.

33 TOURISM AND RECREATION

Tanzania has great natural resources in its Indian Ocean coastline and 12 national parks, especially the 14,763 square-kilometer (5,700 square-mile) Serengeti National Park, famed for its abundance of wildlife. There were 4,673 hotel beds in 1985. Tourist visits average 150,000 per year.

34 FAMOUS TANZANIANS

The most famous 19th-century Zanzibari was Sayyid Sa'id bin Ahmad al-Albusa'idi (b.Oman, 1791–1856), who founded the Sultanate. The foremost modern figure is Julius Kambarage Nyerere (b.1922), the founder and first president of independent Tanganyika (and later of Tanzania) from 1962 to 1985. Salim Ahmed Salim (b.1942) was a president of the UN General Assembly during 1979–80. An internationally known Tanzanian runner is Filbert Bayi (b.1953).

35 BIBLIOGRAPHY

Blaur, E., and J. Lauré. *Tanzania*. Chicago: Children's Press, 1994.
Deeble, Mark, and Victoria Stone. "Deadly Ambush in the Serengeti." *National Geographic*, April 1993, 97–109.
Kaplan, Irving, ed. *Tanzania: A Country Study*. 2d ed. Washington, D.C.: Dept. of the Army, 1987.
Nagel, Rob, and Anne Commire. "Julius K. Nyerere." In *World Leaders, People Who Shaped the World*. Volume I: Africa and Asia. Detroit: U*X*L, 1994.
Yeager, Rodger. *Tanzania: An African Experiment*. 2d ed. Boulder, Colo.: Westview Press, 1989.

THAILAND

Kingdom of Thailand

Prates Thai

CAPITAL: Bangkok (Krung Thep).

FLAG: The national flag, adopted in 1917, consists of five horizontal stripes. The outermost are red; those adjacent are white; the blue center stripe is twice as high as each of the other four.

ANTHEM: There are three national anthems: *Pleng Sansen Phra Barami (Anthem Eulogizing His Majesty)*; *Pleng Chard Thai (Thai National Anthem)*; and *Pleng Maha Chati (Anthem of Great Victory)*, an instrumental composition.

MONETARY UNIT: The baht (B) is divided into 100 satang. There are coins of 1, 5, 10, 25, and 50 stangs and 1, 5, and 10 baht, and notes of 50 satang and 1, 5, 10, 20, 50, 60, 100, and 500 baht. B1 = $0.0396 (or $1 = B25.13).

WEIGHTS AND MEASURES: The metric system is the legal standard, but some traditional units are also used.

HOLIDAYS: New Year's Day, 1 January; Chakkri Day, 6 April; Songkran Day, mid-April; Coronation Day, 5 May; Queen's Birthday, 12 August; Chulalongkorn Day, 23 October; King's Birthday, 5 December; Constitution Day, 10 December. Movable holidays include Makabuja Day, Plowing Festival, and Visakabuja Day.

TIME: 7 PM = noon GMT.

1 LOCATION AND SIZE

Comprising an area of 514,000 square kilometers (198,456 square miles) in Southeast Asia, Thailand (formerly known as Siam) extends almost two-thirds down the Malay Peninsula. Comparatively, the area occupied by Thailand is slightly more than twice the size of the state of Wyoming. It has a total boundary length of 8,082 kilometers (5,022 miles).

Thailand's capital city, Bangkok, is located on the Gulf of Thailand coast.

2 TOPOGRAPHY

Thailand may be divided into five major physical regions: the central valley, front-ing the Gulf of Thailand; the continental highlands of the north and northwest, containing Thailand's highest point, Doi Inthanon (2,565 meters/8,451 feet); the northeast, much of it often called the Khorat Plateau; the small southeast coastal region facing the Gulf of Thailand; and the Malay Peninsula, extending almost 960 kilometers (600 miles) from the central valley in the north to the boundary of Malaysia in the south.

3 CLIMATE

Thailand has a tropical climate. In most of the country, the temperature rarely falls below 13°C (55°F) or rises above 35°C (95°F), with most places averaging

Photo credit: Susan D. Rock.

Hill tribe children sitting on a well at a village near Chiang Mai in northern Thailand.

between 24°C and 30°C (75°F and 86°F). The annual rainfall ranges from 102 centimeters (40 inches) in the northeast to over 380 centimeters (150 inches) in the peninsula.

4 PLANTS AND ANIMALS

Forestlands support hardwoods (notably teak), pine, bamboos, and betel and coconut palms. In the coastal lowlands, mangroves and rattan are plentiful. Among the larger mammals are the bear, otter, and civet cat. Climbing animals include the gibbon and many species of monkeys. There are also sheep, goats, oxen, single-horned rhinoceroses, deer, tapirs, wild cattle, wild hogs, and snakes. There are about 1,000 varieties of native birds, and crocodiles, lizards, and turtles are numerous.

5 ENVIRONMENT

The nation's water supply is at risk due to contamination by industry, farming activity, sewage, and salt water, especially in the Bangkok area. Thailand has 26.3 cubic miles of water. Ninety percent is used for farming activities and 6% for industrial purposes. Thirty-three percent of the nation's city dwellers and 15% of the rural dwellers do not have pure water.

Thailand's cities produce 2.5 million tons of solid waste per year. Industry is responsible for producing 2 million tons of toxic pollutants annually. Urban air and noise pollution was also severe, largely as a result of increasing automobile traffic. Thailand contributes 1.4% of the world's total gas emissions.

Species have been reduced through illegal hunting and trapping. In 1994, 26 of the nation's mammal species and 34 bird species are endangered. Sixty-eight types of plants are also endangered.

6 POPULATION

The 1990 census recorded a population of 56,303,273. A population of 61,202,000 was projected for the year 2000. Average density in 1990 was 111 persons per square kilometer of land (288 per square mile), but there are great regional variations in density.

Bangkok, the capital, is the single major urban area. Metropolitan Bangkok (including suburbs and satellite towns) had a population of 546,937 in 1990.

7 MIGRATION

An immigration quota, introduced in 1947, now limits migration from any one country to 100 persons annually. In 1990, there were only 287,105 registered aliens, of whom 250,043 were Chinese.

As of December 1992, the United Nations estimated that 63,600 refugees were living in Thailand. These represented part of the flood of over 4 million refugees who had left Laos, Cambodia, and Vietnam since the 1970s.

8 ETHNIC GROUPS

Thailand contains more than 30 ethnic groups varying in history, language, religion, appearance, and patterns of livelihood. However, the Thai, related to the Lao of Laos, the Shan of Myanmar (Burma prior to June 1989), and the Thai groupings of southern China, make up about 84% of the total population of Thailand. The Thai may be divided into four major groups: the Central Thai (Siamese) of the Central Valley; the Eastern Thai (Lao) of the Northeast (Khorat); the Northern Thai (Lao) of North Thailand; and the Southern Thai (Chao Pak Thai) of the Malay Peninsula.

Major ethnic minorities are the Chinese (about 11%); Malays (3–4%); Khmers (1%); and Vietnamese or Annamese. Small numbers of residents from India, Europe, and the United States live mainly in urban areas. Principal tribal groups,

LOCATION: 97° to 106°E; 6° to 21°N. **TOTAL BOUNDARY LENGTH:** 8,082 kilometers (5,022 miles).

mainly hill peoples, include the Kui and Kaleung; the Mons; and the Karens.

9 LANGUAGES

The Thai language, with northern, eastern, central (Bangkok or official Thai), and southern dialects, all distantly related to Chinese, prevails throughout the country. Thai, written in a distinctive alphabet, is thought to be part of the Sino-Tibetan language family, although links to Indian languages are also evident. Although the ethnic minorities (including the Malays) generally speak their own languages, Thai is widely understood. The Chinese population is largely bilingual. All official documents are in the central Thai language and script, although English, taught in many secondary schools and colleges, is also used in official and commercial circles.

10 RELIGIONS

Buddhism was the religion of an estimated 95% of the population in 1993. Although virtually all Thai are officially Buddhists, the main form of religion in Thailand might be described as a spirit worship overlaid or mixed in varying degrees with Buddhist and Brahman beliefs imported from India. About 4% of the population, including the Malay ethnic minority, are Muslim. Among the other ethnic minorities, the Chinese practice a traditional mixture of Mahayana Buddhism, Taoism, Confucianism, and ancestor worship. Most Vietnamese are Mahayana Buddhists, and most Indians are Hindus. There were an estimated 305,000 Christians in 1993. There are also small Muslim and Baha'i communities.

11 TRANSPORTATION

Owned and operated by the government, the railways consisted of 3,940 kilometers (2,448 miles) of primarily meter-gauge track in 1991. The highway system, significantly expanded during the 1960s and 1970s, serves many areas inaccessible to railway. In 1991 there were 44,534 kilometers (27,673 miles) of highway. Modern two-lane highways now connect Bangkok with the rest of the country. In 1991, registered motor vehicles totaled 2,727,509, including 825,072 passenger cars.

Waterways, both river and canal, are Thailand's most important means of inland transport. They carry much of the nation's bulk freight over a network of some 4,000 kilometers (2,500 miles). The modern port of Bangkok is the chief port for international shipping. In 1991 there were 154 oceangoing vessels of more than 1,000 gross tons in the Thai merchant fleet, including 106 freighters and 43 tankers.

Since the end of World War II, Bangkok has become an important center of international aviation. Don Muang, a modern airfield outside Bangkok, and Chiang Mai Airport are Thailand's two international air terminals. The government-owned Thai Airways International and Thai Airways Co. handle international and domestic air traffic, respectively. Scheduled airline traffic performed in 1992 included 20,508 million passenger-kilometers and 926 million ton-kilometers of freight.

Photo credit: Corel Corporation.

An express boat carries passengers along the Chao Phraya River near Bangkok.

12 HISTORY

Archaeological excavations have yielded traces of a Bronze Age people dating as far back as 3600 BC. The Thai are racially related to the Chinese and were one of the major peoples who0 migrated from southern China to mainland Southeast Asia.

While in southern China, the Thai had created the powerful Nan-Chao kingdom. Continued pressure from the Chinese and the Tibetans and final destruction by Kublai Khan, founder of the Mongol dynasty in China, forced the Thai southward across the mountain passes into Southeast Asia in 1253. After entering the valley of the Chao Phraya River, they defeated and dispersed the Khmer settlers, ancestors of the Cambodians, and established the kingdom of Thailand.

By the mid-fourteenth century, the Thai had expanded and centralized their kingdom at the expense of the Lao, Burmese, and Cambodians. Although Thailand had trading contacts with the Dutch and Portuguese in the sixteenth century and with the French and British in the seventeenth, it remained a feudal state with a powerful court of nobles. In the nineteenth century, however, Thailand emerged from feudalism and entered the modern world. Commercial treaties of friendship were signed with the British (1855) and with the United States and France (1856). The power of nobles was limited and slavery abolished.

Despite more progressive policies, the Thai government continued as an absolute monarchy. In 1932, however, a bloodless revolution of Westernized intellectuals led to a constitutional monarchy. Since that time, Thailand has had many constitutions, changes of government, and military takeovers. Political parties have tended to cluster around strong personalities rather than political programs.

Political Instability

At the start of World War II (1939–45), Thailand, after taking control of Burmese and Malayan territories, signed a treaty with Japan and declared war on the United States and the United Kingdom. After the war, however, Thailand became an ally of the United States through their common membership in the Southeast Asia Treaty Organization (SEATO), as well as through various other treaties and agreements. In the 1960s, a limited Communist rebellion backed by the People's Republic of China, developed in the north and northeast. It grew in intensity in the late 1960s and early 1970s as the Southeast Asian conflict (Vietnam War) raged on Thailand's northern and northeastern borders.

During the Vietnam War, United States forces were granted the use of air bases in Thailand for bombing raids against North Vietnam and the Vietcong. American forces stationed in Thailand increased to as many as 25,000 by the end of 1972; all but a few military personnel were removed by 1976.

Internally, Thailand weathered a series of political upheavals in the 1970s. There were several different administrations, takeovers or takeover attempts at the beginning and end of the decade, agitation for a more representative government, and periods of martial law.

Contributing to the nation's political instability was the activity of Communist rebels in border areas and the presence of large numbers of refugees from Laos and Cambodia. Following the Vietnamese victory in Cambodia in January 1979, thousands of rebels took advantage of a government offer of amnesty and surrendered to Thai security forces. By the beginning of 1986, there were fewer than 1,000 active Communist rebels, according to government estimates.

General Chatichai Choonhavan, appointed prime minister after the July 1988 victory of the Chart Thai party, took an active role in foreign affairs and made bold initiatives to improve relations with Laos, Vietnam, and Cambodia. In a bloodless military takeover the National Peace Keeping Council (NPKC) removed General Chatichai's government on 23 February 1991 on grounds of corruption. Martial law was declared by the NPKC, the constitution was revoked, and the government was dissolved.

A period of government under a temporary constitution approved in March 1991 ended in massive civil unrest. One hundred demonstrators were killed on 18 May 1992 and thousands were detained.

After intervention by the king, the prime minister, General Suchinda, resigned. In general elections held on 13 September 1992, Chuan Leekpai, leader of the winning Democratic Party, was approved as prime minister.

Refugees and "displaced people" remain a problem for Thailand. In 1994, there were 43,939 immigrants remaining in Thailand from neighboring countries: 32,221 Lao (of whom 28,000 are hill tribe people); 11,603 Vietnamese; and 115 Cambodians. Illegal Myanmar (Burmese) immigrants number 343,235. Prior to 1976, 47,735 came for political reasons. After 1976, 33,000 immigrated for economic reasons. Since 1984, 60,000 arrived fleeing border fighting, and another 200,000 illegal workers and 2,500 students arrived seeking political sanctuary.

13 GOVERNMENT

Thailand has been a constitutional monarchy since 1932. The present king is Bhumibol Adulyadej, who became king in 1946 and was formally crowned as Rama IX on 5 May 1950.

The constitution of 1978 provided for a parliamentary form of government, headed by the king as head of state, chief of the armed forces, and upholder of Buddhism and of all religions. He has the power to declare a state of emergency and rule by decree. The 1978 constitution also provided for a two-chamber legislature consisting of a Senate appointed by the king and a House of Representatives elected by universal voting. In 1986, the House had 347 members and the Senate, 261. The head of government is the prime minister, nominated by the legislature and formally appointed by the king.

On 9 December 1991, the National Peacekeeping Council (NPKC) proclaimed a new constitution, which provided for a National Assembly made up of elected representatives and an appointed Senate, and a cabinet headed by an appointed prime minister. The military group was given power over the Senate.

Thailand is divided into 72 administrative provinces (*changwats*), each under the control of an appointed governor.

14 POLITICAL PARTIES

Constitutional government in Thailand has been hindered by traditional public indifference, and political parties generally have been formed by military personalities rather than around political issues and programs. Leading parties as of the 1992 elections were the Democratic Party (DP), the Chart Thai, the Chart Pattana, the New Aspiration Party, and the Social Action Party (SAP). As of 1994, there were some 20 parties altogether.

15 JUDICIAL SYSTEM

Courts of the first instance, juvenile courts, and magistrates' courts exist in Bangkok and in each of the provincial capitals. A court of appeal, sitting in Bangkok, hears cases for the entire kingdom. The Supreme Court, also in Bangkok, consists of at least three judges and decides only on points of law. There is no trial by jury in Thailand. Islamic courts hear civil cases concerning members of the Muslim minority.

16 ARMED FORCES

The armed forces are organized as 283,000 active duty members (80,000 draftees) and 500,000 reservists. The army, organized into 14 divisions and 33 smaller units, numbered 190,000 members in 1993. The air force, reorganized with American assistance, consisted of 43,000 members with 166 combat aircraft, plus transport, training, and helicopter rescue units. The navy had 50,000 members (including 20,000 marines) and was equipped with 8 frigates, 65 patrol and coastal combatants, and 30 other vessels. In 1992, Thailand spent $2.7 billion on defense.

17 ECONOMY

Thailand experienced a five year economic boom from 1987 to 1992. Since then trouble has appeared on several fronts. The military takeover of February 1991 and the political clashes of May 1992 have affected Thailand's investment and general economic environment. With international reductions in commodity prices, rice and tapioca prices tumbled sharply (Thailand is the world's largest exporter of both), and prices for rubber and sugar, the country's other two leading raw-material exports, dropped as well. Thailand now faces keen export competition from countries such as China, Indonesia, Vietnam, Pakistan and Bangladesh, where labor is cheaper.

Thailand's economic boom is centered in Bangkok. As a result there is an increasing income gap between urban rich and rural poor, with 60% of the population still working on farms cultivating mainly

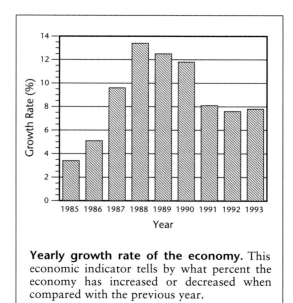

Yearly growth rate of the economy. This economic indicator tells by what percent the economy has increased or decreased when compared with the previous year.

rice. Labor migration has become a key fixture of the Thai economy. A shift in emphasis from export growth to domestic consumption is occurring. In 1994, drought conditions affected rice production and forested areas.

18 INCOME

In 1992, gross national product (GNP) was $106,559 million at current prices, or about $2,110 per person. For the period 1985–92 the average inflation rate was 5.8%, resulting in a real growth rate in GNP of 8.3% per person.

19 INDUSTRY

Since 1979, Thailand's manufacturing sector has increasingly diversified and made the largest contribution to the economy. High-growth industries targeting domestic consumption were construction materials, foods and beverages, and electrical appliances.

As of 1985, most industries still functioned on a modest scale, and Thailand continued to import most manufactured goods. However, growth in some areas has been impressive. In 1971–85, production of food products nearly tripled, textiles grew over 500%, and transportation equipment showed even greater growth. Production of sugar reached 2,678,180 tons in 1982, though it fell off to 2,293,600 tons by 1985.

In 1984, production of synthetic fabrics totaled 904,860 tons, and of cotton fabrics, 937,758 tons. A total of 320,538 motorcycles and 3,547,540 auto, truck, bus, and motorcycle tires were manufactured in the same year. Among chemical products, 6,136,430 cubic meters of nitrogen and 23,799,106 cubic meters of oxygen were produced. Other manufactured goods included 533,346 television sets, 29,407,076 incandescent and fluorescent lamps, and 130,074 tons of galvanized iron plate.

20 LABOR

The labor force in 1992 totaled some 32.4 million. Of the 31 million employed in 1992, about 7.65 million (25%) were engaged in agriculture and related occupations, 4.7 million (15%) in industry, and 18.65 million (60%) in services. In 1990, unemployment amounted to 2.2% of the economically active population.

As of 1 January 1992, the total number of unions was 749 with 194,681 members.

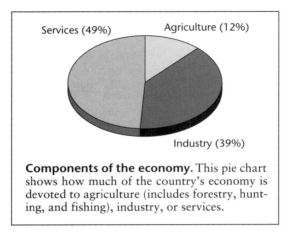

Components of the economy. This pie chart shows how much of the country's economy is devoted to agriculture (includes forestry, hunting, and fishing), industry, or services.

Only 1.6% of the labor force was unionized. Legislation regulating hours and conditions of labor, workers' compensation, and welfare exists.

The minimum age for employment is 13. Children between age 13 and age 15 may be employed in "light work," but employment between the hours of 10:00 p.m. and 6:00 a.m. is prohibited. It is estimated that there are at least 100,000 children between age 13 and age 15 at work in Thailand. The government plans to raise the minimum employment age to 15 by the year 2001. Child labor in Thailand has been the focus of much criticism. Increased enforcement of existing laws had done little to solve the problem. Police raids on workplaces continue to find children under age 13 working illegally, or working under dangerous, unhealthy, or harmful conditions.

21 AGRICULTURE

With some 20 million hectares (49 million acres) of usable land, of which about 13.5

Photo credit: International Labour Office

A young boy on a plantation transporting wood balanced across his shoulders.

million hectares (33.5 million acres) are under cultivation, Thailand continues to rely heavily on agriculture, although the country has suffered from declining export prices in recent years. Thailand is the world's biggest rice exporter, with over 5.1 million tons sent abroad in 1992, for a value of $1,425 million (4% of total exports). Total rice production amounted to 18,500,000 tons in 1992.

Total rubber production in 1992 was 1,400,000 tons, the highest in the world. Sugarcane production reached 46.8 million tons, while output of cassava (tapioca), traditionally important in Thailand, totaled 21.1 million tons. As of 1991,

Thailand provided 95% of the world's cassava exports. Corn production, which has increased significantly in recent decades, reached 3.6 million tons in 1992. Kenaf, tobacco, cotton, and kapok are cultivated mainly for domestic use, but quantities of jute, cocoa, peanuts, soybeans, and medical plants are exported. The Thai government's official policy of encouraging mountain villagers to grow coffee, apples, strawberries, kidney beans, and other temperate crops instead of the profitable opium poppy and marijuana has had some success.

22 DOMESTICATED ANIMALS

Cattle, used for plowing and harrowing, are important to rice farming, and most rural households have some cattle as well as hogs, chickens, and ducks. In 1992, Thailand had 136 million chickens, 17 million ducks, 6.8 million head of cattle, 4.7 million head of buffalo, and 5.1 million swine. Crocodiles, raised for their skins, are a specialty livestock product.

23 FISHING

Fish is a major protein element in the Thai diet. Freshwater fish, abundantly found in rivers and canals, and marine fish (from the waters along the lengthy coastline) produced a catch of 3,065,170 tons in 1991 (as compared with 846,600 tons in 1967). In 1990, Thailand accounted for 16.8% of the world's exports of prepared and preserved fish, valued at over $920 million.

24 FORESTRY

Thailand's forested area declined from 57% of the nation's land area in 1961 to only 27% by 1991, mainly as a result of the continued use of slash-and-burn farming practices by farmers. In 1991, production of roundwood totaled 37.9 million cubic meters, up from 33.6 million cubic meters in 1980. Production of veneer sheets (including teak) in 1991 amounted to 136,000 cubic meters, up from 23,000 cubic meters in 1981. Other important forestry products include charcoal, gums and resins, and kapok fiber and seed.

25 MINING

Thailand is relatively poor in mineral reserves, except for tin and natural gas. In 1991, Thailand was the sixth-largest tin-producing country in the world. In that year, tin ore production totaled 14,937 tons, most of it exported. Deposits of lignite developed with US aid have begun to show a good yield; 14,689,000 tons were produced in 1991. Also in 1991 total iron ore output was 240,075 tons, gypsum production totaled 7,196,390 tons, and cement production was 18,054,000 tons. Rubies, sapphires, topaz, and zircon are also mined.

26 FOREIGN TRADE

Thailand is primarily an importer of petroleum and manufactured goods and an exporter of agricultural products and raw materials. Main exports in 1988 were: rice, rubber, and tapioca products. The United States, Japan, Singapore, the Netherlands, and Germany are main purchasers of Thailand's exports.

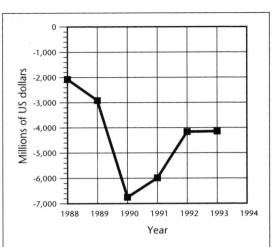

Yearly balance of trade measured in millions of US dollars. The balance of trade is the difference between what a country sells to other countries (its exports) and what it buys (its imports). If a country imports more than it exports, it has a negative balance of trade (a trade deficit). If exports exceed imports there is a positive balance of trade (a trade surplus).

Main imports were machinery and transport equipment, basic manufactures, chemicals, mineral fuels, crude materials except fuels, and food and live animals.

Main trade partners in 1989 were Japan, the United States, Singapore, the United Kingdom, and Hong Kong.

27 ENERGY AND POWER

In 1992, 65% of primary energy consumed came from oil, 20% from natural gas; 13% from coal; and 2% from other sources. Distribution, however, is far from adequate, with only about 20% of the population having access to the system.

Total national output in 1991 was 52,486 million kilowatt hours.

Thailand is heavily dependent on imports of foreign oil. Proven and potential domestic deposits have been estimated at 231 million barrels, but production and development have been inhibited by declining oil prices. Natural gas reserves were estimated at more than 8 trillion cubic feet (225 billion cubic meters) in 1993. Production in 1992 was put at 260 billion cubic feet (7.3 billion cubic meters), double the 1987 amount.

28 SOCIAL DEVELOPMENT

A 1990 law established a social security system which began paying disability and death benefits in 1991, and will pay old age benefits effective 1996. The same law provides for sickness and maternity benefits. Employers are required to provide workers' compensation coverage, including temporary and permanent disability benefits, and medical and survivor benefits.

Women have equal legal rights in most areas, but inequities remain in domestic areas, including divorce and child support.

29 HEALTH

By 1991, 77% of the population had access to safe water and 74% had adequate sanitation.The same year, 26% of children under five years of age were considered malnourished. Life expectancy was 69 years in 1992, and about 90% of the population had access to health care services.

Health care facilities are concentrated in the Bangkok metropolitan area. In 1989, there were 180 private hospitals with 9,377 beds. In 1988, Thailand had 11,260 physicians. In 1991, there were 51,091 nurses and 10,606 midwives. There is one doctor per 4,421 inhabitants. Regional imbalances in the distribution of health facilities and workers persist, with Bangkok and other urban centers being much better supplied than rural areas. Total health care expenditures in 1990 were $4,061 million.

30 HOUSING

Most families in Thailand live in dwellings that compare favorably with living facilities anywhere in Southeast Asia. The Thai government has stimulated housing and community development by means of a housing plan that provides government mortgages for building, renovation, or purchase of government land and houses.

From 1979 to 1984, a total of 1,442,250 housing units were built in Thailand. In 1986, 86% of all living quarters were detached houses, 11% were rowhouses, and 2% were single rooms. The total number of housing units in 1992 was 11,151,000.

31 EDUCATION

Literacy, estimated at 44% in 1947, rose to 93% in 1990: 96.1% for men and 89.9% for women. Compulsory education provisions call for universal school attendance starting at age seven through the fourth year of primary school or through age 15. Both teacher training and technical and vocational training (especially in agri-

Selected Social Indicators

These statistics are estimates for the period 1988 to 1993. For comparison purposes, data for the United States and averages for low-income countries and high-income countries are also given.

Indicator	Thailand	Low-income countries	High-income countries	United States
Per capita gross national product†	$2,110	$380	$23,680	$24,740
Population growth rate	1.7%	1.9%	0.6%	1.0%
Population growth rate in urban areas	3.0%	3.9%	0.8%	1.3%
Population per square kilometer of land	111	78	25	26
Life expectancy in years	69	62	77	76
Number of people per physician	4,421	>3,300	453	419
Number of pupils per teacher (primary school)	17	39	<18	20
Illiteracy rate (15 years and older)	7%	41%	<5%	<3%
Energy consumed per capita (kg of oil equivalent)	673	364	5,203	7,918

† The gross national product (GNP) is the total dollar value of all goods and services produced by a country in a year. The per capita GNP is calculated by dividing a country's GNP by its population. The World Bank defines low-income countries as those with a per capita GNP of $695 or less. High-income countries have a per capita GNP of $8,626 or more. Less than 14% of the world's 5.5 billion people live in high-income countries, while almost 60% live in low-income countries.

> = greater than   < = less than

Sources: World Bank, *Social Indicators of Development 1995,* Baltimore: Johns Hopkins University Press, 1995. Central Intelligence Agency, *World Fact Book,* Washington, D.C.: Government Printing Office, 1994.

culture) have been stressed in recent development plans.

In 1989, about 952,012 students were enrolled in higher education programs. Chulalongkorn University in Bangkok is Thailand's most outstanding university. Also in Bangkok are the University of Thammasart, specializing in social and political sciences, and Kasetsart University, specializing in agriculture.

32 MEDIA

Telephone service now reaches the main towns, with 999,678 telephones in use in 1991.

There are six government and military radio networks and Bangkok alone has five television stations. In 1991, there were 6,300,000 television sets and 10,550,000 radios.

In 1991 there were 40 daily newspapers published in Bangkok, including eight in Chinese and four in English. The provinces have weekly and semiweekly publications, all in Thai, but no daily papers. Among Bangkok's leading daily newspapers published in Thai (with estimated 1991 daily circulation) were *Thai Rath* (800,000), *Daily News* (400,000), *Ban Muang* (150,000), *Matichon* (100,000), *Dao Siam* (100,000), and *Tawan Siam*

(97,000). Leading Chinese papers are *Sing Sian Yit Pao* (40,000) and *Srinakorn Daily News* (30,000). The *Bangkok Post* is published in English, with a circulation of 37,000.

33 TOURISM AND RECREATION

In 1992, tourism, at $4.4 billion, topped the list of the country's total exports. In the late 1960s and early 1970s, the large US troop presence in Southeast Asia produced a growth in Thailand's tourism. Since then, the boom has continued. In 1991, Thailand had 5,086,899 foreign visitors, 3,116,983 from East Asia and 1,207,670 from Europe. There were 190,453 hotel rooms. As hotels increased rates by 41% in 1989, Bangkok, Pattaya, and Phuket became the most expensive destinations in Southeast Asia. Most tourists visit Bangkok and its Buddhist temples (*wats*).

In 1992, the combination of the military takeover, Persian Gulf War, and high incidence of AIDS (600,000 Thais are HIV-positive) combined to yield a drop in tourist arrivals. Tourism from China is increasing, however.

Major sports include soccer and baseball. Thai bull, cock, and fish fighting are also popular (though illegal), along with Thai boxing, golf, badminton, and kite fighting.

34 FAMOUS THAI

Two great Thai monarchs, Mongkut (r.1851–68) and his son Chulalongkorn (r.1868–1910), became famous for introducing Thailand to the modern world. They are, respectively, the king and his young successor in Margaret Landon's *Anna and the King of Siam*. Further progress toward modernization was accomplished in more recent times by three outstanding premiers: Phibul Songgram (1897–1964), Pridi Banomyong (1900–83), and Sarit Thanarat (1900–63).

Prince Wan Waithayakon (1891–1976), foreign minister and Thailand's representative to the UN, played a major role in diplomacy for many years following World War II. Marshal Thanom Kittikachorn (b.1911) was leader of Thailand from 1963 until October 1973, when political protests forced his resignation as prime minister. King Bhumibol Adulyadej (b.US, 1927) took the throne in 1946.

Prince Akat Damkoeng was the author in 1940 of the first modern novel written in Thailand, *Yellow Race, White Race*. Modern styles in painting and sculpture are reflected in the work of Chitr Buabusaya and Paitun Muangsomboon, and the traditional manner in the art of Apai Saratani and Vichitr Chaosanket.

35 BIBLIOGRAPHY

Benedict, Ruth. *Thai Culture and Behavior*. Ithaca, N.Y.: Cornell University Press, 1952.

Kulick, Elliott. *Thailand's Turn: Profile of a New Dragon*. New York: St. Martin's, 1992.

Leonowens, Anna Harriette. *The English Governess at the Siamese Court*. New York: Oxford University Press, 1988.

LePoer, Barbara Leitch, ed. *Thailand, A Country Study*. 6th ed. Washington, D.C.: Library of Congress, 1989.

McNair, S. *Thailand*. Chicago: Children's Press, 1987.

Valli, Eric, and Diane Summers. "Nest Gatherers of Tiger Cave." *National Geographic*, January 1990, 107–133.

TOGO

Republic of Togo
République Togolaise

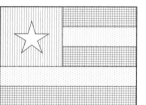

CAPITAL: Lomé.

FLAG: The national flag consists of five alternating horizontal stripes of green and yellow. A five-pointed white star is at the center of a red square which spans the height of the top three stripes.

ANTHEM: *Terre de nos aïeux (Land of Our Fathers).*

MONETARY UNIT: The Communauté Financière Africaine franc (CFA Fr) is a paper currency of 100 centimes. There are coins of 1, 2, 5, 10, 25, 50, 100, and 500 CFA francs and notes of 50, 100, 500, 1,000, 5,000, and 10,000 CFA francs. CFA Fr1 = $0.0018 (or $1 = CFA Fr571).

WEIGHTS AND MEASURES: The metric system is the legal standard.

HOLIDAYS: New Year's Day, 1 January; National Liberation Day, 13 January; Economic Liberation Day, 24 January; Victory Day, 24 April; Independence Day, 27 April; Labor Day, 1 May; Martyrs' Day, 21 June; Assumption, 15 August; All Saints' Day, Anniversary of the failed attack on Lomé, 24 September; 1 November; Christmas, 25 December. Movable religious holidays include Easter Monday, Ascension, Whitmonday, 'Id al-Fitr, and 'Id al-'Adha'.

TIME: GMT.

1 LOCATION AND SIZE

Situated on the west coast of Africa, Togo has an area of 56,790 square kilometers (21,927 square miles), slightly smaller than the state of West Virginia. It has a total boundary length of 1,703 kilometers (1,058 miles). Togo's capital city, Lomé, is located on the Gulf of Guinea coast.

2 TOPOGRAPHY

Togo is traversed in the center by the Togo Mountains, whose highest elevation is Mt. Agou (986 meters/3,235 feet). The Oti River is in the far north. A plateau stretches gradually southward to a coastal plain. The coastline consists of a flat sandy beach partially separated from the mainland by lagoons and lakes.

3 CLIMATE

Togo has a humid, tropical climate, but receives less rainfall than most of the other countries along the Gulf of Guinea. The heaviest rainfall occurs in the hills of the west, southwest, and center, where the precipitation averages about 150 centimeters (60 inches) a year. The coast gets the least rainfall, about 78 centimeters (31 inches) annually. The average maximum and minimum temperatures are 30°C (86°F) and 23°C (73°F) at Lomé, on the southern coast, and 35°C (95°F) and 15°C (59°F) at Mango, in the north.

4 PLANTS AND ANIMALS

Dense belts of reeds are found along the coastal lagoons. Most of the largest wild-

Photo credit: Corel Corporation.

A woman carries a large stack of pots and pans perfectly balanced on her head.

life has been exterminated in the southern area, but in the north, elephants and lions still can be found. Hippopotamuses and crocodiles live in and along the rivers, and monkeys are fairly common. The coastal swamps are full of snakes.

5 ENVIRONMENT

Slash-and-burn agriculture and the cutting of wood for fuel are the major causes of forest depletion. Water pollution is a significant problem in Togo, where 51.5% of the people living in rural areas do not have pure water. The nation's wildlife population is at risk due to poaching and the clearing of land for agricultural purposes.

6 POPULATION

Togo is one of the more densely populated countries in tropical Africa. The estimated 1994 population was 4,246,187, with an average density of 66 persons per square kilometer (171 per square mile). A population of 4,818,000 was projected for the year 2000. The only city of major size is Lomé, the capital, with a 1990 population of 513,000.

7 MIGRATION

There is a steady migration of laborers from rural to urban areas. Members of the Ewe group migrate to and from Ghana. There is also much movement of Ouatchi, Adja, Kabré, and Losso peoples to and from Benin. Some of the illegal aliens expelled from Nigeria in 1983 were Togolese (natives of Togo).

8 ETHNIC GROUPS

Togo's population consists of at least 18 tribal groups possessing neither language nor history in common. The main ethnic group consists of the Ewe and such related peoples as the Ouatchi, Fon, and Adja. They live in the south and constitute at least 40% of the population. Next in size are the Kabrè and related Losso living in the north. Other significant groups are the Mina, Cotocoli, Moba, Gourma, and Akposso. There may be some 2,500 non-Africans in Togo, mostly French.

9 LANGUAGES

French is the official language. It is used in the media and for commerce. However, the public schools combine French with Ewe or Kabiyé, depending on the region.

In all, more than 44 different languages and dialects are spoken in Togo.

10 RELIGIONS

As of 1993, an estimated one-half of Togolese followed African traditional religions. Up to 35% were Christian (about 23% Roman Catholic), and some 15% practiced Islam.

11 TRANSPORTATION

Togo has a relatively well developed road system of about 6,462 kilometers (4,015 miles). In 1991 there were 26,000 passenger cars and 16,000 commercial vehicles. Togo has 516 kilometers (321 miles) of meter-gauge rail.

Togo lacks a natural harbor, but in 1968 a major deepwater port east of central Lomé was completed with a loan from the Federal Republic of Germany (FRG) (then West Germany, now unified Germany). A free port at Lomé serves landlocked Burkina Faso, Niger, and Mali. In 1991 Togo had three oceangoing ships, with a combined gross weight of 21,000 tons. The international airport at Lomé links Togo with other countries of West and Central Africa and with Europe. A second international airport, at Niamtougou, was completed in the early 1980s.

12 HISTORY

Between the twelfth and the eighteenth centuries, the Ewe, Adja, and related peoples came south to this area from the Niger River valley. Portuguese sailors visited the coast in the fifteenth and sixteenth centuries. The French established trading posts in 1626 and again in 1767, but

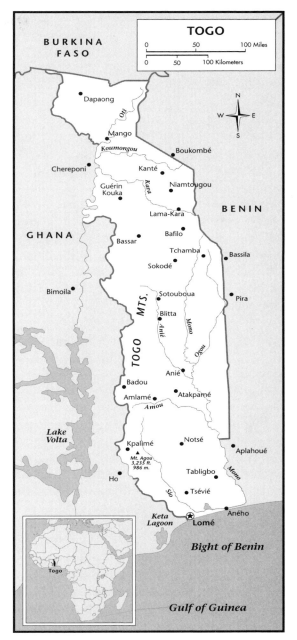

LOCATION: 6°5′ to 11°11′N; 0°5′ to 1°45′E. **BOUNDARY LENGTHS:** Burkina Faso, 126 kilometers (78 miles); Benin, 644 kilometers (400 miles); Gulf of Guinea coastline, 56 kilometers (35 miles); Ghana, 877 kilometers (545 miles). **TERRITORIAL SEA LIMIT:** 30 miles.

abandoned them each time. German traders came to the area that is now Benin as early as 1856, but did not arrive in large numbers until 1880. Germany finally established control over the area, its first African colony, on 5 July 1884. Dr. Gustav Nachtigal signed a treaty establishing a German protectorate over a small coastal area, and its name—Togo—eventually was given to the entire territory. Boundaries between Togo and surrounding territories were set by agreements with the British and French in 1897 and 1899. The boundary arrangements resulted in splitting the Ewe, Adja, Ouatchi, Fon, and other peoples between the Gold Coast (now Ghana), Togo, and Dahomey (now Benin).

Soon after the outbreak of World War I in August 1914, France and Britain gained control of Togo. Between the world wars, the British controlled the coastal area and the railways, and the French took control of the interior.

Beginning in 1947, leaders of the Ewe people repeatedly petitioned the United Nations, first for Ewe unification and subsequently for Togoland unification. At the time, the Ewe were under three different administrations: the Gold Coast, British Togoland, and French Togoland. For nine years the Togoland question was before the United Nations. Finally, a majority of the registered voters in British Togoland decided that the territory should be integrated with an independent Gold Coast. Consequently, when the Gold Coast became the independent state of Ghana, British Togoland ceased to exist.

Independence

On 27 April 1960, the Republic of Togo became an independent nation, with Sylvanus Olympio as president. President Olympio was assassinated on 13 January 1963 by military rebels. Nicolas Grunitzky, the exiled leader of the Togolese Party for Progress, returned to Togo and formed a temporary government. He abandoned the constitution, dissolved the National Assembly, and called new elections. In the May 1963 voting, Grunitzky was elected president, a new 56-member National Assembly was chosen, and a new constitution was approved by national referendum. Grunitzky held office through 1966. On 13 January 1967, the Grunitzky government was overthrown by a military takeover led by Colonel Kléber Dadjo, who was succeeded in April 1967 by Lieutenant Colonel Étienne Éyadéma. The constitution was again suspended and the Assembly dissolved, and Éyadéma declared himself president.

Éyadéma also formed the Togolese People's Rally (Rassemblement du Peuple Togolais—RPT). He was reelected president without opposition on 30 December 1979 and remained firmly in control in the early 1980s, despite the economic problems caused by falling phosphate prices.

On 23–24 September 1986, about 60 rebels tried to seize control of Lomé but were defeated. Éyadéma accused Ghana and Burkina Faso of aiding them. He was elected unopposed to a new seven-year term on 21 December 1986. In March 1991, after police clashes with thousands of anti-government demonstrators, the government agreed to establish a multiparty system. On 28 August 1991, Éyadéma ended 24 years of military rule by surrendering authority to Joseph Kokou Koffigoh. The RPT was to be disbanded and Éyadéma barred from running for the presidency. However, on 3 December 1991, armed forces loyal to Éyadéma attacked the government palace and seized Koffigoh. He was forced to form a coalition government with Éyadéma and legalized the RPT again. The Army, composed largely of Kabyé (Éyadéma's group), never accepted Éyadéma's removal from office. Eventually they were able to place him back in power. On 25 August 1993, he won reelection as president with 97% of the vote.

Éyadéma and his ongoing struggle with the opposition-dominated High Council of the Republic continues to dominate politics in Togo. Legislative elections, held in February 1994, were marred by violence, with armed gangs attacking voting stations and opposition supporters. Of 76 seats being contested, the opposition won 38; the RPT, 37.

13 GOVERNMENT

A new constitution calling for multiparty elections was approved on 27 September 1992. Technically, the president is chosen in a direct, popular, multiparty election. There is an 81-seat National Assembly, chosen in multiparty elections.

14 POLITICAL PARTIES

Since 1969, the nation has been a one-party state. In that year, the Togolese People's Rally (*Rassemblement du Peuple Togolais*—RPT) was founded as the nation's only legal political party. President Éyadéma heads the RPT, which has a Central Committee and a Political Bureau. After opposition parties were legalized on 12 April 1991, other parties began to function, although threatened by pro-Éyadéma forces. Among the new parties are the Togolese Union for Democracy (UTD), the Partí Démocratique Togolais (PTD), and the Action Committee for Renewal (CAR).

15 JUDICIAL SYSTEM

The Supreme Court sits in Lomé. Other judicial institutions include two Courts of Appeal (one civil, the other criminal); courts for first hearings of civil, commercial, and criminal cases; labor and children's courts; and the Court of State Security, set up to judge crimes involving foreign or domestic subversion.

16 ARMED FORCES

In 1993, Togo's 4,800-man army consisted of 5 regiments. The 250-man air force had 16 combat aircraft, and the 200-member naval unit had 2 coastal patrol vessels. Defense spending in 1989 was $43 million.

17 ECONOMY

Togo has an agricultural economy with about 80% of its people engaged in agriculture. The nation also has significant phosphate deposits upon which it depends for foreign trade. International aid was suspended in 1992 to pressure the government towards democratic reforms. Declining prices for Togo's main exports

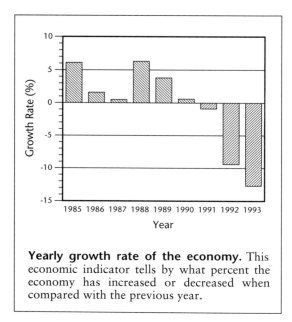

Yearly growth rate of the economy. This economic indicator tells by what percent the economy has increased or decreased when compared with the previous year.

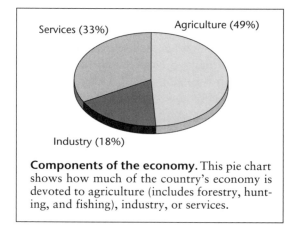

Components of the economy. This pie chart shows how much of the country's economy is devoted to agriculture (includes forestry, hunting, and fishing), industry, or services.

(phosphates, coffee, cocoa, and cotton) continue to have a negative effect on the economy.

18 INCOME

In 1992 Togo's gross national product (GNP) was $1,575 million at current prices, or about $340 per person. For the period 1985–92 the average inflation rate was 2.3%, resulting in a real growth rate in GNP of −1.5% per person.

19 INDUSTRY

Industrial production represents a small part of the economy, with textiles and the processing of agricultural products—palm oil extraction, coffee roasting, cassava flour milling, and cotton ginning and weaving—being the most important sectors. Other industries were developed to provide consumer goods—footwear, beverages, confectionery, salt, and tires.

20 LABOR

About 80% of the 3.4 million inhabitants are engaged in agriculture. Of salaried employees (63,944 in 1987), 48% were in services, 13% in commerce, 8% in manufacturing.

The minimum age for employment is 14, with a higher minimum of 18 for certain types of industrial and technical work. The law is well enforced in the formal sector, although young children traditionally help with family-based businesses, especially in rural areas.

21 AGRICULTURE

Togo is mainly an agricultural country, with about four-fifths of the population engaged in farming. Main food crops in 1992 (in tons) included manioc, 480,000; yams, 393,000; corn, 239,000; and sorghum and millet, 191,000. Certain grains—notably wheat, which cannot be grown in Togo—must be imported.

Leading export crops are coffee and cocoa, followed by cotton, palm kernels, copra, peanuts, and shea nuts (karité). Coffee production decreased to 13,000 tons in 1992. In 1992, cocoa production amounted to 7,000 tons, cotton production totaled 41,000 tons of fiber, and production of palm kernels increased to 15,900 tons. About 2,000 tons of copra are produced annually. The peanut crop in 1992 was 22,000 tons (shelled).

22 DOMESTICATED ANIMALS

Livestock in 1992 included an estimated 1,500,000 sheep, 2,000,000 goats, 800,000 hogs, 320,000 head of cattle, and 7,000,000 poultry.

23 FISHING

Production amounted to an estimated 12,524 tons in 1991. About 97% of that was caught in Atlantic waters and the rest inland.

24 FORESTRY

Production of roundwood in 1991 was estimated at 1,234,000 cubic meters, of which 85% was for fuel.

25 MINING

Lime phosphate, found mostly in the coastal region, is Togo's principal mineral resource. In 1991, Togo was the world's tenth largest producer of phosphate rock. Production was about 2,965,000 tons in that year. Other mineral deposits include

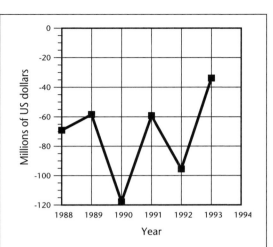

Yearly balance of trade measured in millions of US dollars. The balance of trade is the difference between what a country sells to other countries (its exports) and what it buys (its imports). If a country imports more than it exports, it has a negative balance of trade (a trade deficit). If exports exceed imports there is a positive balance of trade (a trade surplus).

limestone, granite, chromite, bauxite, manganese, gold, copper, and nickel.

26 FOREIGN TRADE

Togo's principal exports are phosphates, cocoa, cotton (ginned), and coffee. The principal imports are cotton textiles; food, beverages, and tobacco; machinery and transport material; petroleum products; and chemical products. China was Togo's leading export partner in 1989 (12.5%) followed by France (8.7%), the former Soviet Union (7.7%), and Italy (7.5%). Togo's imports came primarily from France (29.6%), Netherlands (11.8%), and Germany (7.6%).

Selected Social Indicators

These statistics are estimates for the period 1988 to 1993. For comparison purposes, data for the United States and averages for low-income countries and high-income countries are also given.

Indicator	Togo	Low-income countries	High-income countries	United States
Per capita gross national product†	**$340**	$380	$23,680	$24,740
Population growth rate	**3.2%**	1.9%	0.6%	1.0%
Population growth rate in urban areas	**4.8%**	3.9%	0.8%	1.3%
Population per square kilometer of land	**66**	78	25	26
Life expectancy in years	**55**	62	77	76
Number of people per physician	**8,725**	>3,300	453	419
Number of pupils per teacher (primary school)	**59**	39	<18	20
Illiteracy rate (15 years and older)	**57%**	41%	<5%	<3%
Energy consumed per capita (kg of oil equivalent)	**47**	364	5,203	7,918

† The gross national product (GNP) is the total dollar value of all goods and services produced by a country in a year. The per capita GNP is calculated by dividing a country's GNP by its population. The World Bank defines low-income countries as those with a per capita GNP of $695 or less. High-income countries have a per capita GNP of $8,626 or more. Less than 14% of the world's 5.5 billion people live in high-income countries, while almost 60% live in low-income countries.

> = greater than   < = less than

Sources: World Bank, *Social Indicators of Development 1995*, Baltimore: Johns Hopkins University Press, 1995. Central Intelligence Agency, *World Fact Book*, Washington, D.C.: Government Printing Office, 1994.

27 ENERGY AND POWER

Togo receives about four-fifths of its electricity in the form of hydroelectric power from the Akosombo (or Volta River) Dam in Ghana. Togo's electrical output that year totaled 60 million kilowatt hours; consumption of electricity was 350 million kilowatt hours. An estimated 135,206 tons of petroleum products were imported in 1990.

28 SOCIAL DEVELOPMENT

The government's social welfare program, established in 1973, includes family allowances and maternity benefits; old age, disability, and death benefits; and workers' compensation. The Union of Togolese Women and a women's group connected with the RPT assist in the fight against illiteracy and disease and are involved in child welfare.

29 HEALTH

Medical services include permanent treatment centers and a mobile organization for preventive medicine. Special facilities treat leprosy, sleeping sickness, and mental illness. There is about 1 doctor per 8,725 people, and about 61% of the population had access to health care services.

Photo credit: Corel Corporation.

A boy carries a basket he has just purchased at the local market and heads home.

Yaws, malaria, and leprosy continue to be major medical problems. Average life expectancy is 55 years.

30 HOUSING

The government is attempting to solve the problem of urban overcrowding by promoting housing and establishing sanitation facilities. According to the latest available information for 1980–88, total housing units numbered 470,000 with 6.2 people per dwelling.

31 EDUCATION

The literacy rate in 1990 was estimated at 43%: 56% for men, and 31% for women. Primary education (ages 6–12) is compulsory and free of charge. In 1990, there were 651,962 pupils in 2,494 primary schools, 125,545 pupils in secondary schools, and 8,392 students in technical schools. The University of Benin is at Lomé, and includes colleges of administration, architecture, and urban planning. In 1989, all higher level schools had 7,826 students.

32 MEDIA

The *Journal Official de la République du Togo* is published daily in Lomé; *La Nouvelle Marche*, published in French and Ewe, had a circulation of 10,000 in 1992. The nation had 12,000 telephones in 1991. The radio network broadcasts in

French, English, and local languages. In 1991 there were an estimated 770,000 radios. Television service began in 1973. In 1991, Togo had about 23,000 television sets.

33 TOURISM AND RECREATION

Tourist attractions include the Mandouri hunting reserve, and the beaches and deep sea fishing of the Gulf of Guinea coast. In 1990 there were about 103,246 tourist arrivals, 44% from Europe and 48% from Africa. In 1991, Togo's tourist industry declined due to the Gulf War. The occu-pancy rate in Lomé hotels was 26% in 1992.

34 FAMOUS TOGOLESE

Togo's most prominent statesman was Sylvanus Olympio (1902–63), who led his country's fight for independence and was its first president. Gnassingbé Éyadéma (b.Étienne Éyadéma, 1937) has been president of Togo since 1967.

35 BIBLIOGRAPHY

Decalo, Samuel. *Historical Dictionary of Togo*. 2d ed. Metuchen, N.J.: Scarecrow Press, 1987.

Knoll, Arthur J. *Togo under Imperial Germany, 1884–1914: A Case Study in Colonial Rule.* Stanford, Calif.: Hoover Institution Press, 1978.

TONGA

Kingdom of Tonga
Pule'anga Tonga

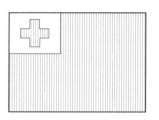

CAPITAL: Nuku'alofa, Tongatapu.

FLAG: The flag, adopted in 1862, is crimson with a cross of the same color mounted in a white square in the upper left corner.

ANTHEM: *Koe Fasi Oe Tu'i Oe Otu Tonga (Tongan National Anthem)* begins "'E 'Otua Mafimafi Ko homau 'Eiki Koe" ("O Almighty God above, Thou art our Lord and sure defense").

MONETARY UNIT: The Tongan pa'anga (T$) of 100 seniti is a paper currency at par with the Australian dollar. There are coins of 1, 2, 5, 10, 20, and 50 seniti, and 1 and 2 Tongan pa'angas, and notes of ½, 1, 2, 5, 10, 20, and 50 pa'angas. T$1 = US$0.7390 (or US$1 = T$1.3532).

WEIGHTS AND MEASURES: The metric system is the legal standard, but some imperial and local weights and measures are also employed.

HOLIDAYS: New Year's Day, 1 January; ANZAC Day, 25 April; Crown Prince's Birthday, 4 May; Independence Day, 4 June; King's Birthday, 4 July; Constitution Day, 4 November; Tupou I Day, 4 December; Christmas, 25–26 December. Movable religious holidays include Good Friday and Easter Monday.

TIME: 1 AM (the following day) = noon GMT.

1 LOCATION AND SIZE

The Tonga archipelago (island group), also known as the Friendly Islands, lies scattered east of Fiji in the South Pacific Ocean. Consisting of 172 islands of various sizes, Tonga has a total area of 748 square kilometers (289 square miles), slightly more than four times the size of Washington, D.C. Nuku'alofa, the capital, is located on the island of Tongatapu.

2 TOPOGRAPHY

The islands run roughly north–south in two parallel chains; the western islands are volcanic, and the eastern are coral encircled by reefs. At 10,800 meters (35,400 feet) deep, the Tonga Trench (ocean floor around Tonga) is one of the lowest parts of the ocean floor. There are few lakes or streams.

3 CLIMATE

The mean annual temperature is 23°C (73°F), ranging from an average daily minimum of 10°C (50°F) in winter to an average maximum of 32°C (90°F) in summer. Mean annual rainfall ranges from 178 centimeters (70 inches) on Tongatapu to 279 centimeters (110 inches) on Vava'u.

4 PLANTS AND ANIMALS

Coconut palms, hibiscus, and other tropical trees, bushes, and flowers are plentiful. Tonga is famous for its flying foxes.

5 ENVIRONMENT

The forest area is declining because of land clearing. Water pollution is also a significant problem due to salinization, sewage, and toxic chemicals from farming activities. The Fiji banded iguana and three turtle species were classified as endangered in 1987.

6 POPULATION

The 1986 census recorded a population of 94,649. The 1995 population was estimated by the United Nations at 99,000, with an estimated population density of 129 inhabitants per square kilometer (334 per square mile). Nuku'alofa, the capital, had a population of 21,383 in the 1986 census.

7 MIGRATION

Emigration by Tongan workers, both skilled and unskilled, has long been of concern to the government. In 1989 approximately 39,400 Tongans lived in the United States, Australia, and New Zealand.

8 ETHNIC GROUPS

The Tongans are a racially uniform Polynesian people. Less than 2% of the population is of European, part-European, Chinese, or of non-Tongan Pacific island origin.

9 LANGUAGES

Tongan, a Polynesian language, is the language of the kingdom. English is taught as a second language in the schools.

10 RELIGIONS

Over 98% of Tongans are Christian. About 64% belong to the Free Wesleyan Church of Tonga, which is headed by the Tongan monarch. There are also Roman Catholics (14%), Anglicans, Seventh-Day Adventists, and Mormons.

11 TRANSPORTATION

In 1991, Tonga had 272 kilometers (169 miles) of surfaced roads. In 1992 there were 3,757 commercial vehicles and 3,297 automobiles. Tonga has no railways. Nuku'alofa is a port of entry for overseas vessels. In 1991, the merchant fleet consisted of three cargo ships and one liquefied gas tanker, for a total of 11,511 gross registered tons.

Air Pacific, Air New Zealand, Polynesian Airlines, and Hawaiian Air operate scheduled international flights from Fuaamotu International Airport at Tongatapu. In 1991, the airport serviced 98,000 passengers.

12 HISTORY

Since the Tongan language was not written down until the nineteenth century, the early history of Tonga (which means "south") is based on oral tradition. Hereditary absolute kings (*Tu'i Tonga*) date back to the tenth century. The present dynasty was founded in the mid-nineteenth century.

Captain James Cook visited the Tongatapu and Ha'apai groups in 1773 and again in 1777. It was in the waters of the Ha'apai group that the famous mutiny on the British ship *Bounty* occurred in 1789.

The first Wesleyan missionaries landed in Tonga in 1826. By the middle of the century, most Tongans had become Christians, the great majority being Wesleyans. The kingdom became a constitutional monarchy in 1975 under George Tupou I (r.1845–93).

In 1900, a treaty of friendship was signed with the United Kingdom, and the islands became a British protectorate. During World War II (1939–45), Tongan soldiers fought the Japanese in the Solomon Islands, and Tongatapu served as an important Allied shipping point.

On 4 June 1970, Tonga became an independent member of the Commonwealth of Nations. In 1972, Tonga claimed the uninhabited Minerva Reefs (southwest of Africa) to prevent the founding of an independent Republic of Minerva as a tax haven.

Many of the government's strongest critics gained seats in the 1987 legislative elections. The large turnover was thought to reflect changing attitudes toward traditional authority.

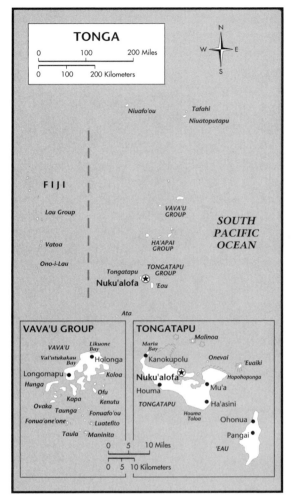

LOCATION: 15° to 23°30's; 173° to 177°w. **TERRITORIAL SEA LIMIT:** 12 miles.

13 GOVERNMENT

Tonga is an independent kingdom. The government is divided into three main branches: the executive, consisting of the king, Privy Council, and cabinet; the Legislative Assembly; and the judiciary. The islands are divided into three districts: Vava'u, Ha'apai, and Tongatapu.

14 POLITICAL PARTIES

There were two political parties as of 1993: the Democratic Reform Movement and the Christian Democratic Party.

15 JUDICIAL SYSTEM

The Supreme Court rules on major civil and criminal cases. Other cases, heard in

Photo credit: Susan D. Rock.

A mother and child at market in Nuku'alofa.

copra and coconut products, bananas, and vanilla bean extract. Unemployment and inflation are major problems.

18 INCOME

In 1992, Tonga's gross national product (GNP) was us$136 million at current prices, or about us$1,530 per person. For the period 1985–92 the average inflation rate was 10.4%, resulting in a real growth rate in GNP of −0.1% per person.

19 INDUSTRY

Encouragement of new industries was a goal of Tonga's five five-year plans (1966–90). Long-established industries are coconut processing, sawmilling, and local handicrafts.

20 LABOR

The total wage labor force in 1990 was about 32,000, of whom 36.5% were employed in agriculture, 14.4% in manufacturing, and 22% in public administration. The unemployment rate was 4.2%. There is no child labor in Tonga.

21 AGRICULTURE

About 69% of Tonga is agricultural land. Main crops for home consumption are yams, taro, sweet potatoes, and manioc. Agricultural exports in 1984/85 included 4,262 tons of coconut oil and 463 tons of desiccated coconut. Estimated production in 1992 included coconuts, 25,000 tons; sweet potatoes, 14,000 tons; cassava, 15,000 tons; oranges, 3,000 tons; and bananas, 1,000 tons.

the Magistrates' Court or the Land Court, may be appealed to the Supreme Court and then to the Court of Appeal, the court of last resort.

16 ARMED FORCES

The Tonga Defense Force consists of regular forces and volunteer reservists. A naval squadron consisting of several fast patrol boats polices territorial waters.

17 ECONOMY

The economy is largely agricultural, depending principally on the export of

22 DOMESTICATED ANIMALS

Livestock in 1992 included 97,000 hogs, 16,000 goats, 12,000 horses, and 10,000 head of cattle.

23 FISHING

Principal species caught are tuna and marlin. The fish catch was 1,889 tons in 1991.

24 FORESTRY

Much wood for construction must be imported. There is a government sawmill on 'Eua. Charcoal is manufactured from logs and coconut shells.

25 MINING

Tonga has few known mineral resources. A limited amount of crushed stone is produced at local quarries.

26 FOREIGN TRADE

Tonga's chief exports are pumpkins, vanilla, woolen knitwear, tuna, leather jackets, coconut oil, and taro. Tonga's major trading partners are New Zealand, Australia, Japan, Fiji, and the United Kingdom.

27 ENERGY AND POWER

All power is derived from thermal sources. Electricity production in 1991 totaled 22 million kilowatt hours.

28 SOCIAL DEVELOPMENT

Every family is provided by law with sufficient land to support itself. Tonga has a family planning program, combined with maternal and child health services. Polynesian cultural traditions have kept most women in subservient roles.

29 HEALTH

In comparison with many other Pacific islands, Tonga is a healthy country. Life expectancy in 1992 was 68 years. Tuberculosis, filariasis, typhoid fever, dysentery, and various eye and skin diseases remain common health problems. In 1985, there were 4 hospitals and 14 health care centers on the islands, with a total of 307 beds. In 1991, Tonga had 49 physicians.

30 HOUSING

Village houses usually have reed sides and a sloping roof thatched with sugarcane or coconut leaves. Modern houses are built of wood, with roofs of corrugated iron. In 1986, the housing stock totaled 15,091 units.

31 EDUCATION

Primary education is compulsory for all Tongans. Adult literacy is estimated at higher than 90%. In 1990 there were 16,522 pupils in Tonga's 115 primary schools and 14,749 in secondary schools. The same year, there were 689 primary school teachers and 832 secondary school teachers. A teacher-training college provides a two-year course.

32 MEDIA

Radio Tonga broadcasts about 75 hours a week in Tongan, English, Fijian, and Samoan. In 1991 there were about 75,000 radio sets on the islands. There is no television. The government publishes a weekly newspaper, the *Tonga Chronicle,*

Selected Social Indicators

These statistics are estimates for the period 1988 to 1993. For comparison purposes, data for the United States and averages for low-income countries and high-income countries are also given.

Indicator	Tonga	Low-income countries	High-income countries	United States
Per capita gross national product†	$1,530	$380	$23,680	$24,740
Population growth rate	1.2%	1.9%	0.6%	1.0%
Population growth rate in urban areas	4.4%	3.9%	0.8%	1.3%
Population per square kilometer of land	129	78	25	26
Life expectancy in years	68	62	77	76
Number of people per physician	2,021	>3,300	453	419
Number of pupils per teacher (primary school)	24	39	<18	20
Illiteracy rate (15 years and older)	<10%	41%	<5%	<3%
Energy consumed per capita (kg of oil equivalent)	184	364	5,203	7,918

† The gross national product (GNP) is the total dollar value of all goods and services produced by a country in a year. The per capita GNP is calculated by dividing a country's GNP by its population. The World Bank defines low-income countries as those with a per capita GNP of $695 or less. High-income countries have a per capita GNP of $8,626 or more. Less than 14% of the world's 5.5 billion people live in high-income countries, while almost 60% live in low-income countries.

> = greater than   < = less than

Sources: World Bank, Social Indicators of Development 1995, Baltimore: Johns Hopkins University Press, 1995. Central Intelligence Agency, World Fact Book, Washington, D.C.: Government Printing Office, 1994.

which has an average circulation of 6,000 copies in Tongan and 1,200 in English.

33 TOURISM AND RECREATION

In 1991 there were 22,006 tourist arrivals, 25% from New Zealand, 24% from Canada, and 16% from Australia. There were 564 hotel rooms. Popular tourist sites are the royal palace and terraced tombs in Nuku'alofa. Fishing, swimming, and sailing are popular, and rugby football is a favorite spectator sport.

34 FAMOUS TONGANS

During the reign of King George Tupou I (Taufa'ahu Tupou, 1797–1893), Tonga became a Christian nation and acquired a constitution. The most famous Tongan of this century was Queen Salote Tupou (1900–1965), whose rule began in 1918. Queen Salote's son, King Taufa'ahau Tupou IV (b.1918), took the throne in 1965 and was formally crowned in 1967.

35 BIBLIOGRAPHY

Bain, Kenneth. The New Friendly Islanders: The Tonga of King Taufa'ahau Tupou IV. London: Hodder & Stoughton, 1993.

Cook, James. The Explorations of Captain James Cook in the Pacific, as Told by Selections of His Own Journals, 1768–1779. Magnolia, Mass.: Peter Smith, n.d.

Marcus, George E. The Nobility and the Chiefly Tradition in the Modern Kingdom of Tonga. Honolulu: University of Hawaii Press, 1980.

TRINIDAD AND TOBAGO

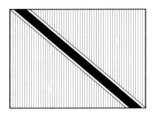

Republic of Trinidad and Tobago

CAPITAL: Port-of-Spain.

FLAG: On a red field, a black diagonal stripe with a narrow white border on either side extends from top left to bottom right.

ANTHEM: Begins, "Forged from the love of liberty, in the fires of hope and prayer."

MONETARY UNIT: The Trinidad and Tobago dollar (TT$) is a paper currency of 100 cents. There are coins of 1, 5, 10, 25, and 50 cents, and 1 dollar, and notes of 1, 5, 10, 20, and 100 dollars. TT$1 = US$0.1720 (US$1 = TT$5.8135).

WEIGHTS AND MEASURES: The metric system is official, but some imperial weights and measures are still used.

HOLIDAYS: New Year's Day, 1 January; Carnival, 14–15 February; Emancipation Day, 1st Monday in August; Independence Day, 31 August; Republic Day, 24 September; Christmas, 25 December; Boxing Day, 26 December. Movable holidays include Carnival, Good Friday, Easter Monday, Whitmonday, Corpus Christi, 'Id al-Fitr, and Dewali.

TIME: 8 AM = noon GMT.

1 LOCATION AND SIZE

Situated off the northeast coast of South America at the extreme southern end of the Lesser Antilles, the islands of Trinidad and Tobago cover an area of 5,130 square kilometers (1,981 square miles), and are slightly smaller than the state of Delaware. Trinidad, the main island, has an area of 4,828 square kilometers (1,863 square miles). Tobago has an area of 300 square kilometers (116 square miles). In addition, 16 small islands are located off the coasts.

Trinidad and Tobago have a coastline length of 470 kilometers (292 miles). The capital city of Trinidad and Tobago, Port-of-Spain, is located on Trinidad's Gulf of Paria coast.

2 TOPOGRAPHY

Trinidad is geologically part of South America, and its topography is similar to that of the adjoining Orinoco section of Venezuela. Three ranges of hills, extending east–west, cross the island. The highest peak of the Northern Range, a continuation of the Venezuelan Paria Peninsula mountains, is El Cerro del Aripo at (940 meters (3,084 feet). Hills in the Central Range rise just over 300 meters (1,000 feet), while those in the Southern Range are somewhat lower. In between these hill ranges is level or gently rolling flatland. Vast swamp areas are found along the east, south, and west coasts. Trinidad has the world's largest natural asphalt bog, the

46-hectare (114-acre) Pitch Lake, on the southwestern coast.

Tobago is geologically part of the Lesser Antilles, and its topography, generally more irregular and rugged than Trinidad's, resembles that of Grenada and other volcanic islands to the north. A central volcanic hill core rising to over 550 meters (1,800 feet) fills most of the island and reaches the sea in many places. Much of the island's limited level land is concentrated in its southwestern tip.

3 CLIMATE

There is little variation in temperature conditions through the year. The mean annual temperature for the entire nation is 21°C (70°F). In Port-of-Spain the annual average is 25°C (77°F). Nights are generally cool. In the northern and central hill areas and on Tobago, annual rainfall exceeds 250 centimeters (98.43 inches). There is a mostly dry season from about January to May and a wet season from June to December.

4 PLANTS AND ANIMALS

The plant and animal life of Trinidad, like the geology of the island, resembles that of neighboring Venezuela. Tobago, by contrast, shows in its flora and fauna its connection with the volcanic Lesser Antilles. Plant life varies with altitude on both islands. The natural vegetation includes wildflowers, many flowering shrubs and trees, palms, giant aroids, and large broad-leaved varieties. Natural animal life includes a few species of mammals, monkeys among them, and many reptiles and birds.

Photo credit: Susan D. Rock.

A quiet beach along Pidgeon Point.

5 ENVIRONMENT

Pollution from oil spills is the country's most serious environmental problem. Water pollution is also caused by mining by-products, pesticides and fertilizers, sewage, and salt water. The nation's cities produce 0.2 million tons of solid waste per year. The land has been damaged by soil erosion due, in part, to the clearing of the land for farming. On the west coast of Trinidad is the Caroni Bird Sanctuary, famed for its marshland and mangroves, where flocks of scarlet ibis roost. Tobago is reputed to be the only place aside from New Guinea where the bird of paradise lives in the wild. Endangered species on Trinidad include the tundra peregrine falcon and loggerhead turtle.

6 POPULATION

At the census of 2 May 1990, the population was 1,234,388 (Trinidad 1,184,106, Tobago 50,282). A population of 1,365,000 was projected for the year 2000. The population density in 1990 was 246 persons per square kilometer (624 persons per square mile). Port-of-Spain, the capital since 1783, had a metropolitan population of about 59,200 in 1988. Most of Trinidad and practically all of Tobago are sparsely settled. Scarborough, the main town of Tobago, has a population of approximately 4,000.

7 MIGRATION

Lack of opportunity has encouraged emigration, mostly to the United Kingdom and United States. In 1990, there were 119,000 people from Trinidad and Tobago in the United States. However, there is also immigration from other islands in the Lesser Antilles, mainly Grenada and St. Vincent, where lack of opportunity is even more serious. Migration from Tobago to Trinidad is common also; there are as many native Tobagonians living on Trinidad as on Tobago.

8 ETHNIC GROUPS

The population is made up of Caucasians, blacks (the descendants of former slaves), East Indians (originally brought to the island as contract laborers from northern

LOCATION: 10°2′ to 11°21′N; 60°30′ to 61°56′W. **TOTAL COASTLINE:** 470 kilometers (292 miles). **TERRITORIAL SEA LIMIT:** 12 miles.

India), Syrians, and Chinese. The total population in 1993 was estimated at 43% black, 40% East Indian, 14% of mixed descent, 1% European, and 2% Chinese and other. Tobago is predominantly black.

While blacks and East Indians on Trinidad are economically interdependent, each community retains its cultural individuality. Intermarriage is rare, and the two groups are physically distinct. They also differ in occupation, diet, religion, residence, agricultural landscape, sometimes dress, and often politics.

9 LANGUAGES

English is the official language. An English patois (dialect), characterized by many foreign words and the special pronunciations of the islands, is understood everywhere. Here and there, a French patois and Spanish are used. In some rural areas, East Indians use Hindi and, less frequently, Urdu, Tamil, and Telegu.

10 RELIGIONS

Christian churches are found on both islands; Hindu temples and Muslim mosques in southern Asian architectural styles are found on Trinidad. In 1985, the population was roughly 36.2% Roman Catholic, 23% Hindu, 13.1% Protestant, 6% Muslim, and 21.7% other or non-observant.

11 TRANSPORTATION

In 1991 there were 8,000 kilometers (4,968 miles) of roads, of which about half were paved. The more densely settled sections of both islands are served by adequate roads, but large sections of Tobago have either no usable roads or poor ones. In 1992, registered motor vehicles included 120,589 passenger cars and 30,126 commercial vehicles. Trinidad has no remaining railways.

The largest passenger and cargo port is at Port-of-Spain. Regularly scheduled coastal vessels connect Port-of-Spain with Scarborough. Air facilities are concentrated at Piarco International Airport, about 26 kilometers (16 miles) southeast of Port-of-Spain. Trinidad and Tobago Airways operates domestic, regional, and international services.

12 HISTORY

Arawak Indians inhabited what they knew as Iere—Land of the Hummingbird—before the arrival on 31 July 1498 of Christopher Columbus, who called the island La Trinidad, or "The Trinity." During the early European period, the island was a supply and shipping center for Spanish traders and fortune seekers in South America. In time, colonists established plantations and imported slave labor from West Africa. The native Indians were eventually wiped out. In 1797, a British expedition from Martinique captured Trinidad, which was ceded formally to Great Britain in 1802 by the Treaty of Amiens and became a crown colony.

During the late Spanish period and through most of the nineteenth century, sugar was the island's main product. The emancipation of slaves in 1834 brought severe labor shortages, and between 1845 and 1917 more than 150,000 contract workers, mostly Hindus and some Muslims from India, were brought to the island as "cheap labor" to replace the slaves. With added labor supplies and new techniques, the cocoa industry thrived, and by the late nineteenth century cocoa had joined sugar as a major export crop. Petroleum was discovered on south Trinidad in 1910 and since then has assumed increasing economic importance.

Tobago was also discovered by Columbus in 1498, but it was ignored by Europeans for many years. From the early seventeenth century, the island changed hands many times among the Dutch, French, and British. Finally, in 1814, the British crown gained possession, which it maintained for a century and a half. Tobago was at first ruled as a separate colony, but during much of the nineteenth century it was administered from the Windward Islands government.

It became a crown colony in 1877 and in 1888 was amalgamated with Trinidad under the colonial name of Trinidad and Tobago. In 1958, the Federation of the West Indies was formed with Jamaica, Barbados, and the British Windward and Leeward Islands. Jamaica and Trinidad and Tobago withdrew in 1961, and the federation collapsed.

On 31 August 1962, Trinidad and Tobago became independent. The country retained membership in the Commonwealth as a British dominion. Eric Williams, the founder of the People's National Movement (PNM), became prime minister in 1961 and held the office until his death in 1981.

In 1976, Trinidad and Tobago declared itself a republic, and a president replaced the British monarch as chief of state. In 1980, Tobago attained a degree of self-government when it was granted its own House of Assembly. After losing its majority standing in the 1986 elections, the PNM returned to power in 1991 under Prime Minister Patrick Augustus Mervyn Manning.

13 GOVERNMENT

Under its 1961 constitution, as amended in 1976, Trinidad and Tobago has a two-chamber legislature, and, as head of state, a ceremonial president chosen by Parliament. The 36-member House of Representatives is the more important of the two houses. The Senate consists of 31 members, all appointed by the president. The chief executive officer is the prime minister, who is leader of the majority party. Cabinet ministers are appointed primarily from the House of Representatives by the president.

Trinidad is divided into eight counties. In 1980, Tobago was granted its own House of Assembly.

14 POLITICAL PARTIES

The People's National Movement (PNM), formed in 1956 by Eric Williams, has dominated politics in Trinidad and Tobago. In 1991, the PNM returned to office after a four-year break, winning 21 of 36 seats. Other parties include the National Alliance for Reconstruction (NAR), and the United National Congress.

15 JUDICIAL SYSTEM

The judicial system is modeled after that of the United Kingdom, with some local variations. The Supreme Court of Judicature is made up of the High Court of Justice and the Court of Appeal. There is a limited right of appeal to the Privy Council, seated in London.

16 ARMED FORCES

The Trinidad and Tobago Defense Force number an estimated 2,000 in one reinforced battalion. There are also a coast guard of 600 and a paramilitary police force numbering 4,800.

17 ECONOMY

Although it is by far the most prosperous of the Caribbean nations, Trinidad and Tobago's high degree of dependence on oil revenues has made it very sensitive to falling oil prices in recent years. Its economy is oriented toward trade and tourism. Inflation remained at single digit levels up to 1992 (6.5%), but it soared in 1993 (11%).

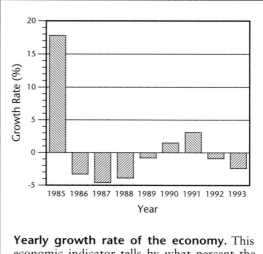

Yearly growth rate of the economy. This economic indicator tells by what percent the economy has increased or decreased when compared with the previous year.

18 INCOME

In 1992, the gross national product (GNP) was $4,995 million at current prices, or about $3,830 per person. For the period 1985–92, the average inflation rate was 5.2%, resulting in a real growth rate in per person GNP of –3.0%.

19 INDUSTRY

Long-established industries are those processing raw materials of the farm, forest, and sea. Foremost are sugar, molasses, and rum, followed by fish, lumber, fats and oils, and animal feed. Manufactured products include furniture, matches, angostura bitters, soap, confections and clay products. Newer industries include concrete products, canned citrus, bottled drinks, glass, drugs, chemicals, clothing, building materials, and metal goods.

20 LABOR

The economically active population in 1991 was estimated at 492,100 persons, of whom approximately 34% were engaged in services; 16.8% in commerce; 17% in construction and electricity, gas, and water supply; 15.5% in mining, quarrying, and manufacturing; 10.4% in agriculture, forestry, hunting, and fishing; 6% in transportation and communications; and 0.3% in other sectors. Unemployment was at 17.4% in 1990. As of 1992, about 25% of the work force was organized into 45 labor unions. Laws regulate the use of child labor, but enforcement appears to be lax.

21 AGRICULTURE

About 23% of the total land area was capable of cultivation in 1991, most of it

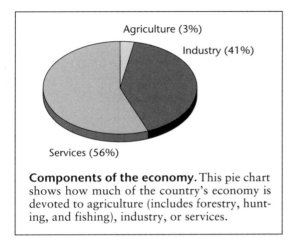

Agriculture (3%)

Industry (41%)

Services (56%)

Components of the economy. This pie chart shows how much of the country's economy is devoted to agriculture (includes forestry, hunting, and fishing), industry, or services.

on Trinidad. There are two distinct types of agricultural operations—the large estate or plantation that employs large numbers of laborers, and the small farm cultivated by the owner (or tenant) and family. Crops include corn, rice, peas, beans, potatoes, other vegetables, and a wide variety of fruits. Normally, 80% or more of the islands' production is exported.

Sugar production was 1,292,000 tons in 1992. Both cocoa and coffee production suffer from inefficiency, crop disease, and uncertain world market conditions. In 1992, cocoa production was 2,000 tons, and coffee output was about 1,000 tons.

22 DOMESTICATED ANIMALS

Livestock plays only a minor role in the nation's agriculture. The water buffalo, brought from India, is the major pack animal in rice cultivation and probably the most productive animal in the country. Trinidad and Tobago rely heavily on dairy imports from Europe to satisfy domestic demand.

In 1992, the livestock population included an estimated 10,000,000 poultry, 60,000 head of cattle, 52,000 goats, 50,000 hogs, 14,000 sheep, and 9,000 water buffalo.

23 FISHING

The fishing industry has great potential, but current production does not begin to meet local demands, and large quantities of fish must be imported. Shrimp and mackerel make up one-third of the overall annual catch, which totaled 10,283 tons in 1991.

24 FORESTRY

Approximately half, or 219,000 hectares (541,000 acres) of the land is forested, but only about 30% is true forest; the rest is farmland. Much of the forest is in hill areas and is not easily accessible for forestry. Several dozen small sawmills are in operation. Roundwood production in 1991 was about 72,000 cubic meters.

25 MINING

Natural asphalt, of which Trinidad has the largest supply in the world, is its second mineral of economic value, after petroleum. Southwest of San Fernando is the island's famous Pitch Lake, a 46-hectare (114-acre) deposit of oozing black asphalt, which has been mined commercially since the nineteenth century. The annual yield has declined from an average of 200,000 tons in the 1960s to 20,000 tons in 1991. Quarrying operations on the islands involve over 1 million tons annually of limestone and cement.

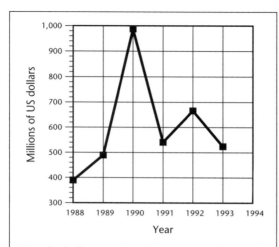

Yearly balance of trade measured in millions of US dollars. The balance of trade is the difference between what a country sells to other countries (its exports) and what it buys (its imports). If a country imports more than it exports, it has a negative balance of trade (a trade deficit). If exports exceed imports, there is a positive balance of trade (a trade surplus).

26 FOREIGN TRADE

The foreign trade of Trinidad and Tobago is very large for a country of its size, due mainly to its petroleum processing industry. Crude oil is imported for processing and then re-exported as gasoline, kerosene, and other petroleum products.

Principal exports are petroleum and petroleum products, chemicals, and manufactured goods. Total exports in 1993 were US$1,400 million. The country's major buyers were the United States, Barbados, Jamaica, Canada, the United Kingdom, and Central and South America.

Imports in 1993 totaled US$1,360 million and consisted mainly of crude petroleum, machinery, transportation equipment, manufactured goods, and fuels. Major suppliers were the United States, the United Kingdom, Canada, Brazil, Venezuela, other European Community countries, and Jamaica.

27 ENERGY AND POWER

Petroleum is the main source of energy and since the 1940s has been the nation's principal industry. Trinidad's oil production was 145,000 barrels a day in 1992. Proven crude oil reserves exceed 600 million barrels. Several untapped offshore fields in the southeast were under exploration in 1992. Natural gas production in 1992 was 5,600 million cubic meters. In 1991, total electrical energy production by public utilities was 3,525 million kilowatt hours.

28 SOCIAL DEVELOPMENT

The National Insurance System provides old age, retirement, and disability pensions; maternity, sickness, and survivors' benefits; and funeral grants. A food stamp program was introduced in 1978. Maternal and child health and family planning rank high among the government's social development priorities. In 1993, women constituted 36% of the labor force, and many women are active in business and the professions.

29 HEALTH

Government health facilities include general hospitals in Port-of-Spain and San Fernando, as well as small district hospitals. In 1991, there were 911 physicians.

Selected Social Indicators

These statistics are estimates for the period 1988 to 1993. For comparison purposes, data for the United States and averages for low-income countries and high-income countries are also given.

Indicator	Trinidad and Tobago	Low-income countries	High-income countries	United States
Per capita gross national product†	$3,830	$380	$23,680	$24,740
Population growth rate	1.1%	1.9%	0.6%	1.0%
Population growth rate in urban areas	1.9%	3.9%	0.8%	1.3%
Population per square kilometer of land	246	78	25	26
Life expectancy in years	72	62	77	76
Number of people per physician	1,355	>3,300	453	419
Number of pupils per teacher (primary school)	26	39	<18	20
Illiteracy rate (15 years and older)	4%	41%	<5%	<3%
Energy consumed per capita (kg of oil equivalent)	4,696	364	5,203	7,918

† The gross national product (GNP) is the total dollar value of all goods and services produced by a country in a year. The per capita GNP is calculated by dividing a country's GNP by its population. The World Bank defines low-income countries as those with a per capita GNP of $695 or less. High-income countries have a per capita GNP of $8,626 or more. Less than 14% of the world's 5.5 billion people live in high-income countries, while almost 60% live in low-income countries.

> = greater than   < = less than

Sources: World Bank, Social Indicators of Development 1995, Baltimore: Johns Hopkins University Press, 1995. Central Intelligence Agency, World Fact Book, Washington, D.C.: Government Printing Office, 1994.

In 1992, 99% of the population had access to health care services. The general health of the population has been improving, and substantial decreases have been recorded in the death rates for malaria, tuberculosis, typhoid, and syphilis.

Improvements in sanitation have reaped impressive health benefits. In 1990, 97% of the population had access to safe water and 79% had adequate sanitation. As a result, reported cases of dysentery and hookworm have declined dramatically. Average life expectancy is estimated at 72 years.

30 HOUSING

There is an acute shortage of adequate housing, and high rents have contributed to inflation. A typical rural home for a large family consists of one to three rooms plus an outside kitchen. Slums and tenements are typical of urban life. Nearly all private dwellings, urban or rural, have toilets and piped-in water.

31 EDUCATION

About 96% of the population 10 years of age and older is literate. In 1990, the islands had 476 primary and intermediate schools with 7,473 teachers and 193,992 students. Secondary schools enrolled 98,741 pupils in 1988. Education is compulsory for six years.

The University of the West Indies has a Trinidad campus. There are also government-run technical colleges, a polytechnic institute, and five teachers' colleges, as well as John F. Kennedy College, a liberal arts school outside Port-of-Spain. In 1990, higher education enrollment was estimated at 4,090 students, with 289 teaching staff.

32 MEDIA

Radio broadcasting is provided by the National Broadcasting Service (public) and the Trinidad Broadcasting Co. The Trinidad and Tobago Television Service emphasizes school and adult-education programs. There are two AM and four FM radio stations and five TV stations. In 1991 there were an estimated 394,000 television sets and 615,000 radios in use. As of 1991, there were 211,747 telephones.

Freedom of the press is both constitutionally guaranteed and respected in practice. There are four daily newspapers. The *Trinidad Guardian,* a morning and Sunday paper, had an average daily circulation of 41,500 in 1991. *The Trinidad and Tobago Express,* published daily and Sunday, had a daily circulation of 46,700.

33 TOURISM AND RECREATION

Outstanding tourist attractions include mountains, beaches, and reefs on both islands. Entertainment includes calypso and steel band music, both of which originated in Trinidad. Festive events include Carnival, held annually on the two days before Ash Wednesday; the Muslim festival of Hosein; and the Hindu festival of lights, Dewali, which occurs in October or November. Cricket and soccer (called football) are the most popular sports.

As of 1991, hotels and similar establishments on the islands had a total of 2,928 rooms with a 52.1% occupancy rate. Tourist arrivals in 1991 totaled 219,836, of whom 159,735 came from the Americas and 49,292 from Europe.

34 FAMOUS TRINIDADIANS AND TOBAGONIANS

Eric Eustace Williams (1911–81), the main political figure of his time, was prime minister from 1961 until his death. His successor was George Michael Chambers (b.1928). Notable writers include Samuel Selvon (b.1923) and V.S. (Vidiadhur Surajprasad) Naipaul (b.1932).

35 BIBLIOGRAPHY

Bereton, Bridget. *A History of Modern Trinidad.* Portsmouth, N.H.: Heinemann Educational Books, 1982.

Oxaal, Iva. *Black Intellectuals and the Dilemmas of Race and Class in Trinidad.* Cambridge, Mass.: Schenkman, 1982.

Williams, A. R. "Trinidad and Tobago." *National Geographic,* March 1994, 66–89.

TUNISIA

Republic of Tunisia
Al-Jumhuriyah at-Tunisiyah

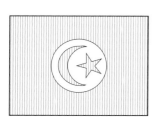

CAPITAL: Tunis.

FLAG: Centered on a red ground is a white disk bearing a red crescent and a red five-pointed star.

ANTHEM: *Al-Khaladi (The Glorious).*

MONETARY UNIT: The Tunisian dinar (D) is a paper currency of 1,000 millimes. There are coins of 1, 2, 5, 10, 20, 50, and 100 millimes and of ½, 1, and 5 dinars, and notes of 1, 5, 10, and 20 dinars. D1 = $1.2763 (or $1 = D0.7835).

WEIGHTS AND MEASURES: The metric system is the legal standard.

HOLIDAYS: New Year's Day, 1 January; Independence Day, 20 March; Martyrs' Day, 9 April; Labor Day, 1 May; Victory Day, 1 June; Republic Day, 25 July; Women's Day, 13 August; Evacuation Day, 15 October; Accession of President Ben Ali, 7 November. Movable religious holidays include 'Id al-Fitr, 'Id al-'Adha', 1st of Muharram (Muslim New Year), and Milad an-Nabi.

TIME: 1 PM = noon GMT.

1 LOCATION AND SIZE

Situated on the northern coast of Africa, Tunisia has an area of 163,610 square kilometers (63,170 square miles), slightly larger than the state of Georgia, and has a total boundary length of 2,445 kilometers (1,519 miles). Tunisia's capital city, Tunis, is located on the Mediterranean Sea coast.

2 TOPOGRAPHY

Mountains divide the country into two distinct regions, the well-watered north and the drier south, which includes Tunisia's highest point, Mt. Chambi (Jebel Chumbi), at 1,544 meters (5,064 feet). The northern region contains extensive cork forests and fertile grasslands. The southern region contains a central plateau and a desert area in the extreme south, which merges into the Sahara Desert. A river system—the Medjerda—drains into the Gulf of Tunis (Golfo de Tunis).

3 CLIMATE

Tunisia consists of two climatic belts, with Mediterranean influences in the north and Saharan in the south. Temperatures are moderate along the coast, with an average annual reading of 18°C (64°F), and hot in the interior south. Temperatures at Tunis range from an average minimum of 6°C (43°F) in January to an average maximum of 33°C (91°F) in August. Precipitation in the north reaches a high of 150 centimeters (59 inches) annually, while rainfall in the extreme south averages less than 20 centimeters (8 inches) a year.

4 PLANTS AND ANIMALS

Tunisia has a great variety of trees, including cork oak, oak, pines, jujube, and gum. More than one-fourth of the country is covered by esparto grass which can be used to make rope. Jackal, wild boar, and several species of gazelle are numerous. Horned vipers and scorpions are common in the Sahara Desert.

5 ENVIRONMENT

Loss of agricultural land to erosion, and damage to range and forest lands from overgrazing and overcutting of timber for fuel are major concerns. Seventy-six percent of the nation's land area is threatened by erosion. Tunisia uses 80% of its water for farming and 7% for industrial purposes. Sixty-nine percent of the people living in rural areas do not have pure water.

There are four national parks. In 1994, 6 of the nation's mammal species, 14 bird species, and 26 types of plants were endangered. A World Wildlife Fund project succeeded in rescuing the Atlas deer from near extinction.

6 POPULATION

The 1994 estimate of Tunisia's population was 8,777,590. A total of 9,781,000 was projected for the year 2000. The average density in 1994 was 52 persons per square kilometer (139 persons per square mile). Tunis, with a metropolitan population of about 2,084,000, was the largest city.

7 MIGRATION

Internal migration is a serious problem in Tunisia. Rural unemployment has caused many country dwellers to move to urban centers, where conditions are often harsh. Many Tunisians also seek employment abroad; in the early 1990s, there were approximately 350,000 Tunisian workers in foreign countries, mostly in Libya and France. Some 207,500 Tunisians lived in France in 1990.

8 ETHNIC GROUPS

Tunisia's population is almost entirely of Arab and Berber descent. The number of Tunisian Jews declined to about 2,500 by 1989. The small European population consists mostly of French and Italians.

9 LANGUAGES

Arabic is the official language. French is used in the schools, in government, and in trade. Small numbers of people speak Berber.

10 RELIGIONS

Nearly all (99%) Tunisians are Sunni Muslims. Small Muslim minorities belong to the Hanafite school or to the Ibadhi sect. The non-Muslims consist mainly of about 12,000 Roman Catholics and a declining number of Jews.

11 TRANSPORTATION

As of 1991, 17,700 kilometers (11,000 miles) of highway, 51% of it paved, connected the major cities and provided access to most regions of the country. In 1991, there were 330,000 passenger cars and 185,000 commercial vehicles. The Tunisian National Railway Company (Société National des Chemins de Fer Tunisiens) operates over 2,000 kilometers

(1,200 miles) of standard- and narrow-gauge track, located mostly in the northern region and central plateau. A metro rail system for Tunis opened in 1985.

Tunisia has excellent shipping facilities at Tunis, the principal port, and at Sfax, Sousse, Bizerte, and Gabes. As of 1991, the merchant fleet had 22 oceangoing ships, totaling 151,000 gross registered tons. Tunis-Carthage Airport provides direct connections to most major cities in Europe and the Middle East. Tunis Air, the national airline, carried 1.2 million passengers in 1992.

12 HISTORY

Between the ninth and thirteenth centuries, a series of warring Arab dynasties ruled Tunisia. In the thirteenth century, the Hafsids restored order, founding a dynasty that, from the thirteenth century to the sixteenth, made Tunisia one of the flourishing regions of North Africa. In the beginning of the sixteenth century, however, Spain's occupation of important coastal locations led to the demise of Hafsid rule. In 1574, the Ottoman Turks occupied Tunisia, eventually ruling it through a series of administrators called "beys." In 1705, the bey Husayn ibn 'Ali established a dynasty, the Husaynids. They ruled Tunisia under the Ottoman Empire until 1881, then under the French until 1956, the year of Tunisia's independence (the dynasty was abolished in 1957). During the nineteenth century, they exercised nearly independent rule. However, their efforts to Westernize the region led to financial ruin, and an international commission made up of British, French,

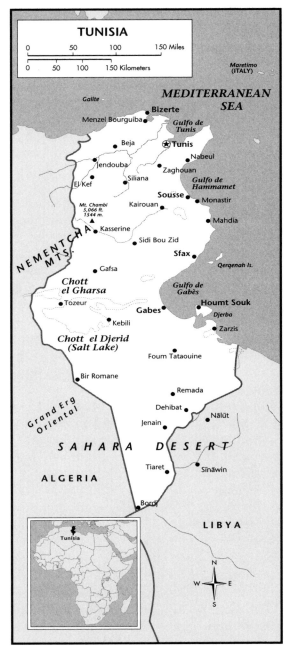

LOCATION: 7°33′ to 11°38′E; 29°54′ to 37°21′N.
BOUNDARY LENGTHS: Mediterranean coastline, 1,028 kilometers (639 miles); Libya, 459 kilometers (285 miles); Algeria, 958 kilometers (595 miles). **TERRITORIAL SEA LIMIT:** 12 miles.

and Italian representatives was set up to supervise Tunisian finances. Rivalry between French and Italian interests led to a French invasion of Tunisia in May 1881. After this, the Tunisian dynasty was allowed to continue, although real power passed to the French, who invested heavily in Tunisia to modernize it. The Tunisians, in turn, supported France in World War I (1914–18).

The Tunisian quest for independence began before World War I and continued through the formation of the moderate Destour Party, which split into factions in 1934. The French held firm against repeated requests for self-rule until, finally, it was promised by French Premier Pierre Mendès-France on 31 July 1954. On 20 March 1956, France recognized Tunisian independence. In April 1956, Habib Bourguiba formed the first government of independent Tunisia. Bourguiba won the first presidential election in 1959 and was reelected in 1964, 1969, and 1974, when the National Assembly amended the constitution to make him president for life.

Economic problems and political oppression during the late 1970s led to protests by students and workers. In 1980, the government started granting more freedom to the people. Trade union leaders were released from jails, and in July 1981 the formation of opposition political parties was permitted. However, in elections that November, candidates of Bourguiba's ruling Destourian Socialist Party won all 136 National Assembly seats and 94.6% of the popular vote. An economic slump in 1982–83 brought a renewal of tensions.

International Relations

After independence, Tunisia pursued a neutral, or nonaligned, course in foreign affairs while maintaining close economic ties with the West. On 19 March 1983, Tunisia and Algeria, whose relations had been strained during the 1970s, signed a 20-year treaty of peace and friendship. Relations with Libya have been stormy since Tunisia backed out of a pact to merge the two countries in 1974. Tunisian-Libyan relations reached a low point in January 1980, when some 30 commandos, aided by Libya, briefly seized an army barracks and other buildings at Gafsa in an attempt to inspire a popular uprising against Bourguiba. Following the evacuation of the Palestine Liberation Organization (PLO) from Lebanon in August 1982, Tunisia admitted PLO Chairman Yasir Arafat and nearly 1,000 Palestinian fighters. An Israeli bombing raid on the PLO headquarters near Tunis killed about 70 persons. By 1987, the PLO presence was down to about 200, all civilians. In 1993, Tunisia welcomed an official Israeli delegation as part of the peace process.

In the late 1980s, President Bourguiba's government cracked down on all forms of dissent. He turned on many of his former political associates, including his wife and son, while blocking two legal opposition parties from taking part in elections. A massive roundup of Islamic fundamentalists in 1987 was the president's answer to what he termed a terrorist conspiracy sponsored by Iran, and diplomatic relations with Tehran were broken. On 27 September 1987, a state security court found 76 defendants guilty of plotting against the government and planting bombs; seven (five in absentia) were sentenced to death.

The trusted Minister of Interior, who had conducted the crackdown, General Zine el-Abidine Ben Ali, was named prime minister in September 1987. Six weeks later, Ben Ali seized power, ousting Bourguiba, who he said was too ill and senile to govern any longer. Ben Ali assumed the presidency himself, promising political liberalization. Almost 2,500 political prisoners were released. The following year, Tunisia's constitution was revised, abolishing the presidency for life. Elections were advanced from 1991 to 1989 and Ben Ali was elected president, running unopposed.

Tunisia has continued to follow a moderate, nonaligned course in foreign relations, complicated by periodic difficulties with its immediate neighbors. Relations with Libya remained tense after ties were resumed in 1987. Algeria signed a border agreement in 1993 and planned a gas pipeline through Tunisia to Italy. Although the United States has provided economic and military aid, Tunisia opposed American support for Kuwait following Iraq's invasion in 1990.

Photo credit: International Labour Office

A young boy tends his father's flock of sheep.

presidential domination. The single-chamber National Assembly (*Majlis al-Ummah*) was expanded in 1993 to 160 members, elected by general, free, direct, and secret ballot. All citizens 20 years of age or older may vote. Presidential ratification is required before a bill passed by the legislature can become law, but the Assembly may override the president's veto by a two-thirds majority.

13 GOVERNMENT

The president initiates and directs state policy and appoints judges, provincial governors, the mayor of Tunis, and other high officials. The cabinet, headed by a prime minister, varies in size and is under

14 POLITICAL PARTIES

The Constitutional Democratic Rally (RCD) dominates the country's political life. Its leader from 1934, the year of its founding as the Neo-Destour Party, to

1987 was Habib Bourguiba. From 1959 to 1994, the RCD held a monopoly on Assembly seats. Banned in 1963, the Communist Party was the first opposition group to be fully legalized in 1981. Two other parties, the Movement of Social Democrats (Mouvement des Démocrates Socialistes) and the Movement (or Party) of Popular Unity (Mouvement (Parti) de l'Unité Populaire) were formally legalized in 1983. The principal Islamist party, An Nahda, has been outlawed.

15 JUDICIAL SYSTEM

Magistrates are appointed by the president upon recommendation of the Supreme Council of the Magistracy. In the mid-1980s there were 51 cantonal, or district, courts, 13 courts of first instance, and 3 courts of appeal. The ultimate court of appeal is a Court of Cassation, which has three civil sections and one criminal section. In addition, a High Court is set up for the sole purpose of prosecuting a member of the government accused of high treason. A Military Tribunal, consisting of a presiding civilian judge from the Court of Cassation and four military judges, hears cases involving military personnel as well as national security cases concerning civilians.

16 ARMED FORCES

As of 1993, Tunisia had an army of 27,000, mostly draftees. The navy had 4,500 men, 1 frigate and 20 patrol and coastal combatants. The air force had 3,500 personnel and 38 combat aircraft. There is obligatory 12-month military service. The national police (Public Order

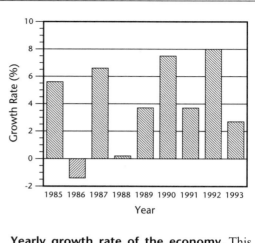

Yearly growth rate of the economy. This economic indicator tells by what percent the economy has increased or decreased when compared with the previous year.

Brigade) has 3,500 men, and the national guard 10,000.

17 ECONOMY

Agriculture, which engages about one-third of the labor force, is still the mainstay of the Tunisian economy, although minerals (especially crude oil and phosphates) and tourism are the leading sources of income from abroad. Industrial development has increased rapidly since the 1960s. Nevertheless, unemployment continues to plague Tunisia.

18 INCOME

In 1992 Tunisia's gross national product (GNP) was $14,615 million at current prices, or about $1,720 per person. For the period 1985–92, the average inflation rate was 6.6%, resulting in a real growth rate in per person GNP of 2.1%.

19 INDUSTRY

Food industries include flour milling; fish, fruit, and vegetable canning; olive oil processing; and sugar refining. In 1991, Tunisia produced 1.8 million tons of wheat, 225,000 tons of citrus fruit, and 650,000 tons of tomatoes. Manufacturing is dominated by textiles and leather and accounted for 38.5% of merchandise exports in 1993.

In 1990, fertilizer production included triple superphosphate, 792,000 tons, and phosphoric acid, 777,000 tons. Other manufactured goods included cement, 3.12 million tons, and iron and steel, 291,000 tons. Several plants assemble vehicles: auto production was 860 units in 1988; pick-ups, 630; trucks, 430; and tractors, 290. Handicrafts industries produce clothing, rugs, pottery, and copper and leather goods for both local and export markets.

20 LABOR

The labor force was estimated at 2,500,000 in 1992, including seasonal agricultural workers. Full employment has been a goal of successive development plans; however, unemployment still ranges from 15% to 25% (16% in 1992). The largest and most powerful trade union is the General Union of Tunisian Workers (Union Générale des Travailleurs Tunisiens—UGTT).

Minimum wage rates, which vary by occupation, are fixed by two government

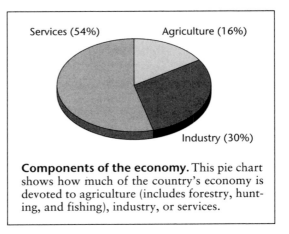

Components of the economy. This pie chart shows how much of the country's economy is devoted to agriculture (includes forestry, hunting, and fishing), industry, or services.

commissions. Disputes are settled by the secretary of state for social affairs. The Agricultural Labor Code governs working conditions for farmers. For other workers there are fixed five-day workweeks of 40 and 48 hours. All workers are entitled to annual paid leave of up to 18 working days; women receive maternity leave of 4 to 6 weeks.

Child labor is regulated, but children still appear to be widely employed in agriculture, small businesses, craft work, and as domestic help.

21 AGRICULTURE

Harvests have traditionally yielded sizable surpluses for export, chiefly to France. Crops fluctuate greatly in size, however, depending upon the weather. Chief grain crops in 1992 were wheat, 1,584,000 tons, and barley, 570,000 tons. Olive trees number some 55 million; output in 1992 comprised 121,000 tons of olive oil. Other important commodities (with 1992 production figures, in thousands of tons) were tomatoes, 550; citrus fruits, 185; sugar beets, 291; potatoes, 218; wine, 41; dates, 82; table grapes, 113; pears, 36; and cantaloupes and other melons, 82. The government has undertaken irrigation and soil conservation projects to improve agricultural production and raise the living standard of rural areas.

22 DOMESTICATED ANIMALS

In 1985 there were an estimated 6.4 million sheep, 1.3 million goats, 636,000 head of cattle, 311,000 mules and asses, 230,000 camels, and 41 million poultry.

23 FISHING

Commercial fishing takes place along the Mediterranean coast and in the Lake of Tunis and Lake Achkel. The 1991 catch was 90,710 tons.

24 FORESTRY

Forest and wooded lands covered about 668,000 hectares (1,651,000 acres) in 1991. The oak and pine forests of the northern highlands provide cork for export (some 7,500 tons produced annually) and firewood for local use. Estimated forestry output in 1991 included wood for fuel, 3,152,000 cubic meters; wood-based panels, 97,000 cubic meters; paper and paperboard, 78,000 tons; and sawn wood, 16,000 cubic meters.

25 MINING

Crude petroleum and phosphate rock are the two most important commodities. Known reserves of phosphate are estimated at 3.5 to 4 billion tons (5% of world reserves), and, as of 1991, Tunisia

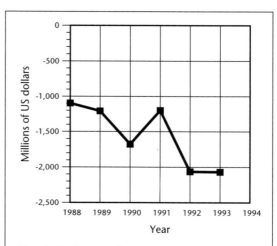

Yearly balance of trade measured in millions of US dollars. The balance of trade is the difference between what a country sells to other countries (its exports) and what it buys (its imports). If a country imports more than it exports, it has a negative balance of trade (a trade deficit). If exports exceed imports there is a positive balance of trade (a trade surplus).

ranked fifth in the world in phosphate production. In 1991, mineral production included calcium phosphate, 6,400,000 tons; iron ore, 295,000 tons; zinc concentrates, 9,353 tons; and lead concentrates, 1,285 tons. Cement production was 3,300,000 tons and marine salt, 441,000 tons. In 1991, Tunisia also produced 322,366 tons of barite, 100,000 tons of gypsum, 37,580 tons of fluorspar, and 900 kilograms of silver.

26 FOREIGN TRADE

Tunisia's foreign trade is based upon the export of mineral and agricultural products, textiles, and chemicals in exchange for consumer goods, raw and processed

Selected Social Indicators

These statistics are estimates for the period 1988 to 1993. For comparison purposes, data for the United States and averages for low-income countries and high-income countries are also given.

Indicator	Tunisia	Low-income countries	High-income countries	United States
Per capita gross national product†	$1,720	$380	$23,680	$24,740
Population growth rate	2.3%	1.9%	0.6%	1.0%
Population growth rate in urban areas	3.2%	3.9%	0.8%	1.3%
Population per square kilometer of land	52	78	25	26
Life expectancy in years	68	62	77	76
Number of people per physician	1,537	>3,300	453	419
Number of pupils per teacher (primary school)	26	39	<18	20
Illiteracy rate (15 years and older)	35%	41%	<5%	<3%
Energy consumed per capita (kg of oil equivalent)	576	364	5,203	7,918

† The gross national product (GNP) is the total dollar value of all goods and services produced by a country in a year. The per capita GNP is calculated by dividing a country's GNP by its population. The World Bank defines low-income countries as those with a per capita GNP of $695 or less. High-income countries have a per capita GNP of $8,626 or more. Less than 14% of the world's 5.5 billion people live in high-income countries, while almost 60% live in low-income countries.

n.a. = data not available   > = greater than   < = less than

Sources: World Bank, *Social Indicators of Development 1995,* Baltimore: Johns Hopkins University Press, 1995. Central Intelligence Agency, *World Fact Book,* Washington, D.C.: Government Printing Office, 1994.

materials, and agricultural and industrial equipment. Textiles are now the largest component of both exports and imports. By 1991, textiles' share of total exports expanded to 35%, and of imports to 21%. Western Europe is the focus of Tunisia's foreign trade, and its largest trading partner is France.

27 ENERGY AND POWER

Petroleum reserves were estimated at 1,700 million barrels in 1992; total production in 1992 was reported as 5,189,000 tons. Natural gas plant liquids production totaled 5,000 barrels per day in 1992. Since 1962, the government-owned Tunisian Electric and Gas Company has controlled all electrical power. Electricity production in 1991 was 5,555 million kilowatt hours, with 99% of the total supplied by conventional thermal plants.

28 SOCIAL DEVELOPMENT

The Agricultural Labor Code of 20 April 1956 grants agricultural workers family allowances and old age pensions. During 1960–64, the government instituted a social security system to which both employers and workers contribute. It is administered by the National Social Security Fund, which provides benefits including maternity payments, family allowances, disability and life insurance, and old age insurance. Polygamy was prohibited in 1957, and Tunisian women enjoy full civil and political rights under the law.

29 HEALTH

Health conditions have shown significant improvement in recent years, although diet and sanitation remain deficient. Epidemics have virtually disappeared, and the incidence of contagious diseases has been considerably reduced. Average life expectancy was 68 years in 1992. There are an estimated 65 doctors per 100,000 people. In the same year, there were 12 hospital beds per 1,000 people. Free health services are available to about 70% of the population, with about 90% of the population having access to health care services in 1992. Total expenditures in 1990 for health care were $614 million.

30 HOUSING

The natural increase of population, augmented by the migration of rural dwellers to urban areas, has caused serious housing problems. Squatter communities, called gourbvilles, have sprung up in urban regions. The rate of housing construction lags far behind the need.

As of 1984, 71% of housing units were traditional structures, or "dar," 14% were "villas" (detached homes), 9% were the squatter homes called "gourli," and 5% were apartments. Housing construction

for 1993 was projected at approximately 40,100 units, up from 38,600 units in 1992.

31 EDUCATION

In 1984, almost all school-age boys and 87% of eligible girls attended school; the proportions for secondary schools, however, were only 37% of boys and 26% of girls. Arabic is the language of instruction in early primary grades but is later replaced by French. In 1991, there were 1,426,215 students and 54,013 teachers in 3,971 primary schools; there were 589,674 pupils and 34,808 instructors in secondary institutions. The University of Tunis was founded on 31 March 1960. Tunisians studying at foreign universities numbered about 10,000 in 1985. All higher level institutions in 1991 had 76,097 students and 4,941 instructors. The 1990 adult literacy rate was 65%. Of this rate, men were estimated at 74.2% and women at 56.3%.

32 MEDIA

Tunisia's well-developed postal, telephone, and telegraph system is government-operated and links all the important cities. In 1991, there were 333,185 telephones. The government-owned Tunisian Radio-Television Broadcasting (ERTT) broadcasts in Arabic, French, and Italian. There are four television channels, and a fifth was being set up in Sfax in 1993. In 1991, there were an estimated 1,640,000 radios and 650,000 television sets in use. The leading daily newspapers, with 1991 circula-

An artisan's ornate pots and whimsical figures on display at a local market.

tions, were *As-Sabah* (70,000), *Le Temps* (42,000), and *La Presse* (40,000).

33 TOURISM AND RECREATION

Tourism is Tunisia's leading net earner of money from abroad. Hotel rooms numbered 61,594 in 1991, and the occupancy rate was 37.6 percent. In 1991, 3,224,015 visitors went to Tunisia, 1,086,564 from Europe and 911,836 from Africa. Tourist expenditures reached $685 million that year. Tunisia's cosmopolitan capital city, Tunis, the ruins of Carthage, and the modern coastal resorts in the vicinity of Monastir are among the main tourist attractions.

34 FAMOUS TUNISIANS

Ancient Carthage was located near the site of modern Tunis. Its most famous leader was Hannibal (247–183 BC), the general who campaigned in Italy for several years (218–211 BC) but who was defeated by the Romans under Scipio Africanus at Zama in 202 BC. The dominant figure of modern Tunisia is Habib Bourguiba (Habib bin 'Ali ar-Rugaybah, b.1903); he led Tunisia to independence, formed its first government, and was president from 1957 to 1987. Mongi Slim (1908–69) served as president of the 16th session of the UN General Assembly (1961–62). Gen. Zine el 'Abidine Ben 'Ali (b.1936) assumed the presidency in 1987.

Tunisia's noteworthy literary figures include Albert Memmi (b.1915), the author of *The Statue of Salt* (1957), who writes in French; and Mahmoud Messadi (b.1911), who writes in Arabic. Prominent Tunisian painters are Ammar Farhat (b.1911) and Jallah bin 'Abdallah (b.1921).

35 BIBLIOGRAPHY

Fox, M. *Tunisia*. Chicago: Children's Press, 1990.

Nelson, Harold D., ed. *Tunisia: A Country Study*. 3d ed. Washington, D.C.: Dept. of the Army, 1988.

Perkins, Kenneth J. *Historical Dictionary of Tunisia*. Metuchen, N.J.: Scarecrow Press, 1989.

Salem, Norma. *Habib Bourguiba, Islam, and the Creation of Tunisia*. Wolfeboro, N.H.: Longwood, 1984.

TURKEY

Republic of Turkey

Türkiye Cumhuriyeti

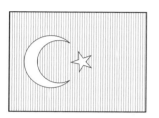

CAPITAL: Ankara.

FLAG: The national flag consists of a white crescent (open toward the fly) and a white star on a red field.

ANTHEM: *Istiklâl Marşi (March of Independence).*

MONETARY UNIT: The Turkish lira (TL) is a paper currency of 100 kuruş. There are coins of 1, 5, 10, 20, 25, 50, and 100 liras, and notes of 5,000, 10,000, 20,000, 50,000, 100,000, 250,000, and 500,000 liras. TL1 = $0.000045 (or $1 = TL22,159.8).

WEIGHTS AND MEASURES: The metric system is the legal standard.

HOLIDAYS: New Year's Day, 1 January; National Sovereignty and Children's Day, 23 April; Spring Day, 1 May; Youth and Sports Day, 19 May; Victory Day, 30 August; Independence Day (Anniversary of the Republic), 29 October. Movable religious holidays include Şeker Bayrami (three days) and Kurban Bayrami (four days).

TIME: 3 PM = noon GMT.

1 LOCATION AND SIZE

The Republic of Turkey consists of Asia Minor, the small area of eastern Turkey in Europe, and a few offshore islands in the Aegean Sea. It has a total area of 780,580 square kilometers (301,384 square miles), which is slightly larger than the state of Texas. Turkey has a total boundary length of 9,827 kilometers (6,106 miles). Its capital city, Ankara, is located in the northwest part of the country.

2 TOPOGRAPHY

Turkey consists of the low, rolling hills of Turkish Thrace, the fertile river valleys that open to the Aegean Sea, the warm plains of Antalya and Adana on the Mediterranean, the narrow coastal region along the Black Sea, and the rugged mountain ranges that surround and intersect the high, desert-like Anatolian plateau. The highest point is Mount Ararat (Ağri Daği) at (5,165 meters (16,945 feet). Other than the Tigris and Euphrates, which have their sources in eastern Anatolia, rivers are relatively small.

Most of Turkey lies within an earthquake zone, and recurrent tremors are recorded. The record destructive earthquake was that of 29 December 1939 which killed 30,000 persons.

3 CLIMATE

The mean temperature range on Turkey's southern and Aegean coasts is 17–20°C (63–68°F), and the annual rainfall ranges from 71 to 109 centimeters (28–43 inches). The Black Sea coast is also relatively mild (14–15°C/57–59°F) and very moist, with 71–249 centimeters (28–98 in) of rainfall. On the central Anatolian plateau the average annual temperature is 8–12°C (46–54°F), and annual precipitation is 30–75 centimeters (12–30 inches). The eastern third of Turkey is colder (4–9°C / 39–48°F), and rainfall averages 41–51 centimeters (16–20 inches).

4 PLANTS AND ANIMALS

Evergreens are found in the mountains of southern, southwestern, and northern Turkey. Licorice, valonia oaks, and wild olive trees grow in the southwest. Principal varieties of wild animals are wild boar, hare, Turkish leopard, brown bear, red fox, gazelle, beech marten, pine marten, wildcat, lynx, otter, badger, and several species of deer. There is a large variety of birds, including the snow partridge, quail, great bustard, little bustard, widgeon, woodcock, snipe, and a variety of geese, ducks, pigeons, and rails. Bees and silkworms are grown commercially.

5 ENVIRONMENT

Among Turkey's principal environmental problems is air pollution in Ankara and other cities. The nation's rivers are polluted with industrial chemicals; among them, mercury has created a serious threat. Soil erosion affects both coastal and internal areas.

In 1994, five of Turkey's mammal species and 18 of its bird species were endangered. Eighteen types of plants were threatened with extinction.

6 POPULATION

According to the 1990 census, Turkey's population was 56,473,035. A popula-

tion of 68,165,000 was projected for the year 2000. Population density is about 75 persons per square kilometer (194 persons per square mile). Istanbul (formerly Constantinople), the largest city, had a 1990 population of 6,620,241.

7 MIGRATION

Much Turkish emigration has consisted of workers under contract for employment in European Community countries. Germany alone had 1,779,600 Turks at the end of 1991. There are also large numbers of Turks in prosperous Muslim countries such as Sa'udi Arabia, the Gulf states, and Libya. In 1985, 2,282,000 Turkish nationals were living abroad, and the number has grown since then.

8 ETHNIC GROUPS

About 85% of the population is Turkish. The major ethnic minority (by mother tongue), the Kurds, is estimated at 12% of the population. Arabs, Turkmen, Circassians, Greeks, and others make up about 3% of the population. Hundreds of thousands of Armenians were either killed or forced to flee Turkey during and immediately following World War I; bitterness between Armenians and Turks continues to this day.

9 LANGUAGES

Turkish, which belongs to the Ural-Altaic group, is the official language. A 1928 language reform substituted the Roman alphabet for the Arabic script, which had been used by the Turks since their conversion to Islam.

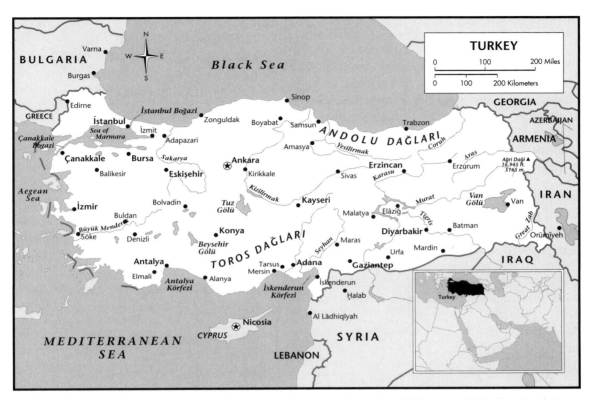

LOCATION: 25°40′ to 44°48′E; 35°51′ to 42°6′N. **BOUNDARY LENGTHS:** Armenia, 268 kilometers (167 miles); Azerbaijan, 9 kilometers (5 miles); Georgia, 252 kilometers (157 miles); Iran, 499 kilometers (311 miles); Iraq, 331 kilometers (206 miles); Syria, 822 kilometers (500 miles); Greece, 206 kilometers (128 miles); Bulgaria, 240 kilometers (150 miles); total coastline, 7,200 kilometers (4,482 miles). **TERRITORIAL SEA LIMIT:** 6 miles, Aegean Sea; 12 miles, Mediterranean and Black seas.

Kurdish is a language of the Iranian group and is written in Arabic script in Turkey. Two of the three major dialects are spoken in Turkey.

10 RELIGIONS

Although about 99% of the population is Muslim, there is no official state religion. The vast majority of Turkish Muslims are Sunni, but there is a substantial Shi'ite minority. In 1986, religious minorities included an estimated 100,000 Christians and 20,000 Jews.

11 TRANSPORTATION

Turkey's size and difficult terrain, together with limited economic resources, have proved great obstacles to the construction of transportation facilities. By 1991, 8,401 kilometers (5,217 miles) of railroad track connected most of the important points in the country with Ankara, Istanbul, and the Black Sea and Mediterranean ports. Railways carried 129.4 million passengers and 14.85 million tons of freight in 1991.

Animal transportation in most of the country has gradually given way to trucks and buses that use roads provided by extensive construction programs since World War II. As of 1991, 1,864,344 automobiles, 202,605 buses and minibuses, and 554,300 trucks, were registered. The Turkish merchant fleet in 1991 consisted of 347 vessels of all types totaling 4.08 million gross registered tons. The leading ports were Mersin, Istanbul, Izmir, Iskenderun, and Izmit.

Two international airports—Istanbul and Ankara—are served by some 20 international air carriers.

12 HISTORY

In ancient times, Turkey was known as Asia Minor or Anatolia. Among the many inhabitants were the Hittites (c.1800–c.1200 BC), the first people to use iron; the Greeks, who, according to legend, destroyed Troy (or Ilium) about 1200 BC; the Persians (546–333 BC); and the Romans, beginning in the second century BC.

Roman Emperor Constantine I (the Great) changed the name of the city of Byzantium to Constantinople (now Istanbul) and made it his capital in AD 330. Constantinople, seat of the Byzantine Empire, became the center of Eastern Orthodox Christianity, which officially separated from Roman Catholicism in 1054, when the pope and the patriarch of Constantinople excommunicated each other.

The forerunners of the inhabitants of present-day Turkey, known as the Seljuk Turks, defeated the Byzantines and attained a highly developed Muslim culture in their great capital at Konya, in central Turkey. The Turkish conquest of Syria, including Palestine, led to the Crusades (1096–1270), a series of inconclusive wars between various Christian and Muslim nations. The sack of the Christian city of Constantinople by Christian Crusaders in 1204, followed by the establishment of the Latin Kingdom there (1204–61), tended to discredit the Crusading movement.

The Ottoman Empire

Seljuk power was shattered when the Mongols swept across Asia Minor in 1243. As the Mongols withdrew, Turkish power revived and expanded under the Ottoman Turks, who conquered and occupied Constantinople in 1453 and made it their capital. At its peak, in the sixteenth century, the Ottoman Empire encompassed an estimated 28 million inhabitants and included Asia Minor, much of the Arabian Peninsula, part of North Africa, the islands of the eastern Mediterranean, the Balkans, the Caucasus, and the Crimea.

During the seventeenth, eighteenth, and nineteenth centuries, as a result of the rise of nationalism and competition by European powers, the Ottoman Empire gradually shrank in size. The Illustrious Rescript of 1856, which was part of the settlement of the Crimean War (1853–56)—a clash between the Russian and Ottoman Empires—ensured equal rights for non-

Muslims, provided for prison reform and the codification of Turkish laws, and opened Turkey to the West.

World War I

In 1913, leaders of the Committee for Union and Progress took effective control of the government under Sultan Mehmet V (r.1909–18) and, at the outbreak of World War I (1914–18), threw what little remained of Ottoman strength behind the Central Powers. Although the Turks were unable to make any headway against British forces defending the Suez Canal, they did offer a heroic defense at the famous battle of Gallipoli, which lasted from February 1915 to January 1916 and took the lives of about 100,000 soldiers on each side.

In 1917, Turkish resistance collapsed, and the British pushed Turkey out of Syria, Palestine, Iraq, and Arabia. An armistice was concluded on 30 October 1918. Before and during the war, Armenians sought to establish their independence and were brutally repressed by the Turks. Over a million people are said to have died, being driven from their homes, although many others survived in exile.

On the basis of a series of earlier Allied agreements, the Ottoman Empire was stripped of all non-Turkish areas, and much of what remained—Asia Minor—was divided among the United Kingdom, France, Greece, and Italy. On 1 November 1922, the sultanate was abolished by a provisional government led by Mustafa Kemal (later called Atatürk). On 29 October 1923, a republic was proclaimed, with

Photo credit: Susan D. Rock.

Ruins of the Library of Celcus located in the ancient city of Ephesus.

Ankara as its capital, and on 3 March 1924, the caliphate was abolished and all members of the dynasty banished.

Post-WWI Reforms

During the next few years, a series of social, legal, and political reforms were accomplished that became known as the Atatürk Reforms. They included the substitution of secular law for religious law, the writing of a republican constitution based on popular sovereignty, suppression of religious education in Turkish schools, introduction of a Roman alphabet to replace the Arabic script, and the legal upgrading of the position of women. With minor exceptions, political power resided in a single party, the Republican People's Party, and to a very substantial extent in Mustafa Kemal personally, until his death in 1938.

World War II

Turkey remained neutral during most of World War II (1939–45), but early in 1945 it declared war on the Axis and became a charter member of the United Nations. After the war, Turkey became firmly committed to the Western alliances—the North Atlantic Treaty Organization (NATO) and the Central Treaty Organization, or CENTO (Baghdad Pact).

The Democrat Party, which came to power in 1950, stressed rapid industrialization and economic expansion at the cost of individual liberties. By 1960, the Menderes government had restricted judicial independence, university autonomy, and the rights of opposition parties. On 27 May 1960, Prime Minister Menderes and other government leaders were arrested by a newly formed Committee of National Unity.

General Cemal Gürsel became acting president and prime minister and was later elected president by the New Grand National Assembly under a new constitution. The opposition Justice Party (JP) gained control of the government from 1965 until 1971, when it was ousted by the military. Martial law was imposed from June to September 1970, and reimposed from 1971 to 1973.

The Stuggle for Cyprus

A succession of weak coalition governments, headed alternately by Süleyman Demirel and Republican leader Bülent Ecevit, held office between 1973 and 1980.

Ecevit's government was in power during the Greco-Turkish war on Cyprus in July–August 1974. On 15 July, Cypriot President Makarios was overthrown. Fearing the island would be united with Greece, Turkish forces invaded on 20 July. A United Nations cease-fire came into effect two days later, but after peace talks at Geneva broke down, Turkish troops consolidated their hold over the northern third of the island by 16 August. As the result of this action, the United States embargoed shipments of arms to Turkey until 1978; as of 1994, an estimated 25,000 or more Turkish troops remained on Cyprus to support the Turkish Republic of Northern Cyprus, which only Turkey recognizes.

Maintaining Democracy

During the late 1970s, escalating acts of violence by political groups of the extreme left and right, coupled with economic decline, threatened the stability of Turkey's fragile democracy. A five-man military National Security Council (NSC), headed by General Kenan Evren, took power in a bloodless coup on 12 September 1980, imposed martial law, and arrested thousands of suspected terrorists.

In a national referendum on 7 November 1982, Turkish voters overwhelmingly approved a new constitution under which

General Evren became president of the republic for a seven-year term. Following parliamentary elections in 1983, Jurgut Özal, leader of the victorious Motherland Party, was installed as prime minister.

Özal's Motherland Party retained its parliamentary majority in November 1987 elections, and, in 1989, Özal was elected president. His ambition was to tie Turkey closely to Europe but, despite improvements in Turkey's human rights record, its application for full membership in the European Union was deferred indefinitely. During the Gulf War, he joined the embargo against Iraq, closed Iraq's oil pipelines, provided facilities for allied air raids, and later supported protective measures for Iraqi Kurds. In compensation, Turkey received increased Western aid worth $300 million.

Former prime minister Demeral succeeded to the presidency in May 1993, following the 1991 electoral victory of his the True Path and Social Democratic Party coalition, and the death of Özal. Tansu Ciller, True Path chairperson, became Turkey's first female Prime Minister in July 1993.

In 1994, Ciller faced three major tasks: dealing with the problems of high inflation (about 70%) and unemployment, and reducing government regulations; pacifying the rebellious Kurdish areas of eastern Turkey, where large numbers of troops have been tied down in a conflict that has taken thousands of lives; as well as responding to the rising challenge to Turkey's secular nationalism from politically militant Islamic groups.

13 GOVERNMENT

The constitution ratified in November 1982 declares Turkey to be a democratic and secular republic. It vests executive powers in the president of the republic and the Council of Ministers. Legislative functions are delegated to the single-chamber National Assembly, consisting of 400 members elected for five-year terms.

The chief administrative official in each of Turkey's 73 provinces (*vilayets* or *ils*) is the provincial governor (*vali*).

14 POLITICAL PARTIES

Since the 1991 elections, a coalition of the True Path Party (Dogru Yol Partisi—DYP) and the Social Democratic Populist Party (Sosyal Demokrasi Halkçi Partisi—SDHP) has been in power, having defeated the Motherland Party (Anatavan Partisi—ANAP). Outside the established political system are the Kurdistan Workers Party (PKK) and other smaller separatist parties that have been banned.

15 JUDICIAL SYSTEM

There are four branches of courts: civil, administrative, military, and constitutional. Civil courts are specialized into five sections: civil, enforcement, criminal, commercial, and labor. Decisions of civil courts are appealable to a High Court of Appeals in Ankara.

Administrative courts include courts of first instance, regional appeals courts, and a Council of State at the top. The Military Courts have jurisdiction over military personnel. The Constitutional Court reviews the constitutionality of legislation at the time of passage.

The constitution guarantees defendants the right to a public trial. The bar association is responsible for providing free counsel to indigent defendants. There is no jury system.

16 ARMED FORCES

The total armed forces strength in 1993 was 560,300 (including 481,000 draftees), plus 1.1 million reserves. The army had 450,000 men (410,000 draftees) in 5 infantry divisions (1 mechanized), 7 armored brigades, and 18 infantry divisions (1 mechanized), 7 armored brigades, and 18 independent specialized brigades.

The navy had 52,300 personnel. Naval strength included 2 submarines, 12 destroyers, 8 frigates, 47 patrol and coastal combatants, 37 mine warfare vessels, and about 35 auxiliary ships. The defense budget for 1992 was $5.2 billion. An estimated 30,000 Turkish soldiers were stationed on Cyprus.

17 ECONOMY

Continued high population growth and income gaps between the rich and poor have left much of the population unaffected by economic growth. Between 1988 and 1993, the annual rate of inflation was always in the 60–70% range.

Since the end of World War II, agriculture's share of the economy has declined, while that of industry (including construction) and services has expanded. This shift in economic activity is in part the result of deliberate government policy. In early

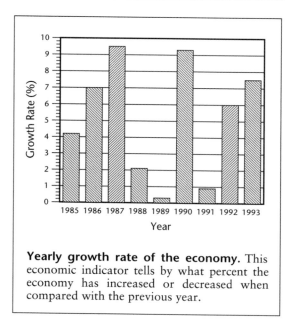

Yearly growth rate of the economy. This economic indicator tells by what percent the economy has increased or decreased when compared with the previous year.

1994, the lira was devalued, leading to even higher inflation.

18 INCOME

In 1992, Turkey's gross national product (GNP) was $114,234 million at current prices. The average national income is about $2,970 per person. For the period 1985–92, the average inflation rate was about 60%, resulting in a real growth rate in per person GNP of 3%.

19 INDUSTRY

The textile industry, the largest industrial unit in Turkey next to petroleum refineries, is centered in Izmir, Istanbul, Adana, and Kayseri. Major industrial complexes include a government-owned iron and steel mill. The sugar-beet industry ranks first among food-processing industries and

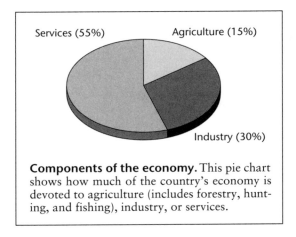

Services (55%)   Agriculture (15%)

Industry (30%)

Components of the economy. This pie chart shows how much of the country's economy is devoted to agriculture (includes forestry, hunting, and fishing), industry, or services.

produces more than domestic consumption requires.

Textile enterprises in 1992 produced 180 million meters of cotton and wool fabrics. Other industrial commodities in 1992 (in thousands of tons) included coke, 3,252; steel castings, 10,343; crude iron, 4,508; cement, 28,560; sugar, 1,572; and newsprint, 119. Selected consumer items produced in 1992 were home refrigerators, 1,093,776; washing machines, 870,888; sewing machines, 197,100; television receivers, 2,320,464; and passenger cars, 265,092. Output of petroleum products (in thousands of tons) included gasoline, 2,946; kerosene, 150; fuel oil, 8,441; and motor oil, 6,565.

20 LABOR

Of the total civilian labor force of 20,319,000 in 1992, 18,700,000 persons were employed. Of these, 44% worked in agriculture (including forestry and fishing); while the industrial labor force amounted to 18% of the working popula-

tion. The unemployment rate was 7.8% in 1992, down from 8.2% in 1991.

A detailed labor code administered by the Ministry of Labor controls many aspects of labor-management relations. In 1992, there were 98 strikes, with 62,189 workers involved and 1,53,578 workdays lost.

Use of child labor appears to be fairly widespread, despite existing laws, although the government has lately increased its number of inspectors.

21 AGRICULTURE

Wheat is the principal crop, accounting for 66% of total grain production in 1992. In that same year, 19,318,000 tons of wheat were grown, followed by barley with 6,900,000 tons. Turkey also produced 14,800,000 tons of sugar beets and about 3,460,000 tons of grapes. Other agricultural products were grown in lesser but still important quantities in 1992: maize, 2,100,000 tons; sunflower seeds, 950,000 tons; cotton, 605,000 tons; and oranges, 420,000 tons.

Turkish tobacco is world famous for its lightness and mildness. Tobacco represented 9% of total agricultural exports in 1992 and 2% of all Turkish exports that same year (versus 6% in 1982). Some 320,000 tons of tobacco were produced in 1992. Other crops of commercial importance include olives (950,000 tons in 1992), tea (142,000 tons), fruits, nuts, and vegetable oil. Turkey usually leads the world in the production and export of hazelnuts (about 520,000 tons produced in 1992) and pistachio nuts, and as of

1991 also ranks first (ahead of the United States) in the production of raisins.

22 DOMESTICATED ANIMALS

Many animals are used for transport and draft purposes as well as to supply meat and dairy products. The principal animals of commercial importance are mohair goats and sheep. The sheep wool is used mainly for blankets and carpets, and Turkey is a leading producer of mohair.

In 1992 there were 51.1 million sheep and goats, 11.9 million head of cattle, and 139 million hens and roosters. Production of wool was estimated at 42,000 tons in 1992. Other livestock products included milk, 6.1 million tons; meat, 1,009,000 tons; and hen eggs, 390,000 tons. Turkey produced some 55,000 tons of honey in 1992, fourth in the world after China, the United States, and Mexico.

23 FISHING

The total ocean catch by Turkey's deep-sea fishermen was 317,424 tons in 1991, most of it tuna and sardines. In addition, 47,216 tons of freshwater fish were caught.

24 FORESTRY

Forests occupy 20,199,000 hectares (49,913,000 acres), or 26% of Turkey's total area. Roundwood production in 1991 included 26,000 cubic meters of sawnwood, and 781,000 cubic meters of wood-based panels. Other forestry products were firewood, 9,796,000 cubic meters; wood pulp, 96,000 tons; and paper and paperboard, 833,000 tons.

Photo credit: Corel Corporation.

Market day in Kas, a city along the Mediterranean coast.

25 MINING

Turkey has a wide variety of known minerals, but its resources are only partially developed. Among the minerals actively exploited and marketed are copper, chromite, iron ore, sulfur, pyrite, manganese, mercury, lead, zinc, barite, and meerschaum. Production of chrome ores and concentrates in 1991 fell to about 652,000 tons. Iron ore output increased to a reported 3,942,254 tons in 1991.

Other minerals produced in 1991 (in thousands of tons) were lignite, 46,029; boron minerals, 1,815; sulfur, 135; and strontium, 65. Eskişehir, in northwestern

Selected Social Indicators

These statistics are estimates for the period 1988 to 1993. For comparison purposes, data for the United States and averages for low-income countries and high-income countries are also given.

Indicator	Turkey	Low-income countries	High-income countries	United States
Per capita gross national product†	$2,970	$380	$23,680	$24,740
Population growth rate	2.1%	1.9%	0.6%	1.0%
Population growth rate in urban areas	4.5%	3.9%	0.8%	1.3%
Population per square kilometer of land	75	78	25	26
Life expectancy in years	67	62	77	76
Number of people per physician	983	>3,300	453	419
Number of pupils per teacher (primary school)	29	39	<18	20
Illiteracy rate (15 years and older)	12%	41%	<5%	<3%
Energy consumed per capita (kg of oil equivalent)	983	364	5,203	7,918

† The gross national product (GNP) is the total dollar value of all goods and services produced by a country in a year. The per capita GNP is calculated by dividing a country's GNP by its population. The World Bank defines low-income countries as those with a per capita GNP of $695 or less. High-income countries have a per capita GNP of $8,626 or more. Less than 14% of the world's 5.5 billion people live in high-income countries, while almost 60% live in low-income countries.

> = greater than   < = less than

Sources: World Bank, *Social Indicators of Development 1995*, Baltimore: Johns Hopkins University Press, 1995. Central Intelligence Agency, *World Fact Book*, Washington, D.C.: Government Printing Office, 1994.

Anatolia, is the world center of meerschaum, and Turkey is famous for its meerschaum pipes. Production has fallen in recent years from the 1989 level of 10,350 kilograms to 2,800 kilograms in 1991.

26 FOREIGN TRADE

The principal exports in 1992 were apparel and textiles, and fruits and vegetables. The principal imports were machinery, fuel, chemicals, and vehicles. In 1992, European Community countries supplied about 44% of Turkey's imports and received about 52% of its exports. Islamic countries of the Middle East and North Africa accounted for approximately 15% of Turkey's total imports and 19% of its exports.

27 ENERGY AND POWER

Turkey provides about 60% of its own energy needs overall; but in recent years, it has had to import several times as much petroleum as it produced. In 1992, output of coal totaled 50.6 million tons (89% soft coal). In 1991, production of crude oil came to a reported 4.3 million tons, while consumption totaled 22.1 million tons that year.

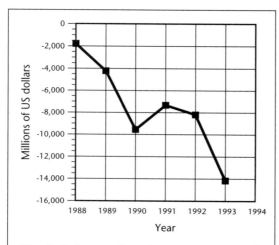

Yearly balance of trade measured in millions of US dollars. The balance of trade is the difference between what a country sells to other countries (its exports) and what it buys (its imports). If a country imports more than it exports, it has a negative balance of trade (a trade deficit). If exports exceed imports there is a positive balance of trade (a trade surplus).

Hydroelectric and thermal power plants in 1991 produced 60,338 million kilowatt hours of electricity (38% hydro). Of the total electrical output in 1991, lignite-burning plants accounted for 34%; natural gas, 21%; fuel oil, 5.5%; and hard coal, 2%.

28 SOCIAL DEVELOPMENT

Since 1936, various forms of social security have been introduced, all administered by the Social Insurance Institution, and which include industrial accident and disease, old age, sickness, disability, and maternity insurance. In some localities, the social insurance organization operates its own hospitals and other facilities. The social organization, Bağ-kur, pays monthly benefits to artisans, craftsmen, and other self-employed workers. Government workers are covered by the Government Employees Retirement Fund.

The Turkish government has supported family-planning services within the context of an integrated maternal and child health program.

29 HEALTH

Free medical treatment, given at state hospitals or health centers, is provided by the state to any Turkish citizen who obtains a certificate of financial need from a local administrator. In 1992, there were 941 hospitals with 139,606 beds (2.4 per 1,000 people). In 1990, the Ministry of Health employed 23,254 doctors (0.9 per 1,000 people) with a further 17,750 in other public institutions. Total health care expenditures for 1990 were $4.281 billion.

Malaria, cholera, and trachoma have been effectively controlled by large-scale public preventive measures. Average life expectancy was 67 years in 1992. Between 1984–92, there were approximately 5,000 war-related deaths in the Kurd rebellion.

30 HOUSING

A traditional village house consists of sun-dried brick (adobe) or rough-hewn stone walls across which are laid timbers piled with brush and then topped with packed earth. The flat roof is often used for storage of feed grain. Urban housing varies from houses similar to those in villages to modern, centrally heated apartment buildings.

In the period 1981–85, 305,890 new residential buildings containing 929,104 apartments were completed; virtually all these apartments had electricity, piped water, kitchens, and baths. As of 1985, 71% of all housing units were detached houses, 23% were apartments, and 6% were squatters' houses. Under 1% were marginal dwellings.

31 EDUCATION

In 1990, the literacy rate was about 88%; 89% for males and 71.1% for females. Primary, secondary, and much of higher education is free. Education is compulsory for children aged 6 to 14 or until graduation from primary school (grade 5). However, owing to the inadequate number and distribution of schools and teachers, only about two-thirds of the children of primary-school age attend school. Secondary schooling is for six years.

The regular school system consists of five-year primary schools, three-year junior high schools, and three-year high schools. Parallel to this system is a variety of technical, trade, and commercial schools. Among private schools in operation are a number of foreign schools, and those maintained by ethnic or religious minorities. Among Turkey's 28 universities are the universities of Istanbul (founded 1453) and Ankara (founded 1946), the Technical University of Istanbul (founded 1773), and the Middle East Technical University at Ankara (founded 1957).

In 1991, there were 50,669 primary schools, with 234,961 teachers and 6,878,923 students. In 1991, enrollment in all secondary-level schools was 3,987,423 students, with 170,611 teachers. Of these, 12,607 students and 1,116 teachers were enrolled or teaching at teacher training schools, and 976,916 students and 54,999 teachers were from vocational schools. The universities and other public higher institutions had 810,781 students and 35,123 faculty members that same year.

32 MEDIA

Postal, telephone, and telegraph service is owned and operated by a semi-independent government enterprise under the jurisdiction of the Ministry of Transport and Communications. Telephones in 1991 numbered about 7,467,151. The state operates AM and FM radio stations and television broadcasting. The number of radio sets in 1991 was 9,200,000; and registered television sets numbered 10,000,000.

Although the 1982 constitution guarantees freedom of expression, it also authorizes newspaper confiscations and closures in the cases of crimes against the unity, security, or republican principles of the state. After the 1980 coup, the military government, which had placed control of the press in the provincial martial law administrators, repeatedly closed down newspapers it claimed had published material damaging to the national interest. The independent leftist Istanbul daily *Cumhuriyet* (1991 circulation, 76,300) has been closed a number of times. Other leading Istanbul dailies (with 1991 circulation figures) are *Sabah* (737,000), *Hurriyet* (588,200), *Milliyet* (396,400), *Bugun* (228,000), and *Turkiye* (160,200).

33 TOURISM AND RECREATION

In 1991, 5,517,897 visitors arrived in Turkey, including 14% from Germany, 13% from the former Soviet Union, and 9% from Romania. Tourism receipts totaled $2.6 billion. There were 94,383 hotel rooms with a 37% occupancy rate.

In addition to the museums and monuments of Istanbul, places of interest include the Aegean port of Izmir, the ancient cities of Troy (Ilium), Ephesus, Tarsus, Konya, Samsun, Erzurum, and Trabzon; Mt. Ararat (Ağri Daği), traditionally considered the landing place of Noah's Ark, the remains of which some expeditions have tried to find; the ski resort of Uludağ, 36 kilometers (22 miles) south of Bursa; and the sea resort of Antalya, on the Mediterranean coast.

Water sports, mountaineering, and football (soccer) are popular forms of recreation, as are such traditional Turkish sports as grease wrestling (yağli güreş), camel fighting (deve güreşi), and a horseback javelin competition (cirit oyonu) played mainly in eastern Turkey.

34 FAMOUS TURKS

The most famous rulers before the coming of the Turks were Croesus (r.560–546 BC), a king of Lydia noted for his wealth and for the loss of his kingdom to the Persians; Constantine I (the Great; Flavius Valerius Aurelius Constantinus, b.Moesia, AD 280?–337), the first Roman emperor to accept Christianity and to use Constantinople as a capital; and Justinian I (the Great).

Twentieth-century leaders include Enver Paşa (1881–1922), a Young Turk leader who was the ruler of Turkey during World War I; and Mustafa Kemal Atatürk (1881–1938), a World War I military commander, nationalist leader, and first president of the republic.

Outstanding religious figures include Haci Bektaş Veli (1242–1337), founder of the Bektashi dervishes. Revered literary figures include the mystical poets Yunus Emre (1238?–1320?) and Süleyman Çelebi (d.1422), author of *Mevlidi Sherif (Birth Song of the Prophet)*.

Sinasi (1826–71), a dramatist, journalist, and essayist, was the first Turkish writer in the Western tradition. The poet Ziya Paşa (1825–80) was the outstanding literary figure of the reform period. Significant contemporary novelists include Halide Edib Adivar (1884–1966) and Yasar Kemal Gokceli (b.1922).

35 BIBLIOGRAPHY

Ahmad, Feroz. *The Making of Modern Turkey*. New York: Routledge, 1993.

Allen, Thomas B. "Turkey Struggles for Balance." *National Geographic*, May 1994, 2–36.

Palmer, Alan Warwick. *The Decline and Fall of the Ottoman Empire*. New York: M. Evans, 1993.

Pitman, Paul M., ed. *Turkey: A Country Study*. 4th ed. Washington, D.C.: Library of Congress, 1988.

Shaw, Stanford J., and Ezel Kural. *History of the Ottoman Empire and Modern Turkey*. 2 vols. Cambridge, England: Cambridge University Press, 1977.

Zurcher, Erik Jan. *Turkey: A Modern History*. New York: I.B. Tauris, 1993.

TURKMENISTAN

Republic of Turkmenstan

Туркменистан

Turkmenistan

CAPITAL: Ashgabat (Ashkhabad).

FLAG: Green field with claret stripe of five carpet patterns; white crescent and five white stars symbolizing five major conditions of life on earth—light, sound, sense of smell, sense of touch, and sense of balance—to the right of the stripe.

ANTHEM: *Independence Turkmenistan.*

MONETARY UNIT: Manat, the unit of currency, was introduced by the government in November 1993. As of fall 1994, 60 manat = $1, but exchange rates are likely to fluctuate widely.

WEIGHTS AND MEASURES: The metric system is used.

HOLIDAYS: Independence Day, 27 October.

TIME: 5 PM = noon GMT.

1 LOCATION AND SIZE

Located in southern Asia, bordering the Caspian Sea between Iran and Uzbekistan, Turkmenistan is slightly larger than the state of California, with a total area of 488,100 square kilometers (188,456 square miles). Its boundary length totals 3,736 kilometers (2,322 miles).

Turkmenistan's capital city, Ashgabat (Ashkhabad), is located in the central part of the country.

2 TOPOGRAPHY

The topography features flat to rolling desert with dunes to the Caspian Sea.

3 CLIMATE

The mean temperature is 28°C (82°F) in July and –4°C (25°F) in January. Daytime temperatures of 122°F in the Garagum desert are not unusual. Rainfall averages 25 centimeters (9.8 inches) a year.

4 PLANTS AND ANIMALS

The Garagum desert covers 90% of the country, and there is little plant or animal life. Herders raise goats, camels, and sheep in the desert.

5 ENVIRONMENT

The most significant environmental problems in Turkmenistan include salt in the soil and water pollution. The nation's water supply is threatened by chemical contaminants from farming and by the lack of adequate sewage treatment plants.

6 POPULATION

The population of Turkmenistan was estimated at 4,075,316 in 1995. A population of 4,479,000 was projected for 2000. The estimated population density in 1995 was 8 persons per square kilometer (22 per square mile). Ashgabat (Ashkhabad), the capital, had an estimated population of 517,200 at the end of 1992.

7 MIGRATION

Emigration to other former Soviet Union republics exceeded immigration by 20,600 during 1979–90. More than 40,000 people fled from Tajikistan to Turkmenistan in 1992 to escape civil war.

8 ETHNIC GROUPS

In 1989, 72% of the population consisted of Turkmens (or Turkomans). Some 9.5% were Russians, 9% Uzbeks, and 2.5% Kazakhs. Like the Turkmens, the Uzbeks and Kazakhs are Turkic-speaking peoples.

9 LANGUAGES

Turkmen is mandatory in the schools. It is a Turkic language of the Oghez group. Russian remains in common use in government and business.

10 RELIGIONS

The population is primarily Sunni Muslim, with strong elements of local Shamanism and Sufi mysticism included in its practices.

11 TRANSPORTATION

Nebit-Dag, Ashgabat (Ashkhabad), Mary, and Chardzhou are connected by railroad to the nation's main port of Krasnovodsk on the Caspian Sea. In 1990, there were some 23,000 kilometers (14,283 miles) of highways, of which 80% were hard-surfaced.

12 HISTORY

The territory of present-day Turkmenistan has been inhabited since the Stone Age, with evidence of agricultural communities as early as 6000 BC. The region was conquered by Alexander the Great at the end of the fourth century BC. Arabs invaded in 716 AD, and began to introduce Islam. Turks first entered Turkmenistan in the ninth century and took control in 1040. The entire region was conquered by Mongols in 1219–1221, and Turkmenistan came under the control of various kingdoms for several hundred years.

Russia began to make commercial contacts with the Turkmens as early as the sixteenth century; by the eighteenth century, almost all trade between Europe and Central Asia passed through Turkmenistan. Between 1865 and 1885, Russia annexed the region, which was the last portion of the Russian Empire to be conquered.

Turkmen remained in general rebellion throughout the period of the Russian Bolshevik revolution and civil war. Muslim and nationalist opposition resisted the Bolsheviks until 1924, when the area was made part of the Trans-Caspian Republic. In 1925, the present-day territory became a Soviet Socialist Republic.

Throughout the Soviet period, Turkmenistan was among the poorest and least assimilated of the republics. In October 1990, when Turkmenistan became independent, Sapamurat Niyazov, appointed

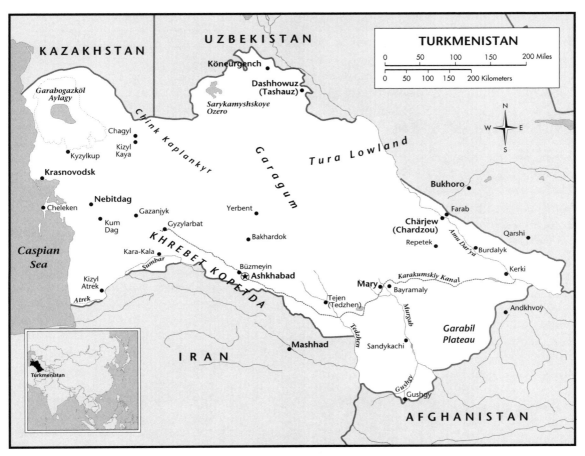

LOCATION: 40°0′N; 60°0′E. **BOUNDARY LENGTHS:** Total boundary lengths, 3,736 kilometers (2,322 miles); Afghanistan, 744 kilometers (462.3 miles); Iran, 992 kilometers (616.4 miles); Kazakhstan, 379 kilometers (236 miles); Uzbekistan, 1,621 kilometers (1007.3 miles).

during the Gorbachev regime, was elected president by the republic's Supreme Soviet. Turkmenistan declared independence on 27 October 1991.

13 GOVERNMENT

The executive branch of government is the responsibility of a prime minister and his cabinet. The legislative branch comprises two bodies, a 50-member Majlis, or Assembly, and the Halk Maslahaty, or People's Council. Although Turkmenistan is officially a democratic republic, in fact the republic is strictly controlled by its president, Sapamurat Niyazov.

There are five large regional subdivisions called velayets. Beneath these are shekhers, then etraps, then ovs.

14 POLITICAL PARTIES

The only legally registered party in the republic is the Democratic Party of Turkmenistan, which is what the Communist Party renamed itself in September 1991.

15 JUDICIAL SYSTEM

There are 61 district and city courts, 6 provincial courts, and a Supreme Court. There are also military courts and a Supreme Economic Court which hears cases involving disputes between business enterprises and ministries.

16 ARMED FORCES

A Russian air-ground force of 34,000 is under joint control with Turkmenistan. The government has organized a Republic Security Force and National Guard for law enforcement.

17 ECONOMY

Although Turkmenistan boasts rich mineral deposits, including oil, gas, potassium, sulfur, and salts, per person net material product (NMP) was only 60% of the average Soviet republic's production in the late 1980s, and Turkmenistan's social welfare indicators are among the lowest in the former Soviet Union.

18 INCOME

In 1992, Turkmenistan's gross national product (GNP) was $4,895 million at current prices, or about $1,390 per person. For the period 1985–92 the average annual inflation rate was 13.2%.

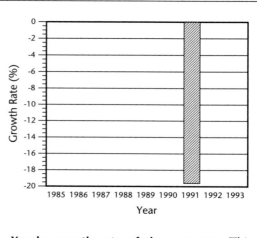

Yearly growth rate of the economy. This economic indicator tells by what percent the economy has increased or decreased when compared with the previous year.

19 INDUSTRY

In 1992, total industrial output declined by 15%. Food processing (especially meat and dairy processing), construction materials, and electricity generation accounted for 14%, 6%, and 5%, respectively, of total industrial output value in 1991. Turkmen carpets are known worldwide for their quality. In 1991, 1.38 million square meters of carpets and tapestry were produced.

20 LABOR

Of an estimated 2.2 million inhabitants of working age in 1991, agriculture engaged 43%; personal services, 26%; manufacturing, mining, and utilities, 11%; construction, 10%; trade, 6%; and other sectors,

4%. Minimum age laws regulate the use of child labor.

21 AGRICULTURE

Cotton is the main crop. Reported cotton production in 1992 ranges from 395,000 to 1.4 million tons. In 1992, reports of wheat production ranged from 400,000 to 470,000 tons.

22 DOMESTICATED ANIMALS

The livestock population in 1992 included sheep, 5,380,000; chickens, 8,000,000; pigs, 300,000; and goats, 220,000. In 1992, 17,000 tons of greasy wool and 860,000 karakul skins were produced.

23 FISHING

The Caspian Sea provides fishing resources; fishing is an important export activity.

24 FORESTRY

Desert-like conditions block the development of commercial forestry.

25 MINING

Turkmenistan has the world's third-largest reserves of sulfur. Other mineral deposits include potassium and polymetallic ores.

26 FOREIGN TRADE

Exports and imports are heavily dominated by inter-republic trade, which accounted for 86% of the country's total trade in 1990 (in domestic prices). Principal foreign markets for the country's goods (mainly cotton fibers and some fuel) were Germany, Bulgaria, and the Czech Republic. Germany, Poland and the Czech Republic were the three largest international import sources, mainly for machinery, foods, and consumer goods.

27 ENERGY AND POWER

In 1991, 84 billion cubic meters of natural gas were produced making Turkmenistan the second-largest natural gas producer in the former Soviet Union region. In 1991, Turkmenistan produced 5.4 million tons of oil. About 70% of electricity generation is powered by natural gas. In 1990, 14,900 million kilowatt hours of electricity were generated.

28 SOCIAL DEVELOPMENT

Under the constitution, women are protected from discrimination in employment, inheritance, marriage rights, and other areas.

29 HEALTH

In 1992, there was about 1 doctor for every 278 people, and 11.3 hospital beds per 1,000 inhabitants. Health care expenditures for 1990 were $459 million. Average life expectancy is 65 years.

30 HOUSING

In 1990, Turkmenistan had 11.1 square feet of housing space per person. As of 1 January 1991, 108,000 households (or 31%) were on waiting lists for urban housing.

31 EDUCATION

The adult literacy rate was estimated at 98% in 1990, with men estimated at 98.8% and women at 96.6%. Education is compulsory from the age of 7 to 17. The

Selected Social Indicators

These statistics are estimates for the period 1988 to 1993. For comparison purposes, data for the United States and averages for low-income countries and high-income countries are also given.

Indicator	Turkmenistan	Low-income countries	High-income countries	United States
Per capita gross national product†	$1,390	$380	$23,680	$24,740
Population growth rate	2.4%	1.9%	0.6%	1.0%
Population growth rate in urban areas	2.4%	3.9%	0.8%	1.3%
Population per square kilometer of land	8	78	25	26
Life expectancy in years	65	62	77	76
Number of people per physician	278	>3,300	453	419
Number of pupils per teacher (primary school)	n.a.	39	<18	20
Illiteracy rate (15 years and older)	2%	41%	<5%	<3%
Energy consumed per capita (kg of oil equivalent)	2,268	364	5,203	7,918

† The gross national product (GNP) is the total dollar value of all goods and services produced by a country in a year. The per capita GNP is calculated by dividing a country's GNP by its population. The World Bank defines low-income countries as those with a per capita GNP of $695 or less. High-income countries have a per capita GNP of $8,626 or more. Less than 14% of the world's 5.5 billion people live in high-income countries, while almost 60% live in low-income countries.

n.a. = data not available   > = greater than   < = less than

Sources: World Bank, *Social Indicators of Development 1995,* Baltimore: Johns Hopkins University Press, 1995. Central Intelligence Agency, *World Fact Book,* Washington, D.C.: Government Printing Office, 1994.

government reports 1,764 schools with enrollment of 850,000. In 1990, higher-level institutions had a total of 41,800 pupils enrolled.

32 MEDIA

Turkmen Radio and Television broadcast transmissions from Moscow. In 1989, 66 newspapers and 34 periodicals were published, mostly in Ashgabat (Ashkhabad).

33 TOURISM AND RECREATION

Turkmenistan is open to both business travelers and tourists. The principal accommodations are hotels that formerly belonged to the Soviet Intourist system.

34 FAMOUS TURKMENISTANIS

Saparmuryad A. Niyazov has been president of Turkmenistan since December 1991. Abdulhekin Qulmukam Medoghlia was a writer, researcher, and political activist who was killed in 1937 during one of the Soviet purges. The poet and intellectual Maktum Kuli envisioned an independent Turkmenistan.

35 BIBLIOGRAPHY

Maslow, Jonathan Evan. *Sacred Horses: The Memoirs of a Turkmen Cowboy.* New York: Random House, 1994.

TURKS AND CAICOS ISLANDS

CAPITAL: Grand Turk.

FLAG: The flag is a British blue ensign with the shield of the colony in the fly; the shield is yellow with a conch shell, lobster, and Turk's head cactus represented in natural colors.

ANTHEM: *God Save the Queen.*

MONETARY UNIT: The US dollar of 100 cents (US$) has been the official currency since August 1973. The Turks and Caicos crown is also in circulation.

WEIGHTS AND MEASURES: The imperial system is used.

HOLIDAYS: New Year's Day, 1 January; Commonwealth Day (May); Queen's Official Birthday (June); Emancipation Day, 1st Monday in August; Constitution Day, 30 August; Columbus Day, 2d Monday in October; Human Rights Day (October); Christmas, 25 December; Boxing Day, 26 December. Movable religious holidays include Good Friday and Easter Monday.

TIME: 7 AM = noon GMT.

1 LOCATION AND SIZE

Situated in the Atlantic Ocean southeast of the Bahamas, the Turks and Caicos Islands consist of two island groups separated by the Turks Island Passage. The Turks Islands group comprises two inhabited islands, Grand Turk and Salt Cay, and six uninhabited cays (small low islands), surrounded by a roughly triangular reef bank. The Caicos group includes six principal islands (North Caicos, Middle Caicos, East Caicos, South Caicos, West Caicos, and Providenciales) plus numerous rocky islets, all surrounded by the Caicos Bank, a triangular shoal. The total land area of the Turks and Caicos Islands is 430 square kilometers (166 square miles), slightly less than 2.5 times the size of Washington, D.C. The Turks and Caicos Islands have a coastline length of 389 kilometers (242 miles). The capital city, Grand Turk, is in the Turks Islands.

2 TOPOGRAPHY

The Turks Islands are low and flat, and surrounded by reefs. The land mass is limestone; the coastlines are indented with shallow creeks and mangrove swamps. The highest elevation is only 50 meters (164 feet) above sea level on Providenciales. On the north coast of Middle Caicos (which is also known as Grand Caicos), are limestone cave formations.

3 CLIMATE

Days are sunny and dry and nights are cool and clear throughout the year. Temperatures on the islands range from a low of 16°C (61°F) to a high of 32°C (90°F), with the hottest period generally occurring between April and November. Rainfall averages 53 centimeters (21 inches) per year, and hurricanes occur frequently.

4 PLANTS AND ANIMALS

The ground cover is scrubby and stunted tropical vegetation, with sea oats, mangrove, casuarina, and palmetto. There is little natural wildlife other than birds and butterflies. West Caicos island is especially noted as a sanctuary for birds. Spiny lobster, conch, clams, bonefish, snapper, grouper, and turtle are plentiful.

5 ENVIRONMENT

Fresh water is a scarce commodity, and most islanders rely on private cisterns. In 1992, the government developed legislation that would create 12 national parks, 8 nature reserves, 5 sanctuaries, and 9 historic sites.

6 POPULATION

The population in 1990 was 11,696. The majority of people were living on Grand Turk (3,720), South Caicos (1,220), and North Caicos (1,305) islands. The 1990 population density was 27 persons per square kilometer (70 per square mile). The major towns are Grand Turk on Grand Turk Island, and Cockburn Harbour on South Caicos.

7 MIGRATION

Because of the islands' limited job opportunities, it has become common for young men to emigrate to Caribbean islands (including Puerto Rico) or to the United States in search of work. In the mid-1980s, many Haitian and Dominican immigrants came to Turks and Caicos to work in low-wage hotel jobs unattractive to local residents.

8 ETHNIC GROUPS

About 90% of the population is of black African descent, the remainder being of mixed, European, or North American origin.

9 LANGUAGES

The official and universal language of the Turks and Caicos Islands is English, which is blended with some local expressions.

10 RELIGIONS

Most islanders are Christian; the main denominations are Baptist (25.5% in 1990), Methodist, and Anglican. Other Protestant groups and the Roman Catholic Church, which comprises 18% of the population, are also represented.

11 TRANSPORTATION

There are about 121 kilometers (75 miles) of roads on the islands. The main roads on Grand Turk and South Caicos are paved.

The main seaports are at Grand Turk, Cockburn Harbour on South Caicos, Providenciales, and Salt Cay. There are four paved runways of more than 1,220 meters (4,000 feet) on Grand Turk, South Caicos, and Providenciales.

12 HISTORY

Archaeological expeditions have found Arawak implements and utensils on Turks and Caicos Islands. When Juan Ponce de León arrived in 1512, Lucayan Indians inhabited the islands. The first settlements were by Bermudians, who arrived in the 1670s, and began extracting salt from the islands. Bahamian, Bermudan, Spanish, French, and British rivalry over the prospering salt trade resulted in numerous invasions through the first half of the eighteenth century. In 1787, Loyalists fleeing the American Revolution established settlements and cotton and sisal plantations on several of the larger Caicos Islands. Ten years later, the islands came under the jurisdiction of the Bahamas colonial government. Slavery was abolished in 1834. In 1848, the Turks and Caicos islanders were granted a charter of separation from the Bahamas.

From 1848 to 1873, the islands were largely self-governing, under the supervision of the British governor of Jamaica. Following the decline of the salt industry, the islands became a Jamaican dependency until 1958, when they joined the Federation of the West Indies. When the federation dissolved and Jamaica achieved independence in 1962, Turks and Caicos became a British crown colony. Although independence for Turks and Caicos in 1982 had been agreed upon in principle in 1979, a change in the islands' government brought a reversal in policy. The islands are still a crown colony.

The islands were shaken by scandals in the mid-1980s, including the conviction of top government officials on drug charges in the United States. The government was disbanded in July 1986 until new elections could be called. The islands have returned to their previous form of government, and remain a dependent territory of the United Kingdom.

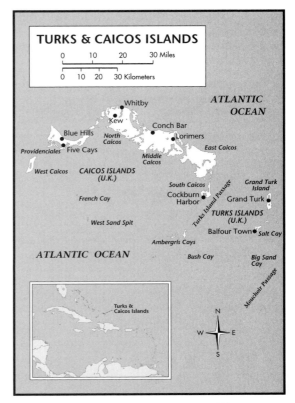

LOCATION: 21° to 22°N; 71° to 72°30'W.

13 GOVERNMENT

Under the 1976 constitution, the governor, representing the crown, is responsible for external affairs, defense, and internal security. The governor presides over an Executive Council of seven members. In order to remain in office, the chief minister must command a majority of the 20-seat Legislative Council.

14 POLITICAL PARTIES

The Progressive National Party (PNP) and the People's Democratic Movement (PDM) are the two major parties in the system. They differ primarily over the question of independence.

15 JUDICIAL SYSTEM

The administration of justice is in the hands of a magistrate who presides weekly in Grand Turk and may sit in each of the other islands as necessary. Appeals are heard by the Eastern Caribbean Supreme Court.

16 ARMED FORCES

The Turks and Caicos Islands have no military force. Defense is provided by the United Kingdom.

17 ECONOMY

Tourism and lobster fishing have replaced salt raking as the main economic activities of the islands, which are very poor. Fishing and subsistence farming are the principal occupations; underemployment and unemployment are estimated at over 40%.

18 INCOME

In 1989, the gross domestic product (GDP) was estimated at US$68.5 million, or $5,857 per person.

19 INDUSTRY

The main industry is the processing of lobster and conch for export. South Caicos and Providenciales have a combined total of four seafood processing plants.

20 LABOR

Government is the largest employer, followed by the tourist sector and financial services. Most self-employed persons engage in fishing or subsistence farming.

There is one labor organization, the St. George's Industrial Trade Union, with a membership of approximately 250.

21 AGRICULTURE

Of the total area of Turks and Caicos, only about 2%, or 1,000 hectares (2,500 acres), is devoted to agriculture. Crop output is small. Rainfall is low, and the cost of transporting produce from island to island is not competitive with imports. Corn, beans, and other food crops are grown entirely for local or household consumption. Fruit and many other foods must be imported, with Haiti as the principal supplier.

22 DOMESTICATED ANIMALS

Cattle, hogs, and poultry are raised by householders to supplement food supplies. There is little commercial production of meat or dairy products.

23 FISHING

Fishing is the traditional occupation of the islanders. The harvesting of lobster and conch for export to the United States and Haiti is an organized commercial operation that in 1991 yielded 210 tons of lobster and 431 tons of conch.

24 FORESTRY

There are no significant forests.

25 MINING

There is no mineral wealth other than salt. With the decline of foreign markets, all salt operations for export were closed down, and salt has not been mined in commercial quantities since 1974.

Photo credit: Anne Kalosh

A resort hotel in Providenciales.

26 FOREIGN TRADE

The United States and United Kingdom are the islands' principal trade partners. In 1991, the country registered US$4.4 million in exports, mainly composed of lobstertails, conch, and fish meat. Imports recorded US$39.8 million, including food, beverages, manufactured goods, fuel, building supplies, and tobacco.

27 ENERGY AND POWER

Electrical output in 1991 amounted to nine million kilowatt hours, entirely from conventional thermal sources; slightly more than half of this output came from public sources.

28 SOCIAL DEVELOPMENT

The central government provides few welfare services or benefits. Churches and benevolent societies are the principal sources of charitable aid.

29 HEALTH

A modern cottage hospital (30 beds) and an outpatient and dental clinic are located on Grand Turk, and there are 11 outpatient clinics throughout the islands. In 1992, there were 1.25 doctors per 1,000 people.

30 HOUSING

Wooden shacks—easily damaged by hurricanes—have been replaced by concrete block structures, especially in the towns. However, some traditional nineteenth-century Bermudian architecture remains.

31 EDUCATION

Education is free and compulsory between the ages of 4½ and 15. In 1985/86, primary schools had a combined total of 1,429 students, and three government secondary schools had 815 students. Expenditure on education in 1985 was US$1.4 million. There are no higher educational institutions on the islands.

32 MEDIA

Telephone service operates on Grand Turk, South Caicos, and Providenciales; there were 1,450 telephones in 1993. There are 3 AM radio stations and several TV stations; in 1991, there were approximately 6,000 radios. Newspapers include the *Turks and Caicos News,* a weekly; the *Turks and Caicos Current,* published every two months; the *Turks and Caicos Chronicle,* a quarterly; and *The Voice,* a monthly.

33 TOURISM AND RECREATION

A total of 54,616 tourists visited the islands in 1991, 43,390 from North America. There were 1,051 hotel rooms with a 61% occupancy rate. Revenues from tourism were US$43 million. In 1992, tourist arrivals declined slightly to 52,000, primarily due to the US recession and the demise of Pan Am, the principal airline that served the islands. Visitors are attracted by the beautiful beaches and by opportunities for snorkeling, diving, and sport fishing. The windmills on Salt Cay and the nineteenth-century architecture on Grand Turk, along with horse carriages, provide quaint settings.

34 FAMOUS PERSONS

J.A.G.S. MacCartney (1946?–1980), referred to by his countrymen as "Chief," was the first chief minister of the Turks and Caicos Islands, serving from 1976 until his death.

35 BIBLIOGRAPHY

Augier, F. R. *The Making of the Indies.* London: Longmans, 1965.
Boultbee, Paul G. *Turks and Caicos Islands.* Santa Barbara, Calif.: Clio Press, 1991.

TUVALU

CAPITAL: Funafuti.

FLAG: The national flag has the Union Jack in the upper quarter nearest the hoist; nine yellow stars on a light blue field are arranged in the same pattern as Tuvalu's nine islands.

ANTHEM: *Begins "Tuvalu for the Almighty"*

MONETARY UNIT: Both the Australian dollar (A$) and the Tuvaluan dollar (T$) of 100 cents are legal tender. There are coins of 1, 2, 5, 10, 20, and 50 Tuvaluan cents; 1 and 5 Tuvaluan dollars; and notes of 5, 10, 20, 50, and 100 Australian dollars. T$1 = US$0.7008 (or US$1 = T$1.4269).

WEIGHTS AND MEASURES: The metric system is being introduced, but imperial measures are still commonly employed.

HOLIDAYS: New Year's Day, 1 January; National Children's Day, first Monday in August; Tuvalu Day, 1 October; Christmas Day, 25 December; Boxing Day, 26 December. Movable holidays include Commonwealth Day (March), Queen's Official Birthday (June), and Prince of Wales's Birthday (November); movable religious holidays include Good Friday and Easter Monday.

TIME: Midnight = noon GMT.

1 LOCATION AND SIZE

Tuvalu (formerly the Ellice Islands) is a cluster of nine islands located in the southwestern Pacific Ocean, with a total land area of 26 square kilometers (10 square miles)—about one-tenth the size of Washington, D.C.—and a coastline of 24 kilometers (15 miles). Tuvalu's capital city, Funafuti, is located on the island of Funafuti.

2 TOPOGRAPHY

Tuvalu consists entirely of low-lying coral atolls.

3 CLIMATE

The annual mean temperature of 30°C (86°F) is moderated by trade winds from the east. Rainfall averages over 355 centimeters (140 inches).

4 PLANTS AND ANIMALS

Vegetation consists of coconut palm, pandanus, and imported fruit trees. Pigs, fowl, and dogs flourish on the islands. There are 22 known species of butterfly and moth.

5 ENVIRONMENT

The environment is threatened by the crown of thorns starfish, which destroys coral; erosion of beachheads by the use of sand for building materials; and excessive clearance of forest undergrowth for firewood.

6 POPULATION

The 1995 population was estimated at 9,995 by the United States Bureau of the

Census but at 13,000 by the United Nations. Funafuti, the capital, had a 1985 mini-census population of 2,810.

7 MIGRATION

During the nineteenth century, emigration by Tuvaluans to work abroad reduced the population from about 20,000 to 3,000.

8 ETHNIC GROUPS

The islanders are almost entirely Polynesian and have strong ties with the Samoans and Tokelauans.

9 LANGUAGES

English and Tuvaluan, the latter a Polynesian tongue related closely to Samoan, are the principal languages.

10 RELIGIONS

Today 98% of Tuvaluans are members of the Church of Tuvalu, a Congregationalist group. There are small Roman Catholic, Seventh-Day Adventist, and Baha'i communities.

11 TRANSPORTATION

Most roads are little more than tracks. Funafuti and Nukufetau are the only seaports, and all the islands are served by Tuvalu's one inter-island ferry. Funafuti has one airport, a grass strip that cannot be used for jet aircraft.

12 HISTORY

Between 1850 and 1875, the islands were raided by ships forcibly recruiting plantation workers for South America, Fiji, Hawaii, Tahiti, and Queensland (Australia). The Ellice Islands (as Tuvalu was then known), together with the Gilbert Islands (now Kiribati), became a British protectorate in 1892 and a colony in 1916. In 1943, United States forces occupied the Ellice Islands in order to drive the Japanese from the Gilberts.

After World War II (1939–45), the ethnic differences between the Micronesians of the Gilberts and the Polynesians of the Ellice Islands led the Ellice Islanders to demand separation. A referendum held during August–September 1974 produced an overwhelming majority of 3,799 to 293 for separation, and on 1 October 1975, the Ellice Islands were established as the separate British colony of Tuvalu.

Tuvalu became an independent member of the Commonwealth of Nations on 1 October 1979. In a poll held in 1985, Tuvaluans rejected the idea that Tuvalu should become a republic.

13 GOVERNMENT

Tuvalu is an independent constitutional monarchy. The head of state is the British monarch, whose representative on the islands is the governor-general. There is a single-chamber legislature, the House of Assembly, with 12 members elected to four-year terms by universal adult suffrage. Funafuti's town council and the other seven island councils each have six elected members.

14 POLITICAL PARTIES

There are no political parties, and political life and elections are dominated by personalities.

15 JUDICIAL SYSTEM

Eight island courts deal with land disputes and other local matters, and a High Court of Justice hears appeals from district courts. Appeals from the High Court may go to the Court of Appeals in Fiji and ultimately to the United Kingdom Privy Council in London.

16 ARMED FORCES

Tuvalu has no armed forces except for the local police. For defense, the islands rely on Fiji and Papua New Guinea.

17 ECONOMY

Economic life is simple, but there is no extreme poverty. There is intensive use of limited resources, namely coconuts and fish; copra (dried coconut meat) is the only cash crop.

18 INCOME

Tuvalu's gross domestic product (GDP) in 1990 was the smallest of any independent state. Major sources of income are British aid and the earnings of Tuvaluan workers abroad.

19 INDUSTRY

There is no industry apart from handicrafts, baking, and small-scale construction.

20 LABOR

Most of the active labor force is engaged in farming. Minimum age laws effectively regulate the use of child labor.

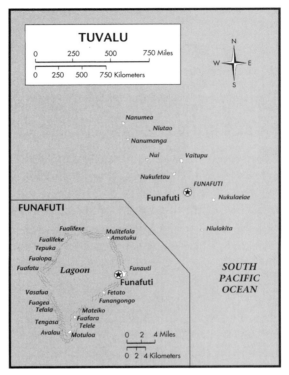

LOCATION: 5° to 11°S; 176° to 180°E. **TOTAL COASTLINE:** 24 kilometers (15 miles). **TERRITORIAL SEA LIMIT:** 12 miles.

21 AGRICULTURE

Coconuts are the main crop for both sale and consumption; the coconut yield in 1992 was about 3,000 tons. Other food crops are pulaka (taro), pandanus fruit, bananas, and pawpaws.

22 DOMESTICATED ANIMALS

In 1992, there were some 13,000 pigs on the islands.

23 FISHING

Sea fishing, especially for tuna and turtle, is excellent. The fish catch in 1991 was 526 tons.

24 FORESTRY

There is little useful timber on the islands.

25 MINING

There is no commercial mining.

26 FOREIGN TRADE

Most food, fuel, and manufactured goods are imported. Total imports and exports of Tuvalu and Kiribati were valued at US$27 million in 1990. About 48% of total trade in 1982 was with Fiji, 40% with Australia, and 5% with New Zealand.

27 ENERGY AND POWER

Very few private households have electrical service. Electricity production in 1990 amounted to 3 million kilowatt hours, or 330 kilowatt hours per capita.

28 SOCIAL DEVELOPMENT

Villages are organized on a communal rather than a clan basis and have a customary system of social welfare.

29 HEALTH

There are no serious tropical diseases on the islands except for a dwindling number of leprosy and dysentery cases. In 1990, there were 1.8 hospital beds per 1,000 people.

30 HOUSING

Most islanders live in small villages and provide their own housing from local materials. There is a critical housing shortage on Funafuti and Vaitupu.

31 EDUCATION

All children receive free primary education from the age of six. The Tuvalu school system has seven years of primary and six years of secondary education. In 1990, 1,485 students were enrolled in primary schools while secondary schools had 345 students. In 1979, the University of the South Pacific (Fiji) established an extension center at Funafuti.

32 MEDIA

The Tuvalu Broadcasting Service, on Funafuti, transmits daily in Tuvaluan and also broadcasts news in English. There is efficient inter-island radio communication. There is no commercial press, but *Tuvalu Echoes* is published biweekly by the government.

33 TOURISM AND RECREATION

Tuvalu's remoteness has discouraged tourism. In 1991, 976 tourists visited Tuvalu, 82% of them from Eastern Asia and the Pacific. There were 26 hotel rooms.

34 FAMOUS TUVALUANS

Tuvalu's first prime minister was Toaripi Lauti (b. Papua New Guinea, 1928).

35 BIBLIOGRAPHY

Geddes, W. H., et al. *Atoll Economy: Social Change in Kiribati and Tuvalu.* Canberra: Australian National University Press, 1982.

MacDonald, Barrie. *Cinderellas of the Empire.* Canberra: Australian National University Press, 1982.

GLOSSARY

aboriginal: The first known inhabitants of a country. A species of animals or plants which originated within a given area.

acid rain: Rain (or snow) that has become slightly acid by mixing with industrial air pollution.

adobe: A brick made from sun-dried heavy clay mixed with straw, used in building houses. A house made of adobe bricks.

adult literacy: The ability of adults to read and write.

afforestation: The act of turning arable land into forest or woodland.

agrarian economy: An economy where agriculture is the dominant form of economic activity. A society where agriculture dominates the day-to-day activities of the population is called an agrarian society.

air link: Refers to scheduled air service that allows people and goods to travel between two places on a regular basis.

airborne industrial pollutant: Pollution caused by industry that is supported or carried by the air.

allies: Groups or persons who are united in a common purpose. Typically used to describe nations that have joined together to fight a common enemy in war.

In World War I, the term Allies described the nations that fought against Germany and its allies. In World War II, Allies described the United Kingdom, United States, the USSR and their allies, who fought against the Axis Powers of Germany, Italy, and Japan.

aloe: A plant particularly abundant in the southern part of Africa, where leaves of some species are made into ropes, fishing lines, bow strings, and hammocks. It is also a symbolic plant in the Islamic world; anyone who returns from a pilgrimage to Mecca (Mekkah) hangs aloe over his door as a token that he has performed the journey.

Altaic language family: A family of languages spoken in portions of northern and eastern Europe, and nearly the whole of northern and central Asia, together with some other regions. The family is divided into five branches: the Ugrian or Finno-Hungarian, Smoyed, Turkish, Mongolian, and Tunguse.

althing: A legislative assembly.

amendment: A change or addition to a document.

Amerindian: A contraction of the two words, American Indian. It describes native peoples of North, South, or Central America.

amnesty: An act of forgiveness or pardon, usually taken by a government, toward persons for crimes they may have committed.

Anglican: Pertaining to or connected with the Church of England.

animism: The belief that natural objects and phenomena have souls or innate spiritual powers.

annual growth rate: The rate at which something grows over a period of 12 months.

annual inflation rate: The rate of inflation in prices over the course of a year.

anthracite coal: Also called hard coal, it is usually 90 to 95 percent carbon, and burns cleanly, almost without a flame.

anti-Semitism: Agitation, persecution, or discrimination (physical, emotional, economic, political, or otherwise) directed against the Jews.

apartheid: The past governmental policy in the Republic of South Africa of separating the races in society.

appeasement: To bring to a state of peace.

appellate: Refers to an appeal of a court decision to a high authority.

applied science: Scientific techniques employed to achieve results that solve practical problems.

aquaculture: The culture or "farming" of aquatic plants or other natural produce, as in the raising of catfish in "farms."

aquatic resources: Resources that come from, grow in, or live in water, including fish and plants.

aquifer: An underground layer of porous rock, sand, or gravel that holds water.

arable land: Land that can be cultivated by plowing and used for growing crops.

arbitration: A process whereby disputes are settled by a designated person, called the arbitrator, instead of by a court of law.

archipelago: Any body of water abounding with islands, or the islands themselves collectively.

archives: A place where records or a collection of important documents are kept.

arctic climate: Cold, frigid weather similar to that experienced at or near the north pole.

aristocracy: A small minority that controls the government of a nation, typically on the basis of inherited wealth.

armistice: An agreement or truce which ends military conflict in anticipation of a peace treaty.

artesian well: A type of well where the water rises to the surface and overflows.

ASEAN *see* Association of Southeast Asian Nations

Association of Southeast Asian Nations: ASEAN was established in 1967 to promote political, economic, and social cooperation among its six member countries: Indonesia, Malaysia, the Philippines, Singapore, Thailand, and Brunei. ASEAN headquarters are in Jakarta, Indonesia. In January 1992, ASEAN agreed to create the ASEAN Free Trade Area (AFTA).

atheist: A person who denies the existence of God or of a supreme intelligent being.

atoll: A coral island, consisting of a strip or ring of coral surrounding a central lagoon.

atomic weapons: Weapons whose extremely violent explosive power comes from the splitting of the nuclei of atoms (usually uranium or plutonium) by neutrons in a rapid chain reaction. These weapons may be referred to as atom bombs, hydrogen bombs, or H-bombs.

austerity measures: Steps taken by a government to conserve money or resources during an economically difficult time, such as cutting back on federally funded programs.

Australoid: Pertains to the type of aborigines, or earliest inhabitants, of Australia.

Austronesian language: A family of languages which includes practically all the languages of the Pacific Islands—Indonesian, Melanesian, Polynesian, and Micronesian sub-families. Does not include Australian or Papuan languages.

authoritarianism: A form of government in which a person or group attempts to rule with absolute authority without the representation of the citizens.

autonomous state: A country which is completely self-governing, as opposed to being a dependency or part of another country.

autonomy: The state of existing as a self-governing entity. For instance, when a country gains its independence from another country, it gains autonomy.

average inflation rate: The average rate at which the general prices of goods and services increase over the period of a year.

average life expectancy: In any given society, the average age attained by persons at the time of death.

Axis Powers: The countries aligned against the Allied Nations in World War II, originally applied to Nazi Germany and Fascist Italy (Rome-Berlin Axis), and later extended to include Japan.

bagasse: Plant residue left after a product, such as juice, has been extracted.

Baha'i: The follower of a religious sect founded by Mirza Husayn Ali in Iran in 1863.

Baltic states. The three formerly communist countries of Estonia, Latvia, and Lithuania that border on the Baltic Sea.

Bantu language group: A name applied to the languages spoken in central and south Africa.

banyan tree: An East Indian fig tree. Individual trees develop roots from the branches that descend to the ground and become trunks. These roots support and nourish the crown of the tree.

Baptist: A member of a Protestant denomination that practices adult baptism by complete immersion in water.

barren land: Unproductive land, partly or entirely treeless.

barter: Trade practice where merchandise is exchanged directly for other merchandise or services without use of money.

bedrock: Solid rock lying under loose earth.

bicameral legislature: A legislative body consisting of two chambers, such as the U.S. House of Representatives and the U.S. Senate.

bill of rights: A written statement containing the list of privileges and powers to be granted to a body of people, usually introduced when a government or other organization is forming.

bituminous coal: Soft coal; coal which burns with a bright-yellow flame.

black market: A system of trade where goods are sold illegally, often for excessively inflated prices. This type of trade usually develops to avoid paying taxes or tariffs levied by the government, or to get around import or export restrictions on products.

bloodless coup: The sudden takeover of a country's government by hostile means but without killing anyone in the process.

boat people: Used to describe individuals (refugees) who attempt to flee their country by boat.

bog: Wet, soft, and spongy ground where the soil is composed mainly of decayed or decaying vegetable matter.

Bolshevik Revolution. A revolution in 1917 in Russia when a wing of the Russian Social Democratic party seized power. The Bolsheviks advocated the violent overthrow of capitalism.

bonded labor: Workers bound to service without pay; slaves.

border dispute: A disagreement between two countries as to the exact location or length of the dividing line between them.

Brahman: A member (by heredity) of the highest caste among the Hindus, usually assigned to the priesthood.

broadleaf forest: A forest composed mainly of broadleaf (deciduous) trees.

Buddhism: A religious system common in India and eastern Asia. Founded by and based upon the teachings of Siddhartha Gautama, Buddhism asserts that suffering is an inescapable part of life. Deliverance can only be achieved through the practice of charity, temperance, justice, honesty, and truth.

buffer state: A small country that lies between two larger, possibly hostile countries, considered to be a neutralizing force between them.

bureaucracy: A system of government that is characterized by division into bureaus of administration with their own divisional heads. Also refers to the inflexible procedures of such a system that often result in delay.

Byzantine Empire: An empire centered in the city of Byzantium, now Istanbul in present-day Turkey.

CACM *see* Central American Common Market.

candlewood: A name given to several species of trees and shrubs found in the British West Indies, northern Mexico, and the southwestern United States. The plants are characterized by a very resinous wood.

canton: A territory or small division or state within a country.

capital punishment: The ultimate act of punishment for a crime, the death penalty.

capitalism: An economic system in which goods and services and the means to produce and sell them are privately owned, and prices and wages are determined by market forces.

Caribbean Community and Common Market (CARICOM): Founded in 1973 and with its headquarters in Georgetown, Guyana, CARICOM seeks the establishment of a common trade policy and increased cooperation in the Caribbean region. Includes 13 English-speaking Caribbean nations: Antigua and Barbuda, the Bahamas, Barbados, Belize, Dominica, Grenada, Guyana, Jamaica, Montserrat, Saint Kitts-Nevis, Saint Lucia, St. Vincent/Grenadines, and Trinidad and Tobago.

CARICOM *see* Caribbean Community and Common Market.

carnivore: Flesh-eating animal or plant.

carob: The common English name for a plant that is similar to and sometimes used as a substitute for chocolate.

cartel: An organization of independent producers formed to regulate the production, pricing, or marketing practices of its members in order to limit competition and maximize their market power.

cash crop: A crop that is grown to be sold rather than kept for private use.

cassation: The reversal or annulling of a final judgment by the supreme authority.

cassava: The name of several species of stout herbs, extensively cultivated for food.

caste system: One of the artificial divisions or social classes into which the Hindus are rigidly separated according to the religious law of Brahmanism. Membership in a caste is hereditary, and the privileges and disabilities of each caste are transmitted by inheritance.

Caucasian: The white race of human beings, as determined by genealogy and physical features.

Caucasoid: Belonging to the racial group characterized by light skin pigmentation. Commonly called the "white race."

cease-fire: An official declaration of the end to the use of military force or active hostilities, even if only temporary.

CEMA *see* Council for Mutual Economic Assistance.

censorship: The practice of withholding certain items of news that may cast a country in an unfavorable light or give away secrets to the enemy.

census: An official counting of the inhabitants of a state or country with details of sex and age, family, occupation, possessions, etc.

Central American Common Market (CACM): Established in 1962, a trade alliance of five Central American nations. Participating are Costa Rica, El Salvador, Guatemala, Honduras, and Nicaragua.

Central Powers: In World War I, Germany and Austria-Hungary, and their allies, Turkey and Bulgaria.

centrally planned economy: An economic system all aspects of which are supervised and regulated by the government.

centrist position: Refers to opinions held by members of a moderate political group; that is, views that are somewhere in the middle of popular thought between conservative and liberal.

cession: Withdrawal from or yielding to physical force.

chancellor: A high-ranking government official. In some countries it is the prime minister.

cholera: An acute infectious disease characterized by severe diarrhea, vomiting, and, often, death.

Christianity: The religion founded by Jesus Christ, based on the Bible as holy scripture.

Church of England: The national and established church in England. The Church of England claims continuity with the branch of the Catholic Church that existed in England before the Reformation. Under Henry VIII, the spiritual supremacy and jurisdiction of the Pope were abolished, and the sovereign (king or queen) was declared head of the church.

circuit court: A court that convenes in two or more locations within its appointed district.

CIS *see* Commonwealth of Independent States

city-state: An independent state consisting of a city and its surrounding territory.

civil court: A court whose proceedings include determinations of rights of individual citizens, in contrast to criminal proceedings regarding individuals or the public.

civil jurisdiction: The authority to enforce the laws in civil matters brought before the court.

civil law: The law developed by a nation or state for the conduct of daily life of its own people.

civil rights: The privileges of all individuals to be treated as equals under the laws of their country; specifically, the rights given by certain amendments to the U.S. Constitution.

civil unrest: The feeling of uneasiness due to an unstable political climate, or actions taken as a result of it.

civil war: A war between groups of citizens of the same country who have different opinions or agendas. The Civil War of the United States was the conflict between the states of the North and South from 1861 to 1865.

climatic belt: A region or zone where a particular type of climate prevails.

Club du Sahel: The Club du Sahel is an informal coalition which seeks to reverse the effects of drought and the desertification in the eight Sahelian zone countries: Burkina Faso, Chad, Gambia, Mali, Mauritania, Niger, Senegal, and the Cape Verde Islands. Headquarters are in Ouagadougou, Burkina Faso.

CMEA see Council for Mutual Economic Assistance.

coalition government: A government combining differing factions within a country, usually temporary.

coastal belt: A coastal plain area of lowlands and somewhat higher ridges that run parallel to the coast.

coastal plain: A fairly level area of land along the coast of a land mass.

coca: A shrub native to South America, the leaves of which produce organic compounds that are used in the production of cocaine.

coke: The solid product of the carbonization of coal, bearing the same relation to coal that charcoal does to wood.

cold war: Refers to conflict over ideological differences that is carried on by words and diplomatic actions, not by military action. The term is usually used to refer to the tension that existed between the United States and the USSR from the 1950s until the breakup of the USSR in 1991.

collective bargaining: The negotiations between workers who are members of a union and their employer for the purpose of deciding work rules and policies regarding wages, hours, etc.

collective farm: A large farm formed from many small farms and supervised by the government; usually found in communist countries.

collective farming: The system of farming on a collective where all workers share in the income of the farm.

colloquial: Belonging to ordinary, everyday speech: often especially applied to common words and phrases which are not used in formal speech.

colonial period: The period of time when a country forms colonies in and extends control over a foreign area.

colonist: Any member of a colony or one who helps settle a new colony.

colony: A group of people who settle in a new area far from their original country, but still under the jurisdiction of that country. Also refers to the newly settled area itself.

COMECON see Council for Mutual Economic Assistance.

commerce: The trading of goods (buying and selling), especially on a large scale, between cities, states, and countries.

commercial catch: The amount of marketable fish, usually measured in tons, caught in a particular period of time.

commercial crop: Any marketable agricultural crop.

commission: A group of people designated to collectively do a job, including a government agency with certain law-making powers. Also, the power given to an individual or group to perform certain duties.

commodity: Any items, such as goods or services, that are bought or sold, or agricultural products that are traded or marketed.

common law: A legal system based on custom and decisions and opinions of the law courts. The basic system of law of England and the United States.

common market: An economic union among countries that is formed to remove trade barriers (tariffs) among those countries, increasing economic cooperation. The European Community is a notable example of a common market.

commonwealth: A commonwealth is a free association of sovereign independent states that has no charter, treaty, or constitution. The association promotes cooperation, consultation, and mutual assistance among members.

Commonwealth of Independent States: The CIS was established in December 1991 as an association of 11 republics of the former Soviet Union. The members include: Russia, Ukraine, Belarus (formerly Byelorussia), Moldova (formerly Moldavia), Armenia, Azerbaijan, Uzbekistan, Turkmenistan, Tajikistan, Kazakhstan, and Kirgizstan (formerly Kirghiziya). The Baltic states—Estonia, Latvia, and Lithuania—did not join. Georgia maintained observer status before joining the CIS in November 1993.

Commonwealth of Nations: Voluntary association of the United Kingdom and its present dependencies and associated states, as well as certain former dependencies and their dependent territories. The term was first used officially in 1926 and is embodied in the Statute of Westminster (1931). Within the Commonwealth, whose secretariat (established in 1965) is located in London, England, are numerous subgroups devoted to economic and technical cooperation.

commune: An organization of people living together in a community who share the ownership and use of property. Also refers to a small governmental district of a country, especially in Europe.

communism: A form of government whose system requires common ownership of property for the use of all citizens. All profits are to be equally distributed and prices on goods and services are usually set by the state. Also, communism refers directly to the official doctrine of the former U.S.S.R.

compulsory: Required by law or other regulation.

compulsory education: The mandatory requirement for children to attend school until they have reached a certain age or grade level.

conciliation: A process of bringing together opposing sides of a disagreement for the purpose of compromise. Or, a way of settling an international dispute in which the disagreement is submitted to an independent committee that will examine the facts and advise the participants of a possible solution.

concordat: An agreement, compact, or convention, especially between church and state.

confederation: An alliance or league formed for the purpose of promoting the common interests of its members.

Confucianism: The system of ethics and politics taught by the Chinese philosopher Confucius.

coniferous forest: A forest consisting mainly of pine, fir, and cypress trees.

conifers: Cone-bearing plants. Mostly evergreen trees and shrubs which produce cones.

conscription: To be required to join the military by law. Also known as the draft. Service personnel who join the military because of the legal requirement are called conscripts or draftees.

conservative party: A political group whose philosophy tends to be based on established traditions and not supportive of rapid change.

constituency: The registered voters in a governmental district, or a group of people that supports a position or a candidate.

constituent assembly: A group of people that has the power to determine the election of a political representative or create a constitution.

constitution: The written laws and basic rights of citizens of a country or members of an organized group.

constitutional monarchy: A system of government in which the hereditary sovereign (king or queen, usually) rules according to a written constitution.

constitutional republic: A system of government with an elected chief of state and elected representation, with a written constitution containing its governing principles. The United States is a constitutional republic.

consumer goods: Items that are bought to satisfy personal needs or wants of individuals.

continental climate: The climate of a part of the continent; the characteristics and peculiarities of the climate are a result of the land itself and its location.

continental shelf: A plain extending from the continental coast and varying in width that typically ends in a steep slope to the ocean floor.

copra: The dried meat of the coconut; it is frequently used as an ingredient of curry, and to produce coconut oil. Also written *cobra, coprah,* and *copperah.*

Coptic Christians: Members of the Coptic Church of Egypt, formerly of Ethiopia.

cordillera: A continuous ridge, range, or chain of mountains.

corvette: A small warship that is often used as an escort ship because it is easier to maneuver than larger ships like destroyers.

Council for Mutual Economic Assistance (CMEA): Also known as Comecon, the alliance of socialist economies was established on 25 January 1949 and abolished 1 January 1991. It included Afghanistan*, Albania, Angola*, Bulgaria, Cuba, Czechoslovakia, Ethiopia*, East Germany, Hungary, Laos*, Mongolia, Mozambique*, Nicaragua*, Poland, Romania, USSR, Vietnam, Yemen*, and Yugoslavia. Nations marked with an asterisk were observers only.

counterinsurgency operations: Organized military activity designed to stop rebellion against an established government.

county: A territorial division or administrative unit within a state or country.

coup d'ètat or coup: A sudden, violent overthrow of a government or its leader.

court of appeal: An appellate court, having the power of review after a case has been decided in a lower court.

court of first appeal: The next highest court to the court which has decided a case, to which that case may be presented for review.

court of last appeal: The highest court, in which a decision is not subject to review by any higher court. In the United States, it could be the Supreme Court of an individual state or the U.S. Supreme Court.

cricket (sport): A game played by two teams with a ball and bat, with two wickets (staked target) being defended by a batsman. Common in the United Kingdom and Commonwealth of Nations countries.

criminal law: The branch of law that deals primarily with crimes and their punishments.

crown colony: A colony established by a commonwealth over which the monarch has some control, as in colonies established by the United Kingdom's Commonwealth of Nations.

Crusades: Military expeditions by European Christian armies in the eleventh, twelfth, and thirteenth centuries to win land controlled by the Muslims in the middle east.

cultivable land: Land that can be prepared for the production of crops.

Cultural Revolution: An extreme reform movement in China from 1966 to 1976; its goal was to combat liberalization by restoring the ideas of Mao Zedong.

Cushitic language group: A group of Hamitic languages that are spoken in Ethiopia and other areas of eastern Africa.

customs union: An agreement between two or more countries to remove trade barriers with each other and to establish common tariff and nontariff policies with respect to imports from countries outside of the agreement.

cyclone: Any atmospheric movement, general or local, in which the wind blows spirally around and in towards a center. In the northern hemisphere, the cyclonic movement is usually counter-clockwise, and in the southern hemisphere, it is clockwise.

Cyrillic alphabet: An alphabet adopted by the Slavic people and invented by Cyril and Methodius in the ninth century as an alphabet that was easier for the copyist to write. The Russian alphabet is a slight modification of it.

decentralization: The redistribution of power in a government from one large central authority to a wider range of smaller local authorities.

deciduous species: Any species that sheds or casts off a part of itself after a definite period of time. More commonly used in reference to plants that shed their leaves on a yearly basis as opposed to those (evergreens) that retain them.

declaration of independence: A formal written document stating the intent of a group of persons to become fully self-governing.

deficit: The amount of money that is in excess between spending and income.

deficit spending: The process in which a government spends money on goods and services in excess of its income.

deforestation: The removal or clearing of a forest.

deity: A being with the attributes, nature, and essence of a god; a divinity.

delta: Triangular-shaped deposits of soil formed at the mouths of large rivers.

demarcate: To mark off from adjoining land or territory; set the limits or boundaries of.

demilitarized zone (DMZ): An area surrounded by a combat zone that has had military troops and weapons removed.

demobilize: To disband or discharge military troops.

democracy: A form of government in which the power lies in the hands of the people, who can govern directly, or can be governed indirectly by representatives elected by its citizens.

denationalize: To remove from government ownership or control.

deportation: To carry away or remove from one country to another, or to a distant place.

depression: A hollow; a surface that has sunken or fallen in.

deregulation: The act of reversing controls and restrictions on prices of goods, bank interest, and the like.

desalinization plant: A facility that produces freshwater by removing the salt from saltwater.

desegregation: The act of removing restrictions on people of a particular race that keep them socially, economically, and, sometimes, physically, separate from other groups.

desertification: The process of becoming a desert as a result of climatic changes, land mismanagement, or both.

détente: The official lessening of tension between countries in conflict.

devaluation: The official lowering of the value of a country's currency in relation to the value of gold or the currencies of other countries.

developed countries: Countries which have a high standard of living and a well-developed industrial base.

development assistance: Government programs intended to finance and promote the growth of new industries.

dialect: One of a number of regional or related modes of speech regarded as descending from a common origin.

dictatorship: A form of government in which all the power is retained by an absolute leader or tyrant. There are no rights granted to the people to elect their own representatives.

diplomatic relations: The relationship between countries as conducted by representatives of each government.

direct election: The process of selecting a representative to the government by balloting of the voting public, in contrast to selection by an elected representative of the people.

disarmament: The reduction or depletion of the number of weapons or the size of armed forces.

dissident: A person whose political opinions differ from the majority to the point of rejection.

dogma: A principle, maxim, or tenet held as being firmly established.

domain: The area of land governed by a particular ruler or government, sometimes referring to the ultimate control of that territory.

domestic spending: Money spent by a country's government on goods used, investments, running of the government, and exports and imports.

dominion: A self-governing nation that recognizes the British monarch as chief of state.

dormant volcano: A volcano that has not exhibited any signs of activity for an extended period of time.

dowry: The sum of the property or money that a bride brings to her groom at their marriage.

draft constitution: The preliminary written plans for the new constitution of a country forming a new government.

Druze: A member of a Muslim sect based in Syria, living chiefly in the mountain regions of Lebanon.

dual nationality: The status of an individual who can claim citizenship in two or more countries.

duchy: Any territory under the rule of a duke or duchess.

due process: In law, the application of the legal process to which every citizen has a right, which cannot be denied.

durable goods: Goods or products which are expected to last and perform for several years, such as cars and washing machines.

duty: A tax imposed on imports by the customs authority of a country. Duties are generally based on the value of the goods (*ad valorem* duties), some factors such as weight or quantity (specific duties), or a combination of value and other factors (compound duties).

dyewoods: Any wood from which dye is extracted.

dynasty: A family line of sovereigns who rule in succession, and the time during which they reign.

earned income: The money paid to an individual in wages or salary.

Eastern Orthodox: The outgrowth of the original Eastern Church of the Eastern Roman Empire, consisting of eastern Europe, western Asia, and Egypt.

EC *see* European Community

ecclesiastical: Pertaining or relating to the church.

echidna: A spiny, toothless anteater of Australia, Tasmania, and New Guinea.

ecological balance: The condition of a healthy, well-functioning ecosystem, which includes all the plants and animals in a natural community together with their environment.

ecology: The branch of science that studies organisms in relationship to other organisms and to their environment.

economic depression: A prolonged period in which there is high unemployment, low production, falling prices, and general business failure.

economically active population: That portion of the people who are employed for wages and are consumers of goods and services.

ecotourism: Broad term that encompasses nature, adventure, and ethnic tourism; responsible or wilderness-sensitive tourism; soft-path or small-scale tourism; low-impact tourism; and sustainable tourism. Scientific, educational, or academic tourism (such as biotourism, archetourism, and geotourism) are also forms of ecotourism.

elected assembly: The persons that comprise a legislative body of a government who received their positions by direct election.

electoral system: A system of choosing government officials by votes cast by qualified citizens.

electoral vote: The votes of the members of the electoral college.

electorate: The people who are qualified to vote in an election.

emancipation: The freeing of persons from any kind of bondage or slavery.

embargo: A legal restriction on commercial ships to enter a country's ports, or any legal restriction of trade.

emigration: Moving from one country or region to another for the purpose of residence.

empire: A group of territories ruled by one sovereign or supreme ruler. Also, the period of time under that rule.

enclave: A territory belonging to one nation that is surrounded by that of another nation.

encroachment: The act of intruding, trespassing, or entering on the rights or possessions of another.

endangered species: A plant or animal species whose existence as a whole is threatened with extinction.

endemic: Anything that is peculiar to and characteristic of a locality or region.

Enlightenment: An intellectual movement of the late seventeenth and eighteenth centuries in which scientific thinking gained a strong foothold and old beliefs were challenged. The idea of absolute monarchy was questioned and people were gradually given more individual rights.

enteric disease: An intestinal disease.

epidemic: As applied to disease, any disease that is temporarily prevalent among people in one place at the same time.

Episcopal: Belonging to or vested in bishops or prelates; characteristic of or pertaining to a bishop or bishops.

ethnolinguistic group: A classification of related languages based on common ethnic origin.

EU *see* European Union

European Community: A regional organization created in 1958. Its purpose is to eliminate customs duties and other trade barriers in Europe. It promotes a common external tariff against other countries, a Common Agricultural Policy (CAP), and guarantees of free movement of labor and capital. The original six members were Belgium, France, West Germany, Italy, Luxembourg, and the Netherlands. Denmark, Ireland, and the United Kingdom became members in 1973; Greece joined in 1981; Spain and Portugal in 1986. Other nations continue to join.

European Union: The EU is an umbrella reference to the European Community (EC) and to two European integration efforts introduced by the Maastricht Treaty: Common Foreign and Security Policy (including defense) and Justice and Home Affairs (principally cooperation between police and other authorities on crime, terrorism, and immigration issues).

exports: Goods sold to foreign buyers.

external migration: The movement of people from their native country to another country, as opposed to internal migration, which is the movement of people from one area of a country to another in the same country.

fallout: The precipitation of particles from the atmosphere, often the result of a ground disturbance by volcanic activity or a nuclear explosion.

family planning: The use of birth control to determine the number of children a married couple will have.

Fascism: A political philosophy that holds the good of the nation as more important than the needs of the individual. Fascism also stands for a dictatorial leader and strong oppression of opposition or dissent.

federal: Pertaining to a union of states whose governments are subordinate to a central government.

federation: A union of states or other groups under the authority of a central government.

fetishism: The practice of worshipping a material object that is believed to have mysterious powers residing in it, or is the representation of a deity to which worship may be paid and from which supernatural aid is expected.

feudal estate: The property owned by a lord in medieval Europe under the feudal system.

feudal society: In medieval times, an economic and social structure in which persons could hold land given to them by a lord (nobleman) in return for service to that lord.

final jurisdiction: The final authority in the decision of a legal matter. In the United States, the Supreme Court would have final jurisdiction.

Finno-Ugric language group: A subfamily of languages spoken in northeastern Europe, including Finnish, Hungarian, Estonian, and Lapp.

fiscal year: The twelve months between the settling of financial accounts, not necessarily corresponding to a calendar year beginning on January 1.

fjord: A deep indentation of the land forming a comparatively narrow arm of the sea with more or less steep slopes or cliffs on each side.

fly: The part of a flag opposite and parallel to the one nearest the flagpole.

fodder: Food for cattle, horses, and sheep, such as hay, straw, and other kinds of vegetables.

folk religion: A religion with origins and traditions among the common people of a nation or region that is relevant to their particular life-style.

foreign exchange: Foreign currency that allows foreign countries to conduct financial transactions or settle debts with one another.

foreign policy: The course of action that one government chooses to adopt in relation to a foreign country.

Former Soviet Union: The FSU is a collective reference to republics comprising the former Soviet Union. The term, which has been used as both including and excluding the Baltic republics (Estonia, Latvia, and Lithuania), includes the other 12 republics: Russia, Ukraine, Belarus, Moldova, Armenia, Azerbaijan, Uzbekistan, Turkmenistan, Tajikistan, Kazakhstan, Kyrgizstan, and Georgia.

fossil fuels: Any mineral or mineral substance formed by the decomposition of organic matter buried beneath the earth's surface and used as a fuel.

free enterprise: The system of economics in which private business may be conducted with minimum interference by the government.

free-market economy: An economic system that relies on the market, as opposed to government planners, to set the prices for wages and products.

frigate. A medium-sized warship.

fundamentalist: A person who holds religious beliefs based on the complete acceptance of the words of the Bible or other holy scripture as the truth. For instance, a fundamentalist would believe the story of creation exactly as it is told in the Bible and would reject the idea of evolution.

game reserve: An area of land reserved for wild animals that are hunted for sport or for food.

GDP *see* gross domestic product.

Germanic language group: A large branch of the Indo-European family of languages including German itself, the Scandinavian languages, Dutch, Yiddish, Modern English, Modern Scottish, Afrikaans, and others. The group also includes extinct languages such as Gothic, Old High German, Old Saxon, Old English, Middle English, and the like.

glasnost: President Mikhail Gorbachev's frank revelations in the 1980s about the state of the economy and politics in the Soviet Union; his policy of openness.

global greenhouse gas emissions: Gases released into the atmosphere that contribute to the greenhouse effect, a condition in which the earth's excess heat cannot escape.

global warming: Also called the greenhouse effect. The theorized gradual warming of the earth's climate as a result of the burning of fossil fuels, the use of man-made chemicals, deforestation, etc.

GMT *see* Greenwich Mean Time.

GNP *see* gross national product.

grand duchy: A territory ruled by a nobleman, called a grand duke, who ranks just below a king.

Greek Catholic: A person who is a member of an Orthodox Eastern Church.

Greek Orthodox: The official church of Greece, a self-governing branch of the Orthodox Eastern Church.

Greenwich (Mean) Time: Mean solar time of the meridian at Greenwich, England, used as the basis for standard time throughout most of the world. The world is divided into 24 time zones, and all are related to the prime, or Greenwich mean, zone.

gross domestic product: A measure of the market value of all goods and services produced within the boundaries of a nation, regardless of asset ownership. Unlike gross national product, GDP excludes receipts from that nation's business operations in foreign countries.

gross national product: A measure of the market value of goods and services produced by the labor and property of a nation. Includes receipts from that nation's business operation in foreign countries

groundwater: Water located below the earth's surface, the source from which wells and springs draw their water.

guano: The excrement of seabirds and bats found in various areas around the world. Gathered commercially and sold as a fertilizer.

guerrilla: A member of a small radical military organization that uses unconventional tactics to take their enemies by surprise.

gymnasium: A secondary school, primarily in Europe, that prepares students for university.

hardwoods: The name given to deciduous trees, such as cherry, oak, maple, and mahogany.

harem: In a Muslim household, refers to the women (wives, concubines, and servants in ancient times) who live there and also to the area of the home they live in.

harmattan: An intensely dry, dusty wind felt along the coast of Africa between Cape Verde and Cape Lopez. It prevails at intervals during the months of December, January, and February.

heavy industry: Industries that use heavy or large machinery to produce goods, such as automobile manufacturing.

hoist: The part of a flag nearest the flagpole.

Holocaust: The mass slaughter of European civilians, the vast majority Jews, by the Nazis during World War II.

Holy Roman Empire: A kingdom consisting of a loose union of German and Italian territories that existed from around the ninth century until 1806.

home rule: The governing of a territory by the citizens who inhabit it.

homeland: A region or area set aside to be a state for a people of a particular national, cultural, or racial origin.

homogeneous: Of the same kind or nature, often used in reference to a whole.

Horn of Africa: The Horn of Africa comprises Djibouti, Eritrea, Ethiopia, Somalia, and Sudan.

housing starts: The initiation of new housing construction.

human rights activist: A person who vigorously pursues the attainment of basic rights for all people.

human rights issues: Any matters involving people's basic rights which are in question or thought to be abused.

humanist: A person who centers on human needs and values, and stresses dignity of the individual.

humanitarian aid: Money or supplies given to a persecuted group or people of a country at war, or those devastated by a natural disaster, to provide for basic human needs.

hydrocarbon: A compound of hydrogen and carbon, often occurring in organic substances or derivatives of organic substances such as coal, petroleum, natural gas, etc.

hydrocarbon emissions: Organic compounds containing only carbon and hydrogen, often occurring in petroleum, natural gas, coal, and bitumens, and which contribute to the greenhouse effect.

hydroelectric potential: The potential amount of electricity that can be produced hydroelectrically. Usually used in reference to a given area and how many hydroelectric power plants that area can sustain.

hydroelectric power plant: A factory that produces electrical power through the application of waterpower.

IBRD *see* World Bank.

illegal alien: Any foreign-born individual who has unlawfully entered another country.

immigration: The act or process of passing or entering into another country for the purpose of permanent residence.

imports: Goods purchased from foreign suppliers.

indigenous: Born or originating in a particular place or country; native to a particular region or area.

Indo-Aryan language group: The group that includes the languages of India; also called Indo-European language group.

Indo-European language family: The group that includes the languages of India and much of Europe and southwestern Asia.

industrialized nation: A nation whose economy is based on industry.

infanticide: The act of murdering a baby.

infidel: One who is without faith or belief; particularly, one who rejects the distinctive doctrines of a particular religion.

inflation: The general rise of prices, as measured by a consumer price index. Results in a fall in value of currency.

installed capacity: The maximum possible output of electric power at any given time.

insurgency: The state or condition in which one rises against lawful authority or established government; rebellion.

insurrectionist: One who participates in an unorganized revolt against an authority.

interim government: A temporary or provisional government.

interim president: One who is appointed to perform temporarily the duties of president during a transitional period in a government.

internal migration: Term used to describe the relocation of individuals from one region to another without leaving the confines of the country or of a specified area.

International Date Line: An arbitrary line at about the 180th meridian that designates where one day begins and another ends.

Islam: The religious system of Mohammed, practiced by Moslims and based on a belief in Allah as the supreme being and Mohammed as his prophet. The spelling variations, Muslim and Muhammed, are also used, primarily by Islamic people. Islam also refers to those nations in which it is the primary religion.

isthmus: A narrow strip of land bordered by water and connecting two larger bodies of land, such as two continents, a continent and a peninsula, or two parts of an island.

Judaism: The religious system of the Jews, based on the Old Testament as revealed to Moses and characterized by a belief in one God and adherence to the laws of scripture and rabbinic traditions.

Judeo-Christian: The dominant traditional religious makeup of the United States and other countries based on the worship of the Old and New Testaments of the Bible.

junta: A small military group in power of a country, especially after a coup.

khan: A sovereign, or ruler, in central Asia.

khanate: A kingdom ruled by a khan, or man of rank.

kwashiorkor: Severe malnutrition in infants and children caused by a diet high in carbohydrates and lacking in protein.

kwh: The abbreviation for kilowatt-hour.

labor force: The number of people in a population available for work, whether actually employed or not.

labor movement: A movement in the early to mid-1800s to organize workers in groups according to profession to give them certain rights as a group, including bargaining power for better wages, working conditions, and benefits.

land reforms: Steps taken to create a fair distribution of farmland, especially by governmental action.

landlocked country: A country that does not have direct access to the sea; it is completely surrounded by other countries.

least developed countries: A subgroup of the United Nations designation of "less developed countries;" these countries generally have no significant economic growth, low literacy rates, and per person gross national product of less than $500. Also known as undeveloped countries.

leeward: The direction identical to that of the wind. For example, a *leeward tide* is a tide that runs in the same direction that the wind blows.

leftist: A person with a liberal or radical political affiliation.

legislative branch: The branch of government which makes or enacts the laws.

leprosy: A disease that can effect the skin and/or the nerves and can cause ulcers of the skin, loss of feeling, or loss of fingers and toes.

less developed countries (LDC): Designated by the United Nations to include countries with low levels of output, living standards, and per person gross national product generally below $5,000.

literacy: The ability to read and write.

Maastricht Treaty: The Maastricht Treaty (named for the Dutch town in which the treaty was signed) is also known as the Treaty of European Union. The treaty creates a European Union by: (a) committing the member states of the European Economic Community to both European Monetary Union (EMU) and political union; (b) introducing a single currency (European Currency Unit, ECU); (c) establishing a European System of Central Banks (ESCB); (d) creating a European Central Bank (ECB); and (e) broadening EC integration by including both a common foreign and security policy (CFSP) and cooperation in justice and home affairs (CJHA). The treaty entered into force on November 1, 1993.

Maghreb states: The Maghreb states include the three nations of Algeria, Morocco, and Tunisia; sometimes includes Libya and Mauritania.

maize: Another name (Spanish or British) for corn or the color of ripe corn.

majority party: The party with the largest number of votes and the controlling political party in a government.

mangrove: A tree which abounds on tropical shores in both hemispheres. Characterized by its numerous roots which arch out from its trunk and descend from its branches, mangroves form thick, dense growths along the tidal muds, reaching lengths hundreds of miles long.

manioc: The cassava plant or its product. Manioc is a very important food-staple in tropical America.

maquis. Scrubby, thick underbrush found along the coast of the Mediterranean Sea.

marginal land: Land that could produce an economic profit, but is so poor that it is only used when better land is no longer available.

marine life: The life that exists in, or is formed by the sea.

maritime climate: The climate and weather conditions typical of areas bordering the sea.

maritime rights: The rights that protect navigation and shipping.

market access: Market access refers to the openness of a national market to foreign products. Market access reflects a government's willingness to permit imports to compete relatively unimpeded with similar domestically produced goods.

market economy: A form of society which runs by the law of supply and demand. Goods are produced by firms to be sold to consumers, who determine the demand for them. Price levels vary according to the demand for certain goods and how much of them is produced.

market price: The price a commodity will bring when sold on the open market. The price is determined by the amount of demand for the commodity by buyers.

Marshall Plan: Formally known as the European Recovery Program, a joint project between the United States and most Western European nations under which $12.5 billion in U.S. loans and grants was expended to aid European recovery after World War II.

Marxism *see* Marxist-Leninist principles.

Marxist-Leninist principles: The doctrines of Karl Marx, built upon by Nikolai Lenin, on which communism was founded. They predicted the fall of capitalism, due to its own internal faults and the resulting oppression of workers.

Marxist: A follower of Karl Marx, a German socialist and revolutionary leader of the late 1800s, who contributed to Marxist-Leninist principles.

massif: A central mountain-mass or the dominant part of a range of mountains.

matrilineal (descent): Descending from, or tracing descent through, the maternal, or mother's, family line.

Mayan language family: The languages of the Central American Indians, further divided into two subgroups: the Maya and the Huastek.

mean temperature: The air temperature unit measured by the National Weather Service by adding the maximum and minimum daily temperatures together and diving the sum by 2.

Mecca (Mekkah): A city in Saudi Arabia; a destination of pilgrims in the Islamic world.

Mediterranean climate: A wet-winter, dry-summer climate with a moderate annual temperature range.

mestizo: The offspring of a person of mixed blood; especially, a person of mixed Spanish and American Indian parentage.

migratory birds: Those birds whose instincts prompt them to move from one place to another at the regularly recurring changes of season.

migratory workers: Usually agricultural workers who move from place to place for employment depending on the growing and harvesting seasons of various crops.

military coup: A sudden, violent overthrow of a government by military forces.

military junta: The small military group in power in a country, especially after a coup.

military regime: Government conducted by a military force.

military takeover: The seizure of control of a government by the military forces.

militia: The group of citizens of a country who are either serving in the reserve military forces or are eligible to be called up in time of emergency.

millet: A cereal grass whose small grain is used for food in Europe and Asia.

minority party: The political group that comprises the smaller part of the large overall group it belongs to; the party that is not in control.

missionary: A person sent by authority of a church or religious organization to spread his religious faith in a community where his church has no self-supporting organization.

Mohammed (or Muhammedor Mahomet): An Arabian prophet, known as the "Prophet of Allah" who founded the religion of Islam in 622, and wrote *The Koran*, the scripture of Islam. Also commonly spelled Muhammed, especially by Islamic people.

monarchy: Government by a sovereign, such as a king or queen.

money economy: A system or stage of economic development in which money replaces barter in the exchange of goods and services.

Mongol: One of an Asiatic race chiefly resident in Mongolia, a region north of China proper and south of Siberia.

Mongoloid: Having physical characteristics like those of the typical Mongols (Chinese, Japanese, Turks, Eskimos, etc.).

Moors: One of the Arab tribes that conquered Spain in the eighth century.

Moslem (Muslim): A follower of Mohammed (spelled Muhammed by many Islamic people), in the religion of Islam.

mosque: An Islam place of worship and the organization with which it is connected.

mouflon: A type of wild sheep characterized by curling horns.

mujahideen (mujahedin or mujahedeen): Rebel fighters in Islamic countries, especially those supporting the cause of Islam.

mulatto: One who is the offspring of parents one of whom is white and the other is black.

municipality: A district such as a city or town having its own incorporated government.

Muslim: A frequently used variation of the spelling of Moslem, to describe a follower of the prophet Mohammed (also spelled Muhammed), the founder of the religion of Islam.

Muslim New Year: A Muslim holiday. Although in some countries 1 Muharram, which is the first month of the Islamic year, is observed as a holiday, in other places the new year is observed on Sha'ban, the eighth month of the year. This practice apparently stems from pagan Arab times. Shab-i-Bharat, a national holiday in Bangladesh on this day, is held by many to be the occasion when God ordains all actions in the coming year.

NAFTA (North American Free Trade Agreement): NAFTA, which entered into force in January 1994, is a free trade agreement between Canada, the United States, and Mexico. The agreement progressively eliminates almost all U.S.-Mexico tariffs over a 10–15 year period.

nationalism: National spirit or aspirations; desire for national unity, independence, or prosperity.

nationalization: To transfer the control or ownership of land or industries to the nation from private owners.

native tongue: One's natural language. The language that is indigenous to an area.

NATO see North Atlantic Treaty Organization

natural gas: A combustible gas formed naturally in the earth and generally obtained by boring a well. The chemical makeup of natural gas is principally methane, hydrogen, ethylene compounds, and nitrogen.

natural harbor: A protected portion of a sea or lake along the shore resulting from the natural formations of the land.

naturalize: To confer the rights and privileges of a native-born subject or citizen upon someone who lives in the country by choice.

nature preserve: An area where one or more species of plant and/or animal are protected from harm, injury, or destruction.

neutrality: The policy of not taking sides with any countries during a war or dispute among them.

Newly Independent States: The NIS is a collective reference to 12 republics of the former Soviet Union: Russia, Ukraine, Belarus (formerly Byelorussia), Moldova (formerly Moldavia), Armenia, Azerbaijan, Uzbekistan, Turkmenistan, Tajikistan, Kazakhstan, and Kirgizstan (formerly Kirghiziya), and Georgia. Following dissolution of the Soviet Union, the distinction between the NIS and the Commonwealth of Independent States (CIS) was that Georgia was not a member of the CIS. That distinction dissolved when Georgia joined the CIS in November 1993.

news censorship see censorship

Nonaligned Movement: The NAM is an alliance of third world states that aims to promote the political and economic interests of developing countries. NAM interests have included ending colonialism/neo-colonialism, supporting the integrity of independent countries, and seeking a new international economic order.

Nordic Council: The Nordic Council, established in 1952, is directed toward supporting cooperation among Nordic countries. Members include Denmark, Finland, Iceland, Norway, and Sweden. Headquarters are in Stockholm, Sweden.

North Atlantic Treaty Organization (NATO): A mutual defense organization. Members include Belgium, Canada, Denmark, France (which has only partial membership), Greece, Iceland, Italy, Luxembourg, Netherlands, Norway, Portugal, Spain, Turkey, United Kingdom, United States, and Germany.

nuclear power plant: A factory that produces electrical power through the application of the nuclear reaction known as nuclear fission.

nuclear reactor: A device used to control the rate of nuclear fission in uranium. Used in commercial applications, nuclear reactors can maintain temperatures high enough to generate sufficient quantities of steam which can then be used to produce electricity.

OAPEC (Organization of Arab Petroleum Exporting countries): OAPEC was created in 1968; members include: Algeria, Bahrain, Egypt, Iraq, Kuwait, Libya, Qatar, Saudi Arabia, Syria, and the United Arab Emirates. Headquarters are in Cairo, Egypt.

OAS (Organization of American States): The OAS (Spanish: Organizaciûn de los Estados Americanos, OEA), or the Pan American Union, is a regional organization which promotes Latin American economic and social development. Members include the United States, Mexico, and most Central American, South American, and Caribbean nations.

OAS *see* Organization of American States

oasis: Originally, a fertile spot in the Libyan desert where there is a natural spring or well and vegetation; now refers to any fertile tract in the midst of a wasteland.

occupied territory: A territory that has an enemy's military forces present.

official language: The language in which the business of a country and its government is conducted.

oligarchy: A form of government in which a few people possess the power to rule as opposed to a monarchy which is ruled by one.

OPEC *see* OAPEC

open economy: An economy that imports and exports goods.

open market: Open market operations are the actions of the central bank to influence or control the money supply by buying or selling government bonds.

opposition party: A minority political party that is opposed to the party in power.

Organization of Arab Petroleum Exporting Countries *see* OAPEC

organized labor: The body of workers who belong to labor unions.

Ottoman Empire: An Turkish empire founded by Osman I in about 1603, that variously controlled large areas of land around the Mediterranean, Black, and Caspian Seas until it was dissolved in 1918.

overfishing: To deplete the quantity of fish in an area by removing more fish than can be naturally replaced.

overgrazing: Allowing animals to graze in an area to the point that the ground vegetation is damaged or destroyed.

overseas dependencies: A distant and physically separate territory that belongs to another country and is subject to its laws and government.

Pacific Rim: The Pacific Rim, referring to countries and economies bordering the Pacific Ocean.

pact: An international agreement.

Paleolithic: The early period of the Stone Age, when rough, chipped stone implements were used.

panhandle: A long narrow strip of land projecting like the handle of a frying pan.

papyrus: The paper-reed or -rush which grows on marshy river banks in the southeastern area of the Mediterranean, but more notably in the Nile valley.

paramilitary group: A supplementary organization to the military.

parasitic diseases: A group of diseases caused by parasitic organisms which feed off the host organism.

parliamentary republic: A system of government in which a president and prime minister, plus other ministers of departments, constitute the executive branch of the government and the parliament constitutes the legislative branch.

parliamentary rule: Government by a legislative body similar to that of Great Britain, which is composed of two houses—one elected and one hereditary.

parochial: Refers to matters of a church parish or something within narrow limits.

patriarchal system: A social system in which the head of the family or tribe is the father or oldest male. Kinship is determined and traced through the male members of the tribe.

patrilineal (descent): Descending from, or tracing descent through, the paternal or father's line.

pellagra: A disease marked by skin, intestinal, and central nervous system disorders, caused by a diet deficient in niacin, one of the B vitamins.

per capita: Literally, per person; for each person counted.

perestroika: The reorganization of the political and economic structures of the Soviet Union by president Mikhail Gorbachev.

periodical: A publication whose issues appear at regular intervals, such as weekly, monthly, or yearly.

petrochemical: A chemical derived from petroleum or from natural gas.

pharmaceutical plants: Any plant that is used in the preparation of medicinal drugs.

plantain: The name of a common weed that has often been used for medicinal purposes, as a folk remedy and in modern medicine. *Plaintain* is also the name of a tropical plant producing a type of banana.

poaching: To intrude or encroach upon another's preserves for the purpose of stealing animals, especially wild game.

polar climate: Also called tundra climate. A humid, severely cold climate controlled by arctic air masses, with no warm or summer season.

political climate: The prevailing political attitude of a particular time or place.

political refugee: A person forced to flee his or her native country for political reasons.

potable water: Water that is safe for drinking.

pound sterling: The monetary unit of Great Britain, otherwise known as the pound.

prefect: An administrative official; in France, the head of a particular department.

prefecture: The territory over which a prefect has authority.

prime meridian: Zero degrees in longitude that runs through Greenwich, England, site of the Royal Observatory. All other longitudes are measured from this point.

prime minister: The premier or chief administrative official in certain countries.

private sector: The division of an economy in which production of goods and services is privately owned.

privatization: To change from public to private control or ownership.

protectorate: A state or territory controlled by a stronger state, or the relationship of the stronger country toward the lesser one it protects.

Protestant Reformation: In 1529, a Christian religious movement begun in Germany to deny the universal authority of the Pope, and to establish the Bible as the only source of truth. (*Also see* Protestant)

Protestant: A member or an adherent of one of those Christian bodies which descended from the Reformation of the sixteenth century. Originally applied to those who opposed or protested the Roman Catholic Church.

proved reserves: The quantity of a recoverable mineral resource (such as oil or natural gas) that is still in the ground.

province: An administrative territory of a country.

provisional government: A temporary government set up during time of unrest or transition in a country.

pulses: Beans, peas, or lentils.

purge: The act of ridding a society of "undesirable" or unloyal persons by banishment or murder.

Rastafarian: A member of a Jamaican cult begun in 1930 as a semi-religious, semi-political movement.

rate of literacy: The percentage of people in a society who can read and write.

recession. A period of reduced economic activity in a country or region.

referendum: The practice of submitting legislation directly to the people for a popular vote.

Reformation *see* Protestant Reformation.

refugee: One who flees to a refuge or shelter or place of safety. One who in times of persecution or political commotion flees to a foreign country for safety.

revolution: A complete change in a government or society, such as in an overthrow of the government by the people.

right-wing party: The more conservative political party.

Roman alphabet: The alphabet of the ancient Romans from which the alphabets of most modern western European languages, including English, are derived.

Roman Catholic Church: The designation of the church of which the pope or Bishop of Rome is the head, and that holds him as the successor of St. Peter and heir of his spiritual authority, privileges, and gifts.

romance language: The group of languages derived from Latin: French, Spanish, Italian, Portuguese, and other related languages.

roundwood: Timber used as poles or in similar ways without being sawn or shaped.

runoff election: A deciding election put to the voters in case of a tie between candidates.

Russian Orthodox: The arm of the Orthodox Eastern Church that was the official church of Russia under the czars.

sack: To strip of valuables, especially after capture.

Sahelian zone: Eight countries make up this dry desert zone in Africa: Burkina Faso, Chad, Gambia, Mali, Mauritania, Niger, Senegal, and the Cape Verde Islands. *Also see* Club du Sahel.

salinization: An accumulation of soluble salts in soil. This condition is common in desert climates, where water evaporates quickly in poorly drained soil due to high temperatures.

Samaritans: A native or an inhabitant of Samaria; specifically, one of a race settled in the cities of Samaria by the king of Assyria after the removal of the Israelites from the country.

savanna: A treeless or near treeless plain of a tropical or subtropical region dominated by drought-resistant grasses.

schistosomiasis: A tropical disease that is chronic and characterized by disorders of the liver, urinary bladder, lungs, or central nervous system.

secession: The act of withdrawal, such as a state withdrawing from the Union in the Civil War in the United States.

sect: A religious denomination or group, often a dissenting one with extreme views.

segregation: The enforced separation of a racial or religious group from other groups, compelling them to live and go to school separately from the rest of society.

seismic activity: Relating to or connected with an earthquake or earthquakes in general.

self-sufficient: Able to function alone without help.

separation of power: The division of power in the government among the executive, legislative, and judicial branches and the checks and balances employed to keep them separate and independent of each other.

separatism: The policy of dissenters withdrawing from a larger political or religious group.

serfdom: In the feudal system of the Middle Ages, the condition of being attached to the land owned by a lord and being transferable to a new owner.

Seventh-day Adventist: One who believes in the second coming of Christ to establish a personal reign upon the earth.

shamanism: A religion of some Asians and Amerindians in which shamans, who are priests or medicine men, are believed to influence good and evil spirits.

shantytown: An urban settlement of people in flimsy, inadequate houses.

Shia Muslim: Members of one of two great sects of Islam. Shia Muslims believe that Ali and the Imams are the rightful successors of Mohammed (also commonly spelled Muhammed). They also believe that the last recognized Imam will return as a messiah. Also known as Shiites. (*Also see* Sunnis.)

Shiites *see* Shia Muslims.

Shintoism: The system of nature- and hero-worship which forms the indigenous religion of Japan.

shoal: A place where the water of a stream, lake, or sea is of little depth. Especially, a sand-bank which shows at low water.

sierra: A chain of hills or mountains.

Sikh: A member of a politico-religious community of India, founded as a sect around 1500 and based on the principles of monotheism (belief in one god) and human brotherhood.

Sino-Tibetan language family: The family of languages spoken in eastern Asia, including China, Thailand, Tibet, and Burma.

slash-and-burn agriculture: A hasty and sometimes temporary way of clearing land to make it available for agriculture by cutting down trees and burning them.

slave trade: The transportation of black Africans beginning in the 1700s to other countries to be sold as slaves—people owned as property and compelled to work for their owners at no pay.

Slavic languages: A major subgroup of the Indo-European language family. It is further subdivided into West Slavic (including Polish, Czech, Slovak and Serbian), South Slavic (including Bulgarian, Serbo-Croatian, Slovene, and Old Church Slavonic), and East Slavic (including Russian Ukrainian and Byelorussian).

social insurance: A government plan to protect low-income people, such as health and accident insurance, pension plans, etc.

social security: A form of social insurance, including life, disability, and old-age pension for workers. It is paid for by employers, employees, and the government.

socialism: An economic system in which ownership of land and other property is distributed among the community as a whole, and every member of the community shares in the work and products of the work.

socialist: A person who advocates socialism.

softwoods: The coniferous trees, whose wood density as a whole is relatively softer than the wood of those trees referred to as hardwoods.

sorghum (also known as Syrian Grass): Plant grown in various parts of the world for its valuable uses, such as for grain, syrup, or fodder.

Southeast Asia: The region in Asia that consists of the Malay Archipelago, the Malay Peninsula, and Indochina.

staple crop: A crop that is the chief commodity or product of a place, and which has widespread and constant use or value.

state: The politically organized body of people living under one government or one of the territorial units that make up a federal government, such as in the United States.

steppe: A level tract of land more or less devoid of trees, in certain parts of European and Asiatic Russia.

student demonstration: A public gathering of students to express strong feelings about a certain situation, usually taking place near the location of the people in power to change the situation.

subarctic climate: A high latitude climate of two types: *continental subarctic*, which has very cold winters, short, cool summers, light precipitation and moist air; and *marine subarctic*, a coastal and island climate with polar air masses causing large precipitation and extreme cold.

subcontinent: A land mass of great size, but smaller than any of the continents; a large subdivision of a continent.

subsistence economy: The part of a national economy in which money plays little or no role, trade is by barter, and living standards are minimal.

subsistence farming: Farming that provides the minimum food goods necessary for the continuation of the farm family.

subtropical climate: A middle latitude climate dominated by humid, warm temperatures and heavy rainfall in summer, with cool winters and frequent cyclonic storms.

subversion: The act of attempting to overthrow or ruin a government or organization by stealthy or deceitful means.

Sudanic language group: A related group of languages spoken in various areas of northern Africa, including Yoruba, Mandingo, and Tshi.

suffrage: The right to vote.

Sufi: A Muslim mystic who believes that God alone exists, there can be no real difference between good and evil, that the soul exists within the body as in a cage, so death should be the chief object of desire, and sufism is the only true philosophy.

sultan: A king of a Muslim state.

Sunni Muslim: Members of one of two major sects of the religion of Islam. Sunni Muslims adhere to strict orthodox traditions, and believe that the four caliphs are the rightful successors to Mohammed, founder of Islam. (Mohammed is commonly spelled Muhammed, especially by Islamic people.) (*Also see* Shia Muslim.)

Taoism: The doctrine of Lao-Tzu, an ancient Chinese philosopher (about 500 B.C.) as laid down by him in the *Tao-te-ching.*

tariff: A tax assessed by a government on goods as they enter (or leave) a country. May be imposed to protect domestic industries from imported goods and/or to generate revenue.

temperate zone: The parts of the earth lying between the tropics and the polar circles. The *northern temperate zone* is the area between the tropic of Cancer and the Arctic Circle. The *southern temperate zone* is the area between the tropic of Capricorn and the Antarctic Circle.

terracing: A form of agriculture that involves cultivating crops in raised banks of earth.

terrorism: Systematic acts of violence designed to frighten or intimidate.

thermal power plant: A facility that produces electric energy from heat energy released by combustion of fuel or nuclear reactions.

Third World: A term used to describe less developed countries; as of the mid-1990s, it is being replaced by the United Nations designation Less Developed Countries, or LDC.

topography: The physical or natural features of the land.

torrid zone: The part of the earth's surface that lies between the tropics, so named for the character of its climate.

totalitarian party: The single political party in complete authoritarian control of a government or state.

trachoma: A contagious bacterial disease that affects the eye.

treaty: A negotiated agreement between two governments.

tribal system: A social community in which people are organized into groups or clans descended from common ancestors and sharing customs and languages.

tropical monsoon climate: One of the tropical rainy climates; it is sufficiently warm and rainy to produce tropical rainforest vegetation, but also has a winter dry season.

tsetse fly: Any of the several African insects which can transmit a variety of parasitic organisms through its bite. Some of these organisms can prove fatal to both human and animal victims.

tundra: A nearly level treeless area whose climate and vegetation are characteristically arctic due to its northern position; the subsoil is permanently frozen.

undeveloped countries *see* least developed countries.

unemployment rate: The overall unemployment rate is the percentage of the work force (both employed and unemployed) who claim to be unemployed.

UNICEF: An international fund set-up for children's emergency relief: United Nations Children's Fund (formerly United Nations International Children's Emergency Fund).

universal adult suffrage: The policy of giving every adult in a nation the right to vote.

untouchables: In India, members of the lowest caste in the caste system, a hereditary social class system. They were considered unworthy to touch members of higher castes.

urban guerrilla: A rebel fighter operating in an urban area.

urbanization: The process of changing from country to city.

USSR: An abbreviation of Union of Soviet Socialist Republics.

veldt: In South Africa, an unforested or thinly forested tract of land or region, a grassland.

Warsaw Pact: Agreement made 14 May 1955 (and dissolved 1 July 1991) to promote mutual defense between Albania, Bulgaria, Czechoslovakia, East Germany, Hungary, Poland, Romania, and the USSR.

Western nations: Blanket term used to describe mostly democratic, capitalist countries, including the United States, Canada, and western European countries.

wildlife sanctuary: An area of land set aside for the protection and preservation of animals and plants.

workers' compensation: A series of regular payments by an employer to a person injured on the job.

World Bank: The World Bank is a group of international institutions which provides financial and technical assistance to developing countries.

world oil crisis: The severe shortage of oil in the 1970s precipitated by the Arab oil embargo.

wormwood: A woody perennial herb native to Europe and Asiatic Russia, valued for its medicinal uses.

yaws: A tropical disease caused by a bacteria which produces raspberry-like sores on the skin.

yellow fever: A tropical viral disease caused by the bite of an infected mosquito, characterized by jaundice.

Zoroastrianism: The system of religious doctrine taught by Zoroaster and his followers in the Avesta; the religion prevalent in Persia until its overthrow by the Muslims in the seventh century.